Praise for
MEDIA AND CULTURE

"Thanks to Dr. Campbell for writing, and Bedford/ St. Martin's for publishing, what I consider an ideal introductory textbook!"

—Sharon R. Mazzarella,
Ithaca College

"I thought the level of writing was outstanding, perhaps the best I have seen in a mass media text."

—Steven Alan Carr,
Indiana University–Purdue University Fort Wayne

"*Media and Culture* allows students to build upon their own experiences with various media they use, to see the ways in which those media are active constructors of culture. Students can begin to see their roles in the society at large, and the many ways in which they use the media (and the media use them) in constructing that culture."

—John L. Hochheimer,
Ithaca College

"*Media and Culture* is the single best textbook I've seen for introductory courses on media and society. The writing is appealing—clear without being stuffy, hip without pandering. The recurring questions about democracy are an excellent way to invite students to think more critically about media. It gets much closer to student experiences of media than any other text I've seen, without simply affirming those experiences. The textbook is visually appealing and up-to-date in its examples. In my view, it strikes the right balance for beginning students—it doesn't scare them away with outspoken radicalism, but neither does it celebrate the media system as it currently exists."

—John Durham Peters,
University of Iowa

"This is a very student friendly text without giving up one historical point or recent example. It connects the past to the present by hooking students with what they know best: new technology, popular music, television, and movies—and then showing how these technologies built on older print media."

—*Journalism and Mass Communication Educator*
(Spring 1998)

"The topics covered are the right ones. Nothing is missing. *Media and Culture* is a great book."

—Douglas Gomery,
University of Maryland

"*Media and Culture* is a terrific tool because it directs our attention to the media environment in which we must survive, discusses issues and incidents that occurred within students' memories, and engages students' critical thinking faculties."

—Enid Sefcovic,
Florida Atlantic University

"*Media and Culture* is, in my opinion, the best text resource for a course that examines the historical, social, cultural, philosophical, and economic impact of media. The book is a concise and informative reference on the influential nature of media communication from Gutenberg to Gates. . . . A superb example of excellent writing, solid research, and descriptive content that deconstructs the myths of media perpetuated in other mass communication texts."

—David Marc McCoy,
Kent State University

"I adopted the book because it does everything a more objective treatment does, and it also provides a critical perspective. . . . The critical perspective has enlightened the work of all of us who study media, and Campbell has the power to infect students with his love of the subject."

—Roger Desmond,
University of Hartford

"I've been using the critical process of description-analysis-interpretation-evaluation in my course for many years but only this text seems to adhere to this effective format. This is a major reason why I selected *Media and Culture* for my course."

—Clifford E. Wexler,
Columbia-Greene Community College

"I give the text high marks for currency and accuracy. I especially appreciate the 'Global Village' material, since it focuses attention beyond the narrow frame of most American audiences, especially students."

—John Pantalone,
University of Rhode Island

MEDIA AND CULTURE

An Introduction to

Mass Communication

MEDIA AND CULTURE

An Introduction to

Mass Communication

Second Edition

Richard Campbell
Middle Tennessee State University

with

Christopher R. Martin
University of Northern Iowa

and

Bettina Fabos
University of Iowa

Bedford/St. Martin's
Boston ◆ New York

For Bedford/St. Martin's

Executive Editor: Patricia Rossi
Developmental Editor: Michael Gillespie
Associate Developmental Editor: Simon Glick
Production Editor: Jessica Zorn
Editorial Assistant: Regan Park
Senior Production Supervisor: Cheryl Mamaril
Senior Marketing Manager: Charles Cavaliere
Art Direction and Cover Design: Lucy Krikorian
Text Design: Robin Hoffmann/Brand X Studios
Copy Editor: Carol Anderson
Indexer: Riofrancos & Co. Indexes
Graphics: Burmar Technical Corp.
Photo Research: Alice Lundoff
Cover Art: Kay Petronio
Composition: Robin Hoffmann/Brand X Studios
Printing and Binding: R. R. Donnelly & Sons Co.

President: Charles H. Christensen
Editorial Director: Joan E. Feinberg
Editor in Chief: Nancy Perry
Director of Editing, Design, and Production: Marcia Cohen
Managing Editor: Erica T. Appel

Library of Congress Catalog Card Number: 99-62220

For information, write: Bedford/St. Martin's, 75 Arlington Street, Boston, MA 02116 (617-399-4000)

ISBN: 0-312-20200-8

Acknowledgments
Acknowledgments and copyrights appear on pages 537–538, which constitute an extension of the copyright page.

"WE ARE NOT ALONE."

For my family—Chris, Caitlin, and Dianna

Brief

PART I MASS MEDIA AND THE CULTURAL LANDSCAPE

Chapter 1 Mass Communication: A Critical Approach 2
Chapter 2 Information and New Technology: Media at the Crossroads 34

PART II SOUNDS AND IMAGES

Chapter 3 Sound Recording and Popular Music 64
Chapter 4 Popular Radio and the Origins of Broadcasting 100
Chapter 5 Television and the Power of Visual Culture 134
Chapter 6 Cable and the Specialization of Television 170
Chapter 7 Movies and the Impact of Images 202

PART III WORDS AND PICTURES

Chapter 8 Newspapers and the Rise of Modern Journalism 238
Chapter 9 Magazines in the Age of Specialization 270
Chapter 10 Books and the Power of Print 308

PART IV THE BUSINESS OF MASS MEDIA

Chapter 11 Advertising and Commercial Culture 342
Chapter 12 Public Relations and Framing the Message 376
Chapter 13 Media Economics and the Global Marketplace 404

PART V DEMOCRATIC EXPRESSION AND THE MASS MEDIA

Chapter 14 The Culture of Journalism: Values, Ethics, and Democracy 426
Chapter 15 Media Effects and Cultural Approaches to Research 458
Chapter 16 Legal Controls and Freedom of Expression 484

CONTENTS

The twentieth century is not ending quietly or easily. And our mass media have been right in the middle of the action. Since the first edition of *Media and Culture* was published in 1997, the media have helped propel us from one major event to the next. Throughout 1998 and early 1999, Americans were transfixed by the sordid details and political firestorm surrounding President Bill Clinton's affair with White House intern Monica Lewinsky, his ensuing impeachment by the House of Representatives, and his eventual acquittal in the Senate. Spring 1999 brought the world to Kosovo and Serbia, where we learned about a horrific campaign of ethnic cleansing and watched footage of NATO's hi-tech war. Seemingly far from the killing fields in the former Yugoslavia, spring 1999 also gave us the tragic shooting rampage at Columbine High School in Littleton, Colorado, where two teenagers shot and killed twelve classmates and a teacher before turning their guns on themselves. And in the summer of 1999, we experienced both the joy of watching the U.S. soccer team win the Women's World Cup before a large, global audience, and the sadness of witnessing another Kennedy family tragedy unfold on television as we learned of the fatal airplane crash of John F. Kennedy Jr., his wife, and his sister-in-law.

Clearly, the mass media play a central role in representing national and global culture. But they also, over our lifetimes, play a more intimate role. We watch TV and go to movies to find stories that resonate with our own experience or transport us to someone else's life. We read books and magazines for clues to the past and help with the present. We scan newspapers for information and search the Internet for the future. We go to the mass media for stories about our neighbors, our world, and ourselves.

This revised edition of *Media and Culture* is a trip through that landscape. It is both a personal and a global journey. As a textbook, it aims to provide maps for navigating the cultural terrain. It asks that we participate in the critical work of evaluating mass media and shaping their direction. In this journey, we have choices. We can watch the media as detached outsiders. As observers, we can praise them when they perform well and blame them for our social predicaments. Or we can become active participants. We can analyze the impact and investigate the consequences of the stories that media industries tell and sell. As involved citizens, we can challenge our media to perform at high levels and steer them to serve and preserve democratic ideals.

The journey through the media landscape is different for each of us and for each generation. As part of everyone's autobiography, the mass media are cast as significant players. But to understand our lives in the context of a larger world, we need some distance from personal history. We need to stand back from our experience and view the media's impact on the world through a larger lens.

That's where this book comes in.

The second edition of *Media and Culture* asks students to become critical consumers of the media and engaged citizens in the society that the media shape. *Media and Culture* offers maps for surveying the cultural landscape and tools for critiquing the media's influences on democratic life and consumer culture. In probing historical events and contemporary trends in mass communication, *Media and Culture* invites students to become cultural activists ready to investigate and challenge the power of mass media in daily life.

Five key perspectives and themes guide *Media and Culture:*

A Critical Viewpoint

Media and Culture introduces students to four stages of the critical thinking and writing process—description, analysis, interpretation, and evaluation. The text uses these stages as a lens for examining the historical context and current processes that shape mass media as part of American culture. This framework guides chapter content and informs the writing of each chapter as well as the Critical Process exercises at the end of each chapter.

A Cultural Perspective

This textbook uses a narrative approach to investigate media as part of the rituals of everyday culture. Most mass media, whether news, prime-time television, magazines, film, paperback novels, or advertising, make use of storytelling to tap into our shared beliefs and values, and so does *Media and Culture*. Each chapter presents the events and issues surrounding media culture as intriguing and informative narratives rather than a series of unconnected facts and feats. *Media and Culture* presents the history of mass media as compelling and complicated stories that map the uneasy and parallel developments of consumer culture and democratic society.

Media Technology and Convergence

Media and Culture examines key technological developments that have changed the world: from the telegraph, our first binary communication system (with its electronic dots and dashes), to the Internet, our latest binary system (with its digital ones and zeroes). The text studies our journey from the Industrial Age to the Information Age, featuring the phenomenon of media convergence: the confluence of home, school, and business computers, TV sets, telephones, radio, CD players, VCRs, email, video games, newspapers, fax machines, magazines, and communication satellites.

The organization of *Media and Culture* takes into account the dramatic influences of electronic and digital forms of communication on the social world. Since converging forms of mass communication integrate aspects of print, electronic, and digital culture in our daily lives, we begin with the stories of convergence. Rather than starting chronologically with the book, our oldest mass medium, the industry chapters open with the media students know best: the Internet, music, radio, television, cable, and film. Placing past and present communication developments within contemporary contexts, *Media and Culture* looks at older media against the backdrop of new forms that have reshaped printed culture.

Values and Ethics

To develop a critical perspective toward mass media, students must think about values and ethics as a routine and integrated part of the way they experience media in daily life. Media books often ghettoize the subject of ethics by treating it as a separate, isolated chapter near the end. *Media and Culture*, on the other hand, weaves into the larger story discussions about the values depicted in mass communication and the ethical implications faced by media practitioners.

Media Economics and Democracy

To become better citizens and discerning consumers, students must pay attention to the complex relationship between democracy and capitalism, between the marketplace of ideas and the global consumer market. To that end, *Media and Culture* addresses the significance of the dramatic rise in multinational media systems. It invites students to explore the implications of the 1996 Telecommunications Act and the vast control that a handful of mammoth international companies exercise over the production and distribution of commercial mass media. Ownership issues are an integral part of the individual media chapters. Additionally, Chapter 13 looks critically at the global picture and encourages students to participate in the debates over ownership. Each chapter ends with a discussion of the role of various mass media on the nature of democratic life.

new to this edition

The second edition of *Media and Culture* has been fully revised and updated to reflect the ongoing changes within mass media and society as well as to strengthen the features that make the book such an effective learning tool—its unique critical approach and cultural perspective. Using the most contemporary examples and current industry information available, *Media and Culture* gets students to think and talk critically about the messages and images that media bombard them with daily.

An Improved Critical Approach

- **New two-tiered Critical Process questions** at the end of each chapter offer both short assignments that can be done in class and longer, more complex assignments that can be assigned for homework. The Critical Process is explained in Chapter 1 and applied throughout the text. Additional Critical Process questions are available at <www.mediaculture.com>.

- **New Case Studies invite students to sharpen critical thinking skills,** examining such topics as how the rival media empires of Rupert Murdoch and Ted Turner have affected entertainment, economics, and free expression worldwide; the evolution of photojournalism from its nineteenth-century origins to today's digital images and questions of image-tampering; and the rise of e-commerce and its impact on traditional shopping.

- **New Examining Ethics boxes explore current issues,** such as the need for codes of ethical conduct in online journalism, and how ABC News reports on its corporate owner, Disney.

An Improved Cultural Perspective

- **Expanded coverage of global issues.** Additional Global Village boxes—twice as many as in the previous edition—cover filmmaking in India, Hong Kong, and Japan and how it influences Hollywood; how tobacco companies target emerging Asian markets with advertising; and the international syndication of TV shows like *The X-Files, Baywatch, Xena: Warrior Princess,* and *Hercules: The Legendary Journeys.*

- **Expanded coverage of new technology and its impact.** Thoroughly updated coverage of the Internet in Chapter 2 charts the development of this phenomenal new medium and explores its cultural impact. Additional coverage within the industry chapters investigates the Internet's effects on other mass media, such as radio and newspapers. Campbell also explores the latest technological developments in the media landscape—including MP3, e-books, e-commerce, broadcasting via the Internet, HDTV, and digital filmmaking.

- **Increased coverage of alternative media.** Alternative Voices—an all-new section in chapters 2–10—reports on individuals who adapt one of the mass media to bypass traditional, corporate-owned outlets in order to create their own messages. Subjects include community-owned cable systems that compete with corporate providers, the free computer operating system Linux, newspapers produced by homeless people, unlicensed "pirate radio," and independent recording labels.

The Most Current Text Available

- **Fully updated examples, facts, and statistics** keep students on top of the most recent media industry developments and corporate mergers in the rapidly changing world of mass communication, such as the partnering of Netscape and AOL, AT&T's cable acquisitions, and Viacom's recent acquisition of CBS.

- **50 percent of all feature boxes are new or heavily revised.** Of *Media and Culture*'s thirty-nine feature boxes, fourteen are new and seven are significantly revised.

- **The best coverage of trends and new technology.** This edition includes more coverage of alternative media, the Internet and its impact on traditional media, and all the latest technological developments shaping media today.

- **More than half the photographs are new to this edition.** Widely praised for its design and visual material, this edition of *Media and Culture* continues to visually engage students.

- **Related Web sites** are listed at the end of every chapter to guide students toward relevant Internet resources.

- **Updated instructional aids and links, plus essays by Richard Campbell at <www.mediaculture.com>.** Appearing are "Media Critic" essays written by *Media and Culture* author Richard Campbell, as well as updated chapter study guides, chapter quizzes, Web links, additional Critical Process questions, and instructor resources.

supplements

Media and Culture Instructor's Resource Manual

Bettina Fabos, University of Iowa, and Christopher R. Martin, University of Northern Iowa;
ISBN 0-312-25011-8

This extensive manual provides sample course syllabi for a range of teaching approaches, tips for facilitating in-class discussions, suggestions for incorporating more writing assignments into your course, chapter outlines, lecture topics, lecture spin-offs, Critical Process exercises, classroom media resources, and an annotated list of more than two hundred video resources.

Multimedia Presentations CD-ROM
ISBN 0-312-25045-2

This multimedia CD-ROM lets you build classroom presentations around three case studies: *Popular Music and the Freedom of Expression* (Paul Fischer, Middle Tennessee State University), *Newspapers: From Print to the Web* (Craig Brandon, Keene State College), and *Photojournalism: Photography and the Coverage of War* (Jim Kelley, Southern Illinois University). These presentations include visual and textual material that instructors can either use as assembled for lectures or can customize with additions from the Web or from the instructor's own materials.

www.mediaculture.com

Fully revised and updated, this companion site offers valuable resources for students and instructors. Student resources include detailed chapter overviews, sample chapter quizzes, Critical Process exercises, timely Media Critic essays by Richard Campbell and other media scholars, exercises related to the issue of *Brill's Content* bundled with the text, career resources, an online glossary, and research resources, links, and tutorials. Instructor resources include downloadable PowerPoint slides, sample syllabi, and sample assignments.

Bundle with *Brill's Content*

Each student and instructor using *Media and Culture*, Second Edition, receives a free copy of *Brill's Content*, the media watchdog magazine that critically assesses the performance of today's media. Questions on our Web site, <www.mediaculture.com>, will help students make connections between articles in the magazine and topics covered in *Media and Culture*. Students and instructors are eligible to receive the lowest price subscription rate available so they can benefit from the magazine all year.

Media Career Guide: Preparing for Jobs in the 21st Century, **Second Edition**
James Seguin, Robert Morris College; ISBN 0-312-25016-9

Practical and student-friendly, this revised guide includes a comprehensive directory of media jobs, practical tips, and career guidance for students considering a major in communication studies and mass media.

Untangling the Web: A Guide to Mass Communication on the Web, **Second Edition**
Deborah Greh, St. John's University; ISBN 0-312-25014-2

This updated guide offers practical advice for novices and experts on accessing information from the Internet, conducting searches, and evaluating and citing sources. It can be packaged with *Media and Culture* at no extra charge.

The Bedford/St. Martin's Video Resource Library

Over a dozen contemporary and historical media-related videos are organized around the issues explored in *Media and Culture.* Instructors are eligible to select video materials from the library upon adoption of *Media and Culture.*

Testing Program
Thomas Beell, Iowa State University
Computerized Test Bank ISBN 0-312-25630-2; Print Test Bank ISBN 0-312-25012-6

A complete testing program is available in print and as software formatted for Windows and Macintosh, with multiple choice, true/false, fill-in-the-blank, and short and long essay questions.

PowerPoint Presentation
Pamela Wilson, Reinhardt College
Windows ISBN 0-312-25091-6; Macintosh ISBN 0-312-25090-8

Available for both Macintosh and Windows, these PowerPoint slides highlight key information from the text, allowing instructors to make classroom presentations with greater visual impact. Instructors can customize the slides to fit their own needs.

What's Next in Communication?: Readings on Media and Culture
Christopher Harper, Ithaca College; ISBN 0-312-16743-1

This engaging collection of readings reflects the transformation of mass media and covers hot topics of the digital age, such as "computer gaps" based on race, age, or income; the longevity of television and newspapers; the pros and cons of public journalism; online vs. printed magazines; trends for niche publications; advertising campaigns of the future; and privacy in cyberspace.

acknowledgments

I am very grateful to everyone at Bedford/St. Martin's who supported this project through its many stages. I wish that every textbook author could have the kind of experience I had with these people: Chuck Christensen, Joan Feinberg, Tisha Rossi, Alice Lundoff, and Brian McGrath. I also worked with a superb and supportive developmental editor: Michael Gillespie. Thanks especially to the creativity of Simon Glick, associate developmental editor. I particularly appreciate the tireless work of Jessica Zorn, project editor, who made sure I got the details right, and of Cheryl Mamaril, senior production supervisor.

I also want to thank the many fine and thoughtful reviewers who contributed ideas to the second edition of *Media and Culture*: Susan B. Barnes, Fordham University; Margaret Bates, City College of New York; Steven Alan Carr, Indiana University–Purdue University, Fort Wayne; William G. Covington Jr., Bridgewater State College; Roger Desmond, University of Hartford; Jules d'Hemecourt, Louisiana State University; Cheryl Evans, Northwestern Oklahoma State University; Douglas Gomery, University of Maryland; Colin Gromatzky, New Mexico State University; John L. Hochheimer, Ithaca College; Sheena Malhotra, University of New Mexico; Sharon R. Mazzarella, Ithaca College; David Marc McCoy, Kent State University; Beverly Merrick, New Mexico State University; John Pantalone, University of Rhode Island; John Durham Peters, University of Iowa; Lisa Pieraccini, Oswego State College; Susana Powell, Borough of Manhattan Community College; Felicia Jones Ross, Ohio State University; Enid Sefcovic, Florida Atlantic University; Keith Semmel, Cumberland College; Augusta Simon, Embry-Riddle Aeronautical University; Clifford E. Wexler, Columbia-Greene Community College.

I would also like to thank the reviewers who helped shape the first edition: Paul Ashdown, University of Tennessee; Terry Bales, Rancho Santiago College; Russell Barclay, Southern Methodist University; Thomas Beell, Iowa State University; Fred Blevens, Southwest Texas State University; Stuart Bullion, University of Maine; William G. Covington Jr., Bridgewater State College; Robert Daves, *Minneapolis Star Tribune*; Charles Davis, Georgia Southern University; Thomas Donahue, Virginia Commonwealth University; Ralph R. Donald, University of Tennessee at Martin; John P. Ferre, University of Louisville; Donald Fishman, Boston College; Elizabeth Atwood Gailey, University of Tennessee; Bob Gassaway, University of New Mexico; Anthony Giffard, University of Washington; Zhou He, San Jose State University; Barry Hollander, University of Georgia; Sharon Hollenbeck, Syracuse University; Anita Howard, Austin Community College; James Hoyt, University of Wisconsin at Madison; Joli Jensen, University of Tulsa; Frank Kaplan, University of Colorado; William Knowles, University of Montana; Michael Leslie, University of Florida; Janice Long, University of Cincinnati; Kathleen Maticheck, Normandale Community College; Maclyn McClary, Humboldt State University; Robert McGaughey, Murray State University; Joseph McKerns, Ohio State University; Debra Merskin, University of Oregon; David Morrissey, Colorado State University; Michael Murray, University of Missouri at St. Louis; Susan Dawson O'Brien, Rose State College; Patricia Bowie Orman, University of Southern Colorado; Jim Patton, University of Arizona; John Pauly, St. Louis University; Ted Pease, Utah State University; Janice Peck, University of Colorado; Tina Pieraccini, University of New Mexico; Peter Pringle, University of Tennessee; Sondra Rubenstein, Hofstra University; Jim St. Clair, Indiana University Southeast; Jim Seguin, Robert Morris College; Donald Shaw, University of North Carolina; Martin D. Sommernes, Northern Arizona State University; Linda Steiner, Rutgers University; Jill Diane Swensen, Ithaca College; Sharon Taylor, Delaware

State University; Hazel Warlaumont, California State University at Fullerton; Richard Whitaker, Buffalo State College; Lynn Zoch, University of South Carolina.

There are many other people to thank. When I left high school teaching for graduate work in media studies, I fell in with a number of fine teachers at both the University of Wisconsin–Milwaukee and Northwestern University who helped shape the way I think about many of the issues raised in this book. Thanks in particular to Earl Grow and Leah Vande Berg. I am especially grateful to David Eason and Douglas Gomery, who have kept in touch over the years and whose ideas continue to influence how I think about *Media and Culture*.

I want to also thank my former students at Marquette University, the University of Wisconsin–Milwaukee, Mount Mary College, the University of Michigan, and my current students at MTSU, especially Laurie Woods, who worked as a graduate research assistant on this revision. Some of my former students have contributed directly to this text, and thousands have endured my courses over the years—and made them better. My all-time favorite former students, Chris Martin and Bettina Fabos, have become important contributors to this book. I am forever grateful for their fine writing, research support, and funny phone conversations. Their daughter Olivia was born in the middle of all the revisions.

I am most grateful, though, to the people I most love: my son Chris; my daughter Caitlin; and, most of all, my wife Dianna, whose inspired insights, shared interests, and daily support are constant resources.

CONTENTS

Preface xii

PART I
Mass Media and the Cultural Landscape

chapter 1

mass communication: a critical approach 2

culture and the evolution of mass communication 5
  oral and written communication 6
  printed communication 6
  electronic and digital communication 8

mass media and the process of communication 9
  a linear model of mass communication 10
  an alternative approach to mass communication 11
  the role and impact of the mass media 11

surveying the cultural landscape 13
  culture as a hierarchy 16
  culture as a map 19
    Traveling Back to the Good Old Days • *Familiar Landmarks and
    Unexplored Territory*
  shifting values in modern culture 20
  shifting values in postmodern culture 22

critiquing media and culture 26
  steps in the critical process 27
    Description • *Analysis* • *Interpretation* • *Evaluation*
  benefits of a critical perspective 29

EXAMINING ETHICS Trash, Teens, and TV Talk Shows 14

CASE STUDY The Material Girl as Postmodern Icon 24

THE GLOBAL VILLAGE Bedouins, Camels, Transistors,
and Coke 30

REVIEW QUESTIONS • *QUESTIONING THE MEDIA* • *SEARCHING THE INTERNET* •
THE CRITICAL PROCESS 31

chapter 2

information and new technology: media at the crossroads 34

origins of the information highway 37
the evolution of a new mass medium 38
the birth and growth of the internet 39

information access on the information highway 41
converging media and technology breakthroughs 44
converging media and content 45
mapping the internet 46
The World Wide Web • *Internet Service Providers* • *Browsers* •
Search Engines

ownership issues on the internet 49
a clash of values 50
future control of the internet 50
alternative voices 52

citizens, cyberspace, and democracy 52
free expression and security nightmares 53
competing highways and the knowledge gap 57
problems and possibilities 58

CASE STUDY E-commerce: Sale of the Century? 42

TRACKING TECHNOLOGY WebCams: The Whole World Is Watching 51

EXAMINING ETHICS Regulating the Internet 54

REVIEW QUESTIONS • *QUESTIONING THE MEDIA* • *SEARCHING THE INTERNET* •
THE CRITICAL PROCESS 61

PART II
Sounds and Images

chapter 3

sound recording and popular music 64

early technology and the development of sound recording 67
wax cylinders and flat disks 67
audiotape and cds 68
surviving the threat of radio 70

popular music and the formation of rock 71

the rise of pop music 71

rock and roll: here to stay 72

rock muddies the water 73

    High and Low Culture • *Masculine and Feminine* • *Black and White* • *North and South* • *The Sacred and the Secular*

battles in rock and roll 76

    Cover Music and Race • *Payola, Records, and Radio* • *Taming the Music*

a changing industry: reformations in popular music 81

the british are coming! 81

soul music and motown   82

folk, blues, politics, and drugs 83

    Folk-Rock and Dylan • *Rock's Psychedelic Turn* • *Rock as Mainstream Culture*

alternative sounds of punk and grunge 85

rap redraws musical lines 87

the business of sound recording 88

the major labels 89

independent labels 89

the business of making a recording 90

    Selling a Recording • *Dividing the Profits*

bootlegging 94

alternative voices 95

recordings, free expression, and democracy 95

CASE STUDY Chuck D Got Game 78

THE GLOBAL VILLAGE The International Beat 91

TRACKING TECHNOLOGY MP3 and the Spread of Music 96

REVIEW QUESTIONS • *QUESTIONING THE MEDIA* • *SEARCHING THE INTERNET* • *THE CRITICAL PROCESS 97*

chapter 4

popular radio and the origins of broadcasting 100

the origins and development of broadcasting 102

the underlying technology 103

    Marconi and Wireless Telegraphy • *De Forest and Radio*

early broadcasting regulations 106

the formation of the rca monopoly 106

the evolution of commercial radio 108

dissension in the ranks 108

sarnoff and nbc 109

the end of the rca monopoly 110

paley and cbs 111

the mutual broadcasting system 111
chaos and the radio act of 1927 112
the golden age of radio 112

radio reinvents itself 116

new technologies 117
The Transistor • Armstrong and FM
changes in programming 118
The Rise of Format and Top 40 Radio • Payola

the sounds of radio today 121

the economics of broadcast radio 121
*Commercial Radio and Specialization • Contemporary Music
Formats • Resisting the Top 40*
nonprofit radio 126
alternative voices 128

radio, ownership, and democracy 128

EXAMINING ETHICS NPR and Support for Noncommercial
Radio 113

CASE STUDY The Appeal of Talk Radio 124

TRACKING TECHNOLOGY Pirate Radio with a Digital
Twist 129

*REVIEW QUESTIONS • QUESTIONING THE MEDIA • SEARCHING THE INTERNET •
THE CRITICAL PROCESS 131*

chapter 5

television and the power of visual culture 134

early technology and the development of television 137

the formative years 137
Technical Standards • The TV Freeze
television booms in the fifties 141
The Collapse of Sponsorship • The Quiz-Show Scandals

key programming trends in the tv age 143

tv's information culture 143
*NBC News • CBS News • ABC News • Contemporary Trends in
Network News*
tv's entertainment culture 145
Televised Comedy • Televised Drama

the decline of the network era 152

technological transformations 153
regulating the networks 154
emerging new networks 155

the economics of television 156
    prime-time production 157
        Independent Programs • *Network Programs*
    prime-time distribution 158
    how syndication works 159
        Off-Network and First-Run Syndication • *Hybrid Syndication* •
        Barter vs. Cash
    measuring television by ratings and shares 162
    alternative voices 164

the public, television, and democracy 164
    TRACKING TECHNOLOGY DTV: The Digital Revolution 140
    THE GLOBAL VILLAGE TV and International Syndication 160
    CASE STUDY Anatomy of a TV "Failure" 165
    REVIEW QUESTIONS • *QUESTIONING THE MEDIA* • *SEARCHING THE INTERNET* •
    THE CRITICAL PROCESS 167

chapter 6

cable and the specialization
of television 170

early technology and the development of cable 173
    catv—community antenna television 173
    a threat to broadcasting 174

cable's franchising and regulation wars 175
    franchising frenzy 175
    regulation nightmares and federal cable laws 176
        Common Carrier or Electronic Publisher? • *The Repeal of Syndex Rules* •
        The Cable Acts of 1984 and 1992 • *The Telecommunications Act of 1996*

narrowcasting challenges broadcasting 182
    basic cable 183
        CNN's Window to the World • *"I Want My MTV"*
    premium cable 191
        The HBO Alternative • *Pay-per-View and Interactive Cable* • *Cable Radio*
    direct-broadcast satellites: cable without wires 193

ownership and business issues in cable 195
    at&t and time warner—the major players 195
    the business of cable 197
    alternative voices 197

cable, dbs, and implications for democracy 198
    TRACKING TECHNOLOGY Communication Satellites
    Open Doors to the Future 177

CASE STUDY Ted Turner and Rupert Murdoch: Match of the Media Moguls 186

REVIEW QUESTIONS • QUESTIONING THE MEDIA • SEARCHING THE INTERNET • THE CRITICAL PROCESS 199

chapter 7

movies and the impact of images 202

early technology and the evolution of movies 205
the development of film 205
the power of stories in the silent era 207

the arrival of nickelodeons 207

the power of the studio system 208
controlling production 209
controlling distribution 210
controlling exhibition 211
Movie Palaces • Mid-City Theaters

the triumph of hollywood storytelling 212
the "sound" of movies 212
classic hollywood cinema 213
Hollywood Narratives • Hollywood Genres • Hollywood "Authors"
outside the hollywood system 221
Foreign Films • The Documentary Tradition • The Rise of Independent Films

the transformation of the hollywood system 226
the hollywood ten 226
the paramount decision 227
moving to the suburbs 228
television changes hollywood 228
hollywood adapts to video 229

the economics of the movie business 230
production, distribution, and exhibition today 231
the major players 233
alternative voices 234

popular movies and implications for democracy 235
CASE STUDY Breaking Through Hollywood's Race Barrier 214

THE GLOBAL VILLAGE Beyond Hollywood: Asian Cinema 223

REVIEW QUESTIONS • QUESTIONING THE MEDIA • SEARCHING THE INTERNET • THE CRITICAL PROCESS 235

PART III
Words and Pictures

chapter 8

newspapers and the rise
of modern journalism 238

the evolution of american newspapers 241
colonial newspapers and the partisan press 241
the penny-press era 242
the age of yellow journalism 244
    Pulitzer and the New York World • *Hearst and the* New York Journal

american print journalism in the modern period 246
the advent of modern journalism 246
    Ochs and the New York Times • *"Just the facts, please."*
interpretive journalism 248
    The Limits of Objectivity • *The Press-Radio War*
literary forms of journalism 250
    The Attack on Objectivity • *Journalism as Art*

contemporary journalism 251

categorizing news and u.s. newspapers 253
consensus vs. conflict 253
ethnic, minority, and oppositional newspapers 254
    The Immigrant and Ethnic Press • *African American Newspapers* •
    Spanish-Language Newspapers • *Native American Newspapers* •
    The Underground Press
economic demands vs. editorial duties 257
    Business Operations • *News Responsibilities* • *Wire Services and Feature*
    Syndication

issues of ownership, economics, and technology 259
circulation woes 259
joint operating agreements 260
newspaper chains 262
changes in technology 263
alternative voices 264

newspapers and democracy 266
CASE STUDY The Alternative Journalism of Dorothy Day
and I. F. Stone   260

EXAMINING ETHICS Codes of Conduct for Online Journalism 265

REVIEW QUESTIONS • QUESTIONING THE MEDIA • SEARCHING THE INTERNET • THE CRITICAL PROCESS 267

chapter 9

magazines in the age of specialization 270

the early history of magazines 273
colonial magazines 274
the first u.s. magazines 274
the arrival of national magazines 275
pictorial pioneers 276

the development of modern american magazines 276
social reform and the muckrakers 277
the rise of general-interest magazines 278
Saturday Evening Post • Reader's Digest • Time • Life
the fall of general-interest magazines 282
TV Guide *Is Born* • Life *and* Look *Expire* • People *Puts* Life *Back into* Magazines

the domination of specialization 285
regional editions 286
demographic editions 286
magazine categories and types 287
the fragmented magazine marketplace 289
Leisure, Sport, and Music Magazines • Travel and Geography Magazines • Magazines for the Ages
elite magazines and cultural minorities 292
The New Yorker • *Redefining Cultural Minorities*
supermarket tabloids 294
webzines and media convergence 295

the organization and economics of magazines 296
departments and duties 296
Production and Technology • Editorial Content • Advertising and Sales • Circulation and Distribution
major magazine chains 302
alternative voices 304

magazines in a democratic society 304
CASE STUDY The Evolution of Photojournalism 280
TRACKING TECHNOLOGY The Personal Zine Explosion 297

EXAMINING ETHICS Sex, Lies, and Advertising 300

*REVIEW QUESTIONS • QUESTIONING THE MEDIA • SEARCHING THE INTERNET •
THE CRITICAL PROCESS 305*

chapter 10

books and the power of print 308

the history of books from papyrus to paperbacks 312
  manuscript culture 313
  the gutenberg revolution 313
  book production in the united states 314

modern publishing and the book industry 315
  the formation of publishing houses 315
  types of books 316
    *Trade Books • Professional Books • Textbooks • Mass-Market
    Paperbacks • Religious Books • Reference Books • University-Press Books*

the organization and ownership of the book industry 325
  the structure of book publishing 325
  book clubs and mail order 327
  bookstores 328
  online bookstores 330
  ownership patterns 331

trends in book publishing 332
  influences of television and film 332
  blockbusters and licenses 334
  talking books 335
  book preservation 335
  alternative voices 336

books and the future of democracy 336
CASE STUDY Comic Books: Alternative Themes,
but Superheroes Prevail 318

TRACKING TECHNOLOGY E-books and the Future
of Reading 333

EXAMINING ETHICS Censorship Issues in Book
Publishing 338

*REVIEW QUESTIONS • QUESTIONING THE MEDIA • SEARCHING THE INTERNET •
THE CRITICAL PROCESS 339*

PART IV
The Business of Mass Media

chapter 11

advertising and commercial culture 342

early developments in american advertising 346
the first advertising agencies 346
advertising in the 1800s 347
 Trademarks and Packaging • Patent Medicines and Department Stores
promoting social change and dictating values 350
early ad regulation 351

the shape of american advertising today 351
the influence of visual design 352
the mega-agency 352
the boutique agency 353
the structure of ad agencies 353
 Market Research and VALS • Creative Development • Media
 Selection • Account and Client Management

persuasive techniques in contemporary advertising 359
conventional persuasive strategies 360
the association principle 360
myth analysis 363

commercial speech and regulating advertising 364
critical issues in advertising 365
 Children and Advertising • Advertising in Schools • Health and Advertising
watching over advertisers 369
 Comparative Advertising • Puffery and Deceptive Ads
advertising's threat to journalism 370
advertising and the internet 371

advertising and democracy 372
EXAMINING ETHICS Fighting Over Sneakers 354
CASE STUDY Women, Ads, and Stereotypes 362
THE GLOBAL VILLAGE Smoking Up the Global Market 367

REVIEW QUESTIONS • QUESTIONING THE MEDIA • SEARCHING THE INTERNET •
THE CRITICAL PROCESS 373

chapter 12

public relations and framing the message 376

early developments in public relations 379
p. t. barnum, buffalo bill, and the railroads 380
the modern public relations agent 381
"Poison Ivy" Lee • Edward Bernays
pseudo-events and manufacturing news 384

the practice of public relations 385
approaches to organized pr 385
Independent Agencies • In-House Services
performing public relations 386
*Writing and Editing • Media Relations • Special
Events • Research • Community and Consumer Relations •
Government Relations and Lobbying*

tensions between pr and the press 392
elements of professional friction 393
*Undermining Facts and Blocking Access • Promoting Publicity and
Business as News*
managing the press 395

public relations, social responsibility, and democracy 397
CASE STUDY GM Trucks and NBC's *Dateline* Disaster 391
EXAMINING ETHICS Levi Strauss and Anti-Sweatshop
Public Relations 398

*REVIEW QUESTIONS • QUESTIONING THE MEDIA • SEARCHING THE INTERNET •
THE CRITICAL PROCESS 401*

chapter 13

media economics and the global marketplace 404

analyzing the media economy 407
the structure of media organizations 407
the performance of media organizations 408

the transition to an information economy 410
deregulation trumps regulation 410
consolidation and mergermania 412
flexible markets 412
global markets and specialization 413
disney: a postmodern media conglomerate 416

social issues in media economics 419
the limits of antitrust laws 419
consumer choice vs. consumer control 420
cultural imperialism 421

the media marketplace and democracy 422
CASE STUDY Consumer Ratings and TV Economics 414

REVIEW QUESTIONS • QUESTIONING THE MEDIA • SEARCHING THE INTERNET • THE CRITICAL PROCESS 424

PART V
Democratic Expression and the Mass Media

chapter 14

the culture of journalism: values, ethics, and democracy 426

modern journalism in the information age 428
what is news? 429
neutrality and other values in american journalism 430

ethics and the news media 432
ethical predicaments 433
Deploying Deception • Invading Privacy • Conflict of Interest
resolving ethical problems 436

reporting rituals and the legacy of print journalism 439
focusing on the present 439
Getting a Good Story • Getting a Story First
relying on experts 441
balancing story conflict 444
acting as adversaries 445

journalism in the age of television 445
differences between print and television news 446
Sound Bitten • Pretty-Face and Happy-Talk Culture
visual language and critical limits 448

conventional news, public journalism, and democracy 449
the future of news 449
What Is Public Journalism? • Criticizing Public Journalism
public journalism reimagines reporting's role 454
Social Responsibility • Deliberative Democracy

EXAMINING ETHICS Why Those Hidden Cameras Hurt Journalism 434

CASE STUDY The Case of *60 Minutes* 442

*REVIEW QUESTIONS • QUESTIONING THE MEDIA • SEARCHING THE INTERNET •
THE CRITICAL PROCESS 455*

chapter 15

media effects and cultural approaches to research 458

early developments in media research 460

*Propaganda Analysis • Public-Opinion Research • Social-Psychology
Studies • Marketing Research*

research on media effects 463

key phases in research approaches 464
*Hypodermic-Needle Model • Minimal-Effects Model • Uses and
Gratifications Model*
approaches to media effects 466
Experiments • Surveys • Content Analysis
explaining media effects 470
Agenda-Setting • The Cultivation Effect
evaluating research on media effects 471

cultural approaches to media research 472

cultural studies 473
Textual Analysis • Audience Studies • Political Economy
evaluating cultural approaches 475

media research, ivory towers, and democracy 477

THE GLOBAL VILLAGE Television Promotes Literacy and
Mutes Class Divisions in Brazil 476

CASE STUDY Violence Study Shows Television's Mental
Block 478

*REVIEW QUESTIONS • QUESTIONING THE MEDIA • SEARCHING THE INTERNET •
THE CRITICAL PROCESS 482*

chapter 16

legal controls and freedom of expression 484

the origins of free expression and a free press 487

models for expression and speech 488
censorship as prior restraint 489
The Pentagon Papers Case • The Progressive *Magazine Case*

unprotected forms of expression 491
    Libel • *Defenses against Libel Charges* • *The Right of Privacy* • *Obscenity*
first amendment vs. sixth amendment 499
    Gag Orders and Shield Laws • *Cameras in the Courtroom* • *Curbing the
Law's Chilling Effect*

film and the first amendment 502
social and political pressure on the movies 503
    Film-Review Boards • *Industry Self-Regulation*
the motion-picture production code 504
rating movie content 505

expression over the airwaves 506
fcc rules, broadcasting, and indecency 507
    Print vs. Broadcast Rules • *Dirty Words and Indecent Speech*
political broadcasts and equal opportunity 509
the demise of the fairness doctrine 510

cyberspace, expression, and democracy 511
communication policy in cyberspace 511
watchdog citizens 513

CASE STUDY "Pretty Woman," Rap, and Copyright Law 492

EXAMINING ETHICS How ABC News Covers Disney 514

REVIEW QUESTIONS • *QUESTIONING THE MEDIA* • *SEARCHING THE INTERNET* •
THE CRITICAL PROCESS 515

Notes 519

Glossary 527

Index 539

About the Author 557

MEDIA AND CULTURE

An Introduction to

Mass Communication

Mass Communication

A Critical Approach

On April 20, 1999, Columbine High School in Littleton, Colorado, became part of American history. On that day, heavily armed and outfitted in trench coats, two outcast teenage boys from this Denver suburb attacked their school, planting as many as fifty bombs and killing twelve fellow students and a respected teacher. Cornered by SWAT teams, the two boys—one an eighteen-year-old who had recently been rejected by the Marines and the other a seventeen-year-old college-bound senior—killed themselves in the high school library. The sad event was the worst school-related student killing spree in our nation's history.

In the aftermath of the tragedy, we tried to make sense of senselessness. We looked for explanations. We looked for clues to violent teen behavior. We looked to blame—and there was plenty to go around. Some of us blamed the parents for not recognizing their sons' anger and alienation. Some blamed the school system for failing to address the concerns and pathologies of its marginalized students. Some blamed traditional teen cliques that help make outcasts of their peers. Some blamed the boys' possible connection to the "Trench Coat Mafia"—a group of paranoid teen outsiders who apparently hated Christians, Jews, blacks, and athletes. Some blamed lax gun-control laws that allowed eighteen-year-olds to buy assault weapons as easily as they buy baseball cards. (A major 1996 study has pointed out that the overall gun-related death rate for U.S. children under age fifteen is twelve times higher than the combined rate of twenty-five other advanced and affluent nations.)

And a lot of people blamed the mass media and our popular culture—fraught with images that can desensitize individuals to the consequences of violence—for their role in the Colorado catastrophe. The media even blamed the media, wildly speculating that the killers immersed themselves in the black-clad Goth culture and the dark lyrics of shock rocker Marilyn Manson (who cancelled several shows immediately after the tragedy). Other media and critics pointed to violent video and computer games such as Doom, a game actually being used by the military to train soldiers to kill. Still others looked to the influence of films like *The Basketball Diaries*, in which a drugged-out, trench-coated teenager (played by Leonardo DiCaprio) imagines shooting a teacher and his classmates. And still others pointed to the boys' interest in the Internet as their source for bomb-making information and their outlet for the hate speech they directed at those they despised. (In fact, the two boys were part of a group that controlled the school's official Web site, and if adults had monitored the site more closely they may have been able to confront earlier the anger and hatred that consumed these young killers.)

In the weeks and months following the tragedy, the causes and effects of this complex event continued to spark conversations about our nation's major social problems. Many suggestions for solving them surfaced and continue to emerge. These have included holding parents more accountable legally for their children's behavior, devising task forces that identify teens in trouble, and making it more difficult for young people to buy guns. Some critics called on schools to devote more attention to issues of character, giving young students more responsibility as citizens who help to solve a community's problems. On the media front, critics and politicians once again encouraged the business moguls who run entertainment empires to curb products that glorify death and violence.

So what exactly are the media's role and responsibility in tragedies like Littleton? How do we demand higher standards from our mass media and popular culture? In this book, we take up such questions. Clearly, the mayhem in Colorado resulted from a number of tangled forces—some explainable, some inexplicable. Mass media certainly played several roles—as manufacturers of youth culture, as reporters of tragic events, as intruders into families' private grief, and as definers of how we think about social issues. Even as the tragedy unfolded, local TV news anchors spoke on air to terrified students using their cell phones—students trapped in classrooms who could have accidentally given away their hidden locations to the killers watching television coverage on school monitors.

At their worst, the media's appetite for telling and selling stories leads them not only to document tragedy, but also to capitalize on it. While it is important and legitimate to cover events like the Littleton shooting, many social critics are uneasy with the way our culture seems to hurtle from one media circus to another, devouring the next big event to fill the news vacuum. Network and cable television immediately packaged the high school shooting as "Terror in the Rockies" or "Lessons from Littleton." When such a newsworthy event occurs, the media intensely focus our attention upon the event, saturating the airwaves with 24-hour coverage, live updates, and specially chosen theme music. Just as quickly, the media seem to disappear as soon as the sound bites or images become less compelling.

In this book, we examine media as a central force in shaping our culture and democracy. We investigate issues such as the media coverage of Littleton to see ways the mass media fail us as well as the ways they succeed. After all, they have an impact beyond telling tragic stories or influencing troubled teenagers. The media—in all their various forms, from mainstream newspapers to radio talk shows to Internet chat rooms—tried to help bring understanding to this national event that affected all of us that early spring day in 1999. At their best, our media reflect and sustain the values and traditions of a vital democracy. They not only engage and entertain diverse audiences, but they also watch over society's institutions, making sense of its important events and chronicling the ebb and flow of daily life.

The growth of media industries, commercial culture, and new technologies— fiber-optic cable, computers, televisions, satellites—offers a challenge to all of us. If we can learn to examine and critique the powerful dynamics of the media, we will be better able to monitor the rapid changes going on around us. In the chapters that follow, we will investigate the history and structure of media's major institutions. In the process, we will develop an informed and critical view of the multiple impacts these institutions have had on community and global life. Our goal is to become not only more critical as consumers of mass media but also more engaged as citizens who accept responsibility for the shape and direction of media culture.

culture and the evolution of mass communication

One way to understand the role and impact of the media in our lives is to understand the cultural context in which the media operate. Often, culture is symbolically spelled with a capital *C* and is associated with *art*, the unique forms of representational expression that give pleasure and raise awareness about what is true, good, and beautiful. Culture, however, can also begin with a small *c*. According to this view, culture is a broad category that identifies the ways in which people live and represent themselves at particular historical times. This idea of culture encompasses fashion, sports, architecture, education, religion, and science, as well as mass media. Although we can study permanent cultural forms, such as novels or songs from various historical periods, culture is always changing. It includes a society's art, beliefs, customs, games, technologies, traditions, and institutions. It also encompasses a society's modes of **communication**: the process of creating symbol systems that convey information and meaning (for example, language systems, Morse code, film, or computer codes).

Culture is made up of both the *products* that a society fashions and, perhaps more important, the *processes* that forge those products and reflect a culture's diverse values. Thus, **culture** may be defined as the symbols of expression that individuals, groups, and societies use to make sense of daily life and to articulate their values. According to this definition, when we listen to music, read a book, or watch television, we are not asking "Is this art?" but are instead trying to identify or connect with something or someone. In other words, we are assigning meaning to the song, book, or TV program. Culture, therefore, is a process that delivers the values of a society through products or other meaning-making forms. For instance, the American ideal of rugged individualism has been depicted for decades through a tradition of book, movie, and television westerns and detective stories.

> "The important thing to keep in mind is that tragedies like [Littleton] are caused by a constellation of factors, and the first place to look for explanations is a child's home and family life, the quality of parenting they've received, the types of friendships they've formed. But, that said, the media [is] one very strong catalyst for pushing marginal kids over the edge." —Gary Edgerton, media scholar, 1999

Culture embodies a society's values, and the mass media help distribute those values. We may say, then, that the **mass media** are the cultural industries—the channels of communication—that produce and distribute songs, novels, newspapers, movies, online computer services, and other cultural products to large numbers of people. The historical development of media and communication can be traced through several overlapping eras in which newer forms of technology and knowledge disrupted and modified older forms. These eras, which still affect society, are *oral, written, print, electronic,* and *digital.* The first two eras refer to the primary communication of tribal or feudal communities and agricultural economies. The last three phases feature the development of **mass communication**: the process of designing and delivering cultural messages and stories to large and diverse audiences through media channels as old as the book and as new as the Internet. Hastened by the growth of industry and modern technology, mass communication accompanied the gradual shift of rural populations to urban settings and the rise of a consumer culture.

oral and written communication

In most early societies, information and knowledge first circulated slowly through oral traditions passed on by poets, teachers, and tribal storytellers. As alphabets and the written word developed, however, a manuscript culture began to complement and then overshadow oral communication. Documented and transcribed by philosophers, monks, and stenographers, the manuscript culture served the ruling classes. Working people were generally illiterate, and the gap between peasants and rulers was vast. These eras of oral and written communication occurred over many centuries. Although exact time frames are disputed, historians generally consider these eras to be a part of civilization's premodern period, spanning the epoch from 1000 B.C. to the mid-fifteenth century.

Early tensions between oral and written communication played out among ancient Greek philosophers and writers. Socrates (470–399 B.C.), for instance, made his arguments through public conversations and debates. This dialogue style of communication became known as the *Socratic method,* and it is still used in university law schools and college classrooms. Many philosophers who supported the superiority of oral tradition feared that the written word would threaten public discussion by offering fewer opportunities for the give and take of conversation. In fact, Socrates' most famous student, Plato (427–347 B.C.), sought to banish poets, whom he saw as purveyors of thoughts less rigorous than those generated in oral, face-to-face, question-and-answer discussions. These debates foreshadowed similar discussions in the twentieth century regarding the dangers of television and the Internet. Do contemporary technologies, such as TV talk shows and anonymous online chat rooms, cheapen public discussions and prevent us from forming face-to-face associations and talking to one another more personally?

printed communication

The invention of the printing press and movable metallic type in the fifteenth century provided the industrial seed that spawned modern mass communication. From the time of Johannes Gutenberg's invention, it took about four hundred years for the print era to evolve and to eclipse oral and written traditions.

The printing press, among its many contributions, introduced a method for mass production. Presses and publications spread rapidly across Europe in the late 1400s and

Probably the most revolutionary development in media history, the printing press and the mass production of books paved the way for both a consumer market and the democratic spread of knowledge. This page from the Psalter, or Book of Psalms (*left*), was printed by Gutenberg's partner, Johann Fust, in 1457. Beside it is a re-creation of a plate that could have been used to print it.

early 1500s. Many early books were large, elaborate, and expensive, taking months to illustrate and publish. They were usually purchased by wealthy aristocrats, royal families, church leaders, and prominent merchants and politicians. Gradually, however, printers reduced the size and cost of books, making them available to more people.

With the print revolution, the book became the first mass-marketed product in history. The printing press combined three elements necessary for this innovation. First, duplication, or copying, replaced the tedious manuscript system in which scribes hand-copied a text several times to produce multiple copies. Second, duplication could be done rapidly, producing mass quantities of the same book. Third, the faster processing of multiple copies brought down the cost of each unit, making books more affordable to less affluent people. These three basic innovations would provide the impetus for the Industrial Revolution, assembly-line production, modern capitalism, and the rise of consumer culture in the twentieth century.

The printing press also paved the way for major social and cultural changes by transmitting knowledge across national boundaries. Mass-produced printed materials spread information faster and farther than ever before, extending communication outside the realm of isolated community life. Such widespread information ushered in the concept of nationalism, allowing people to think of themselves not merely as members of families or tribes but as part of a country whose interests were broader than local or regional concerns.

With the revolution in industry came the rise of the middle class and an elite business class of owners and managers who gained the kind of clout once held only by the nobility or the clergy. Whereas oral and writing societies featured decentralized local governments, the print era marked the ascent of more centralized nation-states. As print media lessened the role of oral and manuscript communication, they also became key tools for commercial and political leaders to distribute information and maintain social order.

As with the Internet today, however, it was difficult for a single business leader or political party in democratic societies to gain total control over books and technology (although the king did control printing-press licenses in early-nineteenth-century England). Instead, the mass publication of pamphlets, newspapers, magazines, and books helped to spread and democratize knowledge. Literacy rates rose among the working and middle classes as publications of all sorts became affordable. Industrialization required a more educated workforce, but printed literature and textbooks also encouraged compulsory education, thus extending learning beyond the world of wealthy upper-class citizens.

Just as the printing press fostered nationalism, it also nourished the competing ideal of individualism, which would become a fundamental value in American society in the nineteenth and twentieth centuries. With all sorts of ideas and treatises available, people came to rely less on their local community and their commercial, religious, and political leaders for guidance. By challenging tribal life, the printing press "fostered the modern idea of individuality," disrupting "the medieval sense of community and integration."[1] In urban and industrial environments, many individuals became severed from the traditions of rural life, which had encouraged community cooperation in premodern times.

By the mid-nineteenth century, the ideal of individualism had permeated the rise of commerce and increased resistance to government interference in the affairs of self-reliant entrepreneurs. The democratic impulse of individualism also undermined religious authority. Printers and writers circulated views counter to traditional doctrine. Ultimately, the printing press and the wide distribution of knowledge facilitated large social movements, including the Protestant Reformation and the Industrial Revolution.

electronic and digital communication

In Europe and America, the impact of industry's rise was enormous: Factories replaced farms as the main centers of work and production. During the 1880s, roughly 80 percent of Americans lived on farms and in small towns; by the 1920s and 1930s, most of this population had shifted to urban areas, where new industries and economic opportunities beckoned. The city had overtaken the country as the focus of national life. A relatively stable rural existence gave way to urban and suburban lifestyles that were more unsettled, mobile, and diverse.

"We are in great haste to construct a magnetic telegraph from Maine to Texas; but Maine and Texas, it may be, have nothing important to communicate. . . . We are eager to tunnel under the Atlantic and bring the old world some weeks nearer to the new; but perchance the first news that will leak through into the broad flapping American ear will be that Princess Adelaide has the whooping cough."
—Henry David Thoreau, *Walden*, 1854

In America, the gradual transformation from an industrial, print-based society to an informational era began with the arrival of the telegraph in the 1840s. The telegraph made four key contributions to communication. First, it separated communication from transportation, making media messages instantaneous—unencumbered by stagecoaches, ships, or the pony express.[2] Second, the telegraph, in combination with the rise of newspapers, transformed "information into a commodity, a 'thing' that could be bought or sold irrespective of its uses or meaning."[3] By the time of the Civil War, news had become a valuable product, foreshadowing its contemporary role as a phenomenon that is both enormously profitable and nearly unavoidable. Third, the telegraph made it easier for military, business, and political leaders to coordinate commercial and military operations, especially after the installation of the transatlantic cable in the late 1860s. Finally, the telegraph was an omen of future technological developments, such as the fax machine and the cellular phone. Although modern telegraphy marked the full-blown arrival of the print era, it also planted the earliest seeds for even faster forms of electronic and digital communication to develop.

The rise of film at the turn of the century and the development of radio in the 1920s were early signposts, but the electronic phase of the Information Age really began in the 1950s and 1960s. The dramatic impact of television on daily life, beginning in the 1950s, marked the arrival of a new visual and electronic era. With the coming of the latest communication gadgetry—ever smaller personal computers, cable television, direct-broadcast satellites, cellular phones, beepers, faxes, and electronic mail (email)—the Information Age passed into a digital phase. *Electronic* innovations, for instance, included hand-cranked and later rotary-dial telephones, whereas *digital* innovations brought Touch-Tone technology. In digital communication, images, texts, and sounds are converted (encoded) into electronic signals (represented as varied combinations of binary numbers—ones and zeros), which are then reassembled (decoded) as a precise reproduction of a TV picture, a magazine article, a CD recording, or a telephone voice. On the Internet's various World Wide Web pages, image, text, and sound are all digitally reproduced and transmitted globally.

New electronic and digital technologies, particularly cable television and the Internet, have developed so quickly that traditional leaders in communication have lost some of their control over information. For example, network news lost a portion of its influence and audience in the 1992 and 1996 presidential election to CNN's Larry King, the Comedy Channel, MTV, radio talk shows, and various Internet newsgroups and chat lines. The technology of email, which has assumed some of the functions of the postal service, is outpacing attempts to control it within national borders. A professor sitting at her desk in Murfreesboro, Tennessee, can instantly send a message to a research scientist in Warsaw, Poland, who can now respond without fear of government agents opening his mail. As recently as 1990, written letters between the two might have taken months to reach their destinations.

mass media and the process of communication

As far back as 1935, the Lindbergh baby kidnap-murder trial raised concerns about electronic news and the impact of the media. In the 1990s, the mass media reported the sordid sagas of the British royal family, the mysterious Unabomber, and President Clinton and Monica Lewinsky. Of course, for impact, nothing approached the criminal trial of former football star O.J. Simpson. With its universal theme of the fallen sports hero, the case drew an enormous amount of media attention, including gavel-to-gavel coverage on CNN and Court TV.

Although often labeled and discussed disparagingly as "the media," mass communication institutions are not a single entity. The mass media constitute a wide variety of industries and merchandise, from documentary news programs about tragic famines in Africa to infomercials about personal hygiene products. The word *media* is, after all, a Latin plural form for the singular noun *medium*. Although television, newspapers, music, movies, magazines, books, billboards, direct mail, broadcast satellites, and the Internet are all part of the media, they remain largely discrete segments, each quite capable of producing worthy products as well as pandering to society's worst desires, prejudices, and stereotypes.

Painting all media with the same broad brush is not only inaccurate but also reflects the distrustful view that many people hold toward prominent social institutions, from local governments to daily newspapers. Of course, when our president has

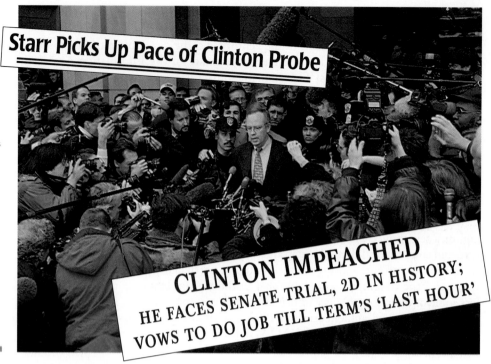

The center of intense media attention in 1998, independent counsel Kenneth Starr headed an unprecedented $40–$60 million investigation of President Clinton. What started as an inquiry into the president's alleged involvement in an Arkansas land-fraud deal eventually led to the discovery of the president's affair with Monica Lewinsky. Starr's investigation and its fallout—impeachment of President Clinton by the House of Representatives and the ensuing Senate trial, which resulted in acquittal—preoccupied the media and the nation throughout 1998.

Starr Picks Up Pace of Clinton Probe

CLINTON IMPEACHED
HE FACES SENATE TRIAL, 2D IN HISTORY; VOWS TO DO JOB TILL TERM'S 'LAST HOUR'

an extramarital affair with a young intern—and the story saturates the media—our distrust is understandable. In this book, we will attempt to replace a sometimes misdirected and cynical perception of the media with an attitude of genuine criticism.

a linear model of mass communication

To develop an interpretive or critical perspective toward the media, we need insight into how the mass-communication process works. One of the most influential ideas about the way media work is depicted in the linear model of communication. In this model, mass communication is conceptualized as the process of producing and delivering messages to large audiences. According to the linear model, mass communication is a component system, made up of **senders** (the authors, producers, agencies, and organizations) who transmit **messages** (the programs, texts, images, sounds, and advertisements). Through a mass-media **channel** (newspapers, books, magazines, radio, television, or the Internet), senders pitch their messages to large groups of **receivers** (readers, viewers, citizens, and consumers). In the process, **gatekeepers**, such as editors, producers, and other media managers, function as message filters. Media gatekeepers make decisions about what messages actually get produced for particular audiences. The process occasionally allows **feedback**, in which citizens and consumers return messages to senders or gatekeepers through letters to the editor, phone calls, email, Web-site postings, or as audience members of talk shows.

Although the linear model explains certain aspects of the communication process, media messages usually do not flow smoothly from a sender at point A to a receiver at point Z. Like fish in turbulent water, words and images are in flux, spilling into each other and crisscrossing in the flow of daily use. Media messages are encoded and sent in written and visual forms, but senders often have very little control over how their messages are decoded, or whether the messages are ignored by readers and viewers.

an alternative approach
to mass communication

Moving beyond a simple sender-message-receiver model, it is important to recognize that individuals and societies bring diverse meanings to cultural messages because of factors such as gender, age, educational level, ethnicity, and occupation. For instance, when the rapper Ice-T's heavy-metal group Body Count produced the song "Cop Killer" in the early 1990s, police organizations and urban teens interpreted the lyrics in dramatically different ways. Some police groups wanted to ban the song, arguing that it would lead to violence, while fans of the band asserted that the song correctly portrayed the power of police authority in urban America.

It is sometimes easy to assume that producers of media messages are the active creators of communication and that audiences are merely passive receptacles. This may describe some situations, but as the "Cop Killer" example illustrates, audiences also shape and bend media messages to fit their own values and viewpoints. This phenomenon is known as *selective exposure:* Audiences seek messages and produce meanings that correspond to their beliefs and values. Thus, in the process of mass communication, audiences are actively interpreting, refashioning, or rejecting messages that flow through various media channels.

At its most significant level, the mass-communication process can alter a society's perception of events and attitudes. Throughout the twentieth century, for instance, courageous print journalists covered world wars and other armed conflicts, helping the public to comprehend the magnitude and tragedy of such events. In the 1950s and 1960s, television news reports on the civil-rights movement led to crucial legislation that transformed the way many white people viewed the problems and aspirations of African Americans. In the early 1990s, the televised testimony of Anita Hill at the Clarence Thomas Senate-confirmation hearings placed the usually private issue of sexual harassment on the larger public agenda. In the mid-1990s, the best media coverage in the aftermath of the first Simpson trial stirred public discussion regarding both legal reform and domestic abuse. And in the late 1990s, the Clinton-Lewinsky affair and the Starr report sparked heated debates over private codes of behavior and public abuses of authority. In each of these instances, the mass media played a key role in changing awareness, attitudes, and even policy.

the role and impact
of the mass media

Concerns about popular forms of culture have often upset the status quo and led to periodic public outcries. At the turn of the century, newly arrived immigrants who spoke little English gravitated toward cultural events (such as boxing, vaudeville, and the new medium of silent film) whose enjoyment did not depend solely on understanding the English language. Consequently, these popular events occasionally became a flash point for many groups, including the Daughters of the American Revolution, local politicians, religious leaders, and police vice squads, who not only resented the commercial success of immigrant culture but feared that these "low" cultural forms would undermine traditional American values.

Debates about culture and media are not new. The earliest discussions date from the ancient Greeks. Socrates, himself accused of corrupting youths, worried that children exposed to stories "without distinction" would "take into their souls teachings that are wholly opposite to those we wish them to be possessed of when they are grown up."[4] The playwright Euripides, on the other hand, believed that art should

In the 1950s, television images of early civil-rights struggles, which visually documented the inequalities faced by black citizens, had a profound effect on the United States. In 1957, the governor of Arkansas refused to allow black students like Elizabeth Eckford *(left foreground)* to enter Little Rock's Central High School, even though segregation had been outlawed by the Supreme Court in 1954. In response, President Dwight Eisenhower sent in the army to integrate the school and control angry white mobs.

imitate life, that characters should be real, and that artistic works should reflect the actual world even when that reality was sordid.

In *The Republic*, Plato developed the classical view of art: It should aim to instruct and uplift. He worried that some staged performances glorified evil and that common folk watching might not be able to distinguish between art and reality. Aristotle, Plato's student, occupied a middle ground in these debates, arguing that art should provide insight into the human condition but should entertain as well.

Since the early Greeks, concerns about the impact of culture have continued. In the United States in the 1950s, the emergence of television and rock and roll generated countless points of contention. For instance, the phenomenal popularity of Elvis Presley set the stage for many of today's debates over rap lyrics and television's negative influence. In 1956 and 1957, Presley made three appearances on the *Ed Sullivan Show*. The public outcry against Presley's "lascivious" hip movements was so great that by the third show camera operators were instructed to shoot the singer from the waist up. Thousands of protective parents refused to allow their children to watch Presley's performances. In some communities, objections to Presley were motivated by class bias and racism. Many white adults believed that this "poor white trash" singer from Mississippi was spreading rhythm and blues, a "dangerous" form of black popular culture.

Today, the stakes are even higher. Given the reach and spread of print, electronic, and digital communication, culture and its myriad mutations play an even more controversial role in society. People used to share their common interests in radio or TV characters and major news stories in backyard, barroom, and coffee-shop conversations, but the proliferation of specialized publications and personalized channels has fragmented the media audience. Many citizens have become critical of the lack of quality in so much contemporary culture and are concerned about the overwhelming amount of information now available. Even the computer, once heralded as the educational salvation for children, has created confusion. When kids announce that they are "on the computer," parents may wonder whether they are writing a term paper, playing a video game, talking to a cyberspace pen pal, shopping for sneakers, or downloading pornography.

In recent years, it has become common for political candidates to question and attack various forms of the mass media for their negative impact. In 1992, for example, Vice President Dan Quayle denounced the "family values" portrayed on a *Murphy Brown* episode, which championed single motherhood. In 1995, presidential candidate Bob Dole condemned media conglomerate Time Warner for its partial ownership of a controversial rap-music label. Congress got into the act in 1996, an election year, by rewriting the nation's telecommunications laws. These laws require all TV manufacturers to equip sets with the V-chip, a technology that allows adults to block inappropriate TV programs from the view of children.

By the mid-1990s, the mass media had given the public much to be concerned about. Talk shows exploited personal problems for commercial gain (see "Examining Ethics: Trash, Teens, and TV Talk Shows" on page 14). Television research once again documented the connection between aggression in children and violent entertainment programs. Children watched nearly forty thousand TV commercials each year. Debates also raged about curbing kids' exposure to pornography and adult subject matter on the Internet. Yet, although media depictions may worsen social problems, research has seldom demonstrated that they directly *cause* our society's major afflictions. For instance, when a young middle-school student kills a fellow student over a pair of basketball shoes, should society blame the ads that glamorized the shoes and the network that carried the ad? Or are parents, teachers, and religious leaders failing to instill strong moral values? Or are economic and social issues involving gun legislation, consumerism, and income disparity at work here as well? While the shoe manufacturer bears responsibility as a corporate citizen, did the ad itself cause the tragedy, or is the ad symptomatic of larger problems?

> "Skyscrapers were citadels of the new power of finance capitalism. . . . Far above the thronging sidewalks, they elevated the men who controlled much of the capital that lubricated the workings of organized cultural enterprises— publishing companies, film studios, theatrical syndicates, symphony orchestras. Culture . . . was becoming increasingly organized during the twentieth century. And the model for that organization was the hierarchical, bureaucratic corporation."
> —Jackson Lears, historian

With American mass-media industries earning $200 billion annually, the economic stakes are high. Large portions of media resources now go into studying audiences, capturing their attention, and taking their consumer dollars. This process involves trying to influence everything from how people vote to how they relax and how they shop. Like the air we breathe, the fallout from the mass media surrounds us. But to monitor the media's "air quality," a responsible citizenry must attend to diverse media messages that are too often taken for granted.

surveying the cultural landscape

Some cultural phenomena gain wide popular appeal, and others do not. Some appeal to certain age groups or social classes; some, such as rock and roll, jazz, and classical music, are popular worldwide. Other cultural forms, such as Tejano, salsa, or Cajun music, are popular only in certain regions or communities. Some aspects of culture are considered elite in one place (opera in the United States) and popular in another (opera in Italy). Throughout history, however, most societies have arranged culture into hierarchical categories.

Jerry Springer Show

"LOVING" YOU IS TORTURE!"

In 1998, the *Jerry Springer Show*, according to Nielsen rating statistics, passed *Oprah* as the most-watched daytime TV talk show. For some critics, this omen signaled the end of civilization as we know it. For many, Springer—a former TV news anchor and once the mayor of Cincinnati—had become a symbol of the worst aspects of American popular culture. Edited outtakes from his show—too racy or explicit for television—are now marketed as semi-pornographic videos. The *Springer* show, which debuted in 1991, has routinely encouraged fighting among family members and groups of former friends. At its worst, Springer's program exploits personal problems and pathologies for commercial gain and public spectacle. But as low as Springer has sunk, the record low point for daytime TV programming strategy is probably held by another program.

In March 1995, the *Jenny Jones Show* taped a program in Chicago about secret admirers. One participant, Scott Amedure, who identified himself as gay, revealed his affections for another guest, Jonathan Schmitz, a heterosexual. Humiliated by the revelation, Schmitz returned to Michigan, bought a shotgun, and three days later killed Amedure. Although the program never aired, the story intensified public concern over talk shows, which were already under attack for exploiting sexual topics and ambushing gullible guests.

As a result, some local TV stations dropped the most offensive programs, and large advertisers such as Philip Morris and Proctor & Gamble reduced their advertising sup-

14

port. Meanwhile, the *Jenny Jones Show* disavowed legal responsibility, claiming that guests had been told their admirers might be of either sex. In 1996, after doctors and his family documented Schmitz's precarious psychological history, he was convicted of second-degree murder; Amedure's family immediately filed a $25 million civil suit against the *Jenny Jones Show*, arguing that the program's producers did a poor job of screening its guests. The family won their suit but the appeal by the program's lawyers was still working its way through the courts in 1999. Meanwhile, Schmitz's psychiatrist was negotiating a movie deal and writing a book about the case.

Although this incident was tragic and atypical, such talk-show topics and tactics have become standard daytime fare, especially on *Springer*. These practices raise serious ethical questions. Complicating any discussion of ethics, however, are the competing values that govern how talk shows handle topics and guests. Most media organizations have ethical codes that guide how professionals should behave in different situations. But beyond self-regulatory codes, how can consumers criticize and shape the ethics of media institutions?

Arriving at ethical decisions is a particular kind of criticism involving several steps. These include (1) laying out the case; (2) pinpointing the key issues; (3) identifying the parties involved, their intent, and their competing values; (4) studying ethical models and theories; (5) presenting strategies and options; and (6) formulating a decision or policy.[1] As a test case, we will look at the topic of teenagers, sex, and talk shows. Our goal will be to make some ethical decisions and to lay the groundwork for a policy that programs might implement

TALK TV'S TOP SHOWS

Jerry Springer (Universal TV)
Oprah Winfrey (Kingworld)
Judge Judy (Universal TV)
Jenny Jones (Warner Bros. TV)
Sally Jessy Raphael (Universal TV)
Ricki Lake (Columbia TriStar)
Montel Williams (Paramount)
Rosie O'Donnell (Universal TV)

Source: Nielsen Syndication Service

regarding suitable subject matter and the treatment of guests. We will follow the six steps just mentioned. (See Chapter 14, pages 436–38, for details on solving ethical problems.)

Examining Ethics Activity: As a class or in smaller groups, design a policy to guide talk shows on topics involving teens and sex. Start by researching the topic; find as much information as possible. For example, you might want to examine the guidelines from other talk shows.

Do they provide appropriate counseling for guests, and what form does the counseling take? Indicate whether the ethics policy should be government mandated or an industrywide guideline. Finally, send the policy to various talk shows; ask for their evaluations and whether they would consider implementing it.

Talk Show Titles

- Honey, I have a secret.
- Housewives vs. Strippers
- Should parents do time for their kids' crimes?
- Low-life Teenagers
- My teen can't go without sex.
- Irresponsible Teen Moms
- My daughter looks like a slut!
- My mom is a slut.
- Mother ran off with her daughter's fiancé.
- You're too old to be dating a teen.

culture as a hierarchy

In twentieth-century America, critics and audiences have established a hierarchy of culture. At the top is what is frequently labeled **high culture**, such as ballet, the symphony, art museums, and classical literature. At the bottom of the ladder is popular or **low culture**, such as soap operas, rock and rap music, talk radio, comic books, and monster truck pulls (see Figure 1.1). High culture, which stands for "good taste" and is often supported by wealthy patrons and corporate donors, has become associated with "fine art," which is available primarily in libraries, theaters, or museums. In contrast, low or popular culture has become aligned with the questionable tastes of the "masses," who enjoy the commercial "junk" circulated by the mass media. Whether or not we agree with this cultural ladder, the high-low hierarchy has become entrenched, often determining or limiting the ways culture is discussed today.[5]

Some critics are concerned that popular culture in the form of contemporary movies, television, and rock music distracts students from serious literature and philosophy, thus ruining their imagination and undermining their ability to recognize good art.[6] Discounting a person's ability to value Aristotle and Aerosmith concurrently, this critical view pits popular culture against the more traditional forms of high art and culture. The assumption is that because popular forms of culture are made for profit, they cannot be experienced with the same personal intensity as more elite art forms.

Another concern is that popular culture exploits classic works of literature and art. The best example may be Mary Wollstonecraft Shelley's dark Gothic novel *Frankenstein*, written in 1818 and ultimately transformed into multiple popular

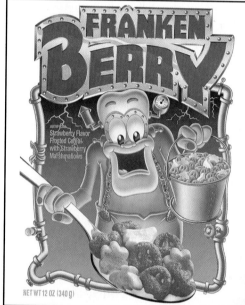

Today, Mary Shelley, the author of *Frankenstein*, might not recognize popular culture's mutations of her Gothic classic. First published in 1818, the novel has inspired more than twenty-five film adaptations and sparked the creation of everything from the 1960s sitcom *The Munsters* to a sugar-coated cereal.

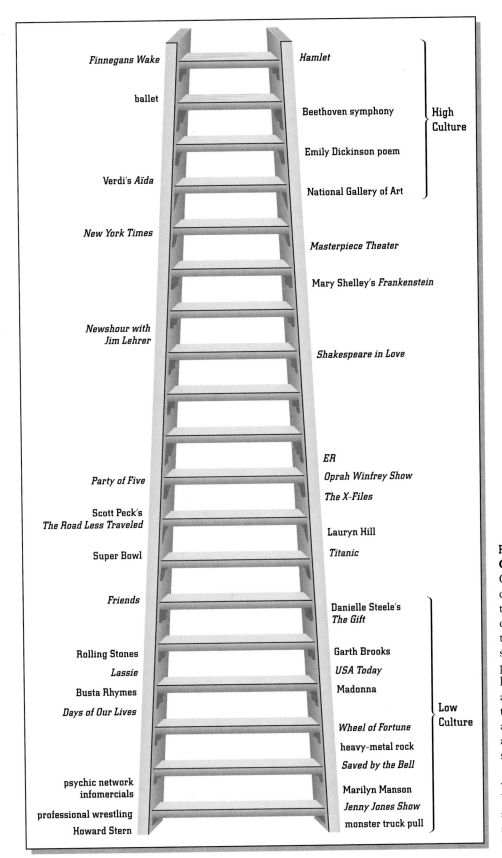

Finnegans Wake

Hamlet

ballet

Beethoven symphony

Emily Dickinson poem

High
Culture

Verdi's *Aïda*

National Gallery of Art

New York Times

Masterpiece Theater

Mary Shelley's *Frankenstein*

*Newshour with
Jim Lehrer*

Shakespeare in Love

ER

Oprah Winfrey Show

Party of Five

The X-Files

Scott Peck's
The Road Less Traveled

Lauryn Hill

Super Bowl

Titanic

Friends

Danielle Steele's
The Gift

Rolling Stones

Garth Brooks

Lassie

USA Today

Busta Rhymes

Madonna

Days of Our Lives

Wheel of Fortune

Low
Culture

heavy-metal rock

Saved by the Bell

psychic network
infomercials

Marilyn Manson

Jenny Jones Show

professional wrestling

monster truck pull

Howard Stern

Figure 1.1
Culture as a Hierarchy
Culture is diverse and difficult to categorize. Yet throughout the twentieth century we have tended to think of culture not as a social process but as a set of products sorted into high, low, or middle positions on a cultural ladder. Look at this highly arbitrary arrangement and see if you agree or disagree. Write in some of your own examples.

Why do so many people view culture this way? What are the strengths and limitations of thinking about culture in these terms?

"OH, WE NEVER WATCH TELEVISION, WE'RE PSEUDOINTELLECTUALS."

forms. Today, the tale is best remembered by virtue of a 1931 film version starring Boris Karloff as the towering monster. In addition to the movies, television turned the tale into *The Munsters*, a mid-1960s situation comedy. Eventually, the monster was resurrected as sugar-coated Frankenberry cereal. In the recycled forms of the original story, Shelley's themes about abusing modern science and judging people based on appearances are often lost or trivialized.

Unlike an Italian opera or a Shakespearean tragedy, many elements of mass culture have a short life span. The average newspaper circulates for about twelve hours, then lands in a recycle bin or at the bottom of a bird cage; the average magazine circulates for about five to seven days; a Top 40 hit on the radio lasts about one month; and the average TV series survives for less than ten weeks. Although endurance does not necessarily denote quality, in the view of many critics, better forms of culture have staying power. These critics argue that popular forms promote a culture that is unstable and fleeting, that they follow rather than lead public taste. In the television industry, this is known as "least objectionable programming," or LOP: Network gatekeepers pander to mediocrity by putting on bland, disposable programming that will not disturb or challenge a typical viewer.

A final concern of critics is that popular culture not only undermines or exploits high culture but has inundated the cultural environment, driving out higher forms of culture and cheapening public life.[7] This concern is supported by data showing that TV sets are in use in the average American home for more than seven hours a day, exposing adults and children each year to thousands of hours of TV commercials and popular culture. According to the critics, the prevalence of media products prevents the public from experiencing genuine art. Forty or more radio stations are available in most cities; cable systems with at least seventy-two channels are in place in nearly 70 percent of all U.S. households; and CD players, computer online services, VCRs, and DVD players are increasing in popularity. Thus, the chance of more refined culture transforming the media environment or even finding a substantial audience has become unlikely.

There is also concern that the impact of popular culture, especially its visual forms, has undermined democratic reasoning. According to this view, popular media may inhibit social progress by transforming audiences into cultural dupes, seduced by the promise of products. A few multinational conglomerates, which make large profits from media products, may be distracting citizens from examining economic disparity and implementing change. Seductive advertising images contradict the actual lives of many people, who cannot afford the products offered in the marketplace. In this environment, art and commerce have become blurred, damaging the audience's power to make cultural distinctions. Sometimes called the "Big Mac" theory, this view suggests that people are so addicted to popular media fare that they have lost not only the will to challenge social inequities but also their discriminating taste for finer things.

culture as a map

To depict culture as an ongoing process and to account for individuality, it is helpful to imagine culture as a map. Maps represent large, unwieldy spaces that spread out in all directions. Maps highlight main highways and familiar urban centers, but they also include scores of side roads and small towns, diverting our focus to unexplored areas.

A map model of culture demonstrates that, on the one hand, cultural phenomena may seem conventional, recognizable, stable, and comforting. On the other hand, they may tend toward the innovative, unfamiliar, unstable, and challenging. Most forms of culture, however, demonstrate both of these tendencies. For example, we may buy the CD of a favorite artist for its innovation *and* familiarity. We may listen to a particular song to complement a mood, to distance ourselves from problems, or to reflect critically on the song's lyrics.

We know that people have complex cultural tastes, needs, and interests based on their particular backgrounds. It is not surprising, then, that our cultural forms—from blues music and opera to comic books and classical literature—contain a variety of messages. Just as Shakespeare's plays were packed with both obscure and popular references, TV episodes of *The Simpsons* today include allusions to the Beatles, Kafka, the *Adventures of Ozzie & Harriet*, Tennessee Williams, talk shows, and *Citizen Kane*. In other words, cultural products and their meanings are "all over the map," suggesting that, in spite of many critics' tendencies to rank culture vertically, we should not think about our cultural environment merely as a product hierarchy.

> "TV is a genre of reruns, a formulaic return to what we already know. Everything is familiar. Ads and old programs are constantly recycled. It's like mythology, like the Homeric epics, the oral tradition, in which the listener hears passages, formulae, and epithets repeated over and over again. There is a joy in repetition, as children know when they say, 'Mommy, tell me that story again.' "
>
> —Camille Paglia,
> *Harper's*, 1991

Traveling Back to the Good Old Days. Some critics of popular culture assume that society was better off before the latest developments in mass media. They resist the idea of redrawing established cultural maps. The nostalgia for some imagined "better past" has often operated as a device for condemning new cultural phenomena. In the nineteenth century, in fact, a number of intellectuals and politicians worried that rising literacy rates among the working class might create havoc. How would the aristocracy maintain its authority and status if others could read? Throughout history, a call to return to familiar terrain, to "the good old days," has been a frequent response to new, "threatening" forms of popular culture, which over the years have included the waltz, silent movies, jazz, comic books, rock and roll, soap operas, rap music, and tabloid newspapers.

Familiar Landmarks and Unexplored Territory. The appeal of culture is often its ring of familiarity, pulling audiences toward the security of repetition and common landmarks. Consider, for instance, television's *Lassie* series. More than five hundred episodes now exist in syndication; many had a familiar and repetitive plot line: Timmy, who arguably possessed the poorest sense of direction and suffered more concussions than any TV character in history, gets lost or knocked unconscious. After finding Timmy and licking his face, Lassie goes for help and saves the day. Adult critics might mock this melodramatic formula, but many children find comfort in the predictability of the story. This quality is also illustrated when night after night children ask their parents to read Margaret Wise Brown's *Good Night, Moon*. Like children, adults also seek a kind of comfort, often returning to the same songs, the same plays, the same poems, and the same television programs.

On the other hand, we also seek the new—aspects of culture that demonstrate originality and complexity. For instance, James Joyce's *Finnegans Wake* (1939) created language anew and challenged readers, as the novel's poetic first sentence illustrates: "riverrun, past Eve and Adam's, from swerve of shore to bend of bay, brings us by commodius vicus of recirculation back to Howth Castle and Environs." A revolutionary work, crammed with historical names and topical references to events, myths, songs, jokes, and daily conversation, Joyce's novel remains a challenge to decode.

shifting values in modern culture

In contemporary life, cultural boundaries are being tested; the lines between information and entertainment have blurred. Consumers now read newspapers on their computer screens. Media corporations do business across vast geographic boundaries. We are witnessing *media convergence* wherein satellite dishes, TV screens, and computer modems easily access new and old forms of mass communication. For a fee, everything from magazines to movies is channeled into homes through computer modems and TV cables. To place these shifts and convergences in historical context, scholars have traced the meandering route of cultural values through the *modern* period (from the full-blown arrival of the Industrial Revolution in the nineteenth century) to one that is frequently labeled *postmodern*, or contemporary.

What it means to be *modern* is complicated. As we have seen, the process of modernization involved individuals and societies responding to changing economic circumstances. Captains of industry employed workforces and new technology, creating efficient manufacturing centers and inexpensive products aimed at making everyday life better and more profitable. Printing presses and assembly lines made major contributions in this transformation, and modern advertising spread the word about new gadgets to American consumers.

Cultural responses to modernization often manifest themselves in the mass media. For example, Aldous Huxley, in *Brave New World* (1932), created a fictional world in which he cautioned readers that modern science and technology posed a threat to individual dignity. Charlie Chaplin's film *Modern Times* (1936), set in a futuristic manufacturing plant, also told the story of the dehumanizing impact of modernization and machinery. Writers and artists, in their criticisms of the modern world, often point to technology's ability to alienate us from one another, capitalism's tendency to foster greed and consumerism, and government's inclination to create bureaucracies that oppress rather than help people. Among the major values of the modern period, four have manifested themselves frequently in the cultural environment: *celebrating the individual, believing in rational order, working efficiently*, and *rejecting tradition*.

These values of the modern period were originally embodied in the printing press and later in newspapers and magazines. The print media encouraged the vision

In the 1936 film *Modern Times*, director Charlie Chaplin satirized modern industry and confronted the dehumanizing aspects of a futuristic manufacturing plant. In the 1980s, IBM produced a television commercial using the character of Chaplin's Little Tramp to tout the intimacy of the company's latest line of personal computers.

of individual writers, publishers, and readers who circulated new ideas. Whereas the premodern period was guided by strong beliefs in a natural or divine order, becoming modern meant elevating individual self-expression to a central position. Along with democratic breakthroughs, however, individualism and the Industrial Revolution triggered modern forms of hierarchy, in which certain individuals and groups achieved higher standing in the social order. For example, those who managed commercial enterprises gained more control over the economic ladder, but an intellectual class of experts, who mastered specialized realms of knowledge, gained increasing power over the nation's social, political, and cultural agendas.

To be modern meant to value the capacity of organized, scientific minds to solve problems efficiently. Progressive thinkers maintained that the printing press, the telegraph, and the railroad in combination with a scientific attitude would foster a new type of informed society. At the core of this society, the printed mass media, particularly newspapers, would educate the citizenry, helping to build and maintain an organized social framework.[8] Journalists strove for the modern ideal through a more objective approach to reporting. They discarded ornate or decorative writing and championed a lean and neutral look. The modern style of front-page news de-emphasized descriptive detail, humor, commentary, and historical context. The lead sentences that reported a presidential press conference began to look similar, whether they were on the front page in Atlanta, Georgia, or Zap, North Dakota. Just as modern architecture made many American skylines look alike, the front pages of newspapers began to resemble one another (see Figure 1.2).

Finally, to be modern meant to throw off the rigid mores of the past, to break with tradition. Modern journalism became captivated by timely and immediate events. As a result, the more standardized forms of front-page journalism, which championed facts and current events, often failed to analyze sufficiently the ideas underlying these events.

Figure 1.2
**Premodern vs.
Modern News**

These two stories, separated by 161 years, illustrate some differences between premodern and modern news. The 1834 story includes asides, humor, and opinion by the writer; the 1995 story seems objective, stripped of any direct evidence of the reporter's viewpoint. The 1834 story is more dramatic in its description of the crime; the 1995 story focuses on facts—who, what, when, where—revealing that even specific ages and the exact address of the motel are important. The 1834 story treats the crime irreverently; the 1995 story treats the crime seriously. What are the pros and cons of each style? What attitudes toward the victims are represented by the different styles of reporting?

NEW YORK SUN

VOLUME II.   NEW YORK, JULY 4, 1834   NUMBER 23.

POLICE OFFICE

Patrick Ludwick was sent up by his wife, who testified that she had supported him for several years in idleness and drunkenness. Abandoning all hopes of a reformation in her husband, she bought him a suit of clothes a fortnight ago and told him to go about his business, for she would not live with him any longer. Last night he came home in a state of intoxication, broke into his wife's bedroom, pulled her out of bed, pulled her hair, and stamped on her. She called a watchman and sent him up. Pat exerted all his powers of eloquence in endeavoring to excite his wife's sympathy, but to no purpose. As every sensible woman ought to do who is cursed with a drunken husband, she refused to have anything to do with him hereafter—and he was sent to the penitentiary.

ANN ARBOR NEWS POLICE BEAT

November 19, 1995

Ann Arbor police expect to arraign on Monday an Allen Park man who is accused of assaulting his female companion in a local hotel room early Friday morning after she refused to have sex with him.

The 48-year-old man was arrested Saturday in Allen Park by police there, Ann Arbor police said Saturday. The 33-year-old woman, who lives in Wyandotte, told investigators that the man struck her in the head with a bottle and punched her when she would not consent to sex.

Employees at the Ramada Inn Ann Arbor, 3750 Washtenaw Ave., said the man and woman checked in around 2 a.m. Friday.

shifting values in postmodern culture

For many, the changes occurring in contemporary, or postmodern, society are identified only by a confusing array of examples: remote controls, Nike ads, shopping malls, fax machines, David Letterman, South Park, *USA Today*, car phones, MTV, hip-hop, and Madonna (see "Case Study: The Material Girl as Postmodern Icon" on page 24). Some critics argue that postmodern culture represents a way of seeing—a condition (or malady) of the human spirit. Chiefly a response to the modern world, controversial postmodern values are playing increasingly pivotal roles in our daily lives. Four values, in particular, have surfaced in the so-called postmodern period: *opposing hierarchy, diversifying and recycling culture, questioning scientific reasoning,* and *embracing paradox* (see Table 1.1).

One of the main values of contemporary culture is an opposition to hierarchy. Many are challenging the sometimes arbitrary line between high and low culture, while others are blurring the distinctions between fact and fiction or art and commerce. For example, a new television vocabulary now includes *docudrama* (NBC's 1999 two-part

TABLE 1.1
Trends across Historical Periods*

	Premodern (roughly pre-1800s)	Modern (roughly post-1800s)	Postmodern (since 1950s)
Range of work hierarchies	peasants/merchants/rulers	factory workers/managers/national CEOs	temp workers/managers/global CEOs
Major work sites	field/farm	factory/office	office/home/"virtual" or mobile office
Communication reach	local	national	global
Communication transmission	oral/manuscript	print/electronic	electronic/digital
Communication channels	storytellers/elders/town criers	books/newspapers/magazines/radio/television	television/cable/Internet/multimedia
Communication at home	quill pen	typewriter/computer	personal computer or laptop computer

* The examples in this table identify some of the significant trends in the premodern, modern, and postmodern periods of society.

Source: For a slightly different view, see Charles Jencks, "The Three Eras of Civilization," in *What Is Post-Modernism?* 3rd ed. (New York: St. Martin's Press, 1989), 47.

miniseries *The 60s*), *infotainment* (*Entertainment Tonight*), and *infomercials* (fading celebrities selling everything from cosmetics to psychic connections). In magazines, arresting clothing or cigarette ads sometimes combine stark social commentaries with low-key sales pitches. At the movies, the fusion of comedy and tragedy in *Pulp Fiction* (1994) or *Fargo* (1996) is representative of the postmodern style.

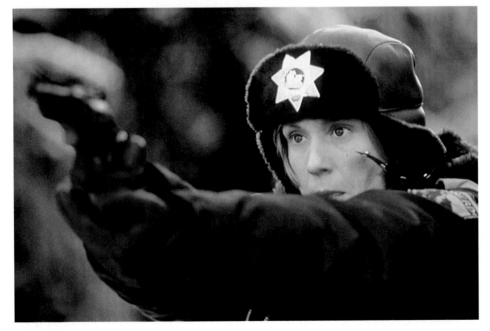

Cited as an example of postmodernism for fusing silly and macabre themes, the independent film *Fargo* became a surprise hit in 1996. The movie won a best-actress Oscar for Frances McDormand, pictured here playing the heroic and very pregnant Minnesota sheriff who tracks down two bad guys. The film was produced by Joel Coen and directed by Ethan Coen, and the brothers won an Oscar for their original screenplay.

The Material Girl as Postmodern Icon

poseur?

feminist?

savvy business woman?

in control?

Whether you think she is a genius or a crass self-promoter, a savvy feminist business woman or a tasteless poseur, it is impossible to deny that Madonna has cultural and commercial staying power. In 1998, the same year she turned forty, the singer's single "Ray of Light" became her fortieth Top 40 hit in the United States. By 1999, only the Beatles and Elvis Presley outranked her for accumulating Top 40 hit recordings during the rock era. Between 1984 and 1994, eleven of Madonna's singles reached No. 1 on the charts (the Beatles had 20 No. 1 hits between 1964 and 1970; Presley scored 18 No. 1 hits between 1956 and 1969). Madonna's *Ray of Light* album has sold more than three million copies and brought her three more Grammy Awards in March 1999, the first she had ever won for best song and best album.

Born the daughter of devout Catholics in Bay City, Michigan, in 1958, Madonna Louise Ciccone has arguably commanded more international attention than any cultural figure since the Beatles. Since the Vatican condemned her 1990 *Blonde Ambition* world tour and an early 1990s release sold "only" two million copies, critics have been writing her

obituary as a pop superstar. However, the parade of Letterman and Leno jokes and the academic treatises that have been trying to uncover her meaning suggest that she remains a controversial symbol for both positive and negative aspects of postmodern culture.

In 1989, Pepsi-Cola withdrew an expensive two-minute TV ad starring Madonna on the day after her controversial "Like a Prayer" music video premiered on MTV. Almost immediately after its release, Italy banned the video when a Catholic group threatened court action. The same song, used as background in the commercial, netted $5 million of Pepsi's money for Madonna. The video tells a fairly conventional story of a woman who sees a white man commit a crime while an innocent black man takes the rap. As an eyewitness, Madonna's character comes forward to tell the truth. Beyond the basic plot, however, the video blurs the border between the sacred and the secular, between religious fervor and sexual energy. When various groups protested the video and its use of Christian symbols (burning crosses and Madonna kissing a black saintlike figure), Pepsi decided to withdraw the ad. Although the ad used none of the footage from the music video, Pepsi feared the negative publicity and potential boycotts.

Over the years, such boundary blurring has been Madonna's hallmark. She has been, in her words, "pushing buttons" to provoke cultural disputes since her 1984 single "Like a Virgin" became the year's biggest pop hit. In 1990, a sexually explicit video, "Justify My Love," was banned by MTV. The video tested the borders between heterosexuality and homosexuality and again mixed religious symbols with sexual images. Later, Madonna appeared on *Nightline* to defend herself and to promote the independent release of the banned video. *Nightline* slyly decided to air the video and drew one of its largest audiences ever.

genius?

tasteless?

crass self-promoter?

working mother?

Although Madonna's personal conduct has been heavily criticized, her defenders argue that she has become one of the premier entrepreneurs in a media world where men have historically called the shots. She has also contributed to social causes, and she appeared in voter-education promotions for MTV in the early 1990s, which helped register millions of young voters (although Madonna herself was not registered).

Critics chide her for her imitativeness. Perhaps no one has been assailed more often than Madonna for not being original. One writer criticized her for continually imitating old movie icons, "inventing herself as a mutable being, a container for a multiplicity of images."[1]

Other critics argue that there's more than photocopying going on in Madonna's work. Although her music videos deliberately recall pop culture goddesses from Greta Garbo to Marilyn Monroe, Madonna reinvents them with a contemporary spin. Unlike the original icon, for instance, the Monroe of Madonna's 1985 "Material Girl" coquettishly rejects her wealthy suitors at will. During a *Saturday Night Live* appearance in 1993, Madonna appeared in a "Wayne's World" skit to make fun of her own music and image.

Madonna has continually split the feminist and critical community. Some assess her as a no-talent master of self-promotion, who perpetuates the stereotype of women as sex objects and "boy toys." Culture critic and Madonna fan Camille Paglia believes that many feminists are simply threatened by Madonna's overt celebration of eroticism: "Madonna is a true feminist. . . . [She] has taught young women to be fully female and sexual while still exercising total control of their lives."[2]

Another media critic, Michael McWilliams, makes a different case. He says that Madonna is despised because her fans are not the conventional adults and mainstream critics who condemn her: "What [the mainstream] never understood about Madonna was her thrill in role playing—changes in hair color, costumes, body tones, complete images—in much the same way that her greatest fans [gays, blacks, kids, and teens] have had to role play in order to survive."[3]

One of the strongest critiques of Madonna comes from African American scholar bell hooks, who has written about the postmodern paradox of the singer's cultural image in "Madonna: Plantation Mistress or Soul Sister?" Hooks admires Madonna for "creating a cultural space where she can invent and reinvent herself and receive public affirmation and material reward."[4] Yet hooks notes that Madonna's many personas often subordinate the black and gay characters she uses in her white-girl-makes-good dramas, perpetuating conventional hierarchies. In *Truth or Dare*, the film documenting her 1990 concert tour, Madonna surrounded herself with what she described as "emotional cripples" (mostly racial minorities, gay men, and other members of oppressed groups) so that she could fulfill her need "to be a mother."

Now Madonna is over forty and a real mother; in 1996 she gave birth to a daughter, Lourdes, after one of the most publicized pregnancies in media history. After the birth of her child, Madonna continues to reinvent herself as she explores her spirituality through eastern religions and the Cabala, a form of Jewish mysticism. She has also stayed on the cutting edge of trends musical, economic, and iconic; in 1999 she contributed a single to the hit soundtrack for *Austin Powers: The Spy who Shagged Me*, recorded a duet with latin music superstar Ricky Martin, and continued her film acting career. In the end, contradictions surround Madonna: Her music seems to champion oppressed groups at the same time that it has made her wealthy and a global icon for consumer culture.

Another contemporary value (or vice) of the so-called postmodern era emphasizes diversity and fragmentation, including the wild juxtaposition of old and new cultural styles. In a suburban shopping mall, for instance, Waldenbooks and Gap clothes border a Vietnamese, Italian, and Mexican food court, while a Muzak version of the Beatles' "Revolution" plays in the background. Part of this stylistic diversity involves borrowing and then transforming earlier ideas from the modern period. In music, rap deejays and performers like Puff Daddy sample old R&B, soul, and rock classics to reinvent songs. Borrowing in rap is often so pronounced that the original artists and record companies have frequently filed for copyright infringement. Critics of postmodern style contend that it borrows too heavily and devalues originality, emphasizing surface over depth and recycled ideas over new ones. Throughout the twentieth century, for example, films have been adapted from books and short stories. Now, films often derive from popular TV series: *The Brady Bunch*, *The Fugitive*, *Beavis and Butt-head*, *X-Files: The Movie*, *Mission Impossible*, and *The Mask of Zorro*, to name just a few. To capitalize on and keep pace with TV's large audience, other media often promote the copy over the original.

Another tendency of postmodern culture is to raise doubts about scientific reasoning. Rather than seeing science purely as enlightened thinking, postmodernists view it as laying the groundwork for modern bureaucratic problems. They reject rational thought as "the answer" to every social problem, lauding instead the premodern values of small communities. Internet users, for example, are seen as reclaiming in electronic form lost conversational skills and letter-writing habits. Even the current popularity of radio and TV talk shows, according to this view, is partly an attempt to recover lost aspects of oral traditions. Given the feelings of powerlessness and alienation that mark the contemporary age, one attraction of the talk-show format has been the way it encourages ordinary people to participate in discussions with celebrities and experts.

Although some forms of contemporary culture raise questions about rational science, other postmodern cultural forms warmly embrace technology. Blockbuster films such as *Jurassic Park* and *Titanic* do both, doubting modern science but depending on technological wizardry for their execution. During the modern period, art and literature frequently criticized the potential dangers of machines. The postmodern style, however, does not seem as critical of new technologies. For example, MTV offers its popular *Unplugged* program, which spurns electronic sounds for rock music's acoustic heritage, but also serves up high-tech wizardry in its music videos and in such programs as *Celebrity Deathmatch*.

Many forms of contemporary culture generally accept technology. There is, however, a fundamental paradox in this uneasy postmodern alliance. As modern writers and artists have pointed out, new technologies often eliminate jobs and physically isolate us from one another. Conversely, new technologies can draw people together to discuss politics on radio talk shows, electronic town-hall meetings or Internet newsgroups. Our lives today are full of such incongruities.

critiquing media and culture

Just as communication is not always reducible to the linear sender-message-receiver model, many forms of media and culture are not easily represented by the high-low metaphor. We should, perhaps, strip culture of such adjectives as *high*, *low*, *popular*, and *mass*. These modifiers may artificially force media forms into predetermined categories.

Instead of focusing on these labels, we should be looking at a wide range of issues generated by culture, from the role of storytelling in the mass media to the global influences of media industries on consumer culture. We should also be moving toward a critical perspective that takes into account the intricacies of the cultural landscape.

A fair critique of any cultural form requires a working knowledge of the particular book, poem, program, or music under scrutiny. For example, to understand W. E. B. Du Bois's essays, critics immerse themselves in his work and in the historical context in which he wrote. Similarly, if we want to develop a meaningful critique of *The Simpsons* or *South Park*, it is essential to understand the contemporary context in which both programs are produced. The critical process helps us grasp why particular writers or programs have a distinctive influence on culture.

To begin this process of critical assessment, we must imagine culture as more complicated and richer than the high-low model allows. We must also assume a critical stance that enables us to get outside our own preferences. We may like or dislike Ricky Martin's Latin rhythms, Chuck D's political rap, or Marilyn Manson's Goth rock, but if we want to criticize this music intelligently, we should understand what various types of music have to say and why their messages have appeal for particular audiences. The same approach applies to other cultural forms. If we critique a newspaper article, we must account for the language that is chosen and what it means; if we analyze a film or TV program, we need to slow down the images in order to understand what they mean.

steps in the critical process

It is easy to form a cynical view of the stream of advertising, talk shows, rock stars, and tabloids that flood the cultural landscape. But cynicism is no substitute for solid criticism. Our goal is to strike a balance between taking a *critical* position (developing knowledgeable interpretations and judgments) and becoming *tolerant* of diverse forms of expression (appreciating the distinctive variety of cultural products and processes). A cynical view usually involves some form of intolerance and either too little or too much information. For example, after enduring the glut of news coverage devoted to President Clinton and Monica Lewinsky in 1998 and 1999, we might easily have become cynical about our political system. However, *information* in the form of news facts and *knowledge* about a complex social process such as an impeachment trial are

Calvin and Hobbes   by Bill Watterson

not the same thing. The critical process stresses the subtle distinctions between amassing information and becoming knowledgeable.

Developing a critical perspective involves mastering four overlapping stages that build on each other:

- *Description:* paying close attention, taking notes, and researching the subject under scrutiny

- *Analysis:* discovering and focusing on significant patterns that emerge from the description stage

- *Interpretation:* asking and answering the "What does that mean?" and "So what?" questions about one's findings

- *Evaluation:* arriving at a judgment about whether something is good, bad, or mediocre, which involves subordinating one's personal taste to the critical assessment resulting from the first three stages

Let us look at each of these stages in greater detail.

Description. If we decide to focus on how well the news media serve democracy, we might critique the fairness of several programs or stories from *60 Minutes* or the *New York Times*. We start by describing the programs or articles, accounting for their reporting strategies, and noting what persons are featured as interview subjects. We might further identify central characters, conflicts, topics, and themes. From the notes taken at this stage, we can begin comparing what we have found to other stories on similar topics. We can also document what we think is missing from these accounts—the questions, viewpoints, and persons that were not included—and other ways to tell the story.

Analysis. In the second stage of the critical process, we isolate *patterns* that call for closer attention. At this point, we decide how to focus the critique. Since *60 Minutes* has produced thousands of hours of programs, our critique might spotlight just a few key patterns. For example, many of the program's reports are organized like detective stories, reporters are almost always visually represented at a medium distance, and interview subjects are generally shot in tight close-ups. In studying the *New York Times*, on the other hand, we might limit our analysis to countries that get covered more regularly than others, recurring topics chosen for front-page treatment, or the number of quotes from the same set of experts.

Interpretation. In the interpretive stage, we try to determine the *meanings* of the patterns we have analyzed. The most difficult stage in criticism, interpretation demands an answer to the "So what?" question. For instance, the visual space granted *60 Minutes* reporters—compared with the close-up shots used for interview subjects—might mean that the reporters appear to be in control. They are given more visual space in which to operate, while interview subjects have little room to maneuver within the visual frame. As a result, the subjects often look guilty, and the reporters look heroic—or, at least, in charge. If we look again at the *New York Times*, its attention to particular countries might mean that the paper tends to cover nations in which the United States has more vital economic interests, even though the *Times* might claim to be neutral in its reporting of international news.

Evaluation. The fourth stage of the critical process focuses on making an informed judgment. Building on description, analysis, and interpretation, we are better able to evaluate the fairness of a group of *60 Minutes* or *New York Times* reports. At this stage, we can grasp the strengths and weaknesses of the news media under study and make critical judgments measured against our own frames of reference—what we like and dislike as well as what seems good or bad about the topics we analyzed.

This fourth stage differentiates the reviewer (or *previewer*) from the critic. Most newspaper reviews, for example, are dictated by daily time constraints and space limits. Although these reviews may give us important information about particular programs, they often begin and end with personal judgments—"This is a quality show" or "That was a piece of trash"—which should be the final stage in any substantial critical process. Regrettably, most reviews do not reflect such a process; they do not move much beyond the writer's own frame of reference.

benefits of a critical perspective

Developing an informed critical perspective allows us to participate in a debate about media culture as a force for *both* democracy and consumerism. On the one hand, the media can be an impetus for democratic tendencies. Consider the role of television in documenting racism and injustice in the 1960s; the use of video technology to reveal oppressive conditions in China and Eastern Europe or to document crimes by urban police departments; and the appearance of political rap music, as black-produced commerce drawing attention to social injustice. The media have also helped to renew interest in diverse cultures around the world (see "The Global Village: Bedouins, Camels, Transistors, and Coke" on page 30).

On the other hand, competing against these democratic tendencies is a powerful commercial culture that reinforces a world economic order controlled by fewer and fewer multinational corporations. For instance, when Poland threw off the shackles of the Soviet Union in the late 1980s, one of the first things its new leaders did was buy and dub the American soap operas *Santa Barbara* and *Dynasty*. For some Poles, these shows were a relief from sober Soviet political propaganda, but other Poles worried that their country had inherited another kind of indoctrination, starring American consumer culture.

This example illustrates that contemporary culture cannot easily be characterized as one thing or another. Binary terms such as *liberal* and *conservative* or *high* and *low* have less meaning in an environment where so many boundaries have been blurred, so many media forms have converged, and so many diverse cultures exist. Modern distinctions between print and electronic culture have begun to break down largely because of the increasing number of individuals who have come of age in *both* a print *and* an electronic culture.[9] Either/or models of culture, such as the high-low view, are making room for more inclusive models, similar to the map metaphor for culture discussed earlier.

What are the social implications of the new, blended, and merging cultural phenomena? How do we deal with the fact that public debate and news about everyday life now seem as likely to come from Oprah, Larry King, or popular music, as from the *New York Times, Nightline,* or *Newsweek?*[10] Clearly, such changes challenge us to reassess and rebuild the standards by which we judge our culture. The search for answers lies in recognizing the significant links between cultural expression and daily life. The search also involves monitoring how well the mass media serve democratic practices and involve a rich variety of people, not just as consumers but also as citizens.

Democracy requires the active participation of interested citizens. Part of this involvement means watching over the role and impact of the mass media, a job that belongs to each citizen, not just to paid media critics. In this textbook, we will begin the job by examining the historical contexts and current processes that shape media

"A **cynic** is a man who, when he smells flowers, looks around for a coffin."
—H. L. Mencken

THE GLOBAL VILLAGE

Bedouins, Camels, Transistors, and Coke

Upon receiving the Philadelphia Liberty Medal in 1994, President Václav Havel of the Czech Republic described postmodernism as the fundamental condition of global culture, "when it seems that something is on the way out and something else is painfully being born." He described this "new world order" as a "multicultural era" or state in which consistent value systems break into mixed and blended cultures:

> For me, a symbol of that state is a Bedouin mounted on a camel and clad in traditional robes under which he is wearing jeans, with a transistor radio in his hands and an ad for Coca-Cola on the camel's back. . . . New meaning is gradually born from the . . . intersection of many different elements.[1]

Many critics, including Havel, think that there is a crucial tie between global politics and postmodern culture. They contend that the people who overthrew the former Yugoslavia and the Soviet Union were the same people who valued American popular culture—especially movies, rock music, and television—for its free expression and democratic possibilities.

As modern communist states were undermined by the growth and influence of transnational corporations, citizens in these nations capitalized on the developing global market, using portable video and audio technology to smuggle out tapes of atrocities perpetrated by totalitarian regimes. Thus it was difficult for political leaders to hide repressive acts from the rest of the world. In *Newsweek*, CBS news anchor Dan Rather wrote about the role of television in the 1989 student uprising in China:

Television brought Beijing's battle for democracy to Main Street. It made students who live on the other side of the planet just as human, just as vulnerable as the boy on the next block. The miracle of television is that the triumph and tragedy of Tiananmen Square would not have been any more vivid had it been Times Square.[2]

At the same time, we need to examine the impact on other nations of the influx of popular culture—the second-biggest American export (after military and airplane equipment). Has access to an American consumer lifestyle fundamentally altered Havel's Bedouin on the camel? What happens when CNN or MTV is transported to remote African villages that share a single community TV set? These questions still need answers. A global village, which through technology shares culture and communication, can also alter traditional rituals forever.

To try to grasp this phenomenon, we might imagine how we would feel if the culture from a country far away gradually eroded our established habits. This, in fact, is happening all over the world as American culture becomes the world's global currency. Although newer forms of communication such as email have in some ways increased citizen participation in global life, in what ways have they muted the values of older cultures? Our current postmodern period is double-coded: It is an agent both for the renewed possibilities of democracy and for the worldwide spread of consumerism and American popular culture.

CNN's Larry King made his mark on cable television by interviewing politicians and celebrities. But many journalists resented King's role in the 1992 presidential elections, especially when the Texas business tycoon Ross Perot used his appearances with King to bypass the conventional news media and launch his third-party candidacy. King's cable power had diminished by 1998, however, as CNN's ratings dropped in the face of new 24-hour cable-news imitators.

products. By probing various media industries, we can then develop a framework for tracking the ways in which media industries perform. By becoming more critical consumers and engaged citizens, we will be in a better position to influence the relationships among mass media, democratic participation, and the cultural landscape that we inhabit.

REVIEW QUESTIONS

Culture and the Evolution of Mass Communication

1. Define *culture, mass communication,* and *mass media,* and explain their interrelationships.

2. What does it mean to spell and define culture with a small *c* or with a capital *C?*

3. What are the key technological breakthroughs that accompanied the transition to the print and electronic eras? Why were these technologies significant?

Mass Media and the Process of Mass Communication

4. Explain the linear model of mass communication and its limitations.

5. In looking at the history of popular culture, explain why newer forms of media seem to threaten status quo values?

Surveying the Cultural Landscape

6. Describe the hierarchical model of culture. What are its strengths and limitations?

7. Describe the map model of culture. What are its strengths and limitations?

8. What are the chief differences between modern and so-called postmodern values?

Critiquing Media and Culture

9. What are the four steps in the critical process? Which of these is the most difficult and why?

10. What is the difference between cynicism and criticism?

11. Why is the critical process important?

31

QUESTIONING THE MEDIA

1. Using music or television as an example, identify a performer or program you once liked but began to dislike as you grew older. Your tastes changed. Why did this happen?

2. From your own experience, cite examples in which you think the media have been treated unfairly. Draw on comments from parents, teachers, religious leaders, friends, news media, etc. Discuss whether these criticisms have been justified.

3. Pick an example of a popular media product that you think is harmful to children. How would you make your concerns known? Should the product be removed from circulation? Why or why not? If you think the product should be banned, how would you do it?

4. Make a critical case either defending or condemning Comedy Central's *South Park*, a TV talk show, professional wrestling, a rap group, or a soap opera. Use the four-step critical process to develop your position.

5. Although in some ways postmodern forms of communication, such as email, MTV, and CNN, have helped citizens participate in global life, in what ways might these forms harm more traditional or native cultures?

SEARCHING THE INTERNET

http://www.mediahistory.com
The Media History Project was founded to discover and understand trends in practices in various media. You'll find information about media research and theory, historical time lines, and links to related sites.

http://library.advanced.org/10455/
Established by two teens in Holland, the Mass Media and Global Communications site offers general information and statistics about the media as well as suggestions about how to think critically about the role media plays in our lives.

http://interact.uoregon.edu/MediaLit/HomePage
The Media Literacy Online Project is a comprehensive media-literacy resource that encourages an informed and critical understanding of the media.

http://danenet.wicip.org/ntc/
This site is the online version of *Telemedium*, a scholarly journal that studies issues related to media literacy.

THE CRITICAL PROCESS

In Brief

Develop another model or metaphor for categorizing culture, other than the ladder or map models offered on pages 16–20. How would your model help us to better understand the ways in which culture works? Discuss your model with classmates.

In Depth

In small groups, or as a class, write the headings *quality* and *trash* on the board or on a sheet of paper. As a group, agree on one or two television shows that serve as examples of trashy programs and quality programs. In another column, if necessary, place any programs that are in dispute—those that may divide group opinion. (Films, books, magazines, and advertisements could be used here as well.) Your column headings should look like this:

Quality   *Trash*   *In Dispute*

1. For each set of programs, gather ammunition and evidence. On a separate piece of paper, *describe* the programs by listing their narrative features: basic plots, central conflicts or tensions, typical subject matter, major themes, main characters, and how tensions are resolved.

2. Now return to your listing of programs. Under each category, name and *analyze* the attributes that led your group to classify the programs as you did. Identify as many characteristics as you can and then summarize which virtues are essential to a quality show, which vices make a show trashy, and which elements make a particular show hard to classify.

3. Examine the patterns among the characteristics you have chosen, and *interpret* what this means. Why did you pick the characteristics you did for each category? Why did you associate particular features with quality or with trash? What made your disputed programs a problem for different members of your group? Why do some viewers (or readers) gravitate toward trashy shows? What might the programs mean to those audiences? For the programs you could not easily categorize, what led to their disputed standing?

4. *Evaluate* the progams on your lists. Assess whether these shows are good or bad for society. Should restrictions be placed on some programs even if this means testing the First Amendment protection of the press and free speech?

   Discuss the differences that were evident in your group between individual tastes and the critical standards used to make judgments. Are more categories needed to evaluate programs adequately? If so, what categories should be added?

   What standards did your group use to judge merit? Why is it important to make critical judgments of this kind?

Information and New Technology
Media at the Crossroads

"Intelligent Island"—it's not a spin-off of an old television program but a real place. "Intelligent Island" is what Singapore wants its country to become, with information technology "pervasive in every aspect of society, at work, home, and play." With a population of nearly three million, the modern city-nation in Southeast Asia—physically less than one-fifth the size of Rhode Island—is planning its place in the twenty-first century economy as a global hub in Internet commerce. The centerpiece of Singapore's plan is the creation of a new, high-capacity Internet system that promises to be an interactive multimedia showplace, with real-time, broadcast-quality sound and video transmissions. The Singapore ONE (One Network for Everyone) initiative, developed with the assistance of more than a dozen multinational companies, including IBM, Microsoft, NEC, Oracle, Sun Microsystems, and Yahoo!, had brought high-speed Internet service to nearly every business, school, government agency, and household in Singapore by the end of 1998, making Singapore perhaps the most Internet-intensive, if not intelligent, country in the world. Although almost everyone in Singapore has access to the Singapore-ONE system, by 1999 only one in four households was using it. Among the top concerns were the high monthly access charges (in part because Singapore's government-sponsored system has no competition) and the lack of quality multimedia Internet content.

Singapore isn't the only place with Internet dreams. Chile, Brazil, Japan, Korea, Malaysia, Taiwan, Canada, and Western Europe have begun programs to create a faster second-generation Internet. The United States, too, is upgrading its Internet system with two major efforts that began in 1996. The Next Generation Internet Initiative is a federal program designed to funnel money through the National Science Foundation, NASA, the Department of Energy, and other agencies to develop new networks and applications that will allow users to send and receive information at up to a thousand times the current speed of the Internet. A second initiative, called Internet2, consists of more than 130 universities and corporations and has a similar mission of creating a multimedia-friendly Internet that will make video conferencing, digital libraries, distance education, and three-dimensional shared virtual-reality environments all more possible and common. The Internet2 initiative, funded with both government and private investment, is nicknamed the Abilene Project, after the railroad that opened up the American frontier beyond Kansas in the 1860s.

Although Internet2 completed its coast-to-coast backbone in 1999, chances are that most Americans won't be able to get on this multilane superhighway—at least not now. Unlike Singapore's government-supported "one network for everyone," the second generation of the Internet in the United States is largely privately held and is currently available only to certain scientists and commercial users, leaving most Americans struggling with the traffic jams on the original information highway. Researchers who are familiar with Internet2 say that most Americans won't have access to the improved Internet until 2002. By that time, the scientific and corporate communities plan to have moved on to Internet3.

Frontier metaphors have often been used to explain the complexity and potential of the Information Age. In fact, new media observers Daniel Burstein and David Kline have argued that *cyberspace*, the mysterious regions where the global networks of communication take their users, is "like the Old West," nourishing "a culture of zealous individualism and entrepreneurialism. It has its gold rushes (Wall Street), its uncharted land (the Internet), its territories newly opened to farmers and homesteaders (the World Wide Web), a pony express (electronic mail), plenty of outlaws (hackers) but nary a sheriff (security), and its few settled towns (e.g., America Online and Prodigy) where decent folk can enjoy some of the comforts of civilization."[1] Of the "uncharted land" of that highway section called the **Internet**—the vast central network of high-speed telephone lines and satellite relays designed to link and carry computer information worldwide—Burstein and Kline write: "Simply put, the Internet is ungovernable . . . you can pretty much do what you want—and, for the most part, there's no sheriff or posse to stop you."

Although the Old West metaphor offers one way to view contemporary media development, the vocabulary of the new communication technology has actually fixed on a highway metaphor, which works well with the map model of culture introduced in Chapter 1. Imagine the traditional media—books, newspapers, television, and radio—as an older interstate highway system now intersected by a sprawling, poorly planned major freeway, much of which is still under construction and is fed by thousands of new capillary roads, some paved, some dirt, some extending into remote locations around the globe.

Unlike interstate highways built by federal and state governments, however, the *information highway* has been taken over and expanded by private enterprise, although it was initially established and subsidized by the government. What difference will this make? It may be too early to tell, but we do know that when private commercial managers took over radio broadcasting in the 1920s and 1930s, they helped build the United States into the world's foremost producer of communication technology and content. At the same time, though, they dramatically thwarted the growth of non-profit and educational broadcasting.

Predictions about the cultural and social impact of the Information Age veer in many different directions. One view suggests that the information highway will lead to a utopian global village, shattering outdated geographic boundaries and building worldwide communities linked by computers. Another prediction suggests that although information may be more accessible on the Internet, growing reams of data will make it hard to distinguish information from misinformation. Some Net-watchers worry that the information highway will lead to false communities, where people will spend more time online and less time interacting with others face-to-face. Finally, some view the Internet as a tool that will reflect the global economy, where development is unequal and some people will be left out or left behind.

The full impact of the Internet and the expanding information highway, like all emerging mass media, will evolve over time. Cable TV, for example, which operated in only 13 percent of American households in 1975, took nearly twenty years to reach 60 percent of U.S. homes. Although it's difficult to fully assess how the Internet will change the world, it is quite clear that the use of the Internet is growing at a tremendous rate and its impact is being felt economically, politically, socially, and culturally. In the last two years, this impact has been dramatic, from the economic growth of Internet companies such as Yahoo! and Amazon.com into new power players on Wall Street to the political shock waves emanating from the unprecedented global Web release of independent counsel Kenneth Starr's report on the President Clinton/Monica Lewinsky scandal.

In later chapters we will explore the impact of traditional media—such as books, radio, and television—and how they evolved to their current state. But right now we are in the middle of the ongoing Internet revolution, both witnessing and participating in the emergence of this dynamic medium. As governments, corporations, and public and private interests vie to shape the evolution of the information highway, answers to many questions remain ambiguous. Who will have access to the information highway and who will be left behind? Who or what will manage the highway, and what are the implications for the future and for democracy? The task for critical media consumers is to sort through competing Internet and new technology predictions, analyzing and determining how the "new and improved" Information Age can best serve the majority of citizens and communities.

> "The medium, or process, of our time—electric technology—is reshaping and restructuring patterns of social interdependence and every aspect of our personal life."
> —Marshall McLuhan, 1967

origins of the information highway

Although many branches of the information highway still resemble dirt roads, the rapid technological advances that accompany the new routes pose a major challenge to cable TV and to the more traditional media. By the 1990s, the information highway had become increasingly interactive, allowing immediate two-way communication (like telephones) between senders and receivers of media messages. In addition, many side roads along the highway were virtually unregulated, open to all kinds of opportunities and mischief. The Internet alone comprises more than fifty thousand informal and global computer networks, connected by telephone lines. These networks can access books, newspapers, magazines, music, movies, interactive games, email, thousands of information databases, and many other items. With its ability to transport both mass communication and personal conversation, the information highway has also begun to break down conventional distinctions among various media and between private and public modes of communication.

the evolution of a
new mass medium

The term Industrial Age usually refers to the period spanning the development of the steam engine in the 1760s to mass assembly-line production in the 1900s, an era that transformed manufacturing and consumer culture. By a similar measuring stick, the Information Age has barely begun. It has passed through an early phase marked by broadcasting to a phase that features the convergence of personal computers, telephone lines, electronic mail, cable television, and communication satellites.

Most mass media evolve through various stages, which are initiated not only by the diligence of great inventors, such as Thomas Edison, but by social, cultural, political, and economic circumstances. For instance, both telegraph and radio developed as new industrialized nations sought to expand military and economic control over colonies and to transmit information more rapidly. The phonograph, too, emerged because of the social and economic conditions of a growing middle class with more money and leisure time. Today, the information highway is a contemporary response to similar sets of concerns: transporting messages more rapidly while appealing to middle- and upper-middle-class consumers.

Within the appropriate conditions, media innovations emerge in three stages. First is the *novelty* or *development stage*, in which inventors and technicians try to solve a particular problem, such as making pictures move, transmitting voices through the air without wires, or sending mail electronically. Second is the *entrepreneurial stage*, in which inventors and investors determine a practical and marketable use for the new device. For example, early radio or wireless technology relayed messages to and from places where telegraph wires and cables could not go, such as military ships at sea. Part of the information highway also had its roots in the ideas of military leaders who devised a communication system—now known as the Internet—that could survive nuclear wars or natural disasters.

The third phase in a new medium's development involves a breakthrough to the *mass-medium stage*. At this point, businesses figure out how to market the new device as an appealing product for home or office. Although the government and the navy played a central role in radio's early years, commercial entrepreneurs eventually took radio into its broadcasting phase, where it began reaching millions of people. In the same way, Pentagon and government researchers developed the prototype for the Internet, but commercial interests began taking over, extending its reach nationally and globally. With the development of the World Wide Web throughout the 1980s, and the introduction of user-friendly graphic browsers like Mosaic and Netscape in the early 1990s, the Internet entered its mass-medium phase.

Making it easier for users to navigate and exchange information, the development of the World Wide Web in the 1980s catapulted the Internet into its mass-medium stage. Today, the whole world is literally a few keystrokes away, and the Internet has become the most interactive mass medium in history.

By the late 1980s and 1990s, online computer services and the Internet had begun featuring all sorts of mass-communication—and advertising—services and marketing them through computers, modems, and phone lines. Following this innovation, the Internet grew rapidly, becoming "the most wide-ranging interactive mass medium in history."[2] By 1998, about 150 million people worldwide (more than half of them in the United States) used the Internet regularly. Global Internet use is expected to rise to 320 million by 2000, and to 720 million by 2005.[3]

the birth and growth
of the internet

The real national highway system and the contemporary information highway have similar military origins. During the Eisenhower administration in the 1950s, military and government leaders originally planned an interstate highway grid to make transporting military vehicles across the country easier in the event of a national emergency. An interconnected network of freeways enabled a driver to take several different routes to get from point A to point B in the continental United States. Like the national highway system, the Internet originated with military-government planning and with national security as one of its goals.

Begun in the late 1960s by the Defense Department's Advanced Research Projects Agency (ARPA), the original Internet—called ARPAnet and nicknamed the Net—allowed military and academic researchers to communicate on a *distributed network* system (see Figure 2.1). The network design of what would become the Internet differed from the centralized style of telephone communication at the time,

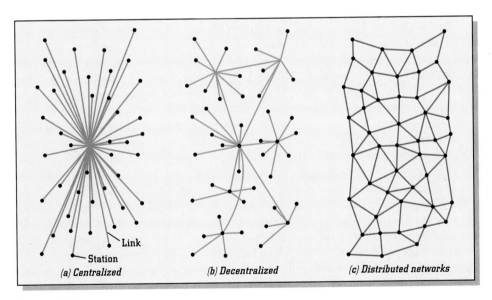

Link
Station
(a) Centralized   *(b) Decentralized*   *(c) Distributed networks*

Figure 2.1
Distributed Networks
Paul Baran, a young computer scientist working at the Rand Corporation in the Cold War era, worked on developing a national communication system that could survive a nuclear attack. Centralized networks (a) are vulnerable because all the paths lead to a single nerve center. Decentralized networks (b) are less vulnerable because they contain several main nerve centers (our long-distance phone system today is mostly decentralized). But in a distributed network (c), which resembles a net, there are no nerve centers; if any connection is severed, information can be immediately rerouted and delivered to its destination.
Source: Katie Hafner and Matthew Lyon, *Where Wizards Stay Up Late* (New York: Simon & Schuster, 1996).

where all calls were routed through a central switcher. A distributed network system offered two advantages to the researchers and military units developing the Net. First, because multiple paths linked one computer site to another, communications "traffic" would be less likely to get clogged at a single point. This helped to convince computer researchers in the 1960s to sign on to the network project—they could share research and data on the new network without their computers becoming overrun by the traffic of others' messages. Second, because the network was like an interconnected web, the Internet offered a communication system that was more impervious to technical screwups, natural disasters, or military attacks. If a "bridge" was out on one "road" of the highway, Net traffic could take another path.

In developing one of the Net prototypes for the military, the Rand Corporation, a Cold War think tank, conceptualized a communications network that had no central authority. Ironically, one of the most hierarchically structured and centrally organized institutions in our culture, the national-defense industry, created the Internet, possibly the least hierarchical and most decentralized social network ever conceived. Each computer hub in the Internet has similar status and power, so nobody can own the system outright and nobody has the power to kick others off the network. There isn't even a master power switch, so authority figures cannot shut off the Internet during an emergency.

During its developmental stage, the military computer network permitted different people in separate locations to communicate with one another. By simply leasing existing telephone lines, they used the system to send *email*—electronic letters and memos—and to post information on computer *bulletin boards*, which are sites that list information about particular topics, such as health issues, computer programs, or employment services. At this stage, the Internet was primarily used by universities and government research labs, and later by corporations, especially companies involved in computer software and other high-tech products, to transmit and receive text information.

By 1982, the Net had hit its entrepreneurial stage: The National Science Foundation invested in a high-speed communication network designed to link computer centers around the country. This innovation led to a dramatic increase in Internet use. Then, after the dissolution of the Soviet Union in the late 1980s, the ARPAnet military venture officially ended. By that time, however, a growing network of researchers, computer programmers, commercial interests, and amateur hackers had tapped into the Net, creating tens of thousands of decentralized intersections. As the military had predicted, the absence of a central authority meant that the Net could not be knocked out. By 1993, the Net had developed basic multimedia capability, allowing users to transmit pictures, sound, and video.

Just as most radio pioneers did not foresee the potential of radio, many pioneers of the Net did not predict how rapidly its mass appeal would spread beyond national and military interests. The Internet system comprises worldwide computer networks that communicate directly through Internet Protocol (IP), a computer language that allows any computer on any network to send data electronically to any other computer on an equal basis.[4] By mid-1998, the worldwide Internet consisted of more than one hundred thousand regional computer networks, and more than thirty-six million hosts—computers also known as **servers**, which are run (or hosted) by universities, corporations, and government agencies. The hosts serve as entry points for Internet traffic and are interconnected by special high-speed data lines.

The Net allows users to find information on virtually any subject, to talk with computer pen pals all over the world, and to participate in discussions about favorite hobbies and social issues. Over the Net, users can also trade software, organize clubs, play games, arrange dates, find internships, and download articles, documents, and books. In the beginning, such connections took place in **newsgroups**, which now account for tens of thousands of loosely organized computer conferences that consist of bulletin boards and individual messages, or postings, which are circulated to subscribers twenty-four hours a day. Recent technological innovations allow users to access and download high-resolution pictures, digital-quality sound recordings, graphic animations, and video files.

Within the last decade, Internet users have doubled each year, and this growth has drawn the attention of commercial interests. Companies are searching for ways to profit from the increased traffic on the Internet, and they are hoping to turn users into consumers by offering product information, selling products, providing services, and selling advertising space. With a computer and an Internet connection, users can go online to purchase a CD, search for hotels in Paris, sell a stock, or buy a car.

Governments are establishing an Internet presence as well, providing information online, posting important documents, and distributing such items as tax forms. Conversely, some governments have tried to limit access to the Internet or control the kind of information that's available. However, transcending geographic borders, the millions of Net users worldwide have generally circumvented the authority of anyone who seemed bent on regulating it. In fact, many users take advantage of the Net's ability to cross borders, circulating banned or controversial writing or art that may have been suppressed by authoritarian governments in other nations.

> "The Internet . . . works like a nonprofit food co-op; it has no owner, is managed by volunteers and derives operating costs from its members, who pay connection fees to large regional computer hubs that direct the system's traffic. . . ."
> —Steve Stecklow, *Wall Street Journal*, 1993

information access on the information highway

What generally distinguishes the information highway from older media is not only the revolutionary ways in which data are stored and retrieved but also the increasing convergence of mass media. Three innovations make the information highway a particularly distinct mass medium. First, it is interactive, enabling receivers to respond almost immediately to senders' messages. Prior to the digital age, traditional print media had few feedback avenues, relying mainly on letters to the editor, which might or might not be acknowledged. Now, however, online editors can respond more quickly to thousands of individual users. Whereas magazine and newspaper editors have traditionally restricted the number of letters they print due to space limitations, the information highway makes it possible to post most feedback letters.

The second way in which the information highway is innovative is that it enables many traditional media to appear on computer screens. Users can call up a magazine story, a music video, a banned book, or a radical newsletter. Previously, one mass-media company delivered a product—a newspaper or a TV program—to a mass audience. Now, however, the Internet multiplies the channels of delivery, thus transforming consumers' traditional interactions with the mass media. The Internet not only connects consumers to other media but also personalizes this experience by allowing them to call up mass media on demand.

Last, the information highway allows individuals to create and distribute their own messages. More easily than other media, the Internet allows people to become *producers* rather than just *consumers* of media content. For example, the cost of owning and operating a television station or newspaper is prohibitive for most people, but the cost of buying a computer, a modem, and Internet access is relatively modest. In addition, because the Internet is decentralized and unhierarchical, there are no gatekeep-

Recall the holiday shopping season of 1998: The nation's mega-malls were crowded with people jostling through the aisles and waiting impatiently in lines; and these were the ones lucky enough to find a parking space. Many found their shopping experiences to be fruitless—hours and hours of poking through stores only to discover that they couldn't find that special gift: the extra-large salad shooter, the barking dogs Christmas carol CD, or a new Furby.

A different version of the 1998 holiday shopping experience took place at home. The shopper sat in a cozy desk chair, perhaps with a warm cup of cocoa and wearing fuzzy slippers. With no parking hassles and no long lines, the consumer window-shopped on the computer screen, comparing prices, finding unique gifts, and making purchases with a few clicks of the mouse.

The emerging phenomenon of electronic commerce, or e-commerce, came of age in the 1998 buying season, when more than 40 percent of online U.S. households spent $3 billion in the months of November and December alone. Moreover, Net shoppers spent more money online, totaling an average of $629 in holiday transactions

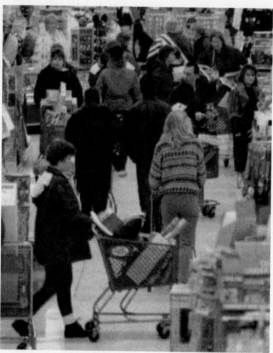

Store shopping . . .

in 1998, compared with $214 in 1997. Those e-shoppers accounted for a majority of the nearly $5 billion spent online in 1998. Users grew accustomed to the increasingly standardized online buying experience, which includes clicking items into their "shopping cart," proceeding to "checkout," entering their contact information and credit-card number, and hitting the send button to complete the transaction. The only person online shoppers might have encountered in the entire process was a parcel worker delivering the purchase a few days later.

And what were the online holiday shoppers buying? Software, books, and CDs topped the list, and reflected the wares of the busiest Web retail sites, including Amazon.com, Outpost.com, Dell Computer, Egghead.com, Gateway, and Disney. For product items that are harder to sell via the Net, such as clothing, companies tried to simulate an actual retail-store visit. The Gap, for example, used a virtual fitting room so that potential customers could mix and match apparel on a cartoon model.

The advantages of online shopping are becoming increasingly familiar: round-the-clock shopping seven days a week; easy price comparisons, especially with sites like Shopper.com, which generates instant lists of outlets and prices; e-coupons with deep discounts that can be printed at home or delivered to the user via regular mail; access to stores around the world with a huge array of products; and even online auctions at sites like eBay.com, where shoppers can find rare goods ranging from coins and stamps to collectible toys and action figures.

Yet, with all its promise, the story of e-commerce also includes cautionary tales. Even with the addition of secure server software that uses encryption technology to scramble personal and credit-card information, there is still a chance that the transaction may not be completely secure. In addition, fraudulent businesses have tapped into e-commerce, marketing pyramid schemes and selling products that may never materialize. There is also concern with the areas of online securities, investments, and stock trading. The familiar "pump and dump" stock scam has been adapted to the Internet, where the owner of a speculative penny stock will pump up the price of the stock through exaggerated claims in financial chat rooms, then dump (sell) the stock when the price becomes inflated. Even for legitimate stock transactions, there is concern that companies don't execute electronic stock trades quickly enough, or that online traders may experience a lag between stock prices listed onscreen and the actual prices in the market.

Other problems for e-commerce, at least in the short term, are technological. The rush of new customers into e-commerce caught a number of new online retailers off-guard. Popular sites like Macys.com, Toys "R" Us, Barnes & Noble, and the Yankee Candle Company broke down under the crush of orders, and even e-commerce pioneer Amazon.com had problems getting gifts delivered on time for Christmas.

Yet the biggest complaint about e-commerce seems rather old-fashioned: the need for better customer service. Online buyers are willing to make the purchase orders themselves, but they still want to be able to talk to a real person if they encounter difficulties. The problem with e-commerce sites is that many of them have not met this demand and consumer complaints online often go ignored. A survey by Internet research firm Jupiter Communications, completed after the 1998 holiday season, found that 42 percent of the leading e-commerce sites either took more than five days to respond to an email inquiry, neglected to respond at all, or listed no email address for customers to use. The risk of such poor communication is that online buyers often take their business to a competing site.

Although the Internet has clearly reached a turning point as a retail medium, most e-commerce operations are still not financially viable. In fact, one Internet consulting company predicts that only 5 percent of retail Web sites will turn a profit in the year 2000. The most famous of unprofitable e-commerce sites is Amazon.com, which continues to spend heavily as it expands and branches out from its core bookselling business. Nevertheless, investors in companies like Amazon.com had astounding faith in the future of e-commerce; in the first quarter of 1999, Amazon.com was worth an astonishing $22.1 billion in stock, exceeding the on-paper value of Kmart and J. C. Penney combined.

This example, in which an unprofitable but forward-looking e-commerce company is valued higher than two established and profitable companies, shows e-commerce at a fascinating precipice. At the end of 1998, online sales of $5 billion made up less than 2 percent of the estimated $2.6 *trillion* of all retail goods purchased in the United States that year. By comparison, Wal-Mart, the leading retailer in the United States, had sales of $137 billion in 1998. Yet analysts project that e-commerce sales will grow into the hundreds of billions of dollars by 2004. But for e-commerce to grow into the new millennium, it may have to adjust in order to entice a culture that often views shopping as entertainment; beyond just convenience and 24-hour access, shopping online needs to compete with the entertainments and attractions of America's malls and shopping districts. As Michael Solomon, a professor of consumer behavior at Auburn University, noted, "When people go shopping in groups, they buy more than when they're on their own. Until you can simulate that, you're losing some sales potential."[1]

or online shopping?

ers to prevent individuals from creating and displaying their own messages. The Internet is inherently democratic and messy. Anyone can use it to express his or her ideas, and all ideas seem functionally equal: An individual's home page sits shoulder-to-shoulder with the home pages of billion-dollar corporations, research universities, and national governments.

converging media and technology breakthroughs

The information highway has blurred the boundary between point-to-point communication and mass communication. The highway has linked home, school, and business computers, TV sets, radios, CD and DVD recorders and players, VCRs, digital cameras, email, video games, scanners, newspapers, fax machines, magazines, and communication satellites. This capability makes it possible for anyone to become a player on the information highway—from cable TV companies and regional telephone providers to computer-software firms and individual entrepreneurs. But the new convergences have had the greatest impact on two communication media—the telephone and the personal computer—which developed primarily as forms of point-to-point or personal communication, not as mass communication. Both, however, have become central players in the Information Age and mass-communication revolutions.

Three key technological developments have made today's intersection of mass media along the information highway possible. The first innovation involved **digital** communication, which was central to the development of the first computers in the 1940s. In digital technology, an image, text, or sound is converted into electronic signals represented as a series of binary numbers—ones and zeros—which are then reassembled as a precise reproduction of an image, text, or sound. Digital signals operate as pieces, or *bits* (from *BI*nary digi*TS*), of information representing two values, such as yes/no, on/off, or 0/1. For example, a typical compact-disk track uses a binary-code system in which zeros are microscopic pits in the surface of the disk, while ones are represented on the unpitted surface. Used in various combinations, these digital codes can duplicate, store, and play back the most complex kinds of sounds.

The words in books, the images on television, and the voices over phone lines can all be converted into digital ones and zeros that computers can "read," or process. With books, magazines, music, TV programs, movies, and phones all beginning to "speak the same language," they are merging onto a congested highway.

The second technological breakthrough, microtechnology, has enabled companies to produce miniature circuits that can process and store electronic signals. In 1971, the introduction of **microprocessors** allowed the integration of thousands of transistors and related circuitry into thin strands of silicon along which binary codes traveled. With this innovation, manufacturers were able to introduce the first *personal computers* (PCs), relatively inexpensive machines that consumers could purchase for home use. PCs were smaller, cheaper, increasingly more powerful, and were no longer just a tool for the office. According to Moore's Law (coined by Gordon Moore, a former chairman of Intel, which is a leading builder of microprocessors), computer-chip power doubles every eighteen months. Because of microtechnology, a single PC that now fits on an individual's lap is far more powerful than the bulky computer systems that occupied entire floors of office buildings during the 1960s. In addition, while computing power has increased, the cost of personal computers has dropped dramatically in the last fifteen years, allowing more consumers to purchase them for home use.

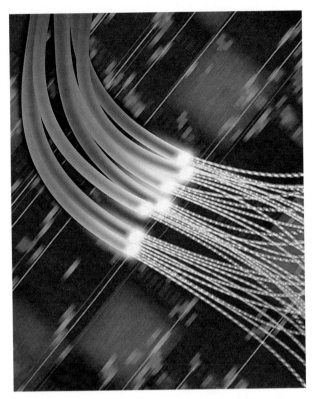

Fiber-optic laser beams carry more than 150,000 times as much information as do older copper phone wire and coaxial TV cables. About forty fiber-optic strands together can carry more than a million digitally compressed telephone conversations, or two thousand cable TV channels.

In the mid-1980s, the third technological development, **fiber-optic cable**, featured thin glass bundles of fiber capable of transmitting thousands of messages that have been digitally converted into shooting pulses of light. Fiber-optic technology has allowed information to be transported via lasers. With their ability to carry broadcast channels, telephone signals, and all sorts of digital codes, thin fiber-optic cables began replacing the older, bulkier copper wire used by phone and cable companies. Nicholas Negroponte, the founding director of MIT's Media Lab, points out that "a fiber the size of a human hair can deliver every issue ever made of the *Wall Street Journal* in less than one second."[5] With the increased speeds of the new media technology, few limits exist with regard to the amount of information digital technology can transport. The chief problems now center around what to put on the information highway, who will run it, and who will have access.

converging media and content

Digital technology now permits multiple and immediate computer access to traditional media such as newspapers, magazines, television programs, movies, and sound recordings. The term for this phenomenon is **media convergence**, whereby old and new media are available via the integration of personal computers, high-speed data links, and digital storage formats. For example, *multimedia content*—mixing audio, video, and data—can be delivered in a number of forms, including through telephone lines, high-bandwidth cable, and digital satellite services.

The multimedia format brings an unprecedented number of content choices and styles to the user, all at once. For example, an Internet site like ESPN.com carries the latest sports scores and full-length text reports on games, streams live audio from sources like ESPN Radio, and offers downloadable video highlights of sporting events. It's also the place to purchase ESPN sportswear and participate in scheduled live chats with sports personalities. Similarly, a multimedia DVD like the *Encyclopaedia Britannica* offers more than seventy-three thousand articles, three hours of video and two hours of sound samples, a full built-in dictionary, and thousands of hypertext links to Internet sources, including *Encyclopaedia Britannica*'s own continuously updated Web site. Thus, an entry on rock and roll's 1964 British Invasion is able to present text-based articles on groups like the Beatles, the Kinks, and the Rolling Stones, samples of songs, sound effects of screaming crowds, picture albums of mod 1960s clothing, and interactive flow charts of several groups' musical influences.

Once created or received, the digital content can be stored in a number of formats that are widely available. A word-processed school paper can easily be stored on a traditional 3.5-inch high-density disk. A whole semester's worth of papers can be stored on a Zip disk, which holds about seventy times more information than a high-density disk. A Zip disk can also hold audio samples, or even a short video clip. For other multimedia content, a **CD-ROM** holds as much information as seven hundred conventional disks. However, CD-ROM stands for *Compact-Disk Read-Only Memory*, and users cannot enter or store new data. This has made CDs an excellent format for stored data, such as encyclopedias, music recordings, video games, and software programs. A new generation of CDs called CD-Rs (recordable) and CD-RWs (rewriteable) allows users to put their own content on CDs. To handle the increasing ability of computer users to create and play back multimedia content, other recent portable storage formats, such as Jaz cartridges, work like souped-up Zip disks.

The greatest leap in digital storage comes with the long-awaited DVD (digital versatile disk, or digital videodisk), which made its retail debut in 1997. The DVD uses digital compression to store a great deal of information—enough space for a two-hour Hollywood movie—on a disk that looks similar to a standard CD. The DVD is the likely successor to the home VCR for playing movie rentals, because it offers higher resolution and never needs to be rewound. In 1998, retailer Circuit City introduced the Divx (pronounced div-ix), a disposable, less expensive version of the DVD that offers a limited number of movie playbacks. Like the CD, the DVD will eventually be recordable, which means that it will branch out from home-entertainment uses to include business and computer storage.

Add to this mix digital DAT tapes and CD Mini-Disks for audio projects, digital still and video cameras, and free media players that can be downloaded from the Web, and it becomes clear that people have a formidable array of tools for experiencing and creating media convergence.

mapping the internet

One of the major problems of the information highway, especially Internet intersections, has been its complexity and disorganization. Originally lacking any basic directory services, the networks were like an enormous free-floating library without a Dewey decimal system. This situation has changed. By the mid-1990s, four major mapping systems existed for negotiating the Internet's sprawling terrain. The first map featured the **World Wide Web**, initially a free and open system for organizing and standardizing information on the Internet. The Web moved the Internet from a message-delivery system to a mass medium. A second mapping system was implemented by commercial Internet Service Providers, such as America Online (AOL), CompuServe, Prodigy, and the Microsoft Network. At the third level are browsers, software environments that help users navigate the Web. Finally, Web search engines help users to find the right Web sites among the millions that are available.

> "In less than three years, the Internet's World Wide Web has spawned some **10 million electronic documents** at a quarter million Web sites. By contrast, the Library of Congress has taken 195 years to collect 14 million books."
>
> —Tim Miller,
>   New Media Resources,
>   1995

The World Wide Web. By the early 1990s, the World Wide Web had become the most frequently visited region of the Internet. (Other regions of the Net include Usenet groups, email service, and gopher information files.) Developed in the 1980s by software engineer Tim Berners-Lee, the Web was initially a text-only data-linking system that allowed computer-accessed information to associate with, or link to, other information no matter where it was on the Internet. Known as *hypertext*, this data-linking feature of the Web was a breakthrough for those attempting to use the Internet. Hypertext is a non-linear way of organizing information, allowing a user to click on a highlighted word, phrase, picture, or icon and skip directly to other files related to that subject in other computer systems.

By using standardized software, today users can navigate through most features of the Internet, including text data such as email, photo-image files, and video and audio clips. *HTML* (*HyperText Markup Language*), the written code that creates Web pages and links, is a language that all computers can read, so computers with varying operating systems, such as Windows and Macintosh, can communicate easily. *Java*, an HTML-compatible language developed by Sun Microsystems in the mid-1990s, is also universally readable by computers and allows small interactive programs to run on Web pages, creating moving graphic elements such as three-dimensional animations and menus that pop up as a mouse pointer passes over them.

The millions of "pages," or sites, on the Web promote everything from a point of view to a job résumé to a wide variety of consumer products. A Web page can be designed on an ordinary word-processing program that has a feature for writing hypertext commands. Almost all national TV commercials now include the product's Web-site address, where more information about a company or its product can be found. The number of sites on the Web jumped from just 130 in 1993 to more than 2.5 million in 1998.[6]

Internet Service Providers. Although most individuals access the Internet through their university or business accounts, home users often purchase a commercial online service, also called an **Internet Service Provider (ISP)**. Four or five companies have dominated in providing these services. Begun in the mid-1980s, America Online (AOL), partially owned by the Tribune Company, is the largest. Late in 1996, when the company lowered its rate to a monthly flat fee of $19.95, service was so backed up that it took hours for customers to log on, creating a brief public-relations nightmare. By 1999, though, AOL had more than fifteen million subscribers. In addition to providing access to the Internet and to thousands of software applications, AOL offers inroads to newspapers, magazines, and the TV networks. Other major online services include CompuServe, bought in the late 1970s by the tax firm H&R Block and acquired by AOL in 1997, and Prodigy, originated by IBM and Sears in the late 1980s. The computer-software giant Microsoft entered the online business in 1995. Given the company's control of 90 percent of the home-computer software market, the Microsoft Network (MSN) quickly became a major player. It teamed up with NBC in 1996 to create MSNBC, the first national news channel available simultaneously on cable TV systems and on the World Wide Web. Alongside the national online services, hundreds of local services, many of them operated by regional telephone companies, also compete to offer consumers access to the Internet.

By the mid-1990s, online services offered access not only to other media but also to financial planning, stock information, weather reports, sports scores, computer games, travel planning, health tips, electronic shopping, and reference works. The availability of online services, accessible with a home computer, a telephone modem or cable line, and a monthly fee, has increased dramatically because of digital technology.

Browsers. The software packages that help users navigate the Web are called **browsers**. The most popular browsers, Netscape's Communicator and Microsoft's Explorer (which displaced Netscape as the most popular browser in 1998, leading to further criticisms about Microsoft's industry dominance), handle Web files and links, and translate them into a more user-friendly graphic layout. Commercial ISPs such as America Online offer their own built-in browser software. Many people use browsers to access popular content pages, such as HotWired (the multimedia version of *Wired* magazine), Expedia (the Microsoft Network travel service), Pathfinder (the Time Warner news and information service), or ESPN.com (an Internet extension of the popular national cable sports channels).

Search Engines. Browsers can take Web surfers to Web sites, but how does one find the appropriate pages to visit? Web **search engines** allow users to enter key words or queries to find related sites on the Web. Because of their great utility, search engines such as Yahoo!, Excite, Infoseek (now called Go), Webcrawler, and Lycos, have become some of the most popular starting points on the Web. Search engines work in two different ways: Some, such as AltaVista or HotBot, send out computer "spider" programs that automatically visit and record site data, creating huge but somewhat unfiltered lists for searches. Others, such as Lycos and Yahoo!, have actual staff people review and catalogue Web sites. While cataloguing engines may not return as many Web sites for each search request, chances are that the sites provided will be more relevant to the search terms. Because search engines are popular entry points, or *portals*, to the Web, the home pages of search engines now offer not only a search button but also several "channels" that provide shortcuts to the day's news stories, up-to-the-minute sports scores, and links to advertisers' Web sites. The idea behind these channels is to keep users connected to the search-engine site for as long as possible, and thus be able to offer an attentive audience to Web advertisers.[7]

As computers and Internet connections have become more affordable, and as fiber-optic connections have replaced copper wire in cable and phone lines, the "side streets" to new information have proliferated. Just as the interstate highway system helped create and expand suburban communities half a century ago, the information highway has produced what are frequently called **virtual communities**. These are groups of users who are separated geographically but connected nationally and globally by their shared interests or business and their access to an online service or to the Internet. But there is also reason for concern that virtual communities are not a good substitute for face-to-face human interaction. In fact, the first major study of the social-psychological effects of Internet use at home, conducted in the Pittsburgh area by Carnegie Mellon University researchers, found that even an hour a week spent online led to an increased amount of depression and a loss of contacts in the user's social circle.[8] Such complaints are similar to those about television—that parents often use television as a baby-sitter instead of personally interacting with their children. Although the conclusions of the Internet study are still being debated,[9] it is a reminder that media technology may not always make life qualitatively better.

ownership issues on the internet

Our contemporary era is distinguished not only by the revolutionary ways in which data are transmitted but also by the increasing convergence of owners and players in mass-media industries. Large media firms, such as Disney, Time Warner, and Microsoft, are buying up or investing in smaller companies and spreading their economic interests among books, magazines, music, movies, radio, television, cable, and Internet channels.

At this point, the economics of newly emerging and converging media remains open and freewheeling. Like the automobile or film industries of an earlier era, many players and companies are jockeying for position. With the passage of the Telecommunications Act of 1996, most regional and long-distance phone companies can now participate in both cable and Internet-access businesses. The phone companies, like cable TV firms, have the added advantage of controlling the wires into most American homes and businesses. As cable and phone companies gradually convert older wiring into high-speed fiber-optic lines, they are wrestling for control of Internet circuitry and intensifying the battle over mass-communication delivery systems.

Given the paucity of regulations governing the emerging Internet industry, and the industry's rapid growth, it is not surprising to see a recent spate of mergers, joint ventures, consolidations, and power grabs. By 1999, for example, telephone giant AT&T had begun to position itself as a one-stop communications company, bringing telephone, Internet, cable service, and entertainment content to its customers across the country. First, AT&T acquired TCI, Inc., the largest cable-television system operator, in 1998, giving AT&T a direct cable link into millions of households. A few months later, At Home, a high-speed cable-based Internet service controlled by TCI, Inc. (and now AT&T), bought Excite, a leading Internet search engine and portal. Adding to AT&T's penetration into the market is its 1999 deal to offer telephone service in thirty-three states over Time Warner's cable systems. Time Warner cable, too, has expanded its cable television service to include a high-speed Internet connection called Road Runner (after the familiar Warner Brothers cartoon character).

America Online (AOL), already the largest ISP, acquired Web-browser company Netscape in 1998. Disney acquired search engine Infoseek and used it to create the Go Network in 1999, an umbrella site for all of Disney's Web services, including the ABC television network and ESPN. Yahoo!, one of the leading Web destinations, sought to solidify its position and remain independent in the flurry of takeovers by purchasing GeoCities, a company that operates a popular site that hosts free Web pages for individuals.

Although all of these mergers were an attempt to find a dominant position in the Information Age, some companies still loomed larger than others. In the late 1990s, Microsoft fought an antitrust lawsuit brought by the U.S. Justice Department that argued Microsoft used its near-monopoly dominance of its Windows operating systems to illegally sabotage its competitors, including Netscape. The court decision will undoubtedly have a major impact on the leading players of the information highway, as

"One of the more **remarkable features** of the computer network on which much of the world has come to rely is that **nobody owns it**. That does not mean, however, that no one controls it."
— Amy Harmon,
New York Times,
1998

well as on the evolution of the Internet in the twenty-first century. The desire of corporations to tap into the Internet economy is clear. Controlling a popular Internet portal also means owning a lucrative Internet advertising location. In 1998, businesses spent an estimated $1 billion to advertise on the Net, one of the primary growth areas in advertising. The increasing dominance of commercial interests on the Internet is affecting the way in which the information highway—once a nonprofit, government-subsidized medium known for freely accessible information—is evolving.

a clash of values

Discussing the economic implications of the information highway, critics Daniel Burstein and David Kline associate the Internet with a series of personality traits: "Free. Egalitarian. Decentralized. Ad hoc. Open and peer-to-peer. Experimental. Autonomous. Anarchic." They contrast these traits with the personality of modern business organizations: "For profit. Hierarchical. Systematized. Planned. Proprietary. Pragmatic. Accountable. Organized and reliable."[10] Given this clash of values, the development of the Internet should remain unstable and dynamic over the next several years, despite the attempts to commercialize access to the Net's vast regions. Unlike phone, movie, broadcast-network, and cable TV businesses, where ownership has become increasingly consolidated in the hands of a few powerful firms, many parts of the Internet have so far eluded centralization. In fact, the Internet is less likely to suffer from the same economic limitations of other mass media because it was not designed to be an efficiently managed, tightly controlled, and secure system.

An antiauthoritarian spirit resides in the Net, from the easily downloadable shareware and freeware to the recent work of the self-described "hacktivists," who use their hacker skills to bring political protest to the Internet.[11] Not all efforts to commercialize the Internet have been effective, and to a large extent the Internet ethos of free information is alive and well. For example, *Slate*, the high-profile online magazine sponsored by Microsoft, decided to forgo its $19.95 annual subscription charge in 1999 after acknowledging that too few people were willing to pay for it.

future control of the internet

The Federal Communications Commission (FCC) was originally set up in the late 1920s and early 1930s to protect the public's interest in broadcasting. Ultimately, however, this government body mainly served the interests of private entrepreneurs and narrowed access to the public airwaves. This pattern is being repeated with the Internet. In the late 1980s, the government officially bowed out as the Internet's major operator and was superseded by a wide variety of public and private concerns.

With many pathways along the information highway now dictated by corporate and commercial interests, critics predict that Internet programs in particular will increasingly favor those who have the money to develop content or technology. The favored ones are likely to be business firms and university research institutes, which depend on large corporations for funding. By 1994, several noncommercial university consortiums, which had been running regional computer hubs and Internet services, had begun selling the rights to manage their services to private corporations. Businesses maintain that they can provide improved services at affordable costs. Critics, however, warn that the increasing privatization of Internet services could threaten their continued development as a democratic network of relatively equal individuals and institutions, free from government or corporate control.

WebCams: The Whole World Is Watching

The first WebCam in the world was trained on the Trojan Room coffeepot. In the primitive days of the Internet in 1991, even before the World Wide Web had been developed, a group of computer researchers at Cambridge University in England had a problem to solve: how to avoid walking flights of stairs to the other side of the building only to find an empty coffeepot. Being resourceful types, the researchers focused a video camera on the coffeepot and created a system that sent captured coffeepot images to each colleague's computer three times a minute. The Coffeepot Cam began to gain notoriety among Internet developers, so the computer scientists at Cambridge linked their real-time coffeepot images to the emerging World Wide Web. Thus, an ordinary drip coffeepot in the hallway outside the Trojan Room became the most-watched coffeepot in the world.

Next came the Amazing Fish Cam. The frequently updated images of tropical fish in a large aquarium reportedly attract an average of ninety thousand hits a day to this second-oldest WebCam. The Web has since been host to the Amazing Ferret Cam, the Amazing Ironing Cam, a cam shot of the genuinely amazing Niagara Falls, and live camera shots of hundreds more things and places around the world.

The most popular WebCam site of all is JenniCAM, which offers continuously updated camera shots of the first person to be the subject of a WebCam. Jennifer Ringley started JenniCAM in 1996 from her dorm room at

Mon, Nov 9, 1998 4:56 PM   http://www.jennicam.org ©JKR

SOME WEBCAM SITES

Trojan Room Coffee Machine
   http://www.cl.cam.ac.uk/coffee/coffee.html
The Amazing Fish Cam
   http://home.netscape.com/fishcam
JenniCAM
   http://www.jennicam.org
Cammunity
   http://www.cammunity.com
EarthCam
   http://www.earthcam.com

Dickinson College, in Carlisle, Pennsylvania, to do sort of a Fish Cam, but with a person instead. Since then, she has truly lived in a fish bowl, with major portions of her life (now from a Washington, D.C., apartment) captured on camera for millions to see. The effect is somewhat like the 1998 movie *The Truman Show*, except that in this case the subject willingly consents to the voyeurs. Visitors to JenniCAM can see shots of Jenni sitting in front of her computer, reading, entertaining guests, and sleeping. Viewers sometimes also see her without clothing, and engaging in sexual activity, which Ringley defends as part of "real life." Yet Ringley argues that she isn't giving up her privacy: "Just because people can see me doesn't mean it affects me—I'm still alone in my room no matter what."

With publicity from interviews on National Public Radio, the *Today* show, and *Entertainment Tonight*, Jenni now attracts more than four million visitors to her site each day, and may have more fans than most television shows.[1] Guests of the site can see images refreshed every twenty minutes for free. Thousands more have paid a $15 annual membership fee for the privilege of seeing updated JenniCAM images every two minutes. Ringley—who has shunned advertisers' offers—says that she was forced to develop JenniCAM subscriptions to cover the cost of upgrading and maintaining her site. In other ventures, Ringley is involved in "JenniShow," a biweekly RealVideo broadcast affiliated with a separate Web site; the site also sells bumper stickers that read: "I'd rather be watching JenniCAM."

The U.S. government is already trying to privatize the assignment of domain names. From 1993 to 1998—the first five years of the Web's phenomenal growth—the United States' National Science Foundation supervised the assignment of World Wide Web domain names through a private contractor, and gave rise to the now-familiar Web-name extensions (e.g., ".com," ".net," and ".org"). In 1998, as the U.S. government moved to establish a new international authority to administer and expand Net domain names, the future of the Net's control still seemed unclear. Further privatization is assured for Internet2; the U.S. federal government is providing the seed money to start this next generation of the Net but has vowed to let business control it eventually.

Although the government has taken a less central role in developing and maintaining the Internet, what is still to be determined is who will manage the information and communication systems of the future. For a while in the mid-1990s, some traditional broadcasters and cable operators, often at odds in the past, joined forces, linked by a common purpose: to ensure that telephone companies were challenged in the race to convert copper wire to fiber-optic systems and to sign subscribers to the newest media services. But the 1996 Telecommunications Act altered the landscape again, encouraging mergers and joint ventures among phone companies and cable operators.

alternative voices

As the information highway becomes increasingly jammed with commercial traffic and interests, the pioneering spirit of its early days endures. Microsoft has become the predominant corporation of the Information Age, but independent software creators persist in developing alternate visions of the information highway. One of the best examples of this is the development of *open-source software*. In the early days of computer code writing, amateur hackers collectively developed software, freely sharing the program source code and ideas to upgrade and improve programs. Beginning in the 1970s, Microsoft put an end to much of this activity by making software development a business in which programs were developed privately and users were required to pay for them—and all the necessary upgrades.

Some hackers are still developing noncommercial, open-source software. As Microsoft fought an antitrust lawsuit by the U.S. Justice Department in 1999, some experts argued that Linux (pronounced linn-ucks), a free, open-source software operating system, could be a significant challenger to Windows.[12] Linux was established in 1991 by a twenty-one-year-old student at the University of Helsinki. Since then, professional computer programmers and hobbyists around the world have emailed improvements back and forth, creating a sophisticated software system that even Microsoft has acknowledged is a credible alternative to expensive commercial programs. The Linux developers illustrate that although the information highway has become a mass medium, it is evolving in such an open way that a small number of individuals can still make an enormous impact and outfox even the largest of corporations.

citizens, cyberspace, and democracy

Throughout the twentieth century, Americans have closely examined emerging mass media for their potential contributions to democracy and culture. As radio became more affordable in the 1920s and 1930s, we hailed the medium for its ability to reach and entertain even the poorest Americans caught in the Great Depression. When television developed in the 1950s and 1960s, it also held promise as a medium that could reach everyone, even those who were illiterate or cut off from printed information. But as broadcasting evolved, the growth of commercial channels far outpaced the emergence of viable nonprofit channels as fewer and fewer corporations gained more and more control. In the 1980s and 1990s, these issues resurfaced. Many praise the Internet sector of the information highway for its democratic possibilities and for its accessibility. Some advocates even tout it as the most decentralized social network ever conceived.

Unlike many media industries, the Internet has developed largely from the bottom up. Just as amateur radio operators influenced the growth of wireless communication in the early twentieth century, the development of the Internet owes a large debt to amateurs—students, engineers, and assorted computer buffs.

There are several disadvantages, however, to the decentralized nature of the Internet. One drawback has been the increased circulation of data and "news," sometimes called cyberspace litter—the Internet equivalent of unwanted junk mail or newspaper advertising supplements. Unlike traditional news media, which routinely employ editors as information gatekeepers, many individuals and newsgroups on the Internet send out data that are not checked by anyone. Most news media screen material for accuracy, fairness, appropriateness, and decency, but such screening is more difficult to accomplish on the Internet.

Given that there is far less editorial interference in cyberspace, far more misinformation tends to leak through. Urban myths have spread like wildfire as email hoaxes go unchecked and are naively forwarded around the globe. One widespread hoax in the late 1990s involved an email message that typically began "I'm sure many of you watched the recent taping of the *Oprah Winfrey* show where her guest was Tommy Hilfiger." The message details how the popular clothing designer uttered racist comments on the show, and then calls for a boycott of Hilfiger's line of clothing. Many people forwarded the message on to friends before checking the facts: Hilfiger was never on Oprah's show, and she has never even met him. Winfrey ignored the rumor for two years, and finally, after the story refused to go away, denounced it on the air in 1999 as groundless. [13]

Although the Internet is subject to misinformation, it is also a source of unique and valuable information—for example, Web sites that catalog and discredit online hoaxes and urban legends.[14] As such, the Internet offers a diverse array of communication models. In such a decentralized system, millions of message groups send out bits of information, allowing millions of other interested users to receive and respond. Instead of the few-to-many model of traditional media, the Internet offers more opportunities for both one-to-one and many-to-many communication encounters.

"[The Internet] is a way for . . . the struggle in our country, and the many other countries where there are a lot of human rights abuses, to be brought out into the open."
—Janai Robert Orina, Kenyan human rights worker, 1998

■free expression and security nightmares

In the 1990s, no Internet issue commanded more attention than arguments about the suitability of cyberspace material. The Communications Decency Act (CDA), a controversial provision in the 1996 Telecommunications Act, banned indecent and obscene cyberspace material that children might be able to access. The CDA was eventually ruled unconstitutional in a unanimous U.S. Supreme Court decision, but not before a major grassroots movement swept the worldwide Net community. Led by a nonprofit public-interest organization in San Francisco called the Electronic Frontier Foundation (EFF), hundreds of thousands of Web sites added a blue-ribbon logo to their pages, set their background color on black, and linked to the EFF's home page as symbols of opposition to online censorship. The Electronic Frontier

By *Michael M. Epstein*

As the number of Internet users increased exponentially in the mid-1990s, politicians and social activists were faced with a complicated question: Should the government regulate the flow of information on the Internet and, if so, how? The question is complicated, because the laws of the United States have always treated telephone calls, broadcasts, and printed words very differently when it comes to censorship of inappropriate or indecent speech. Although people who make obscene or harassing calls can be prosecuted, the telephone company that carries the call is not held responsible for the misdeeds of the caller. Radio and television broadcasters, who are licensed to use government-owned airwaves in the public interest, are subject to greater regulation of speech content. Networks and individual stations are frequently held legally responsible for inaccuracy and indecency under federal law and the rules of the Federal Communications Commission, even if the transgression was committed by a third party. Printed materials such as books, newspapers, and magazines are virtually free of regular censorship by government, except in the relatively rare instance when obscene statements or images are deemed to have violated local community standards.

Concerned that unrestricted access to the Internet would put children at risk, the U.S. Congress passed the Communications Decency Act (the CDA) in early 1996. With the CDA, Congress made it a felony to transmit obscene, indecent, or harassing material on computer networks where children might see it. Over the objections of free-speech advocates like the American Civil Liberties Union, the American Library Association, and the Center for Technology and Democracy, President Clinton signed the CDA into law on February 8, 1996.

With enactment of the CDA, Congress and the president declared that the Internet should be regulated like a broadcast medium, or so it seemed. On June 12, 1996, a federal court in Philadelphia decided otherwise. Concluding that the CDA violated the First Amendment because it was "overly broad," the court found that the Internet's "unique and democratic nature" required it to be treated differently from broadcast media. Supporters of the CDA ultimately expected to present their case before the Supreme Court, while opponents of the act maintained that the Internet should not be treated any differently from bookstores, libraries, and record shops, where most adult-oriented material is available without restriction. In June 1997, the Supreme Court affirmed the reasoning of the lower court and declared the CDA unconstitutional in the case known as *ACLU v. Reno*.

In 1998, Congress passed a second measure regulating online content known as the Children's Online Protection Act (COPA). Instead of censoring indecent Internet speech

> The Internet's "unique and democratic" nature requires it to be treated differently from broadcast media.

Foundation reports that its blue-ribbon page became the fourth most-linked-to site on the Internet, and received a peak of more than one million visits per day when President Clinton signed the CDA into law in 1996. In 1998, after President Clinton signed a new version of the CDA entitled the Child Online Protection Act (COPA), the blue-ribbon campaign was relaunched (see "Examining Ethics: Regulating the Internet," above). A federal court judge blocked COPA, arguing that like the CDA it was unconstitutional.

Battles over inappropriate material have been part of the story of most mass media, from debates over lurid pulp fiction in the nineteenth century to opposition to sexually explicit themes and images during film's early years. More recently, the demand for X-rated movies helped drive the VCR–video store boom of the 1980s, and outright, COPA requires commercial Internet sites with adult content to restrict access to the site so that children cannot view or read inappropriate material. In October 1998, President Clinton signed COPA into law. Concerned that access restrictions, which include requiring users to log on with a credit card, would have a chilling effect on legitimate adult use, the ACLU and twenty-three Web publishers, including the *New York Times*, filed suit in federal court. On February 1, 1999, federal District Judge Lowell A. Reed Jr. issued a preliminary injunction to block enforcement of COPA, noting that the act would probably be held unconstitutional if the ACLU's lawsuit were given a full trial.

While the Supreme Court will probably have to make a decision about COPA, the technology and culture of the Internet have advanced to the point where U.S. indecency initiatives may have little or no impact on the medium. Opponents of COPA, for instance, point out that because the act applies only to American commercial sites, purveyors of adult content based in other countries will be able to continue to offer easy access to adults and kids alike. Since the Internet knows no geographic boundaries, it is essentially impossible for one or a few countries to act as content gatekeepers for a world community. The concept of a community without borders was put to the test in *U.S. v. Thomas*, a 1996 case involving a California couple who ran a commercial adult Internet site that was available to sub-

> It is essentially impossible for one country to act as content gatekeeper for a world community.

scribers in Tennessee. Although the site did not violate the couple's local community standards for obscenity, a federal district court held that it did violate Tennessee's more stringent obscenity standards and convicted the Thomases. Even though the defendants never set foot in Tennessee, the court ruled that because they knew people in Tennessee were downloading adult content, they would be treated as if they had been operating their business in Tennessee.

The complexities of Internet technology have been augmented by significant changes in American culture at the turn of the new century. In the wake of the Clinton-Lewinsky affair of 1998, distinctions between indecency and political discourse have become blurred. When major news organizations regularly publish or broadcast content that describes or analyzes sexual acts in detail, it is hard to justify holding Internet content to a more restrictive standard. Even the U.S. Congress is not immune to the reality that indecent speech cannot be easily curtailed. Faced with releasing independent counsel Kenneth Starr's sexually explicit grand-jury report in September 1998, Congress chose to disseminate the report widely on the Internet. Ironically, this was exactly the type of conduct Congress had sought to criminalize when it passed the original Communications Decency Act only two years earlier.

Michael M. Epstein is a professor at Southwestern University School of Law and an attorney with a Ph.D. in American studies.

today eliminating some forms of sexual content from television remains a top priority for many politicians and public-interest groups.

Although the "back alleys of sex chat" and the "off-road environment" of the Internet have drawn considerable public attention, early studies estimated that less than 1 percent of all communication on the Internet was pornographic.[15] Many commercial online services and some informal newsgroups have instituted rules aimed at curbing inappropriate language and material at sites that children might visit. Nonetheless, <www.searchterms.com> suggests that topics related to sex are still among the most widely used search terms on the World Wide Web. And by 1999, pornographic sites were among the most profitable regions of the Internet. Another area of concern are Internet sites that carry potentially dangerous information, such

While the Internet has the potential to spread ideas worldwide, it can also be used to spread pornography, hate speech, and other closed-minded ideas. Lewis Lapham, the editor of *Harper's,* warns us that the digital highway can be a place that *excludes* as often as it *includes:* "We need never see or talk to anybody with whom we don't agree."

■ SCIENCE & SOCIETY

Hatemongering on the data highway

Bigotry carves out a niche in cyberspace

Chicago computer buff Bob Arbetman was happily surfing through cyberspace one night when his attention was drawn to a bulletin board offering titled HOLOHOAX.TXT. Tapping in, Arbetman found himself in touch with a professional Holocaust denier whose message, he says, was rabidly antisemitic. "It was straight neo-Nazi propaganda," recalls the 37-year-old electrical engineer.

Outraged by what he was downloading, Arbetman alerted the Simon Wiesenthal Center, the Los Angeles-based institute that exposes neo-Nazis and other bigots. His tip and calls from others who had encountered similar online, often violent, antiblack, antigay, antisemitic hate messages triggered an extensive three-year investigation by Wiesenthal researcher Rick Eaton. The result, *U.S. News* has learned, is a massive dossier of cyberspace hatemongering that the Wiesenthal Center has just submitted to FCC Chairman Reed Hundt. "It may be time for the FCC to place a cop on the superhighway of information," says Rabbi Abraham Cooper, Wiesenthal Center associate dean.

A right to hate. But any attempt to police cyberspace is fraught with practical and legal issues.

television or radio, and so subject to control, or more like the telephone system or the mail, which have greater freedoms over the content of the messages. Unless hate mail directly interferes with civil liberties, insists Godwin, "I can't conceive

invitations to violence and hate. A file called HOMOBASH describes shooting a gay person in the face with a handgun. A graphic titled MONKEY pictures blacks copulating with animals and suggests this was the start of the AIDS epidemic. Another shows a bare-chested, hooknosed Jew holding a bloody knife and standing in a sea of gentile blood.

Some commercial networks, such as Prodigy, say they have taken steps to ban the use of their systems by propagandists of bias. Vinton Cerf, president of the Internet Society, a user organization, says he and his colleagues are preparing a set of voluntary norms they hope will put restraints on racists and other objectionable E-mailers. But guidelines may have little effect in a freewheeling venue such

---

as directions for making bombs, or that advocate violence, such as an antiabortion site called "The Nuremberg Files," which posted personal information about abortion providers in the form of Old West–style "wanted" posters.

Another key issue that people are concerned about is Internet security. Both private users and public institutions worry that government agencies can easily invade their privacy through home and business computers. With the growing use of personal computers in the 1980s, concerns have increased over intrusion into bank accounts, hospital records, and other private matters. A high-profile 1995 case highlighted another problem. A computer hacker stole twenty thousand credit-card numbers from a subscriber list of one of the country's largest Internet-access providers. To counter cyberspace theft, MasterCard and BankAmericard joined with the software firm Netscape in the mid-1990s to develop a system that would allow consumers to buy products online without their credit-card numbers being hijacked.

Although consumers were initially reluctant to divulge credit-card account numbers and other information over the Web, they have quickly warmed to the idea as more rigorous data-encryption standards have been developed and as more companies offer products online. Internet sales that totaled $3 billion in 1997 almost doubled to $5 billion in 1998 and were expected to explode tenfold, to $30 billion, by 2000. Women, who had at first been more skeptical than men about buying products online, are now more likely to make multiple purchases and spend more. Still, more than 60 percent of Internet shoppers are men.

With the growth in e-commerce, however, comes the growth of online marketing strategies and attempts to collect information on Web users. One increasingly common method of gathering information on users is through "cookies"—information profiles about a user that are usually automatically accepted by the Web browser and stored on the user's own computer hard drive. Cookies work as "spies," sending back information to track the user's subsequent visits within that Web site. In a relatively benign situation, cookies can tell a Web site that the user is cleared for access to an authorized site, such as a library database that is open only to university faculty and students. More intrusive are Web sites that use cookies to record the user's Internet account, the last several Web pages visited, and other information that is stored in that person's Web-browser directory. In these cases, the Web sites create a marketing profile of the user and can target certain advertisements to the user. Cookies are automatically accepted by most browsers, although preference commands can be set to reject cookies or provide warnings when a Web site is trying to set such a system. Still, some Web sites, such as that of the *New York Times*, require the user to accept cookies in order to gain access to the site.

competing highways and the knowledge gap

By the mid-1990s, two economic models had emerged to represent the future of the information highway. One model features a one-way communication framework with traditional cable and broadcast TV services that provide content on vast five-hundred-channel systems. For example, a viewer at home could watch and monitor congressional proceedings on cable's two C-Span channels. According to this model, consumers and citizens are rather passive players in the mass-communication process, choosing from a smorgasbord of available services that others have designed. The second framework offers a telephone or computer model. It has an interpersonal, or two-way, channel system, in which users play more active roles in the information process, often designing their own Web sites and picking their conversational partners. In this model, users participate in producing and delivering program services. Through email or a newsgroup, they can contact representatives in Congress and receive quick responses, either directly from legislators or from an office staffer. In this model, anyone in the system can theoretically contact anyone else.

From the vantage point of which model best serves democracy, many observers predict that by the beginning of the twenty-first century the best ideas from both models will emerge. In such a scenario, telephone companies, computer services, cable operators, broadcast interests, powerful leaders, elite entrepreneurs, and ordinary citizens would all play a role in extending the highway and ensuring enough entry ramps for everyone who wants to ride. Under a combination model, a large chunk of the highway would operate more like cable public-access channels, in which viewers and citizens actively participate in the development and direction of programming and content.

One key economic issue is whether the cost of the information highway will undermine equal access. For example, converting the current system to fiber optics will cost an estimated $15 to $20 billion by the end of the twentieth century. Paying for this conversion could result in an ever-widening **knowledge gap**. Mimicking the economic disparity between rich and poor that grew more pronounced during the 1980s, the knowledge gap refers to the growing contrast between "information haves," or digital highway users who can afford to acquire multiple media services, and "information have-nots," users who cannot afford a computer, much less the many options now available on the highway. Although monthly programming services might become relatively inexpensive, the combined costs of computer technology and cable programming may make easy access to the highway less realizable for less affluent citizens.

Media critic Marc Gunther offers an analogy for access to virtual and real highways: "If the information highway becomes a vital communications link in the 21st Century, who will be able to ride? . . . The interstates of the 1950s helped relocate jobs to the suburbs and beyond, leaving city folks stranded unless they owned cars."[16] Whereas traditional media made the same information available to everyone who owned a radio or a TV set, the information highway could create economic tiers and classes of service. It could become a toll road rather than a freeway, with wealthy users buying many tiers of service. Policy groups, media critics, and concerned citizens continue to debate the implications of media access for democratic societies, which have traditionally valued the equal opportunity to acquire knowledge.

Also, for reasons of access, Internet use is uneven across demographic groups. Although by 1998 blacks, Native Americans, Asians, and women over fifty were among the fastest-growing groups of users, whites were much more likely to have access to computers and to use the Internet—even across all income levels—and men made up 57 percent of the Internet community, leaving women in the minority.

problems and possibilities

Current developments on the information highway, including the expanding roles of broadcasting and cable companies, are at a crossroads comparable to that of the early development of radio. In the 1920s, corporate interests in radio pushed aside many noncommercial and civic interests. Similarly, in today's digital environment corporate interests, not government agencies, are building and programming the new systems. The passage of the 1996 Telecommunications Act cleared the way for cable TV systems, computer firms, and telephone companies to merge their interests in advancing communication technology. Companies such as AT&T and the regional Bell phone companies, for instance, have the ready capital to invest in the new information systems.

It is estimated that 50 percent of adults in the United States and Canada will be using the Internet by 2000, thus greatly increasing its possibilities and intensifying problems for agencies that are trying to regulate it. If the past is any predictor, it seems realistic to expect that the Internet's potential for wide democratic use could be partially preempted by narrower commercial interests. As media economist Douglas Gomery warns, "Technology alone does not a communication revolution make. Economics trumps technology every time."[17]

With economic interests trumping technological innovation, a major concern about the information highway relates to corporate downsizing. To reduce payroll overhead, many companies are using sophisticated computer technologies, managed by legions of part-time and full-time computer wizards. This change has reduced traditional job possibilities:

> [T]op down corporate hierarchies are flattening into horizontal, decentralized networks of self-governing work teams. But this flattening process is also crushing and marginalizing millions of once productive citizens. Whole strata of blue-collar and white-collar workers are being downsized into oblivion, their work now performed more efficiently by networked information systems or farmed out to cheap-labor production centers in new global markets overseas.[18]

In the early to mid-1990s, when Internet use began its steep climb, U.S. companies eliminated nearly three million jobs under restructuring plans; much of the downsizing was made possible by the speed and efficiency of new communications technologies.[19]

On the more positive side of the ledger, the new technologies offer at least the potential for enriching democratic processes. Books, newspapers, magazines, radio, film, and television widened and expanded the reach of media, but they did not generate equivalent avenues for response and debate. Defenders of the digital age argue that newer media forms—from radio talk shows to televised town-hall meetings and Internet newsgroups—allow greater participation. Individuals can create their own Web sites and seek the Web sites of others, joining and encouraging conversations about movies, politics, or the meaning of God. In response to these new media forms, older print media are using Internet technology to increase their access to and feedback from varied audiences, soliciting email from users and fostering discussions in chat rooms.

Despite the potential of new media forms, skeptics raise doubts about the participatory nature of discussions on the Internet. For instance, critics warn that Internet users may be searching out only those people whose beliefs and values are similar to theirs. Although it is important to be able to communicate across vast distances with people who have similar viewpoints, these kinds of cyberspace discussions may not serve to extend the diversity and tolerance that are central to democratic ideals.

Access to information also remains a problem. More than 98 percent of all U.S. homes have TV sets, but 7 percent of American households, most of them poor, still do not have basic telephone service, much less the modems and computers needed to join the Internet. By 1999, about half of all American homes had personal computers,

"Unfortunately, there has been far too little discussion of the deeper citizenship issues that stir like fault pressures beneath the bedrock surface of the emerging Information Highway."
—Mitch Kapor, founder, Lotus software, 1993

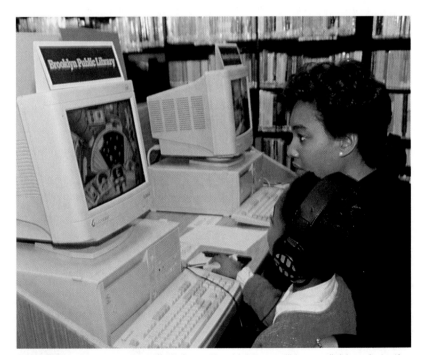

With serious concerns that the information highway will be available only to the most affluent or educated in society, many communities have begun offering access to Internet and World Wide Web services through public libraries, like this one in Brooklyn, New York.

and about 35 percent used modems.[20] In addition, even with a computer and a modem, connecting to an online service and the Internet generally required another substantial monthly fee.

Some communities and organizations are beginning to address the access problem by installing computers equipped with Internet connections in libraries, banks, schools, and other public locations; this gives most community members entry to the Internet, thus encouraging public discussions about taxes, homelessness, rent control, unemployment, and other pressing issues of the day. To aid Internet access, in 1997 the Gates Learning Foundation (which is endowed with more than a billion dollars by Microsoft Corporation chairman Bill Gates and his wife, Melinda) began to donate money for public-access computers to libraries across the United States. While libraries are free to purchase any kind of computer equipment they choose, the foundation provides technical support only for machines that operate with the Microsoft Windows operating system, causing some to label Gates's philanthropy as self-serving.

Globally, though, the have-nots have an even greater obstacle to overcome in connecting to the Internet. Although the Web claims to be worldwide, countries like the United States, Norway, Sweden, Finland, Japan, Israel, Australia, Britain, and Germany account for most of its international flavor. In nations such as Iran, Jordan, Saudi Arabia, Syria, Iraq, China, and Myanmar, the governments permit limited or no access to the Web. In countries like Argentina, Columbia, Brazil, and Mexico, a poor telecommunications infrastructure means that consumers must endure painfully long waits in order to participate. In other countries, phone lines and computers are almost nonexistent.[21] Africa has a substantial population but is particularly technology-poor; the *New York Times* notes that Manhattan has more telephone lines than the thirty-six countries of Sub-Saharan Africa.[22]

To take a critical position on the information-highway debates, we must analyze and judge its possibilities and limitations. Such a position should be grounded in the knowledge that the media are converging nationally and globally, changing the nature of mass communication. One of these changes is *mass customization*, whereby product companies and content providers can customize a Web page or media form for an

As a delicate peace between Israel and Palestine emerged in the late 1990s, a more stable political situation and a stronger economy allowed many Palestinians to take advantage of the World Wide Web at home and at Internet cafes, such as this one in Ramallah, Israel.

individual consumer. For example, NewsEdge Corporation, a Massachusetts firm, operates a Web site and online service called NewsPage. Potential customers who "hit" the site can choose from more than fourteen hundred business-related news issues and categories. After a user completes a consumer profile, the NewsPage software scours fifteen thousand daily and weekly stories generated by six hundred magazines, newspapers, and newsletters, and provides a personalized electronic newspaper for use. The basic service is free, unless the user requests a higher-level premium service. Internet firms such as Excite, Yahoo!, and Netscape also provide similar free personalized front-page services for clients. Such services blur the boundary between one-to-one communication, which we generally associate with an office conversation or a telephone call, and mass communication, which we associate with daily newspapers or TV programs.

It is also no longer very useful to discuss print media and electronic or digital media as if they were completely segregated forms. We live in a world in which a ten-year-old can simultaneously watch an old TV rerun on cable and read the latest *Fear Street* book, where a twenty-year-old student can make sense of a nineteenth-century poem while wearing a Walkman tuned to alternative rock. Moreover, it is now possible to access old reruns, horror thrillers, classic literary texts, and alternative music all through a home computer and Internet connection. Today, developments in word processing, email, books on tape, cable-access channels, children's pictorial literature, magazine advertising, and Internet newsgroups are integrating aspects of both print and electronic culture at the crossroads of everyday life. By 1998, more than seventy million Americans over the age of sixteen—one-third of the country's adult population—used the Internet on a regular basis, many of them as producers as well as consumers of mass communication.[23]

REVIEW QUESTIONS

Origins of the Information Highway

1. What are the three stages in the development of a mass medium?

2. How did the Internet originate? What does its development have in common with earlier mass media?

Information Access on the Information Highway

3. What is media convergence? How does this phenomenon distinguish a different phase in mass-media history?

4. What three key technological developments have made today's intersection of mass media along the information highway possible?

5. How does the World Wide Web work? Why is it significant in the development of the Internet?

6. What are the four major mapping systems of the Internet? How do they make the Internet more organized for the user?

Ownership Issues on the Internet

7. What are the key issues involving ownership of the Internet? How do these issues differ from earlier ownership issues in other mass media?

8. Who are the major players vying for control of the Internet?

Citizens, Cyberspace, and Democracy

9. What are the central concerns about the Internet regarding freedom of expression?

10. What is the knowledge gap, and what does it have to do with the information highway?

11. What are the key problems involving the expansion of the information highway? How can the information highway make democracy work better?

1. If you have been on the Internet, what was your first encounter like? If you have not used the Internet, go to your school or local library and sign on so that you can participate in the following questions.

2. What features of the information highway are you most excited about? Why? What features are most troubling? Why?

3. What are the advantages of an electronic-digital highway that links together televisions, computers, phones, audio equipment, homes, schools, and offices?

4. Do you think virtual communities are genuine communities? Why or why not?

5. As we move from a print-oriented Industrial Age to a digitally based Information Age, how do you think individuals, communities, and nations will be affected?

SEARCHING THE INTERNET

http://www.cdt.org
The Center for Democracy and Technology, a non-profit group, works to promote "democratic values and constitutional liberties in the digital age" by tracking industry and legislative action that affect such issues as privacy, bandwidth, domain names, and free expression.

http://www.cnet.com
Founded in 1995, the commercial site of the Computer Network (CNET) offers a wealth of information about computers, the Internet, and digital technologies.

http://www.eff.org
The Electronic Frontier Foundation was formed to protect civil liberties on the Internet and "to help civilize the electronic frontier; to make it truly useful and beneficial not just to a technical elite, but to everyone."

http://www.internet2.edu
Detailing the latest developments of Internet2, this site offers information on the private consortium of more than 130 universities and corporations that are building and testing the Internet's multimedia-friendly second generation.

http://www.ngi.gov
The federal government site for the NGI Initiative, which coordinates the efforts of federal agencies that are helping to create a new high-capacity Internet.

http://www.zdnet.com
Provided by Ziff-Davis, the leading publisher of computer magazines, Zdnet.com is a comprehensive site for computer and Internet news.

In Brief

This "think-pair-share" exercise focuses on the Internet and its content.

Think: On your own, spend two to three minutes writing down what kind of content—if any—you think should not be on the World Wide Web. Be sure to consider pornography, hate speech, and potentially violent information, such as how to make bombs.

Pair: Turn to your neighbor and compare notes. Do your concerns about certain kinds of Internet content matter only if children might see it? Did either of you list excessive commercialism as a problem? What are the most valuable things about the Internet?

Share: As a class, consider the content of the Internet. Should anything on the Internet be censored? What is the value of the Internet to our society? The Internet is fairly new—does it seem to be developing in a positive direction? If you could rethink the direction and uses of the Internet, what would they be?

In Depth

Create a one- to two-page profile of a typical Internet user. Interview five to ten people—students, friends, teachers, employers, or other users—who travel the Internet at least two or three times each week. Find out what sites they visit and how much time they spend on the Internet per day. What do these users have in common? Are there different types of Net users? Consider their gender, age, education, occupation, and other pertinent background information. What do the users consider to be the benefits and drawbacks of the Internet?

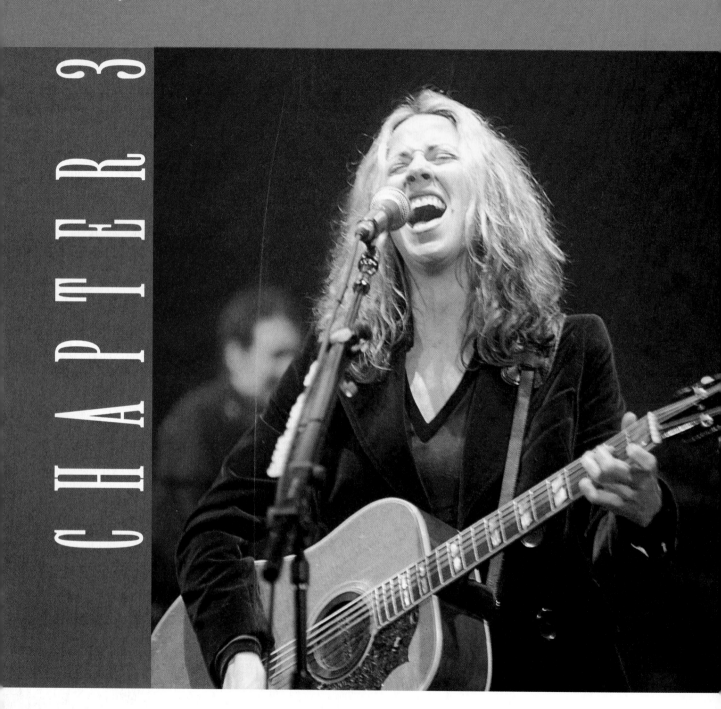

Sound Recording

and Popular Music

CHAPTER 3

There was little in her background to suggest that by her mid-thirties her music would not be welcome in one of the nation's largest retail chains. Born in Kennett, Missouri, in 1962, she twirled batons and ran track in high school. A gifted singer, she learned to play the piano, the accordion, and the guitar. At the University of Missouri, she performed in a band called Cashmere and earned enough credits to land a job teaching music at a St. Louis grade school. At age twenty-four, she left Missouri for Los Angeles, where she worked as a backup singer for Michael Jackson, Don Henley, Eric Clapton, and Rod Stewart.[1]

Then, in 1993, Sheryl Crow launched a solo career. In 1994, her single "All I Wanna Do" soared to the top of the pop charts, making her a star. Crow's first album, *Tuesday Night Music Club*, sold nine million copies. In 1995, she won three Grammy Awards, including one for best new artist.

In 1996, the singer hit a snag. "Love Is a Good Thing," a song from her new CD, upset executives at Wal-Mart, the nation's largest retail store and biggest seller of popular music. The song contained the following lyrics: "Watch out sister / watch out brother / watch our children as they kill each other / with a gun they bought at the Wal-Mart Discount stores."

Wal-Mart banned the album.

Throughout the 1990s, Wal-Mart had won praise from parents and politicians for refusing to sell music that had explicit sexual or violent lyrics. With seventy million customers walking its aisles each year, the retailer decided not to stock recordings that contained advisory labels and has even altered questionable covers. But the *Sheryl Crow* CD contained neither an advisory nor a controversial cover. Although Wal-Mart does not sell guns to minors, in a few incidents involving juveniles police have traced weapons and ammunition to isolated Wal-Mart stores. In fact, in 1994 the company stopped selling handguns in its stores. For her part, Crow worried that without Wal-Mart her fans in remote areas would be unable to find her music. In a few cities during the Crow affair, imaginative deejays distributed copies of the singer's CD in Wal-Mart parking lots. Meanwhile, at Crow's concerts fans continued to call out for "the Wal-Mart song."

Throughout history, popular music has been banned by parents, business outlets, radio stations, school officials, and even governments seeking to protect young people from the raw language and corrupting excesses of the music world. At a time when various forms of rock music have become an ever-present annoyance to many, we forget that in the late 1700s authorities in Europe, thinking that it was immoral for young people to dance so close together, outlawed the waltz as "savagery." A hundred years later, the Argentinian upper class tried to suppress the tango, whose urban roots could be traced to the bars and bordellos of Buenos Aires. The first Latin music and dance to gain international popularity, the tango migrated to Paris in the early twentieth century, and was condemned by the clergy for its impact on French youth. During the 1920s, some adults criticized the Charleston, a dance that featured cheek-to-cheek contact by partners. Rock and roll in the 1950s and rap in the 1990s added their chapters to the age-old battle between generations.

The medium of sound recording has had an immense impact on our culture. The music that helps to shape our identities and comfort us during the transition from childhood to adulthood resonates throughout our lives. It stirs debate among parents and teenagers, teachers and students, politicians and performers. To place the impact of popular music in context, we will begin by investigating the origins of recording's technological "hardware." We will review Thomas Edison's early phonograph, Emile Berliner's invention of the flat disk record, and the development of audiotape and compact disks. We will study radio's early threat to sound recording and the subsequent alliance between the two media when television arrived in the 1950s.

In this chapter, we will also examine the content and culture of the music industry. The predominant role of rock music is a key point of reference. Many important forms of music have become popular—including classical, tango, jazz, salsa, country, blues, gospel, rap, and folk—but no other musical expression has had such an extraordinary impact on other mass-media forms. With the introduction of music videos in the early 1980s, rock music dramatically changed the cable and TV landscapes. More significantly, rock music simultaneously linked and transformed the fundamental structure of *two* mass-media industries: sound recording and radio. Beginning in the 1950s, rock music created an enormous and enduring consumer youth market for sound recordings, and it provided much-needed content for radio at a time when television had "borrowed" most of radio's longtime programming. Rock music has influenced a diverse array of international cultures, operating as a kind of common ground for fans worldwide. In this chapter, we will look at rock and other contemporary forms of popular music as we survey the growth of sound recording as a mass medium. Finally, we will examine economic and democratic issues facing the recording industry.

> "If people knew what this stuff was about, we'd probably all get arrested."
>
> —Bob Dylan, 1966

early technology and the development of sound recording

New mass media have often been defined in terms of the communication technology that preceded them. For example, movies were initially called *motion pictures*, a term from photography that stuck; radio was referred to as *wireless telegraphy;* and television was often called *picture radio.* Sound recording instruments were initially labeled *talking machines* and later called *phonographs*, when Thomas Edison made a recording device in 1877 that played back voices. Edison's invention was the result of tinkering with existing innovations, the tele*phone* and the tele*graph*. The origin of *tele-* is the Greek word for "far off"; *phono-* and *-graph* come from the Greek words for "sound" and "writing." This early blending of technology foreshadowed our contemporary era, in which media as diverse as newspapers and movies are converging on the information highway. Before the Internet, however, the first major media convergence involved the relationship between the sound recording and radio industries.

wax cylinders and flat disks

In the 1850s, the French printer Leon Scott de Martinville conducted the first experiments with sound recording. Using a hog's hair bristle as a needle, he tied one end to a thin membrane stretched over the narrow part of a funnel. When the inventor spoke into the funnel, the membrane vibrated, and the free end of the bristle made grooves on a revolving cylinder coated with a thick liquid called *lamp black*. Different sounds made different trails in the lamp black. However, de Martinville could not figure out how to play back the sound. That is what Thomas Edison did in 1877. He recorded his voice by using a needle to press his voice's sound waves onto tinfoil wrapped around a metal cylinder about the size of a cardboard toilet-paper roll. After recording his voice, Edison played it back by repositioning the needle to retrace the grooves in the foil, a material he later replaced with wax.

As we discussed in Chapter 2, most new media pass through three developmental stages. The first is the novelty stage, in which inventors experiment to solve a particular problem, such as how to play back recorded music. In the second or entrepreneurial stage, inventors and investors work out a practical and marketable use for the new device. Edison, for example, initially thought of his phonograph as a kind of answering machine; he envisioned a "telephone repeater" that would "provide invaluable records, instead of being the recipient of momentary and fleeting communication."[2]

In the third stage, entrepreneurs figure out how to market the new device as a consumer product. For sound recording, a key breakthrough at this stage came from Emile Berliner, a German engineer who had immigrated to America. In the late 1880s, he began using a flat spinning five-inch disk to trace voices. Through a photo-engraving process, he recorded the sounds onto disks made of metal and shellac. These disks became the first records. Using Edison's ideas, Berliner developed a machine for playing his disks on the first turntable, which he called a *gramophone*.

Berliner also developed a technique that allowed him to stamp and mass-produce his round records. Previously, using Edison's cylinder, performers had to play or sing into the speaker for *each* separate recording. Berliner's technique featured a master recording from which copies could be easily duplicated in mass quantities. In addition, the industry realized that disks needed to have places for labels, so that the music could be differentiated by title, performer, and songwriter. This led to the development of a "star system," because fans could identify and choose their favorite sounds and artists.

Now is the time to select your Victrola for Christmas

Victrola Instruments and Victor Records are so much in demand for gifts that there is a shortage every Christmas. Place your order now while all the twenty-one instrument styles at from $25 up and complete record stocks are available.

Ask your dealer or write to us for illustrated catalogs.

Victrola

Look under the lid and on the labels for these Victor trade marks

Victor Talking Machine Company, Camden, N.J.

This ad for a Victrola ran in magazines in 1922. RCA bought the Victrola company in the late 1920s and adopted its famous "His Master's Voice" trademark, which became one of the most famous trademarks of the twentieth century.

Another breakthrough occurred in the early twentieth century, when the Victor Talking Machine Company placed the hardware, or "guts," of the record player inside a piece of furniture. These early record players, known as Victrolas, were mechanical and had to be primed with a crank handle. Electric record players, first available in 1925, gradually replaced Victrolas in the late 1920s as more homes were wired for electricity.

In the 1940s, since shellac was needed for World War II munitions production, the record industry turned to a polyvinyl plastic record. The vinyl recordings turned out to be more durable than shellac records, which broke easily. In 1948, CBS Records introduced the 33⅓ revolutions-per-minute (rpm) *long-playing record* (LP), with about ten minutes of music on each side. This was an improvement over the three to four minutes of music contained on the existing 78-rpm records. The next year, RCA developed a competing 45-rpm record, featuring a quarter-size hole (best suited for jukebox use). The two new standards were technically incompatible, meaning they could not be played on each other's machines. A five-year marketing battle ensued, similar to the VHS and Beta war over consumer video standards in the 1980s, or the Macintosh vs. Windows battle over computer-operating-system standards in the 1980s and 1990s. In 1953, CBS and RCA compromised. The 33⅓ record became the standard for long-playing albums and collections of music, and 45s became the format for two-sided singles. Record players were designed to accommodate 45s, 33⅓ LPs, and, for a while, 78s. The 78-rpm record, however, eventually became obsolete, doomed to antique collections along with Edison's wax cylinders.

audiotape and cds

Berliner's flat disk would be the key recording advancement until the advent of **audiotape** in the 1940s, when German engineers developed plastic magnetic tape (which U.S. soldiers confiscated at the end of the war). Lightweight magnetized strands of ribbon finally allowed sound editing and multiple-track mixing, in which instrumentals or vocals could be recorded at one location and later mixed onto a master recording in another studio.

The first machines developed to play magnetized audiotape were bulky reel-to-reel devices. But by the mid-1960s, engineers had placed reel-to-reel audiotapes inside small plastic cassettes. Audiotape also permitted "home dubbing": Consumers could copy their favorite records onto tape or record songs from the radio. This practice denied sales to the worried recording industry; during the period from the mid to late 1970s, record sales dropped by 20 percent. Meanwhile, blank audiotape sales doubled. Some thought audiotape would kill record albums because of its superior sound and editing capability, but commercial sales of albums did not plummet until the compact disk came along in the 1980s.

In 1958, engineers developed stereophonic sound, or **stereo**, which eventually made monophonic (one-track) records obsolete. Stereo permitted the recording of two separate channels, or tracks, of sound. Recording-studio engineers, using audio-tape, could now record many instrumental or vocal tracks, which they "mixed down" to the two stereo tracks. Playing the channels back through two loudspeakers creates a more natural sound distribution that fills a room.

The biggest recording advancement came in the 1970s, when electrical engineer Thomas Stockham developed **digital recording**, in which music is played back by laser beam rather than by needle or magnetic tape. Digital recorders translate sound waves into computer-like on/off impulses and store the impulses on disks in binary code. When played back, the laser decodes, or "reads," the stored impulses; a microprocessor translates these numerical codes into sound and sends them through the loudspeakers. This technique began replacing Edison's **analog recording** technique, which merely captured the fluctuations of the original sound waves and stored those signals on records or cassettes as a continuous stream of magnetism—*analogous* to the actual sound. Incorporating purer, more precise digital techniques (which do not add noise during recording and editing sessions), **compact disks**, or **CDs**, hit the market in 1983.

By 1987, CD sales had doubled LP album sales (see Figure 3.1). Although audiocassette sales outnumbered CD sales two to one as recently as 1988, by 1998 CDs outsold cassettes nearly four to one. To compete with CDs, some manufacturers introduced digital cassette tapes with improved sound quality. One such format, **digital audiotape (DAT)**, was developed by Japanese engineers in the early 1990s. DAT featured CD-quality sound on a machine that could record as well as play back tapes. As a consumer product, the new tape format, even with its recording and dubbing capacity, could not overcome the head start of CDs. By 1997, more than 65 percent of all American households had a CD player, and consumers seemed reluctant to invest in new, incompatible formats. Sony's Mini-Disc format (which can record sound and play it back) and the forthcoming all-audio DVD format (with greater storage capacity) offer additional capabilities but are also compatible only with certain CD-player systems. In the late 1990s, CDs solidified their position as the leading music format with the introduction of CD-Rs (recordable CDs, which consumers can record on only once) and CD-RWs (rewriteable CDs, which can be recorded over many times). With the aid of desktop computers and the Internet, music fans began to download music files and "burn" them onto blank CDs. The technology allowed individuals to record music using the more durable digital CD format rather than cassettes. This development upset the major recording companies (see "Tracking Technology: MP3 and the Spread of Music" on page 96).

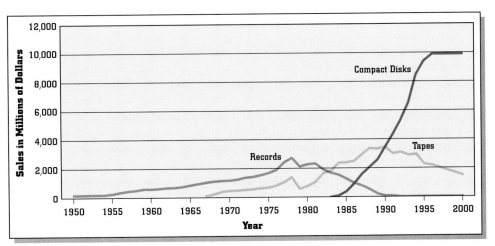

**Figure 3.1
Annual Record,
Tape, and CD Sales**
Source: Recording
Industry Association
of America.

surviving the threat of radio

By 1915, the phonograph had become a popular form of entertainment. The recording industry sold thirty million records that year, and by the end of the decade sales more than tripled each year. By 1924, though, record sales were only half of what they had been the previous year. Radio had arrived as a competing mass medium.

To avoid paying the record industry for copyrighted music, many radio stations started their own in-house orchestras. The American Society of Composers, Authors, and Publishers (ASCAP), founded in 1914 to collect copyright fees for publishers and writers, charged that radio was contributing to plummeting record and sheet-music sales. By 1925, before radio advertising had fully emerged, small and large stations were asked to pay between $250 and $2,500 a week for music rights. Between 1922 and 1925, six hundred stations left the air, in part because they could not pay for content.

But radio would ultimately win this early round. Throughout the late 1920s and the onset of the Depression, record and phonograph sales continued to fall. Meanwhile, music on radio remained free. When the Twenty-first Amendment repealed the thirteen-year constitutional ban on alcohol in 1933, however, the record industry got a boost. Music clubs and neighborhood taverns mushroomed in popularity. The introduction of the jukebox permitted bar owners to play records without hiring live bands—a hardship during the Depression. The record industry welcomed the new business. Although the 1930s marked a period of intense struggle between the radio and recording industries, the decade also launched the two media on an extended courtship.

By the 1950s, with television pilfering many of its variety shows, crime dramas, and comedy programs, as well as its advertising revenue, radio turned to the record industry for a cheap source of content. When songs were played on the air, record sales rose. By the end of the 1950s, the adversarial history of recording and radio had come full circle. Once the threatened medium in the 1930s, the music industry saved radio in the 1950s. The marriage of the two media would eventually enable both to prosper economically at record levels.

Just as radio would later improve its sound quality (through FM and stereo) to retain an edge over television, the recording industry survived during radio's golden age by continually improving sound reproduction. With RCA's acquisition of the Victrola company in 1929 came the development of radio-phonograph players. Then, in the 1930s, RCA began experimenting with *high-fidelity* systems, which improved phonographic sound dramatically. In the 1950s these "hi-fi" systems were introduced to the consumer market. Designed to produce the best fidelity (faithfulness to the music or voice without noise or distortion), the systems came in two varieties: *console* and *component*.

A variation on the Victrola, *console systems* combined several elements—radio tuner, turntable, speakers, and amplifier—all hardwired inside a piece of furniture. Hi-fis looked like dining-room sidebars and, based on the market research of the day, were marketed primarily to women. By the 1950s, when this consumer market was saturated, manufacturers "unpacked" the furniture, introducing *component systems,* which allowed consumers to mix and match different models and parts. They also permitted easier replacement of various elements. Once again, based on research that tapped into existing gender stereotypes, component systems featured lots of dials, chrome, and control panels—new marketing ploys aimed at men. Today, companies have created another market by melding the console and component concepts into *entertainment systems*. These systems allow users to stack various components, including a CD and a tape player, a television, a radio, and a VCR, into a large piece of furniture.

popular music and the formation of rock

Although popular music today refers to styles as diverse as blues, country, Tejano, salsa, jazz, rock, reggae, and rap, popular American music existed prior to these genres. In general, **pop music** appeals either to a wide cross section of the public or to sizable subdivisions within the larger public based on age, region, or ethnic background (for example, teenagers, southerners, Mexican Americans). The word *pop* has also been used to distinguish popular music from classical music, which is written primarily for ballet, opera, ensemble, or symphony. Although we sometimes assume that popular music depended on the phonograph and the radio for success, it actually existed prior to the development of these media.

the rise of pop music

In the late nineteenth century, the sale of sheet music for piano and other instruments spread rapidly in an area of Manhattan along Broadway known as Tin Pan Alley. During the popular ragtime era in the early 1900s, "tin pan" was a derisive term used to describe the way that quickly produced tunes supposedly sounded like cheap pans clanging together. The tradition of song publishing that began in Tin Pan Alley in the late 1800s continued throughout the 1950s, with such rock-and-roll writing teams as Jerry Lieber–Mike Stoller and Carole King–Gerry Goffin. Major influences during the earlier period included the marches of John Philip Sousa, the ragtime piano pieces of Scott Joplin, and the show tunes and vocal ballads of Irving Berlin, Hoagy Carmichael, George Gershwin, and Cole Porter.

> "Music should never be **harmless**."
> —Robbie Robertson, The Band

At the turn of the century, with the newfound ability of song publishers to mass-produce sheet music for a growing middle class captivated by a piano craze, popular songs moved from novelty stage to business enterprise. With the emergence of the phonograph, song publishers also discovered that recorded tunes boosted interest in and sales of sheet music. Although the popularity of sheet music would decline rapidly with the development of the radio in the 1920s, songwriting along Tin Pan Alley played a key role in transforming popular music into a mass medium.

As sheet music grew in popularity, **jazz** developed in New Orleans. An improvisational and mostly instrumental musical form, jazz absorbed and integrated a diverse body of musical styles, including African rhythms, blues, and gospel. Jazz influenced many bandleaders throughout the 1930s and 1940s. Groups led by Louis Armstrong, Count Basie, Tommy Dorsey, Duke Ellington, Benny Goodman, and Glenn Miller were among the most popular of the jazz, or "swing," bands, whose music also dominated radio and recording in their day.

The first vocal stars of popular music in the twentieth century were products of the vaudeville circuit (which radio, movies, and the Depression would kill in the 1930s). In 1929, Rudy Vallee wrapped himself in a raccoon coat and sang popular songs into a megaphone. In the 1930s, the bluesy harmonies of a New Orleans vocal trio, the Boswell Sisters, influenced the Andrew Sisters, whose boogie-woogie style helped them sell more than sixty million records in the late 1930s and 1940s. Also in the 1930s, Bing Crosby pioneered a relaxed, intimate style called crooning; he popularized Irving Berlin's "White Christmas," one of the most **covered** (recorded or performed by other artists) songs in recording history. In one of the first mutually beneficial alliances between sound recording and radio, many early pop vocalists had network or regional radio programs, which vastly increased their exposure. Ironically,

From the 1800s to the 1950s, New York's Tin Pan Alley was home to a successful songwriting tradition that played a key role in transforming popular music into a mass medium. Before the rise of radio, printed song sheets brought music into the home. Colorful examples of sheet music include the New Orleans–based jazz of Ferd "Jelly Roll" Morton; the wildly popular 1920s dance craze, the Charleston; and the influential ragtime of Scott Joplin.

their record sales, promoted on radio, boosted sound recording at a time when the record industry was threatened by the growing popularity of radio.

Frank Sinatra arrived in the 1940s. His romantic ballads foreshadowed the teen love songs of rock and roll's early years. Nicknamed "The Voice" early in his career, Sinatra, like Crosby, parlayed his music and radio exposure into movie stardom. (Both singers made more than fifty films apiece.) Helped by radio, Vallee, the Andrew Sisters, Crosby, and Sinatra were among the first vocalists to become popular with a large national teen audience. Their record sales helped stabilize the industry, and in the early 1940s, Sinatra's concerts alone caused the kind of audience riots that would later characterize rock-and-roll performances.

> "Frank Sinatra was categorized in 1943 as 'the glorification of ignorance and musical illiteracy.' "
> —Dick Clark,
> *The First
> 25 Years
> of Rock & Roll*

rock and roll: here to stay

The cultural storm called **rock and roll** hit in the 1950s. (Like the early meaning of *jazz, rock and roll* was a blues slang term that sometimes meant "sex.") It combined the vocal and instrumental traditions of popular music with the rhythm-and-blues sounds of Memphis and the country beat of Nashville. Early rock and roll was therefore considered the first "integrationist music," merging the black sounds of rhythm and blues, gospel, and Robert Johnson's screeching blues guitar with the white influences of country, folk, and pop vocals.[3] Only a few musical forms have ever sprung from such a diverse set of influences, and no new style of music has ever had such a widespread impact on so many different cultures. From an economic perspective, no single musical form prior to rock and roll had ever simultaneously transformed the structure of two mass-media industries: sound recording and radio.

Many social, cultural, economic, and political factors contributed to the growth of rock and roll in the 1940s and 1950s. First, radio, which saw its network programs converting to television, was seeking inexpensive forms of content. Radio deejays, particularly Alan Freed in Cleveland (and later on WINS in New York), began exposing more white people to black music. Some white teens cruising the radio dial had already discovered black-oriented stations, however, and had adopted the different rhythms as dance music. The migration of southern blacks to northern cities in search of better jobs during the first half of the twentieth century also spread different popular music styles.

During this time, **rhythm and blues**, or **R&B**, developed in various cities. Featuring "huge rhythm units smashing away behind screaming blues singers," R&B merged urban blues and big-band sounds.[4] As with rap today, young listeners were fascinated by the explicit (and forbidden) sexual lyrics in songs like "Annie Had a Baby," "Sexy Ways," and "Wild Wild Young Men." Although banned on some stations, R&B by 1953 aired on 25 percent of all radio stations for at least a few hours each week. In those days, black and white musical forms were segregated: Trade magazines tracked R&B record sales on "race" charts, which were kept separate from white record sales tracked on "pop" charts.

Second, in the repressive and uneasy atmosphere of the 1950s, with the constant concern over the atomic bomb, the Cold War, and communist witch-hunts, young people were seeking forms of escape from the menacing world created by adults. Teens have traditionally sought out music that has a beat—music they can dance to. In Europe in the late 1700s they popularized the waltz, and in America during the 1890s they took up a dance called the cakewalk. The trend continued during the 1920s with the Charleston, in the 1930s and 1940s with the jazz swing bands and the jitterbug, in the 1970s with disco, and in the 1980s and 1990s with hip-hop. Each of these twentieth-century musical forms began as dance and party music before their growing popularity eventually energized both record sales and radio formats.

Third, and most significant, the border that had separated white and black cultures began to break down. This process started with music and among the young, but it got a boost during the Korean War in the early 1950s, when President Truman signed an executive order integrating the armed forces. Young men drafted into the service were thrown together with others from very different ethnic and economic backgrounds. The biggest legal change, though, came with the *Brown v. Board of Education* decision in 1954. With this ruling, the Supreme Court officially ended "separate but equal" laws, which had kept white and black schools, hotels, restaurants, rest rooms, and drinking fountains segregated for decades. Thus mainstream America began to wrestle seriously with the legacy of slavery and the unequal treatment of its African American citizens. A cultural reflection of the times, rock and roll would burst from the midst of these social and political tensions.

rock muddies the waters

In the 1950s, legal integration accompanied a cultural shift, and the industry's race and pop charts blurred. White deejay Alan Freed had been playing black music for his young audiences since the early 1950s, and such white performers as Johnnie Ray and Bill Haley had crossed over to the race charts to score R&B hits. Black artists like Chuck Berry were performing country songs, and for a time Ray Charles even played in an otherwise all-white country band. Revitalizing record sales and changing the sound of radio, rock and roll exploded old distinctions and tested traditional boundaries in five critical ways.

High and Low Culture. In 1956, Chuck Berry's song "Roll Over Beethoven" introduced rock and roll to high culture: "You know my temperature's risin' / the jukebox is blowin' a fuse . . . Roll over Beethoven / and tell Tchaikovsky the news." Although such early rock-and-roll lyrics seem tame by today's standards, at the time, rock and rollers were challenging music decorum and the rules governing how musicians should behave (or misbehave): Berry's "duck walk" across the stage; Elvis Presley's pegged pants and gyrating hips, influenced by blues performers he admired; and Bo Diddley's use of the guitar as a phallic symbol, another old blues tradition. An affront to well-behaved classical-music audiences, such acts and antics would be imitated endlessly throughout rock's history. In fact, rock and roll's live exhibitions and the legends about them became key ingredients in promoting record sales.

> "Listening to my idol Nat [King] Cole prompted me to sing sentimental songs with distinct diction. The songs of Muddy Waters impelled me to deliver the down-home blues in the language they came from, Negro dialect. When I played hillbilly songs, I stressed my diction so that it was harder and whiter. All in all it was my intention to hold both the black and white clientele."
>
> —Chuck Berry,
> *The Autobiography,*
> 1987

Masculine and Feminine. Rock and roll was also the first popular music that overtly confused issues of sexuality. Although early rock largely attracted males as performers, the most fascinating feature of Elvis Presley, according to the Rolling Stones' Mick Jagger, was his androgynous appearance.[5] During this early period, though, the most sexually outrageous rock-and-roll performer was Little Richard (Penniman), who influenced a generation of extravagant rock stars.

Wearing a pompadour hairdo and assaulting his Steinway piano, Little Richard was considered rock's first drag queen, blurring the boundary between masculinity and femininity (although his act had been influenced by a flamboyant six-and-a-half-foot-tall gay piano player named Esquerita, who hosted drag-queen shows in New Orleans in the 1940s).[6] Little Richard has said that, given the reality of American racism, he feared the consequences of becoming a sex symbol for white girls: "I decided that my image should be crazy and way out so that adults would think I was harmless. I'd appear in one show dressed as the Queen of England and in the next as the pope."[7] By the end of the 1950s, although white parents may not have been overly concerned about their daughters falling for Little Richard, most adults did not view rock and roll as harmless.

Black and White. Rock and roll also blurred geographic borders between country and city, between black urban rhythms from Memphis and white country & western music from Nashville. Early white rockers such as Buddy Holly and Carl Perkins combined country or hillbilly music, southern gospel, and Mississippi Delta blues to create a sound called **rockabilly.** Raised on bluegrass music and radio's Grand Old Opry, Perkins (a sharecropper's son from Tennessee) mixed these influences with music he heard from black

Among the most influential and innovative American guitarists, Robert Johnson (1911–38) played the Mississippi Delta blues and was a major influence on early rock and rollers, especially the Rolling Stones and Eric Clapton. His intense slide-guitar and finger-style playing also inspired generations of blues artists, including Muddy Waters, Howlin' Wolf, Bonnie Raitt, and Stevie Ray Vaughan.

Although his unofficial title, "King of Rock and Roll," has been challenged by Little Richard and Chuck Berry, Elvis Presley remains the most popular solo artist of all time. From 1956 to 1962, he recorded seventeen No. 1 hits, from "Heartbreak Hotel" to "Good Luck Charm." According to Little Richard, Presley's major legacy was that he opened doors for many young performers and made black music popular in mainstream America.

cotton-field workers and blues singers like Muddy Waters and John Lee Hooker, both of whom used electric guitars in their performances. In 1956, Perkins recorded "Blue Suede Shoes"; a Presley cover version made the song famous.

Conversely, rhythm and blues spilled into rock and roll. The urban R&B influences on early rock came from Fats Domino ("Blueberry Hill"), Willie Mae "Big Mama" Thornton ("Hound Dog"), and Big Joe Turner ("Shake, Rattle, and Roll"). Many of these songs, first popular on R&B labels, crossed over to the pop charts during the mid to late 1950s (although many were performed by more widely known white artists). Chuck Berry, who originally played country music to supplement his day jobs as a beautician and carpenter, obliterated these boundaries. His first hit was "Maybellene," modeled on an old country song called "Ida Red." To earn royalties, since the country version was too old for copyright, Chess Records asked Berry to make some changes, and he renamed the song after a popular cosmetic product. Chess gave the record to Alan Freed, who attached his name to the credits in exchange for radio play. "Maybellene" became a No. 1 R&B hit in July 1955 and crossed over to the pop charts the next month, where it climbed to No. 5.

Although rock lyrics in the 1950s may not have been especially provocative or overtly political, soaring record sales and the crossover appeal of the music itself represented an enormous threat to long-standing racial and class boundaries. In 1956, the secretary of the North Alabama White Citizens Council bluntly spelled out the racism and white fear concerning the new prominence of African American culture: "Rock and roll is a means of pulling the white man down to the level of the Negro. It is part of a plot to undermine the morals of the youth of our nation."[8]

North and South. Not only did rock and roll muddy the urban and rural terrain, but in doing so it combined northern and southern influences as well. In fact, with so much blues, R&B, and rock and roll rising from the South, this region regained some of the cultural standing that it had lost after the Civil War. With many young northern middle-class teens influenced by southern "lower-class" music, rock and roll challenged stereotypes regarding class as well as race. Just as many white male teens today are fascinated by rap (buying more than 50 percent of the rap CDs on the commercial market by the late 1990s), Carl Perkins, Elvis Presley, and Buddy Holly—all from the rural South—were fascinated with and influenced by the black urban styles they had heard on the radio or seen in nightclubs.

But the key to record sales and the spread of rock and roll, according to famed record producer Sam Phillips, of Sun Records, was to find a white man who sounded black. Phillips found that man in Elvis Presley. Commenting on Presley's cultural importance, one critic wrote: "White rockabillies like Elvis took poor white southern mannerisms of speech and behavior deeper into mainstream culture than they had ever been taken, at the same time he was being reviled for seducing white youth with black music."[9]

> "[Elvis Presley's] kind of music is deplorable, a rancid smelling aphrodisiac."
>
> —Frank Sinatra, 1956

> "There have been many accolades uttered about his talent and performances through the years, all of which I agree with wholeheartedly."
>
> —Frank Sinatra, 1977

The Sacred and the Secular. Just as it confronted racial, sexual, regional, and class taboos, the new music for many mainstream adults also constituted an offense against God. Many early rock figures had close ties to religion. As a boy, Elvis Presley had dreamed of joining the Blackwoods, one of country-gospel's most influential groups. As a teen, Jerry Lee Lewis was thrown out of a Bible institute in Texas. Also influenced by church gospel music, Ray Charles changed the lyrics of an old gospel tune: "I've got a Savior / way over Jordan / he's saved my soul, oh yeah?" became "I got a woman / way over town / she's good to me." A top R&B hit in 1955, "I Got a Woman" became one of Charles's signature songs. The recording drew criticism from many African American church leaders and members, who worried about the impact of such worldly music on black youths.

Many people in the 1950s thought that rock and roll violated the boundary between the sacred and the secular. In the late 1950s, public outrage was so great that it even convinced Little Richard and Jerry Lee Lewis, both sons of southern preachers, that they were playing the "devil's music." By 1959, Little Richard had left rock and roll to become a minister. Lewis, too, feared that rock was no way to salvation. He had to be coerced into recording "Great Balls of Fire," a song by Otis Blackwell that turned an apocalyptic biblical phrase into a highly charged sexual teen love song. The tune, banned by many radio stations, nevertheless climbed to No. 2 on the pop charts late in 1957.

battles in rock and roll

With the blurring of racial lines, performers and producers played a tricky game as they tried to get R&B music accepted in the 1950s. Two prominent white disc jockeys used different methods. Alan Freed, credited with popularizing the term *rock and roll*, played original R&B songs from race charts and the black versions of early rock and roll. In contrast, Philadelphia deejay Dick Clark believed that making black music acceptable to white audiences required cover versions by white artists.

Some music historians point to Jackie Brenston's "Rocket 88" and other R&B songs from the early 1950s as the first rock and roll. But Bill Haley and the Comets, a former country group, scored the first No. 1 rock-and-roll hit on the *Billboard* pop chart in May 1955 with "Rock Around the Clock." The record had been an R&B hit in 1954, but it gained popularity and notoriety in the 1955 teen rebellion movie *Blackboard Jungle.* The song became a symbol of juvenile delinquency for many parents and raised concerns about negative influences in the changing recording industry.

Cover Music and Race. Since the integration of popular music in the 1960s, black and white artists have recorded and performed each other's original tunes. For example, Otis Redding, an established R&B songwriter, covered the Rolling Stones' "Satisfaction" in 1966. Both the Rolling Stones and Eric Clapton covered Robert Johnson's 1930s blues songs, and Clapton had a No. 1 hit in 1974 with Bob Marley's reggae tune "I Shot the Sheriff." More recently, Nirvana covered an old Leadbelly folk-blues tune, "In the Pines," and in 1998 Lauryn Hill covered Frankie Valli's hit from the 1960s, "Can't Take My Eyes Off of You."

Although today we take such rerecordings for granted, in the 1950s cover music was racially coded. Almost all popular covers were attempts by white producers and artists to capitalize on popular songs from the R&B charts and transform them into hits on the pop charts. Occasionally, white producers would list white performers like Elvis Presley, who never wrote songs himself, as co-writers for the tunes they covered. More often, dishonest producers would buy the rights to potential hits from naive songwriters, who seldom saw a penny in royalties or received credit as the writers.

During this period, black R&B artists, working for small record labels, saw many of their popular songs covered by white artists working for major labels. These cover records, boosted by better marketing and ties to white deejays, usually outsold the original black versions. Covers also slowed sales of the original releases and hampered smaller labels. For instance, the 1954 R&B song "Sh-Boom," by the Chords on Atlantic's Cat label, was immediately covered by a white group, the Crew Cuts, for the major Mercury label. Record sales declined for the Chords, although jukebox and R&B radio play remained strong for their original version. As rock critic Ed Ward suggested, "With 'Sh-Boom,' the pop establishment had found itself a potent weapon to use against R&B records—whiten them up and use the corporate might of a major label to get them to places a hapless [small label] caught with a hit on its hands could never reach."[10]

By 1955, R&B hits regularly crossed over to the pop charts. LaVern Baker's 1955 hit "Tweedlee Dee" for Atlantic was quickly covered by Mercury's Georgia Gibbs. Baker's version went to No. 14; two weeks later, Gibbs's cover reached No. 2 and stayed in the Top 40 for nineteen weeks. Pat Boone's cover of Fats Domino's "Ain't That a Shame" went to No. 1 and stayed on Top 40's pop chart for twenty weeks, while Domino's original made it only to No. 10.

During this time, Pat Boone ranked as the king of cover music, with thirty-eight Top 40 songs between 1955 and 1962. His records were second in sales only to Presley's. Slowly, however, the cover situation changed. After watching Boone outsell his song "Tutti-Frutti" in 1956, Little Richard wrote "Long Tall Sally," which included lyrics written and delivered in such a way that he believed Boone would not be able to adequately replicate them. "Long Tall Sally" went to No. 6 for Little Richard and charted for twelve weeks; Boone's version got to No. 8 and lasted nine weeks.

Overt racism lingered in the music business well into the 1960s. When the Marvelettes scored a No. 1 hit with "Please Mr. Postman" in 1961, their Tamla/Motown label had to substitute a cartoon album cover because many record-store owners feared customers would not buy a recording that pictured four black women. A turning point, however, came in 1962, the last year that Pat Boone, then age twenty-eight, ever had a Top 40 rock-and-roll hit. That year Ray Charles covered "I Can't Stop Loving You," a 1958 country song by the Grand Old Opry's Don Gibson. This marked the first time that a black artist, covering a white artist's song, had notched a No. 1 pop hit. With Charles's cover, the rock-and-roll merger between gospel and R&B and white country and pop became complete. In

Richard Wayne Penniman (Little Richard) was inducted into the Rock and Roll Hall of Fame in 1986. Little Richard played a key role in getting black music played on white radio stations and sold in mainstream record stores. His flamboyant, gender-tweaking style has been a major influence on many performers—notably Elton John and David Bowie in the 1970s, Culture Club and Prince in the 1980s, and Marilyn Manson and Dennis Rodman in the 1990s.

Buffalo Springfield's 1967 hit song "For What It's Worth" became an anthem of sorts for the antiestablishment youth movement of the 1960s. The melancholy melody opens with a slow two-note guitar intro that builds to an instantly recognizable chorus: "Stop, hey what's that sound, everybody look what's going down . . ."

The song may well have remained a baby-boomer rock classic had Chuck D, the creative voice behind the influential hip-hop group Public Enemy, not decided to revive it in a new form. Chuck D took "For What It's Worth" and carefully built a bass-heavy hip-hop groove beneath the song's original instruments, added a steady stream of new rap lyrics, and bolstered the chorus with a gospel choir. Like the rap-rock collaboration of Run-DMC and Aerosmith in 1986 for a groundbreaking new version of Aerosmith's "Walk This Way," and the 1998 Puff Daddy hit "Come with Me," featuring Led Zeppelin guitarist Jimmy Page, Chuck D invited the singer-songwriter Stephen Stills to add his voice to the chorus and perform on the music video. Stills, a founding

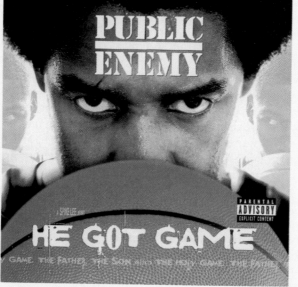

member of the short-lived group Buffalo Springfield (and later part of the more famous Crosby, Stills and Nash) had written and performed the original Buffalo Springfield hit.

In Chuck D's version, "For What It's Worth" became "He Got Game," the title cut on the sound track of Spike Lee's 1998 film of the same name. The movie, starring Denzel Washington and NBA player Ray Allen, is about a talented high-school basketball prospect who is hounded by

agents, shoe companies, and universities. The best of rap and hip-hop combines musical sampling with social or political messages, and in "He Got Game," Chuck D's rap critiques the game's overcommercialism: "It might feel good, it might sound a little somethin' / but damn the game if it don't mean nothing." Not surprisingly, the political sentiments from the 1960s youth movement—the need to expose existing power inequities and eloquently express outrage—apply equally to the ongoing exploitation of African Americans in the sports industry and the many existing forms of racism in society. In writing "He Got Game," Chuck D symbolically linked the 1960s generation of social consciousness with the present and created a new song that expertly crossed over generation, race, and genre. Besides the film's title song, Chuck D contributed to the film's entire sound track, with other songs such as "Politics of Sneaker Pimps" (which rails specifically against shoe companies) and "Super Agent" (a not-so-subtle attack on sports agents). *He Got Game* marked the first time that a hip-hop group contributed an entire sound track to a feature-length movie.

Public Enemy established itself as one of hip-hop's most influential and politically explosive groups with a string of seminal albums on the Def Jam label in the late 1980s and early 1990s, including *Yo! Bum Rush the Show* (1987); *It Takes a Nation of Millions to Hold Us Back* (1988); *Fear of a Black Planet* (1990); and *Apocalypse '91 . . . The Enemy Strikes Back* (1991). The group's singles are some of hip-hop's most memorable: "Don't Believe the Hype," "911 Is a Joke,"

fact, the relative acceptance of black crossover music provided a more favorable cultural context for the political activism that spurred important civil-rights legislation in the mid-1960s.

Payola, Records, and Radio. Rock and roll helped the recording and radio industries confront racism, but in other ways rock and roll has not benefited these two media. During the late 1950s, both industries faced the payola scandals. In the music

"Fight the Power" (the theme of Spike Lee's controversial 1989 movie *Do the Right Thing*), and "Can't Truss It." With Chuck D's especially incisive and creative lyrics critiquing racial injustice, economic oppression, and black-on-black racism, Public Enemy pushed hip-hop forward and gave it a strong political conscience. *Nation of Millions* is considered by some critics to be the best hip-hop album of all time.

Chuck D (then Carleton Ridenhour) first experimented with rap in the mid-1980s while he was a student of graphic design and a campus radio personality at Adelphi University, on Long Island, New York. His group, Public Enemy, also came to include Flavor Flav (William Drayton), who contrasts Chuck D's aggressive rap style with comic antics and posturing, and DJ Terminator X (Norman Rogers), who runs the turntables and rhythm tracks.

Sometimes referred to as the godfather of rap, Chuck D is known as an eloquent spokesman for his group and for rap itself, describing his music as "the CNN for black culture" and recognizing the potential of rap and hip-hop to unify and inform black audiences. Even as Chuck D called for greater diversity among rap artists, rap split into various camps in the 1990s— "old school" hip-hop, represented by Public Enemy; "gangsta rap," represented by such artists as NWA and Snoop Doggy Dog; and "pop," or "mainstream," hip-hop, represented by such artists as Puff Daddy and Will Smith. In the early 1990s, so-called gangstas began outselling alternative hip-hop three to one, and gangsta rap came to define the rap genre. By 1995, Public Enemy had disbanded after their 1994 album, *Muse Sick-N-Hour Mess Age*, was panned by critics and Flavor Flav went into drug rehabilitation. Chuck D recorded an underappreciated solo album in 1996, *Autobiography of Mista Chuck*. Yet after a four-year hiatus,

Chuck D

Public Enemy was on tour again with the *He got Game* sound-track album.

If Public Enemy had resurrected a rock classic with *He Got Game*, the group's members were in some ways resurrecting themselves as well. "The whole thing is to keep taking a lot of shots at the rim," Chuck D told the *Houston Chronicle*. "You keep doing it for the love of the art. I think it's a good thing that a group like Public Enemy can disappear for three or four years and then come back and still be relevant. We're trying to give hip-hop the longevity of a Led Zeppelin or a Rolling Stones."

Public Enemy's comeback takes place at a time when hip-hop is moving away from gangsta style and back to a more experimental sound, incorporating elements of R&B, soul, reggae, and rock. This diversity of sound and lyric is evident in the broad hip-hop spectrum represented by the recent successes of old and new artists such as Jay-Z, DMX, Lauryn Hill, Missy Elliott, Busta Rhymes, and the Beastie Boys. Chuck D has rejoined the fray, re-politicizing hip-hop with socially relevant lyrics and spurning the traditional ways of the music industry.

In an attempt to give artists and fans more control over music, Chuck D has brought his fighting spirit to the Internet, putting downloadable songs and remixes on his Public Enemy Web site <www.public-enemy.com> in the MP3 format. Public Enemy's music label, Def Jam (a unit of Universal/Polygram), pressured Public Enemy to remove the music from its Web site, but Chuck D left Def Jam rather than compromise. In early 1999, released from his label, Chuck D launched a live Internet radio site, <www.bringthenoise.com>, and became the first major performer to release a digital album both online (in MP3) and as a CD.

industry, **payola** is the practice of record promoters paying deejays or radio programmers to play particular songs. As recorded rock and roll became central to commercial radio in the 1950s, independent promoters hired by record labels pressured deejays to play the artists whom they represented. In the 1950s, as today, less than 10 percent of new releases became hits or sold more than the fifty thousand copies needed for a major label to make money. With the industry releasing a hundred new singles per week by the end of the 1950s, the demand for airplay—essential to establishing hit-record sales—was enormous. Although payola was considered unethical and a form of bribery, no laws prohibited its practice.

Following closely on the heels of television's quiz-show scandals, congressional hearings on radio payola began in December 1959. After a November announcement of the upcoming hearings, stations across the country fired deejays, and many others resigned. The hearings were partly a response to generally fraudulent business practices and partly an opportunity to blame deejays and radio for rock and roll's negative impact on teens (in the same manner that some politicians today routinely blame television or movies for escalating crime).

In 1959, shortly before the hearings, a Chicago deejay decided to clear the air. He broadcast secretly taped discussions in which a small independent record label acknowledged that it had paid $22,000 to ensure that a record would get airplay. The deejay, Phil Lind of WAIT, got calls threatening his life and had to have police protection. At the hearings in 1960, Alan Freed admitted to participating in payola, although he said he did not believe there was anything illegal about such deals. His career soon ended. Dick Clark, then an influential twenty-nine-year-old deejay and the host of TV's *American Bandstand*, would not admit to practicing payola. But the committee chastised Clark and alleged that a number of his complicated business deals were ethically questionable. Congress eventually added a law concerning payola to the Federal Communications Act, prescribing a $10,000 fine and/or a year in jail for each violation of the law. However, given the interdependent relationship between radio and recording, payola scandals persist. Along with MTV, radio still has enormous influence in making or breaking songs, careers, and a record label's investment.

A promotional strategy called *pay-for-play* emerged in 1998 as a legal alternative to payola. Like the paid programming of infomercials, pay-for-play involves up-front payments from record companies to radio stations to play a song a specific number of times. Some in the music industry find pay-for-play to be a safeguard against payola, since buying airtime eliminates the need to constantly pressure programmers to play certain music. Others argue that radio programmers abdicate their responsibility for the playlist with pay-for-play, and that listeners may not be completely aware of the financial payments to the radio station.

Taming the Music. By late 1959, many key figures in rock and roll had been tamed, partly by mounting social pressure against the music so often accused of undermining America's youths. Jerry Lee Lewis was exiled from the industry, labeled southern "white trash" for marrying his thirteen-year-old third cousin; Elvis Presley was drafted into the army; Chuck Berry was run out of Mississippi and eventually jailed for gun possession and transporting a minor (with a prostitution record) across state lines; and Little Richard left rock and roll to sing gospel music. Then, in February 1959, a plane crash in Iowa killed Buddy Holly ("Peggy Sue"), Richie Valens ("La Bamba"), and the Big Bopper ("Chantilly Lace"), a tragedy mourned in Don McLean's 1971 hit "American Pie" as "the day the music died."

Although rock and roll did not die in the late 1950s, the recording industry decided that it needed a makeover. To protect the enormous profits the new music had been generating, record companies began to discipline some of rock's rebellious impulses. In the early 1960s, in particular, the industry tried to clone Pat Boone by featuring a new generation of clean-cut white singers, including Frankie Avalon, who made beach-movie musicals for teenagers, and Ricky Nelson, the youngest son from TV's popular comedy series the *Adventures of Ozzie & Harriet*. Rock and roll's explosive violations of class and racial boundaries were, for a time, transformed into simpler generation-gap problems. By the early 1960s, the music had developed a milder reputation for merely fostering disagreements among parents and teens.

a changing industry: reformations in popular music

As the 1960s began, rock and roll was tamer and "safer," as reflected in the surf and road music of the Beach Boys and Jan & Dean. Rock music, however, was beginning to branch out in several directions. For instance, the success of producer Phil Spector's so-called all-girl groups, such as the Crystals ("He's a Rebel") and the Ronettes ("Be My Baby"), and other groups, such as the Shangri-Las ("Leader of the Pack"), challenged the male-dominated world of early rock. In addition, rock music and other popular styles went through cultural reformations that significantly changed the industry. These included the internationalization of sound recording during the "British invasion," the development of soul and Motown, the political impact of folk-rock, the rejection of music's mainstream by punk and grunge performers, and the reassertion of black urban style in the phenomenon of rap.

the british are coming!

Rock recordings today remain among America's largest economic exports, bringing in more than $15 billion a year from abroad. The origin of rock's global impact can be traced to England in the late 1950s, when the young Rolling Stones listened to the urban blues of Robert Johnson and Muddy Waters and the young Beatles tried to imitate Chuck Berry and Little Richard.

Until 1964, rock-and-roll recordings had traveled on a one-way ticket to Europe. While American artists regularly reached the top of the charts overseas, *no* British performers had yet appeared on any Top 10 pop lists in the States. This changed almost overnight. In 1964, the Beatles invaded with their mop haircuts and pop reinterpretations of American blues and rock and roll. By the end of the year, more than thirty British hits had landed on American Top 10 lists.

Ed Sullivan, who booked the Beatles several times on his TV variety show in 1964, helped promote their early success. Sullivan, though, reacted differently to the Rolling Stones, who had initially been rejected by British television because lead singer Mick Jagger sounded "too black." Before the Stones performed on Sullivan's program in 1964, he made them change a lyric from "let's spend the night together" to "let's spend some time together"; then he issued an apology to viewers following their performance. The Stones

Leading the British invasion of America's pop charts in 1964, the Beatles made several appearances on the *Ed Sullivan Show*. In addition to opening America's doors to other British artists in the mid-1960s, the Beatles championed musical innovations that are still found in music today, such as thematic albums, multitrack recording, and looping (a forerunner to sampling).

were not invited back. Performing black-influenced music and struggling for acceptance, the band was cast as the "bad boys" of rock in contrast to the "good" Beatles. Despite Sullivan's lack of support, the Stones would go on to inspire harder versions of rock music in the 1970s, what one conservative critic called "a relentless percussive assault on the human ear."[11]

With the British invasion, rock and roll unofficially became *rock*, sending popular music and the industry in two directions. On the one hand, the Stones, influenced by both blues and 1950s rock and roll, emphasized hard rhythms and vocals in their performances. Their music would influence a generation of hard-rock and heavy-metal performers, two of the many subgenres of rock that developed in the 1970s. The Beatles, on the other hand, influenced by Frank Sinatra as well as by rock and roll, more often stressed melody. Their music inspired rock's softer digressions. With the Beatles arriving shortly after the assassination of John F. Kennedy, America welcomed their more melodic and innocent recordings.

"Hard rock was rock's blues base electrified and upped in volume . . . heavy metal wanted to be the rock music equivalent of a horror movie— **loud, exaggerated, rude**, out for thrills only."　—Ken Tucker,
Rock of Ages,
1986

In the end, the British invasion verified what Chuck Berry and Little Richard had already demonstrated—that rock-and-roll performers could write and produce popular songs as well as Tin Pan Alley had. The success of British groups helped change an industry arrangement in which most pop music was produced by songwriting teams hired by major labels and matched with selected performers. Even more important, however, the British invasion showed the recording industry how older American musical forms, especially blues and R&B, could be repackaged as rock and exported around the world.

soul music and motown

Ironically, the British invasion, which drew much of its inspiration from black influences, siphoned off many white listeners from a new generation of black performers. Gradually, however, throughout the 1960s, black singers like James Brown, Sam Cooke, Aretha Franklin, Ben E. King, and Wilson Pickett found large diverse audiences. Transforming the rhythms and melodies of older R&B, pop vocals, and early rock and roll into what became labeled as *soul*, they countered the British invaders with powerful vocal performances. It is hard to define soul music, which mixes gospel, blues, and urban and southern black styles, with slower, more emotional and melancholic lyrics. Soul contrasted sharply with the emphasis on loud, fast instrumentals that had become so important to rock music.[12]

The main independent label to nourish soul and black popular music was Motown, started by former Detroit autoworker and songwriter Berry Gordy with a $700 investment in 1960. (In 1988, Gordy would sell Motown to MCA for $60 million.) Beginning with Smokey Robinson and the Miracles, whose "Shop Around" hit No. 2 late in 1960, Motown groups rivaled the pop success of British bands throughout the decade.

Born and raised in Detroit, the members of the Primettes changed their name to the Supremes in 1961, when they signed with Motown's Tamla label. They became Motown's most popular singing group, scoring the first of twelve No. 1 hits with "Where Did Our Love Go?" in 1964. The group's lead singer, Diana Ross, left the Supremes in 1969 to begin a successful solo career.

Robinson, who later became a vice president of Motown, also wrote "My Girl" for the Temptations and "My Guy" for Mary Wells—both No. 1 hits in the mid-1960s. In the 1960s and 1970s, Motown produced the Four Tops, Martha and the Vandellas, and the Jackson 5. But the label's most successful group was the Supremes, featuring Diana Ross. Between 1964 and 1969, this group scored twelve No. 1 singles. These Motown groups had a more stylized, softer sound than the grittier southern soul (or funk) of Brown and Pickett. Motown producers realized at the outset that by cultivating romance and dance over rebellion and politics, black music could attract a young, white audience. But this music did not remain politically quiet. Popular Motown hits like Marvin Gaye's "What's Goin' On" (1970) and Edwin Starr's "War" (1970) dealt with the ongoing trauma of the Vietnam War.

folk, blues, politics, and drugs

Other forms of black music also had an impact on the 1960s, including the folk-blues of the legendary Leadbelly (Huddie Ledbetter). In its broadest sense, **folk music** in any culture refers to songs performed by untrained musicians and passed down mainly through oral traditions. Folk encompasses old-time music from the banjo and fiddle tunes of Appalachia to the accordion-led zydeco of Louisiana. Given its rough edges and amateur quality, folk is considered a more democratic and participatory musical form. Unlike most 1960s soul, surfer music, and early Beatles recordings, folk music also had a political edge. Folk, in fact, inspired many writers and performers of popular music to become more socially aware.

By the early 1900s, **blues** music had emerged as a category separate from folk. Influenced by African American spirituals, ballads, and work songs in the rural South, the music of Robert Johnson, Son House, and Charley Patton exemplified early blues. Their sound came from the misnamed Mississippi Delta—"a flat, fertile leaf-shaped plain" that stretches south two hundred miles from Memphis, Tennessee, to Vicksburg, Mississippi, but is north of the river's actual delta in Louisiana.[13] The music traveled to northern cities during the migration of black workers in search of industrial jobs before and after World War I. In the late 1930s, the electric guitar—a major contribution to rock music—made it easier for musicians "to cut through the noise in ghetto taverns" and gave southern blues its urban style, popularized in the work of Muddy Waters, Howlin' Wolf, B.B. King, and Buddy Guy.

During the 1930s, folk became defined by a white musician named Woody Guthrie ("This Land Is Your Land"). Like many blues singers, Guthrie also brought folk music from the country to the city. He wrote his own songs, promoted social reforms, and played acoustic guitar. Groups such as the Weavers, featuring labor activist and songwriter Pete Seeger, carried on Guthrie's legacy. In 1950, before rock and roll, the Weavers' cover of Leadbelly's "Good Night, Irene" stayed at the top of the pop charts for thirteen weeks. Although the group was regularly blacklisted for political activism, the Weavers' comeback concert at Carnegie Hall in 1955 reenergized folk and inspired a new generation of singer-songwriters, including Joan Baez, Bob Dylan, Simon & Garfunkel, James Taylor, Carly Simon, and Joni Mitchell.

Significantly influenced by the blues, Bob Dylan identified folk as "finger pointin'" music that addressed current social circumstances, such as the growing civil-rights movement and the Vietnam War. For many folk followers who had grown up on less overtly political rock and roll, acoustic folk music represented both a maturing process and a return to traditional, de-amplified values.

Folk-Rock and Dylan. When the Byrds electrified folk recordings in the 1960s, they invented **folk-rock**, a sound that went on to influence a long list of performers, from the Grateful Dead to R.E.M. and the Indigo Girls. Partly a response to the

British invasion, amplified folk-rock earned the Byrds a No. 1 hit in 1965 with a cover of Dylan's folk song "Mr. Tambourine Man." The Byrds had grabbed the attention of Dylan, who had also been influenced by a British group, the Animals, and their 1964 hit "The House of the Rising Sun."

Dylan's career as a folk artist had begun with his performances in New York's Greenwich Village in 1961. His notoriety as a songwriter was spurred by his great energy and his unique mumbly, nasal voice. Then, at a key moment in popular music's history, Dylan walked onstage at the 1965 Newport Folk Festival with an electric guitar and took rock music in a more political direction. Accompanied by a backup group later known as The Band, Dylan was booed and cursed by traditional "folkies," who saw amplified music as a sellout to the commercial recording industry. For many critics, however, Dylan's move to rock was aimed at reaching a broader and younger constituency. For Dylan, who would later experiment with country and gospel music before returning to the blues, it was a matter of changing with the times and finding sounds that matched his interests. By 1965, Dylan had his first major hit, "Like a Rolling Stone," a six-minute blues-rock tune boosted by new "progressive rock" radio stations that played longer cuts.

Rock's Psychedelic Turn. Alcohol and drugs have long been associated with the private lives of blues, jazz, country, and rock musicians. These links, however, became much more public in the late 1960s and early 1970s, when authorities busted members of the Rolling Stones and the Beatles. With the increasing role of drugs in youth culture and the availability of LSD (not made illegal until the mid-1960s), more and more rock musicians experimented with and sang about drugs in what were frequently labeled rock's psychedelic years. A number of performers believed, as did various writers and artists from other eras, that artistic expression could be enhanced by mind-altering drugs. The music of this period fed on liberal drug laws and a large college-student population, the targeted consumers for much of this music. In the past, musicians had not publicized their drug and alcohol habits. The 1960s drug explorations, however, coincided with the free-speech movement, in which taking drugs was seen by some artists as a form of personal expression and a public challenge to traditional values.

The rock-drug connection was also a cultural response to the perceived failure of traditional institutions to deal with social problems such as racism and the Vietnam War. Students and musicians used drugs not only to experiment or get high, or out of boredom or addiction, but to drop out of conventional society. Some dropped all the way out. During this time, incidents involving drugs or alcohol claimed the lives of several artists, including Janis Joplin, Jimi Hendrix, and the Doors' Jim Morrison.

At the time, the recording industry generally did little to confront the diseases of drug dependency and alcoholism among musicians. As long as artists produced hits, record companies either ignored the problem or, in a few cases, made sure that musicians were supplied with drugs to sustain their routines and energy levels. With the rise in cocaine and heroin addiction among musicians in the 1980s and 1990s, the industry faced a new set of challenges. Critics and scholars alike have linked the 80 percent rise in drug use among twelve- to seventeen-year-olds between 1992 and 1996 to increased drug use among their rock-group role models.[14] This time around, however, the National Academy of Recording Arts and Sciences, which runs the Grammy Awards, brought together hundreds of industry managers and agents to discuss drug issues. Many critics contend, however, that until record companies are willing to terminate contracts and drop their support of artists unwilling to take responsibility for their addictions, problems and tragedies will persist.

Rock as Mainstream Culture. Following the historic Woodstock concert in August 1969, which drew more than 400,000 fans to a New York farm, the deaths of

Joplin and Hendrix in 1970, and the announcement late in 1970 that the Beatles had officially disbanded, rock music reached a crossroads. Considered a major part of the rebel counterculture in the 1960s (despite its profits), rock music in the 1970s was increasingly viewed as the centerpiece of mainstream consumer culture. With major music acts earning huge profits, rock soon became another product line for manufacturers and retailers to promote, package, and sell.

Nevertheless, some rock musicians continued the traditions of early rock. In the 1970s, stars like Bruce Springsteen emerged to carry on rock's integrationist legacy, combining the influences of Chuck Berry and Elvis Presley with the folk-rock poetry of Bob Dylan. Britain's Elton John drew upon the outrageous stage performances of Little Richard and the melodic influences of the Beatles. Generally, though, in the 1970s business concerns steered rock and its stars toward a new form of segregation, one that divided popular music along class and race lines. Both the recording industry and album-oriented rock formats on radio began to aggressively market and program harder rock music and to aim it primarily toward middle-class white male teens.

Another sign that rock and roll had become synonymous with mainstream culture was the continued blurring of the distinction between the sacred and the secular. By the 1970s, rock and roll's earliest foes—religious institutions—had begun to embrace forms of rock as a means of retaining and attracting young churchgoers. In some Catholic churches, rock infiltrated via special church services that featured folk guitar versions of hymns. In many Protestant churches, where gospel music was already a familiar style, contemporary Christian gospel and Christian rock emerged, melding Bible-based lyrics with music that mimicked R&B, Top 40 pop, and even heavy metal. By the mid-1990s, Christian rock boasted a number of acts that featured newly minted contracts with major labels. It was the fastest-growing segment of the music industry. Bands like Jars of Clay, Audio Adrenaline, and dc Talk crossed over into mainstream radio and MTV, charting million-selling CDs.

alternative sounds of punk and grunge

In the United States and Britain in the mid-1970s, **punk rock** challenged the orthodoxy and commercialism of the record business. Punk has generally been characterized by its loud, unpolished distortions, jackhammer beat, primal vocal screams, crude aggression, and defiant or comic lyrics. By this time, the glory days of rock's competitive independent labels had ended, and rock music was controlled by six major companies: CBS, Warner, Polygram, RCA, Capitol-EMI, and MCA. According to critic Ken Tucker, this situation gave rise to "faceless rock—crisply recorded, eminently catchy," featuring anonymous hits by bands with "no established individual personalities outside their own large but essentially discrete audiences" of young white males.[15]

In avoiding rock's consumer popularity, punk attempted to recover the early amateurish and offensive energies of rock and roll. Essentially, any teenager with a few weeks of guitar practice could learn the sound, making music that was both more democratic and discordant than rock. In the early 1970s, pre-punk groups like the Velvet Underground set the stage for the Ramones and the Dead Kennedys. In England, the music of the Sex Pistols ("Anarchy in the U.K."), one of the most controversial groups in rock history, was eventually banned for offending British decorum.

Punk, of course, was not a commercial success in the United States in the 1970s, lack of wide popularity being one of punk's goals. Nevertheless, punk made contributions, especially by "defining the big business of the rock industry and then condemning it." Punk also offered women the opportunity "to participate fully in the rock world for the first time in the history of the music."[16] In the United States, for instance, poet

"Through their raw, nihilistic singles and violent performances, the [Sex Pistols] revolutionized the idea of what rock and roll could be."
—Stephen Thomas Erlewine, *All-Music Guide,* 1996

Rising from the streets of late-1960s New York City, the pre-punk sounds of the Velvet Underground helped set the stage for punk groups like the Ramones and the Sex Pistols. While much of the U.S. focused on psychedelic music and the hippie movement, the Velvet Underground played as the house band for Andy Warhol's Factory and became synonymous with downtown bohemian chic. Although the group never became commercially successful, its sonic experimentation and gritty realism influenced generations of performers, including Joy Division, R.E.M., and Nirvana.

and rocker Patti Smith helped pioneer punk in the mid-1970s, and in Britain, Siouxsie & the Banshees assaulted commercial rock's fixation on all-male groups.

Taking the spirit of punk and infusing it with attention to melody, **grunge** represented a significant development in rock in the 1990s. Grunge's commercial breakthrough can be traced to the "Smells Like Teen Spirit" cut on the album *Nevermind* by Nirvana, led by songwriter and vocalist Kurt Cobain. In 1992, *Nevermind* was the top-selling album in America, its popular success ironically built on satirizing some of the rock music of the 1970s and 1980s. One critic described a Cobain song as "stunning, concise bursts of melody and rage that occasionally spilled over into haunting, folk-styled acoustic ballad."[17] Suffering from stomach problems, drug addiction, and severe depression, Cobain committed suicide in 1994.

Influenced by punk, grunge groups adopted an alienated performing style that was in direct contrast to the slick theatrics of 1970s and 1980s rock. Taking a cue from low-key folk singers and 1960s rock bands like the Grateful Dead, grunge spoke the low-maintenance language of the garage: torn jeans, T-shirts, long underwear, worn sneakers, and old flannel shirts. But with the music's success, grunge's antistyle became commercially viable as hundreds of new garage bands emulated it.

Nirvana's influences paved the way for a variety of punk and alternative groups in the 1990s, including Nine Inch Nails, Smashing Pumpkins, Soundgarden, Stone Temple Pilots, and Pearl Jam. In 1993, trying to play down its commercial success, Pearl Jam refused to release any music-video singles from its new No. 1 album, *Vs.*, which had sold more than five million copies. It also chose to perform in smaller arenas and on college campuses rather than in the gigantic, impersonal sports stadiums preferred by established rock bands. Then, in 1994, the band canceled a national tour to protest the high service charges and alleged monopolistic practices of Ticketmaster, a company that often dictates a concert's ticket prices. By 1998, with the release of its fifth album, *Yield*, Pearl Jam yielded to some of the realities of being a popular rock act by consenting to a music video (although it was animated, with no images of the group) and appearing at tour venues that sold tickets through Ticketmaster.

In some critical circles, both punk and grunge are considered subcategories or fringe movements of **alternative rock**. This vague label describes many types of experimental rock music that offered a departure from the theatrics and staged extravaganzas of 1970s *glam rock*, which showcased such performers as David Bowie and Kiss. Appealing chiefly to college students, alternative rock has traditionally opposed the sounds of Top 40 and commercial FM radio. In the 1980s and 1990s, U2 and R.E.M. emerged as successful groups often associated with alternative rock. A key dilemma for successful alternative performers, however, is that their popularity results in commercial success, ironically a situation that their music often criticizes.

"Everyone feels good about selling a million records compared to selling eight or nine million. It's made our lives a lot saner, and besides, the fans who really like us still go out and buy the records."
—Stone Gossard, guitarist, Pearl Jam, 1998

rap redraws musical lines

With the growing segregation of radio formats and the dominance of mainstream rock by white male performers, the place of black artists in the rock world diminished. By the late 1990s, no major popular black successor to Chuck Berry or Jimi Hendrix had emerged in rock. These trends, combined with the rise of "safe" dance disco by white bands (the Bee Gees), black artists (Donna Summer), and integrated groups (the Village People), created a space for the culture that produced rap music.

In some ways a black counterpart to the spirit of white punk, **rap music** also stood in direct opposition to the polished, professional, and less political world of soul. Rap's combination of social politics, male swagger, and comic lyrics carried forward long-standing traditions in blues, R&B, soul, and rock and roll. Like punk, rap was driven by a democratic, nonprofessional spirit—accessible to anyone who could talk in street dialect and cut (or sample) records on a turntable. Rap deejays emerged in Jamaica and New York, scratching and re-cueing old reggae, disco, soul, and rock albums. As dance music, rap developed MCs (masters of ceremony), who used humor, boasts, and "trash talking" to entertain and keep the peace at parties.

When the Sugarhill Gang released "Rapper's Delight" in 1979, the music industry viewed it as a novelty song, even though the music was rooted in a long tradition of party deejays playing soul and funk music through powerful sound systems. Then, in 1982, Grandmaster Flash and Furious Five released "The Message" and infused rap with a political take on ghetto life. Rap also continued the black musical tradition of elevating the spoken word over conventional instruments, which were displaced by turntables. Although rap was at first considered party music, its early political voices, including Public Enemy and Ice-T, addressed civil-rights issues and the worsening economic conditions facing urban America.

Rap exploded as a popular genre in 1984 with the commercial successes of groups like Run-DMC, the Fat Boys, and LL Cool J. That year, Run-DMC's album *Raising Hell* became a major crossover hit, the first No. 1 rap album on the popular charts (thanks in part to a collaboration with Aerosmith on a rap version of the group's 1976 hit "Walk This Way"). Like punk and early rock and roll, rap was cheap to produce, requiring only a few mikes, speakers, amps, turntables, and vinyl record albums. With CDs displacing LPs as the main recording format in the 1980s, partially obsolete hardware was "reemployed" for use by rap artists, many of whom had trained in vocational colleges for industrial jobs that evaporated in the 1970s and 1980s.

Since most major labels and many black radio stations rejected the rawness of rap, the music spawned hundreds of new independent labels. Although initially dominated by male performers, rap was open to women, and some—Salt-N-Pepa and Queen Latifah (Dana Owens) among them—quickly became major players. Soon white groups like the Beastie Boys and 3rd Bass were also combining rap and punk influences in commercially successful music.

Rap, like punk, defies mainstream culture. Some rap has drawn criticism from both white and black communities for lyrics that degrade women or applaud violence. Rappers respond that punk has often been more explicit and offensive but that punk's lyrics are less discernible under the guitar distortion. The conversational style of rap, however, makes it a forum in which performers can debate such issues as gender, class, and drugs. A few rappers have also fought extended battles over copyright infringement, since their music continues to sample rock, soul, funk, and disco records. The 1997 hit "I'll Be Missing You" by Puff Daddy (Sean "Puffy" Combs) and Faith Hill, for instance, samples a loop from the 1983 Police single "Every Breath You Take." Sampling isn't restricted to hip-hop, though. The alternative British rock group the Verve sampled an orchestral recording of the Rolling Stones' 1965 hit "The Last Time" without permission in their 1998 song "Bittersweet Symphony." The Verve's

> "We're like reporters.
> We give them [our listeners] the truth. People where we come from hear so many lies that the truth stands out like a sore thumb."
> —Eazy-E, N.W.A., 1989

87

Lauryn Hill's 1998 debut solo album, *The Miseducation of Lauryn Hill,* was an eclectic mix of hip-hop beats, fluid rap, reggae bass lines, and Motown soul. The recording was a multimillion seller and a hit with critics as well, winning *Rolling Stone* magazine's best album of the year award and five Grammys—the most ever for a female recording artist. Hill, also a member of the Fugees, said she wanted to make "a hip-hop album that has the roots, the integrity, and sound of an old record."

success with "Bittersweet Symphony" was itself bittersweet, since the Rolling Stones and their former managers successfully sued for songwriting credits and all publishing royalties for the song.

Although rap encompasses many different styles, including various Latin offshoots, its most controversial subgenre is probably **gangsta rap**. This style developed in Los Angeles in 1987, partly in response to drug-related news stories that represented, at least for many African American communities, a one-sided portrait of life in urban America. This offshoot of rap drew major national attention in 1996 with the shooting death of Tupac Shakur, a performer, actor, and ex-con who lived the violent life he sang about on albums like *Thug Life.* But although Shakur was criticized for his criminal lifestyle, he was revered by many fans for telling hard truths about urban problems and street life. In 1997, Notorious B.I.G. (Christopher Wallace, a.k.a. Biggie Smalls), whose followers were prominent suspects in Shakur's death, was shot to death in Hollywood. He was considered Shakur's main gangsta-rap rival.[18]

In the wake of Shakur's and B.I.G.'s deaths, the business and sound of rap changed. Los Angeles–based Death Row Records (once a top rap label with such artists as Shakur, Snoop Doggy Dogg, and label cofounder Dr. Dre), fell apart with the imprisonment of its leader, Marion "Suge" Knight, for parole violations, and lost distribution support from its parent company (Interscope/Universal Music Group).[19] With the loss of one of its leading artists in Notorious B.I.G., rival New York hip-hop label Bad Boy Entertainment (owned by Sean "Puffy" Combs and Arista Records) has led the movement away from gangsta rap to a more danceable hip-hop that combines singing and rapping with musical elements of rock and soul.[20]

Throughout rap's history, artists have occasionally characterized themselves as street reporters who tell alternative stories of city life. Chuck D of Public Enemy has maintained that most rap music offers interpretations of urban experience and the war on drugs that are very different from network-news portrayals. Despite the conflicts generated around rap, it remains a major development in popular music. Like early rock and roll, rap's crossover appeal, particularly to white male adolescents, seems rooted in a cultural style that questions class and racial boundaries and challenges status quo values.

"The creative and commercial **emergence of women** has been rivaled only by the **growth of hip-hop** as the most vital development in pop music in the '90s."
—Robert Hilburn,
New York Times,
1999

the business of sound recording

One key issue raised by alternative movements in the recording industry is the uneasy relationship between music's business and artistic elements. The lyrics of rap or alternative rock, for example, often question the commercial values of popular music. Both rock and rap are built on the assumption that musical integrity requires a separation between business and art. But, in fact, the line between commercial success and artistic expression grows hazier each day. When the questioning of commercialism resonates with enough fans, popular artists stand to make a lot of money. In order to understand this situation, we need to look at the business of sound recording.

By the late 1990s, sales of recorded music had posted several years of slow but stable growth, generating about $12.2 billion a year in the United States and more than $38 billion worldwide. In economic terms, the music business generates more revenue than all other media except television. It also constitutes a global **oligopoly**: a business situation in which a few firms control most of an industry's production and distribution resources. Such global reach gives these firms enormous influence over what types of music gain worldwide distribution and popular acceptance.

the major labels

From the 1970s to the late 1990s, six companies controlled popular music. Then, in 1998, Canada's Seagram Company bought PolyGram from Netherlands-based Philips Electronics, leaving five corporations that produce about 85 percent of all American CDs and cassettes and control 80 percent of the global market. In addition, while virtually all major labels were once American-owned, by the late-1990s only one major company, Warner Music (a subsidiary of Time Warner), claimed the United States as its home base. The largest music corporation by far is Seagram, once known mainly as a beverage company that produced such brands as Chivas Regal, Absolut, and Captain Morgan Rum. Seagram first moved toward the entertainment industry in 1995 with the purchase of MCA, better known as Universal Studios. With both MCA-Universal and PolyGram as subsidiaries, Seagram shifted its corporate focus from distilled beverages to the entertainment industry, and gained control of nearly 23 percent of the American and global music markets. The other global players are Sony, the Japanese company that bought CBS Records in the 1980s; EMI, owned by Britain's EMI Group; and BMG, owned by Bertelsmann in Germany, which bought RCA Records in the 1980s (see Figure 3.2). Each "major" owns and operates several labels, most of them formerly independent companies. Majors produce and distribute some twenty-five hundred CD and cassette albums each year.

Figure 3.2
The Major Labels in the Recording Industry
Source: Los Angeles Times, May 22, 1998.

17.9%
Time Warner
(Atlantic, Elektra)

22.7%
MCA-Universal/
PolyGram
(A&M, Geffen)

18.3%
Sony
(Columbia, Epic)

11.9%
Bertelsmann
(Arista, BMG, RCA)

15.9%
Independents

13.3%
EMI
(Capitol, Virgin)

independent labels

The rise of rock and roll in the 1950s and early 1960s showcased a rich diversity of independent labels, all vying for a share of the new music. These labels included Sun, Stax, Chess, Motown, and Atlantic. Today, most of these independents have folded or been absorbed by majors. However, in contrast to the five global players, some five thousand large and small production houses—sometimes called *indies*—record less commercially viable music, or music they hope will become commercially viable. Often struggling enterprises, indies require only a handful of people to operate them. They identify forgotten older artists and record new innovative performers. To keep costs down, indies usually depend on wholesale distributors to promote and sell their music. Producing about 16 percent of America's music in the late 1990s, indies often enter into deals with majors to gain the widest distribution for their artists. They may also entrust their own recordings or contracts to independent distributors, who ship new recordings to various retail outlets and radio stations. The Internet has also become a low-cost distribution and promotion outlet for independent labels, which often use Web sites for recording and merchandise sales, fan discussion groups, and regular email updates of tour schedules and new releases.

In the music business, the majors frequently rely on indies to discover and initiate distinctive musical trends that first appear on a local level. For instance, although rap was and still is rejected by many radio stations and major labels, indies such as Sugarhill, Tommy Boy, and Uptown emerged in the 1980s to produce this music for regional markets. In the early 1990s, punk faced similar problems and relied on labels such as Kill Rock Stars, Liquid Meat, and Aargh! Records. As another example, two small southern companies—Fat Possum Records and Rooster Blues Records—have been scouring the South in the 1990s for forgotten or ignored blues artists. Indies play a major role as the music industry's risk-takers, since major labels are reluctant to invest in lost or commercially unproven artists.

Once indies become successful, the financial inducement to sell out to a major label is enormous. Seattle indie Sub Pop (Nirvana's initial recording label), faced with the commercial success of alternative rock, sold 49 percent of its stock to Time Warner for $20 million in 1994. PolyGram, Sony, and EMI aggressively pursued the punk label Epitaph, which once rejected takeover offers as high as $50 million. Today, all five majors are busy looking for and picking off independent labels that have successfully developed artists with national or global appeal (see "The Global Village: The International Beat" on page 91).

the business of making a recording

Like most mass media, the music business is divided into several areas, including artist development, technical facilities, sales and distribution, advertising and promotion, and administrative operations. Recording companies, whether major or minor, are generally driven by **A&R (artist & repertoire) agents**: the talent scouts of the music business, who discover, develop, and sometimes manage artists. A&R executives listen to demonstration tapes, or *demos*, from new artists; and they decide whom to hire and which songs to record. Before Chuck Berry, Little Richard, and rock's British invasion, few commercially successful performers wrote their own music, so A&R agents had to match them with songs and writers—a practice still prevalent in country music.

The technical group at a recording label oversees the entire production process. A typical recording session is a complex process that involves musicians and audio technicians, and is directed by a session engineer and a producer. George Martin, for example, served as both chief engineer and producer for the Beatles' sessions in the 1960s. He is credited with introducing orchestral sounds to rock music, a trend many rock groups copied in the 1970s.

Today, the engineer and producer roles usually fall to different people. A chief engineer oversees the technical aspects of the recording session, everything from choosing recording equipment to arranging microphone placement. In charge of the overall recording process, the producer handles most nontechnical elements of the session, including reserving studio space and hiring musicians. During recording, the producer takes command and in most cases decides whether certain vocal or instrumental parts work well or need to be rerecorded.

Most popular CDs and tapes are now produced part by part. Using separate microphones, the vocalists, guitarists, drummers, and other musical sections are digitally recorded onto audio tracks. To produce one song, as many as two or three dozen tracks might be recorded, often at different times and in different studios. Controlling the overall sound quality, the chief engineer mixes the parts onto a two-track stereo master tape. Mixing engineers specialize in other postproduction editing; they mix the multiple tracks after the recording sessions. Mastering engineers prepare the song for transfer to a final version on audiotape and CD. Remix engineers work with tapes that are

THE GLOBAL VILLAGE

The International Beat

Celia Cruz   Ricky Martin

Since the late 1980s, most good music stores have added a section designated as "world music." Although it is sometimes confused with ethnic or folk music, *world music* was specifically coined as a marketing term to distinguish it from these two other genres. While it includes releases from African, Latin American, Indian, and other international artists, world music is notable for assimilating Western music without sacrificing what makes it unique in the first place.

Nigerian artist Fela, for example, was so influenced by James Brown's rock and roll when it was introduced to West Africa that he began to include baritone saxophones and large horn sections in his music, creating a compelling mix of Western and non-Western styles. Likewise, singer Oumou Sangare, from Mali, juxtaposes feminist lyrics with her indigenous Wassoulou music. From the African continent also comes the high-life and roots rhythms of Ghana; the soukous and dance music of Zaire; and the pennywhistle and bubblegum sounds of South Africa. Europe offers Celtic tunes from Ireland, Scotland, and Wales; Magyar and Gypsy traditional music from Hungary; folk and punk sounds from the Alps; and flamenco from southern Spain. The diverse regions of the Caribbean have produced rumba, salsa, merengue, calypso, and reggae. The Americas offers its own contributions to world folk forms with bluegrass, cajun, zydeco, and Tejano.

Oftentimes world musicians are relatively unknown in their own countries but get discovered on the world-music scene, as did Cape Verdean singer Cesaria Evora, now wildly popular in France. At other times, they are national stars who finally get "discovered" by Western audiences. Indian songstress Lata Mongashkar has recorded more than thirty thousand songs in twenty languages, and may be the most recorded singer in the world. The Dominican Republic's Juan Luis Guerra's

WORLD MUSIC STARS

merengue recordings have sold more than five million copies. Other top world-music figures include Cuban singer Celia Cruz, known as the queen of salsa; Nigeria's King Sunny Ade; and East Indian movie star Asha Bhosle, a mainstay on cable's International Channel, who also makes claims as the world's most-recorded singer.

Although American rock has influenced global culture since the 1950s, much of this music has in turn been influenced by sounds from around the world. For example, the music of India's famed sitar player Ravi Shankar influenced the Beatles' recordings in the late 1960s; and in the 1980s, South Africa's Ladysmith Black Mambazo changed the sound of folk-rock on Paul Simon's *Graceland* album. World-music critics have argued, however, that throughout this century other musical styles, particularly Argentina's tango and Cuba's mambo and rumba, have had a larger global impact than such styles as American rock.

While music stores are making room for world-music sections on their shelves, the category is still not clearly defined. Singers like Italian tenor Andrea Bocelli or Canadian singer-composer Loreena McKennitt, for example, top certain world-music charts, yet they might just as easily fall into the classical or New Age categories, respectively. Other world-music artists are popularized through such U.S.-produced movie sound tracks, like Ireland's Gaelic Storm, featured in *Titanic*, and Hungary's Màrta Sebestyén, whose haunting voice opened and closed *The English Patient*. The bottom line is that almost all musical styles are complex mixes rooted in a variety of cultures. Given the ongoing development of global communication systems, different *musical* forms will continue to bump one another, and this democratic tendency will become more pronounced in the twenty-first century. With the music industry's constant desire for "the next big thing," the biggest stars of the next hundred years may emerge from the world-music genre.

already mastered, removing flaws or adding new instrumental or vocal parts. Since digital keyboard synthesizers are able to reproduce most instrumental sounds, engineers can now duplicate many instrumental parts without recalling studio musicians.

Throughout the recording and postproduction process, the marketing department plans strategies for packaging, promoting, and selling a recording. In addition to arranging advertising in various media, this department might design point-of-purchase displays that use signs, posters, and other eye-catching gimmicks to encourage in-store impulse buying, which accounts for nearly 15 percent of all CD and audiotape sales.

Selling a Recording. Distributing and selling CDs and tapes is a tricky part of the business. Most recordings are sold at *direct retail* stores, which offer variety and account for more than 50 percent of all record sales. Like the bookstore business, the major economic trend in music sales is toward large chain stores such as Sam Goody or Tower Records, each of which operates hundreds of stores nationally, mostly in shopping malls, urban centers, and near college campuses. Direct retailers specialize in music, carefully monitoring new releases by major labels and independents. Like chain bookstores, direct music retailers keep a large inventory. Their staffs can also track down and order obscure recordings that the store may not have on hand. In addition, used-CD stores and inventories have developed as a by-product of the durability of digital recordings. Book chains such as Barnes & Noble and Borders also sell recordings as part of their "superstore" product mix.

To ease potential music buyers' hesitations, in the 1990s most major music retailers added in-store music listening stations so customers could sample CDs. The CD Listening Bar stores in California started the trend when music distributors realized that in-store listening opportunities could enhance sales of featured artists. The listening posts were a throwback to the isolation booths of some record stores of the 1950s, where customers could listen to the latest 45-rpm single before purchasing it.

Gaining on record stores are general retail outlets, which have recently captured more than 30 percent of CD and tape sales. Because music is not the main focus of these stores, outlets like Kmart contract with *rack jobbers* to stock their stores' music racks or shelves with the latest CDs, audiocassettes, and music videos. Rack jobbers either lease shelf space from the stores or sell recordings directly to them. By managing inventories and orders, rack jobbers perform record-keeping tasks that many retailers prefer to avoid. To earn the highest profits, rack jobbers generally stock the most popular music, screen controversial titles for some of their clients, and ignore obscure musical forms.

Another 10 percent of recording sales each year come from *music clubs* such as BMG and Columbia. Like book clubs, music clubs use direct mail and inserts in Sunday newspapers to promote or advertise new and old releases. They might offer prospective members ten CDs for the price of one as an incentive to join. In exchange, consumers agree to buy three or four CDs at the regular price (about $17–$20 in 1999, plus a typical $2 shipping charge) over the next three or four years. Like major book clubs, music clubs sort through many possible new releases, identifying the commercial hits or "hot" groups. Through clubs, consumers are generally offered music by only the most popular and profitable performers.

In 1997, the recording industry began to track Internet sales of music for the first time. Although Net-based sales accounted for only 0.3 percent of music purchases that year (less than the 0.9 percent of music purchases made through TV offers), the industry predicted rapid growth in this area. Most of the sales on the Internet are made via Web-page order forms through such retailers as CDnow, Music Boulevard, and Amazon.com. But the industry expects that music downloaded from the Internet in digital formats such as MP3 and recorded onto a CD will become a viable sales and distribution network (see "Tracking Technology: MP3 and the Spread of Music" on page 96).

With the appearance of MTV in the early 1980s, music videos created another level of complexity for the music business. Virtually every artist today who introduces a new CD or cassette also makes an accompanying video for distribution on cable channels such as MTV, Country Music Television (CMT), Black Entertainment Television (BET), or VH1. In the late 1990s, a typical music video cost a recording company and its artists between $100,000 and $300,000 to produce. However, some major stars and their labels spend in excess of a million dollars for a single video; the record amount is $7 million for Michael Jackson's 1995 video "Scream," laden with special effects and featuring Michael and Janet Jackson in an austere, weightless space-ship environment. Initially, MTV was important to recording companies and new artists. If artists had difficulty getting radio play, the cable channel became another venue for launching performers. MTV has become so influential today, however, that videos are often a must: Radio stations may choose not to play a particular rock artist until a demand has been created by MTV airings.

Dividing the Profits. A look at the various costs and profits from a typical CD reveals how money circulates in the recording industry. For a CD that retails at Tower Records for $15.99, the wholesale price is about $8—the actual cost of producing and promoting the recording. The remaining half constitutes the profit margin, which is split among the record company, the distributor, and retailers. The record company reaps the highest profit (close to $4 on a typical CD) but, along with the artist, bears the bulk of the expenses: manufacturing costs, packaging and CD design, advertising and promotion, and artists' royalties (see Figure 3.3).

A singer-songwriter who has negotiated a 12 percent royalty rate would earn just under $1 for a CD or cassette whose wholesale price is $8. So a CD that "goes gold"— sells 500,000 units—would net the artist around $500,000. Out of this amount, the artist repays the record company the money it has advanced to him or her—approximately $150,000—for recording and music-video costs, tour expenses, and so forth. Another $150,000 or so might have to be set aside in a reserve account to cover any unsold recordings returned by record stores. This would leave the artist with about $200,000, some of which would be divided among band members.[21]

New artists usually earn a royalty rate of between 5 and 10 percent on the wholesale price of a cassette or CD. A more established performer might negotiate a

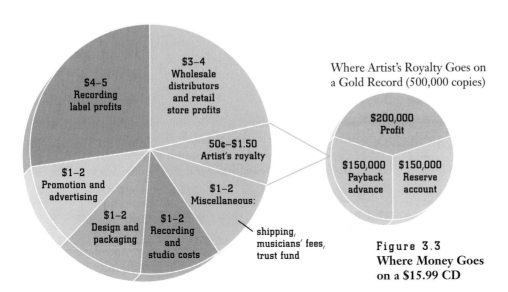

Figure 3.3
**Where Money Goes
on a $15.99 CD**

10 to 15 percent rate, and popular artists might get more than 15 percent. However, most lesser-known songwriters and performers remain in debt. For every Alanis Morissette (whose debut album, *Jagged Little Pill*, has sold more than sixteen million copies in the United States and twenty-eight million worldwide since 1995), there are thousands of songwriters and performers who cannot overcome their debts to various managers, producers, and record labels.

Independent producers or labels sign songwriters, singers, or groups and then advance them money to cover expenses, hoping for a hit song or album. The Jayhawks, for example, a country-rock group whose 1992 album sold 200,000 copies, had debts in 1995 totaling $1 million. Because of the stress caused by this debt, one member left the group to make furniture, which he began selling to wealthy musicians he had met while touring as a Jayhawk. This story is not unusual: More than 95 percent of all musicians who receive advances do not recoup them through recording sales.

In addition to sales royalties received by artists from their recording companies, two other kinds of royalty payments exist: mechanical and performance royalties. Songwriters protect their work by obtaining an exclusive copyright on each song, ensuring that it will not be copied or performed without permission. To protect their copyrights, songwriters assign their creations to a publisher, who represents the songs by trying to sell them in printed form or by having them recorded by a major label or indie. Songwriters and publishers receive a *mechanical royalty* when they allow a song to be recorded. They are paid at a rate of about one half cent for each CD or audiotape sold.

The owner of a song's copyright, which is not always the songwriter, also receives a *performance royalty* whenever the music is used on radio or television. Since songwriters are seldom wealthy enough to underwrite the original costs of producing a CD or tape, they often sell their copyrights to recording companies. On behalf of songwriters and recording labels, performance royalties are collected by several national licensing associations, the largest of which are ASCAP and Broadcast Music, Inc. (BMI). These groups keep track of recording rights, collect copyright fees, and license music for use in TV commercials or films. Radio stations annually pay licensing fees of between 1 and 2 percent of their gross annual revenues, and they generally play only licensed music, which makes it difficult for alternative or independent music to gain a broad following.

bootlegging

In the late 1980s, the collapse of communist governments throughout Eastern Europe and the growth of wide-open economies worldwide led to a flourishing illegal market in the music industry. In the absence of international policing of copyright laws, manufacturing plants were set up, especially throughout China and other parts of Asia, to copy, or bootleg, unauthorized CDs and cassettes. These illegal firms sold recordings at cut-rate prices, with no profits going to the original recording companies or to the artists themselves.

Three forms of **bootlegging** have been a part of the music industry for much of the twentieth century. First, as just described, are *counterfeits*, who duplicate the content of a record as it appeared in its original form. Second are *pirates*, who reissue rare or out-of-print material without official permission from the songwriter or copyright holder.[22] Finally, the most common bootlegging occurs from unauthorized or stolen tape recordings of live concerts, informal studio sessions, or live radio or TV appearances. Individuals duplicate these recordings and then sell them for profit without paying fees to the artists.

Although bootlegging has been a part of musical lore ever since tape recorders appeared in the 1930s, it reached its heyday in the sixties. With informal folk and rock concerts increasing, many musicians paid scant attention to those who recorded their performances. The most famous bootleg album from this period was a Bob Dylan collection, *The Great White Wonder*, a set of demo tapes and informal sessions that surfaced during the late 1960s while Dylan was recovering from a motorcycle accident. The Grateful Dead, arguably the most-taped artists in music history, were unable to stop the illegal recording of their lengthy concerts and eventually encouraged fans to tape their performances.

In general, although the first two forms of bootlegging have often been practiced but seldom condoned, the third type has generated arguments. Record companies and their artists claim that bootlegging denies them a share of revenue that, by law, belongs to them. Bootleggers, however, contend that most fans already own all the "legal" music of the artists and that bootlegging adds a personal touch to fans' music collections. Fans also contend that bootlegging provides free publicity and a commercial payoff for artists, since the clandestine music circulates among people who may not otherwise hear it. With the advent of recordable and rewriteable CDs and Internet sites offering illegal downloads of copyrighted music in the MP3 format, the recording industry's battle against the bootleggers has become even more complicated.

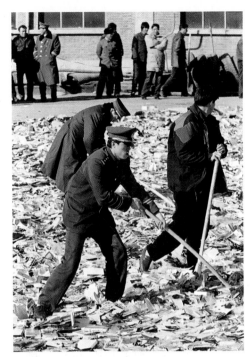

In 1996, police officers in China shoveled pirated CDs and videotapes into the path of a steamroller. Despite such public acts and a 1996 China-U.S. agreement to protect intellectual property rights, China remains the world's largest producer of pirated CDs and cassettes.

alternative voices

A few artists, concerned that they would lose complete creative control if they signed with a major label, have demonstrated an alternative path to success in the music industry. The Washington, D.C., punk band Fugazi has become nationally prominent while shunning offers from the majors and running its own label. Likewise, Canadian artist Loreena McKennitt has slowly built audiences for her blend of Celtic style and world music through touring, public-radio airplay, and word of mouth. She now has a string of recordings that have gone gold on her own Quinlan Road label. But perhaps the artist to push the boundaries of economic independence the furthest is folk rocker Ani DiFranco, who has sold more than 1.5 million recordings on her Righteous Babe label, and whose live-show ticket sales have generated more than $4 million in recent years. DiFranco established her small record label in her native Buffalo, New York, in 1990 and created a thriving mini-industry in a city sometimes known for its bleak economy. She makes it a point to contract with local businesses to manufacture her CDs, posters, newsletters, and T-shirts, even when those items could be produced less expensively elsewhere. DiFranco has now attained such a level of success and self-sufficiency that she doesn't need the help of a major label.

recordings, free expression, and democracy

In the mid-1980s, the newly formed Parents Music Resource Center (PMRC) triggered Senate hearings on explicit sexual and violent themes in rock music. Although opposed to the *direct* censorship of music, PMRC sought to pressure recording companies to add warning stickers on CDs and tapes. The group appeared at subcommittee hearings that also took testimony from such rock and pop figures as Frank Zappa, Donny Osmond, and John Denver. Opposed to labeling as a violation of free speech, the musicians argued that advisory warnings would merely attract attention to music that curious adolescents might otherwise overlook. Soon after the 1985 hearings, the

95

by Lisa Napoli

To understand why the music industry is so concerned about the file format called MP3, it helps to talk to someone like Ben May, twenty-one, a computer-science major at Columbia University.

It is young, technologically savvy consumers like him who have forced the industry to rethink the way it delivers music. May downloads songs from the Internet in the form of MP3 files, most of which are created by music collectors who trade songs online.

"There's this weird sort of culture, sort of parallel to the hacker culture," he said in an interview. "People think it's really cool that they have lots of stuff they didn't pay for."

At last count, May had about 1,700 MP3 files, most of which he has transferred to compact disk using a low-cost CD "burner" that he bought when the music he was downloading began to fill up too much of his hard drive.

"I'm sort of compulsive," he explained. "I have a short attention span. Music has a very heavy rotation for me. We're the sound-bite generation."

The fact that no money is changing hands for this music is what troubles the Recording Industry Association of America (RIAA), a trade group that works to protect artists' rights and royalties. Some of what is downloaded is free and legal, like songs from unsigned bands that are eager to get their music in the hands of as many people as possible. But a lot of what is on the Internet is there in violation of copyright law, which means that the record companies and the artists are not getting their profits.

Thanks to the high-speed Internet connections available to many dorm-dwelling students these days, the process of grabbing and playing these files is fairly fast and simple, once the necessary software is downloaded and a user tracks down the files he or she wants.

Using a CD "burner," people can store about ten hours of MP3 files in a portable format.

Finding interesting music is a form of recreation on which May spends a considerable amount of time.

"What I do is sit and stare at the lists on FTP servers and newsgroups, looking for stuff I've heard that interests me," he said. "I can download an entire album from someone else in the dorm in two minutes. From someone else, ten minutes."

May said that he has bought more music, not less, since he started trading MP3 files.

The opportunity for people to hear a wider variety of music is just one of the arguments put forth in a manifesto called "Free Music," written by Ram Samudrala, a twenty-six-year-old Ph.D. candidate at Stanford University.

A musician himself, Samudrala believes MP3 is an important step in a radical transformation of the music business, and he opposes the attempts by the RIAA to fight MP3.

"The music industry restricts copying and other uses of music in order to maximize profit, but this comes at a great cost, that of abridging the spread of creativity," he writes on his Web page. "Music is about creative and passionate ideas. Not product."

The MP3 traders said they don't mind paying for music; they just don't want to pay as much as the industry charges.

May believes that he should be able to pay a fee to download music off the Internet—rather than going to a store and buying it, and paying for packaging and the like.

"You're not paying for the disk; you're paying for the right to use the software," he said.

For a certain generation of people who see the Internet as one part record store, one part trading ground, one part music player, there's no turning back.

"Everyone who's into computers does the MP3 thing," May said, "whether or not they admit it."

Source: Lisa Napoli, "Fans of MP3 Forced the Issue," *New York Times*, December 16, 1998.

record industry established a voluntary system, stamping disks and tapes containing explicit lyrics with parental-advisory stickers. However, gangsta rap came along in the late 1980s and became another lightning rod for free-expression controversies. In the 1990s, public pressure forced Time Warner to sell its 50 percent share of the controversial gangsta-rap label Interscope Records.

The battle over popular music's controversial lyrics speaks to the heart of democratic expression. On the one hand, popular recordings have a history of confronting stereotypes (by integrating urban and country styles, for instance) and questioning conventions (by the explicit use of political or sexual lyrics). At the same time, however, popular music has often reproduced old stereotypes: limiting women's access as performers in the recording world, fostering racist or homophobic stereotypes, and celebrating violence or misogyny.

Popular musical forms that test cultural boundaries face a dilemma: how to uphold a legacy of free expression while resisting co-optation by giant companies bent on consolidating independents and maximizing profits. For example, since the 1950s forms of rock music have been teetering on the edge of what's acceptable, becoming commercial, pulling back, reemerging as rebellious, and then repeating the pattern. This dynamic between popular music's clever innovations and capitalism's voracious appetite is crucial. Record companies sign a handful of stars for enormous sums of money, negotiating such transactions as Janet Jackson's record-setting $80 million megadeal with EMI's Virgin label in 1996, while other forms of innovative music are never heard by many mainstream audiences.

Still, the major labels need resourceful independents to develop new talent. Ironically, successful commerce requires periodic infusions of the diverse sounds that come from ethnic communities, backyard garages, dance parties, and neighborhood clubs. At the same time, musicians need the major labels if they want wide distribution or national popularity. Such an interdependent pattern is common in contemporary media economics.

No matter how it is produced and distributed, popular music endures because it speaks to both individual and universal themes, from a teenager's first romantic adventure to a nation's outrage over social injustice. Music often reflects the personal or political anxieties of a society. It also breaks down artificial or hurtful barriers better than many government programs. Despite its tribulations, music at its best continues to champion a democratic spirit. Writer and free-speech advocate Nat Hentoff addressed this issue in the 1970s when he wrote: "Popular music always speaks, among other things, of dreams—which change with the times."[23] The recording industry continues to capitalize on and spread those dreams globally, but in each generation musicians and their fans keep imagining new ones.

> "The distribution of **music on the Internet** may ultimately alter the way it is made, released, sold, stored, and valued."
> —Jon Pareles, *New York Times,* 1998

REVIEW QUESTIONS

Early Technology and the Development of Sound Recording

1. The technological configuration of a particular medium sometimes elevates it to mass-market status. Why did Emile Berliner's flat disk replace Edison's wax cylinder, and why did this reconfiguration of records matter in the history of the mass media? Can you think of other mass-media examples in which the size and shape of the technology have made a difference?

2. How did sound recording survive the advent of radio?

Popular Music and the Formation of Rock

3. How did rock and roll significantly influence two mass-media industries?

4. Although many rock-and-roll lyrics from the 1950s are tame by today's standards, this new musical development represented a threat to many parents and adults at that time. Why?

5. What moral and cultural boundaries were blurred by rock and roll in the 1950s?

6. Why did cover music figure so prominently in the development of rock and roll and the record industry in the 1950s?

A Changing Industry: Reformations in Popular Music

7. Explain the British invasion. What was its impact on the recording industry?

8. How did soul music manage to survive the British invasion in the 1960s?

9. What were the major influences of folk music on the recording industry?

10. Why did rap and punk rock emerge as significant musical forms in the late 1970s and 1980s? What do their developments have in common, and how are they different?

The Business of Sound Recording

11. What companies control the bulk of worldwide music production and distribution?

12. Why are independent labels so important to the music industry?

13. What accounts for the cost of a typical CD recording? Where do the profits go?

Recordings, Free Expression, and Democracy

14. Why is it ironic that so many forms of alternative music become commercially successful?

QUESTIONING THE MEDIA

1. Who was your first favorite group or singer? How old were you at the time? What was important to you about this music?

2. If you ran a noncommercial campus radio station, what kind of music would you play and why?

3. Think about the role of the 1960s drug culture in rock's history. How are drugs and alcohol treated in contemporary and alternative forms of rock and rap today?

4. Is it healthy for or detrimental to the music business that so much of the recording industry is controlled by five large international companies? Explain.

5. Do you think the global popularity of rock music is mainly a positive or a negative cultural influence? What are the pros and cons of rock's influence?

SEARCHING THE INTERNET

http://www.cdnow.com
Established in 1994, CDnow offers more than 300,000 music-related items, with song excerpts, music reviews, and cover art to sample prior to online purchases.

http://www.riaa.com
The official site of the Recording Industry Association of America, the trade group that promotes U.S. recording companies. It is loaded with statistics and industry legislation issues.

http://www.mp3.com
The major site on the Internet for information on the MP3 music format, including downloadable MP3 players and a huge variety of free MP3 music files.

http://www.beastieboys.com
One of the best online sites for a music group, with links to Beastie Boys merchandise, tour dates, email lists, music samples in Real Audio and MP3 formats, and the group's Grand Royal Records label.

http://www.rockhall.com
The site includes a virtual tour of the Rock and Roll Hall of Fame museum, audio files and biographies of inductees, and a list of the 500 Songs that Shaped Rock and Roll.

http://www.public-enemy.com
Public Enemy's official site offers an eclectic mix of press releases, band information, occasional live talks by Chuck D, and downloadable new releases in the MP3 and MP4 formats.

In Brief

As an individual or group exercise, compare the way in which magazine advertisements sold consumer audio equipment in the 1950s or 1960s with how they sell today. You or your instructor will need to find ads to analyze in magazines like *Rolling Stone*, *Spin*, and *Stereo Review*. Look for a range of ads, from console and component stereo systems to portable radios and Walkmans.

1. What are the similarities and differences between today's audio ads and those from the 1950s and 1960s?

2. For each ad you have collected, can you describe what kind of consumers the ad seems to be targeting?

3. Do the ads tend to show only audio equipment, or do they show people using the equipment? If people are pictured, do the ads produce or reproduce stereotypes about race, class, gender, and age?

4. Do the ads suggest anything about the role of music in society? (Is it emotionally liberating? Is it rebellious? Is it about self-definition?)

In Depth

In small groups, take on the investigation of a small independent recording company (of which there are thousands throughout the United States). In your investigation, try to find answers to the following questions:

1. What kind of music does this label specialize in? What is the profile of a typical fan?

2. How does this label go about identifying artists and getting a recording to the consumer?

3. What sorts of commercial obstacles does this independent label face?

4. Is the goal of this label to eventually sell to a major label or to remain independent?

5. From the perspective of those who run the label, what are the major problems facing the recording industry?

6. According to those who work at this label, how easy or difficult is it to enter the industry? Are there student internship possibilities at the label or at other independent labels?

Add other questions and information as you go along. Meet with the members of your group to discuss your findings. Your group might want to prepare a chart or provide information on your label that can be shared with the rest of the class.

(Note: This assignment can be adapted to other media industries covered in this text.)

CHAPTER 4

Network radio solved Tom Joyner's problem. A popular urban radio personality in Chicago in the 1970s, Joyner moved to Dallas in the 1980s to work at another radio station. Then Chicago called again: Would Joyner give up his morning show in Dallas to do an afternoon show in Chicago? "A light went on," says Joyner. "Mornings, afternoons. I can do this."

So, for eight years Joyner was the "Fly Jock," waking up at 3 A.M. to go on air in Dallas at 5:30 A.M., flying to Chicago at 9:30 A.M., and arriving at twelve noon. After a 2 to 6 P.M. shift in the Windy City, he would catch a flight that got him back to Dallas by 9 P.M. In 1994, seven million frequent-flier miles later, Joyner was travel-weary. The solution, and a way to reach even larger audiences, was the offer he accepted from ABC Radio to do a live, nationally syndicated morning show from Dallas. Joyner's program has since grown to include five million listeners in more than ninety broadcast markets, including Chicago, Dallas, Detroit, Miami, Washington, D.C., and Los Angeles. Joyner now has the nation's No. 1 urban radio show, targeting African Americans between the ages of twenty-five and fifty-four with a mix of comedy, soap-opera sketches, social activism, and old-school R&B music.

Joyner's program is part of a larger trend in radio toward airing national content—a trend fueled by the unprecedented consolidation in radio-station ownership since the 1996 Telecommunications Act. Under the new, relaxed ownership rules—

where consolidation reigns—it is much less expensive for one corporate owner to circulate a syndicated program on all its stations than to provide local programming that serves only a particular region. Proponents of this system argue that nationally syndicated programs link the country together, creating deejay and talk-radio stars like Joyner, the Fabulous Sports Babe, Howard Stern, Rush Limbaugh, and Dr. Laura Schlessinger, all of whom reach large, nationwide audiences. But when radio segments are filled by national programming, local deejays and talk anchors who emphasize regional ideas and interests are displaced. Some stations forsake local programs altogether, running automated syndicated programming services twenty-four hours a day. While this increasing reliance on syndicated programming may be cost-effective for owners, in many ways the radio industry is beginning to resemble the fast-food industry: less local flavor, fewer choices for listeners, and more national chains offering the same fare to popular demographic groups that advertisers target throughout the country.

The impact of radio in the twentieth century has been immense, and from all indications its influence has not faded. From the early days of network radio, which gave us "a national identity" and "a chance to share in a common experience,"[1] to the more customized, demographically segmented medium today, radio's influence continues to reverberate throughout the airwaves. Though television has displaced radio as our most common experience, radio has specialized and survived. The daily music and persistent talk that resonate from radios all over the world continue to play a key role in contemporary culture.

The story of radio from its invention at the turn of the century to its survival in the age of television is one of the most remarkable in media history, and it will be the focus of this chapter. We will examine the cultural, political, and economic factors surrounding radio's development and perseverance. We will explore the origins of broadcasting, from the early theories about mysterious radio waves to the critical formation of RCA as a national radio monopoly. We will then probe the evolution of commercial radio, including the rise of NBC as the first network, the development of CBS, and the establishment of the first federal radio acts. Reviewing the fascinating ways in which radio reinvented itself in the 1950s, we will also examine television's impact on radio programming and its advertising base, focusing on the invention of FM radio, radio's convergence with sound recording, and the influence of various formats. Finally, we will survey the economic health, increasing conglomeration, and cultural impact of commercial and noncommercial radio today.

> "The telegraph and the telephone were instruments for private communication between two individuals. The radio was democratic; it directed its message to the masses and allowed one person to communicate with many.
>
> "The new medium of radio was to the printing press what the telephone had been to the letter: it allowed immediacy. It enabled listeners to experience an event as it happened."
>
> —Tom Lewis,
> *Empire of the Air*

the origins and development of broadcasting

The wired and electronic transmissions of media messages have always required three ingredients: power (electricity); symbols (Morse code, music, or language); and a transmission-reception system (such as radio and TV stations and sets). With these requirements, radio did not emerge as a full-blown mass medium until the 1920s, though it had been evolving for a number of years.

the underlying technology

The invention of the telegraph in the 1840s ushered in the modern age of mass media. American artist-inventor Samuel Morse developed the first practical system, sending electrical impulses from a transmitter through a cable to a reception point. Using a symbol system that became known as Morse code—a series of dots and dashes that stood for letters in the alphabet—telegraph operators transmitted news and messages simply by interrupting the electrical current along a wire cable. By 1844, Morse had set up the first telegraph line between Washington, D.C., and Baltimore, Maryland. By 1861, lines ran coast to coast. By 1866, the first transatlantic cable ran between Newfoundland and Ireland along the ocean floor. Although it transmitted only about six words per minute, this cable was the forerunner of today's global communication technologies, including the Internet, faxes, and satellite transmissions.

Along with this revolution came a recognition of the telegraph's limitations. For instance, the telegraph dispatched complicated language codes, but it was unable to transmit the human voice. Armies benefited from telegraphed information, but ships still had no contact with the rest of the world. As a result, navies could not find out that wars had ceased on land and often continued fighting for months. Commercial shipping interests also lacked an efficient way to coordinate and relay information from land and between ships. What was needed was a telegraph without the wires.

The key development in wireless transmissions came from James Maxwell, a Scottish physicist who in the mid-1860s elaborated on some earlier ideas about electricity and magneticism. Maxwell theorized that there existed **electromagnetic waves**: invisible electronic impulses similar to visible light. Maxwell's equations showed that electricity, magnetism, light, and heat are part of the same electromagnetic spectrum and radiate in space at the speed of light, about 186,000 miles per second (see Figure 4.1). Maxwell further theorized that a portion of these phenomena, later known as radio waves, could be harnessed so that signals could be sent from a transmission point and obtained at a reception point. As one historian commented on the significance of Maxwell's ideas: "Every appliance we have today, from an electric generator to the microwave oven in the kitchen—and, of course, the radio—operates according to his fundamental equations. As Newton revolutionized mechanical science in the seventeenth century, so Maxwell revolutionized electrical science in the nineteenth."[2]

Figure 4.1
The Electromagnetic Spectrum
Source: The World Book Encyclopedia, Chicago, 1988.

The electromagnetic spectrum extends from short gamma rays through light waves to long radio waves. The spectrum diagrammed below gives the frequency and wavelength for the various waves. Frequencies are given in hertz and wavelengths in meters. The raised figures with the 10's are a way of abbreviating numbers. For example, 10^{15} hertz equals 1 followed by 15 zeros, or 1,000,000,000,000,000 hertz. The numbers with a minus sign tell how many places the decimal point must be moved in front of the number. For example, 10^{-7} meters equals 0.0000001 meter.

It was German physicist Heinrich Hertz, however, who in the 1880s proved Maxwell's theories. Hertz created a crude device that permitted an electrical spark to leap a small gap between two steel balls. As the electricity jumped the gap, it emitted electromagnetic waves and marked the first recorded transmission and reception of a radio wave. Hertz's experiments profoundly influenced two inventor-entrepreneurs, Guglielmo Marconi and Lee De Forest, who at the turn of the century began marketing wireless communication systems for businesses.

Marconi and Wireless Telegraphy. In 1894, Guglielmo Marconi, a twenty-year-old, self-educated Italian engineer, read Hertz's work and set about trying to make wireless technology practical. Marconi understood that developing a way to send high-speed messages over great distances would transform communication, the military, and commercial shipping. Although revolutionary, the telephone and the telegraph were limited by their dependence on wires.

Marconi improved on Hertz's experiments in a number of important ways. First, to the spark-gap transmitter he attached a Morse telegraph key, which could send out dot-dash signals. The electrical impulses traveled into a Morse inker, the machine telegraph operators used to record the dots and dashes onto narrow strips of paper. Second, Marconi discovered that *grounding*—connecting the transmitter and receiver to the earth—greatly increased the distance he could send signals.

The Italian government, not understanding what Marconi had accomplished, refused to patent his invention. Thus, in 1896 he left for England, where he finally received a patent on *wireless telegraphy*, a form of voiceless point-to-point communication. In London, in 1897, he formed the Marconi Wireless Telegraph Company, later known as British Marconi, and began installing wireless technology on British naval and private commercial ships. In 1899, he opened a branch in the United States, establishing a company nicknamed American Marconi. That same year, he sent the first wireless Morse code signal across the English Channel to France, and in 1901 he relayed the first wireless signal across the Atlantic Ocean.

Although Marconi was a successful innovator and entrepreneur, his vision was limited. He saw wireless telegraphy only as point-to-point communication, much like the telegraph and the telephone, and not as a one-to-many mass medium. He also confined his applications to military and commercial ships. In limiting his patents to Morse-code transmission, Marconi left it to others to explore the transmission of voice and music via the wireless.

De Forest and Radio. In 1899, inventor Lee De Forest, who liked to call himself "the father of radio," wrote the first Ph.D. dissertation on wireless technology. Understanding the extent and influence of Marconi's innovations,

French engineers transmitted an early wireless signal from the Eiffel Tower in 1898. Their Morse-code transmission was picked up almost three miles away. Two years earlier, twenty-two-year-old Guglielmo Marconi had sent a signal two miles across his parents' estate in Bologna, Italy.

De Forest decided that he could ensure his future livelihood and place in history by going beyond Marconi. In 1901, De Forest challenged the Italian inventor, who had contracted with the Associated Press to cover New York's International Yacht Races. De Forest signed up to report the races for a rival news service. The two rivals' transmitters jammed each other's signals so badly, however, that officials ended up relaying information on the races the premodern way—with flags and hand signals. The event symbolized a problem that would persist throughout radio's early development: noise and interference from too much competition for a finite supply of radio waves.

In 1902, De Forest set up the Wireless Telephone Company to compete head-on with American Marconi, by then the leader in the field of wireless communication. A major difference between Marconi and De Forest was the latter's interest in wireless voice and music transmissions, which became known as *wireless telephony* and, later, as *radio*. The key distinction is that both wireless telegraphy and telephony are forms of point-to-point communication, either wireless operator to wireless operator or phone to phone. Radio or broadcasting, however, became a form of mass communication—one to many. Radio offered the possibility of sending accessible messages to thousands of people who did not need training in Morse code.

Although occasionally accused of stealing ideas, De Forest went on to patent more than three hundred inventions. He claimed as his biggest breakthrough the development of the Audion, or triode, vacuum tube. Until the arrival of transistors and solid-state circuits, the Audion powered radios by detecting signals and then amplifying them. De Forest's improvements in detection, conduction, and amplification greatly increased listeners' ability to hear dots and dashes and, later, speech and music on a receiver set. His modifications were essential to the development of voice transmission, long-distance radio, and eventually television. In fact, many historians consider De Forest's improvements to the vacuum tube the beginning of modern electronics.

The credit for the first voice broadcast belongs to Canadian engineer Reginald Fessenden, formerly a chief chemist for Thomas Edison. Fessenden went to work for the U.S. Navy and eventually for General Electric (GE), where he played a central role in improving wireless signals. Both the navy and GE, however, were interested in the potential for simple voice transmissions that did not require Morse code. On Christmas Eve in 1906, after GE had built Fessenden a powerful transmitter, he gave his first public demonstration, sending a voice through the airwaves from his station at Brant Rock, Massachusetts. A radio historian describes what happened:

> That night, ship operators and amateurs around Brant Rock heard the results: "someone speaking! . . . a woman's voice rose in song. . . . Next someone was heard reading a poem." Fessenden himself played "O Holy Night" on his violin. Though the fidelity was not all that it might be, listeners were captivated by the voices and notes they heard. No more would sounds be restricted to mere dots and dashes of the Morse code.[3]

Ship operators, who had not seen the publicity announcing Fessenden's broadcast, were astonished to hear voices rather than the familiar Morse code. (Some operators actually thought they were having a supernatural encounter.)

Broadcasting, once an agricultural term that referred to the process of casting seeds over a large area, would come to mean the transmission of radio waves (and, later, TV signals) to a broad public audience. Prior to radio broadcasting, the wireless was considered only a form of **narrowcasting**, the kind of person-to-person communication that was possible via the telegraph and telephone. Today, narrowcasting has come to mean any specialized electronic programming or media channel aimed at a target audience, such as cable's Golf Channel or an Internet newsgroup for the medical profession.

In 1907, De Forest followed Fessenden's first broadcast by sending radio voices and music—actually a performance by Metropolitan Opera tenor Enrico Caruso—to

"I discovered an **Invisible Empire of the Air**, intangible, yet solid as granite."
—Lee De Forest, inventor

his friends in New York. The next year, De Forest and his wife, Nora, played records into a microphone from atop the Eiffel Tower. The signals were picked up four hundred miles away. Radio had passed from an inventor's toy to a business venture; it was now set to explode as a mass medium.

early broadcasting regulations

The first international conference on the wireless convened in Germany in 1903. Besides signal-interference issues, the conference addressed wireless requirements for ships at sea. The U.S. government had initially refused to ratify international rules because American manufacturers thought this would stifle national growth. But ultimately, in 1910, Congress passed the Wireless Ship Act, which required that all major U.S. seagoing ships carrying more than fifty passengers and traveling more than two hundred miles off the coast be equipped with wireless equipment with a one-hundred-mile range.

Two years later, in response to increased noise and interference on the airwaves, and in the wake of the *Titanic* tragedy, Congress passed the Radio Act of 1912. A brand-new British luxury steamer, the *Titanic* sank in 1912, killing fifteen hundred people; wireless reports had played a critical role in pinpointing the *Titanic's* location, enabling rescue ships to save seven hundred lives. A short policy guide, this first Radio Act required all wireless stations to obtain radio licenses from the Commerce Department. Since radio waves crossed state and national borders, legislators determined that broadcasting constituted a "natural resource"—a kind of interstate commerce. With this act, America also formally adopted the SOS Morse-code distress signal that other countries had been using for several years. The Radio Act of 1912 governed radio's development and regulated the new medium until 1927.

the formation of the
rca monopoly

By 1915, more than twenty American companies sold point-to-point communication systems, primarily for use in ship-to-shore communication. Having established a reputation for efficiency and honesty, American Marconi was the biggest and best of these companies. But in 1914, with World War I beginning in Europe and with America warily watching the conflict, the U.S. Navy questioned the wisdom of allowing a foreign-controlled company to wield so much power. American corporations in competition with Marconi, especially General Electric and AT&T, capitalized on the navy's xenophobia and succeeded in undercutting Marconi's influence.

Wireless telegraphy played an increasingly large role in military operations as the navy sought tight controls on information. When the United States entered the war in 1917, the navy closed down all amateur radio operations and took control of key radio transmitters to ensure military security. When the war ended in 1919, corporate heads and government leaders conspired to make sure radio communication would serve American interests. They planned to dominate communication worldwide by controlling the manufacture of radio transmitters and receivers.

At a meeting in May 1919, GE decided not to sell Marconi $5 million worth of vacuum tubes and potent new alternators, the best available power source for long-range radio transmissions. The military, influenced by Franklin Roosevelt, at that time the navy's assistant secretary, did not want such equipment under foreign control. Roosevelt was guided by President Woodrow Wilson's goal of developing the United States as an international power, a position greatly enhanced by American military successes during the war. Wilson believed that in the postwar era, a world power needed international dominion over shipping, or oil, or communication. Great Britain had long controlled the first two and had dominated transatlantic telegraph operations and the world's supply of cable since the 1860s. Wilson and the navy saw an opportunity to slow Britain's influence over communication and to promote a U.S. plan for control of wireless operations.

Some members of Congress and the corporate community opposed federal legislation that would grant the government or the navy a radio monopoly. Consequently, Owen Young, head of GE's legal department (and later GE's chairman), hatched a compromise plan that would pool wireless patents and technology to form a new American company. To secure the alternators that it needed, British Marconi was forced to sell its American subsidiary. GE then bought American Marconi at the urging of the navy and formed the Radio Corporation of America (RCA), the chosen instrument for the expansion of American communication technology throughout the world.[4]

With the formation of RCA, the patents pool expanded. Under the new arrangement, wireless patents from the navy, AT&T, GE, and the former American Marconi were combined to ensure U.S. control over the manufacture of transmitters and receivers. Initially, AT&T manufactured most transmitters, while GE (and later Westinghouse) made radio receivers. RCA administered the pool, collecting and distributing patent royalties to pool members. To protect individual profits from existing patents, the government did not permit RCA to manufacture equipment or to operate radio stations under its own name for several years. Instead, RCA's initial function was to ensure that radio parts were standardized by manufacturers and to control frequency interference by amateur radio operators, which became an increasing problem after the war.

At this time, the control of patents, amateurs, and foreigners were among RCA's major concerns. A government restriction mandated that no more than 20 percent of RCA—and eventually any U.S. broadcasting facility—could be owned by foreigners. This restriction, later raised to 25 percent, became a 1934 law that applied to all U.S. broadcasting stocks and facilities. Because of this rule, in 1985 Rupert Murdoch, the head of Australia's giant News Corp., became a U.S. citizen so that he could buy a number of TV stations as well as form the Fox television network.

Even after defusing Marconi's power in 1919, the navy worried that other important patents might come under foreign control. During the next two years, RCA entered into a series of cross-licensing agreements that brought Westinghouse and a number of smaller companies into the monopoly. These agreements further strengthened the cozy relationship between government and radio's corporate leaders that had begun during World War I. RCA's most significant impact, however, was that it gave the United States almost total control over the emerging mass medium of broadcasting, which at the time had not been anticipated by most wireless executives. By pooling more than two thousand patents and sharing research developments, RCA ensured the global dominance of the United States in mass communication, a position it maintained in electronic hardware into the 1960s and in program content through the 1990s.

At the time, the United States was the only country that placed broadcasting under the care of commercial, rather than military or government, interests. RCA's head start and protected status would enable America to become the world's largest exporter of information services and popular culture.

the evolution of commercial radio

When Westinghouse engineer Frank Conrad set up a crude radio studio above his Pittsburgh garage in 1919, placing a microphone in front of a phonograph to broadcast music and news to his friends (whom Conrad supplied with receivers) two evenings a week, he unofficially became the medium's first disc jockey. In 1920, a lightbulb went on in the head of a Westinghouse executive who had become intrigued by Conrad's curious hobby: "The efforts that were being made to develop radio telephone as a confidential means of communication were wrong . . . instead its field was really one of wide publicity."[5] In other words, the executive had realized the potential of radio as a mass medium. Westinghouse then established station KDKA, which aired national returns from the Cox-Harding presidential election on November 2, an event most historians consider the first professional broadcast. Almost overnight, the age of point-to-point wireless became the age of broadcast radio.

In 1921, the U.S. Commerce Department officially licensed five radio stations for operation, although a number of engineering schools had been operating experimental stations for several years. By early 1923, more than six hundred commercial and noncommercial stations were operating. Some stations were owned by AT&T, GE, and Westinghouse, but many were run by amateurs or were independently owned by universities or businesses. Later, the government permitted RCA to acquire its own stations. By the end of 1923, 550,000 radio receivers, most manufactured by GE and Westinghouse, had been sold for about $55 each. Just as the "guts" of the phonograph had been put inside a piece of furniture to create a consumer product, the vacuum tubes, electrical posts, and bulky batteries that made up the radio receiver were placed inside stylish furniture and marketed to the home. By 1925, 5.5 million radio sets were in use across America, and radio was a mass medium.

dissension in the ranks

In 1922, in a major power grab, AT&T, which already had a government-sanctioned monopoly in the telephone business, decided to break its RCA agreements in an attempt to monopolize radio as well. Identifying the new medium as the "wireless telephone," AT&T argued that broadcasting was merely an extension of its control over the telephone. Ultimately, the corporate giant complained that RCA had gained too much monopoly power. In violation of its early agreements with RCA, the phone company began making and selling its own radio receivers.

Then, in New York in 1922, AT&T started WEAF (now WNBC), the first radio station to sell commercial time to advertisers. The phone company

From this crude radio studio above his garage, Frank Conrad broadcast the first wireless message in the United States, ushering in the age of broadcast radio. Conrad's employer, Westinghouse, used this broadcasting equipment to create KDKA, one of the country's first radio stations.

claimed that under the RCA agreements it had the exclusive right to sell ads, which AT&T called *toll broadcasting*. Most people in radio at the time recoiled at the idea of using the medium for crass advertising, viewing it, instead, as a public information service. But by August 1922, AT&T had nonetheless sold its first ad to a New York real-estate developer for $50. The idea of promoting the new medium as a public service, along the lines of today's noncommercial National Public Radio (NPR), ended when executives realized that radio ads offered another opportunity for profits. Advertising revenue would in fact ensure profits long after radio-set sales had saturated the consumer market.

The initial strategy behind AT&T's toll broadcasting idea, however, was the phone company's effort to conquer radio. By virtue of its agreements with RCA, AT&T retained the rights to interconnect the signals between two or more radio stations via telephone wires. In 1923, when AT&T aired a program simultaneously on its flagship WEAF station and on WNAC in Boston, the phone company created the first **network**: a cost-saving operation that links, through special phone lines (and, later, satellite relays), a group of broadcast stations that share programming produced at a central location. By the end of 1924, AT&T had interconnected twenty-two stations in order to air a talk by President Calvin Coolidge. Some of these stations were owned by AT&T, but most of them simply consented to become AT&T "affiliates," agreeing to air the phone company's programs. These network stations informally became known as the *telephone group* and later as the Broadcasting Corporation of America (BCA).

In response, GE, Westinghouse, and RCA interconnected a smaller set of competing stations, known as the *radio group*. Initially, their network linked WGY in Schenectady, New York (then GE's national headquarters), and WJZ in Manhattan. The radio group had to use inferior Western Union telegraph lines when AT&T denied them access to telephone wires. By this time, AT&T had sold its stock in RCA and refused to lease its lines to competing radio networks. The telephone monopoly was now enmeshed in a battle to defeat RCA for control of radio. This, among other problems, eventually led to a government investigation and an arbitration settlement in 1925. In the agreement, the Justice Department, irritated by AT&T's power grab, redefined patent agreements. AT&T received a monopoly on providing the wires, known as *long lines*, to interconnect stations nationwide. In exchange, AT&T sold its BCA network to RCA for $1 million and agreed not to reenter broadcasting for eight years (a banishment that actually extended into the mid-1990s).

sarnoff and nbc

After Lee De Forest, David Sarnoff was among the first to envision the wireless as a modern mass medium. From the time he served as Marconi's fifteen-year-old personal messenger, Sarnoff rose rapidly at American Marconi. He became a wireless operator, helping to relay information about the *Titanic* survivors in 1912. Promoted to a series of management positions, Sarnoff was closely involved in RCA's creation in 1919, when most radio executives saw wireless merely as point-to-point communication. But with Sarnoff as RCA's first commercial manager, radio's potential as a mass medium was quickly realized. At age thirty, Sarnoff became RCA's general manager in 1921.

After RCA acquired AT&T's telephone-group stations, Sarnoff created a new subsidiary in September 1926 called the National Broadcasting Company (NBC). Its ownership was shared by RCA (50 percent), General Electric (30 percent), and Westinghouse (20 percent). This loose network of stations would be hooked together by AT&T long lines. Shortly thereafter, the original telephone group became known as the NBC-Red network, and the radio group became the NBC-Blue network.

> "I believe the **quickest way to kill** broadcasting would be to use it for direct advertising."
> —Herbert Hoover, Secretary of Commerce, 1924

Although NBC owned a number of stations by the late 1920s, many independent stations began affiliating with the networks to receive programming. An **affiliate** station, though independently owned, signs a contract to be part of a network and receives money to carry the network's programs. In exchange, the network reserves time slots, which it sells to national advertisers. By 1933, NBC-Red had twenty-eight affiliates; NBC-Blue had twenty-four.

The rationale behind a network is an economic one: A network allows stations to control program costs and avoid unnecessary duplication. As early as 1923, AT&T realized that it would be cheaper to produce programs at one station and broadcast them simultaneously over a network of owned, or affiliated, stations than for each station to generate its own programs. Such a network centralized costs and programming by bringing the best musical, dramatic, and comedic talent to one place, where programs could be produced and then distributed all over the country.

In essence, network radio helped modernize America by de-emphasizing the local and the regional in favor of national programs broadcast to nearly everyone. In fact, when Charles Lindbergh returned from the first solo transatlantic flight in 1927, an estimated twenty-five to thirty million people listened to his welcome-home party on the six million radio sets then in use. At the time, it was the largest shared audience experience in the history of any mass medium.

David Sarnoff's leadership at RCA was capped by two other negotiations that solidified Sarnoff's stature as the driving force behind radio's development as a modern medium. In 1929, Sarnoff cut a deal with General Motors for the manufacture of car radios, which had been invented a year earlier by William Lear (later the designer of the Learjet), who sold the radios under the name Motorola. Sarnoff also merged RCA with the Victor Talking Machine Company. Afterward, until the mid-1960s, the company was known as RCA Victor, adopting as its corporate symbol the famous terrier sitting alertly next to a Victrola radio-phonograph. The merger gave RCA control over Victor's records and recording equipment, making the radio company a major player in the sound recording industry. In 1930, David Sarnoff became president of RCA and ran the company for the next forty years.

the end of the rca monopoly

As early as 1923, the Federal Trade Commission had charged RCA with violations of antitrust laws but allowed the monopoly to continue. By the late 1920s, the government, concerned about NBC's growing control over radio content, intensified its scrutiny. Then, in 1930, when RCA bought out the GE and Westinghouse interests in the two NBC networks, federal marshals charged RCA/NBC with a number of violations, including exercising too much control over manufacturing and programming. Although the government had originally sanctioned a closely supervised monopoly for wireless communication, RCA products, its networks, and the growth of the new mass medium had dramatically changed the radio industry by the late 1920s. After the collapse of the stock market in 1929, the public became increasingly distrustful of big business. In 1932, the government revoked RCA's monopoly status.

RCA acted quickly. In exchange for the government's canceling half of the corporation's nearly $20 million debt, which had accumulated during the early years of the Depression, Sarnoff's company bought out GE's and Westinghouse's remaining shares in RCA's manufacturing business. Now RCA would compete directly against GE, Westinghouse, and other radio manufacturers, but to encourage new competition Sarnoff agreed not to make radio equipment for thirty months. Ironically, in the mid-1980s, General Electric bought back RCA, a shell of its former self and no longer competitive with foreign electronics firms. GE was chiefly interested in RCA's brand-name status and its still-lucrative subsidiary, NBC.

paley and cbs

Even with RCA's head start and its favored status, the company's two NBC networks faced competitors in the late 1920s. The competitors all found it tough going. One group, United Independent Broadcasters (UIB), even lined up twelve prospective affiliates and offered them $500 a week for access to ten hours of station time in exchange for quality programs. UIB was cash-poor, however, and AT&T would not rent the new company line services to link the affiliates. Enter the Columbia Phonograph Company, which was looking for a way to preempt RCA's merger with the Victor Company, then Columbia's major competitor. With backing from the record company, UIB and the new Columbia Phonograph Broadcasting System launched a wobbly sixteen-affiliate network in 1927, nicknamed CPBS. But after losing $100,000 in the first month, the record company pulled out. Later, CPBS dropped the word *phonograph* from the title, creating CBS.

In 1928, William Paley, the twenty-seven-year-old son of Sam Paley, owner of a Philadelphia cigar company, bought controlling interest in CBS to sponsor the cigar manufacturer's La Palina brand. One of Paley's first moves was to hire the public-relations pioneer Edward Bernays, Sigmund Freud's nephew, to polish the new network's image. Paley and Bernays modified a concept called **option time**, in which CBS paid affiliate stations $50 per hour for an option on any portion of their time. The network provided programs to them and sold ad space or sponsorships to various product companies. In theory, CBS could now control up to twenty-four hours a day of its affiliates' radio time. Some affiliates received thousands of dollars per week merely to serve as conduits for CBS programs and ads. Since NBC was still *charging* some of its affiliates as much as $90 a week to carry network programs, the CBS offer was extremely appealing.

By 1933, Paley had more than ninety affiliates, many of them defecting from NBC. Paley also concentrated on developing news programs and entertainment shows, particularly soap operas and comedy-variety series. In the process, CBS successfully raided NBC, not just for affiliates but for top talent as well. Throughout the 1930s and 1940s, Paley lured a number of radio stars from NBC, including Jack Benny, Frank Sinatra, George Burns and Gracie Allen, and Groucho Marx. During World War II, Edward R. Murrow's powerful firsthand news reports from bomb-riddled London established CBS as the premier radio-news network, a reputation it carried forward to television. In 1949, near the end of big-time network radio, CBS finally surpassed NBC as the highest-rated network. Although William Paley had intended to run CBS only for six months to help get it off the ground, he ran it for more than fifty years.

the mutual broadcasting system

While the major networks were building their dynasties during the 1930s, not all radio stations sought affiliations with them; many stations were content to produce their own regional and local programs. In 1934, four powerful independent stations—WGN in Chicago, WOR in Newark, WLW in Cincinnati, and WXYZ in Detroit—formed the Mutual Broadcasting System. Sharing programs and functioning more as a cooperative venture than as a regular network, three of these stations operated fifty-thousand-watt "clear channels" that reached most of North America. Among the first AM stations established in the United States, clear channels claimed the most powerful AM signals. Other stations operating on the same channels were required to reduce their signal power at night, allowing clear channel stations to broadcast with a minimum of interference across distances of hundreds of miles, giving them huge potential audiences.

Mutual offered a small central news service and a few entertainment programs, and it mostly served smaller stations, often in remote areas that were ignored by NBC and CBS. In 1968, Mutual became the first network to offer a news service, the Mutual Black Network, which raised issues of interest to black listeners. Today, Mutual serves thousands of radio affiliates by providing a variety of national news services and other programs, including rebroadcasts of many old radio programs from the 1930s.

chaos and the radio act of 1927

In the 1920s, as radio moved from narrowcasting to broadcasting, the battle for more frequency space and less channel interference intensified. Manufacturers, engineers, station operators, network executives, and the listening public demanded action. Many wanted more sweeping regulation than the simple licensing function granted under the Radio Act of 1912, which gave the Commerce Department little power to deny a license or to unclog the airwaves.

Beginning in 1924, commerce secretary Herbert Hoover conducted a series of national radio conferences, which included industry representatives, to fix the channel problems. He ordered radio stations to share time and to set aside certain frequencies for entertainment and news and others for farm and weather reports. To challenge Hoover, a station in Chicago jammed the airwaves, intentionally moving its signal onto an unauthorized frequency. In 1926, the courts eventually decided that, based on the existing Radio Act, Hoover had the power only to grant licenses, not to restrict stations from operating. Within the year, two hundred new stations clogged the airwaves, creating a chaotic period in which nearly all radios had poor reception. By early 1927, sales of radio sets had declined sharply.

In an attempt to restore order to the airwaves, Congress passed the Radio Act of 1927, the precursor to the Federal Communication Act of 1934. The 1927 act stated that licensees did not *own* their channels but could license them as long as they operated in order to serve the "public interest, convenience, or necessity." To oversee licenses and negotiate channel problems, the 1927 act created the Federal Radio Commission (FRC), appointed by the president. Although the FRC was intended as a temporary committee, it grew into a powerful regulatory agency. In 1934, with passage of the Federal Communication Act, the FRC became the Federal Communication Commission (FCC). Its jurisdiction covered not only radio but also the telephone and the telegraph (and later television, cable, and the Internet).

In 1941, an activist FCC went after the networks. Declaring that NBC and CBS could no longer force affiliates to carry programs they did not want, the government outlawed the practice of option time that Paley had used to build CBS into a major network. The FCC also demanded that RCA sell one of its two NBC networks. RCA and NBC claimed that the rulings would bankrupt them. The Supreme Court sided with the FCC, however, and RCA eventually sold NBC-Blue to a group of businessmen for $8 million in the mid-1940s. It became the American Broadcasting Company (ABC). These government crackdowns brought long-overdue reform to the radio industry. But they had not come soon enough to prevent considerable damage to noncommercial radio (see "Examining Ethics: NPR and Support for Noncommercial Radio" on page 113).

"Four years ago we were dealing with a **scientific toy**; today we are dealing with a vital force in American life."
—Herbert Hoover, 1925

the golden age of radio

Many ingredients in television today were initially formulated for radio. The term *veejay*, or video jockey, used on cable's MTV and VH1, derives from *deejay*, or *disc jockey*, a term first used in 1941 to describe someone who played recorded music on radio

Since Thomas Paine declared government a "necessary evil" in the 1700s, Americans have had a healthy skepticism toward government-funded projects. That makes the success of National Public Radio (NPR) a surprise. Supported since 1970 by the federal government and individual donations, NPR—which now has about five hundred affiliate public radio stations across the United States—is usually touted for fulfilling radio's promise as a mass medium. Most critics argue that NPR programs, particularly its syndicated *All Things Considered* (1971–) and *Morning Edition* (1980–), have outperformed the commercial sector in bringing quality and variety to radio; NPR's many interview and news-feature series are considered unrivaled in broadcast news.

So why is it that in every decade since NPR's creation, politicians have threatened to cut off its support? One reason is a perceived liberal bias, which makes NPR a target of political conservatives. Most critics, however, regard NPR as much more evenhanded than the commercial news networks. NPR's own audience studies indicate that slightly more than one-third of its listeners are conservatives, just under one-third are liberals, and the other third are moderates.[1]

NPR's shaky status had its origins in radio history. By the late 1920s, corporate interests had wrested control of radio away from the noncommercial sector: farmers, labor unions, educators, religious leaders, and other citizen groups operating radio stations. Even prior to this time, the government had long been granting favors to commercial radio, including requests for rules to control amateur operators and signal interference. In a bit of slippery reasoning, radio lobbyists representing the networks claimed that the coverage of education, religion, and labor available on noncommercial radio (and often broadcast today on NPR) were propaganda serving special interests. They also claimed that the profit motives of the networks represented the real public interest.

Based on this logic, the newly created Federal Radio Commission (FRC) forced many nonprofit stations off the air during evening hours, turning their frequencies over to commercial stations. This limited a nonprofit station's air time and diminished its audience reach (since most radio listening occurred after dinner). Many nonprofit stations also had their daytime power severely curtailed. A signal that once traveled thousands of miles now went only a few miles. In addition, every three months broadcasters could challenge each other for air space, with network stations and their technical superiority given FRC preference. Slowly, commercial stations began buying up the nonprofits, which struggled to meet expenses during the Depression. Overall, noncommercial stations declined from more than two hundred in 1927 to sixty-five by 1934.[2]

During the last major battle over radio reform, the Wagner-Hatfield Amendment to the 1934 Communication Act would have set aside 25 percent of all broadcast frequencies for a wide range of nonprofit groups. The arguments of commercial lobbyists, however, defeated the measure. By describing capitalism (an economic system) as a simple synonym for democracy (a political system), corporate interests prevailed, curtailing most future debates on broadcast ownership. Commercial broadcasting came to be viewed as natural—the American way.

NPR continues to struggle with the fallout from these early arguments, which still raise a number of ethical and economic questions. Should NPR receive money from the government? Should NPR get money from commercial broadcasters, as happens in other countries, to ensure that diverse voices are heard—even though such voices may not be profitable to commercial radio? NPR and the Corporation for Public Broadcasting (CPB), with the help of the grassroots efforts of listeners across the country, defeated the bill for complete privatization of public broadcasting that Congress pushed in the mid-1990s. In fact, federal funding for the CPB actually increased in the late 1990s. Yet the threats to defund public radio have had lingering effects. For example, in 1998, NPR affiliates were required for the first time ever to meet minimum standards in either audience ratings or private fundraising in order to be eligible for CPB funding. Some worry that these quasi-commercial standards will make public radio programmers pay too much attention to ratings and moneymaking, and discourage public radio's tradition of unique programming.

> "Most critics regard NPR as much more evenhanded than the commercial news networks."

113

programs. In addition, the first weather forecasts and farm reports on radio began in the 1920s. Regularly scheduled radio news analysis started the same year, with H. V. Kaltenborn, a reporter for the *Brooklyn Eagle*, providing commentary on AT&T's WEAF. The first regular *network* news analysis began on CBS in 1930, featuring Lowell Thomas, who would remain on radio for forty-four years. Thomas's first report began, "Adolph Hitler, the German fascist chief, is snorting fire. There are now two Mussolinis in the world, which seems to offer a rousing time."[6]

> "The Shadow, mysterious aide to the forces of law and order is, in reality, Lamont Cranston, wealthy young man about town who, years ago in the Orient, learned the hypnotic power to cloud men's minds so that they could not see."
> —opening line,
> *The Shadow,* 1931

Radio, like television today, commanded a central position in most American living rooms in the 1930s and 1940s. At the time, only a handful of stations operated in most large radio markets, and popular stations were affiliated with either CBS or one of the two NBC networks. Many large stations employed their own in-house orchestras and aired live music daily. Listeners had favorite evening programs, usually fifteen minutes long, which they would tune in each night. Families gathered around the radio to hear such shows as *Amos 'n' Andy*, *The Shadow*, *The Lone Ranger*, *The Green Hornet*, and *Fibber McGee and Molly*, or one of President Franklin Roosevelt's fireside chats.

Among the most popular early forms on radio, the *variety show* served as the forerunner to such popular TV shows as the *Ed Sullivan Show*. The variety show, developed from stage acts and vaudeville, began with the *Eveready Hour* in 1923 on

During America's golden age of radio, large audiences tuned in to the suspense of the crime thriller *The Shadow*, the daily drama of the *Guiding Light*, and the antics of ventriloquist Edgar Bergen and dummy Charlie McCarthy.

Originally, white comedians Charles Correll and Freeman Gosden created *Amos 'n' Andy* as a blackface vaudeville act and in 1925 took their stage act to Chicago's WGN radio station. In 1929, NBC picked up the program, and it became the prototype for future situation comedies on both radio and TV. Deemed racist by some black newspapers in the 1930s, the program was arguably the most popular in the history of radio among both white and black audiences. *Amos 'n' Andy* made a short run on network television in the early 1950s, featuring TV's first all-black cast.

WEAF. Considered experimental, the program presented classical music, minstrel shows, comedy sketches, and dramatic readings. Stars from vaudeville, musical comedy, and New York theater and opera would occasionally make guest appearances.

By the 1930s, studio-audience *quiz shows—Professor Quiz* and the *Old Time Spelling Bee*—had emerged. Other quiz formats, used on *Information Please* and *Quiz Kids*, featured guest panelists. The quiz formats were later copied by television, particularly in the 1950s. *Truth or Consequences*, based on a nineteenth-century parlor game, began in 1940 and presented guests performing goofy stunts. It ran for seventeen years on radio and another twenty-seven on television, influencing TV stunt shows like CBS's *Beat the Clock* in the 1950s and cable's *Double Dare* in the 1980s.

Dramatic programs, mostly radio plays that were broadcast live from theaters, developed as early as 1922. Historians mark the appearance of *Clara, Lu, and Em* on WGN in 1931 as the first *soap opera*. One year later, Colgate-Palmolive bought the program, put it on NBC, and began selling the soap products that gave this dramatic genre its distinctive nickname. Early "soaps" were fifteen minutes in length and ran five or six days a week. It wasn't until the mid-1960s on television that soaps were extended to thirty minutes, and by the late 1970s they had expanded to sixty minutes. Still a fixture on CBS, the *Guiding Light* actually began on radio in 1937 and moved to television in 1952 (the only radio soap to successfully make the transition). By 1940, sixty different soap operas occupied nearly eighty hours of network radio time each week.

The *situation comedy*, a major staple of TV programming today, also began on radio in the mid-1920s. By the early 1930s, the most popular comedy was *Amos 'n' Andy*, which started on Chicago radio in 1925 before moving to NBC-Blue in 1929. By today's standards, *Amos 'n' Andy* was a nineteenth-century minstrel show that often stereotyped black characters as shiftless and stupid. Created as a blackface stage act by two white comedians, Charles Correll and Freeman Gosden, the program was criticized as racist. But NBC and the program's producers claimed that *Amos 'n' Andy* was as popular among black audiences as among white listeners.

A pioneering program in many ways, *Amos 'n' Andy* launched the idea of the *serial* show: a program that featured continuing story lines from one day to the next. The format was soon copied by soap operas and other radio dramas. *Amos 'n' Andy*

On Halloween in 1938, Orson Welles's radio dramatization of *War of the Worlds* created a panic up and down the East Coast, especially in Grover's Mills, New Jersey—the setting for the fictional Martian invasion that many listeners assumed was real. Here, a seventy-six-year-old Grover's Mills resident guards a warehouse against alien invaders.

aired six nights a week from 7:00 to 7:15. During the show's first year on the network, radio-set sales rose nearly 25 percent nationally. To keep people coming to restaurants and movie theaters, owners broadcast *Amos 'n' Andy* in lobbies, rest rooms, and entryways. Early radio research estimated that the program aired in more than half of all radio homes in the nation during the 1930–31 season, making it the most popular radio series in history. From 1951 to 1953, it made a brief transition to television (Correll and Gosden sold the rights to CBS for $1 million), becoming the first TV series to have an entirely black cast.

While *Amos 'n' Andy* was the most popular series in radio, the most famous single broadcast featured an adaptation of H. G. Wells's *War of the Worlds* on the radio series *Mercury Theater of the Air*. Orson Welles produced, hosted, and acted in this popular series, which adapted science fiction, mystery, and historical adventure dramas for radio. On Halloween eve in 1938, the twenty-three-year-old Welles aired the 1898 Martian invasion novel in the style of a radio news program. For people who missed the opening disclaimer, the program sounded like a real news report, with eyewitness accounts of pitched battles between Martian invaders and the U.S. Army.

The program created a panic that lasted several hours. In New Jersey, some people walked through the streets with wet towels around their heads for protection from deadly Martian heat rays. In New York, young men reported to their National Guard headquarters to prepare for battle. Across the nation, calls jammed police switchboards. Afterward, Orson Welles, once the radio voice of *The Shadow*, used the notoriety of this broadcast to launch a film career. Meanwhile, the FCC called for stricter warnings both before and during programs that imitated the style of radio news.

Radio in this golden age was not the portable medium it would later become, however. Prior to transistors and solid-state integrated circuits, most radio sets required large glass tubes housed in heavy wooden pieces of furniture. Most programs in those days had a single sponsor who created and produced each show. The networks distributed these programs live around the country, charging the sponsors advertising fees. Many shows—the *Palmolive Hour*, *General Motors Family Party*, the *Lucky Strike Orchestra*, and the *Eveready Hour* among them—were named after the sole sponsor's product.

radio reinvents itself

The history of American mass media reveals that older media forms do not disappear when confronted by newer forms. Instead, mass media adapt. Although radio threatened sound recording in the 1920s, and television threatened radio in the 1950s, both older forms adjusted to the economic and social challenges posed by the arrival of a newer medium. Remarkably, the arrival of television in the 1950s marked the only time in media history in which a new medium virtually stole every national programming and advertising strategy from the older medium. Television snatched radio's advertisers, its program genres, its major celebrities, and its large evening audiences. In the process, the TV set physically displaced the radio as the living-room centerpiece across America.

new technologies

The story of radio's evolution and survival provides a fascinating look at the impact of one medium on another. This is especially important today, as newspapers and magazines enter the information highway and as publishers produce Web sites and books on tape for new generations of "readers." In contemporary culture, we have grown accustomed to such media convergence as the norm. To understand this blurring of the boundaries between media forms, it is useful to look at the 1950s and the ways in which radio responded to the advent of television.

The Transistor. A key development in radio's adaptation occurred with the invention of the *transistor* by Bell Laboratories in 1947. Transistors, like De Forest's vacuum tubes, could receive and amplify radio signals. However, they used less power and heat and were more durable and less expensive. Best of all, they were tiny. Transistors, which also revolutionized hearing aids, represented the first step in replacing bulky and delicate tubes, leading eventually to today's siliconchip integrated circuits. Texas Instruments marketed the first transistor radios in 1953, at about $40 apiece. Using even smaller transistors, Sony introduced the pocket radio in 1957. But it wasn't until the 1960s that transistor radios became cheaper than conventional tube and battery radios. For a while, the term *transistor* became a synonym for a small, portable radio.

The development of transistors permitted radio to go where television could not—to the beach, the office, into bedrooms and bathrooms, and nearly all new cars. (Before the transistor, car radios were a luxury item.) By the 1960s, most radio listening actually took place *outside* the home. For economic reasons, radio turned to the recording industry for content to replace the shows it had lost to television.

Armstrong and FM. By the time the broadcast industry launched commercial television in the 1950s, many, including David Sarnoff of RCA, were predicting radio's demise. To fund television's development and protect his radio holdings, Sarnoff had even delayed a dramatic breakthrough in broadcast sound, what he himself called a "revolution"—FM radio.

Edwin Armstrong, who first discovered and developed FM radio in the 1920s and early 1930s, is often considered the most prolific and influential inventor in radio history. He alone understood the impact of De Forest's vacuum tube, and he used it to invent an amplifying system that enabled radio receivers to pick up distant signals. Armstrong's innovations rendered obsolete the enormous alternators used for generating power in early radio transmitters. In 1922, he sold a "super" version of his circuit to RCA for $200,000 and sixty thousand shares of RCA stock, making him a millionaire as well as RCA's largest private stockholder.

Armstrong also worked on the major problem of radio reception—electrical interference. Between 1930 and 1933, the inventor filed five patents on **FM**, or frequency modulation. Offering static-less radio reception, FM supplied greater fidelity and clarity than AM, making FM ideal for music. **AM**, or amplitude modulation, stressed the volume, or height, of radio waves; FM accentuated the pitch, or distance, between radio waves (see Figure 4.2). Although David Sarnoff, by then the chairman

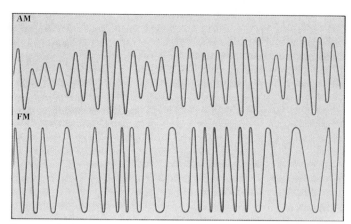

Figure 4.2
AM and FM Waves
Source: Adapted from David Cheshire, *The Video Manual*, 1982.

of RCA, thought that television would replace the older medium, he helped Armstrong set up the first experimental FM station atop the Empire State Building. Eventually, though, the RCA chief thwarted FM's development (which he was able to do, since RCA had an option on Armstrong's new patents). In 1935, Sarnoff threw RCA's considerable weight behind the development of television. With the FCC allocating and reassigning scarce frequency spaces, RCA wanted to ensure that channels went to television before they went to FM. But most of all, Sarnoff wanted to protect RCA's existing AM empire. Given the high costs of converting to FM and the revenue needed for TV experiments, Sarnoff decided to close down Armstrong's station.

Armstrong plunged ahead without RCA. He founded a new FM station and advised other engineers, who started more than twenty experimental stations between 1935 and the early 1940s. In 1941, the FCC approved limited space allocations for commercial FM licenses. During the next few years, FM grew in fits and starts. Between 1946 and early 1949, the number of commercial FM stations expanded from forty-eight to seven hundred. But then the FCC moved FM's frequency space to a new band on the electromagnetic spectrum, rendering some 400,000 prewar FM receivers useless. FM's future became uncertain, and by 1954 the number of FM stations had fallen to 560.

On January 31, 1954, Edwin Armstrong, weary from years of legal skirmishes over patents, wrote a note apologizing to his wife, removed the air conditioner from his thirteenth-story New York apartment, and jumped to his death. A month later, David Sarnoff announced record profits of $850 million for RCA, with TV sales accounting for 54 percent of the company's earnings. In the early 1960s, the FCC opened up more spectrum space for the superior sound of FM, infusing new life into radio. Although AM stations had greater reach, they could not match the crisp fidelity of FM, which would gradually make FM the preferred broadcast medium for music. In the early 1970s, about 70 percent of listeners tuned almost exclusively to AM radio. By the 1980s, however, FM had surpassed AM in profitability. By the 1990s, more than 75 percent of all listeners reportedly preferred FM, and more than 5,500 commercial and 1,900 noncommercial FM stations were in operation. The expansion of FM represented one of the chief ways radio survived television and Sarnoff's gloomy predictions.

changes in programming

Live and recorded music had long been radio's single biggest staple, accounting for 48 percent of all programming in 1938. Although network affiliates in large markets carried many drama, comedy, and variety series, smaller independent stations had always relied heavily on music. As noted earlier, in the 1920s, many stations even hired their own house bands and studio musicians. In the 1930s and 1940s, lean economic times forced more stations to play recorded music, either older music in the public domain (not under copyright) or music that was marginally popular and was not closely monitored by ASCAP. (See Chapter 3.)

Although live music on radio was generally considered superior to recorded music, early disc jockeys made a significant contribution to the latter. They demonstrated that music alone could drive radio. In fact, when television snatched radio's program ideas and national sponsors, radio's dependence on recorded music became a necessity and helped the medium survive in the 1950s.

The Rise of Format and Top 40 Radio. As early as 1949, station owner Todd Storz, in Omaha, Nebraska, experimented with formula-driven, or **format radio**. Under this system, management rather than deejays controlled programming each hour. When Storz and his program manager noticed that bar patrons and waitresses repeatedly played their favorite songs from the forty records available in a jukebox, they began researching record sales to identify the most popular tunes. From observing jukebox culture, Storz hit on the idea of *rotation:* playing the top songs many times during the day. By the mid-1950s, the management-control idea had combined with the rock-and-roll explosion. The *Top 40 format* was born. Although the term *Top 40* derived from the number of records stored in a jukebox, this format came to refer to the forty most popular hits in a given week as measured by record sales.

As format radio grew, program managers combined rapid deejay chatter with the best-selling songs of the day and occasional *oldies*—popular songs from a few months earlier. By the early 1960s, to avoid "dead air," managers asked deejays to talk over the beginning and the end of a song so that listeners would feel less compelled to switch stations. Ads, news, weather forecasts, and station identifications were all designed to fit a consistent station environment. Listeners, tuning in at any moment, would recognize the station by its distinctive sound.

In format radio, management carefully coordinates, or programs, each hour, dictating what the deejay will do at various intervals throughout each hour of the day (see Figure 4.3). Management creates a program log—once called a *hot clock* in radio jargon—that deejays must follow. By the mid-1960s, one study had determined that in a typical hour on Top 40, listeners could expect to hear about twenty ads; numerous weather, time, and contest announcements; multiple recitations of the station's call letters; about three minutes of news; and approximately twelve songs.

Radio managers further sectioned off programming into *day parts*, which typically consisted of 6 to 10 A.M., 10 A.M. to 3 P.M., 3 to 7 P.M., and 7 P.M. to 12 midnight time blocks. Each day part, or block, was programmed through ratings research according

Figure 4.3
Radio Program Log for an Oldies Station
Source: WQKL-FM, Ann Arbor, MI, 1997.

to who was listening. For instance, a Top 40 station would feature its top deejays in the morning and afternoon periods when audiences, many riding in cars, were largest. From 10 A.M. to 3 P.M., research determined that women at home and secretaries at work usually controlled the dial, so program managers, capitalizing on the gender stereotypes of the day, played more romantic ballads and less hard rock. Teenagers tended to be heavy evening listeners, so program managers often discarded news breaks at this time, since research showed that teens turned the dial when news surfaced.

Critics of format radio argued that only the top songs received play and that lesser-known songs deserving air time received meager attention. Although a few popular star deejays continued to play a role in programming, many others quit when managers introduced formats. Owners approached programming as if it were a science, but deejays considered it an art form. In format radio, record picks were simply based on jukebox inventories, record-store sales, and trade-publication charts. Program managers argued that deejays were probably smarter and more affluent than the average listener and therefore could not be fully trusted to know popular audience tastes. The owners' position, which generated more revenue, triumphed.

Payola. According to management, format radio had another big advantage over deejays who simply played their favorite music. It helped curb **payola**, the practice by which record promoters paid deejays to play particular records. As we noted in Chapter 3, payola was rampant during the 1950s, as record companies sought to guarantee record sales. When management took control of programming, however, individual deejays had less impact on what records would be played and became less susceptible to bribery. In response to this situation, record promoters often turned their attention to a few influential, high-profile deejays, whose backing could make or break a record nationally, or to key program managers in charge of Top 40 formats in large urban markets.

Despite congressional hearings and new rules designed to eliminate the problem, payola persisted. In the 1970s, for example, payola scandals involved exchanging airplay for drugs as well as cash. Although a 1984 congressional hearing determined that there was "no credible evidence" of payola practices in the recording industry, NBC News broke a story in 1986 about independent promoters who had alleged ties to the Mafia. One of NBC's sources on the story, Miami deejay Don Cox, was severely beaten right after the news story aired. Cox had told NBC that he had turned away promoters who offered cash and cocaine for guaranteeing airplay. A subsequent investigation led major recording companies to break most of their ties with independent promoters. Prominent record labels had been paying such promoters up to $80 million per year to help records become hits. Format radio eliminated the payola problem on a large scale, but charges of exchanging airplay for money, drugs, and sex continue to haunt both the radio and the recording industry.

In 1998, a legal alternative to payola emerged, and was hotly debated in the radio and recording industries. The promotional strategy, called *pay-for-play*, involves up-front payments from record companies to radio stations to play a song a specific number of times.[7] Stations that use pay-for-play sidestep FCC regulations by broadcasting disclosures that state that the song has been sponsored or paid for by the record company. In effect, the time to play the song is being purchased, not unlike the paid programming of television infomercials. If the station's listeners ultimately like the pay-for-play song, the song can become part of the station's regular, unsponsored lineup. For example, Flip/Interscope Records paid a Portland, Oregon, radio station $5,000 to play a song by hip-hop/metal band Limp Bizkit fifty times during a five-week period. The band ultimately gained a listenership in the market, and later played a concert in Portland. Although some see pay-for-play as a direct, honest way to introduce new music on radio stations, others object to having commercial interests blatantly tamper with playlists and the weekly *Billboard* music charts.

the sounds of radio today

Contemporary radio sounds very different from its predecessors. In contrast to the few stations per market in the 1930s, most large markets today include more than forty receivable signals that vie for listener loyalty. With the exception of national network-sponsored news segments and nationally syndicated programs, most programming is locally produced and heavily dependent on the music industry for content. Although a few radio personalities, such as Howard Stern, Rush Limbaugh, Don Imus, Tom Joyner, Dr. Laura Schlessinger, and the Fabulous Sports Babe are nationally prominent, local deejays and their music are the stars at most radio stations.

However, unlike listeners in the 1930s, who tuned in their favorite shows at set times, listeners today do not say, "Gee, my favorite song is coming on at 8:00 P.M., so I'd better be home to listen." Instead, radio has become a secondary, or background, medium that follows the rhythms of daily life. In the 1930s, radio often dictated those rhythms, particularly with its popular evening programs. Today, radio programmers worry about channel cruising, that habit listeners have, especially while in their cars, of searching the dial until they find a song they like.

Today, stations are more specialized. Listeners in the 1940s were loyal to favorite programs, but now we are loyal to favorite stations, music formats, and even radio personalities. We generally listen to only four or five stations that target us, usually based on our age, gender, or race. Television long ago took over the role of reaching the larger mass audience. In the 1930s, peak listening time occurred during evening hours—dubbed *prime time* in the TV era—when people were home from work and school. Today, the heaviest radio listening occurs during *drive time*, those periods between 6 and 9 A.M. and 4 and 7 P.M. when people are commuting to and from work or school. All of these changes were well under way by the late 1950s. For a time, critics thought radio might collapse under the weight of TV's growing popularity. In 1944, near the peak of radio's renown, only about a thousand stations were on the air. More than fifty years later, more than twelve thousand radio stations operate in the United States, customizing their sounds to reach mobile niche audiences. With radio as a truly portable medium, Americans are still tuning in, on average, for more than three hours on weekdays and nearly six hours on weekends.

The Fabulous Sports Babe, America's first nationally syndicated female sports talk-show host, is known for her extensive sports knowledge, outrageous personality, and in-your-face opinions.

the economics of broadcast radio

More than 10 percent of all U.S. spending on media advertising goes to radio stations. Like newspapers, radio generates its largest profits by selling local and regional ads. Thirty-second radio-spot ads range from $1,500 or more in large markets to just a few dollars in the smallest markets. Gross advertising receipts were $13 billion in 1997 (more than $10 billion in local ad sales, with the remainder in national network and non-network sales), up from about $10 billion in 1995. The industry is economically healthy and employs more than 150,000 people. Unlike television, where nearly 40 percent of a station's expenses goes to buy syndicated programs, local radio stations get much of their content free from the recording industry. Therefore, only about 20 percent of a typical radio station's budget goes to cover programming costs.

When radio stations want to purchase programming, they often turn to national network radio, which generates more than $500 million in ad sales annually by offering dozens of specialized services. For example, Westwood One, a major radio network service managed and partly owned by CBS, syndicates more than 150 programs, including regular news features (e.g., CBS Radio News, CNBC Business Radio), entertainment programs (e.g., *Country Countdown USA*, *House of Blues Radio Hour*, SPIN Radio Network), talk shows to fill entire day parts (e.g., *Imus in the Morning*, *Loveline*, and the *Tom Leykis Show*), and complete 24-hour formats (e.g., Adult Rock & Roll, Bright Adult Contemporary, Hot Country, Mainstream Country, Westwood One 70s, and CNN Headline News). By the late 1990s, more than sixty companies offered national program and format services, typically providing local stations with programming in exchange for time slots for national ads. The most successful radio network programs are the shows broadcast by affiliates in the Top 20 markets, which offer advertisers half of the country's radio audience. As mergers and buyouts continue, creating huge national radio groups in the wake of the 1996 Telecommunications Act, national network radio is expected to produce a larger portion of radio revenues.

Commercial Radio and Specialization. Although Top 40 managers pioneered format radio, stations today use a variety of formats based on managed program logs and day parts, as explained earlier. All told, more than twenty different radio formats, plus variations, serve diverse groups of listeners. To please advertisers, who want to know exactly who's listening, formats are usually targeted at audiences according to their age and income, gender, or race/ethnicity. Radio's specialization allows advertisers to reach smaller target audiences at costs that are much less than those for television. This process has become extremely competitive, however, because there may be forty or fifty stations available in a large radio market. In the 1990s, according to the Center of Radio Information, more than one thousand stations a year (roughly 10 percent of all stations) switched formats, in an effort to find the formula that would generate more advertising money. Some stations, particularly those in large cities, have also been renting blocks of time to various local ethnic and civic groups, allowing them to dictate their own formats and sell ads.

Although Top 40 radio—also called contemporary hit radio (CHR)—is in decline, it still appeals to many teens and young adults, and advertisers continue to buy time from Top 40 stations. Since the mid-1980s, however, these stations have lost ground steadily as younger generations have followed music on MTV rather than on radio. In addition, Top 40 music in the 1990s has become so diverse, encompassing everything from gangsta rap to children's songs, that "no commercial radio station could ever play it all and hold on to an audience."[8]

In contrast, the nation's fastest-growing format throughout much of the 1990s was the news/talk format. (See "Case Study: The Appeal of Talk Radio" on page 124.) In 1987, only 170 radio stations operated formats dominated by either news programs or talk shows, which tend to appeal to adults over thirty-five (except for sports talk programs, which draw both younger and older mostly male sports fans). By 1996, buoyed by the notoriety and popularity of Howard Stern and Rush Limbaugh, more than a thousand stations used some combination of news and talk. A news/talk format, though

TABLE 4.1 The Twelve Most Popular Radio Formats			
1987		**1998**	
Format	Number of Stations	Format	Number of Stations
Country	2,468	Country	2,630
Adult contemporary (AC)	2,213	AC	1,955
Top 40/CHR	825	Oldies	1,153
Nostalgia/adult standards	719	News/talk	1,083
Religious	554	Religious	968
Easy listening	375	News	809
Album-oriented rock (AOR)	319	Talk	686
Oldies	261	Sports	603
News/talk	171	Rock/AOR	582
Spanish-language	163	Contemporary hit/Top 40	561
Black/gospel	162	Gospel	559
Soft rock	152	Christian	509

Source: The Center for Radio Information Broadcasting and Cable Yearbook.

more expensive to produce than a music format, appeals to advertisers looking to target working- and middle-class adult consumers. Nevertheless, most radio stations continue to be driven by a variety of less expensive music formats. (See Table 4.1.)

Contemporary Music Formats. Known first as middle-of-the-road, or MOR, the *adult contemporary* (AC) format is among radio's oldest and most popular, reaching between 17 and 20 percent of all listeners, most of whom are older than forty. In the early 1970s, *Broadcasting* magazine described AC's eclectic mix of news, talk, oldies, and soft rock music as "not too soft, not too loud, not too fast, not too slow, not too hard, not too lush, not too old, not too new."

Many formats target by age or gender, but some also appeal to particular ethnic or racial groups. For example, *Spanish-language* radio targets large Cuban populations in Miami, Puerto Rican listeners in New York, and Mexican American audiences in California and Texas (where KCOR, the first all-Spanish-language station, originated in San Antonio in 1947). Besides talk shows and news segments in Spanish, these formats feature a variety of Spanish, Caribbean, and Latin American musical styles, including calypso, flamenco, mariachi, merengue, reggae, samba, and salsa.

In terms of African American listeners, formats featuring jazz, gospel, rhythm and blues, hip-hop, and dance music have targeted various audience segments over the years. In 1947, WDIA in Memphis was the first station to program exclusively for black listeners. Now called *urban contemporary* (UC), this format targets a wide variety of African American listeners, primarily in large cities. UC, which typically plays popular dance, rap, and blues music, also subdivides by age, featuring an adult UC category with performers like Luther Vandross and Anita Baker. A number of stations that refuse to play rap use what the industry calls a *black/R&B* format.

Pitched to older listeners and used as background sound, instrumental radio music is played in many offices, supermarkets, retail stores, and homes. Characterized by critics as "elevator music," the *easy listening* (EZ) format is aimed at adult listeners, predominantly female and white. Sometimes also called *wall-to-wall music*, or *musical wallpaper*, these formats were the first to acknowledge that radio had become a secondary

The Appeal of Talk Radio

Talk radio, the fastest-growing radio format since Top 40 in the 1950s, comes in two varieties (excluding sports talk): the personal and the political. Much like the programs of Dr. Laura Schlessinger, Howard Stern, Rush Limbaugh, or Don Imus today, the earliest talk shows in radio mixed personal stories and political intrigue, with an emphasis on the former. The genre developed in the 1920s around syndicated newspaper columnists Louella Parsons and Walter Winchell. Parsons, who wrote gossip columns about the movie industry for the powerful Hearst newspaper chain, used her position to coerce film stars who could not afford bad publicity to appear on radio. Winchell, one of the most popular commentators in radio history, discussed both celebrity culture and the day's top news stories.

The forerunner of today's talk-therapy programs was the shady Medical Question Box, featuring Dr. John Brinkley in the 1920s. Brinkley had purchased a mail-order diploma for $100 from the Eclectic Medical University in Missouri. On his program, which aired from a

Dr. Laura Schlessinger

powerful Kansas station, a caller would mail in symptoms (at $2 per inquiry), and over the radio Brinkley would diagnose and offer a cure (at $1 per prescription). He also dispensed bottled medicines without ever having seen the patient. His advertising promoted a surgery that he claimed would restore sexual potency by implanting goat glands in a man's scrotum, an operation that Brinkley performed many times. Not recognizing Brinkley's medical degree, the American Medical Association protested. In 1930, the Federal Radio Commis-

sion eventually revoked his radio license for failing to serve the "public interest," whereupon Brinkley took his show across the border to Mexican radio.

Franklin Roosevelt's radio conversations during his thirteen years as president are some of the most important in the history of political talk radio. Roosevelt's staff used radio to promote Social Security, rural electrification, and the Tennessee Valley Authority, among other New Deal reforms. FDR's own fireside chats on radio helped a struggling nation survive the Depression, the menace of Hitler, and a second world war. When Roosevelt announced Japan's December 7, 1941, attack on Pearl Harbor, more than sixty-two million listeners were tuned in—still the single largest audience for any radio talk.

Father Charles Coughlin, the "radio priest," began broadcasting from the Shrine of the Little Flower in Royal Oak, Michigan, in the late 1920s. In addition to religion, the charismatic Coughlin discussed politics and economics. He also used his radio pulpit to support FDR. As Coughlin's national reputation expanded and the Depression deepened, however, he turned against FDR's New Deal and became more reactionary. He railed against labor unions and began singing the praises of Nazism, using his anti-Semitism to attract donations for his small parish. Although scolded by the Catholic hierarchy, Coughlin stayed on the air until 1940, when broadcasters stopped selling him time.

Louisiana senator Huey Long also used radio to spread his message. Long turned against Roosevelt in the 1930s and

activity: background "noise" in the television age. In the past few years, however, EZ formats have declined, losing ground to *nostalgia/big-band* formats (also called *adult standards*). Aimed at listeners who care about the original versions of the music from their youth, nostalgia/big-band formats emphasize early pop and jazz vocalists and the swing era, including music by Frank Sinatra, Ella Fitzgerald, Louis Armstrong, and Glenn Miller.

The *country* format does not reach as many total listeners as AC or news/talk radio, but country claims by far the most stations—more than twenty-six hundred by 1998. Many of these stations are in tiny markets where country has traditionally demanded more radical economic reforms to ease the Depression. Using radio to promote his Share-the-Wealth Society, which promised a minimum income for American families, Long soon earned a loyal national following. His populist motto, "Every man a king," and folksy southern charm worked well on radio. In 1935, Long announced his candidacy for the presidency, a move that threatened to split the Democratic Party, but he was assassinated later that year.

Rush Limbaugh led the trend of popular conservative talk-radio hosts in the 1990s. His success created scores of imitators (G. Gordon Liddy, Oliver North, and Michael Reagan among them). In 1998, the National Association of Radio estimated that 75 to 80 percent of radio talk-show hosts were taking a conservative stance. But the tide in talk radio began to shift by the late 1990s, as listeners seemed to tire of endless political talk on the airwaves. Dr. Laura Schlessinger surpassed Limbaugh and shock jock Howard Stern with her national call-in program (syndicated in 1994), which deals with the more personal issues of love, marriage, and family responsibility. Some critics pointed out that Schlessinger's doctorate degree is in physiology, not psychology, yet other critics felt that Schlessinger's more than two decades as a talk-show therapist equipped her with the ability to

make quick, unyielding moral judgments about her callers' problems.

There are many reasons for the staying power of talk shows. First, broadcast talk represents an electronic extension of an older oral past. As more impersonal forms of print culture displaced the more intimate forms of oral culture, modern societies lost something. Talk shows, though electronically filtered, may be one attempt to recover those important lost traditions of daily conversation. Second, in an age that has become increasingly bureaucratic and impersonal, radio talk at least creates the feel, and frequently the illusion, of intimacy. Although it often exploits the personal pain and problems of individuals, talk radio suggests that someone out there in the world will listen and react to our everyday troubles and anxieties.

Whether the talk is personal or political, whether it takes place in coffee shops, cars, via email, or over the backyard fence, we tune in to participate. We may be looking for people whose bizarre lives make our daily problems pale in comparison. We may be searching for solutions to larger social dilemmas and ways to make democracy work better. Or we may be seeking a little company. When talk radio airs a diversity of viewpoints, it keeps all forms of democratic conversation alive.

reigned as the default format for communities with only one radio station. Country music has old roots in radio, starting in 1925 with the influential Grand Old Opry program on WSM in Nashville. Although Top 40 drove country music out of many radio markets in the 1950s, the growth of FM in the 1960s brought it back as station managers looked for market niches not served by rock music. As diverse as rock, country music today includes such subdivisions as old-time, progressive country, country-rock, western swing, country-gospel, and Tejano (a blend of Texas country, Mexican folk melodies, and German accordion music).

Resisting the Top 40. Accompanying the expansion of the FM spectrum in the mid-1960s, *progressive rock* emerged as an alternative to conventional formats. Many of the noncommercial stations broadcast from college campuses, where student deejays and managers, unencumbered by ads and format radio, rejected the commercialism associated with Top 40 tunes. Instead, they began playing lesser-known alternative music and longer album cuts. Until that time, most rock on radio had been consigned almost exclusively to Top 40 AM formats, with song length averaging about three minutes.

The expansion of FM created room for experimenting, particularly with classical music, jazz, blues, and non–Top 40 rock songs. Experimental FM stations, both commercial and noncommercial, served as a venue for Bob Dylan's 1965 song "Desolation Row," which ran eleven minutes. In 1967, the Doors' "Light My Fire," a No. 1 hit, featured a seven-minute version for FM and a three-minute Top 40 AM version. The same year, some FM stations played Arlo Guthrie's "Alice's Restaurant," an eighteen-minute satiric antiwar folk ballad. FM offered a cultural space for hard-edged political folk and for rock music that commented on the civil-rights movement and protested America's involvement in the Vietnam War. By the 1970s, progressive rock had been copied, tamed, and absorbed by mainstream radio under the format label *album-oriented rock* (AOR). By 1972, AOR-driven album sales already accounted for more than 85 percent of the retail record business. By the 1980s, as first-generation rock and rollers aged and became more affluent, AOR had become less political and played mostly white post-Beatles music featuring such groups as Pink Floyd, Led Zeppelin, Cream, and Queen.

A number of critics have denounced AOR for limiting the definition of rock music. They argue that the strictly controlled AOR format displaced progressive rock by aiming "programming at an extremely specific, limited listenership," mostly white males in the thirteen to twenty-five age range. AOR programming guidelines initially ignored most black and female performers, whom program directors claimed held little appeal for AOR's target audience. By discouraging certain kinds of music, AOR formats encouraged a type of "institutionalized racism and sexism." These guidelines were later adopted by MTV in its formative years, making it harder for black and female artists to crack the video scene in the early 1980s.[9]

Today, there are several spin-offs from AOR. *Classic rock* serves up rock oldies to the baby-boom generation from the mid-1960s through the 1980s and is aimed primarily at listeners who have outgrown the conventional Top 40. The *oldies* format serves adults who grew up on 1950s and early 1960s rock and roll. Begun in California in the mid-1960s, oldies formats recall the integrationist impulse of early rock as well as emphasize soul and Motown music from the 1960s. Listening habits and record research indicate that most people identify closely with the music they listened to as adolescents and young adults. This tendency partially explains why oldies and classic rock stations have surpassed Top 40 stations today. It also helps to explain the recent nostalgia for music from the 1980s.

nonprofit radio

In the 1930s, the Wagner-Hatfield Amendment was intended to set aside 25 percent of radio for a wide variety of nonprofit stations. When the amendment went down in defeat in 1935, the future of educational and noncommercial radio looked bleak. Many nonprofits had sold out to for-profit owners during the Depression. The stations that remained were often banished from the air during the evening hours or assigned weak signals by federal regulators who favored commercial owners and their lobbying agents. Still, nonprofit public radio survived. More than seventeen hundred such stations now operate, many of them low-wattage stations on college campuses.

During the 1960s, nonprofit broadcasting found a Congress sympathetic to an old idea: using radio and television as educational tools. As a result, National Public Radio (NPR) and the Public Broadcasting Service (PBS) were created as the first noncommercial networks. Under the auspices of the Public Broadcasting Act of 1967 and the Corporation for Public Broadcasting (CPB), NPR and PBS were mandated to provide alternatives to commercial broadcasting. NPR's popular news and interview programs, *Morning Edition* and *All Things Considered*, draw three to four million listeners per day. Over the years, however, more time and attention have been devoted to public television than to public radio. When government funding tightened in the late 1980s and 1990s, television received the lion's share. In 1994, a conservative majority in Congress cut financial support and threatened to scrap the CPB, the funding authority for public broadcasting. Consequently, stations became more reliant than ever on private donations and corporate sponsorship. While depending on handouts, especially from big business, public broadcasters steered clear of some controversial subjects, especially those that critically examined corporations.

Like commercial stations, nonprofit radio has also adopted the format style. Unlike commercial radio, however, the dominant style in public radio is a loose variety format whereby a station may actually switch from jazz, classical music, and alternative rock to news and talk during different parts of the day. Some college stations, too small to affiliate, have kept alive the spirit of early 1950s radio, when deejays chose the music. Noncommercial radio still remains the place for both tradition and experimentation, for programs that do not draw enough listeners for commercial success.

By the late 1990s, religious programs, classical music, and jazz had become the primary formats in public and nonprofit radio. Of these, religious broadcasting is the format that most frequently relies on commercials as a source of revenue. Although about 350 stations nationally are devoted to religious programming full-time, another thousand stations devote at least fifteen hours a week to religious shows, double the number from the early 1980s.[10] Research from 1995 indicated that women constituted about 60 percent of the audience for religious programs and that the average annual income of listeners was about $30,000 a year. Although many religious stations and programs are noncommercial and depend solely on listener donations, roughly half of these broadcasts rely on advertising to pay the bills. In general, religious stations do not advertise controversial products (such as alcohol) that might undercut the values promoted on the programs. Major advertisers on religious programs—clothing retailers, department stores, food companies, and car dealers—believe that associating their products with religious values gives their ads a kind of credibility that cannot be found as easily on for-profit, commercial stations. The continuing growth of the religious radio format reflects the general cultural resurgence of spirituality in America since the 1960s. Religious radio formats also serve as an increasingly popular way for religious organizations to raise funds.

Although the proposed Wagner-Hatfield Amendment failed to redistribute radio resources in the mid-1930s, public and nonprofit radio have managed to maintain a presence on the radio dial. First, in 1948 the FCC approved the ten-watt FM station. Prior to this time, radio stations had to have at least 250 watts to get licensed. A 10-watt station with a broadcast range of only about seven miles took very little capital to operate, so more people could participate in the new FM phenomenon. These stations not only promoted Edwin Armstrong's invention but became training sites for students interested in broadcasting. Although the FCC stopped licensing new 10-watt stations in 1978, and low-power stations aren't eligible for funding from the Corporation for Public Broadcasting, by the 1990s more than a thousand 10-watters were still in operation.

A second development that aided public radio also occurred in 1948. For the first time, the government authorized a noncommercial license for a noninstitutional

"Although noncommercial radio seems to have turned the corner of public awareness, it has not yet overcome **decades of disorganization** and neglect and abuse by the federal government."
—Peter Fornatale and Joshua Mills, *Radio in the Television Age*, 1980

operation. In other words, the FCC granted a nonprofit license to a station not affiliated with labor, religion, education, or a civic group. The license went to Lewis Kimball Hill, a radio reporter and pacifist during World War II, who started the Pacifica Foundation to run experimental public stations. Pacifica stations, like Hill himself, have often challenged the status quo in radio as well as in government. Most notably, in the 1950s they aired the poetry, prose, and music of performers—considered radical, left-wing, or communist—who were blacklisted by television and seldom acknowledged by AM stations. Over the years, Pacifica has also been fined and reprimanded by the FCC and Congress for airing programs that critics considered inappropriate for public airwaves. By 1999, Pacifica had seventy affiliate stations.

alternative voices

Activists in hundreds of communities across America have recently protested the exclusivity of radio broadcasting by starting up their own noncommercial "pirate" radio stations. Broadcasting over a radius of just a few miles with low-power FM signals of one to ten watts, the pirate radio stations challenge corporate broadcasters' dominance of public airwaves. The National Association of Broadcasters and other industry groups have pressed to have the pirate broadcasters closed down, citing their illegality and their potential to create interference with existing stations. Between 1995 and 1998, more than five hundred illegal micropower radio stations were shut down. Still, an estimated one hundred to one thousand pirate stations are in operation in the United States, in both large urban areas and small rural towns.

> "Radio affects most people intimately, person-to-person, offering a world of unspoken communication between writer-speaker and listener. That is the immediate aspect of radio. A private experience."
> —Marshall McLuhan, *Understanding Media*, 1964

The low-power radio-station operators (who prefer the moniker "community" to "pirate" radio) argue that they could operate with licenses, but the FCC doesn't even grant broadcast licenses to stations under one hundred watts. Free-speech advocate Stephen Dunifer, founder of Free Radio Berkeley in California, says that community radio provides a real alternative to cookie-cutter commercial formats: "Community radio is consistent with the diverse community it reflects. Communication is radio's primary use. By promoting civic discourse, we can create a vibrant community."[11] Dunifer's Free Radio Berkeley began serving its California community in 1993, and grew to a staff of one hundred volunteers before a legal battle with the FCC shut it down in 1998. Shortly afterward, another group continued the community broadcasting effort and began transmitting its radio signal from the Berkeley Hills. Although the FCC has shut down hundreds of pirate broadcasters, the protests have also begun to make a difference. In 1999, the FCC issued a proposal for licensing low-power community FM radio stations. The agency reported that it had received more than thirteen thousand inquiries in the previous year from individuals and groups who were interested in starting low-power radio stations.

radio, ownership, and democracy

In recent years, the rules concerning the ownership of the public's airwaves have changed substantially. With the passage of the 1996 Telecommunications Act, the FCC eliminated most ownership restrictions on radio. As a result, in 1996 alone some 2,100 stations switched owners, as $15 billion changed hands. Previously, any single person or company could own up to twenty AM and twenty FM stations nationwide,

Pirate Radio with a Digital Twist

by Robert Occhialini

It's a story you've heard before: Law enforcement agents bust into a house, arresting the miscreants they find inside and hauling their illegal equipment off to an impound yard. A crack den? No, just a pirate radio station. But after being busted twice by the Federal Communications Commission (FCC), the operators of Tampa's Party Pirate 102.1 FM have had enough—they're switching to the Internet <www.ldbrewer.com/pirate.html>.

More consumers have broadband Internet access than ever before, which means the quantity and quality of audio and video streaming on the World Wide Web is increasing rapidly. More and more commercial radio stations are simulcasting over the Web, and Internet-only broadcast stations such as Broadcast.com and Spinner.com have sprung up. Television stations are also making the move in increasing numbers, and other nonbroadcast media, such as magazines and newspapers, are adding audio broadcasts and interviews to their Web-site offerings.

Not to be outstripped by their commercial and legally licensed counterparts, pirate radio broadcasters—those who illegally use broadcast frequencies to transmit unregulated radio programs—are making the move too. Who can blame them? They can no longer be threatened with FCC seizure of their equipment, since the United States government does not regulate Internet content. The Web does not use the radio frequencies that make pirate radio broadcasters "pirates," so moving to cyberspace transforms them into legal Webcasters. As one pirate broadcaster put it, "I don't see how the FCC has the authority to regulate Internet broadcasts—they aren't radio transmissions."

Some pirates, like Steal This Radio on New York's Lower East Side, move from apartment to apartment with tiny hand-rigged transmitters whose range is no more than a few city blocks; others, like Israel Offshore Radio, broadcast from ships in international waters and can be heard for thousands of miles. Needless to say, pirates also refuse to follow the rules of content and scheduling set up by the FCC—they specialize in beyond-alternative music as well as decidedly nonmainstream political and religious viewpoints. There are hundreds of pirates in the U.S. and perhaps thousands of others overseas.

In fact, it's now possible to listen to pirate broadcasts from all over the world through your computer. From a trance show on Holland's Freewave <www.deejay.demon.nl/main.html> to the Texas-twanger broadcasts of Texas Twister Radio <www.effectweb.com/twister/howdy.htm> to a born-again Christian diatribe from Free Radio Free Rock <www.freeradiofreerock.com/index.htm>, a wide variety of content not normally available can be readily viewed or listened to via the Internet.

Loose networks of Internet pirates are now being formed around the country. "The Net has made it much easier to communicate with other operators," says Chris Smolinski, who maintains a popular index of pirate radio pages at <www.access.digex.net/~cps>, "and to find information on operating stations." These networks allow several different broadcasters to share the cost of maintaining a single server that streams their content over the Web. Unlike a transmitter, the server can be anywhere, not necessarily near the source of the programming. As with traditional broadcasting, programs can be transmitted live or recorded to play at a scheduled time. Most pirate stations available on the Internet are remaining true to their roots and broadcasting over their illegal frequencies as well, despite the threat of government persecution.

Smolinski believes that "the Web will keep becoming more popular" for pirate broadcasters, but adds, "I don't think it will replace over-the-air transmitting, just coexist with it," since many pirates believe that abandoning old-fashioned broadcasting would be betraying their belief in democratizing the airwaves. If FCC pressure on pirates continues, however, more and more of them are likely to follow the example of Tampa's Party Pirate and migrate to the new medium.

Source: Robert Occhialini, "Bandwidth with Byte," *Swing,* November 1998.

Stephen Dunifer, who founded Radio Free Berkeley in 1993, is a vocal advocate for low-power community FM radio stations. Through his pirate radio station and his writing, he continues to battle the FCC and the National Association of Broadcasters, charging them with "grand theft larceny—stealing the public airwaves." For information about pirate radio stations throughout the world, access <http://www.radio4all.org>.

and only two of these could be in the same market. The new law allows individuals and companies to acquire as many stations as they want, with relaxed restrictions on the number of stations a single broadcaster may own in the same city: The larger the market or area, the more stations a company may own within that market. For example, in areas where forty-five or more stations are available to listeners, a broadcaster may own up to eight stations, but not more than five of one type (AM or FM). In areas with fourteen or fewer stations, a broadcaster may own up to five stations (three of any one type). In very small markets with a handful of stations, a broadcast company may not own more than half the stations. By 1998, 70 percent of radio stations were either co-owned with other stations or under contract with a program supplier in a time-brokerage agreement (purchasing blocks of time to air certain programs), making stations that are independently owned and programmed increasingly rare.[12] Between March 1996 and June 1998 alone, seven hundred stations shifted from individual to chain ownership.[13]

There were twice as many radio stations operating in the mid-1990s as in the mid-1980s, but the total number of owners remained the same. The FCC once tried to encourage diversity in broadcast ownership. From the 1950s through the 1980s, a media company could not own more than seven AM, seven FM, and seven TV stations nationally, and not more than one radio station per market. But today the commission embraces the consolidation schemes pushed by the powerful NAB (National Association of Broadcasters) lobbyists in Washington, D.C., in which fewer and fewer owners control more and more of the airwaves. For instance, in 1995 its buyout of CBS briefly made Westinghouse the largest single owner of radio stations in the United States. Then, in 1996 Westinghouse/CBS extended its reach by merging its radio holdings with Infinity Broadcasting. By the late 1990s, the group operated more than one hundred stations nationwide.

Westinghouse/CBS was eclipsed by an enormous network created in 1998, when the Chancellor Media Corporation (a two-station company in 1994), based in Irving, Texas, purchased Capstar Broadcasting to form a radio group of 463 stations with an estimated $1.6 billion in combined revenue. With so many stations at its disposal, Chancellor also formed its own AM/FM Radio Network, and delivered a blow to rival CBS by wooing the durable Top 40 countdown personality Casey Kasem away from the CBS-managed Westwood One. In another enormous radio purchase in 1998, Clear Channel Communications, the fourth-largest group owner, swallowed up Jacor Communications, the fifth-largest radio chain, to create the nation's second-largest group, with 454 stations in 101 cities. As a result of these consolidations, in many American cities only three companies control about 80 percent of the local radio market.[14]

Given broadcasters' reluctance to raise questions about these economic arrangements, public debate regarding radio as a special national resource has remained minuscule. Looking to the future, a big question remains to be answered: With a few large broadcast companies now permitted to dominate radio ownership nationwide, will this consolidation of power in any way restrict the number and kinds of voices permitted to speak over public airwaves? To ensure that mass-media industries continue to serve democracy, the public needs to play a role in developing the answer to this question.

Radio has managed to survive the economic threat posed by television, but its future in the twenty-first century is yet to be determined. With its specialized services, radio remains a diverse mass medium where we can find our culture, our history, our politics, and our music represented. Radio's daily doses of news, talk, and song reverberate throughout the airwaves and across the Internet, helping to define areas of culture that are not readily acknowledged in mainstream newspapers or on prime-time television.

REVIEW QUESTIONS

The Origins and Development of Broadcasting

1. Why was the development of the telegraph important in media history? What were some of the disadvantages of telegraph technology?

2. How is the concept of the wireless different from that of radio?

3. What was Marconi's role in the development of the wireless?

4. What were Lee De Forest's contributions to radio?

5. Why was the RCA monopoly formed?

6. How did broadcasting, unlike print media, come to be federally regulated?

The Evolution of Commercial Radio

7. What was AT&T's role in the early days of radio?

8. How did the radio networks develop? What were the contributions of David Sarnoff and William Paley to network radio?

9. Why did the government-sanctioned RCA monopoly end?

10. What is the significance of the Communication Act of 1934?

Radio Reinvents Itself

11. How did radio adapt to the arrival of television?

12. What was Edwin Armstrong's role in the advancement of radio technology? Why did RCA hamper Armstrong's work?

13. How did music on radio change in the 1950s?

14. What was format radio, and why was it important to the survival of radio?

The Sounds of Radio Today

15. Why are there so many radio formats today?

16. Why has Top 40 radio diminished as a format in the 1980s and 1990s?

17. What is the state of nonprofit radio today?

Radio, Ownership, and Democracy

18. What are the current ownership rules governing American radio?

19. Throughout the history of radio, why did the government encourage diversity among radio owners?

20. What are the arguments that pirate radio operators use to justify the existence of their stations?

QUESTIONING THE MEDIA

1. Describe your earliest memories of listening to radio. Do you remember a favorite song? How old were you? Do you remember the station's call letters? Why did you listen?

2. Count the number and types of radio stations in your area today. What formats do they use? Do a little research and compare today's situation with the number and types of stations available in the 1930s and the 1950s. Describe the changes that occurred.

3. If you could own and manage a commercial radio station, what format would you choose and why?

4. If you ran a noncommercial campus radio station in your area, what services would you provide that are not being met by commercial format radio?

5. How might radio be used to improve social and political discussions in the United States?

SEARCHING THE INTERNET

http://www.abcradio.com/tomjoyner.htm
The promotional site for Tom Joyner, the syndicated urban radio-show host, and one of ABC Radio's national stars.

http://wmbr.mit.edu/stations/list.html
One of the most comprehensive listings of U.S. and worldwide radio station Web pages, including stations that broadcast their audio signal on the Internet.

http://www.pri.org
Public Radio International is a top provider of content for more than six hundred public radio stations, with programs such as Garrison Keillor's *A Prairie Home Companion*, Ira Glass's *This American Life*, and *World Cafe*.

http://www.fcc.gov
The comprehensive FCC site includes a section on radio and the full text of the Telecommunications Act of 1996.

http://www.broadcast.com
Broadcast.com: is a leading site for live, "streaming" media, with continuous Netcasts of nearly four hundred radio stations.

http://www.npr.org
NPR's site includes audio files of special reports and hourly news updates, along with guides to other NPR programming.

THE CRITICAL PROCESS

In Brief

Think-Pair-Share

Think: Take two minutes to write down answers to the following questions about your radio-listening habits: How much radio do you listen to? When do you listen? What attracts you to a particular station?

Pair: Turn to a neighbor and compare notes. Which radio formats (if any) do you agree on? What do you think the stations are doing that is "right"? Are there some aspects of radio programming that bother you? What are they?

Share: Open up the discussion to the entire class. If you could envision the perfect radio station with the perfect format, what would it be? How would it be funded? Whom would it serve? What should be the purpose of this radio station in the community?

In Depth

In small groups (or as a class), listen to a few radio stations and compare two or three radio formats for one hour during the day. (This could also be developed as a written project.) Use a chart and break each hour into a program log. (See Figure 4.3 on page 119.) Track the time devoted to several categories, including:

- music
- deejay chatter and routines
- community announcements
- contests

- news
- ads
- station promotion
- other

Use a pie graph to demonstrate the approximate percentage of time a station devotes to each category. Then, based on your analysis of the formats, answer the following questions:

1. For each station you analyze, construct a profile of the kind of listener you think that station is trying to reach. To develop the profile, look at each category carefully. For example, how is news treated during the hour? When Top 40 developed, station managers tried to make the news and the ads sound like the music they were programming. Was this the case during the hours you listened? Provide evidence to support your position. Call the programming department at each station and ask what audience it is attempting to target. (These departments might also give you information on ad costs and ratings.) Finally, compare your own listener profile with the information each station has given you.

2. According to FCC rules, radio stations are trustees of public airwaves. Based on the limited hours you listened, were these stations doing a responsible job of reaching the public? Did they provide a consistent and identifiable sound? What did they do well? In what ways could they improve?

CHAPTER 5

The X-Files, one of the most fascinating cultural phenomena of our time, is about alien intruders, mutating monsters, government conspiracies, and citizen paranoia. Not only has this program helped raise the national standing of the Fox network to the status of CBS, NBC, and ABC but by 1999 the show's global presence had extended into nearly ninety countries. Apparently citizens from other nations enjoy a good tale about a paranoid and dysfunctional United States.

There is also no better example of media convergence. The book, the *Official Guide to the X-Files*, had expanded to three volumes by 1999. Cultlike "x-philes" fan magazines ranged from polished store-rack glossies to Xeroxed fanzines, and there are more than one thousand Web sites devoted to the program. Among the sites "are dozens specializing in 'fan fiction'—short stories that invent new plots and scenes for the show's two main characters"—FBI agents Fox Mulder and Dana Scully.[1] And in spring 1998, the *X-Files* EXPO, a kind of traveling carnival devoted to the program, toured the country, mainly to hype the release of the *X-Files* movie, yet one more aberration of converging media.

Although the producers of the film said moviegoers did not have to watch the TV show to understand the movie, the *X-Files* movie did continue the story line of the TV program, marking a first in prime-time television history and marketing. A motion-picture version of a network program generated more than $80 million in box-office revenue from the show's TV fans and drew new fans for the program's prime-time launch in 1998–99, its sixth season on television. The movie and the TV program, not coincidentally, are produced by different but cooperative divisions of Fox, a major subsidiary of News Corp., owned and run by the Australian media baron Rupert Murdoch (who also owns *TV Guide* and, in another example of convergence, uses the magazine to promote *X-Files* and other Fox network shows).

The show has been a gold mine for Fox/News Corp. and will generate more than $1.5 billion in profit over its expected eight-year prime-time run. By the 1998–99 season, the program cost Fox about $60 million annually (about $2.8 million for each of its twenty-two to twenty-four episodes per season). In offsetting these production costs, Fox earned well over $200 million in annual revenue from selling advertising during prime time and during rerun episodes on FX, a Fox cable channel. In addition, Fox earned $35 million by selling the first three years of the program into global and national syndication (in which stations bid on the rights to air reruns). After paying off its production costs, then, *X-Files* brought in about $185 million to Fox during the 1998–99 season alone.

With innovative and popular programming such as *The X-Files* and *The Simpsons* (the longest-running prime-time cartoon in TV history), the Fox network demonstrated that in a shrinking marketplace—amid the VCR, cable, and Internet booms—a new network could evolve and prosper. In addition, Fox used a tactic that television once employed against radio—raiding other networks for programming. The big coup came in 1994, when Fox won the four-year broadcast rights to National Football Conference (NFL) games from CBS for $1.5 billion. In several top markets—including Atlanta, Detroit, Milwaukee, and St. Louis—network-affiliated stations defected to the upstart six-year-old Fox shortly thereafter. Football had been on CBS for thirty years, and the loss shook the network. After four years without the NFL, CBS staged a Fox-like raid on NBC, securing the 1998–2002 rights to American Conference League games in a $2 billion–plus deal. CBS hoped the return of football would stem the tide of affiliate abandonment and reverse the ratings slide that plagued the network after the Fox coup in the mid-1990s.

The Fox raid on CBS programming and station allegiances recalled the offensive that television conducted on the radio industry in the 1950s. Throughout the 1950s, television seduced national audiences with scratchy black-and-white moving images. Television eventually took over radio's national sponsors, program ideas, and even its **prime-time** audience, those tuned in between 8 and 11 P.M. (or 7 to 10 P.M. in the Midwest). Old radio scripts began reappearing in TV form. In 1949, for instance, *The Lone Ranger* rode over to television from radio, where the program had originated in 1933. *Amos 'n' Andy*, a fixture on network radio since 1928, became the first TV series to have an entirely black cast in 1951; this circumstance would not be repeated until *Sanford and Son* in 1972. Jack Benny, Red Skelton, George Burns and Gracie Allen, among the most prominent comedians of their day, all left radio for television. Symbolic of the times, the radio news program *Hear It Now* turned into TV's *See It Now*, and *Candid Microphone* became *Candid Camera*.

Since replacing radio in the 1950s as our most popular medium, television's social and cultural impact has repeatedly sparked arguments. During the last decade, for example, teachers, clergy, journalists, and others have waged a public assault on TV's negative impact on children. A 1995 *New York Times* poll suggested that most Americans blamed television as the biggest single factor

> "Television is the medium from which most of us receive our news, sports, entertainment, cues for civic discourse and, most of all, our marching orders as consumers."
>
> —Frank Rich,
> *New York Times*, 1998

underlying teenage sex and violence (although TV viewing during teenage years actually decreases).[2] During election campaigns, television has been a target as well, serving as a lightning rod for frustration regarding what is wrong with American society.

But there is another side to this story. In the 1960s, television was there to expose civil-rights violations in the South, and in the 1980s it did the same in Eastern Europe and China. In the early 1990s, the televised Clarence Thomas–Anita Hill hearings triggered public debate about sexual harassment. In times of crisis, our fragmented and pluralistic society has turned to television as a touchstone, as common ground. We did this during the Army-McCarthy hearings on communism in the 1950s, in the aftermath of the Kennedy and King assassinations in the 1960s, during the political turmoil of Watergate in the 1970s, and after the space-shuttle disaster in the 1980s. When President Bush announced America's attack on Iraq in 1991, most U.S. homes tuned in; when 170 people died in the bombing of the Oklahoma City federal building in 1995, we again turned to television to make sense of senselessness. And in 1998 and 1999, we followed the Clinton impeachment process on our TVs. For better or worse, television has woven itself into the cultural fabric of daily life.

> "The Lewinsky scandal is tawdry, but it also is an irresistible story of sex and power, and television's unblinking focus on it is playing an active role in presidential power and politics."
> —Caryn James,
> *New York Times*, 1998

In this age of increasing market specialization, television is still the one mass medium that delivers content millions can share simultaneously—everything from the Super Bowl to a network miniseries to a presidential election debate. In this chapter, we will examine television's impact: the cultural, social, and economic factors surrounding the most influential media innovation since the printing press. We will begin by reviewing the early experiments with TV technology that led to the medium's development. We will then focus on the TV boom in the 1950s, including the downfall of sponsor-controlled content and the impact of the quiz-show scandals. Most of TV's major programming trends developed during this period, and we will investigate the most significant ones, including news, comedy, and drama. We will then trace the audience decline that has affected the major networks. In addition, we will explore television as a prime-time money factory, examining various developments and costs in the production, distribution, and syndication of programs. Finally, we will look at television's impact on democracy.

early technology and the development of television

Television changed social life, and the change was swift and dramatic. In 1948, only 1 percent of America's households had a television set. By 1953, more than 50 percent had one. By the early 1960s, more than 90 percent of all homes had a TV set. With television on the rise throughout the 1950s, many feared that radio—as well as books, magazines, and movies—would become unnecessary. What happened, of course, is that both radio and print media adapted to this new technology. In fact, today more radio stations are operating and more books and magazines are published than ever before; and ticket sales for movies have remained fairly steady since the 1960s.

the formative years

Although television achieved mass-media status in the 1950s, inventors from a number of nations had been toying with the idea of televised images for nearly a hundred years. Isolating TV and radio waves, part of the electromagnetic spectrum, required two ingredients: a photoelectric sensing material and a technique for encoding pictures for transmission through the air. Inventors needed a medium like film so that when light struck it, an electric current could be generated. In the late 1800s, the invention of the *cathode ray tube*, the forerunner of the modern TV picture tube, combined principles of the camera and electricity. Since television images cannot physically float through the air, technicians and inventors developed a method of encoding them at a transmission point (a TV station) and decoding them at the reception point (a TV set).

In the 1880s, German inventor Paul Nipkow developed the *scanning disk*, a large flat metal disk with a series of small perforations organized in a spiral pattern. As the disk rotated, it separated pictures into pinpoints of light that could be transmitted as a series of electronic lines. As the disk spun, each small hole scanned one line of a scene to be televised. For years, Nipkow's disk served as the foundation for experiments regarding the transmission of visual images.

In 1907, Russian physicist Boris Rosing improved the mechanical scanning device, but it was his lab assistant, Vladimir Zworykin, and an Idaho teenager, Philo Farnsworth, who independently pioneered an electronic TV system. Zworykin left Russia for America in 1919 and went to work for Westinghouse, where he developed the *iconoscope*, the first TV camera tube to convert light rays into electrical signals. By breaking down and converting these signals into radio waves, transmitting them through the air, and reconstructing them in a receiver set, inventors made television a possibility by 1923.

At the 1939 World's Fair in New York, the "guts" of a TV set featured a sealed glass device called a *cathode ray tube*. Such picture tubes were the technical standard in television for more than fifty years. Late in 1996, the FCC approved a new standard—digital, high-definition television. Forty-two stations introduced the new standard late in 1998.

At age sixteen, Farnsworth patented an electronic *image dissector* tube and figured out that mechanical scanning systems would not work for sending pictures through the air over long distances. In 1927, at age twenty-one, Farnsworth transmitted the first TV picture electronically—the image of a dollar sign. Finally, in 1930, he patented the first electronic television. RCA, then the world leader in broadcasting technology, challenged Farnsworth in a major patents battle. He would have to rely on his high-school notebooks as evidence to win against the company. After its court defeat, RCA had to negotiate to use Farnsworth's seventy-three patents. He later licensed these patents to RCA and AT&T for use in the commercial development of television. RCA conducted the first public demonstration of a TV image at the 1939 World's Fair.

Technical Standards. In the late 1930s, the National Television Systems Committee (NTSC), a group representing major electronics firms, began meeting to outline industry-wide manufacturing and technical standards. These meetings were similar to those held in the 1980s and 1990s to develop standards for high-definition television (HDTV) and digital television (see "Tracking Technology: DTV: The Digital Revolution" on page 140). As a result of the NTSC meetings, in 1941 the FCC adopted a 525-line image, scanned electronically at thirty frames per second (fps), which became the standard for all TV sets produced in the United States (until about 2006, when the new digital standard is supposed to phase out old sets). About thirty countries, including Japan, Canada, Mexico, Saudi Arabia, and most Latin American nations, adopted the NTSC system. Great Britain and the former Soviet Union, however, waited for the technology to improve and eventually adopted a slightly superior 625-line,

25-fps system, used for decades throughout most of Europe and Asia. A third standard operated in France, Belgium, Algeria, and a few other countries.

The TV Freeze. In 1941, the FCC set aside thirteen channels (1–13) on the **VHF** (very high frequency) band for black-and-white television. At this time, though, most electronic firms were converting to wartime production, so the commercial development of television was limited: Only ten stations were operating when Pearl Harbor was attacked in December 1941. However, by 1948, the FCC had issued nearly a hundred television licenses. Due to growing concern about channel allocation and frequency interference problems, which needed to be reviewed, the FCC declared a freeze on any new licenses from 1948 to 1952.

The Korean War prolonged the freeze. During this time, cities such as New York, Chicago, and Los Angeles had several TV stations, while other areas, including Little Rock, Arkansas, and Portland, Oregon, had none. Cities with TV stations saw a 20 to 40 percent drop in movie attendance during this period; more than sixty movie theaters closed in the Chicago area alone. But in non-TV cities, movie audiences increased. Taxi receipts and nightclub attendance also fell in TV cities, as did library-book circulation. At the same time, radio listening declined; for example, Bob Hope's network radio show lost half its national audience between 1949 and 1951. By 1951, sales of television sets had surpassed sales of radio receivers.

After a second NTSC conference in 1952 sorted out technical problems, the FCC ended the licensing freeze and issued a major report finalizing technical standards, many of which are still used today—and will be until the new digital standard takes over. Among its actions, the FCC set aside seventy new channels (14–83) on an ultrahigh frequency (**UHF**) band, although few manufacturers in the 1950s made TV sets equipped with UHF reception. As a result, UHF license holders struggled for years, until a 1964 law finally required manufacturers to equip sets with UHF reception. With the expansion of UHF slowed by technical snags, the FCC eventually "took back" channels 70–83 and reassigned those frequencies (plus VHF's Channel 1) to other communication services such as cellular phones.

In communities across the country, nearly 250 channels were initially earmarked for educational or nonprofit status, most of them on the newly created UHF band. Commercial interests, as they did in radio, had gobbled up most of the early VHF assignments with the FCC's blessing. Since the FCC did not establish a method for financing nonprofit stations, a long economic struggle followed for many of the educational TV stations. Even with the creation of the Corporation for Public Broadcasting (CPB) in 1967, which funneled federal funds to nonprofit radio and to more than three hundred public TV stations, the loose, decentralized network of stations that share Public Broadcasting Service (PBS) programming have had to beg listeners for much of their financial support. This has been especially true since the 1990s, when a more fiscally conservative Congress reduced much of the CPB's funding.

Another outcome of the freeze featured deliberations over a color system. In 1952, the FCC tentatively approved the experimental CBS system. Because its signal could not be received by black-and-white sets, however, the system was incompatible with those that most Americans owned. In 1954, RCA's color system, which could also receive black-and-white images, usurped CBS to become the color standard. Although NBC began broadcasting a few shows in color in the mid-1950s, it wasn't until 1966 that all three networks broadcast their entire evening lineups in color.

Almost thirteen hundred communities received TV-channel allocations from the FCC after the freeze ended. Since broadcast signals could interfere with one another, the FCC created a national map and tried to evenly distribute all available channels throughout the country. By the mid-1950s, there were more than four hun-

DTV: The Digital Revolution

Late in 1996, the Federal Communications Commission initiated the first fundamental changes in TV technology in more than fifty years.[1] Since the early 1960s, a search had been undertaken to improve the clarity and resolution of the standard NTSC 525-line TV image established in the 1940s. Most experiments focused on improving existing *analog transmission*, in which images are sent as continuous signals through the airwaves on specific frequencies. By the 1980s, Japanese firms had developed *high-definition television* (HDTV) for their own markets; with 1,100-plus lines of resolution, HDTV was far superior to the NTSC (National Television Systems Committee) standard. HDTV seemed certain to become the new U.S. television standard.

In the late 1980s, however, HDTV ran into the digital revolution. After seeing an impressive Sony HDTV demonstration in 1987, the FCC set up a race among various companies—including Sony—to develop a new American standard that used digital technology, which reduced both images and text to computerized signals. Sony and other Japanese firms created a hybrid of analog and digital HDTV innovations. To meet the Japanese challenge, in 1988 a consortium of broadcasters, electronics and computer manufacturers, and researchers from Europe and America—known as the Grand Alliance—began developing an all-digital system that surpassed the versatility of existing HDTV formats. The digital standard requires much less frequency space to store many more images and holds much more information and computer data than can analog or hybrid systems.

In late 1996, the FCC approved the Grand Alliance digital system, now known as DTV. Under this plan, each existing television station will be allocated a second channel for roughly ten to fifteen years as consumers convert to digital sets. During that time, each station will continue to broadcast programs using traditional analog signals on its old channel. Meanwhile, the same programs, as well as new digitized programs and computer services, will be transmitted on DTV. At the end of the adjustment period, the stations will return their old analog frequencies to the FCC for redistribution, formally ending analog broadcasting sometime after 2006.

As we enter the twenty-first century, several things are clear. DTV will provide lightweight, flat-screen, and even wall-mounted reception and will eventually replace bulky analog picture-tube sets. But over the short run, the next ten to fifteen years will feature a marketplace war between the computer industry and the TV electronics industry, each offering its own version of digital television, especially since the FCC has approved fourteen different digital formats. In addition, many critics believe that the conversion to DTV may last much longer. Since 200 million NTSC TV sets and 60 million NTSC VCRs will be made obsolete, consumers may be reluctant to switch to a new, far more expensive standard. The predictions of each side, made in 1997 at the outset of this manufacturing battle, appear below.

THE CONSUMER ELECTRONICS INDUSTRY SAYS:

- Past experience has shown that when consumers shop for a new TV, they are most interested in picture quality and cost.

- The Web is not yet a mass medium; there are few regular browsers, and they are concentrated in places like Silicon Valley.

- Viewers want to watch traditional movies, sports, and prime-time programming, not interact with televisions.

- Computers are finicky, difficult devices; most people like the simplicity of their TV sets.

THE COMPUTER INDUSTRY SAYS:

- Consumers, no longer satisfied with plain-vanilla television, want rich, interactive viewing experiences.

- Viewers will be as interested in browsing the World Wide Web as in watching traditional TV programming.

- High-definition pictures, while attractive, will not be enough to sell the new digital TV sets.

- The consumer electronics industry is slow-moving and lacking in imagination and innovation.

Source: Joel Brinkley, "Building Your Next TV: Two Industries Fight for a $150 Billion Prize," *New York Times*, March 28, 1997, pp. C1, C2.

dred television stations in operation, a 400 percent surge since the pre-freeze era. Today, about seventeen hundred TV stations are in operation, including more than three hundred nonprofit stations, which increasingly rely on corporate sponsorship for support.

television booms in the fifties

Like radio in the 1930s and 1940s, early television programs were often conceived, produced, and supported by a single sponsor. Many of the top-rated programs in the 1950s even included the sponsor's name in the title: *Texaco Star Theater*, *Buick Circus Hour*, *Camel News Caravan*, *Colgate Comedy Hour*, *Gillette Cavalcade of Sports*, *Kraft Television Theater*, and *Goodyear TV Playhouse*. Today, with the exception of the occasional *Hallmark Hall of Fame* drama, virtually no program on network television is named after and controlled by a single sponsor.

The Collapse of Sponsorship. Throughout the early 1950s, the broadcast networks became increasingly unhappy with the control sponsors exerted over program content. With the growing popularity of television came opportunities to alter prior financial arrangements, especially given the high cost of producing programs on a weekly basis. In 1952, for example, a single one-hour TV show cost a sponsor about $35,000, a figure that had risen to $90,000 by the end of the decade. These weekly costs became increasingly difficult for sponsors to bear.

David Sarnoff, then head of RCA/NBC, and William Paley, head of CBS, saw the opportunity to diminish the role of sponsors. Enter Sylvester "Pat" Weaver (father of actress Sigourney Weaver), who was appointed president of NBC by Sarnoff in 1953. A former advertising executive, Weaver was used to controlling radio content for his clients. When he made the switch to television, Weaver sought to retain that control—by forcing advertisers out of the content game. By increasing program length from fifteen minutes (standard for radio programs) to thirty and sixty minutes, Weaver substantially raised program costs for advertisers. In addition, two new programming changes made significant inroads in helping the networks gain control of content. Both strategies involved producing longer programs, thus making it difficult for a single sponsor to foot the bill.

The first strategy featured the concept of the *magazine program*. In January 1952, NBC introduced the *Today* show, which started as a three-hour morning talk-news program. A few years later, in September 1954, NBC premiered the ninety-minute *Tonight Show*. Since both shows ran daily rather than weekly, studio production costs managed by a single sponsor were prohibitive. Rather than selling the whole concept to one sponsor, NBC sold *spot ads* within the shows: Advertisers paid the network for thirty- or sixty-second time slots.

One of the longest-running programs on television, NBC's *Today* (1952–) has been hosted over the years by Dave Garroway, Tom Brokaw, Jane Pauley, and Bryant Gumbel. With its current hosts, Katie Couric and Matt Lauer (*left*), and a glass-walled studio that looks out onto New York's Rockefeller Plaza, *Today* was rated the No. 1 morning TV talk show in 1999. However, audience numbers for the network morning programs have generally declined with the rise of competing shows on cable channels.

The network, not the sponsor, now owned the programs or bought them from independent producers. More than forty-five years later, shorter versions of the *Today* and *Tonight* shows remain fixtures on NBC.

The second strategy, known originally as the *spectacular*, is today recognized by a more modest term, the *television special*. At NBC, Weaver bought special programs, like Laurence Olivier's filmed version of *Richard III* and the Broadway production of *Peter Pan*, again selling spot ads to many sponsors. The TV version of *Peter Pan* was a particular success, watched by some sixty-five million viewers. More typical specials featured music-variety shows hosted by top singers such as Judy Garland and Frank Sinatra. The combination of these programming strategies—and one juicy television scandal—ended sponsors' control over television content.

The Quiz-Show Scandals. Corporate backers of quiz shows drove the final nail into the coffin of sponsor-controlled TV content. In the mid-1950s, the networks revived the radio *quiz-show* genre. CBS aired the *$64,000 Question*, originally radio's more modest *$64 Question*—symbolic of how much television had raised the economic stakes. Owned by Revlon, which bought a half-hour block of evening prime time from the network in 1955, the program ranked as the most popular TV show in America during its first year. As one historian has suggested, "It is impossible to explain fully the popular appeal of the *$64,000 Question*. Be it the lure of sudden wealth, the challenge to answer esoteric questions, happiness at seeing other people achieving financial success, whatever the program touched in the American psyche at mid-century, this was stunning TV."[3] By the end of the 1957–58 season, twenty-two quiz shows aired on network television.

Revlon followed its success with the *$64,000 Challenge* in 1956. At one point, Revlon's two shows were running first and second in the national ratings, and its name recognition was so effective that the company periodically ran out of products. In fact, the company's cosmetic sales skyrocketed from $1.2 million before its sponsorship of the quiz shows to nearly $10 million by 1959.

Compared with dramas and situation comedies (which we'll look at shortly), quiz shows were cheap to produce, with inexpensive sets and mostly nonactors as guests. In addition, these programs offered the corporate sponsor the opportunity to have its name displayed on the set throughout the program.

The problem was that most of these shows were rigged. To heighten the drama and get rid of guests whom the sponsors or producers did not find appealing, key contestants were rehearsed and given the answers. The most notorious rigging occurred on *Twenty-One*, a quiz show owned by Geritol (whose profits climbed $4 million one year after deciding to sponsor the program in 1956). The subject of Robert Redford's 1994 film, *Quiz Show*, *Twenty-One*'s most infamous contestant was Charles Van Doren, a Columbia University English professor from a famous literary family. In 1957, Van Doren won $129,000 during his fifteen-week run on the program; his fame then landed him a job on NBC's *Today* show. In 1958, after a series of contestants accused the morning show *Dotto* of being fixed, the networks quickly dropped twenty shows. Following further rumors of fixing, a *TV Guide* story, a New York grand-jury probe, and a congressional investigation in 1959 (during which Van Doren admitted cheating), big-money prime-time quiz shows ended.

Although often little more than a compelling footnote in many accounts of television's history, the impact of the quiz-show scandals was enormous. First, the pressure on TV executives to rig the programs and the subsequent fraud effectively put an end to any role sponsors might have in creating television content. Sponsors and their ad agencies gradually accepted the networks' economic strategy of having several companies buy commercial time during a single program or a TV series.

Second, although many Americans had believed in the democratic possibilities of television—bringing inexpensive information and entertainment into every household—this belief was undermined by the sponsors and TV executives who participated in the quiz-show fraud. During the 1950s, many people trusted that pictures were more honest than words. The scandals provided the first dramatic indication that TV images could be manipulated. The seeds, then, for our contemporary cynicism about electronic culture had sprouted full-blown by the late 1950s. By the end of the decade, a growing number of middle-class parents were even refusing to allow their children to watch television.

Third, and most important, quiz shows magnified the separation between the privileged few and the general public, a division between high and low that would affect print and visual culture for at least the next forty years. That Charles Van Doren had come from a literary family of Ivy League intellectuals and "sold his soul" for fame and money drove a wedge between intellectuals and the popular new medium. At the time, many well-educated people aimed a wary skepticism toward television. This was best captured in the famous 1961 speech by FCC commissioner Newton Minow, who labeled game shows, westerns, cartoons, and other popular genres part of commercial television's "vast wasteland." Critics have used the wasteland metaphor ever since to admonish the TV industry for failing to live up to its potential. More than forty years after the quiz-show scandal, non-network, independently produced programs like *Jeopardy* and *Wheel of Fortune*, now called *game shows*, have made a strong comeback in late afternoon time slots. Although cable services like MTV and Comedy Central have experimented with more comic game programs in evening hours, the major broadcast networks remain reluctant to put game shows on again in prime time, even though they are profitable and much cheaper to produce than one-hour dramas or half-hour situation comedies.

> "I was fascinated by the seduction of [Charles] Van Doren, by the Faustian bargain that lured entirely good and honest people into **careers of deception.**"
> —Robert Redford, director, *Quiz Show*

key programming trends in the tv age

The disappearance of quiz shows marked the end of most prime-time network programs originating from New York. From about 1955 through 1957, the three major networks gradually moved their entertainment divisions to Los Angeles for its close proximity to Hollywood production studios. Network news operations, however, remained in New York. Symbolically, these cities came to represent the two major branches of TV programming: entertainment and information. Although there is much blurring between these categories today, at one time the two were much more distinct.

tv's information culture

In terms of television journalism, many local broadcast stations, TV newsmagazines, and cable's CNN have all made key contributions and generated their own controversies. However, in this section the focus will be on the network evening news, which over the years has had the most significant and sustained daily impact on viewers nationwide. Since the 1960s, broadcast journalism has consistently topped print news in national research polls that ask which news medium is more trustworthy. This fact alone makes the evening news a force to be reckoned with in our information culture.

NBC News. Featuring a panel of reporters interrogating political figures, NBC's weekly *Meet the Press* (1947–) remains the oldest news show on television. Daily evening newscasts, though, began on NBC in February 1948 with the *Camel Newsreel Theater*. Originally a ten-minute Fox Movietone newsreel that was also shown in theaters, this filmed news service was converted to a live broadcast one year later. Renamed the *Camel News Caravan* and anchored by John Cameron Swayze (who later became a spokesperson for Timex watches), the NBC newscast showed Swayze reading short news items in a converted radio studio. Toward the end of the fifteen-minute show, he would announce grandly, "Now let's go hopscotching the world for headlines!" and read a list of one- or two-sentence reports, which were occasionally accompanied by filmed newsreel footage.

Sponsored by a cigarette and the first news show to air in color, *Camel News* was succeeded by the *Huntley-Brinkley Report* in 1956. With Chet Huntley in New York and David Brinkley in Washington, this coanchored NBC program became the most popular evening news show on television. To provide a touch of intimacy, the coanchors would sign off their broadcasts, "Good night, Chet."/"Good night, David." This program served as the model for hundreds of local news broadcasts that eventually developed dual anchors to present the news. After Huntley retired in 1970, the program was renamed *NBC Nightly News* and struggled to compete with CBS's emerging star anchor, Walter Cronkite. A series of anchors and coanchors followed before Tom Brokaw settled in as NBC's sole anchor in September 1983.

CBS News. A second regular evening news show, *Television News with Douglas Edwards*, premiered on CBS in May 1948. In 1956, the CBS program became the first news show to be videotaped for rebroadcast on *affiliate* stations (independently owned stations that sign contracts with a network and carry its programs) in western time zones. (Ampex had just developed the first workable videotape recorder.) Walter Cronkite succeeded Edwards in 1962, starting a nineteen-year run as anchor of the renamed *CBS Evening News*. Once a World War II correspondent for a print wire service, Cronkite in 1963 anchored the first thirty-minute network newscast, which featured a live ocean-side interview with President John Kennedy, twelve weeks before his assassination. In 1968, Cronkite went to Vietnam to cover America's involvement in that civil war firsthand. Putting aside his role as an objective news anchor, he concluded on the air that the American public had been misled about Vietnam and that U.S. participation in the war was a mistake. With such a centrist news personality now echoing the protest movement, public opinion against American intervention mounted. Partly because of the influence of Cronkite's criticisms, President Lyndon Johnson decided not to seek reelection in 1968.

Retiring from his anchor position in 1981, Cronkite was succeeded by Dan Rather, a former White House correspondent who had starred on CBS's respected newsmagazine *60 Minutes* since 1975. Despite a $22 million, ten-year contract, Rather could not sustain the program as the highest-rated evening newscast, however. To woo viewers and exude warmth, he tried wearing colorful sweater vests and briefly signed off the news with the slogan "Courage." But neither succeeded in increasing the size of his audience. Rather did score a major coup in 1990, when he obtained an exclusive interview in Baghdad with Saddam Hussein shortly after the Iraqi leader ordered his troops to invade Kuwait, triggering the Persian Gulf War. Ratings for the newscast at CBS, however, remained flat. In the mid-1990s, the network tried an experiment aimed at both recapturing viewers and responding to the long-standing criticism that male anchors controlled the daily network news: CBS paired Rather with former *Today* show host Connie Chung. Unlike CNN and many local news stations, which routinely use male and female news teams, women anchors on the networks have long been relegated to substitute or weekend duty. Ratings continued to sag, however, and CBS terminated Chung after just a few months.

ABC News. Initially, ABC struggled to get a daily news program on the air. Throughout the years, the network tried many anchors and formats as it attempted to cut into the dominance of NBC in the 1960s and CBS in the 1970s. ABC premiered a daily program in 1948, but it folded when few affiliates chose to carry it. The network finally launched a daily news show in 1953, anchored by John Daly, the head of ABC News and also the host of CBS's evening game show *What's My Line?* After Daly left in 1960, a series of personalities sat behind the anchor desk, including John Cameron Swayze and in 1965 a twenty-six-year-old Canadian, Peter Jennings. Dubbed "anchor boy" by critics at the time, Jennings lasted just over two years before returning to London as a foreign correspondent. Another series of rotating anchors ensued, including Harry Reasoner and Howard K. Smith. Then, in 1976, the network hired Barbara Walters away from NBC's *Today* show, gave her a $1 million annual contract, and made her the first woman to regularly coanchor a network newscast. With Walters and Reasoner (the first reporter chosen in 1968 to launch *60 Minutes*) together, viewer ratings rose slightly, but the network was still behind CBS and NBC. In 1977, ABC sports director Roone Arledge took over as head of the newly combined ABC News and Sports division. In 1978, he launched *ABC World News Tonight*, featuring four anchors: Frank Reynolds in Washington, Jennings in London, Walters in New York, and Max Robinson in Chicago. Robinson was the first black reporter to coanchor a network news program. Walters decided to leave her anchor position in the early 1980s and focus on doing celebrity and political interviews. In 1983, ABC chose Jennings as the sole anchor. By the late 1980s, the ABC evening news had become the most-watched network newscast. It was dethroned, however, in 1996, when Brokaw's NBC program took the lead for the next three years.

Contemporary Trends in Network News. Audiences watching the network news contributed to the demise of many afternoon daily newspapers (which had virtually disappeared in most large U.S. cities by 1999). By the 1980s, though, network audiences also began to decline. Facing competition from VCRs and cable, especially CNN, network advertising revenues flattened out. In response, the networks cut back staffs in the late 1980s and early 1990s, eliminating many national and foreign reporter posts. In an effort to duplicate the financial success of *60 Minutes*, the most profitable show in TV history, the networks began developing relatively inexpensive newsmagazines. ABC's *20/20* and *Primetime Live* (which was renamed as a second *20/20* in 1998) became moneymakers, and *20/20* aired four evenings a week by 1999. NBC's successful *Dateline* programs were appearing five nights a week by 1999. Building on the success *60 Minutes* helped create for all three networks, CBS launched *60 Minutes II* in January 1999 to compete with other weeknight newsmagazines. In addition, a number of syndicated non-network newsmagazines were developed by independent producers for the local late-afternoon and late-night markets. These featured more than twenty breezy-sometimes-sleazy syndicated tabloids, including *Entertainment Tonight*, *Hard Copy*, and *A Current Affair*. More recently, Fox started its own 24-hour cable news service, and NBC, which already operated one cable news channel (CNBC), teamed up with Microsoft to launch MSNBC, the first news channel available simultaneously on cable and the World Wide Web.

tv's entertainment culture

While news divisions remained anchored in New York, the networks began to shift their entertainment divisions to Los Angeles, partly due to the success of the pioneering series *I Love Lucy* (1951–57). *Lucy*'s owners and costars, Desi Arnaz and Lucille Ball, began filming the top-rated situation comedy in California near their home. In

"If NBC found five more *Seinfeld*s, there would be two or three fewer *Dateline*s on the air. That's not news. That's filler."

—Don Hewitt,
60 Minutes
founder and
executive
producer,
1998

1951, *Lucy* became the first program filmed in front of a live audience. This was before the days of videotape, when the only way to preserve a live broadcast, other than by filming it like a movie, was through a technique called *kinescope*. In this process, a film camera recorded a live TV show off a studio monitor. The quality of the kinescope technique was generally poor, and most series that were saved this way have not survived. *I Love Lucy*, *Alfred Hitchcock Presents*, and *Dragnet* are among a handful of series from the 1950s that endured because they were originally shot and preserved on film.

Televised Comedy. Even during the quiz-show boom of the mid and late 1950s, the primary staples of television were comedy and drama, both significantly influenced by New York radio, vaudeville, and theater. This period is often referred to as the golden age of television. Television comedy back then (as now) came in three varieties: the sketch comedy (the forerunner of programs such as *Saturday Night Live* and *In Living Color*), the situation comedy (or *sitcom*), and the domestic comedy.

Sketch Comedy. Identified on occasion as *vaudeo*, or the marriage of vaudeville and video, **sketch comedy** was a key element in early vaudeville-like TV variety shows. These programs included singers, dancers, acrobats, animal acts, and ventriloquists as well as comedy skits. The shows "resurrected the essentials of stage variety entertainment" and played to noisy studio audiences.[4] Vaudeville performers dominated television's early history. Stars of sketch comedy included Milton Berle, TV's first major celebrity, in *Texaco Star Theater* (1948–67); Red Skelton in the *Red Skelton Show* (1951–71); and Sid Caesar, Imogene Coca, and Carl Reiner in *Your Show of Shows* (1950–54), for which playwright Neil Simon, filmmakers Mel Brooks and Woody Allen, and writer Larry Gelbart (*M*A*S*H*) all served as sketch writers.

Sketch comedy had major drawbacks, though. Since skits were an integral part of the hour-long variety series, these programs were more expensive to produce than half-hour sitcoms. In addition, skits on weekly variety shows, such as the *Perry Como Show* (1948–63), the *Dinah Shore Chevy Show* (1956–63), and the *Carol Burnett Show* (1967–79), used up new routines very quickly. The ventriloquist Edgar Bergen (the father of *Murphy Brown* star Candice Bergen) once commented that "no comedian should be on TV once a week; he shouldn't be on more than once a month."[5]

With original skits and new sets required each week, production costs mounted, and the vaudeville-influenced variety series faded. The last successful weekly program of this type, *Barbara Mandrell & the Mandrell Sisters*, ended its two-year NBC run in 1982 due to the demanding schedule of doing music and comedy on a weekly basis. In this instance, it was Mandrell, not low ratings, who stopped production of the show. Mandrell said that musical numbers and sketch comedy, which could be used over and over for different audiences on the nightclub circuit, lasted only one week on television. Since the early 1980s, variety shows have appeared only as yearly specials.

Situation Comedy. Over the years, the major staple on television has been the half-hour comedy series, the only genre represented in the Top 10–rated programs every year since 1949. (See Table 5.1.) One type of comedy series, the **situation comedy**, features a recurring cast and set as well as several narrative scenes. It establishes a situation, complicates it, develops increasing confusion among its characters, and alleviates the complications.[6] *I Love Lucy* from the 1950s, the *Beverly Hillbillies* from the 1960s, *Happy Days* from the 1970s, *Night Court* from the 1980s, and *Third Rock from the Sun* from the 1990s are all part of this long tradition.

In most situation comedies, character development is downplayed in favor of zany plot twists and disruptions. Characters are usually static and predictable; they generally do not develop much during the course of a series. Such characters "are never

TABLE 5.1
Selected Situation and Domestic Comedies Rated in the Top 10

The most durable and familiar genre in the history of television has been the sitcom. It is the only genre that has been represented in the Nielsen rating Top 10 lists every year since 1949. Below is a selection of top-rated comedies at five-year intervals, spanning forty years.

1955–56

I Love Lucy (#2)
Jack Benny Show (#5)
December Bride (#6)

1960–61

Andy Griffith Show (#4)
Real McCoys (#8)
Jack Benny Show (#10)

1965–66

Gomer Pyle, U.S.M.C. (#2)
Lucy Show (#3)
Andy Griffith Show (#7)
Bewitched (tie #7)
Beverly Hillbillies (tie #7)
Hogan's Heroes (#9)

1970–71

Here's Lucy (#3)

1975–76

All in the Family (#1)
Laverne & Shirley (#3)
Maude (#4)
Phyllis (#6)
Sanford and Son (tie #7)
Rhoda (tie #7)

1980–81

M*A*S*H (#4)
The Jeffersons (#6)
Alice (#7)
House Calls (tie #8)
Three's Company (tie #8)

1985–86

Cosby Show (#1)
Family Ties (#2)
Cheers (#5)
Golden Girls (#7)
Who's the Boss? (#10)

1990–91

Cheers (#1)
Roseanne (#3)
A Different World (#4)
Cosby Show (#5)
Murphy Brown (#6)
Empty Nest (#7)
Golden Girls (tie #10)
Designing Women (tie #10)

1997–98

Seinfeld (#1)
Veronica's Closet (#3)
Friends (#4)
Union Square (#8)
Frazier (tie #10)
Home Improvement (tie #10)
Just Shoot Me (tie #10)

Sources: Tim Brooks and Earle Marsh, *The Complete Directory to Prime Time Network and Cable TV Shows*, 4th ed. (New York: Ballantine, 1988), 963–75; Susan Sackett, *Prime-Time Hits* (New York: Billboard Books, 1993), 335–48; *Time Almanac 1999* (Boston: Information Please LLC, 1998); 716; and A. C. Nielsen Media Research.

troubled in profound ways." Stress, the result of external confusion rather than emotional anxiety, "is always funny."[7] While watching situation-driven comedies, many viewers usually think of themselves as slightly superior to the characters who inhabit the sitcom world. Much like viewers who are attracted to soap operas, sitcom fans feel just a little bit smarter than characters whose lives seem wacky and out of control.

Domestic Comedy. One spin-off of the sitcom form is the **domestic comedy**, in which characters and settings are usually more important than complicated predicaments. Although any given show might offer a wacky situation as part of a subplot, more typically the main narrative features a domestic problem or family crisis that characters have to solve. There is a greater emphasis on character development than on reestablishing the order that has been disrupted by confusion. Domestic comedies take place primarily at home (*Leave It to Beaver, Good Times*), at the workplace (*Taxi, Cheers*), or at both (*Frazier, Home Improvement*).

Although funny things happen in domestic comedies, the main emphasis is on how the characters react to one another. Family and workplace bonds are tested and strengthened by the end of the show. Generally, viewers identify more closely with the major characters in domestic comedies. One example illustrates the difference between a sitcom and its domestic counterpart. In an early episode of the sitcom

All in the Family (1971–83), starring Carroll O'Connor (*right*) and Jean Stapleton (*left*) as Archie and Edith Bunker, was one of the most popular programs in TV history. Created by Norman Lear, the program explored issues of class, ethnicity, gender, and race, which until then had been considered off-limits in a comedy format.

"Despite the incredibly hostile treatment she has gotten in the press—because she's four things TV women are not supposed to be, working-class, loudmouthed, overweight, and a feminist—Roseanne became a success because her mission was simple and welcome: to take the schmaltz and hypocrisy out of media images of motherhood."

—Susan Douglas,
Where the Girls Are

Happy Days (1974–84), the main characters were accidentally locked in a vault over a weekend. The plot turned on how they were going to free themselves, which they did after assorted goofy adventures. Contrast this with an episode from the domestic comedy *All in the Family* (1971–83), in which archconservative Archie and his ultraliberal son-in-law Mike are accidentally locked in the basement. The physical predicament became a subplot as the main "action" shifted to the characters themselves, who reflected on their generational and political differences.

Today, most programs mix comedic elements. An episode of *Friends* (1994–) might offer a character-driven plot about the generation gap and a minor subplot about a pet monkey gone berserk. Domestic comedies also mix dramatic and comedic elements. An episode of *Roseanne* (1988–97), for example, might juxtapose a dramatic scene in which a main character has a heart attack with another in which the Conner family intentionally offends their stuffy neighbors by decorating their home in a "white trash" holiday motif. This blurring of serious and comic themes marks a contemporary hybrid, sometimes labeled *dramedy*, which has included such series as *Moonlighting* (1985–89), the *Wonder Years* (1988–93), *Northern Exposure* (1990–95), and *Ally McBeal* (1997–).

Televised Drama. Another key staple of television has been the drama. Because the production of TV entertainment was centered in New York in its early days, many of its ideas, sets, technicians, actors, and directors came from New York theater. Young stage actors, including Anne Bancroft, Warren Beatty, Ossie Davis, James Dean, Gene Hackman, Grace Kelly, Paul Newman, Sidney Poitier, Robert Redford, and Joanne Woodward, began their professional careers in early television, often because they could not find stage work in New York. The TV dramas that grew from these early influences fit roughly in two categories: the anthology drama and the episodic series.

Anthology Drama. In the early 1950s, television—like cable in the early 1980s—served a more elite and wealthier audience. The **anthology drama**, which brought live dramatic theater to television, entertained and often challenged that audience. Influenced by stage plays, anthologies offered new teleplays, casts, directors, writers, and sets from one week to the next. Since movie studios owned the rights to major stage plays of the day, anthology television was often based on original material. In fact, this genre launched the careers of such writers as Rod Serling (*Requiem for a Heavyweight)*, William Gibson (*The Miracle Worker*), Reginald Rose (*Twelve Angry*

Men), and Paddy Chayefsky (*Marty*). The teleplays of these writers were often later made into movies. Chayefsky, in fact, would go on to write the screenplay for the 1976 film *Network*, a biting condemnation of television.

In the 1952–53 season alone, there were eighteen anthology dramas competing on the networks. Programs such as *Kraft Television Theater* (1947–58 and actually created to introduce Kraft's Cheez Whiz product), *Studio One* (1948–58), *Goodyear TV Playhouse* (1951–57), the *U.S. Steel Hour* (1953–63), *Alfred Hitchcock Presents* (1955–65), *Playhouse 90* (1956–60), and the *Twilight Zone* (1959–64) mounted original plays each week. However, the demands on the schedule were such that many of these programs alternated slots biweekly with other anthologies or with variety programs.

The commercial networks quit producing anthologies for economic and political reasons. First, although anthologies were popular, advertisers disliked them. Anthologies often presented stories that confronted complex human problems that were not easily resolved. Chayefsky had referred to these dramas as the "marvelous world of the ordinary."[8] The commercials that interrupted the drama, however, told straightforward stories in which problems were easily solved by purchasing a product: "a new pill, deodorant, toothpaste, shampoo, shaving lotion, hair tonic, car, girdle, coffee, muffin recipe, or floor wax."[9] By probing the psychology of the human condition, complicated anthologies made the simplicity of the commercial pitch ring false. Another aspect of the sponsors' dilemma was that these dramas often cast "non-beautiful heroes and heroines,"[10] unlike the stars of the commercials.

Ally McBeal (1997–), starring Calista Flockhart (*left*) as Ally and Lisa Nicole Carson (*right*) as Renee, has been a highly successful dramedy for Fox. Unlike earlier TV legal dramas like *Perry Mason,* which focused on courtroom conflicts, this quirky show about an offbeat law firm in Boston has gained a large following for the creative ways it mixes serious and comic—if not absurd—subplots about the characters' personal lives as well as the law.

"Aristotle once said that a play should have a beginning, a middle and an end. But what did he know? Today, a play must have a first half, a second half, and a station break."
—Alfred Hitchcock, director

By 1954, sponsors and ad agencies were demanding more input into script revisions. For instance, Reginald Rose's teleplay *Thunder on Sycamore Street* was based on a real incident in which a black family moved into an all-white neighborhood and was pressured to leave. CBS, pressured by advertisers who wanted to avoid public controversy, asked that the black family be changed to "something else." To make the teleplay more commercially palatable, Rose rewrote the script, turning the black family into a white ex-convict. Faced with increasing creative battles with the writers and producers of these dramas, sponsors began to move toward less controversial programming, such as quiz shows and sitcoms.

Second, this golden age of television was largely supported by a more affluent audience, particularly in the early 1950s. The people who could afford TV sets at this time could also afford tickets to a play. For these viewers, the anthology drama was an extension of their cultural tastes and simply brought theater directly into their homes. In 1950, less than 10 percent of American households had TV sets, with the heaviest concentration of ownership in New York. By 1956, however, 71 percent of all U.S. households had sets. As the production of sets rose during the post–World War II manufacturing boom, prices dropped as well. Working- and middle-class families were increasingly able to afford televisions. Anthology dramas were not as popular in

149

this expanded market as they were with upscale theatergoers. When the networks began relocating their creative headquarters to Hollywood, such moves also reduced theatrical influences. As a result, by the end of the decade, westerns, which were inexpensively produced by film studios on location near Los Angeles, had become the dominant TV genre.

Third, anthology dramas were expensive to produce—double the price of most other TV genres in the 1950s. In 1949, the average sixty-minute drama cost around $10,000 (compared with $1.5 million today). Although variety series eventually became the most expensive genre, anthologies cost, on average, $35,000 per hour by 1955. In contrast, a thirty-minute quiz show cost just over $10,000 to produce. Each week meant a completely new story line, as well as new writers, casts, and expensive sets. Sponsors and networks came to realize that it would be cheaper to use the same cast and set each week, and it would also be easier to build audience allegiance with an ongoing program. In an anthology series of individual plays, there were no continuing characters with whom viewers could identify over time.

In addition, anthologies that dealt seriously with the changing social landscape were sometimes labeled "politically controversial." This was especially true during the witch-hunts provoked by Senator Joseph McCarthy and his followers to rid media industries and government agencies (including the army) of left-wing influences. (See Chapter 16 on blacklisting.) Ultimately, sponsors and network executives came to prefer less controversial programming such as quiz shows and westerns. By the early 1960s, this once dominant dramatic form had virtually disappeared from network television, although its legacy continues on American public television, especially with the imported British program *Masterpiece Theater* (1971–).

Episodic Series. Abandoning anthologies, producers and writers increasingly developed the **episodic series**, first used in radio in 1929, because it seemed best suited for the weekly grind of televised drama. In this format, main characters continue from week to week, sets and locales remain the same, and technical crews stay with the program. Story concepts in episodic series are broad enough to accommodate new adventures each week, creating an atmosphere in which there are ongoing characters with whom viewers can regularly identify.

The episodic series comes in two general types: chapter shows and serial programs. *Chapter shows* employ self-contained stories that feature a problem, a series of conflicts, and a resolution. This structure can be used in a wide range of dramatic genres, including adult westerns like *Gunsmoke* (1955–75); medical dramas like *Marcus Welby, M.D.* (1969–76) and *ER* (1994–); police/detective shows like *Dragnet* (1951–59, 1967–70) and *Magnum, P.I.* (1980–88); family dramas like *The Waltons* (1972–81) and *Little House on the Prairie* (1974–82); and fantasy/science fiction like *Star Trek* (1966–69) and some episodes of *The X-Files* (1993–).

Culturally, television dramas function as a window into the hopes and fears of the

One of the most highly acclaimed dramas of the 1990s, *ER* (1994–) made history in 1998, when NBC agreed to pay the program's producers a record $13 million per episode to keep it on its Thursday-night lineup.

American psyche. In the 1970s, for instance, police/detective dramas became a chapter staple, mirroring the anxieties of many Americans regarding the urban unrest of the late 1960s. The 1970s brought more urban problems, which were precipitated by the loss of factory jobs and the decline of the manufacturing industry. Our popular entertainment reflected the idea of heroic police and tenacious detectives protecting a nation from menacing forces that were undermining our economy and our cities. During this period, such shows as *The F.B.I.* (1965–74), *Ironside* (1967–75), *Mannix* (1967–75), *Hawaii Five-O* (1968–80), the *Mod Squad* (1968–73), *Kojak* (1973–75), and the *Rockford Files* (1974–80) all ranked among the nation's top-rated programs.

A recent spin-off of the police drama has been the law-enforcement reenactment program, sometimes called *cop docs*. Series like Fox's *Cops* (1989–) are cheap to produce, with low overhead and a big return on a minimum investment. Instead of hiring actors at $25,000 per episode, producers have their crews tag along with real police, whose supervisors often donate police cars and other equipment that the producers of conventional dramas usually have to rent or buy. While an hour of conventional prime-time drama cost about $1.5 million to produce per episode in the late 1990s, an hour of crime reenactments cost less than half that amount. Cop docs, like many contemporary daytime talk shows, generally focus their stories on emotional situations and individual pathology rather than on a critical examination of the underlying social conditions that make such problems possible.

Prior to the rise of the cop was the reign of the cowboy, which marked an earlier period of change in America. The western served as one of the most popular chapter genres in television's early history. The network shift to Hollywood made western movie sets immediately available. When studios such as Warner Brothers began dabbling in television in the 1950s, they produced a number of well-received series for ABC, such as *Cheyenne* (1955–63) and *Maverick* (1957–63). The popular western, with its themes of civilization confronting the frontier, apparently provided a symbol for many Middle Americans relocating to the suburbs—between the country and the city. Thirty prime-time westerns aired in the 1958–59 season alone. From this point through 1961, *Gunsmoke* (1955–75), TV's longest-running chapter series, *Wagon Train* (1957–65), and *Have Gun Will Travel* (1957–63) were the three most popular programs in America.

In contrast to chapter programs like westerns and police dramas, *serial programs* are open-ended episodic shows. That is, in these series most story lines continue from episode to episode. Cheaper to produce, usually employing just a few indoor sets, and running five days a week, daytime soap operas are among the longest-running serial programs in the history of television. Acquiring their name from soap-product ads that sponsored these programs in the days of fifteen-minute radio drama, popular soaps include *Guiding Light* (1952–), *As the World Turns* (1956–), *General Hospital* (1963–), *Days of Our Lives* (1965–), and *One Life to Live* (1968–).

With their cliff-hanging story lines and intimate close-up shots, which are well suited to television (a personal medium located in our living rooms and bedrooms), soap operas have been good at creating audience allegiance. Soaps probably do the best job of any genre at imitating the actual open-ended rhythms of daily life. The fact that many of them have endured for well over thirty years means that story lines and characters span generations of viewers who remain faithful to their favorite programs for many years.

The success of the daytime soap formula opened a door to prime time. Although the first popular prime-time serial, *Peyton Place* (1964–69), ran two or three nights a

"The show's original spirit has become kind of the spirit of the country—if not the world. . . . With the Berlin Wall down, with the global nuclear threat gone, with Russia trying to be a market economy, there is a growing paranoia because . . . there are no easy villains anymore."

—Chris Carter,
X-Files creator,
1998

151

week, producers later shied away from such programs because they had less value as syndicated reruns. Most reruns of old network shows are **stripped**—shown five days a week in almost any order that does not require viewers to watch them on a daily basis. Serials, however, require that audiences watch every day so that they don't lose track of the story lines.

In the 1970s, however, with the popularity of the network *miniseries*—a serial that runs over a two-day to two-week period, usually on consecutive nights—producers and the networks began to look at the evening serial differently. The twelve-part *Rich Man, Poor Man*, adapted from an Irwin Shaw novel, ranked number three in national ratings in 1976. The next year, the eight-part *Roots* miniseries, based on writer Alex Haley's search for his African heritage, became the most-watched miniseries in TV history. Then *Holocaust*, a four-part dramatization of Jewish extermination by the Nazis, drew television's largest audiences in 1978.

These miniseries demonstrated to the networks that viewers would watch a compelling, ongoing story in prime time. The success of these programs spawned such soap opera–style series as *Dallas* (1978–91), *Dynasty* (1981–89), *Knots Landing* (1979–92), and *Falcon Crest* (1981–90), which in the 1984–85 season all ranked among America's Top 10 most-viewed programs. In fact, as the top-rated shows in America in the early 1980s, *Dallas* and *Dynasty* both celebrated and criticized the excesses of the rich and spoiled. These shows reached their popular peak during the early years of the Reagan administration, a time when the economic disparity between rich and poor widened dramatically.

Another type of contemporary serial is a hybrid form that developed in the early 1980s with the appearance of *Hill Street Blues* (1981–87). Mixing comic situations and grim plots, this multiple-cast show looked like an open-ended soap opera. On occasion, as in real life, crimes were not solved and recurring characters died. As a hybrid form, *Hill Street Blues* combined elements of both chapter and serial television. Juggling multiple story lines, *Hill Street* featured some self-contained plots that were brought to resolution in a single episode as well as other plot lines that continued from one week to the next. This technique was copied by several successful dramatic hybrids, including *St. Elsewhere* (1982–88), *L.A. Law* (1986–94), *NYPD Blue* (1993–), *The X-Files* (1993–), and *ER* (1994–).

> "I think for a while during the Reagan years it was OK to be **ostentatiously wealthy** and **glitzy**."
> —David Jacobs, executive producer, *Knots Landing*

the decline of the network era

Most historians mark the period from the late 1950s, when the networks gained control over TV's content, to the end of the 1970s as the *network era*. Except for British and American anthology dramas on PBS, this was a time when CBS, NBC, and ABC dictated virtually every trend in prime-time programming (see Figure 5.1). This network dominance was significant because it offered America's rich and diverse ethnic population a cultural center and common topics for daily conversation. Television is often credited, for example, with helping to heal the collective national consciousness after the assassination of President Kennedy in 1963 by creating time and space for shared mourning. During this period of supremacy, the networks collectively accounted for more than 95 percent of all prime-time TV viewing. By 1999, however, this figure had dropped below 50 percent. What happened? To understand the decline of the network era, we will look at three factors: technological changes, government regulations, and the development of new networks.

Day	7	7:30	8	8:30	9	9:30	10	10:30	11 PM	
SUN	THE HARDY BOYS MYSTERIES 3		BATTLESTAR GALACTICA		MOVIE					ABC
	60 MINUTES 11		MARY		ALL IN THE FAMILY 9	ALICE	KAZ 3			CBS
	THE WONDERFUL WORLD OF DISNEY 25		THE BIG EVENT (I)				LIFELINE 2			NBC
MON			WELCOME BACK, KOTTER 4	OPERATION PETTICOAT 2	NFL MONDAY NIGHT FOOTBALL				9	ABC
			WKRP IN CINCINNATI	PEOPLE	M*A*S*H 7	ONE DAY AT A TIME 4	LOU GRANT		2	CBS
			LITTLE HOUSE ON THE PRAIRIE 5		MOVIE					NBC
TUE			HAPPY DAYS 6	LAVERNE AND SHIRLEY 4	THREE'S COMPANY 3	TAXI	STARSKY AND HUTCH		4	ABC
			THE PAPER CHASE		MOVIE					CBS
			GRANDPA GOES TO WASHINGTON		THE BIG EVENT (II)				2	NBC
WED			EIGHT IS ENOUGH 3		CHARLIE'S ANGELS 3		VEGAS			ABC
			THE JEFFERSONS 5	IN THE BEGINNING	MOVIE					CBS
			DICK CLARK'S LIVE WEDNESDAY		MOVIE					NBC
THU			MORK & MINDY	WHAT'S HAPPENING!! 3	BARNEY MILLER 5	SOAP 2	FAMILY		4	ABC
			THE WALTONS		HAWAII FIVE-0 7		BARNABY JONES 11		7	CBS
			PROJECT U.F.O.		QUINCY 2		W.E.B. 3		2	NBC
FRI			DONNY AND MARIE		MOVIE 4					ABC
			WONDER WOMAN		THE INCREDIBLE HULK 3		FLYING HIGH 2			CBS
			THE WAVERLY WONDERS	WHO'S WATCHING THE KIDS	THE ROCKFORD FILES		THE EDDIE CAPRA MYSTERIES 5			NBC
SAT			CARTER COUNTRY 2	APPLE PIE	THE LOVE BOAT		FANTASY ISLAND 2		2	ABC
			RHODA 5	GOOD TIMES	THE AMERICAN GIRLS 6		DALLAS		2	CBS
			CHIPS		SPECIALS 2		SWORD OF JUSTICE			NBC

1978–1979

Figure 5.1
The Fall Prime-Time Schedule toward the End of the Network Era, 1978–79
Programs that are shaded were canceled either during or at the end of the 1978–79 season.
Source: Alex McNeil, *Total Television: A Comprehensive Guide to Programming from 1948 to the Present*, 3rd ed. (New York: Penguin, 1991), 938.

technological transformations

Two major technological developments contributed significantly to the erosion of network dominance: the arrival of communication satellite services for cable television and the home-video market. Prior to the early 1970s, broadcast lobbyists and local stations, fearing advertising competition, had effectively limited the growth of cable television, which had been around since the late 1940s. But a series of moves by the FCC sprung cable loose in 1972. That same year, when Time Inc. launched HBO into satellite orbit, serving movies to hotels and motels, the first crack in the network dam appeared. In 1975, HBO became available to individual cable markets throughout the country, offering the "Thrilla from Manila"—the heavyweight boxing match between Muhammad Ali and Joe Frazier via satellite from the Philippines.

Then, in December 1976, Ted Turner beamed, or *uplinked*, the signal from WTBS, his **independent station** (not affiliated with a network) in Atlanta, to a satellite where cable systems and broadcast stations around the country could access, or *downlink*, it. To encourage interest, the signal was initially provided free, supported only by the ads Turner sold during WTBS programs. But as Turner expanded services, creating new channels like CNN, he also earned revenue by charging monthly fees for his cable services. In its early days, WTBS delivered a steady stream of old TV reruns, wrestling, and live sports from the Atlanta Hawks and the Atlanta Braves (both owned by Turner). Turner and a number of investors would eventually buy the MGM film library to provide additional programming. In the mid-1970s, only about 15 percent of American households received cable. As this figure steadily grew (to 70 percent by 1999), the TV networks, for the first time, began to face serious competition.

The second technological breakthrough also came in 1975–76 with the consumer marketing of videocassette recorders (**VCRs**), which allowed viewers to record and play back programs from television. Earlier in the 1970s, Japan's Sony Corporation had introduced the TV industry to a three-quarter-inch-wide videocassette format that quickly revolutionized television news; until that time, TV news crews had relied solely on shooting film, which often took hours to develop and edit. Then, in 1975, Sony introduced consumers to a home version, *Betamax*, a half-inch format that allowed viewers to tape programs off the air for the first time. The next year, JVC in Japan introduced a slightly larger half-inch consumer format, *VHS* (Video Home System), which was incompatible with Beta. This triggered a marketing war, which helped drive the costs down and put VCRs in more and more homes.

Beta, though a smaller format and technically superior to VHS, ultimately lost the marketplace battle due to a cultural miscalculation by designers. Early Betamax tapes accommodated only about an hour and a half of programming. However, most American consumers used tapes primarily to record movies, usually two hours in length. This meant that *two* tapes, which cost around $15 apiece in the late 1970s, were necessary. When JVC developed the slightly larger VHS format, one standard tape accommodated two hours of programs, enough for an entire movie. Even with technical improvements that compressed more programming onto a single tape, Betamax could never match the recording time or appeal of the longer VHS tapes.

The VCR also got a big boost from a failed suit brought against Sony by Disney and MCA (now Universal) in 1976: The two film studios alleged that home taping violated their movie copyrights. In 1979, a federal court ruled in favor of Sony and permitted home taping for personal use. In response, the defeated but industrious movie studios quickly set up videotaping facilities so that they could rent and sell movies via video stores, which exploded onto the scene in the early 1980s. By the mid-1980s, VHS had pretty much won the war for the video consumer market, and Sony concentrated on developing *Betacam*, a high-quality half-inch industrial format that in the late 1980s began replacing the bulkier three-quarter-inch format in TV newsrooms.

The impact of videocassettes on the networks was enormous. By 1997, nearly 90 percent of American homes were equipped with VCRs that were used for two major purposes: time shifting and movie rentals. *Time shifting* occurs when viewers tape shows and watch them later, when it is convenient for them. This has been a boon, for example, for daytime soap-opera fans who work outside the home; they record their favorite soaps and watch them on weeknights or weekends. Before VCRs, advertisers and networks worried that consumers used TV ad time to fix a snack or go to the bathroom. After VCRs, they had bigger things to worry about. For example, recording TV programs for viewing at a more convenient time produced more complex audience measurement problems. Along with the remote control, which allowed viewers to mute the sound during ads, time shifting made it possible for consumers to avoid ads altogether, either by *zapping*, or cutting, them out of the program with the pause button during recording or by *zipping*, or fast-forwarding, through the ads during the recorded viewing. Predictably, these practices upset ad and network executives, who could no longer assume that "well-behaved" consumers were conscientiously viewing their ads. On top of this was the lure of VCR movies: By the mid-1990s, more than half of all households in America watched a rented movie during prime time at least once a week. The impact of VCRs and movie rentals shook the TV industry; when viewers were watching a videotape, they weren't watching network shows or network ads.

regulating the networks

By the late 1960s, a progressive and active FCC, increasingly concerned about the monopoly-like impact of the three networks, passed a series of regulations that began undercutting their power. The first, the passage of the *Prime-Time Access Rule* (PTAR) in April 1970, took the 7:30 to 8:00 P.M. slot (6:30 to 7:00 P.M. central) away from the networks and gave it exclusively to local stations in the nation's fifty largest TV markets. With this move, the FCC had hoped to encourage local news and public-affairs

> "There's about **three great moments** in a man's life: when he buys a house, and a car, and a new color TV. That's what America is all about."
> —Archie Bunker,
> *All in the Family*

programs. However, most stations simply acquired syndicated quiz shows (*The Joker's Wild*, *Wheel of Fortune*) or *infotainment* programs (*P.M. Magazine*, *Entertainment Tonight*). These latter shows packaged human interest and celebrity stories in TV news style, during which local affiliates sold lucrative regional ads.

In a second move, in 1970 the FCC created the *Financial Interest and Syndication Rules*—called *fin-syn*—which "constituted the most damaging attack against the network TV monopoly in FCC history."[11] Throughout the 1960s, the networks had run their own syndication companies. They sometimes demanded as much as 50 percent of the profits that producers earned from airing older shows as reruns in local TV markets. This was the case even though those shows were no longer on the networks and most of them had been developed not by the networks but by independent companies. The networks claimed that since popular TV series had gained a national audience because of their reach, production companies owed the networks compensation even after shows had completed their prime-time runs. In the 1970s, the FCC banned the networks from reaping such profits from program syndication.

A third and separate action was instituted by the Department of Justice in 1975. Reacting to a number of legal claims against monopolistic practices, the Justice Department limited the networks' own production of non-news shows to a few hours a week. Initially, the limit was three hours of prime-time entertainment programs per week, but this was raised to five hours by the late 1980s. In addition, ABC, CBS, and NBC were limited to producing eight hours per week of in-house entertainment or non-news programs outside prime time, most of which was devoted to soap operas (economical to produce and popular with advertisers). This meant that the networks were forced to continue licensing most of their prime-time programs from independent producers and film studios. Given that the networks could produce their own TV newsmagazines and select which programs to license, however, they still retained a great deal of power over the content of prime-time television.

With increasing competition from cable and home video in the 1990s, the FCC gradually phased out the ban limiting network production. In addition, beginning in 1995, the networks were once again allowed to syndicate and profit from rerun programs, but only the ones they had produced in-house. The elimination of fin-syn and other rules opened the door for megamerger deals. For example, Disney, which bought ABC in 1995, is able to use its vast movie-production resources to develop more entertainment programming for its ABC network. This will certainly cut into opportunities for independent producers to create new shows and compete for prime-time slots on ABC. Many independent companies and TV critics point to the return of a new type of oligopoly. Disney, Westinghouse, and General Electric—multinational corporations that now own the networks—are increasingly dictating the program trends and economic terms for prime-time broadcast television.

emerging new networks

In addition to the overwhelming number of cable services now available to consumers, the networks, which lost about 25 percent of their audience during the 1980s alone, faced further challenges from the emergence of new networks. Rupert Murdoch, who heads the multinational company News Corp., launched the Fox network in April 1987 after purchasing several TV stations from another company and buying a major Hollywood film studio, Twentieth Century Fox. Not since 1955, when the old Dumont network collapsed, had there been an attempt to challenge the Big Three networks.

At first, Fox lost money because it had fewer than a hundred affiliated stations to carry its programs around the country. This was less than half the two-hundred-

With successful shows like *Dawson's Creek* (1998–) and *Buffy the Vampire Slayer* (1997–), starring Sarah Michelle Gellar *(left)*, the WB network has struck a chord with young viewers and struck pay dirt with advertisers who target youth markets. A spin-off from the 1992 movie of the same name, the *Buffy* TV series follows the funny and poignant lives of teens in a typical high school—teens who also chase evil vampires and demons through the dark streets of Sunnydale, California.

plus affiliates each that were contracted to ABC, CBS, and NBC. Originally presenting programs just two nights a week, the Fox network began targeting both young and black audiences with shows like *The Simpsons, Beverly Hills 90210, In Living Color, Martin, Roc,* and *Melrose Place.* By 1994, after outbidding CBS for a portion of pro-football broadcasts, Fox was competing every night of the week. It had managed to lure more than sixty affiliates away from the other networks or from independent status. Some of these stations were in major markets where traditional networks suddenly found themselves without affiliates. In fact, Fox's poaching forced CBS to spend millions to buy two unknown independent UHF stations—Channel 62 in Detroit and Channel 69 in Atlanta—to satisfy advertisers, who expected the network to reach audiences in all major markets. By the early 1990s, Fox was making money. By the mid-1990s, the new network's total number of affiliates rivaled the Big Three.

Fox's success continued the erosion of network power and spurred others who were interested in starting new networks. Paramount, which had recently been acquired by Viacom, and Time Warner, the world's largest media company, both launched networks in January 1995: UPN (United Paramount Network) and WB (Warner Brothers). Using the strategy initiated by Fox, the new networks offered original programs two nights a week in 1995, added a third night in 1996, and by 1999 looked almost like the other four networks. Backed by multinational financing, these companies slowly began going after independent outlets and luring other stations from their old network affiliations. However, their main strategy has been to target minority and young viewers with such programs as *Clueless, Moesha, Buffy the Vampire Slayer, Felicity,* and *Dawson's Creek* (the No. 1 show among females between twelve and seventeen years of age in 1998). In fact, by 1998 WB had become the most-watched network for teenagers in this age bracket.

the economics of television

Despite the erosion of their reach, the traditional networks have remained attractive investments in the business world. In 1985, General Electric, which once helped start RCA/NBC, bought back NBC. In 1995, Disney bought ABC for $19 billion; in 1999, Viacom acquired CBS for $37 billion.

Even though their audiences and profits may have declined, the networks continue to attract larger audiences than any cable or online competitor. To understand the television business today, we need to examine the production and distribution of programming. At stake are $50 billion in advertising revenue each year. In fact, one way to define TV programming is as a system that delivers viewers to merchandise displayed in blocks of commercials. By the late 1990s, *national* advertisers alone, led by Procter & Gamble and General Motors, were spending nearly $30 billion a year in TV advertising.

"By 1960 television had become a mature and streamlined business, a great 'cash cow.' The focus now shifted from invention to convention, from carving out an acceptable social role for itself to counting the rewards of investment, planning, and monopoly."

—J. Fred MacDonald,
One Nation under Television

The key to the television industry's appeal resides in its ability to create programs that American households will habitually tune in on a weekly basis. Producers and film studios spend fortunes telling stories that they hope will keep us coming back. In 1988, while film studios produced a large chunk of network television, more than half of the prime-time schedule was created by independent producers. These companies, such as Carsey-Werner (the *Cosby Show*, *A Different World*, *Roseanne*, *Cybill*, *Third Rock from the Sun*), license, or "rent," each episode to a network for two broadcasts, one in the fall or winter and one in the spring or summer. (Usually twenty-two to twenty-four episodes are produced in a TV season.)

Production costs on network television generally fall into two categories: above-the-line and below-the-line. *Below-the-line* costs, which account for roughly 40 percent of a program's production budget, include the technical, or "hardware," side of production: equipment, special effects, cameras and crews, sets and designers, carpenters, electricians, art directors, wardrobe, lighting, and transportation. More demanding are the *above-the-line*, or "software," costs, which include the creative talent: actors, writers, producers, editors, and directors. These costs account for about 60 percent of a program's budget, except in the case of successful long-running series (like *ER*), in which salary demands by actors drive up above-the-line costs.

Independent Programs. Because of their high cost, many prime-time programs today are produced by production companies that are financed or backed by a major film studio such as Sony or Disney. In these arrangements, film studios (if they don't buy out the more successful independent producers) serve as a bank, offering enough capital to carry producers through one or more seasons. In television, after a network agrees to carry a program, keeping it on the air is done through *deficit financing*. This means that the production company leases the show to a network for a license fee that is actually *less* than the cost of production. (The company hopes to recoup this loss later in lucrative rerun syndication.) Typically, in the late 1990s, the networks might lease an episode of a new half-hour sitcom for about $600,000 for two airings. Each episode, however, cost the producers about $800,000 to make. So on each show, they lose between $100,000 and $200,000. After two years of production (about forty-four episodes), an average half-hour sitcom builds up a $4 to $8 million deficit and the average one-hour drama generates a deficit of $12 to $14 million. This is where film studios have been playing an increasingly crucial role: They finance the deficit. In the early 1990s alone, film studios, which provide production facilities as well as money, covered deficits totaling $350 million annually by bankrolling network prime-time television.

The key to erasing the losses generated by deficit financing is **rerun syndication**: Producers and film studios invest in programs that they hope will stay in a network's lineup

The *Cosby Show*, the nation's most popular program from 1985 through 1989, featured (*from left to right*) Phylicia Rashad, Bill Cosby, Earle Hyman, Clarice Taylor, and Lisa Bonet. Initially rejected by ABC and CBS, the show was eventually picked up by NBC. As a result, the *Cosby Show* single-handedly took NBC from third to first place in the network prime-time ratings battle. Hoping for a similar success story in 1996, CBS reunited Cosby and Rashad in *Cosby*, a family-oriented sitcom set familiarly in New York.

long enough to build up enough episodes (usually four seasons' worth) so that they can be sold, or syndicated, to hundreds of TV markets in the United States and overseas. With a successful program, the profits can be enormous. For instance, when Carsey-Werner's *Cosby Show*, the most-watched show in America from 1985 to 1989, sold its first three years into syndication in 1988, the producers netted more than $800 million. Since the show has already been produced and the original production costs have already been covered, the syndication market at home and abroad becomes almost pure profit for the producers and their backers. It is for this reason that the practice of deficit financing endures. Although investors rarely hit the jackpot, when they do, it can more than cover a lot of losses. By 1997, the *Cosby Show* had earned a record $1 billion in syndication.[12] Profits from the show (and from *Roseanne*) have allowed Carsey-Werner to function as one of the few remaining independent companies that do not require the financial backing of a film studio.

Network Programs. Although the networks still purchase or license many prime-time TV programs, they create more of their own prime-time fare thanks to the relaxation of FCC rules in the mid-1990s. The production of newsmagazines, for instance, became one way for networks to save money and control content in the 1990s. Programs such as ABC's *20/20* or NBC's *Dateline* require only about half the outlay (between $600,000 and $800,000 per episode) demanded by an hour's worth of drama. In addition, the networks, by producing projects in-house, avoid paying license fees to independent producers.

> "For the networks, the hit show is the hub in a growing wheel of interests: promotion platforms for related businesses; sales of replays on cable television or even Internet sites; and the creation of direct links between advertisers and viewers."
> —Bill Carter,
> *New York Times*,
> 1999

Over the years, for example, CBS's highly rated program *60 Minutes* has been a money machine. By 1980, a commercial minute on *60 Minutes*, the nation's highest-rated program that year, sold for a then record $230,000. By the late 1990s, *60 Minutes*—like other top-rated shows—commanded nearly $500,000 per minute for its seven minutes of national ad slots. (By comparison, a low-rated program brought in only a quarter of this amount per minute.) This meant that *60 Minutes* generally earned back its production costs and fees to local stations for carrying the program after selling just a couple minutes of ad time. Even newsmagazines with low ratings still recoup their cheaper production costs fairly easily. Don Hewitt, the creator of *60 Minutes*, estimated that in its first twenty-five years on the air, his program grossed well over $1 billion for CBS.[13]

prime-time distribution

The networks have always been the main distributors of prime-time TV programs to their affiliate stations around the country. By 1997, ABC, CBS, NBC, and Fox were each allied with approximately two hundred stations. By 1999, UPN and WB had nearly 150 affiliates each. The networks pay a fee to affiliate stations for carrying their programs. In this arrangement, local stations receive quality national programs that attract large local audiences. In addition, local ad spaces are allocated during prime time so that stations can sell their own time during these slots.

A common misconception is that TV networks *own* their affiliated stations. This is not true. Although networks own a few stations in major markets like New York, Los Angeles, and Chicago, throughout most of the country networks merely sign short-term contracts to rent time on local stations. For example, WDIV (Channel 4) in Detroit has a contract to carry NBC programs but is owned by the Washington Post/Newsweek Company, based in Washington, D.C. Years ago, the FCC placed restrictions on network-owned-and-operated stations, called **O&Os**. Originally, networks and other companies were limited to owning five VHF and two UHF stations, but the limit was raised to twelve total stations during the 1980s. Hoping to ensure more diversity in ownership, the FCC during this time also mandated that an owner's combined TV stations could reach no more than 25 percent of the nation's ninety-million-plus TV households. Then, in 1996, the sweeping new Telecommunications Act, which will be discussed in Chapter 6, abolished the twelve-station limit and most other ownership restrictions.

Although a local affiliate carries network programs, the station may preempt a network's offering by substituting other programs. According to *clearance rules*, established in the 1940s by the Justice Department and the FCC, all local affiliates are ultimately responsible for the content of their channels and must clear, or approve, all network programming.

Over the years, local affiliates have occasionally rejected the networks. In 1956, Nat King Cole (singer Natalie Cole's father) was one of the first African American performers to host a network variety program. As a result of pressure applied by several white southern organizations, though, the program had trouble attracting a national sponsor. When some southern and northern affiliates refused to carry the program, NBC canceled it in 1957. In another instance, Norman Lear's popular CBS sitcom *Maude* (1972–78) aired two controversial episodes in which the title character, in her late forties, decided to abort an unwanted pregnancy. The episodes topped the ratings when they ran in 1972. However, when the episodes came up for network summer rebroadcast in 1973, a number of Catholic organizations led campaigns that generated seventeen thousand protest letters asking CBS to cancel the second airing. Although CBS refused, 39 of its 217 affiliates did not clear the episodes. Seven national sponsors also pulled their ads. The controversy generated an even bigger audience the second time around, as nearly sixty-five million people watched the two shows as reruns in 1973.

how syndication works

Early each year, executives from thousands of local TV stations and cable firms gather at the world's main "TV supermarket" convention, the National Association of Television Program Executives (NATPE). There they buy or barter for programs that are up for syndication, acquiring the exclusive local market rights, usually for two- or three-year periods, to quiz shows, newsmagazines, talk shows, and *evergreens*—popular old network reruns such as the *Andy Griffith Show* or *I Love Lucy*. In such a competitive arena, TV managers have become less concerned with the quality of programs and more concerned with keeping costs low, delivering viewers to advertisers, and drawing higher ratings than their competitors.

Although the networks have long dominated in selecting and distributing prime-time television, syndicators have played a large role in the hours outside prime time. The distribution/syndication company King World, for example, began in 1972 after the fin-syn rules banished the networks from syndication. Starting out by distributing *Little Rascals* film shorts from the 1930s, King World barely survived its first year. By the end of the 1980s, however, it had become the distributor of the top shows in syndication—*Wheel of Fortune*, *Jeopardy*, and the *Oprah Winfrey Show*—and grossed nearly $400 million per year. In 1999, CBS bought King World for $5 billion.

In addition to companies like Viacom and King World, major syndicators of TV programming include film companies such as Twentieth Century Fox, Disney-Touchstone, and Time Warner, all of which are also involved in the production of TV shows. Networks usually select and distribute about three hours of programming each night (four on Sunday) during prime time and another three to four hours of daytime programming, but this still leaves a substantial number of hours to plug. Because it is often cheaper to buy syndicated programs than to produce local programs (other than

TV producers can often recoup the high cost of original programming when they sell shows in the global marketplace. In 1994, for instance, Fox had already sold *The X-Files*, which had premiered only a year earlier, into more than fifty markets outside the United States. And by 1999 *The X-Files* had aired in nearly ninety nations. Like American TV markets, the price per episode varies according to the size of the market. By the early 1990s, according to the trade magazine *Variety*, a half-hour American sitcom was airing in Poland for about $450–$550 per episode, in Peru for $800–$1,500, and in France for $10,000–$20,000.

In many countries, the popularity of American television poses a cultural threat: Television industries in these countries cannot always afford to produce original programming; they find it cheaper to buy made-in-the-USA programs than to produce a new series. American producers, who have already paid for production costs and begun earning profits, can undercut most competition in foreign markets. For instance, today Malaysia, Jamaica, and Singapore can pur-

Xena: Warrior Princess and *Hercules: The Legendary Journeys* are two of the most popular internationally syndicated programs and are seen in eighty countries.

chase some half-hour sitcoms for as little as $200 an episode. As a result, television companies in many developing countries produce few competitive programs. These countries, in trying to promote their own cultural identity, wrestle with issues raised by importing the values of American TV and movie culture.

Many nations, including Canada, have placed quotas on TV imports from the United States in an effort to encourage original, culture-specific productions. The European Community, which carried more than fifty thousand hours of U.S. programming by the late 1980s, placed a 25 percent quota on programs imported from non-European markets. Still, by the 1990s, the series *Baywatch*, a failure on U.S. network television (canceled by NBC in 1991), was the most popular syndicated television program in Europe and the world.

AVERAGE RATES, IN U.S. DOLLARS, PAID BY INTERNATIONAL BROADCASTERS FOR U.S. TELEVISION SYNDICATION		
	TV Movies	Dramas	Sitcoms
Germany	$300,000	$200,000	$60,000
Canada	$100,000	$50,000	$35,000
Mexico	$18,000–20,000	$9,000	$1,500–4,000
South Africa	$17,000	$6,000	$3,500
New Zealand	$12,000–18,000	$4,500–5,000	$2,500
Russia	$5,000	$4,000	$3,000
Korea	$5,000–15,000	$3,000–4,000	$1,000–1,500
Brazil	$4,000	$2,000	$1,000
Egypt	$3,000	$1,500	$650
Singapore	$2,400	$1,000–1,100	$500–550
Hong Kong	$2,500	$1,000	$450
India	$2,000	$1,000	$500–750

Source: Variety, Sept. 28–Oct. 4, 1998, pp. M12–13.

news), many station managers take the most profitable path rather than originate topical shows that focus on their own communities.

Off-Network and First-Run Syndication. For local affiliate stations, syndicated programs are often used or slotted in what is known as **fringe time**. This includes programming immediately before the evening's prime-time schedule, called *early fringe*, and the time following the local evening news or the network's late-night talk shows, called *late fringe*. Syndication to fill these slots comes in two forms. First, there is **off-network syndication**, in which older programs, no longer running during network prime time, are made available for reruns to local stations, cable operators, online services, and foreign markets. A local station may purchase old *Roseanne* or *Home Improvement* episodes as a lead-in to boost the ratings for its late-afternoon news, or it may purchase *Cheers* or *Seinfeld* to boost its ratings after the late-evening news.

A second type, **first-run syndication**, is any program that is specifically produced for sale into syndication markets. Quiz programs such as *Jeopardy* and *Wheel of Fortune* and daytime talk shows like *Ricki Lake* and *Montel Williams* are made *for* syndication. The producers of these programs sell them directly to local markets around the country and the world. When the FCC established the Prime-Time Access Rule in 1971 to turn more prime time over to local stations, it created an immediate market for new non-network programs.

Created by Gene Roddenberry in 1966, *Star Trek* and its multiple offspring have become one of the most profitable franchises in entertainment history. Owned by Paramount, this pop-culture phenomenon has been going strong for more than three decades through five TV series (one animated), nine feature films, hundreds of novels, and countless consumer products. As the flagship program during the launch of UPN, *Voyager* premiered in 1995, starring Kate Mulgrew (*center*) as *Star Trek*'s first female captain.

Hybrid Syndication. The new *Star Trek* programs, which include *The Next Generation*, *Deep Space Nine*, and *Voyager,* are examples of a hybrid form of first-run syndication. These new episodes are descended from the original *Star Trek*, which aired on NBC in the 1960s but was canceled after three years as a result of low ratings. Although network rejection ends the lives of most programs, on occasion a producer may decide to make new episodes for syndication.

Besides *Star Trek*, the most famous hybrid programs are probably *Hee Haw* and the *Lawrence Welk Show*. Beginning on CBS in 1969, *Hee Haw* was canceled in 1971 even though it was a Top 20 program during its two years on prime time. CBS, however, thought the show was drawing children and older rural viewers, who were not as likely to buy many of the network's advertised products. After cancellation, the show's producers continued making and syndicating *Hee Haw* for more than twenty years. In the late 1970s, it was the most-watched non-network program on television.

Lawrence Welk had a much longer network run, appearing on ABC for sixteen years before its cancellation in 1971 by executives who determined that the program's audience was too old to attract new ad revenue. Welk's production company, however, made 1,542 new episodes between 1971 and 1982 and sold them into first-run syndication. The show was one of the only series that ran in more TV markets

"The *Lawrence Welk Show* ran on ABC from July 1955 until September 1971, when the network dropped the broadcasts, claiming its audience was 'too old.' This was probably true, since the sponsors at the time were Geritol and Sominex."

—Susan Sackett, *Prime Time Hits*, 1993

(over 250) in first-run syndication than it did when it aired originally. In fact, PBS bought the syndication rights in the early 1990s, and *Lawrence Welk* continued to run on more than 270 noncommercial stations.

Barter vs. Cash. Most financing of television syndication is based on either cash or barter. In a *cash deal*, the distributor of a program offers a series for syndication to the highest bidder in a market—typically a station trying to fill a particular time slot. Due to exclusive contractual arrangements, programs air on only one broadcast outlet per market. For example, Viacom, which distributes the *Cosby Show*, offers it in hundreds of television markets around the country. Whichever local station bids the most in a particular market gets the rights to that program, usually for a contract period of two or three years. A small-market station in Fargo, North Dakota, might pay a few thousand dollars to air a week's worth of episodes; in contrast, some Top 10 markets paid well over $150,000 a week for *Cosby* in the late 1980s.

One common variation of a cash deal is called *cash-plus*. For shows that are successful in syndication, distributors may retain some time to sell national commercial spots. When *Cosby* went into syndication, for example, Viacom, in addition to receiving cash for the show from various local outlets, also sold a minute of ad time to national advertisers. When the two-hundred-plus local stations received the programs, they already contained a minute's worth of national ads. Some syndicators use cash-plus deals to keep down the cost per episode; in other words, stations pay less per episode in exchange for giving up ad slots to a syndicator's national advertisers.

While syndicators prefer cash deals, *barter deals* are usually arranged for new or untested programs. In a straight barter deal, no money changes hands between the local station and the syndicator. Instead, a syndicator offers a new program to a local TV station in exchange for a split of the advertising revenue. The program's syndicator will try to make an arrangement with the station that attracts the largest number of local viewers, though this is not always possible. The syndicator then sells some ads at the national level, charging advertisers more money if the program has been sold into a large number of markets. This guarantees the wide national distribution that the networks receive for prime-time shows.

As an example, in the early 1990s, *Star Trek: The Next Generation* (before it became a part of the new UPN network) was offered by its producer-distributor, Paramount, in a 7/5 barter deal. Paramount did not charge cash per episode. Instead, during each airing it retained seven minutes of ad time to sell national spots and left stations with five minutes of ad time to sell local spots. The *Jenny Jones Show* also started out as a barter show. As it became a proved product, its syndicator, Time Warner, repackaged the show as a cash-plus deal.

measuring television by ratings and shares

Although the networks wrested control of content from sponsors in the 1950s, advertising still drives the business. TV shows live or die based primarily on whether advertisers are satisfied with the quantity and quality of the viewing audience.

Since 1950, the major organization tracking prime-time viewing has been the A. C. Nielsen Market Research Company, which estimates what shows viewers watch in the nation's major markets. During the 1950s and 1960s, before ratings were fine-tuned statistically, firms like Nielsen estimated only the mass numbers of households tuned to particular programs. By the 1970s, ratings services provided advertisers, networks, and local stations with much more detail about those viewers—from race and gender to age, occupation, and educational background.

The Top 10 Highest-Rated TV Series, Individual Programs (since 1960)

Program	Network	Date	Rating
1. M*A*S*H (final episode)	CBS	2/28/83	60.2
2. Dallas ("Who Shot J.R.?" episode)	CBS	11/21/80	53.3
3. The Fugitive (final episode)	ABC	8/29/67	45.9
4. Cheers (final episode)	NBC	5/20/93	45.5
5. Ed Sullivan Show (Beatles' first U.S. TV appearance)	CBS	2/9/64	45.3
6. Beverly Hillbillies	CBS	1/8/64	44.0
7. Ed Sullivan Show (Beatles' second U.S. TV appearance)	CBS	2/16/64	43.8
8. Beverly Hillbillies	CBS	1/15/64	42.8
9. Beverly Hillbillies	CBS	2/26/64	42.4
10. Beverly Hillbillies	CBS	3/25/64	42.2

Note: The *Seinfeld* finale, which aired in May 1998, drew a rating of 41-plus—not quite Top 10 material.

Sources: The World Almanac and Book of Facts 1997 (Mahwah, NJ: World Almanac Books, 1996), 296; Corbett Steinberg, *TV Facts* (New York: Facts on File Publications, 1985); A. C. Nielsen Media Research.

A **rating** in TV measurement is a statistical estimate expressed as a percentage of households tuned to a program in the local or national market being sampled. (See Table 5.2.) In 1999, one Nielsen national ratings point represented approximately 1,000,000 television households. Another audience measure is the **share**, a statistical estimate of the percentage of homes tuned to a program, compared with those actually using their sets at the time of a sample. Let's say, for instance, that on a typical night of the sample of 5,000 metered homes wired by Nielsen across the country, 4,000 of those households have their TV sets *turned on* to assorted networks, pay channels, and cable channels. Of those 4,000, about 1,000 are tuned to *Friends* on NBC. The *rating* estimate for that show is 5,000 (number of sets) divided by 1,000 (number of households watching *Friends*), which equals 20 percent. The *share* estimate is 4,000 (sets actually in use) divided by 1,000, which equals 25 percent.

Share measurements have become increasingly important because they tell advertising and TV executives approximately what percentage of sets in use are tuned to their programs in a competitive market. Shares are also good measures during fringe time, when most sets may be turned off. For example, on a given night, 1,000 sets may still be on for late-night viewing. If 500 of that 1,000 are tuned to the *Late Show*, its *rating* would be only 10 percent (5,000 divided by 500), but its *share* of the audience still tuned in would be 50 percent (1,000 divided by 500).

In the early 1970s, during the height of the network era, a prime-time series with a rating of 17 or 18 and a share between 28 and 30 was generally a success. By 1997, though, with increasing competition from cable and VCRs, the threshold for success had dropped to a rating of 9 or 10 and a share under 15. Expectations were far less for the new Paramount (UPN) and Time Warner (WB) networks, which had far fewer affiliates in 1995, their first year, than did the four large networks.

The importance of ratings and shares to the survival of specific TV programs cannot be overestimated. (See "Case Study: Anatomy of a TV 'Failure' " on page 165.) Simply stated, audience measurement tells advertisers roughly how many people are watching. Even more important, it tells them what kind of people are watching. Prime-time advertisers are mainly interested in securing affluent eighteen- to forty-nine-year-old viewers, who account for most consumer spending. If a show is attracting viewers from that group, advertisers then decide if they want to buy time during that particular program and pay the network its asking price. In fact, television operates as an industry in which networks, producers, and distributors target, guarantee, and "sell" viewers in blocks to advertisers. About eight of ten new shows introduced each fall either do not attain the required ratings or fail to reach enough of the "right" viewers. The result is cancellation within the year. Unfortunately, over the years many popular programs have been canceled because advertisers considered their audiences too young, too old, or too poor. (We will return to the economics of ratings in Chapter 13.)

alternative voices

While the major networks and their big-city affiliates have dominated mainstream television, alternative programming does exist—particularly at the small, low-power stations or on cable's public access channels. The king of "alt-TV" is probably Paper Tiger Television (PTTV), a loose and changing group of about one hundred producers, activists, artists, technicians, scholars, and "people-off-the-street," who have produced more than two hundred half-hour programs since 1981. PTTV's focus has been providing programs on issues that have either been ignored by mainstream television or oversimplified by traditional news outlets. These mini-TV documentaries, often combining irreverent humor and detailed analysis, specialize in exploring the connections between production, audience, and sponsors: "Paper Tiger . . . aims to disrupt the TV beliefs of its viewers."[14]

Listed among PTTV's catalogue are "Mythmaking: The Balkans," a 1994 production that examines news coverage and government oppression in former Yugoslavian provinces; "Super Barrio," a 1995 production documenting government injustices and economic conditions in Mexico; and "Torn Between Colors," a 1990 student production featuring African American and Latino high school teens who examine the media coverage of several high-profile crimes in New York. In their video (as in many PTTV productions), the students look at the role of language and image in shaping public opinion, using the medium of television to exert some control over their own lives and how they are portrayed.

the public, television, and democracy

Since the 1950s, television has carried the antielitist promise that its technology could bypass traditional print literacy and reach all segments of society. In such a heterogeneous and diverse nation, the concept of a visual, affordable mass medium, giving citizens entertainment and information that they could all talk about the next day, held great appeal. Similarly, we have had this discussion about newspapers in the 1830s, magazines in the 1880s, radio in the 1920s, and the Internet today (although as in television's early days, the first users of new mass media tend to be more educated and affluent). However, since its creation, our system of commercial television has tended to serve the interests of profit rather than those of democracy. And networks have proved time and again that they are more interested in delivering audiences to advertisers than in providing educational programming to citizens and viewers.

Public television (PBS), which developed in the late 1960s, has often filled the role of programming for viewers who are "less attractive" to commercial networks and advertisers. Besides providing programs for the over-fifty viewer, public television has played an important role in programming for viewers under twelve—another demographic not valued by most advertisers and often neglected by the networks. Over the years, such children's series as *Mister Rogers' Neighborhood* (1967–), *Sesame*

Television shows die early deaths for many reasons. Two of the most common are tough, competitive time slots and poor lead-in shows that fail to attract a big enough following. Then there's the story of *Frank's Place* (1987–88), a critically acclaimed entry in the fall 1987 television lineup.

The series starred Tim Reid as a displaced history professor from Boston who inherited his estranged father's modest restaurant in a working-class area of New Orleans. The winner of three Emmys, *Frank's Place* was canceled by CBS just as it was set to produce new episodes for the 1988–89 TV season.

In fact, most new TV series fail. Even such successful series as *All in the Family*, *M*A*S*H*, *Hill Street Blues*, *Cheers*, and *60 Minutes* started out slowly, some at the bottom of the ratings. But they all got a second chance. Why not *Frank's Place*—especially after a strong premiere on a Monday night in 1987, when it beat NBC's *Alf* and ABC's *MacGyver* with a rating of 15 and a 25 share? In the first place, the show lacked a patient executive champion at the network level who would allow *Frank's Place* to "find" its audience gradually in a fixed time slot. During the show's first year, CBS programmers moved it to six different time slots on four different nights. In fact, the program moved so often that its coproducers, Reid and Hugh Wilson, said that even their own mothers could no longer find it. In addition, the show aired initially at 8:00 P.M. "Kids run the eight o'clock Nielsens," Wilson said at the time, but *Frank's Place* was not aimed at children. He wanted the show in a 9:00 or 9:30 slot.[1]

The cast of *Frank's Place*

> *Frank's Place*: "the first program since *Roots* to take Black culture seriously"

—Alvin Poussaint, Harvard psychiatrist and *Cosby* adviser

Bill Cosby as Dr. Cliff Huxtable

A second problem concerned audience expectations. Shot in film style, *Frank's Place* did not look like *Cosby*, the show that Wilson says paved the way for *Frank's Place*. Instead of viewing *Frank's Place* as a series of short stories, as "individual little movies," viewers perhaps kept looking for, but not finding, a more traditional comedy. Intrinsic to this problem were the questions: Was *Frank's Place* too much about black culture to develop an audience among mainstream America? Though it was primarily a comedy, by tackling such issues as drugs, homelessness, corporate greed, alienation, and religion, was it also viewed as *too* serious? No regular network dramatic series featuring a majority black cast had ever succeeded in prime time, although by 1993 there were nine sitcoms on television that had predominantly black actors.

In one of the show's early episodes, the older bartender Tiger tells a disconsolate Frank, who's not a great businessman, "White folks don't come down here much at night." If we extend that thought, clearly not enough people, white or black, watched or were even aware of the program. Unlike *Cosby*, essentially a show about social class, *Frank's Place* was a show about race as well as class. Safer and less threatening, *Cosby* became one of the most popular shows in the history of television. *Frank's Place*, however, while it lasted, allowed mainstream America to see the viewpoints of characters who lived in a black working-class section of New Orleans—in the margins of America, a place where network prime-time television has never been very comfortable.

Debuting in Great Britain in 1997, the *Teletubbies* combine television technology (their stomachs actually contain TVs) with cuddly characters to educate and entertain one- to four-year-old viewers. Aired in more than half a dozen countries, including PBS in the United States, the series follows the adventures of Tinky Winky, Dipsy, Laa-Laa, and Po. Tinky Winky became the subject of news headlines in February 1999, when religious conservative Jerry Falwell warned readers in his newsletter that Tinky Winky stood as a role model for homosexuals—a charge the producers denied.

Street (1969–), *Electric Company* (1971–76), and *Barney* (1991–) have been fixtures on PBS. With the exception of CBS's long-running *Captain Kangaroo* (1955–84), the major networks have pretty much abdicated the responsibility of developing educational series aimed at children under twelve. In 1996, however, Congress passed a law ordering the networks to offer three hours of children's educational programming per week. The networks, however, have sidestepped this congressional mandate by claiming that many of their routine sitcoms and dramatic shows *are* educational. As of the 1998–99 TV season, the networks had not taken a leadership role in developing innovative TV fare that matches the legacy of PBS.

By 1999, the future of PBS and noncommercial television remained cloudy. Ever since the late 1960s, when the Nixon administration began threatening funding cuts for any programming critical of status quo politics and values, our noncommercial system has frequently been held hostage. Since the government never required wealthy commercial broadcasters to subsidize public television (as many other democracies do), politics has played an increasing role in the fate of PBS. As federal funding levels have dropped (especially during the Reagan and Bush administrations), PBS has depended more and more on corporate underwriting. By 1999, nearly 25 percent of all public television was being funded by corporate sponsors. And while this development has certainly helped support many PBS programs, it has had two chilling effects on PBS's traditional independence from corporate America: (1) the appearance of business programs, such as *Wall Street Week* and *Nightly Business Report*, that routinely promote corporate concerns; and (2) the rejection of controversial programming and hard-hitting documentaries, such as *Deadly Deception*, the 1991 Oscar-winning film that criticized General Electric and the nuclear power industry.

In January 1998, PBS decided to "bury" *Surviving the Bottom Line*, a probing documentary produced by the journalist Hedrick Smith, by airing it on successive Friday evenings, which typically draws the smallest TV audience. The film offered "a provocative attack on the kind of Wall Street thinking that places short-term shareholder interests above the welfare of communities." Longtime PBS journalist (and former press secretary to President Johnson) Bill Moyers sharply criticized PBS's scheduling decision, which, he argued, placed the "life of business" before the "business of life."[15]

In addition to problems faced by our public broadcasting system, the original ideal of "universal" television programming serving as our cultural yardstick has also been undercut. The development of cable, the VCR, new networks, and individualized online services has fragmented us by appealing to our individual and special needs. As new technological changes and individualized online services provide more specialized and individual choices, they also weaken television's role as a national touchstone.

But there is some hope. Supplementing PBS's role, diverse cable channels such as Nickelodeon and the Cartoon Network appeal to one end of the age spectrum, and Lifetime and Bravo serve the other end; each has built up loyal audiences that were not being targeted during the network era. To reinvigorate the ideal of television as a prevailing cultural center, local cable access channels and electronic "town hall" meetings—in which citizens participate directly in the programming process—have begun tentatively to restore the idea of a shared national culture. Such promising local developments help counter the economic situation in television today in which a few large multinational companies are controlling the bulk of national and international TV programming. While we certainly have a greater variety of consumer choices today, we still have very little say in what programs (or products) we might like to see.

The future of television is uncertain. Like the other print and broadcast media that it changed, television is also changing. Technologically, digital advances have already made flat-screen, wall-mounted television sets a reality in the next century. However, with online services now offering our favorite TV shows via computer screen, we no longer even need a traditional TV set. And yet companies are now marketing products that allow access to the World Wide Web through our TV sets. In the digital age, distinctions between computer and TV screens will eventually break down. Most television programs are created by a handful of companies, but they rely on independent producers to supply them with the next new idea or story. Although the 1990s featured talk shows and newsmagazines as hot trends (like quiz shows and westerns before them), these genres, too, will fade.

The mainstream allure of television is both its strength and its weakness. As a plus, television offers special moments—inaugurations, debates, space conquests, football, *Roots*, the Olympics, impeachment hearings—that bring large heterogeneous groups together for shared triumphs and mourning, for common experiences. One drawback, though, is that television does not easily explore or adapt to territory outside that common ground. When television aims for the great American middle, it can often mute points of view that are at the edges. As cultural activists and TV critics, we need to ensure that many voices and views have access in the media marketplace.

> "Those who complain about a lack of community among television viewers might pay attention to the vitality and interaction of TV sports watchers wherever they assemble."
> —Barbra Morris, University of Michigan, 1997

REVIEW QUESTIONS

Early Technology and the Development of Television

1. What were the major technical standards established for television in the 1940s?

2. Why did the FCC freeze the allocation of TV licenses between 1948 and 1952?

3. How did the sponsorship of network programs change during the 1950s?

4. What was the impact of the quiz-show scandals on the television industry?

Key Programming Trends in the TV Age

5. How did news develop at the networks in the late 1940s and 1950s?

6. What are the differences among sketch, situation, and domestic comedy on television?

7. Why did the anthology drama fade as a network programming staple?

8. What are the types of episodic TV series? Why did they survive as a TV staple?

Decline of the Network Era

9. What were the technological changes that contributed to the decline of network control over television?

10. What rules and regulations did the government impose to restrict the networks' power?

11. How have new networks managed to grow over the last decade?

The Economics of Television

12. Why has it become more difficult for producers to independently create programs for television?

13. What are the differences between off-network and first-run syndication?

14. Why do syndicated American television shows have advantages in the global marketplace?

15. What is the difference between a rating and a share in audience measurement?

The Public, Television, and Democracy

16. How has television served as a national cultural center or reference point over the years?

QUESTIONING THE MEDIA

1. Describe your earliest memories of watching television. What was your favorite show? Which shows did your family watch together? Were there shows that you were not allowed to watch? Which ones?

2. How much television do you watch today? Which programs do you try to watch regularly? What attracts you to your favorite program(s)?

3. If you were a network television executive, what changes would you try to make in the programs that America watches?

4. If you ran a public television station, what programming would you provide that isn't currently being supplied by commercial television? How would you finance such programming?

5. How can television be used to improve social and political life in the United States?

SEARCHING THE INTERNET

http://www.nab.org
Official Web site for the National Association of Broadcasters, the main trade association and lobbying body for the broadcast industry.

http://www.cpb.org
This Corporation for Public Broadcasting site provides information on PBS programs, member stations, and those who use public TV for education.

http://www.buttle.com/tv/schedule.htm
Buttle Broadcasting provides TV program guides from different nations around the world.

http://www.ultimatetv.com
Ultimate TV provides program information on all major networks and most local TV stations. Also provides information on what kinds of TV systems operate in various countries.

http://www.nbc.com

http://www.abc.com

http://www.cbs.com

http://www.fox.com

http://www.upn.com

http://www.thewb.com

These are the official national network Web sites. They contain information about their programs as well as listings of the local affiliates.

In Brief

Do you think television plays more of a role in uniting us as a culture or in separating us as individuals? Make two lists on the board (or in groups) and discuss them in class.

In Depth

In small groups (or as a class), track two or three TV programs that share the same time period and compete with each other for viewers. Using a chart of your own design, keep track of the following for four to six weeks: (1) the local and national ads on your programs, and (2) the ratings and shares for these shows. (Weekly ratings information can be found in current trade publications, including *Variety, Broadcasting & Cable*, and *Electronic Media*, or in popular publications such as *Entertainment Weekly* and the Wednesday "Life" section of *USA Today*.) Then, briefly describe each of the programs and analyze them by answering the following sets of questions:

1. During a half-hour block, how many minutes are devoted to advertising? Based on an examination of the ads in your programs, who do the sponsors think are watching these shows? Can you generalize about the intended audience? Are the sponsors targeting their money wisely? Based on your analysis, are there any discrepancies between the ads themselves and what the programs seem to be about?

2. Offer interpretations to explain why you think one show is more popular than the other(s) you have tracked. Consider a number of factors here—the quality of the programs (in terms of production, characters, story themes, etc.); economic factors (costs, placement in the time schedule—what shows your programs follow); social and cultural values and issues raised by the programs (for instance, issues of class, race, age, and gender; whether the programs make you feel included or excluded; how you think other audience groups might respond to the program).

In addition, try to contact the programming and sales departments at local affiliates or at the networks to see if you can get demographic information on who the affiliates or networks think is watching. These departments might also be willing to provide information on ad costs and ratings.

Cable
and the Specialization of Television

CHAPTER 6

170

The employees of cable channel Comedy Central probably don't like to think of their network as the channel that was saved by Mr. Hankey, the Talking Christmas Poo. Yet it was the gross-out humor of the animated series *South Park*—especially fan favorites like the Mr. Hankey episode—that secured Comedy Central's position on cable systems across America in the late 1990s.

Formed in 1991 by a merger of HBO's Comedy Central and MTV's Ha! Channel, Comedy Central struggled to find its place in a competitive cable-television business where cable operators quickly bump low-rated channels to make room for more promising or more requested offerings. Through the 1990s, Comedy Central developed a lineup of stand-up comedy shows, *Saturday Night Live* reruns, cult hits like *Mystery Science Theater 3000 (MST3K)*, the talk show *Politically Incorrect*, and the British comedy series *Absolutely Fabulous*. But sustaining a competitive schedule was difficult: Host Bill Maher took his *Politically Incorrect* to bigger audiences at ABC, *Absolutely Fabulous* ended production, and the cult buzz about *MST3K* wore off. Even worse, the largest cable operator in the United States at the time, TCI, dropped Comedy Central from millions of households on cable systems around the country.

From its debut in the summer of 1997, *South Park* quickly gained a huge share of the eighteen- to twenty-four-year-old audience, and a year later trailed only ESPN's Sunday-night NFL game as cable's most-watched program. With the smart-alecky and scatological humor of the show's foul-mouthed third-grade characters (which earns a "mature audiences" rating) and one of the Internet's most active entertainment Web sites, *South Park* developed a heavy following on college campuses, created a multimillion-dollar product-licensing business, and crossed over to movie screens in the summer of 1999. The show's success came despite the fact that less than half of American households even have access to Comedy Central. With *South Park*, and lesser hits like *The Daily Show* and *Win Ben Stein's Money*, Comedy Central has since developed a reputation for what *TV Guide* critic Matt Roush calls "dangerous comedy." This new image, combined with some of cable's most popular television programs, has also given Comedy Central new momentum in getting back on cable systems.

With growing niche channels like Comedy Central and successful premium services like HBO, cable has redefined television worldwide. By offering more channels—filled with old network reruns, 24-hour news services, music videos, and specialized programs on food, sports, history, the weather, and home shopping—cable TV has gradually eroded the status and market share of the once dominant Big Three networks.

Although cable is almost as old as network television, broadcasters inhibited its growth throughout its first twenty-five years. Since the mid-1970s, however, when both HBO (Time Warner's premium movie service) and WTBS (Ted Turner's Atlanta TV station) became available to cable companies across the nation, cable's growth has been rapid. In 1977, only 14 percent of all homes received cable. By 1985, that number had climbed to 46 percent. By the late 1990s, that figure had leveled off at around 68 percent but was expected to peak at 70 percent by 2000.

The cable industry's emergence from the shadow of broadcast television and its rapid rise to prominence was due partly to the shortcomings of broadcast television. For example, cable generally improved signal reception in most communities. In addition, whereas prime-time broadcast television has traditionally tried to reach the largest possible audiences, cable channels—like magazines and radio—focused more on providing specialized services for smaller audiences broadcasters often ignored. Furthermore, cable, through its greater channel capacity, has provided more access. In many communities, various public, government, and educational channels have made it possible for anyone to air a point of view or produce a TV program. When it has lived up to its potential, cable has offered the public greater opportunities to more fully participate in the democratic promises of television.

"New viewers are not coming to network television. How do you build for the future? If I was a young executive, I don't know if I would come into the network business. I'd probably rather program Comedy Central."

—Leslie Moonves,
president of CBS Television,
1998

We will begin this chapter by examining the fallout from "wired" television, starting with cable's early technological development and traditional broadcasters' attempts to restrict its growth. We will discuss the impact of the various rules and regulations aimed at the cable industry, including the Telecommunications Act of 1996, which was the first major revision of communications law since 1934. We will then turn to various programming strategies, including basic service, premium cable, and pay-per-view, as well as the innovative contributions of CNN, MTV, and HBO. We will also explore an alternative technology—direct-broadcast satellite—and its impact on cable. Finally, we will look at business and ownership patterns, particularly the influence of the largest cable operators, AT&T Broadband & Internet Services (formerly TCI) and Time Warner Cable, and investigate cable's role in a democratic society.

early technology and the development of cable

Unlike recording, radio, and television, cable's earliest technical breakthroughs came from a fairly anonymous and practical group of people. Originating in rural and small-town communities in the late 1940s, cable sprang from obstacles that appliance-store owners faced in selling TV sets to people who lived in remote areas. In an effort to increase sales in areas where hills and mountains blocked broadcast signals, TV dealers and electronics firms built antenna relay towers on the outskirts of their communities to pick up blocked signals. They strung wire from utility poles and then ran cables from the towers into individual homes. Essentially, these individuals created a market for their products by ensuring clear TV reception for viewers.

Although today's technology is more advanced, cable continues to operate pretty much the same way. The key distinction between cable and broadcasting remains: Programs reach TV sets through a wire rather than over the air. The advantage of the cable system is that while the airwaves in any given community can accommodate fifteen or so VHF and UHF channels without electrical interference, cable wires can transmit hundreds of channels with no interference. In a cable system, TV signals are processed at a computerized nerve center, or *headend*, which operates various large satellite dishes that receive and process long-distance signals from CNN in Atlanta or MTV in New York. In addition, the headend houses' receiving equipment can pick up an area's local broadcast signals or a nearby city's PBS station. It relays each premium channel (like HBO), local network affiliate, independent station, and public TV signal along its own separate line. These lines are made up of *coaxial cable*, *fiber optics*, or a combination of both. Until the 1980s, when scientists developed fiber-optic technology—sending coded information along beams of laser light—most cable systems transmitted electronic TV signals via coaxial cable, a solid core of copper-clad aluminum wire encircled by an outer axis of braided wires. These bundles of thin wire could accommodate fifty or more separate channels, or lines, running side by side with virtually no interference.

After "downlinking" various channels from satellites and pulling in nearby stations from the airwaves, headend computers relay them in the same way that telephone calls and electric power reach individual households. Most TV channels are relayed from the headend through *trunk* and *feeder cables* attached to existing utility poles. Cable companies rent space on these poles from phone and electric companies. Signals are then transmitted to *drop* or *tap lines* that run from the utility poles into homes. TV signals move from drop lines to cable-ready TV sets or they pass through a cable converter box, which enables older TV sets to receive each channel (see Figure 6.1).

■ catv—community antenna television

The first small cable systems—called **CATV**, or community antenna television—originated in Oregon, Pennsylvania, and Manhattan, where mountains or tall buildings blocked TV signals. The early systems served roughly 10 percent of the country and, because of early technical and regulatory limits, contained only twelve channels. Even at this early stage, though, TV sales personnel, broadcasters, and electronics firms recognized the two big advantages of cable. First, by routing and reamplifying each channel in a separate wire, cable eliminated over-the-air interference. Second, by running signals through coaxial cable, a cable system increased channel capacity.

**Figure 6.1
A Basic Cable
Television System**
Source: Jennifer Stearns,
A Short Course in Cable
(Office of Communi-
cation, United Church
of Christ, 1981), 9.

In the early days, small communities with CATV often received twice as many channels as were available over the air in much larger cities. Since broadcast channels were generally regarded as a limited natural resource, CATV foreshadowed later developments in which cable-channel capacity grew dramatically and the need to operate a broadcast frequency diminished. In combination, the two early technological advantages of cable would soon propel the new cable industry into competition with conventional broadcast television. Unlike radio, which was intended to free mass communication from unwieldy wires, early cable technology sought to restore wires to improve the potential of television.

a threat to broadcasting

Though the technology for cable existed as early as the late 1940s, cable's growth was effectively short-circuited by conventional broadcasters. For nearly thirty years, local broadcasters, the networks, and television's professional organization—the National Association of Broadcasters (NAB)—successfully lobbied to curb cable development in most cities. Throughout the 1950s and 1960s, the FCC operated on behalf of the broadcast industry to ensure that cable would not compete with conventional television. Local broadcasters worried that if towns could bring in distant signals from more glamorous cities like Chicago or New York, viewers would reject their local stations—and their local advertisers—in favor of big-city signals. Early FCC rules therefore blocked cable companies from bringing distant TV stations into cities and towns with local channels.

There was one exception to these lobbying efforts: CATV service for sparsely populated communities. Since CATV generally served towns that had no TV stations of their own, the broadcast industry welcomed the distribution of distant signals to these areas via cable. After all, relaying a commercial signal to rural areas increased the audience reach and potential ad revenue of a broadcast station.

By the early 1970s, it was clear that cable's growth could no longer be limited to small, isolated communities. With cable's capacity for more channels and better reception, the FCC began to seriously examine industry issues. In 1972, the commission updated or enacted a series of rules regarding cable expansion. Established primarily to protect conventional over-the-air broadcasters in the top one hundred TV markets, most of these rules did not apply to cable systems with fewer than thirty-five hundred subscribers.

The FCC initially reaffirmed **must-carry rules**, first established in 1965, which required all cable operators to assign channels to and carry all local TV broadcasts on their systems. This rule ensured that local network affiliates, independent stations (those not carrying network programs), and public television channels would benefit from cable's clearer reception. The FCC guidelines also allowed additional noncommercial channels to be introduced into bigger TV markets, but it limited the number of distant commercial TV signals to two or three independent stations per cable system. In addition, it prohibited cable companies from bringing in a network affiliate from another city when a local station already carried that network's programming. This ensured that a network affiliate in one market would not have to compete for viewers against a similar affiliate imported from another market.

The 1972 FCC rules also required cable operators to carry their own original programming by mandating **access channels** in the nation's top one hundred TV markets. In other words, cable operators were compelled to provide and fund a tier of nonbroadcast channels dedicated to local education, government, and the public. The FCC required large-market cable operators to assign separate channels for each access service, while cable operators in smaller markets (and with fewer channels) could assign education, government, and the public to share one channel. In addition to free public-access channels, the FCC called for **leased channels**. Citizens could buy time on these channels and produce longer programs or present controversial views.

> "No longer must you be satisfied with programming provided by others. You can **videotape your own shows** and cablecast them to your community on channels set aside for public use. Cable has turned sixth graders, senior citizens, homemakers and clergy into **TV producers**."
> —Jennifer Stearns,
> *A Short Course in Cable,*
> 1981

franchising frenzy

By the end of the 1970s, competition over obtaining franchises to supply local cable service had become intense. Essentially, a *cable franchise* was a mini-monopoly awarded by a local community to the most attractive bidder, usually for a fifteen-year period. Although a few large cities permitted two companies to build different parts of its cable system, in most cases communities granted franchises to only one company. Cities and states used the same logic that had granted monopoly status to AT&T for more than a hundred years: They did not want more than one operator trampling over private property to string wire from utility poles or to bury cables underground.

Local municipalities and, in some instances, state governments got involved in overseeing franchise awards. A number of states, for example, guided the franchising process, and a few even retained the authority to approve a city's cable operator. Eight states—including Alabama, Hawaii, and Vermont—defined cable as a public utility (like the telephone or electric company), so their cable franchises needed approval

Figure 6.2
The Rise of Cable Systems, 1970–99
Sources: National Cable Television Association (NCTA), <www.ncta.com>; Warren Publishing, Inc., *Television & Cable Factbook*, Services Volume No. 67, 1999. Estimates as of January 1, 1999. Reprinted with permission.

from public-utility commissions at the state level. In states in which cable was not defined as a utility, town councils and city governments selected the cable operator. This period, from the late 1970s through the 1980s, constituted a unique, if turbulent, era in media history, for it was during this time that most of the nation's cable systems were built (see Figure 6.2).

During the franchising process, a city (or state) would outline its cable needs and request bids from cable operators. Then a number of companies—none of which could also own broadcast stations or newspapers in the community—competed for the right to install and manage the cable system. In the bid, a company would make a list of promises to the city, including information about construction schedules, system design, subscription rates, channel capacity, types of programming, financial backing, deadlines, and a *franchise fee:* the money the cable company would pay the city annually for the right to operate the local cable system.

Few rules or laws existed to regulate the process of franchise negotiations. During the franchising process, competing cable companies made attractive offers and promises to gain monopoly rights in certain areas. In the early 1980s, for example, Sammon Communication bid for the Fort Worth, Texas, franchise by offering that city a multimillion-dollar community-access package, which included three mobile television vans (for producing community programs), $50,000 for student-internship training programs, $175,000 as an annual budget for access channels, and $100,000 to modernize educational buildings and studios. Such offers were typical in large cable markets.

From the late 1970s through the 1980s, lots of wheeling and dealing transpired, along with occasional corruption. Cable companies sometimes offered far more than they could deliver, and some cities and suburbs occasionally made unfair demands on the franchise awardees. Often, battles over broken promises, unreasonable contracts, or escalating rates ended up in court. Frequently, courts had to determine whether cities were requesting unfair franchise fees or violating the First Amendment rights of cable operators by demanding various channel services.

regulation nightmares and federal cable laws

From the very beginning of cable, no one seemed to know who held legal jurisdiction over wired television. Since the 1934 Communications Act had not anticipated cable, its regulatory status was problematic during these growth years. As late as 1969, the

With the rapid expansion of telephone, television, and radio in the 1950s, a demand developed for more and better ways to send and receive mass communication signals. In the mid-1950s, the Soviet Union and then the United States successfully sent satellites into orbit around the earth. In 1960, the United States launched Echo 1, a *passive* metallic sphere that simply received radio signals from an earth station and reflected them back to earth. In 1962, AT&T launched Telstar, the first communication satellite capable of receiving, amplifying, and returning signals. Telstar received transmissions from the ground, beamed into space from an uplink facility, and retransmitted them to a receiving dish called a downlink. An *active* satellite, Telstar was able to process and relay telephone and television signals between the United States and Europe.

The earliest communication satellites worked for only a few hours a day, when they passed over the regions—or *footprints*—they were serving. But in the mid-1960s, scientists figured out how to lock a communication satellite into synchronous or geostationary orbit. In this location—22,300 miles from the equator—satellites traveling at more than 6,800 mph today circle the earth at the same speed the earth revolves on its axis.

The first satellites lasted seven or eight years and had twelve or twenty-four *transponders*, the relay points on a satellite that perform the receive-and-transmit functions. Cable and DBS (*Direct Broadcast Satellite*) program providers rent these transponders from satellite companies for million-dollar monthly fees. One conventional transponder can process one color-TV signal or about three thousand simultaneous long-distance phone calls. By the mid-1990s, the newest satellites had forty-eight transponders. Companies also began experimenting with *digital compression*, a way of increasing the number of signals trans-

mitted simultaneously without disturbing image quality. This process allowed one transponder to handle four to six TV signals. In 1995, PBS began sending *Sesame Street* to various affiliates using digital compression, hoping to free expensive transponder space that the network could then sublet to other firms.

About 65 percent of satellite use is for television, news, and cable services. Telephone, telegraph, and business communication account for the rest of the transponder market. For example, CNN leases Transponder 5 on the Hughes Galaxy 5 satellite. Many cable channels that operate globally rent two transponders on different satellites to reach receiving dishes in the western and eastern hemispheres.

One of the more pressing issues regarding communication satellites, particularly in recent years, has involved who gets to occupy synchronous orbit, which technically is a finite resource. (There are only so many available satellite "parking spaces" 22,300 miles from the earth.) A major global satellite organization, INTELSAT, operates a network of nineteen satellites and has more than 140 government members. INTELSAT launched its first satellite, Early Bird, in 1965 and has plans to launch four more between 2000 and 2001. The organization continues to wrestle with issues of satellite access. Although geostationary orbit has so far accommodated the satellites from industrialized countries, some developing nations worry that by the time they are prepared to launch, there will not be enough room left. Scarce space allocations have generally operated on a common-carrier basic—first come, first served to the highest bidders. But digital compression technology and the new digital TV standard will eventually solve the scarcity problem by increasing transponder capacity the way FM radio increased the radio spectrum, and the way cable expanded TV services.

Satellite

Satellite orbit

Radio waves to satellite

Radio waves to satellite

Earth station

Direction of earth's rotation

North America

Europe

FCC claimed little jurisdiction in this area. However, once cable began importing distant signals into bigger television markets, the FCC's interest perked up. Prior to that time, the FCC functioned primarily to protect the commercial interests of local broadcasters and the national networks.

Common Carrier or Electronic Publisher? Unlike broadcasting, which is under the legal jurisdiction of the federal government, local and state governments are involved in cable, since cable firms rent access rights to property and telephone poles. In the few states where cable is regulated as a public utility, it is technically a *common carrier* and is required to offer part of its service on a first-come, first-served basis to whoever can pay the rate. Common carriers, like taxi services or phone companies, do not get involved in channel content. Telephone operators, for instance, do not question the topics of personal conversations ("Hi, I'm the phone company, and what are you going to be talking about today?"). Most cable operators, however, view themselves as common carriers only with regard to the one or two leased channels they carry, where customers pay for and control their own programs.

In arguing that they are not common carriers, cable companies instead view themselves as *electronic publishers*, entitled to pick and choose which channels to carry. Historically, the cable industry has sought the same speech or "publishing" freedoms and legal protections that broadcast and print media enjoy in selecting content. In 1979, the Supreme Court agreed, siding with the cable industry in the landmark *Midwest Video* case.[1] In the case, Midwest Video, a cable operator, challenged the FCC's authority to mandate that cable systems carry certain programming, including access channels. Midwest Video's lawyers argued that some of the 1972 rules violated their client's First Amendment rights. In other words, the government could not tell a magazine what to print and, therefore, should not be able to tell a cable operator which channels to carry. In siding with cable, the Supreme Court upheld the rights of cable operators to dictate their content and defined the industry as a form of "electronic publishing." Although the FCC could no longer mandate channels, the Court said that it was still okay for communities to "request" access channels as part of contract negotiations in the franchising process. Access channels are no longer a requirement, but most cable firms continue to offer them in order to remain on good terms with their communities.

The Repeal of Syndex Rules. In 1980, to boost cable from its position as a struggling new industry, the FCC repealed its *syndicated exclusivity*, or *syndex*, rules. These rules had given local stations exclusive rights to syndicate TV programs, such as off-network reruns, which they had purchased. In other words, syndex rules had prohibited cable operators from importing reruns like *Happy Days* or *M*A*S*H* from distant markets, thereby offering consumers the same programming already available on their local stations. Local broadcasters feared that such competition would hurt advertising if consumers chose to watch favorite older shows on a distant cable channel rather than on the station carrying local ads. In exchange for the FCC's repeal of the syndex rules, cable operators agreed to pay copyright fees to broadcasters for imported distant signals. By the late 1980s, these fees amounted to more than $100 million collected from thousands of U.S. cable systems and distributed mostly among the nation's three-hundred-plus independent TV stations. With the repeal of syndex, viewers could conceivably watch episodes of *Happy Days* and *M*A*S*H* five or six times a day on five or six different local and distant channels.

The Cable Acts of 1984 and 1992. The first major federal act governing cable was passed in 1984. Coming during the middle of the Reagan presidency, which had been favorable to deregulating business, it represented a victory for the cable industry and a defeat for local communities. The act capped the annual franchise fee a city could charge a cable operator at 5 percent of the company's gross revenues. The act further protected cable by making it difficult for cities to sign with a new company at the end of the regular fifteen-year franchise period. A more controversial aspect of the act called for a two-year phaseout of must-carry rules, which upset local broadcasters. In addition, it ended rate regulation. This meant that cable operators, while constituting a local monopoly, could set their own unregulated monthly subscriber rates beginning in January 1987.

Between 1984 and 1990, the average rate for basic services (excluding premium movie channels like HBO) rose from about $9 to $17 a month. In addition, in 1984 cable operators had effectively argued that must-carry rules violated their free-speech rights (since in many cases they had to assign one-third of their channels to existing broadcast stations). As a result, cable systems began dropping some PBS affiliates and weaker independent stations from their lineups. By the late 1980s, more than 150 public stations had been removed from local cable systems, and some 50 new independent UHF stations, licensed shortly after the 1984 act, were having difficulty getting a cable channel assigned to them. Some large cable operators dropped regular broadcast signals in favor of new satellite-delivered channels on which operators could run their own ads. Displeased with the act, broadcast lobbyists and consumer watchdog groups began calling for cable reform.

With the growing commercial success of cable and the rapid increase in subscription rates, a less sympathetic FCC and Congress changed the law in 1992, reinstating rate regulation. In the mid-1990s, the FCC surveyed the twenty-five largest cable companies, which served roughly 75 percent of all cable subscribers, and found that rates had fallen in fourteen of those systems but had increased in the other eleven systems. In most instances, loopholes allowed cable companies to raise rates on basic service but decrease rates for premium channels such as Showtime. By 1995, the FCC's Cable Bureau estimated that rates had dropped about 5 to 10 percent among the nation's systems, but the FCC was still processing a backlog of six thousand complaints about cable rates.

In terms of must-carry rules, the 1992 act required that commercial broadcasters opt for either must-carry or *retransmission consent* every three years. The latter option meant that broadcasters could now ask cable operators for fees to carry their channels. However, if broadcasters did this, they waived the right to be automatically

Calvin and Hobbes   by Bill Watterson

Calvin & Hobbes, ©1992 Watterson. Dist. by Universal Press Syndicate. Reprinted with permission. All rights reserved.

carried on these cable systems. In other words, local commercial broadcasters who chose must-carry gave up the right to be compensated for their channel but were assured of a channel assignment on their local cable system. By June 1993, each of the eleven-hundred-plus commercial U.S. TV stations (noncommercial stations could choose only must-carry) had to inform all cable systems in their broadcast range whether they were opting for must-carry or retransmission. At the time, only low-rated independent stations on the fringes of a market opted for must-carry.

In 1993, the stations that chose retransmission consent did so because they believed cable operators would not risk alienating customers by dropping the popular broadcast stations that carried network programs. In general, a broadcast station wanted either money from cable operators for carrying its signal or the right to advertise on more cable channels. By 1995, the FCC was still processing more than two hundred must-carry complaints. These were from both local stations that were unable to get on cable and from cable operators that sought to eliminate broadcasters from their lineups in favor of new satellite channels such as the History or Comedy Channels. A few large station owners, such as ABC, struck deals with cable companies that owned a large number of systems. For example, rather than ask for money, ABC requested that cable systems carry its new ESPN2 sports channel. As a result, ESPN2 is now transmitted to more than thirty million homes.

The Telecommunications Act of 1996. After sixty-two years, Congress finally rewrote the nation's communications laws in 1996, bringing cable fully under the federal rules that had long governed the telephone, radio, and TV industries. In its most significant move, Congress used the Telecommunications Act to knock down regulatory barriers, allowing regional phone companies, long-distance carriers, and cable operators to enter one another's markets. For the first time, owners could operate TV or radio stations in the same market where they owned a cable system. Just as the Telecommunications Act allows cable companies to offer telephone services, it also permits phone companies to use fiber-optic wires to offer Internet services. Before passage of the 1996 legislation, the phone and cable industries had long benefited from their regional and national monopoly status. Congress hoped that the new rules would spur competition and lower both phone and cable rates, although this did not always happen. By 1999, at least seven cable operators were offering residential or commercial phone service in dozens of markets across the United States, and five telephone companies began offering cable service.

> "If this [telecommunications] bill is a blueprint, it's written in washable ink. Congress is putting out a picture of how things will evolve. But technology is transforming the industry in ways that we don't yet understand."
> —Mark Rotenberg, Electronic Privacy Information Center, 1996

While broadcasters fought steadily for must-carry rules over the years, cable systems continued to argue that these rules violated their free-speech rights by dictating what signals must be included among their cable offerings. The Telecommunications Act appeared to settle the issue by reaffirming broadcasters' need for must-carry rules. However, cable companies with limited channel capacity still objected to having to carry low-rated stations; operators could make more money carrying satellite-delivered movie services and specialty channels on topics such as history or health. The nation's ten-thousand-plus cable operators continued to periodically ask the courts to repeal must-carry rules and free the cable industry to carry whatever channels best served its commercial interests. In 1997, however, broadcasting won a final victory when the Supreme Court upheld the constitutionality of must-carry rules, assuring that most broadcasters would be carried by their local cable operator.

TABLE 6.1
Impact of the 1996 Telecommunications Act

On Cable	Monthly rates likely to rise
	Act lifted all federal rate regulations in 1999 for large cable systems
	Rate regulations eliminated immediately on systems with less than 1 percent of the nation's subscribers
	Cable companies may enter phone business
On Phone Companies	Mergers and alliances likely among cable and phone companies
	Act allows seven regional Bell companies to offer long-distance services after demonstrating that they have opened up their local markets to competition
	Long-distance companies can compete in local phone-service business
	Local and long-distance companies can enter cable business
	Telephone and cable companies can own up to 10 percent of each other
On TV Broadcasting	Act takes limits off number of TV stations one company can own as long as total number of stations reach less than 35 percent of population
	Requires manufacturers to equip TV sets with V-chip to allow parents to block violent or sexually explicit programming
On the Internet	Act tried to make it a crime for online computer services or users to transmit pornographic and indecent material without restricting access by minors. This Communications Decency Act was found unconstitutional in 1997.

Sources: "Telecom Vote Signals Competitive Free-for-All," *Wall Street Journal*, February 2, 1996, p. B1+; "Who Gets What," *Time*, February 12, 1996, 52.

Among its other features (see Table 6.1), the 1996 Telecommunications Act permits telephone companies to buy or construct cable systems in communities where there are fewer than fifty thousand residents. The legislation also ended government involvement in rate regulation for all premium movie services and for basic services in small cable systems. For larger systems, however, Congress authorized the FCC to monitor monthly cable rates until 1999 before phasing out federal oversight of regulation entirely.

The 1996 act has had mixed effects for cable consumers. Cable companies argue that it has allowed business mergers (such as the one announced in 1998 between telephone giant AT&T and cable giant TCI) that will lead to innovations in programming, services, and technology. But cable consumers often find themselves footing the bill for future interactive and video services that they may not necessarily want. For example, after three consecutive years of 8 percent rate increases, the typical cable household paid more than $31 a month in 1998 for basic cable service.[2] Critics fear that more mergers will further eliminate rate competition in both the phone and cable businesses, and that there will be no government authority to step in and enforce rate freezes or cuts.

In terms of the act's impact on cable programs, advances in technology and new commercial interests will continue to increase the number of cable channels and add more specialized services, especially for affluent customers. As with other aspects of the information highway, of which cable is now a major thoroughfare, many new developments are likely to bypass poorer communities. Local governments and citizen advocate groups will need to play a strong role to ensure that new media developments reach the widest cross section of people in their communities. The cable industry itself has recently responded to such concerns with an initiative to provide schools and public libraries with free high-speed cable modems and Internet connections.

narrowcasting challenges broadcasting

By the early 1990s, 96 percent of all U.S. households could obtain a basic tier of cable channels for an $18 to $20 monthly fee. However, about one-third of this potential audience, most of whom reside in less affluent central-city areas, chose not to subscribe to cable. Although its audience and advertising revenues remain smaller than those of the major TV networks, cable has emerged as a serious challenger to—and partner of—broadcasting. By 1996, the networks had joined the cable world. NBC now operated two cable-news services (CNBC and MSNBC), while both ABC and CBS had agreements with cable channels to share and develop news, sports, and family programming. Fox had also launched Fox News, a 24-hour news service similar to CNN, and Fox SportsNet, a nationwide sports network that emphasized regional coverage in various markets. *Broadcasting*, the trade magazine for television and an opponent of cable's early growth, had become *Broadcasting & Cable* magazine. The O.J. Simpson trials, which might have been covered gavel-to-gavel by the three networks in the 1960s or 1970s, were instead covered in the mid-1990s by three cable services— CNN, Court TV, and the E! channel. And the Clinton-Lewinsky scandal was a ratings boon for cable talk shows on MSNBC, CNBC, Fox News, and CNN.

During the old network era in television, ABC, CBS, and NBC accounted for more than 95 percent of prime-time viewing; independent stations and public television accounted for the rest. By the late 1990s, however, cable channels drew close to 40 percent of the TV-viewing audience during a typical evening, up from only 6 percent in the mid-1980s. On the other hand, the old broadcast networks slid to less than 50 percent of the prime-time audience, down from 90 percent in the mid-1980s. (Fox, the UPN and WB networks, PBS, independent stations, movie videos, and cable drew the rest of the audience.) By the summer of 1997, basic cable channels had captured a larger prime-time audience than the broadcast networks, the first time that had ever happened. The decline in the networks' viewer base appeared to be healthy for both competition and democracy. In fact, early in its development, especially with the arrival of public-access channels, cable was heralded as a voice for the voiceless. In this sense, it offered opportunities for ordinary citizens to deliver messages and produce programs—options that were not available during the network era.

"We used to think the possibility existed that the erosion was going to stop. We were silly. It's never going to stop. As you give consumers greater and greater choices, they are going to make more choices."

— Robert A. Iger,
president of ABC Inc.,
1998

In the new cable era, a redefined concept of **narrowcasting**—providing specialized programming for diverse and fragmented groups—has cut into broadcasting's large mass audience. For the advertising industry, cable programs provide access to specific target audiences that cannot be guaranteed in broadcasting. For example, a golf-equipment manufacturer can buy ads on the Golf Channel and reach only golf enthusiasts. Since the audience is small and specialized, ads are a fraction of the cost of a network ad; they reach only the targeted viewers and not the larger general public. As cable channels have become more and more like specialized magazines or radio formats (see Figure 6.3), they have siphoned off network viewers. As a consequence, the networks' role as the chief programmer of the shared culture has eroded.

Cable consumers usually choose programming from a two-tiered structure: a group of **basic channels**, part of one monthly fee; and **premium channels**, available individually to customers at an extra monthly fee. These channels are the production arm of the cable industry, supplying programming to the nation's nearly eleven thousand cable operators, which function as program distributors by delivering channels

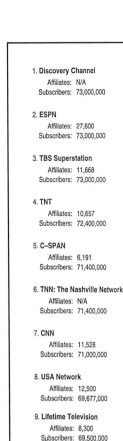

1. Discovery Channel
Affiliates: N/A
Subscribers: 73,000,000

2. ESPN
Affiliates: 27,600
Subscribers: 73,000,000

3. TBS Superstation
Affiliates: 11,668
Subscribers: 73,000,000

4. TNT
Affiliates: 10,657
Subscribers: 72,400,000

5. C–SPAN
Affiliates: 6,191
Subscribers: 71,400,000

6. TNN: The Nashville Network
Affiliates: N/A
Subscribers: 71,400,000

7. CNN
Affiliates: 11,528
Subscribers: 71,000,000

8. USA Network
Affiliates: 12,500
Subscribers: 69,677,000

9. Lifetime Television
Affiliates: 8,300
Subscribers: 69,500,000

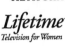

10. Headline News
Affiliates: 6,917
Subscribers: 68,000,000

11. The Weather Channel
Affiliates: 6,500
Subscribers: 68,000,000

12. AMC
Affiliates: N/A
Subscribers: 67,000,000

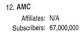

13. The Family Channel
Affiliates: 13,352
Subscribers: 66,900,000

14. A&E Television Network
Affiliates: 12,000
Subscribers: 66,880,000

15. MTV
Affiliates: 9,176
Subscribers: 66,700,000

16. Nickelodeon/Nick at Nite
Affiliates: 11,788
Subscribers: 66,000,000

17. CNBC
Affiliates: 5822
Subscribers: 64,000,000

18. QVC
Affiliates: 6,427
Subscribers: 63,009,873

19. VH1
Affiliates: 6,194
Subscribers: 61,600,000

20. The Learning Channel
Affiliates: N/A
Subscribers: 60,000,000

Figure 6.3
The Top 20 Cable Networks (Ranked by Number of Subscribers)
Source: National Cable Television Association, *Cable Television Developments* (spring 1998): 16–17. Data provided to NCTA by the networks, March–April 1998.
Note: Figures may include non-cable affiliates and/or subscribers. Broadcast viewership is not included.

to cable households. In the late 1990s, a basic-service program package of sixty or more channels cost consumers between $25 and $36 a month nationwide, while a single premium channel like HBO added an additional $8 to $12 per month.

basic cable

A typical basic cable system today includes a thirty-six- to seventy-two-channel lineup composed of local broadcast signals, nonbroadcast access channels (for local government, education, and general public use), a few regional PBS stations, and a variety of services retrieved from national communications satellites. (See "Tracking Technology: Communication Satellites Open Doors to the Future" on page 177.) These basic satellite services include ESPN, CNN, MTV, VH1, the USA Network, Bravo, Nickelodeon, Lifetime, the Fox Family Channel, Comedy Central, CNBC, C-Span and C-Span2, Black Entertainment Television, Telemundo, the Weather Channel, a home-shopping service, and ten to thirty additional channels depending on a cable system's capacity and regional interests. Basic services also include **superstations**, which are merely independent TV stations, such as WTBS in Atlanta or WGN in Chicago, that have uplinked their signal to a satellite to make themselves available nationwide.

Typically, local cable systems pay each of these satellite-delivered services between fifteen and fifty cents a month per subscriber. That fee is then passed along to consumers as part of their basic monthly cable rate. Unlike local broadcasters, which make money almost exclusively through advertising, cable companies earn revenue in a variety of ways: through monthly subscriptions for basic service, local ad sales, pay-per-view programming, and premium movie channels. Most basic satellite services, such as ESPN or Arts & Entertainment, block out time for inexpensive local and regional ads. These local ads are cheaply produced compared with national network ads and reach a smaller audience than do broadcast commercials. Cable, in fact, has permitted many small local companies—from restaurants to clothing stores—that might not otherwise be able to afford TV spots to use television as a means of advertising.

The 1990s witnessed a proliferation of new basic cable networks, increasingly specialized for smaller but more definable audiences. These include the popular Sci-Fi Channel (owned by the USA Network and Viacom/Paramount), the Cartoon Network (owned by Turner/Time Warner and other investors), Comedy Central (owned by Time Warner and Viacom), and fX (owned by Fox and Liberty Media). Newer services featured channels devoted to history, health and fitness, books, games, parenting, pets, therapy, and Indian tribal culture. In 1992, 87 cable networks were in business. By 1999, that number had doubled to more than 175. With so many networks to choose from, cable systems with thirty-six to seventy-two channels (many of them reserved for local broadcasters) carried only the most popular cable networks.

Battling with national cable networks are regional services, which target audiences geographically. About fifty regional channels exist in the United States, and nearly all of them are located in large metropolitan areas that can support such specialized programming. Many of the regional channels are news/talk formats modeled on CNN, but with limited coverage to a single media market. New York, for example, has New York 1 News, a 24-hour service that began in 1992. The New York region also has News 12 cable channels, which cover local markets outside the city, such as Connecticut and New Jersey. Similar services include BayTV (San Francisco), Northwest Cable News (Seattle), NewsChannel 8 (Washington, D.C.), and ChicagoLand Television News. Regional sports channels—many of them affiliates of the national Fox Sports Network—also thrive in many of the same top television markets and regions that are home to multiple professional sports teams.

The general success rate of new services, like many mass-media products, has been about 10 to 15 percent, which means that about 85 to 90 percent of new cable channels fail or are bought out by another cable service. The most difficult challenge new channels face is getting onto enough cable systems—many with limited channel capacity—to become profitable. Although several basic cable services, such as ESPN and the USA Network (both now accessible in seventy million cable households), have been extremely successful, two basic channels—CNN and MTV—have gone beyond being successful: They have made their mark both on American society and on global culture.

CNN's Window to the World. Cable News Network (CNN), a 24-hour TV news channel, premiered in June 1980. CNN was the brainchild of Ted Turner, who helped revolutionize cable when he uplinked his small independent Atlanta station, WTBS, to superstation stature. In 1982, Turner also launched Headline News, adapting the concept of format radio to TV news. Every thirty minutes, Headline News rotates brief versions of the top national and international news stories, followed by sports, business, and entertainment segments. Together, these two cable services—CNN and Headline News—lost nearly $80 million before turning a profit of $13 million in 1985. By the early 1990s, the two news channels were making more than $200 million in annual operating profits. In addition, CNN started a radio news service in 1992 that now provides news to five hundred radio affiliates in the United States. By 1997, CNN was available in more than seventy million U.S. homes. It was also carried part-time by more than 250 local broadcasters who were not affiliated with a regular network or used CNN's 24-hour services to supplement their late-night schedules.

CNN emerged as a serious news competitor to ABC, CBS, and NBC during the Persian Gulf War in 1991, when two of its reporters were able to maintain a live phone link from a downtown Baghdad hotel during the initial U.S. bombing of the Iraqi capital. Even Iraq's military leaders watched the channel to get the American point of view. CNN's ratings soared—from 930,000 U.S. households before the crisis to as many as 10 million homes after the war began. About two hundred local broadcast stations with CNN agreements, including many network affiliates that ordinarily carried regular network coverage, switched to its crisis coverage. (Many of these local stations had already been carrying CNN during the night, when the networks did not offer news to affiliates.) Affecting more than network news, CNN's late-evening reports often made morning newspaper accounts obsolete because the newspapers had deadlines the previous evening.

Before Turner launched CNN in 1980 and well before the meteoric rise of the Internet, there were basically two major news cycles during a given day: in the morning, when many people read the day's newspaper or tuned in to a radio or TV news show, and in the evening, when people listened to the radio on the way home from work or watched the evening news on TV. Most industry experts thought CNN would fail because they didn't believe viewers wanted access to news twenty-four hours a day.

Although economic loss characterized CNN's first five years, Turner eventually proved that his formula for delivering the news had some distinct advantages over the offerings of the broadcast networks. First, CNN emphasized the news itself and created a reporting style that refused to transform news anchors into celebrities. Second, unlike network news departments, which had to edit and condense the day's news into a handful of stories for a half-hour show, the 24-hour format allowed CNN to deliver more timely news in greater detail, often offering live, unedited coverage of news conferences, press briefings, and special events. Third, CNN mastered continuous coverage of breaking news events, such as natural disasters, the 1989 student uprising in Beijing, and the 1991 Persian Gulf War. Liberated from the rigid program scheduling of the broadcast networks, viewers no longer had to wait for the revered evening network news to find a version of what was happening in the world.

"CNN serves as . . . an instant delivery system for dramatic footage from around the globe. In a crisis it becomes a kind of video bulletin board where key players can post messages to one another in full view of the world."

—Jay Rosen,
The Nation,
1991

Christiane Amanpour CNN
Tehran, Iran

Dubbed the "Chicken Noodle Network" by early critics, the Cable News Network built its reputation by scooping the broadcast networks. Today, reaching a potential worldwide audience of more than a billion people, CNN is known for its international presence and access to world leaders. With thirty-five bureaus around the globe—more than ABC, CBS, NBC, and Fox combined—CNN gets its cameras to the site of a story before the competition, and boasts such knowledgeable personnel as award-winning reporter Christiane Amanpour (who also files reports for *60 Minutes*).

Ted Turner and Rupert Murdoch: Match of the Media Moguls

In the 1997 movie *Tomorrow Never Dies*, James Bond's new adversary is Elliot Carver, head of an enormous global media conglomerate called Carver Media Group. With his global domination of news, Carver decides to start World War III to give his media outlets an interesting story to cover and gain a foothold in the huge Chinese media market. The invention of Elliot Carver is not all fiction. In some respects, he is a combination of Ted Turner, founder of CNN and vice chairman of Time Warner, the world's largest media corporation, and Rupert Murdoch, chairman and CEO of the rival News Corp. Although neither media mogul has been accused of trying to incite a world war, it seems their rivalry has had few other limits.

Ted Turner's empire had a modest start with his father's struggling billboard company. In the 1970s, he bought a small UHF station in Atlanta, which he renamed TBS (Turner Broadcasting Service). Then he spent more than $1 million for a satellite uplink to lift his independent signal to superstation stature. To lure a national audience and give his superstation program content, Turner bought the Atlanta Braves and the Atlanta Hawks in 1977; before this move, only broadcast networks controlled professional sports. Then, in 1980, Turner started what many viewed as a joke: a 24-hour cable news channel—CNN.

Rupert Murdoch

Critics called CNN the "Chicken Noodle Network," but when Turner added Headline News and turned a profit in 1985, the traditional networks began to take him more seriously. In the mid-1980s, Turner bought the famed MGM movie studio, including MGM's old movie libraries containing thousands of films, which were then used as programming for TBS—and later TNT (launched by Turner in 1988).

Rupert Murdoch's media conglomerate also began with inherited media holdings. Murdoch expanded his father's struggling Australian newspaper empire, taking over papers in Australia, New Zealand, Britain, and the United States. Murdoch, like Turner, saw television's potential, however, and determined to establish a global entertainment business based in the United States. Shocking the media world, Murdoch applied for (and received) American citizenship in 1985, allowing him to skirt the long-standing rule that prevents foreigners from owning more than 25 percent of any broadcasting facility. As an American citizen, Murdoch was able to purchase a number of TV stations and other media franchises. In 1988, a few years after Turner bought MGM, Murdoch bought the film studio Twentieth Century Fox and by that time had enough TV stations to create the Fox TV network, the first American network to be successfully established since ABC, CBS, and NBC. Then, in an audacious move that dwarfed Turner's purchase of the Braves and the Hawks, Murdoch paid double the going rate for American football broadcasting rights in 1994, forcing out longtime football broadcaster CBS. Fox not only had a steady stream of sports programming but also gained instant prominence as the network favored by the young male sports viewers who make up the audiences most sought after by market advertisers.

It's clear that Turner and Murdoch don't particularly care for each other. By many accounts, both men have legendary egos and ambitions to dominate the global media market. But their personal and political styles constantly clash. The younger Turner (by seven years) is sporty, likes to be photographed, and is a liberal Democrat. By contrast,

Murdoch is a workaholic, is thought to be solely concerned about the bottom line, does not court the media, and is a conservative Republican. Turner has called Murdoch a "very dangerous person, dangerous to democracy, dangerous to this nation." He has challenged Murdoch to a pay-per-view boxing bout and has publicly wished for Murdoch's demise. Murdoch has disparaged his rival's media empire, once attributing a change in CNN programming to Turner's marrying Jane Fonda and giving up lithium, which Turner once took to combat depression.

By the early to mid-1990s, the rivalry had grown a bit unequal, with Murdoch gaining the upper hand. In fact, there were times in the early 1990s when News Corp. considered purchasing the debt-laden Turner Broadcasting. Fortunately for Ted Turner, Time Warner bought his operations in 1995 for $6.5 billion, with Turner staying on as vice chairman of Time Warner and remaining the much wealthier president of Turner Broadcasting. No longer fearing a Murdoch takeover, Turner now had the critical mass of the largest media conglomerate behind him. Three months later, Murdoch retaliated by launching Fox News, a competing 24-hour news service. Not surprisingly, when Murdoch tried to get Time Warner's New York cable TV system (which had one million subscribers) to add his Fox News channel to the cable lineup in 1996, Time Warner declined. Murdoch cried foul play, then fought back by investing $1 billion in the satellite TV service Sky, which offers both cable and local broadcast programming, and bypasses any cable operation in the United States. News Corp. also purchased Asia's satellite news service Star TV. Offering round-the-clock news via satellite, Murdoch became the first worldwide competition to CNN.

Incidentally, with his purchase of Star TV, Murdoch has been accused of trying to court favor with China and gain access to the huge Chinese market. For example, he dropped BBC news service (which has been critical of the Chinese government) from Star TV. In addition, in the publishing realm, Murdoch-owned HarperCollins stopped the presses on *East and West*, the critical memoir written by former Hong Kong governor Chris Patten, and published instead *Deng Xiaoping: My Father*, a glowing biography of the recently deceased former prime minister of China, written by Deng's daughter.

In a deal that possibly stung Turner more than any to date, Murdoch purchased the L.A. Dodgers in 1998, joining Turner in the small fraternity of baseball-team owners. Beyond a mere rivalry, however, both Turner and Murdoch understand the strategic significance of sports as a central component of their media entertainment empires. More than movies or any other event, sports programming is expected to draw subscribers to cable and satellite TV. "We intend to . . . use sports as a battering ram and a lead offering in all our pay-television operations," Murdoch has said. True to his word, Murdoch has made claims on other prized sports institutions, including a thwarted attempt to purchase Manchester United, the most lucrative soccer club in Britain, for $1 billion. He has taken over an entire rugby league in Australia (ruining the game, according to some, by making it too commercial), paid $430 million for rights to broadcast German soccer through Tele-München, and acquired the rights to broadcast four of Italy's top soccer teams.

As media moguls like Murdoch solidify their holdings of both sports teams and the media channels where the competitions are broadcast, some critics have predicted a powerful globalizing trend. Viewers from around the world will be able to watch these games. At the same time, the era of free sports broadcasting may be coming to an end—in the future all games could be broadcast over cable or made into pay-per-view media events.

CNN has also made a big impact on international news coverage, a topic most networks devote little time to. While the networks were cutting costs by closing foreign news operations in the 1980s, CNN was opening them. By the mid-1990s, it operated nine bureaus in the United States and nineteen worldwide, stretching from London to Cairo to Moscow and Tokyo—more foreign news bureaus than any U.S. network. Today, CNN appears in more than 210 countries and territories around the globe. In 1992, its growing presence in Europe expedited the development of a rival news service, Euronews. A consortium of eleven state-owned European TV groups, Euronews emerged for cultural as well as economic reasons. One of its chief executives argued that "CNN is an American channel, an American point of view. The point of Euronews is to give the viewer back his memories."[3] Though Turner's CNN brought the world its first 24-hour TV news service, it continues to reflect American viewpoints and values.

The success of CNN proved that there is both a need and a lucrative market for 24-hour news. Spawning a host of competition in the United States and worldwide, CNN now battles for viewers with other 24-hour news providers, such as MSNBC, CNBC, Fox News, Euronews, Sky Broadcasting, and countless Web sites. But the legacy of CNN remains, and what was first dismissed as a silly idea is now considered a major force in the Information Age.

"I Want My MTV." The second basic cable service to dramatically change the world's cultural landscape is MTV (the Music Television Network), launched by Warner Communication in 1981 and purchased by Viacom in 1985. Now a highly profitable subsidiary of the merger that joined Paramount and Viacom in 1994, MTV and its global offspring—including MTV Asia, MTV Europe, MTV Brazil, MTV Japan, and MTV Latin America—reach nearly 250 million homes worldwide. When Poland escaped Soviet control in the late 1980s, its national television operation immediately began broadcasting MTV. By the late 1990s, more than a quarter of MTV's revenue came from international sources.

Although today MTV exerts a powerful influence on global culture, it was slow to develop in at least one significant way. In its formative years, MTV gave little airtime to African American artists. This history recalls the 1950s and the problems black rock and rollers faced in getting mainstream radio play. In the early 1980s, however, MTV's reluctance to play music videos by black artists was related not to racial tensions but to the economics of the cable system. At that time, most cable companies were operating primarily in affluent white communities in U.S. suburbs. These were the areas that could most easily afford cable. Since rock had been dominated by white male groups throughout the 1970s, MTV determined that white suburban teens probably wanted to see similar groups in their music videos. It took Michael Jackson's *Thriller* album in 1982 to break down music video's early color barrier. The album's large crossover appeal, coupled with the expansion of cable into more urban areas, opened the door to far more diverse videos. With hip-hop's rise in popularity throughout the 1980s and 1990s among both black and white audiences, MTV began to add more rap, soul, and R&B videos to the rotation, as well as programs like *Yo!* and *Jams Countdown*. Through its daily programming, MTV helped sell African American hip-hop culture—with its rap beats, baggy clothes, urban sensibility, and street language—to suburban America and the world at large.

By the end of the 1980s, MTV reported that its annual profits had passed $50 million and that nearly thirty million viewers tuned in at least once during the week. Throughout the 1980s, it sought more and more control over music-video distribution and exhibition, employing two monopoly tactics to ensure dominance. First, MTV paid record companies for exclusive rights to the most popular music videos (for periods ranging from thirty days to one year), thereby preventing access by other music-

Since 1981, MTV has helped shape popular music and youth culture in the United States and around the world. The network has successfully adapted its American formula for viewers in Russia, Japan, Brazil, and elsewhere. Here, Arturo Hernandez, a veejay for MTV Latin America, hosts an event on the beach in Acapulco, Mexico.

video services. Although this was a form of payola, federal laws prohibiting this practice applied only to broadcasting, not to cable. According to *Billboard* magazine, MTV paid CBS Records $8 million in 1984, covering CBS's total music-video production costs for a two-year period. During the mid-1980s, MTV also signed exclusive deals with RCA Records, MCA, Geffen, Warner Music, Atlantic, Polygram, and Capitol Records.[4]

Second, MTV signed agreements with the major cable systems to ensure that it would become the music-video network in all the main cable markets. Those cable companies with limited channel capacity were often reluctant to carry more than one music channel. Competing services, like Ted Turner's attempt to start a music-video channel in 1984, were quickly countered by VH1. After MTV launched this second channel, which was geared toward the baby-boom generation and the parents of the MTV crowd, it was able to buy out Turner within a month. It also began to impose fees on cable services if they refused to carry the new MTV–VH1 package. Late in the 1980s, a service called Hit Video USA, trying to compete with MTV, charged that exclusive contracts constituted an MTV monopoly over music-video distribution and exhibition. The case was settled out of court, and by the late 1990s, MTV remained the only major player in rock videos.

"MTV—Music Television. You may think of it as the channel that rattles your china . . . and hypnotizes your children, but what you may want to know is that MTV is responsible for a complete revolution in the music business."
—Diane Sawyer,
Primetime Live,
1990

Like Euronews, other countries and companies have tried to challenge MTV's dominance. Four major international record companies—EMI, Polygram, Sony, and Warner Music—launched a music channel in Germany in the early 1990s. In the mid-1990s, Mexico started Telehit to compete with MTV Latin America. In 1994, the News Corp. started Channel V for its Star TV service in India, and brought music videos to India that featured a unique regional mix of Hindi film songs and Hinglish. MTV India adapted by regionalizing its service in India and its other Asian markets. Canada, however, represents MTV's toughest challenge to date. Its stricter regulations have blocked MTV's access to many of Canada's cable systems while promoting a Canadian music-video network, MuchMusic (which began offering its service in the United States in 1994).

The major recording labels, spending as much as $50 million a year to produce videos in the 1990s, have grown dependent on MTV's power to certify a hit recording. These companies have also criticized the small group of MTV executives who wade through the hundreds of new videos released each week and judge which 10 to

15 percent are fit for MTV play. The recording companies want to see more of their products on MTV's regular music rotation, which usually accommodates about sixty recordings per week.

Although the plan was scrapped in mid-1995, for a while the major recording labels contemplated challenging MTV by launching a joint American music-video channel controlled by the recording industry. The Justice Department, however, warned that the major labels' involvement in "exhibition" might constitute a "vertical monopoly": tight control of all three arms of a U.S. media industry—production, distribution, *and* exhibition. MTV itself is heavily involved in distributing and exhibiting videos but is not involved in actually *producing* them.

MTV began to stray from a rotation of music videos in the early 1990s to incorporate more original programming, including the reality-based soap opera *The Real World*, the cartoon *Beavis and Butt-head*, and the dating show *Singled Out*. The shift was an effort to provide advertisers with more regular audiences during specific viewing times, but it ended up infuriating record labels and many MTV viewers by further narrowing the channel's video playlists. Numerous anti-MTV sites sprang up on the Internet, along with an alt.mtv-sucks Usenet newsgroup. By the end of the 1990s, the cable channel was attempting to put the music back into MTV by developing new programming that organized video airplay around artist promotion, band biographies, and fan interviews. The retooling, along with an interactive Web site that allows users to sample videos online, join chat rooms, and submit comments to be read on the air, lifted ratings and reenergized the cable channel. In 1998, MTV also launched "The Suite from MTV and VH1" for viewers who want to see a greater variety of music videos. For about $10 a month, a subscriber can receive six specialized music channels—rock, independent label, Spanish-language, country, soul, and jazz/new age/adult-contemporary—via digital compression technology.

As a subsidiary of one of the world's largest media conglomerates, MTV draws more fire for its cultural than for its economic impact. Many critics worry that its influence has eroded local culture-specific traits among the world's young people and substituted an overabundance of U.S. culture in its place. Others argue that MTV has contributed to the decline of conversation and civil discourse through its often sexually suggestive and rapid-fire style. Defenders of the network, however, point out that MTV and cable have created a global village, giving the world a common language. They also applaud a variety of MTV's special programs on issues ranging from drug addiction to racism and social activism. MTV's Rock the Vote campaign, for instance, helped register one million young voters, who may have swung the 1992 presidential election to Bill Clinton. In Hungary, after the decline of Soviet influence, young people started an influential political party that restricted membership to people under thirty years of age, arguing that only young members would not be nostalgic for the return to a more totalitarian regime. Informally, the Hungarians and the press called the new political organization "the MTV party."

The physical style of MTV—from shaky camera footage and quick cuts to bright colors and dazzling visual innovations—has also had, and continues to have, an influence on the media landscape. Touching everything from movies to TV drama and commercials, the MTV style is one that constantly breaks rules and establishes new conventions. Besides turning to MTV for visual inspiration, Hollywood now looks to the channel as a farm league of sorts for its hot new directors; a well-produced music video is considered an ideal audition reel. For many critics, however, MTV has become a virus, its ceaseless succession of disconnected three-minute mini-musicals and compressed narratives infecting most major sound and visual media with plenty of style but little substance.

Beyond the world of music, one of MTV's major programming innovations has been the Nickelodeon channel. Tom Freston, chairman of MTV, says Nickelodeon

"I gotta PBS mind in an MTV world."
—Jimmy Buffett, song lyric, 1999

provides "as wide a variety of television for children as exists anywhere." Freston believes that Nickelodeon has changed the way children and teens think about television: "It's interesting—if you talk to kids who are nine years old, they don't see CBS, NBC, and ABC as being the big places. And that generation is going to grow up a generation in whose mind there's more parity between cable networks and broadcast networks."[5] In an era in which the major networks abandoned children's programming—except for cartoons—because they weren't lucrative enough, competitors such as PBS and Nickelodeon have tried to fill the gap. As Nick at Nite and MTV kids reach adulthood, they no longer view broadcast programs as superior to cable.

premium cable

Besides basic programming, cable offers a wide range of special, or *premium*, services. These include movie channels, such as HBO and Showtime; pay-per-view (PPV) programs; and interactive (two-way) services that allow consumers to use their televisions to bank, shop, play games, and access the Internet. Subscribers to such services pay extra fees in addition to the fee for basic cable. In the early days of cable, there was only a single monthly charge, but with HBO providing movies, a new source of revenue—the premium, or deluxe, tier—was added to the subscription mix. In fact, luring customers to premium channels has plenty of incentives for cable companies: The cost to them is $4 to $6 a month per subscriber to carry a premium channel, but they then charge customers $10 or more per month and reap a nice profit.

The HBO Alternative. By far the oldest and most influential premium service is Home Box Office (HBO), a subsidiary of Time Warner, one of the nation's largest owners of cable companies. HBO launched the first premium cable service in 1972, when it began offering services locally in Wilkes-Barre, Pennsylvania. In 1975, HBO became the first network to use satellites for regular transmission of TV programming. HBO lost money in the beginning. At the time, only two cable systems had invested the $100,000 required for the large earth stations that were technically necessary to retrieve a satellite signal. Between 1975 and 1980, however, the number of cable earth stations grew to seventeen hundred and HBO became a success.

Although HBO reaches less than one-third the audience of a popular basic service, it has remained the dominant premium service, selling monthly subscriptions to twenty-five million homes by 1998. The next closest competitors were another Time Warner service, Cinemax, with almost nine million subscribers, and Viacom's premium services—Showtime, the Movie Channel, and Flix—which combined have 14.8 million subscribers. New premium film channels such as the Sundance Channel (owned by actor Robert Redford, Showtime, and Polygram) and the Independent Film Channel emerged with the growing market of independent films in the mid-1990s. The movie business initially feared that HBO would be a detriment to film attendance in theaters. Eventually, though, HBO and the other premium channels brought a lucrative source of income to the movie studios, which earn roughly a 15 percent share of premium cable's profits. With premium cable locking up the rights to feature-length movies after their initial theater runs, film companies recognized that they could recoup losses from a weak theater run by extending a film's life. This could be done not just via television or neighborhood second-run theaters but through lucrative arrangements with premium cable.

In the early 1980s, when there was little competition, HBO dictated to movie studios which films it wanted and how much it was willing to pay. HBO and other premium channels ran into trouble, however, as videotapes became the preferred method of viewing movies after their theater runs. Both VCRs and PPV (pay-per-view) options brought competition to the movie channels. In the mid-1980s, film studios started releasing movies to PPV and to video stores before offering them to movie channels. The new competition forced the movie channels to expand their services. HBO, for example, began developing its own programming—from children's shows like *Fraggle Rock* to comedies like *The Larry Sanders Show*, an Emmy-winning satire of late-night talk shows.

> "As a pay service, we have to be different. And different doesn't always mean naked bodies, epithets or foul language."
>
> —Seth Abraham, CEO of HBO, 1999

What film studios clearly did not like was HBO's production of its own feature-length films. In 1982, HBO entered into an arrangement with CBS and Columbia Pictures (later bought by Sony) to form a new production house, TriStar Pictures. Many in the movie industry charged that HBO's movie productions constituted vertical integration with involvement in production, distribution, and exhibition. They argued that when Time Inc. (before its merger with Warner) began making movies through HBO and TriStar, the media conglomerate was permitted to do something that film studios could not do. A Supreme Court decision in 1948 had broken up the film industry's vertical structure by forcing the major studios to sell their theaters, the exhibition part of their operations. Time Inc., on the other hand, was the second-largest owner of cable systems—the movie studio equivalent of owning theaters. Since so many cable companies and services existed, though, the government did not seriously challenge HBO's role in movie production.

Pay-per-View and Interactive Cable. *Pay-per-view* services, which began in 1985, allow customers to select a particular movie for a onetime $3 or $4 charge, payable to the local cable service, or $25 to $60 for a special onetime event, such as a championship boxing match, a professional wrestling event, or a rock concert. When these services started in late 1985, they were available in fewer than 150,000 households. By the late 1990s, approximately thirty-two million of the country's sixty-five million cable subscribers had PPV capacity. Generally, the movie studios make a hefty profit from PPV companies, asking as much as 50 percent of what the PPV and cable companies earn from subscribers who view the movies. The studios' cut from PPV is substantially higher than their share from home-movie rentals (about 20 percent) and premium movie channels (about 15 percent). In the 1990s, studios started buying shares of these services, but by the end of the decade it had become clear that consumers still preferred renting videos over viewing PPV movies. This is because video stores can typically release movies about a month and a half before pay-per-view services get a chance to offer them. While the PPV market still generates about $1.5 billion a year with movies, adult content, and special sporting events, it is unclear how long PPV will be around. Request Television, which has dominated PPV services along with Viewer's Choice, folded in 1998 because of uncertain economic viability.

Another type of cable service features *interactive*, or two-way, *channels*. When equipped with two-way technology, such systems allow users to send signals upstream or back to the headend. (Most systems are one-way and can send signals only downstream to homes.) Interactive cable can connect households to their banks, where customers can pay bills or transfer money. Some cable services also permit police burglary units and fire stations to monitor homes and apartments. Like the bulk of cable programming, the most frequent type of two-way service involves entertainment. In 1991, Interactive Network began offering video games to cable consumers, including play-along versions of *Wheel of Fortune* and *Jeopardy*. It also provided services that allowed viewers to guess the next play during a football game or the identity of the villain in *Murder, She Wrote*. The limiting factor for interactive services, though, is bandwidth. Because interactive services require more space to send two-way information on cable (in contrast to the one-way communication of regular cable TV channels), most cable operators are unwilling to offer this feature at the expense of lucrative one-way channels.

Cable Radio. In addition to movies and videos on request, many cable systems now offer CD-quality premium audio services, sometimes called *cable radio*. Routed through a consumer's stereo equipment, cable radio companies like Music Choice and Digital Music Service (DMX) provide 24-hour music channels uninterrupted by ads. Originally known as Digital Cable Radio in the 1980s, Music Choice was the first digital audio service. It featured separate audio channels playing all kinds of prepackaged musical styles ready for home audiotaping, or as background music for business environments. DMX premiered in 1991, and by the mid-1990s it offered sixty channels, twenty-four hours a day, ranging from classical music to rap. Such satellite-delivered channels are another example of media convergence; they link cable, sound recordings, and home-stereo units for a monthly fee of about $9, less than the price of a new CD.

Yet by the late 1990s, interest in premium audio services had peaked. By 1998, DMX served about two million home and business subscribers, with little growth projected. Audio developments on the Internet, such as hundreds of live-streaming radio stations and free downloadable digital music files, further threatened premium cable radio services.

■ direct-broadcast satellites: cable without wires

Because of its dependence on communication satellites, cable TV has always been on the cutting edge of technological developments. Now many of those advances are posing an economic threat to cable in the same ways that cable challenged traditional broadcasting in the 1970s. Of all the emerging technologies, including the Internet, *direct-broadcast satellites* (DBS) present the biggest challenge to the existing cable and television industries.

The earliest earth-station antennas, or dishes—set up in the mid-1970s to receive cable programming—were large, measuring twenty to forty feet in diameter, and expensive (with FCC license fees adding to their high cost). From the beginning, however, engineers worked to reduce the size and cost of the receiving dishes in order to develop a consumer model. In regions and countries with rugged terrain, the installation of cable wiring was not always easy or possible.

To protect the fledgling cable business throughout the 1970s and 1980s, the FCC restricted the development of DBS companies, which get their programming from the same satellite channels (such as CNN, MTV, ESPN, and HBO) that supply the regular cable industry. In the United States, rural communities bypassed FCC restrictions by investing in seven- to ten-foot receiving dishes and downlinking, for free, the same channels that cable companies were supplying to wired communities. These home-satellite dishes, like early cable systems, appeared mostly in sprawling but sparsely populated areas that were too costly for cable companies to wire. Receiving dishes, visible from many interstate highways, began springing up on farms by the late 1970s. Initially, households could pick up channels once they had invested in a large receiving dish, which ranged from $2,000 to $3,000. Not surprisingly, satellite programmers launched a flurry of legal challenges against farmers and small-town residents who were receiving their signals. Rural communities countered that they had the rights to the airspace above their own property; the satellite firms contended that their signals were being stolen. With the law unclear, a number of cable channels began scrambling their signals. As a result, most satellite users had to buy or rent descramblers and subscribe to services, as cable customers did.

From home satellites, the DBS business developed. Signal scrambling spawned companies that provided both receiving dishes and satellite program services for a monthly fee. In 1978, Japanese companies, which had been experimenting with "wire-

> "A buddy of mine with one of them new **satellite dishes** actually gets channels from Neptune."
> —David Letterman, 1996

less cable" alternatives for a number of years, launched the first DBS system in Florida. With gradual improvements in satellite technology, the diameters of satellite receiving dishes decreased from more than twenty feet to three feet in a few years. By 1995, consumers could order satellite dishes the size of a large pizza.

With the emergence of cable as a lucrative industry, the last FCC and technical obstacles gradually fell away, and full-blown DBS services began in 1994. Initially, the FCC authorized a French company, Thomson Consumer Electronics, which had acquired the RCA brand name from General Electric, to sell DBS dishes. After Thomson/RCA sold one million units, the FCC permitted Sony to enter the U.S. DBS market. Gradually, the commission let more licensees into the DBS game. Early rapid sales of Thomson/RCA's DBS systems ranked it among the fastest starting technologies in media history.

By the mid-1990s, DBS companies such as DirecTV/USSB, PrimeStar, and EchoStar offered consumers most of the channels and tiers of service that cable companies carried, often at a slightly lower monthly cost (plus the initial investment of $300 to $1,000 for installing the small-dish antenna). In addition, DBS systems carried more than fifty channels reserved for myriad PPV movies. Thus, DBS presented far more options than what was available on the three or four PPV movie channels offered on most conventional cable systems, which were limited by channel capacity. Buoyed by high consumer interest and competing in large cities as well as rural areas, DBS firms today are challenging the long-standing monopoly status of most cable systems, offering distinct advantages—and disadvantages—compared with cable.

On the upside, DBS's digital technology is superior to standard cable and broadcast signals, providing laser-disk-quality pictures and CD-quality sound. Another big drawing card for DBS is the ability to offer sports packages that give subscribers nationwide access to all the games of professional sports leagues—including football, baseball, soccer, and men's and women's basketball—that aren't carried locally on broadcast networks or basic cable channels. On the downside, along with the initial start-up cost for consumers, DBS systems deliver one satellite signal at a time and do not allow consumers to tape a program on a VCR while they watch another show. In addition, until 1999, when Congress passed legislation allowing DBS to carry local broadcast systems, DBS did not pick up an area's local broadcast signals, which were not uplinked to satellites. This meant that most subscribers had to use a local cable company, an outside TV antenna, or rabbit-ear antennas on their TV set to get the local PBS, independent, and broadcast network programming. Nevertheless, by 1999 DBS services attracted eleven million customers in the United States, although high rates of customer turnover plague the industry. Moreover, mergers began to reduce customer choices, with DirecTV, the No. 1 DBS company, buying out No. 2 PrimeStar in 1999, thus securing nearly 65 percent of the DBS market.

Introducing our newest Digital Satellite System. Imitations are sure to follow.

But don't be fooled. For the most advanced DSS® System available, you want the new

[*Separate favorite channel lists make it easier to find something you want to watch.*]

RCA brand DSS System. Its remote has One-Button Record. Highlight a show on

[*One-Button Record means the end of VCR programming as you know it.*]

the program guide, press record and it programs your VCR for you. And our Personal Profiles feature lets several people create separate favorite channel lists, which you call up by clicking on a picture of yourself. You can also access the most exciting movies and events DIRECTV® and USSB have ever offered, with laser disc quality picture and CD sound capability. The new RCA DSS System. We were the first to introduce it, so who better to improve it? **Changing Entertainment. Again. RCA**

This mid-1990s ad for RCA digital satellite dishes recalls a 1902 advertisement of the Victor Talking Machine Company, which featured a similar dog selling Victrola phonographs. RCA later purchased the Victor company, and the dog peering into the phonograph's megaphone-like speaker (apparently recognizing a lifelike voice) became RCA Victor's enduring symbol.

In the short run, DBS does not appear to threaten cable, which had a clear early advantage in providing the broadcast signals that carried network programming. In addition, telephone companies and cable companies are developing prototype cable channels—through digital compression—that transform standard cable services into five-hundred-channel systems that also include Internet access. This development would counter DBS's main advantage: offering more channels and better-quality images. In the long run, DBS may pose a bigger threat to the home-video and movie-rental market. For consumers who rent a lot of movies, care about the quality of the image, and want to make their own copies, it may eventually be cheaper and more convenient to subscribe to a DBS service.

ownership and business issues in cable

Although there are more than 11,500 cable systems in the United States, most of these systems are controlled by **multiple-system operators** (MSOs), a shrinking number of large corporations that each own many cable systems. By 1998, the Top 12 MSOs controlled the lines into 70 percent of all households wired for cable. (See Table 6.2.) Once again, the economic trend points to an industry slouching toward oligopoly, with a handful of megamedia firms controlling programming for future generations. Like the Internet, however, cable and DBS hold the promise of offering more specialized channels on which the diverse needs of individuals and communities might be met.

at&t and time warner— the major players

Since the early 1980s, two giant companies have dominated the acquisition of smaller cable firms and the accumulation of cable subscribers. TCI (Tele-Communications Inc.), under the long tenure of CEO John Malone, accounted for 2.1 million subscribers in 1982; by 1998, TCI's subscriber base was 13.1 million out of nearly 70 million U.S. cable households. Early in 1999, AT&T, the nation's dominant telephone corporation, acquired TCI as a subsidiary and renamed the cable division AT&T Broadband & Internet Services (BIS). The second-largest MSO, Time Warner Cable, is a division of the world's largest media company. Time Warner had 1.9 million subscribers in 1982. In 1995, when Time Warner bought Cablevision Industries—the eighth-largest MSO—the joint venture meant control of cable circuits in 11.7 million homes. By the late 1990s, after a series of acquisitions that had gone on for fifteen years, AT&T/BIS and Time Warner provided cable service to more than 38 percent of U.S. households.

Beyond their cable-subscriber base, both AT&T and Time Warner are also major providers of programming services. For its part, AT&T—through its Liberty Media Corporation programming subsidiary—owns or has interest in the Discovery Channel, the QVC home-shopping network, Black Entertainment Television (BET), American Movie Classics, Telemundo, the Encore and Starz movie channels, and four professional sports teams, including the New York Knicks. Liberty Media also owns parts of several other cable operations and two-thirds interest in MacNeil/Lehrer Productions, which creates news programming for public television. AT&T's TCI acquisition also includes the AtHome Corporation, a high-speed Internet data service that AT&T hopes to sell in a package with its cable and telephone services.

Rank	Company	Headquarters	Basic Subscriptions
1	Time Warner Cable	Stamford, Conn.	12,600,000
2	AT&T Broadband & Internet Services	Englewood, Colo.	10,843,000
3	MediaOne Group	Boston, Mass.	4,966,000
4	Comcast Cable Communications Inc.	Philadelphia, Pa.	4,551,600
5	Cox Communications Inc.	Atlanta, Ga.	3,855,582
6	Cablevision Systems Corp.	Woodbury, N.Y.	3,438,000
7	Charter Communications Inc.	St. Louis, Mo.	2,364,113
8	Adelphia Communications Corp.	Coudersport, Pa.	2,304,325
9	Century Communications Corp.	New Canaan, Conn.	1,338,000
10	InterMedia Partners	San Francisco, Calif.	1,312,246

Note: AT&T Broadband & Internet Services (ranked No. 2, and incorporating the former TCI, Inc.) will be No. 1 when it completes acquisitions of MediaOne (No. 3) and its remaining interest in Lenfest Communications (No. 11). Other pending acquisitions include AT&T's (in partnership with No. 7 Charter) purchase of InterMedia Partners (No. 10).

Source: Television Digest, June 14, 1999. Copyright © 1999 Warren Publishing, Inc.

In 1995, Time Warner buoyed its position as the world's largest media corporation by offering $6.5 billion to acquire Turner Broadcasting, which included superstation WTBS, CNN, Headline News, TNT, and CNN Radio. Although some FCC staffers raised concerns about sanctioning the extended economic power of Time Warner, the commission formally approved the deal in the fall of 1996. Time Warner—with its magazine, movie, publishing, television, and music divisions—also produces content for its cable services. In addition to acquiring Turner and starting the WB television network, Time Warner is the parent company of Cinemax and HBO, and holds interests in BET, Entertainment Television (E!), Comedy Central, and Court TV. Time Warner is also investing heavily in the Internet with its Road Runner consumer service and a merger with regional phone company U.S. West's Internet service.

A number of cable critics worry that the trend toward fewer owners will limit the number of viewpoints, options, and innovations available on cable. The response from the cable industry is that, given the tremendous capital investment it takes to run cable, DBS, and other media enterprises, media conglomerates are necessary to buy up struggling companies and keep them afloat. This argument suggests that without today's MSOs many smaller cable ventures in programming would not be possible.

Another view maintains that although cable TV firms compete among themselves, it is a limited type of competition, and it protects them against rivals: "That trend is not only a business marketplace issue. It also concerns the U.S. marketplace of ideas. It puts at risk the principle of open access for all citizens to a broad range of competitive information resources."[6] The 1996 Telecommunications Act does allow phone companies to compete for cable's territory. Indeed, telephone conglomerate AT&T acquired TCI in 1999 and in the same year forged a partnership to offer telephone service over Time Warner's cable systems in thirty-three states. The two deals give AT&T—chiefly a long-distance telephone company after an antitrust lawsuit forced it to give up its local phone business in the early 1980s—the ability to offer local phone service via cable to 40 percent of U.S. households. After completion of its merger with MediaOne, another giant cable firm, and other acquisitions, AT&T is expected to have a potential cable-phone customer base of 60 percent of all U.S. households. Concerns have surfaced, though, at least in smaller markets, that cable and telephone services will merge into giant communications overlords, fixing prices without benefit of competition. These concerns raise an important question: In an economic climate in which fewer owners control the circulation of ideas and communication, what happens to new ideas or controversial communication that may not always be profitable to circulate?

the business of cable

In 1970, there were about twenty-five hundred small cable systems operating in the United States; by 1998, about eleven thousand systems were running. In 1976, there were two basic satellite-delivered services, two premium services, and no such thing as pay-per-view. Twenty years later, more than 130 basic services were competing for channel space with twenty premium services and eight PPV companies. Since 1980, basic cable rates have more than quadrupled in price, rising from about $7 per month to more than $31. Monthly prices for premium services, however, have essentially remained the same—less than $9 a month per channel in 1980 and 1996. By the mid-1990s, total revenues from cable rivaled those of broadcasting: $30 billion a year.

The cable industry employed about 23,000 people in 1978 and more than 120,000 by the late 1990s. As in the movie business, the cable workforce serves the production, distribution, and exhibition sectors of the industry. The production end includes the hundreds of providers who either make original programs or purchase older TV programming for national and global distribution. At the local level, production also includes staffers, volunteers, and student interns who create programming on access channels. The distribution sector includes the delivery systems and PPV services that transmit programming via satellite, then via coaxial or fiber-optic cable. The exhibition branch of the industry encompasses thousands of local cable systems, which require programming, sales, technical, and administrative divisions to operate.

alternative voices

After suffering through years of rising rates and limited expansion of service, some of the smallest cities in America have decided to challenge the private monopolies of cable giants like TCI and Comcast by building competing publicly owned cable systems. So far, the municipally owned cable systems number only in the hundreds, and can be found in places like Glasgow, Kentucky; Cedar Falls, Iowa; and Newnan, Georgia. In most cases, they're operated by the community-owned, nonprofit electric utilities. There are more than two thousand such municipal utilities across the United States, serving about 14 percent of Americans and creating the potential for more municipal utilities to expand into communications services.

Cities with public cable systems argue that with no competition, the private cable corporations have been slow to replace older coaxial cables with high-speed fiber-optic networks. Moreover, the lower population densities of small towns and rural areas means that these towns are often the last places to get innovative cable services. By building municipal cable systems, these cities are making sure that they won't be the last stop on the information highway.

TCI derided one proposed municipal cable project in tiny Alta, Iowa (population 1,820), as "creeping socialism." Nevertheless, 88 percent of the voters there approved the establishment of a new municipal cable and telecommunications system in 1997 despite an expensive campaign waged against it by TCI.

The first town to take on an existing private cable provider was Glasgow, Kentucky, which built its own municipal cable system in 1989. The town of fourteen thousand now has seven thousand municipal cable customers. William J. Ray, the

Since its launch on cable's Comedy Central in 1993, *Politically Incorrect with Bill Maher* has paired such diverse guests as shock rocker Marilyn Manson and *The Brady Bunch*'s Florence Henderson. Celebrities debating the news and expressing ardent opinions proved to be enormously successful, offering an alternative to traditional network political coverage. Three years after its debut, ABC bought the rights to the show and began airing it after *Nightline.*

town's Electric Plant Board superintendent and the visionary behind the municipal communications system, argues that municipally run services are not a new idea:

> Cities have long been turning a limited number of formerly private businesses into public-works projects. This happens only when the people making up a local government believe that the service has become so essential to the citizens that it is better if it is operated by the government. In colonial America, it was all about drinking water. In the twentieth century, the issue was electric power and natural gas service. Now, we are facing the same transformation in broadband networks.

For the customer, competition in the local cable market is beneficial. For example, in 1994 in Cedar Falls, Iowa, voters approved the creation of a new municipal broadband fiber-optic cable network, capable of cable and Internet service. With the new challenges of competition, commercial provider TCI then decided to upgrade its own cable system in the city. The benefits of competition in Cedar Falls angered the nearby residents of Waterloo, Iowa, who were served only by TCI. In Waterloo, TCI offered only thirty-six channels for the same monthly fee that brought seventy-six channels to Cedar Falls' TCI customers. Only by threatening to build their own municipal cable system did Waterloo city officials get TCI to rebuild the Waterloo cable system and add more channels.

A 1998 survey stated that almost a quarter of the country's two thousand municipal utilities plan to offer cable and high-speed Internet services. How will commercial cable operators fend off this unprecedented competition? William Ray of Glasgow, Kentucky, has the answer: "If cable operators are afraid of cities competing with them, there is a defense that is impregnable—they can charge reasonable rates, offer consummate customer service, improve their product, and conduct their business as if they were a guest that owes their existence to the benevolence of the city that has invited them in."

cable, dbs, and implications for democracy

When cable emerged to challenge traditional broadcasting in the 1970s, expectations were high, not unlike today's expectations for the Internet. When cable communication mushroomed in the 1980s, network supremacy over television ended. Offering more than new competition, cable's increased channel capacity provided the promise of access. With more channels, it was believed that access on cable would create vibrant debates, allowing ordinary citizens a voice via television. Access channels have, in fact, provided some opportunities for citizens to participate in democracy and even create their own programs. But by the late 1990s, major cities like Kansas City had decided that public-access channels need not even be a requirement for cable franchises. For the most part, cable and DBS have come to follow the one-way broadcast model: Their operators choose the programming from a few service providers, with little input from citizens and consumers.

Most cable channels have become heavily dependent on recycling old television shows and movies to fill up their program schedules. In some ways, this has been beneficial. Cable, particularly through programming like Nickelodeon's Nick at Nite and TVLand, has become a repository for TV shows that are passed along from generation to generation. Ultimately, however, except for C-Span, local access channels, and some interactive services, cable still has not developed its potential to become a clear alternative to traditional broadcasting services. But, with the competition along the information highway and with telephone companies able to deliver TV signals and the Internet through fiber-optic wires, cable's direction seems likely to change.

> "It is not conceivable to me that the revolution we're now going through—which is in my view even deeper, and faster, than the Industrial Revolution—is going to occur smoothly. It cannot." —Alvin Toffler, futurist, 1993

In the broadest sense, the development of cable has always posed a contradiction. On the one hand, cable has dramatically increased the number of channels and offered previously unserved groups the opportunity to address their particular issues on television. On the other hand, cable has undermined the network era during which television worked as a kind of social adhesive, giving most of the population a common bond, a set of shared programs. The concern remains: Does the onslaught of cable and developments such as the Internet create a fragmented culture in which individuals pursue their narrow personal agendas at the expense of larger social concerns?

In the coming years, many communities will experience the convergence of computers and modems, satellites, fax machines, and television sets. Such convergence may make us homebound, freeing us from traditional participation in and travel to workplaces and schools. New technologies have the capacity, of course, to simultaneously bring us together in cyberspace and isolate us physically from one another. Another large issue democracies must face is the increasing control of a few giant media corporations over our means of communication: How will we direct cable, DBS, and new technologies to serve social agendas while they continue to meet consumer and business needs? As with the Internet, the gulf between the information rich and the information poor remains wide, increasing concerns about who will have access to—and who will be able to afford—cable and other new media technologies.

REVIEW QUESTIONS

Early Technology and the Development of Cable

1. What is CATV, and what were its advantages over broadcast television?

2. How did cable pose a challenge to broadcasting, and how did the FCC respond to cable's early development?

Cable's Franchising and Regulation Wars

3. What is the cable franchising process, and how did it work in the 1980s?

4. Why isn't the cable industry treated more like a utility company and a common carrier?

5. What were the syndex rules, and why were they repealed?

6. What were the major differences between the cable acts of 1984 and 1992?

7. How did the Telecommunications Act of 1996 change the economic shape and future of the cable industry?

Narrowcasting Challenges Broadcasting

8. What are the differences between basic cable service and premium services?

9. How have CNN and MTV influenced culture worldwide?

10. How and why did HBO develop? How has HBO threatened the film industry?

11. What are PPV and interactive cable services?

12. What is DBS? How much of a threat are its services to the cable industry?

Ownership and Business Issues

13. Who are the two biggest players in the cable business, and what are some of their major holdings?

14. What are the three basic divisions in the organization of the cable business?

15. In terms of fostering democracy, what are cable's main advantages over traditional broadcasting?

QUESTIONING THE MEDIA

1. How many cable channels do you watch regularly? What programs do you watch? What attracts you to a channel?

2. If you controlled a cable public-access channel in your community, what would be your channel's goal? What could we do to make public-, government-, or educational-access programming more appealing? Should we?

3. Do you think the must-carry rules violate a cable operator's First Amendment rights? Why or why not?

4. CNN and MTV have changed our society as well as global culture. Have these changes been positive or negative? Explain.

5. Do you think DBS will be able to compete with cable? Why or why not?

6. Some critics argue that we no longer participate in traditional neighborhoods and that cable has played a role in fragmenting citizens, keeping us in our homes. Do you agree or disagree? What has cable done well, and in what ways has it adversely affected society?

SEARCHING THE INTERNET

http://www.ncta.com
The site for the cable industry's major trade association, the National Cable Television Association, details cable history, the latest developments in cable technology, and industry news.

http://www.broadcastingcable.com
The online version of *Broadcasting & Cable*, a weekly magazine geared toward executives and managers of the television, radio, and cable industries.

http://www.comcentral.com/southpark
The official *South Park* site, which offers animated *South Park* mini-clips, episode guides and storyboards, interviews with the show's creators, chat room discussions, and the *South Park* store.

http://www.mtv.com
MTV Online offers a comprehensive database of music videos, show information, music news, tips on where to find local bands, music reviews, and chat rooms.

http://www.cnn.com
One of the most sophisticated sites online, *CNN Interactive* offers constantly updated news stories, as well as news archives, a daily almanac, on-air transcripts, and other services.

http://www.tci.com
The Web site of TCI, one of the world's largest cable and telecommunications companies, now part of AT&T Broadband & Internet Services.

THE CRITICAL PROCESS

In Brief

Working alone or in a group, propose a new cable channel that does two things: (1) It should find a unique market niche, and (2) it should be *successful*, meaning it should satisfy the demands of the television industry by drawing an audience that appeals to advertisers. Keep in mind that only 10 to 15 percent of new cable channels succeed. Lists of existing and planned cable channels are available online at the National Cable Television Association's Web site at <www.ncta.com>.

Consider the following questions while creating your proposal: What kinds of programs would run each day? What sort of audience would the channel try to reach? Why would this market be attractive to advertisers?

In Depth

Divide the class into groups of four to six. Each group should prepare an editorial for presentation on public-access cable. The editorial should be roughly four to five minutes in length (750–1,000 words) and should address a controversial or important public issue, such as equal access to the information highway, the state of media education, the impact of talk radio and television talk shows, or the advantages of wealth in the legal process.

1. As a group, draft the editorial. Consult with your instructor for topic ideas and writing strategies. Rewrite the final copy of the editorial.

2. Next, divide each group into subgroups of two or three. One subgroup should approach (either by phone, mail, or face-to-face meeting) a local cable-access channel and request time to read the editorial. The other subgroup should approach a local commercial television station with the same editorial. Tell the station manager or news director that you would like to get your idea onto the public airwaves. Ask how your request might be accommodated.

3. Designate a time for your whole group to meet and write a report about how your editorial was treated by the various media you approached. Address the following questions in your report:

   • How easy or difficult was it to get access to traditional broadcasting vs. cable? How was your group treated?

   • Based on your experience, do broadcast airwaves and cable services "belong" to the public? How democratic is the process of gaining access on cable?

4. During class, the various groups should share and compare reports and experiences. If you were permitted to cablecast or broadcast your editorial, share it with the class.

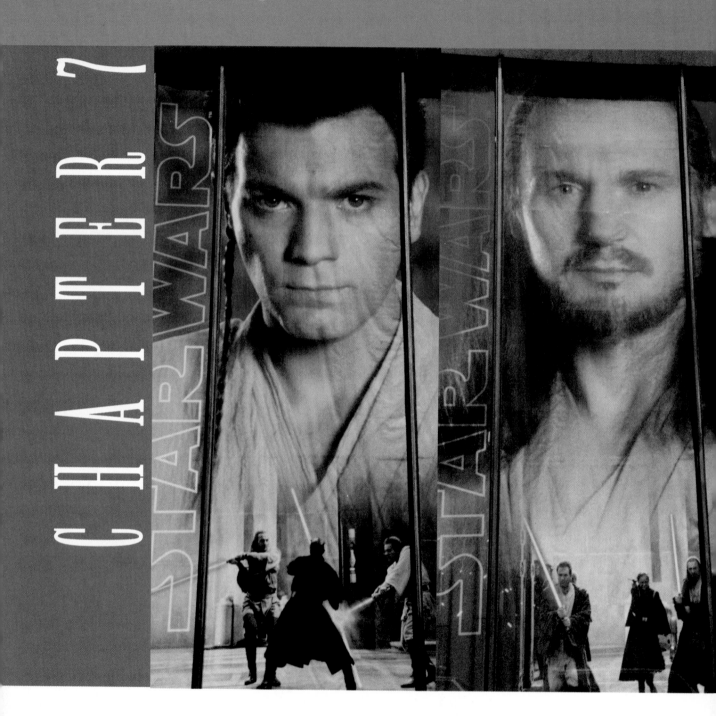

CHAPTER 7

A long time ago, in a film era far, far away, moviegoers first became acquainted with "the Force," with the 1977 release of *Star Wars*. The Force, the world learned, was the supernatural energy field created by all living things—surrounding and penetrating us and binding the galaxy together. Outside of the movie theater, in the parallel universe of the film industry, *Star Wars* writer, producer, and director George Lucas created an entirely different force. *Star Wars* became the most successful movie of its generation, grossing over $320 million in the United States in its original release, and spawning a trilogy that included *The Empire Strikes Back* (1980) and *Return of the Jedi* (1983). Including the re-release of the trilogy in 1997, the three films earned a combined $1.3 billion at the box office, and an unprecedented $4 billion in merchandising, as *Star Wars* images appeared on an astonishing array of products, from Lego X-Wing fighter kits to Darth Vader Pez candy dispensers.

The trilogy dramatically changed the movie industry, bringing special effects to the forefront and creating a complex mythology with broad appeal for movie-goers of all ages. Some critics charge that the *Star Wars* trilogy also helped create the blockbuster mentality in the movie industry, in which action-packed stories are made into big-budget summer hits with merchandising tie-ins and potential for international distribution. Lucas, who also created the popular Indiana Jones series, argues that selling licensing rights is one of the ways he supports his independent filmmaking.

In the summer of 1999, audiences were treated to the release of *The Phantom Menace*, the first of three *Star Wars* prequels. (The original three films were the middle episodes of a nine-part story.) Like its predecessors, this much-anticipated trilogy planned to include three blockbusters with lucrative merchandising tie-ins. Prior to its release, *The Phantom Menace* had already generated a reported $1 billion in licensing revenue, and went on to earn over $400 million in U.S. ticket sales.

More important, with the *Star Wars* prequel trilogy George Lucas again broke new ground in the film industry—this time becoming a force in the emerging era of digital filmmaking. With the help of his renowned Industrial Light and Magic production house, Lucas claimed he could write whatever he wanted in a script, knowing that ILM's digital technology can deliver believable images of any character or environment he imagines—a luxury he did not have in 1977. This kind of extraordinary creative freedom is one of the key aspects of the digital cinema era. Furthermore, digital technology will be increasingly employed in the principle photography of film. Lucas hopes his next film will be shot entirely with digital cameras.

Finally, at several test sites *The Phantom Menace* became the first full-length motion picture from a major studio to use digital electronic projectors in movie theaters to replace standard film projectors. This change in exhibition technology will eventually move motion pictures away from the physical distribution of bulky, expensive film prints and toward a digital distribution system via satellite or optical disks.

As we move into a new century, the American movie industry itself continues to be a powerful global force that not only entertains audiences with compelling stories and breathtaking special effects but actively shapes the culture we live in. Surrounding and penetrating us, movie images and messages have become an indelible part of the media landscape, helping to focus—or distract—our attention from issues and ideals that are important to us as individuals and as a society.

Dating back to the late 1800s, American films have had a substantial social and cultural impact on society. Blockbuster movies such as *Star Wars, E.T., Jurassic Park, The Lion King, Forrest Gump, Independence Day*, and *Titanic* represent what Hollywood has become—America's storyteller. Telling cinematic tales that in 1909 drew us to a nickelodeon theater and in 1999 to our local video store, Hollywood movies have long acted as contemporary mythmakers. At their best, they tell communal stories that evoke and symbolize our most enduring values and our basest desires. The most popular films often make the world seem clearer, more manageable, and more understandable.

Throughout this century, films have helped moviegoers sort through experiences that either affirm or deviate from their own values. Some movies allow audiences to survey "the boundary between the permitted and the forbidden" and to experience, in a controlled way, "the possibility of stepping across this boundary."[1] Popular movies such as *Silence of the Lambs, Menace II Society*, and *Pulp Fiction* examine the distinctions between the normal and the abnormal—a moral border repeatedly fought over by religious leaders, politicians, and entrepreneurs as well as by teachers, parents, and the mass media.

Over and above their immense economic impact (see Table 7.1), movies have always worked on several social and cultural levels. While they distract us from our daily struggles, at the same time they encourage us to take part in rethinking contemporary ideas.

> "The movie is not only a supreme expression of mechanism, but paradoxically it offers as product the most magical of consumer commodities, namely dreams."
> —Marshall McLuhan, *Understanding Media*, 1964

TABLE 7.1
The Top 10 American Box-Office Champions, 1999*

Rank	Title/Date	Domestic Gross** (millions)	Rank	Title/Date	Domestic Gross** (millions)
1	Titanic (1997)	$601	6	Forrest Gump (1994)	330
2	Star Wars (1997)	461	7	The Lion King (1994)	313
3	Star Wars: The Phantom Menace (1999)	423*	8	Return of the Jedi (1983)	307
4	E.T.: The Extra-Terrestrial (1982)	400	9	Independence Day (1996)	306
5	Jurassic Park (1993)	357	10	The Empire Strikes Back (1980)	290

*Most rankings of the Top 10 most popular films are based on American box-office receipts. If international box-office receipts counted, *Jurassic Park* would head the list, with more than $1 billion in worldwide revenues. If these figures were adjusted for inflation, *Gone with the Wind* (1939) would become No. 1 in U.S. theater revenue. (Note: This list was compiled during the release of *The Phantom Menace*.)

**Gross shown in absolute dollars based on box-office sales in the United States and Canada.

Source: "The 50 All Time Highest Grossing Movies," <http://movieweb.com/movie/alltime.html> (September 21, 1999). © 1999 MovieWeb. All Rights Reserved.

We continue to be attracted to the stories that movies tell. It is these stories that keep us going back to movie theaters or to our local video stores.

In this chapter, we will examine the rich legacy and current standing of Hollywood as a national and international mythmaker. We will begin by considering film's early technology and the evolution of film as a mass medium. We will look at the arrival of silent feature films, the emergence of Hollywood, and the development of the studio system with regard to production, distribution, and exhibition. We will then explore the coming of sound and the power of movie storytelling. In the context of Hollywood moviemaking, we will consider major film genres, directors, and alternatives to Hollywood's style, including foreign films and documentaries. Finally, we will look at the movie business today—its major players, economic clout, technological advances, and implications for democracy.

early technology and the evolution of movies

History often credits a handful of enterprising individuals with developing new technologies and mass media. Such innovations, however, are usually the result of extended and simultaneous investigations by a wide variety of people. In addition, the media innovations of both known and unknown inventors are propelled by economic and social forces as well as by individual abilities.[2]

the development of film

Solving the puzzle of making a picture move depended both on advances in photography and on the development of a flexible film stock to replace the heavy metal-and-glass plates used to make individual pictures in the 1800s. In 1889, an American minister, Hannibal Goodwin, developed a transparent and pliable film—called *celluloid*—that could hold a coating, or film, of chemicals sensitive to light. This

Before the arrival of feature-length movies, audiences in the late 1890s were fascinated by the novelty of any moving image. This Edison kinetoscope reel from 1894 featured one of the first close-up shots ever recorded on film—a man sneezing.

breakthrough solved a major problem: It allowed a strip of film to move through a camera and be photographed in rapid succession, producing a series of pictures. In the 1890s, George Eastman (later of Eastman Kodak) bought Goodwin's patents, improved the ideas, and manufactured the first film used for motion pictures.

As with the development of sound recording, Thomas Edison takes center stage in most accounts of the invention of motion pictures. In the late 1800s, Edison initially planned to merge phonograph technology and moving images to create talking pictures (which would not happen in feature films until 1927). Since there was no breakthrough, however, Edison lost interest. But he deputed an assistant, William Kennedy Dickson, to combine advances in Europe with the new celluloid to create an early movie camera, called the *kinetograph*, and a viewing system, called the *kinetoscope*. This small projection system housed fifty feet of film that revolved on spools (similar to a library microfilm reader). It was a kind of peep show, in which viewers looked through a hole and saw images moving on a tiny plate. In 1894, a kinetoscope parlor, featuring two rows of coin-operated machines, opened in New York.

From the start, Edison envisioned movies only as a passing fad or an arcade novelty. Meanwhile, in France, Louis and Auguste Lumière, who ran a photographic-equipment factory, were hard at work. The brothers developed a projection system so that more than one person at a time could see the moving images on a nine- by six-foot projection screen. In a Paris café on December 28, 1895, they projected ten short movies, for viewers who paid one franc each, on such subjects as a man falling off a horse and a child trying to grab a fish from a bowl. Within three weeks, twenty-five hundred people were coming each night to see how, according to one Paris paper, film "perpetuates the image of movement."

With innovators around the world dabbling in moving pictures, Edison's lab and kinetoscope company renewed its interest. Edison patented several inventions and manufactured a new large-screen system called the *vitascope*, which allowed filmstrips of longer lengths to be projected without interruption. Unlike the kinetoscope, vitascope projection improved viewing for large audiences, hinting at the potential of movies as a future mass medium.

Staged at a music hall in New York in April 1896, Edison's first public showing of the vitascope featured shots from a boxing match and waves rolling onto a beach. The *New York Times* described the exhibition as "wonderfully real and singularly exhilarating." Some members of the audience were so taken with the realism of the film images that they stepped back from the screen's crashing waves to avoid getting their feet wet.

Early movie demonstrations such as these marked the beginning of the film industry. At this point, movies consisted of movement recorded by a single continuous camera shot. Early filmmakers had not yet figured out how to move the camera around or how to edit film shots together. Nonetheless, various innovators were beginning to see the commercial possibilities of film. By 1900, short movies had become a part of amusement arcades, traveling carnivals, wax museums, and vaudeville theater.

the power of stories
in the silent era

The shift from early development to the mass-medium stage came with the introduction of *narrative films:* movies that tell stories. Once audiences understood the illusion of moving images, they quickly tired of waves breaking on beaches or vaudeville acts recorded by immobile cameras. To become a mass medium, the early silent films had to offer what books had achieved: the suspension of disbelief. They had to create narrative worlds that engaged an audience's imagination.

Some of the earliest narrative films were produced and directed by French magician and inventor George Melies, who opened the first public movie theater in France in 1896. Melies may have been the first director to realize that a movie was not simply a means of recording reality. He understood that a movie could be artificially planned and controlled like a staged play. By the late 1800s, Melies was producing fairy tales and science-fiction stories—including *Joan of Arc, Red Riding Hood, Cinderella,* and *A Trip to the Moon.* These film shorts lasted less than ten minutes each. By the early 1900s, he had discovered camera tricks and techniques, such as slow motion and cartoon animation, that became key ingredients in future narrative filmmaking.

The first American filmmaker to adapt Melies's innovations to narrative film was Edwin S. Porter. A cameraman who had studied Melies's work in an Edison lab, Porter mastered the technique of editing diverse shots together to tell a coherent story. Early filmmakers plotted and recorded action in a long, continuous filmed sequence. But Porter shot narrative scenes out of order (for instance, some in a studio and some outdoors) and reassembled them in the editing process to make a story. In 1902, he made what is regarded as America's first narrative film, *The Life of an American Fireman.*

Porter also pioneered other innovations in filmmaking. First, he moved the camera and varied its distance from subjects and objects. *American Fireman,* for example, contained the first close-up shot in U.S. narrative film history—a ringing fire alarm. Until then, early moviemakers thought that close-ups cheated the audience of the opportunity to see an entire scene. Second, Porter's most important film, *The Great Train Robbery,* introduced the western as well as chase scenes. In this eleven-minute movie, Porter demonstrated the art of film suspense by alternating shots of the robbers with those of a posse in hot pursuit.

the arrival of nickelodeons

Another major development in the evolution of film as a mass medium was the arrival of movie theaters. They were called **nickelodeons,** a term that combines the admission price with the Greek word for "theater." According to media historian Douglas Gomery, these small and uncomfortable makeshift theaters were often converted cigar stores, pawnshops, or restaurants redecorated to mimic vaudeville theaters: "In front, large, hand-painted posters announced the movies for the day. Inside, the screening of news, documentary, comedy, fantasy, and dramatic shorts lasted about one hour."[3] Because they showed silent narrative film shorts that usually transcended language barriers, nickelodeons flourished during the great European immigration at the turn of the century. These theaters filled a need for many newly arrived people struggling to learn English and seeking an inexpensive escape from the hard life of the city. Often managed by immigrants, nickelodeons required a minimal investment: just a secondhand projector and a large white sheet. Usually a piano player added live music, and sometimes theater operators used sound effects to simulate gun shots or loud crashes.

Although vaudeville theaters continued to feature movies, by 1908 nickelodeons had displaced the vaudeville circuit as the main showplace for films. Since they were less expensive than vaudeville shows and drew fewer well-to-do audiences, nickelodeons were labeled "democracy's theater." Between 1907 and 1909, the number of nickelodeons grew from five thousand to ten thousand. The craze had peaked by 1910, when entrepreneurs began to seek more affluent spectators, attracting them with larger and more lavish movie theaters.

the power of the studio system

By the late 1910s, the movie industry's three basic economic divisions—production, distribution, and exhibition—had been established. In its early phase, control of *production* meant control over camera and projector technology. But as narrative films became central to attracting consumers, production came to mean controlling the making of movies, from writing a script and hiring actors to raising money and filming the story. This is still the case today. *Distribution* constitutes the individuals or companies that deliver films into theaters in various regional, national, and eventually international markets. Finally, *exhibition* refers to where films are displayed—the theaters themselves and the people and companies that own them. Much of film history, as well as the current state of moviemaking, has been significantly affected by the power struggles of film studios vying to dominate one or all of these industry divisions.

"The American cinema is a classical art, but why not then admire in it what is most admirable, i.e., not only the talent of this or that filmmaker, but the genius of the system."

—André Bazin,
film theorist,
1957

Among the first to try his hand at dominating the movie business, Thomas Edison had been observing the growing popularity of film. He formed the Motion Picture Patents Company, a cartel of major U.S. and French film producers, in 1908. Known as the Trust, Edison's company pooled patents in an effort to control film's major technology and, by default, the production of most movies. In addition, the Trust acquired most major film distributorships and signed an exclusive deal with George Eastman, who agreed to supply movie film only to Trust-approved companies.

Some independent producers refused to bow to the Trust's terms. There was too much demand for films, too much money to be made, and too many ways to avoid the Trust's scrutiny. Some producers began to relocate from the early centers of film production in New York and New Jersey to Cuba and Florida. Ultimately, though, Hollywood became a movie magnet and the film capital of the world. Southern California offered cheap labor, diverse scenery for outdoor shooting, barns that could be converted into studios, and a mild climate suitable for year-round production. Far from the Trust, independent companies could also easily slip over the border into Mexico to escape legal prosecution for patent violations.

Two Hungarian immigrants, Adolph Zukor, who would eventually run Paramount Pictures, and William Fox, who would found the Fox Film Corporation (which later became Twentieth Century Fox), played a role in the collapse of Edison's Trust. Zukor's early companies figured out ways to bypass the Trust, and a suit by Fox, a nickelodeon operator turned film distributor, resulted in the Trust's breakup for restraint of trade violations in 1917.

Ironically, although the Trust's monopoly efforts failed, entrepreneurs like Zukor went on to develop other tactics for controlling the industry. The new strategies, many of which are still used today, were more ambitious than just monopolizing patents and technology. They aimed at dominating the movie business at all three essential levels—production, distribution, and exhibition—in a *vertical integration* of power and control. The new tactics ultimately spawned a system that turned the film industry into an *oligopoly*, in which a few firms controlled the bulk of the business.

controlling production

The first movies were sold or rented by the foot; one product was not differentiated from another. Films were novelties, and people were merely curious about the moving images. Gradually, however, producers and distributors recognized that fans sought not only particular kinds of stories—including dramas, westerns, and romances—but particular actors and actresses. This was not unlike what would occur in the 1950s, as radio-station managers noticed that teenagers listened to their favorite performers again and again.

By 1910, film companies were receiving letters from fans inquiring about actors who were not named in the movie credits. (It was an early practice not to list actors in the credits.) Initially, companies were reluctant to identify these individuals because their popularity would force higher salaries; most anonymous film actors were making only $5 to $15 per day. Eventually, though, film studios acknowledged that moviegoers went to certain films because of the performances of their favorite actors.

To meet the tastes of discerning audiences and to better compete against Edison's Trust, Adolph Zukor hired a number of popular actors, forming the Famous Players Company in 1912. Zukor's idea was to exert control over movie production, not through patents but through contracts with the most popular actors of the day. By this time, theater owners were already beginning to demand films featuring the performers who attracted the largest audiences. Zukor signed these performers to exclusive contracts, ensuring that they would make movies only for his company.

> "No, I really cannot afford to work for only $10,000 a week."
> —Mary Pickford to Adolph Zukor, 1915

Zukor also understood the difference between film acting and theater acting, in which actors emphasized "the large gesture" and a "boldly sketched pantomime of emotions."[4] Film acting was more subtle, more intimate, and did not demand that an actor's voice reach the back of a cavernous theater. Film producers began developing talented performers like Mary Pickford, who was "unspoiled" by a theater background and more suited to the new medium. Pickford became one of film's first movie stars. Known as "America's sweetheart" for her portrayal of spunky and innocent heroines, Pickford became so popular that audiences waited in line to see her movies, and producers had to pay her increasingly larger salaries to keep her services.

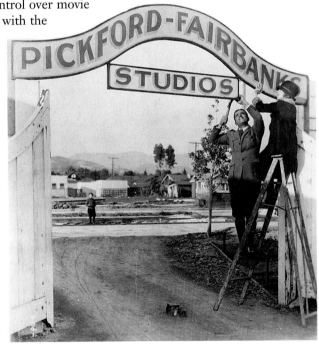

In 1919, Mary Pickford *(right)*, Douglas Fairbanks *(left)*, and Charlie Chaplin, along with director D. W. Griffith, formed the United Artists Corporation. A film-distribution company, UA later became a major studio and merged with MGM.

An astute businesswoman, Mary Pickford was the key figure in elevating the financial status and professional role of film actors. Whereas in 1910 Pickford made about $100 a week, by 1914 she earned $1,000 a week. Eventually, Zukor signed her to Famous Players (which later became part of Paramount Pictures). By 1917, Zukor was paying Pickford a weekly salary of $15,000. Having appeared in nearly two hundred films, Pickford was so influential that in 1919 she broke from Zukor to form her own company, United Artists. Joining her were actor Douglas Fairbanks (her future husband), comedian-director Charlie Chaplin, and director D. W. Griffith.

By the beginning of the 1920s, film production had evolved into the **studio system**. Pioneered by director Thomas Ince and his Hollywood company, Triangle, this system constituted a sort of assembly-line process for moviemaking. It organized a staff of the best technicians and directors schooled in the latest film techniques. According to the system, not only stars but directors, editors, writers, and others worked under exclusive contracts for the major studios. Indeed, those who weren't under contract with some movie company probably weren't working at all. To guide multiple movies through various production stages, Ince gave up directing in 1915 and appointed *producers* to handle hiring, logistics, and finances. In this way, Ince could more easily supervise a number of pictures at one time.

Although United Artists represented a brief triumph of autonomy for a few powerful actors, by the 1920s the studio system firmly controlled creative talent in the industry. In 1927, for example, Paramount director Cecil B. DeMille required the actors playing Jesus and Mary in *The King of Kings* to refrain from such secular activities as playing cards or riding in convertibles off the set. The system was so efficient that each major studio was producing a feature film every week. Pooling talent, rather than patents, was a more ingenious approach for movie studios aiming to dominate film production.

controlling distribution

One of the early forms of movie distribution, *film exchanges* appeared around 1904 as movie companies provided vaudeville theaters with films and projectors. In exchange for their short films, shown between live acts, movie producers received a small percentage of the vaudeville ticket gate receipts. Gradually, as the number of production companies and the popularity of narrative films grew, demand for a distribution system serving national and international markets increased as well. Because few regulations existed in these early days, movies were often stolen or copied. Edison's Trust represented, in part, an attempt to prevent film pirating and to manage the industry by withholding equipment from companies not willing to pay the Trust's patent-use fees.

However, emerging film companies and other independent firms looked to distribution strategies to gain a foothold in the fledgling industry. Early independents like Adolph Zukor, who opposed the Trust, developed several distribution techniques, including *block booking*. Under this system, to gain access to popular films exhibitors had to agree to rent new or marginal films with no stars. Zukor would pressure theater operators into taking a hundred movies at a time to get the few Pickford titles they wanted. Such contracts allowed studios to test-market a new star without much financial risk. Although this practice was eventually outlawed as monopolistic, rising film studios used the tactic effectively to guarantee the success of their films in an open marketplace.

Another distribution strategy involved the marketing of American films in Europe. When World War I disrupted European film production, only U.S. studios were able to meet the demand. The war thus marked a turning point, making the United States the leader in the commercial movie business. Europe never regained its edge. After the war, no other film industry could compete economically with Hollywood. By the mid-1920s, foreign revenue from U.S. films totaled $100 million. Today, in any given week, when the industry trade magazine *Variety* ranks the top-grossing films in foreign countries, U.S. movies (especially easily translatable action/adventure features) continue to dominate the list. For example, in 1997 and 1998 the rereleased *Star Wars* trilogy emerged as top box-office draws in Germany, Spain, Australia, France, and England.

"It's still a business where the hits make up for all the losses along the way. *Star Wars* accentuated that. Everyone wants to reproduce that success, even just once. This tells you about the strength of this kind of franchise."

—Jill Krutick, analyst, Smith Barney, 1997

controlling exhibition

When industrious theater owners began forming film cooperatives to compete with block-booking tactics, producers like Zukor conspired to dominate exhibition. By 1921, Zukor's company owned three hundred theaters, solidifying its ability to show the movies it created. In 1925, a business merger between Paramount and Publix, the country's largest theater chain at the time, with more than five hundred screens, gave Zukor enormous influence over movie exhibition.

Zukor and the heads of several major studios understood that they did not have to own all theaters to ensure that their movies were shown. Over time, the five major studios (which would eventually include MGM, RKO, Warner Brothers, Twentieth Century Fox, and Paramount) merely needed to own about 15 percent of the nation's twenty thousand movie houses. They needed only the first-run theaters, which premiered new films in major downtown areas in front of the largest audiences. Throughout the 1940s, ticket sales from these venues generated 85 to 95 percent of all film revenue.

Movie Palaces. Entrepreneurs ultimately realized that drawing the middle and upper-middle classes to movies required something more attractive than a sheet hung in an abandoned pawnshop. To provide a more hospitable moviegoing environment, exhibitors converted vaudeville theaters into full-time use as movie theaters. In 1914, the three-thousand-seat Strand Theatre, the first movie palace, opened in New York. With elaborate architecture, movie palaces lured spectators who enjoyed entertainment amid the trappings of high-society opera, ballet, symphony, and live theater.

To work their magic on the outside, these theaters often evoked the grandeur of palaces, with massive electric-light displays that announced their presence from blocks away. Linking the moviegoing experience with the trappings of royalty created a powerful attraction. Inside the theater, customers meandered through lavish lobbies, plush promenades, and fancy waiting rooms. Movie exhibitors treated "the movie patron like a king or queen," with ushers, doormen, and services ranging from free child care to "smoking rooms and painting galleries."[5] Taking advantage of new air-cooling systems developed by Chicago's meatpacking industry, movie palaces also featured the first mechanically air-cooled theaters. This perquisite alone transformed summer moviegoing in Chicago into peak viewing time. Doctors even advised pregnant women to escape the heat by spending their afternoons at the movies.

Mid-City Theaters. Another major innovation in exhibition was the development of mid-city movie theaters. The first

With ornate decor, air-conditioning, palatial rest rooms, extensive concession stands, and large film screens, movie palaces became fixtures in major American cities in the 1920s. The palaces typically seated several thousand moviegoers, and often featured elaborate concert organs to accompany films. Despite the rise of state-of-the-art multiplexes in the last twenty years, many movie palaces have been renovated and designated as historic sites and multipurpose arts facilities.

wave of middle-class people moved from urban centers to city outskirts in the 1920s, and mass-transit systems emerged to shuttle these suburbanites to and from work. Movie theaters soon followed, as exhibitors in Chicago began to locate theaters at major transportation intersections in outlying business areas rather than downtown. (For another view of exhibition, see "Case Study: Breaking through Hollywood's Race Barrier" on page 214.) This idea continues today, as large *multiplexes* featuring fifteen to twenty-five screens lure middle-class crowds to interstate crossroads.

Throughout the 1920s, movie attendance climbed steadily. But the Great Depression hit the industry hard, and many customers turned to radio, a cheaper form of entertainment. To compete, theaters began holding contests and prize giveaways. They also offered double features—two movies for the price of one—and started selling candy, soda, and eventually popcorn (which, thanks to the movies, turned corn into a major farm crop in the late 1930s). With jobs restored during World War II, movie attendance surged during the 1940s. In 1946—the industry's all-time peak attendance year—ninety million people went to the movies each week.

By the late 1920s, the major studios had clearly established vertical integration in the industry. What had once been a fairly easy and cheap business to enter had become complex and capital-intensive. What had been many small competitive firms in the early 1900s had become a few powerful studios, including the Big Five—Paramount, MGM, Warner Brothers, Twentieth Century Fox, and RKO—and the Little Three (which did not own theaters)—Columbia, Universal, and United Artists. Together these eight companies formed a powerful oligopoly, which made it increasingly difficult for independent companies to make, distribute, and exhibit commercial films.

the triumph of hollywood storytelling

While early filmmakers like Edwin S. Porter and D. W. Griffith demonstrated the appeal of the film narrative, early stars like Mary Pickford and Charlie Chaplin revealed the audience's attraction to movie actors. Meanwhile, the studios searched for the next technical innovation to enliven the industry and further enhance film's storytelling capabilities. They found it by adding sound to moving images, mixing another powerful ingredient into Hollywood-flavored narratives.

the "sound" of movies

With the studio system and Hollywood's worldwide dominance firmly in place, the next big challenge involved bringing sound to moving pictures. Various attempts at talkies had failed since Edison first tried to link phonograph and moving-picture technologies in the 1890s. During the 1910s, however, technical breakthroughs at AT&T's research arm, Bell Labs, produced prototypes of loudspeakers and sound amplifiers. By the end of the decade, the idea of projecting clear sounds throughout large movie palaces was technically possible, although the cost of outfitting theaters with the necessary equipment remained high.

Experiments with ten-minute sound shorts continued during the 1920s. The four Warner brothers (Harry, Abe, Jack, and Sam), who ran a minor studio at the time, experimented with sound as a novelty, although they did not believe such films would replace silent movies. So Warner Brothers made short "talkers" of vaudeville acts, featuring singers and comedians. The studio packaged them as a novelty along with silent

In 1927, Warner Brothers released *The Jazz Singer,* featuring vaudeville star Al Jolson in the first talkie. The film was supposed to be mostly silent, with just a few musical numbers, but Jolson was so energetic and excitable that he couldn't resist talking between songs.

feature films. Over time, Warner Brothers began outfitting theaters with the necessary sound equipment.

In 1927, Warner Brothers produced a feature-length film, *The Jazz Singer,* starring Al Jolson, a popular vaudeville singer. An experiment, *The Jazz Singer* was basically a silent film interspersed with musical numbers and brief dialogue. At first, there was only modest interest in the movie, which featured just 354 spoken words. But the film grew in popularity as it toured the Midwest, where audiences stood and cheered the short bursts of dialogue. The breakthrough film, however, was Warner Brothers' 1928 release, *The Singing Fool,* which also starred Jolson. Costing $200,000 to make, the film took in $5 million and "proved to all doubters that talkies were here to stay."[6] *The Singing Fool* remained the box-office champ for more than ten years, until 1939, when it was dethroned by *Gone with the Wind.*

By the mid-1920s, Bell Labs had developed the system used by Warner Brothers, which coordinated sound on records with a film projector. Warner Brothers, however, was not the only studio forging into the technology of sound. In April 1927, five months before *The Jazz Singer* opened, the Fox studio had premiered sound-film newsreels. Fox's newsreel company, Movietone, captured the first film footage, with sound, of the takeoff and return of Charles Lindbergh, who piloted the first solo, non-stop flight across the Atlantic Ocean in May 1927. Fox's Movietone system actually photographed sound directly onto the film, running it on a narrow filmstrip that ran alongside the larger, image portion of the film. Superior to the sound-on-record system, the Movietone method eventually became film's standard sound system.

Meanwhile, Fox was sending camera crews around the world in search of talking news. By 1928, the success of newsreels, as popular as most silent features of the day, led to the full conversion to talking pictures. Boosted by the innovation of sound, movie attendance in the United States rose from 60 million in 1927 to 110 million in 1929. By 1931, nearly 85 percent of America's twenty thousand theaters accommodated sound pictures, and by 1935 the world had adopted talking films as the commercial standard.

classic hollywood cinema

By the time sound came to movies, Hollywood dictated not only the business but the style of most moviemaking worldwide. That style, or model, for storytelling developed with the studio system and continues to dominate American filmmaking today. The model comprises three ingredients that give Hollywood movies their distinctive flavor: the narrative, the genre, and the author (or director). The right blend of these ingredients—combined with timing, marketing, and luck—have led to blockbuster movie hits from *Gone with the Wind* to *The Phantom Menace.* Major studios have historically relied on blockbusters to underwrite the 80 to 90 percent of films that fail at the box office.

Oscar Micheaux (1884–1951) was one of the few African American filmmakers to own a production company. He directed, produced, and distributed forty-six films aimed at black audiences.

Despite inequities and discrimination, a thriving black cinema existed in New York's Harlem district during the 1930s and 1940s. Usually bankrolled by white business executives who were capitalizing on the black-only theaters fostered by segregation, independent films featuring black casts were supported by African American moviegoers, even during the Depression. But it was a popular Hollywood film, *Imitation of Life* (1934), that emerged as the highest-grossing film in black theaters during the mid-1930s. The film told the story of a friendship between a white woman and a black woman, whose young daughter denied her heritage and passed for white, breaking her mother's heart.

Despite African Americans' long support of the film industry, their moviegoing experience has not been the same as that of whites. From the late 1800s until the passage of civil-rights legislation in the mid-1960s, many theater owners discriminated against black patrons. In large cities, blacks often had to attend separate theaters where new movies

Gordon Parks

Born in 1912; one of fifteen children; worked as *Life* magazine photographer from 1948 to 1968. His son, Gordon Parks Jr., who directed *Super Fly* (1972), died in a plane crash in Africa while scouting film locations in 1979.

Career Achievements

The Learning Tree (1969): Based on his autobiography about growing up poor on a Kansas farm. Parks wrote, produced, directed, and composed the musical score.

Shaft (1971): The first popular Hollywood action film to feature an African American hero as a central character. Isaac Hayes won an Oscar for the theme song.

Shaft's Big Score (1972): John Shaft (played by Richard Roundtree) takes on the mob in this sequel.

The Super Cops (1974).

Leadbelly (1976): A biography of black blues and folk singer Huddie "Leadbelly" Ledbetter.

Half Past Midnight (1998–2002): A touring retrospective of more than two hundred of Parks's photographs, along with performances of his movies and musical compositions.

might not appear until a year or two after white theaters had shown them. In smaller towns and in the South, blacks were often able to patronize local theaters only after midnight. In addition, some theaters required black patrons to sit in less desirable areas of the theater.[1]

Outside large cities, African Americans often relied on radio sets, church groups, and social clubs for cultural entertainment, especially during the Depression. Changes took place during and after World War II, however, when more middle-class blacks had money to attend movies. When the "white flight" from central cities began during the suburbanization of the 1950s, many downtown and neighborhood theaters began catering to black customers in order to save their businesses. By the late 1960s and early 1970s, these theaters had become major venues for popular commercial films, even featuring a few movies about African Americans, including *Guess Who's Coming to Dinner?* (1967), *In the Heat of the Night* (1967), *The Learning Tree* (1969), and *Sounder* (1972).

Based on the popularity of these films, black photographer turned filmmaker Gordon Parks, who directed *The Learning Tree* (adapted from his own novel), went on to make commercial action/adventure films, including *Shaft* (1971). Popular in urban theaters, especially among black teenagers, the movies produced by Parks and his son—Gordon Parks Jr. (*Super Fly*, 1972)—spawned a number of commercial imitators, labeled *blaxploitation* movies. These films were the subject of heated cultural debates in the 1970s; like some rap songs today, they were both praised for their realistic depictions of black urban life and criticized for glorifying violence. Nevertheless, these films reinvigo-

Spike Lee

Born in 1957; raised in Brooklyn; father a jazz musician, mother a teacher.

Career Achievements

She's Gotta Have It (1986): Lee's first feature won him an Independent Spirit Award for "best first feature film" by an independent filmmaker.

School Daze (1988): A musical score by the director's father, Bill Lee.

Do the Right Thing (1989): A comic/tragic look at racism.

Malcolm X (1992): Chronicles the life of the famed black activist, who was assassinated in 1965.

Crooklyn (1994): Lee co-wrote the story with his sister, Joie Susannah, and his brother, Cinque; set in 1970s Brooklyn.

Get on the Bus (1996): The story of the 1995 Million Man March on Washington.

4 Little Girls (1997): An Academy Award–nominated documentary about a 1963 Alabama church bombing.

He Got Game (1998): The story of a talented high-school basketball player.

Summer of Sam (1999): Based on the "Son of Sam" murders that terrified New York City.

rated urban movie attendance, reaching an audience that had not been well served by the film industry until the 1960s.

Although opportunities for black film directors expanded in the 1980s, by the 1990s mainstream Hollywood was still a formidable place for outsiders to crack. Only one black person, for example, was nominated for an Academy Award in 1995. Still, that same year director Spike Lee asked a number of wealthy black men to bankroll his film *Get on the Bus* (made for one-tenth the cost of the average Hollywood movie). The film depicted the October 1995 Million Man March on Washington, celebrating the kind of black self-reliance that Lee's own moviemaking had long illustrated.

As we move into the twenty-first century, some critics argue that the next step for black filmmakers will be to assume a greater role in the moviemaking process itself, still creating movies that focus on the black experience but also making movies designed for greater mass-market appeal.

Spencer Williams (1893–1969) was a prolific and respected writer-director-actor of black-audience films, with nine feature films to his directorial credit.

215

Hollywood Narratives. American filmmakers from D. W. Griffith to Steven Spielberg have understood the allure of *narrative*, which always includes two basic components: the *story* (what happens to whom) and the *discourse* (how the story is told). Most movies, like most TV shows and novels, feature a number of stories that play out within the larger narrative of the entire film. In Quentin Tarantino's 1994 film *Pulp Fiction*, for instance, one major chronological story traces the adventures of two hit men over a few days. However, Tarantino's discourse deliberately disrupts the story's chronology. One hit man, played by John Travolta, is killed midway through the film but is "brought back" to perform other scenes in the larger narrative (via flashbacks of events that took place before the killing) that the director chose to reveal out of order.

Although there are many ways to tell a story, the cultural style that developed during Hollywood's silent and sound eras has a number of distinct features. For instance, Hollywood movies have traditionally revealed a series of plausible cause-effect relationships that take place in something approximating real time and real space.[7] Like a 50-mm lens in photography that tries to imitate what the eye actually sees, classic Hollywood films, unlike experimental or nonnarrative cinema, attempt to provide models of a believable world. In such films, problems have particular causes, and characters identify those problems and work to establish credible solutions.

To create believable narrative worlds, some standard techniques have developed over the years. For example, *continuity editing* makes space and time seem continuous and seamless. A shift in scenes or spatial arrangement is marked by *edit points*, in which a character appears in a long shot or in an outdoor scene followed by a cut or an edit to a close-up or an indoor scene. Viewers have come to understand that edit points function the way punctuation does in writing; they operate as devices for saving time in the interest of moving the narrative along.

In addition, in narrative films dramatic action and conflict spring mainly from individual characters. Although natural disasters or social issues may spark the film's action, the classic narrative typically "centers on personal psychological causes: decisions, choices, and traits of character."[8] Even in stylized Hollywood musicals (such as *Singin' in the Rain*, 1952; *Grease*, 1978; or *Evita*, 1997), artificial song-and-dance sequences are usually motivated by believable psychological and emotional factors that affect particular characters.

With this focus on character, protagonists and antagonists embody pairs of competing tensions: good vs. evil, male vs. female, young vs. old, city vs. country, or nature vs. civilization. These conflicts play out against a story that typically moves toward a resolution of the tensions that caused the original problem.

Within Hollywood's classic narratives, filmgoers will find an amazing array of intriguing cultural variations. For example, *Jurassic Park*, among the most lucrative films of all time, features the familiar narrative *conventions* of problems, heroes, villains, conflicts, and resolutions. However, the film *differentiates* itself through enhanced *inventions:* computer-animated dinosaurs, which had never been attempted before in a motion picture. This combination of convention and invention—standardized Holly-

> "We tell ourselves **stories** in order to **live**."
> —Joan Didion,
> *The White Album*,
> 1979

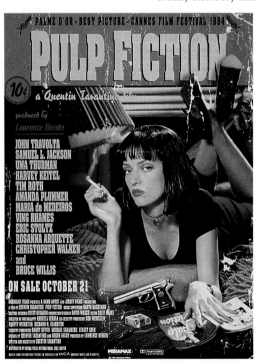

Dubbed the hottest and coolest film of the year, Quentin Tarantino's *Pulp Fiction* ignited Hollywood in 1994 with its inventive plot and smart dialogue. It won Tarantino an Oscar for screenwriting, grossed over $200 million worldwide, resurrected John Travolta's career, and established Miramax as a mini-studio.

wood stories and differentiated special effects—provides a powerful economic package that satisfies most audiences' appetites for both the familiar and the distinctive.

Hollywood Genres. In general, Hollywood narratives fit a *genre*, or category, in which conventions regarding similar characters, scenes, structures, and themes reoccur in combination. Grouping films by category allows the industry to achieve two related economic goals: *product standardization* and *product differentiation.* By making films that fall into popular genres, the movie industry provides familiar models that can be imitated. It is much easier for a studio to promote a film that already fits into a preexisting category with which viewers are familiar. Among the most familiar genres are comedy, drama, romance, action/adventure, mystery/suspense, fantasy/science fiction, musical, horror, gangster, western, and film noir. (See Table 7.2.)

An enduring genre such as the western typically features "good" cowboys battling "evil" bad guys or resolves tension between the natural forces of the wilderness and the civilizing influence of a town. Romances present narratives in which women play more central roles and conflicts are mediated by the ideal of love. Another popular genre, mystery/suspense, usually casts "the city" as a corrupting place that needs to be overcome by the moral courage of a heroic detective. In these movies, the hero searches for clues of criminal violation, then confronts villains, victims, and bystanders, and, finally, explains and resolves the violation or transgression.[9] A durable genre in novels as well as films, mystery movies rely on the introduction of new plots, stars, and directors to differentiate them from their predecessors.

Besides variations of dramas and comedies, which dominate film's long narrative history, another significant genre, the movie musical, added the innovation of on-screen music. Recently, however, the genre has fallen on hard times. Although such musicals as *Jesus Christ Superstar* (1973) and *Hair* (1979) were early influences on the music-video era, they have since been overwhelmed by MTV and other forms of popular music. Furthermore, movie musicals became prohibitively expensive. *Annie,* for instance, cost over $40 million in 1982, far more than the amount of the average feature in the early to mid-1990s.

Musicals are considered risky investments in the film industry today. By 1999, only one musical—*Grease* (1978)—ranked among the top-50-grossing films of all time. Although musicals like *Cats* remain popular as Broadway plays, the staged qualities of such shows are actually a negative when musicals are converted into movies. Since most Hollywood narratives try to create believable worlds, the artificial style of musicals is sometimes a disruption of what many viewers expect. In fact, the movie musicals that have done the best at the box office are the ones with just a few musical numbers that accompany a spoken narrative story, appealing to both adults and children. Disney has skillfully employed this formula in creating a string of hybrid animation-musicals, including *Beauty and the Beast* (1991) and *The Lion King* (1994), both of which later resurfaced as successful Broadway shows after their film achievements.

Another fascinating genre is the horror film, which in 1999 counted only one movie among the top-50-grossing films of all time: *The Exorcist*, from 1973. In fact, from *Psycho* (the original 1960 version) to *Scream*, in the history of the Academy Awards this lightly regarded genre has earned only one Oscar for best picture: *Silence of the Lambs* in 1991. Yet these movies are extremely popular with teenagers, among the largest theatergoing audience, who are in search of cultural choices distinct from adult fare. Critics suggest that the teen appeal of such horror movies as *Halloween* and *Nightmare on Elm Street* (each of which spawned four sequels) is similar to the allure of gangsta rap or heavy-metal music. That is, the horror genre is a cultural form that often carries anti-adult messages or is so gross that no responsible adult would be caught within a mile of its performance. In other words, this genre repels parents while simultaneously attracting their children.

TABLE 7.2
Hollywood Genres

Movies, especially contemporary films, are difficult to categorize because they often combine characteristics from different genres. In 1998, for example, *Armageddon* mixed elements from fantasy/science fiction, action/adventure, and romance, while *The Mask of Zorro* offered comedy, romance, and action/adventure. Shown below are the categories that are generally used by video stores to sort movies. Films from different decades represent the most familiar major genres.

Comedy

The Gold Rush (1925)
Horse Feathers (1932)
Arsenic and Old Lace (1944)
Some Like It Hot (1959)
Dr. Strangelove (1964)
Annie Hall (1977)*
A Fish Called Wanda (1988)
The Birdcage (1995)
Liar, Liar (1997)
There's Something about Mary
 (1998)

Drama

Grand Hotel (1932)
Gone with the Wind (1939)
Citizen Kane (1941)
On the Waterfront (1954)*
A Man for All Seasons (1966)*
One Flew over the Cuckoo's Nest
 (1975)*
Raging Bull (1980)
Do the Right Thing (1989)
Fried Green Tomatoes (1991)
Dead Man Walking (1996)
Good Will Hunting (1997)
Saving Private Ryan (1998)

Romance

It Happened One Night (1934)*
Casablanca (1943)*
Adam's Rib (1949)
Sabrina (1954)
Dr. Zhivago (1965)
The Graduate (1967)
The Goodbye Girl (1977)
Tootsie (1984)
Beauty and the Beast (1993)
Titanic (1997)*
Shakespeare in Love (1998)*

Action/Adventure

The Adventures of Robin Hood
 (1938)
Sands of Iwo Jima (1949)
Ben Hur (1959)*

The Great Escape (1963)
The Sting (1973)*
Die Hard (1988)
Thelma and Louise (1991)
The Lion King (1994)
Lethal Weapon 4 (1998)

Mystery/Suspense

The Lady Vanishes (1938)
Rebecca (1940)*
North by Northwest (1959)
Psycho (1960)
Chinatown (1974)
Witness (1985)
Silence of the Lambs (1991)*
Seven (1996)

Westerns

Cimarron (1931)*
Stagecoach (1939)
The Searchers (1956)
Butch Cassidy and the Sundance Kid
 (1969)
Little Big Man (1970)
The Outlaw Josey Wales (1976)
Silverado (1985)
Unforgiven (1992)*
Posse (1993)
Maverick (1994)

Gangster

Public Enemy (1931)
Scarface (1932)
High Sierra (1941)
Bonnie and Clyde (1967)
The Godfather (1972)*
The Godfather, Part II (1974)*
Scarface (1983)
Goodfellas (1990)
Menace II Society (1993)
Donnie Brasco (1997)

Horror

Phantom of the Opera (1925)
Dracula (1931)
Bride of Frankenstein (1935)

The Wolf Man (1941)
The Blob (1958)
The Birds (1963)
The Exorcist (1973)
Nightmare on Elm Street (1985)
Mary Shelley's Frankenstein (1994)
I Know What You Did Last Summer
 (1997)

Fantasy/Science Fiction

Metropolis (1926)
The Wizard of Oz (1939)
Invasion of the Body Snatchers
 (1956)
2001: A Space Odyssey (1968)
Star Wars (1977)
The Princess Bride (1987)
Terminator 2: Judgment Day (1991)
Independence Day (1996)
Armageddon (1998)

Musicals

Broadway Melody (1929)*
Top Hat (1935)
Meet Me in St. Louis (1944)
An American in Paris (1951)*
West Side Story (1961)*
The Sound of Music (1965)*
Jesus Christ, Superstar (1973)
Annie (1982)
Evita (1997)

Film Noir

Double Indemnity (1944)
Detour (1945)
The Postman Always Rings Twice
 (1946)
The Strange Love of Martha Ivers
 (1946)
Key Largo (1948)
They Live by Night (1948)
Border Incident (1949)
L.A. Confidential (1997)

*Won the Academy Award for that year's best picture.

An interesting and relatively new genre is *film noir* (French for "black film"), which developed in the United States after World War II and continues to influence movies today. Using low-lighting techniques, few daytime scenes, and bleak urban settings that generate a chilling mood, films in this genre explore unstable characters and the sinister side of human nature. These films also often resist the conventional closure of the classic narrative. Although the French critics who first identified noir as a genre place these films in the 1940s, their influence resonates in contemporary films—sometimes called *neo-noir*—including *Raging Bull, Pulp Fiction, Red Rock West, Seven,* and *L.A. Confidential.*

Hollywood "Authors." Film has generally been called a director's medium. Although commercial filmmaking requires hundreds of people to perform complicated tasks, from scriptwriting and casting to set design and editing, the director serves as the main "author" of a film. Certainly the names of Steven Spielberg (*E.T., Schindler's List, Jurassic Park, Saving Private Ryan*) and Spike Lee (*Do the Right Thing, Malcolm X, Get on the Bus, He Got Game*) attract many moviegoers to a film today.

D. W. Griffith, among the first "star" directors, paved the way for future filmmakers. Griffith refined many of the narrative techniques that are still in use today, including varied camera distances, close-up shots, multiple story lines, fast-paced editing, and symbolic imagery. His major work, *The Birth of a Nation* (1915), was a controversial three-hour Civil War epic. Although considered a technical masterpiece, the film glorified the Ku Klux Klan and stereotyped southern blacks. It is nevertheless the movie that triggered Hollywood's ongoing fascination with long narrative films. By 1915, more than 20 percent of films were feature-length (around two hours), and *The Birth of a Nation*, which cost filmgoers a record $2 admission, ran for a year on Broadway.

Successful directors, in general, develop a particular cinematic style or an interest in particular topics that differentiates their narratives from those of other directors. Alfred Hitchcock, for instance, redefined the suspense drama through editing techniques that heightened tension (*North by Northwest*, 1959; *Psycho*, 1960); and Frank Capra championed romantic characters who stood up for the common person (*Mr. Smith Goes to Washington*, 1939; *It's a Wonderful Life*, 1946).

The contemporary status of directors probably stems from two breakthrough films, Dennis Hopper's *Easy Rider* (1969) and George Lucas's *American Graffiti* (1973), which became surprise box-office hits. Their inexpensive budgets, rock-and-roll sound tracks, and big payoffs created opportunities for a new generation of directors. These films exposed cracks in the Hollywood system, which was losing money in the late 1960s and early 1970s. Studio

> "Growing up in this country, the **rich culture** I saw in my neighborhood, in my family—I didn't see that on television or on the movie screen. It was always my ambition that if I was successful I would try to portray **a truthful portrait of African Americans** in this country, negative and positive."
>
> —Spike Lee,
> filmmaker,
> 1996

In one of the most harrowing moments in *North by Northwest*, Cary Grant, playing a Madison Avenue ad executive inadvertently involved with international spies and wrongly framed for murder, is pursued by a crop duster. Director Alfred Hitchcock was masterful at using creative camera shots like this one to heighten audience tension.

executives seemed at a loss to explain and predict the tastes of a new generation of moviegoers. Yet Hopper and Lucas had tapped into the anxieties of the postwar baby-boom generation in its search for self-realization, its longing for an innocent past, and its efforts to cope with the social turbulence of the late 1960s.

Trained in California or New York film schools and products of the 1960s, Francis Ford Coppola (*The Godfather*), Brian De Palma (*Carrie*), William Friedkin (*The Exorcist*), George Lucas (*Star Wars*), Martin Scorsese (*Taxi Driver, Raging Bull*), and Steven Spielberg (*Jaws, Raiders of the Lost Ark*) represented a new wave of Hollywood directors. Combining news or documentary techniques and Hollywood narratives, they demonstrated not only how mass-media borders had become blurred but also how movies had become more dependent on audiences that were products of television and rock and roll. These films signaled the start of a period that Scorsese has called "the deification of the director." A handful of successful men gained the kind of economic clout and celebrity standing that had belonged almost exclusively to top movie stars, and a few of these directors were transformed into big-time Hollywood producers.

Although the status of directors grew in the 1960s and 1970s, recognition for women directors of Hollywood features remained rare.[10] In the history of the Academy Awards, only two women have won an Academy Award nomination for directing a feature film: Lina Wertmuller in 1976 for *Seven Beauties* and Jane Campion in 1993 for *The Piano* (for which Campion won an Oscar for her original screenplay). It's worth noting that both Wertmuller and Campion are from outside the United States, where female directors often receive more funding opportunities for film development. When women in the United States do get an opportunity, it often comes because their prominent standing as popular actors has given them the power to produce or direct. For example, Barbra Streisand's cachet as both a movie star and a popular singer allowed her to produce, co-write, direct, and perform in *Yentl*, a 1983 musical, and to direct and star in *The Mirror Has Two Faces* in 1996. The acting successes of Penny Marshall and Jodie Foster have also aided their later development as movie directors, with such films as *A League of Their Own* (1992) and *Little Man Tate* (1991), respectively.

Although women have made strong contributions in commercial movies as actors, editors, writers, artists, and designers, critics generally attribute their lack of power to the long history of male executives being atop the studio system. With the exception of Mary Pickford, the early studio moguls who ran Hollywood were men.

Building on a film-acting career that includes an Academy Award nomination for her performance in *Taxi Driver* (1976) at age fourteen, and best-actress Oscars for her performances in *The Accused* (1988) and *The Silence of the Lambs* (1991), Jodie Foster is one of the few Hollywood women who have been able to buck industry barriers and successfully work on the opposite side of the camera. Through her production company, Egg Pictures, Foster first directed (and starred in) *Little Man Tate* in 1991, produced (and starred in) *Nell* in 1994, and directed *Home for the Holidays* in 1995.

Even by the late 1990s, among the major studio executives, only a few women held top posts. In the 1995 series *American Cinema*, independent filmmaker Julie Dash (*Daughters of the Dust*, 1992) argued that women's best chances of controlling the movie process, apart from acting, remained outside the Hollywood system.

Living proof of this strategy, TV star Oprah Winfrey began her own production company, Harpo (Oprah spelled backward) Films, in order to produce controversial movies that mainstream Hollywood studios tend to avoid. In 1998, Winfrey's company financed and released *Beloved*, based on Toni Morrison's 1987 Pulitzer Prize–winning novel. Like Streisand before her, Winfrey also starred in the film, playing a runaway slave with a daughter and a secret past in rural Ohio in the mid-1870s.

outside the hollywood system

The contemporary film industry tends to focus on feature-length movies that command popular attention and most of the money. However, shorter narrative films and documentaries dominated cinema's first twenty years and continue to account for most of the movies made today. In addition, movie history has a long tradition in experimental, or avant-garde, films. These types of film, often produced outside the United States, provide opportunities for new filmmakers, both women and men. Below we will look at three alternatives to Hollywood: foreign films, documentaries, and independent films.

> "I haven't been able to convince anyone to finance a film about a young African American woman who's a computer genius." —Julie Dash, film director, 1997

Foreign Films. Although U.S. films earned more than 90 percent of global box-office revenues annually by the late 1990s, they accounted for only 15 percent of the number of commercial films produced worldwide. Despite Hollywood's domination of global film distribution, other countries have a rich history in producing both successful and provocative short-subject and feature films. For example, German expressionism (1919–24), Soviet realism (1924–30), Italian neorealism (1942–51), French new-wave cinema (1959–60), and post–World War II Japanese cinema have all demonstrated alternatives to the Hollywood approach. Today, India has the world's largest film industry (nicknamed Bollywood), producing a whopping eight hundred films a year—mostly romance or adventure musicals in a distinct style, but with Western influences.[11] In comparison, Hollywood moviemakers released 503 films in 1998, and 480 in 1997.

Americans showed early interest in British and French short films and in experimental films such as Germany's *The Cabinet of Dr. Caligari* (1919). The studio moguls, however, held tight reign over the entry of foreign titles into the United States. Foreign-language movies did reasonably well throughout the 1920s, especially in ethnic neighborhood theaters in large American cities. For a time, Hollywood studios even dubbed some popular American movies into Spanish, Italian, French, and German for these theaters. But the Depression brought cutbacks, and by the 1930s the daughters and sons of turn-of-the-century immigrants—many of whom were trying to assimilate into mainstream American culture—preferred their Hollywood movies in English.[12]

Postwar prosperity in the 1950s and 1960s saw a rebirth of interest in foreign-language films by such prominent directors as Sweden's Ingmar Bergman (*Wild Strawberries*, 1957), Italy's Federico Fellini (*La Dolce Vita*, 1960), France's François Truffaut (*Jules and Jim*, 1961), Japan's Akira Kurosawa (*Seven Samurai*, 1954), and India's Satyajit Ray (*Apu Trilogy*, 1955–59). In the 1950s, the gradual breakup of the studios' hold over theater exhibition stimulated the rise of art-house theaters, many specializing in foreign titles. Catering to academic audiences, art houses made a statement against Hollywood commercialism as they sought alternative movies.

Art houses numbered close to a thousand during their peak years in the late 1960s. By the late 1970s, though, the home-video market had emerged, and audiences began staying home to watch both foreign and domestic films. New multiplex theater owners also rejected the smaller profit margins of most foreign titles, which lacked the promotional hype of U.S. films. In addition, many viewers complained that English subtitles distracted them from devoting their attention to the visual images. As a result, between 1966 and 1990 the number of foreign films released annually in the United States dropped by two-thirds, from nearly three hundred to about one hundred titles per year.

With the growth of superstore video chains like Blockbuster in the 1990s, however, more shelf space opened up for diverse kinds of movies, including a larger selection of foreign-language titles. In 1994, the Mexican film *Like Water for Chocolate* became the most successful foreign-language picture ever marketed in the United States. Then, in 1996, it was surpassed by the Italian film *Il Postino (The Postman)*, which also became the first foreign-language film since 1973 to earn an Oscar nomination for best picture. In 1998, Italy's *La Vita è Bella (Life Is Beautiful)* repeated the feat, surpassing *Il Postino*'s revenues while garnering an Oscar nomination for best picture and winning a best actor award for Roberto Benigni, also the film's director. (See Table 7.3.) Still, foreign films, unless produced in cooperative ventures with Hollywood, have difficulty cracking the American market; they accounted for only 2 percent of the U.S. video market in 1995. While there are more movie screens than ever before in the United States (see Figure 7.1), less than 5 percent regularly show foreign-language films. Foreign films are even losing ground at these "alternative" screening sites, as they compete with the expanding independent American film market for screen space. Because of these factors, the foreign-film market in the United States was in crisis by 1998, with no foreign-language films released by the major film companies.[13]

The Documentary Tradition. Both TV news and nonfiction films trace their roots to the movie industry's *interest films* and newsreels in the late 1890s. In Britain, interest films contained compiled footage of regional wars, political leaders, industrial workers, and agricultural scenes. These films accompanied fiction shorts as part of the early moviegoing experience. Pioneered in France and England, *newsreels* consisted of weekly ten-minute magazine-style compilations of filmed news events from around the world organized in a sequence of short reports. A number of international news services began supplying theaters and movie studios with newsreels, and by 1911 they had become a regular part of the moviegoing menu.

A week before Hollywood stages the Oscars, Bollywood, the so-named center of Indian filmmaking in Bombay, India, presents the Lux Zee awards. This ceremony symbolizes the reach of Indian filmmaking, broadcasting to an estimated 200 million viewers in Asia, Africa, Latin America, Eastern Europe, and a number of Arab countries—an audience comparable to that of the Oscars or the Super Bowl. Bollywood produces 800 feature films a year, almost twice as many as Hollywood. The

The Indian classic *Charulata* (*The Lonely Wife*)

films offer an extravagant mixture of melodrama, action, romance, suspense, and musical segments, and are wildly popular in India. The Bollywood formula is generally organized around themes of family reunification, male bonding, and the importance of religious values, and typically features fantastic sets and hordes of extras. There is no kissing on-screen, but many of the films manage to include plenty of wet saris and pelvic-thrusting musical numbers. Bollywood films represent India's largest cultural export. It is not uncommon, for example, for a taxi driver in Greece to hum the sound track of an Indian film, or for a Chinese teenager to follow the trajectory of her favorite Indian movie star.

While Bollywood films haven't been successful in the United States, some think that this will soon change. The influence of satellite television and Western programs is creating an audience demand for higher production values in Indian cinema and different plots that may appeal to an American audience. Meanwhile, Hollywood may become increasingly influenced by a Bollywood aesthetic as it employs Bollywood directors, producers, and actors. Bombay director Shekhar Kapur, for example, directed *Elizabeth*, a stunning epic nominated for seven Oscars, including an Oscar for best picture.

While the influence of Bombay films and directors may be gaining in the first decade of the

Jackie Chan in *Supercop*

2000s, Hong Kong films were the most talked-about—and the most influential—film genre in cinema throughout the late 1980s and early 1990s. The Hong Kong style of highly choreographed action with often breathtaking, ballet-like violence became hugely popular around the world, reaching American audiences and in some cases even outselling Hollywood blockbusters at the box office. In addition, Hong Kong directors like John Woo and Jackie Chan (who also acts in his action movies), arrived in Hollywood to regularly direct action films, while Hong Kong stars like Chow Yun-Fat (*The Replacement Killers*) and Michelle Yeoh (*Tomorrow Never Dies*) are landing starring roles in American action movies.

The unfortunate flip side of this migration to Hollywood is that moviemaking in Hong Kong is in decline. Yet some critics believe that with the old guard moving to Hollywood, young film talents can now be cultivated in Hong Kong, potentially developing new and visionary styles.

Japanese cinema also seems to be in transition. Americans may be most familiar with low-budget monster movies like *Godzilla* and the widely heralded films of influential director Akira Kurosawa, who died in 1998. *Godzilla*'s place in popular culture is firmly established, but Kurosawa's style has had even greater impact: His *Seven Samurai* (1954) was remade by Hollywood as *The Magnificent Seven* (1960), and *The Hidden Fortress* (1958) became George Lucas's inspiration for *Star Wars*.

Japan's leading film export may soon be the work of Hayao Miyazaki, a director of feature-length animated movies who is the country's equivalent to Walt Disney. Ironically, Miyazaki, who created Japan's biggest-grossing film ever—1997's *Mononoke Hime* (*Princess Mononoke*)—signed a global-distribution deal with Disney, which will bring his films to American audiences, but as adult content, not as Disney family films.

223

Figure 7.1
Indoor Theater Screens in the United States, 1975–98
Source: © Motion Picture Association of America, U.S. Economic Review, 1998.

Early filmmakers also produced *travelogues*, which recorded daily life in various communities around the world. Travel films reached documentary status in Robert Flaherty's classic *Nanook of the North* (1922), which tracked a resourceful Eskimo family in the harsh Hudson Bay region of Canada. Flaherty edited his fifty-five-minute film to both tell and interpret the story of his subject. Flaherty's second film, *Moana* (1925), a Paramount-funded study of the lush South Pacific islands and a direct contrast to *Nanook*, inspired the term **documentary** in a 1926 film review by John Grierson, a Scottish film producer. Grierson defined Flaherty's work and the documentary form as "the creative treatment of actuality," or a genre that documents reality by recording real people and settings.

Over time, the documentary developed an identity apart from its commercial presentation. As an educational, noncommercial form, the documentary usually required the backing of industry, government, or philanthropy to cover costs. In support of a clear alternative to Hollywood cinema, various governments began creating special units, such as Canada's National Film Board, to sponsor documentaries. In the United States, art and film received considerable support from the Roosevelt administration during the Depression. Such funding produced Pare Lorentz's *The Plow That Broke the Plains* (1936), which recounted the ecological abuse and erosion of the Great Plains in the 1930s. During World War II, the government continued to turn to filmmakers and to Hollywood to "sell" patriotism. Director Frank Capra produced the seven-part *Why We Fight* documentary series to inspire support for the war effort against Germany and Japan.

By the late 1950s and early 1960s, the development of portable cameras had led to **cinema verité** (a French term for "film truth"). This documentary style allowed filmmakers to go where cameras could not go before and record fragments of everyday life more unobtrusively. Directly opposed to packaged, high-gloss Hollywood features, verité aimed to track reality, employing a rough, grainy look and shaky, handheld camerawork.

Among the key innovators in cinema verité were Drew and Associates, led by Robert Drew, a former *Life* magazine photographer. Through his connection to Time Inc. (which owned *Life*) and its chain of TV stations, Drew shot the groundbreaking documentary *Primary*, which followed the 1960 Democratic presidential primary race

The documentary *Hoop Dreams* chronicles a six-year span in the lives of two gifted African American basketball players from inner-city Chicago as they chase their dreams from eighth grade to the college level, and—they hope—the NBA. At more than three hours in length, *Hoop Dreams* was a surprise box-office hit in 1994, and critic Roger Ebert called it "one of the great moviegoing experiences of my lifetime."

between Hubert Humphrey and John F. Kennedy. Drew's portable cameras went everywhere, capturing glimpses of the political process never seen before, including Humphrey directing rehearsals for a TV appearance and Kennedy in a Milwaukee hotel room nervously awaiting the results of the election.

Since the late 1960s, a leading American practitioner of cinema verité has been Frederick Wiseman, who has filmed a series of documentaries for public television on the misuses of power in American institutions. Unlike traditional TV news, in which the reporter's voice-over narration organizes the story, Wiseman used careful and clever editing to make his point without a reporter's comments. His work includes *Titicut Follies* (1967), which until 1993 was banned from public viewing in Massachusetts for its piercing look at a state-run mental-health facility. Wiseman's films indirectly reveal institutional abuse and waste, and he and the verité tradition have been praised for bringing such corruption to light. They have also been criticized, though, for offering few solutions to the institutional problems they expose.

The documentary form, both inside and outside the United States, extends from turn-of-the-century film shorts to Dziga Vertov's *Man with a Movie Camera* (1927), which demonstrated Soviet-sponsored innovations in film editing. In later eras, the documentary tradition included the French film *Night and Fog* (1955), which reported the atrocities of the Nazi death camps during World War II, and *Hoop Dreams* (1994), a three-hour examination of the rituals of college basketball recruiting in the United States.

Perhaps the major contribution of documentaries has been their willingness to tackle controversial or unpopular subject matter. Oscar-winning documentaries such as Peter Davis's *Hearts and Minds* (1974) examined the complex cultural impact of the Vietnam War and paved the way for Hollywood to confront Vietnam in such fiction features as *The Deer Hunter* (1978) and *Platoon* (1986). In addition, Barbara Kopple's Academy Award–winning film, *Harlan County, U.S.A.* (1977), documented the poignant stories and hard lives of Kentucky coal miners and their families. Connie Field's *The Life and Times of Rosie the Riveter* (1980) sparked a renewed interest in gender and labor issues. Another movie about labor became America's most popular filmed documentary: Michael Moore's *Roger and Me* (1989) presented a comic and controversial look at the complex relationship between the city of Flint, Michigan, and General Motors. To reach a broader audience, Moore and his backers struck a deal with Time Warner to distribute the movie, ensuring audiences beyond college campuses and union halls.

The Rise of Independent Films. The recent success of documentary films like *Roger and Me* and *Hoop Dreams* dovetails with the rise of *indies*, or independently produced films. As opposed to directors working in the Hollywood system, independent filmmakers typically operate on a shoestring budget and show their movies in thousands of campus auditoriums and at hundreds of small film festivals. The decreasing costs of portable technology, including smaller cameras and digital computer editing, has kept many documentarists and other independent filmmakers in business. They make movies inexpensively, relying on real-life situations, stage actors and nonactors, crews made up of friends and students, and local settings outside the studio environment. Successful independents like Todd Solondz (*Welcome to the Dollhouse; Happiness*), Richard Linklater (*Slackers; Dazed and Confused*), and Allison Anders (*Gas, Food, and Lodging; Mi Vida Loca*) continue to find substantial audiences in college, art-house, and some mall theaters that promote work produced outside the studio system.

The rise of independent film festivals in the 1990s—especially the Sundance Film Festival held every January in Park City, Utah—has helped Hollywood rediscover low-cost independent films as an alternative to traditional movies with *Titanic*-size budgets. Films such as *sex, lies, and videotape* (1989); *El Mariachi* (1993); *Shine* (1996); *The Full Monty* (1997); and *Smoke Signals* (1998) were all able to generate industry buzz and major studio distribution deals through Sundance screenings and became star vehicles for several directors and actors. One of the hottest movies of 1999, *The Blair Witch Project*, got its launch at Sundance. The low budget, low tech, faux documentary was filmed by two Florida film students for about $40,000. The young filmmakers sold the distribution rights for $1 million, and the movie went on to earn over $138 million at the box office, riding on a wave of buzz generated via the Internet, on college campuses, and eventually in the mainstream press. As with the recording industry, the major studios have responded to the success of indies either by purchasing successful independent film companies (e.g., Disney's purchase of Miramax) or by developing in-house indie divisions (e.g., Sony's Sony Picture Classics).

> "Climbing Mount Everest naked would seem easy in comparison to making an independent film."
>
> — Claire Panke, independent film director, 1998

the transformation of the hollywood system

Beginning in 1946 and continuing over the next seventeen years, the movie industry lost much of its theatergoing audience. In 1951 alone, more than fifty theaters shut down in New York City. The ninety million people going to movies weekly in 1946 had fallen to less than twenty-five million by 1963. It seemed that the movie industry was in deep trouble, especially in light of television's ascent. Critics and observers began talking about the death of Hollywood. Although Hollywood had diminished as the geographic heart of the industry, a number of dramatic changes altered and eventually strengthened many aspects of the commercial movie business.

By the mid-1950s, significant cultural and social changes—such as suburbanization and television—had begun to reshape the moviegoing experience. By the late 1990s, even though movie attendance per capita had declined dramatically, more indoor theater screens—more than thirty-three thousand—were available in the United States than ever before (see Figure 7.1 on page 224). Theaters, however, have been dramatically downsized from the five-thousand-seat movie palaces that reigned in the 1940s. But despite major social transformations, the commercial film industry remains controlled, as it was earlier, by a few powerful companies. Below, we will review the film industry's adjustments to changing conditions, particularly the impact of political and legal challenges, suburbanization, television, and other technological changes such as cable, VCRs, and DVDs.

the hollywood ten

In 1947, in the wake of the unfolding Cold War with the Soviet Union, conservative members of Congress began investigating Hollywood for alleged subversive and communist ties. That year, the aggressive witch-hunts for political radicals in the film industry by the House Un-American Activities Committee (HUAC) led to the famous Hollywood Ten hearings and subsequent trial. At the time, Congressman J. Parnell Thomas of New Jersey chaired HUAC, which included future president Richard M. Nixon, then a congressman from California, as one of five members of this powerful committee.

During the investigations, HUAC coerced prominent people from the film industry to declare their patriotism and to list those suspected of politically unfriendly tendencies. Upset over labor-union strikes and outspoken writers, many film executives were eager to testify. During the hearings, Jack L. Warner, of Warner Brothers, suggested that whenever film writers made fun of rich men or America's political system, they were engaging in communist propaganda. He reported that movies sympathetic to "Indians and the colored folks" were also suspect.[14] Film producer Sam Wood, who had directed Marx Brothers comedies in the mid-1930s, testified that communist writers could be spotted because they portrayed bankers and senators as villainous characters. Whether they believed it was their patriotic duty or they were afraid of losing their jobs, many film executives and prominent actors "named names" in 1947.

Eventually, HUAC subpoenaed ten unwilling witnesses who were questioned about their membership in various organizations. The so-called Hollywood Ten—nine screenwriters and one director—refused to discuss their memberships or to identify communist sympathizers. Charged with contempt of Congress in November 1947, they were eventually sent to prison. Ironically, two Hollywood Ten members went to the same prison as HUAC chairman Thomas, who would later be convicted of conspiracy to defraud the government in a phony payroll scheme. Although jailing the Hollywood Ten clearly violated their free-speech rights, in the atmosphere of the Cold War many seemingly well-intentioned people worried that "the American way" could be sabotaged via unfriendly messages planted in films.

Upon release from jail, the Hollywood Ten found themselves *blacklisted*, or boycotted, by the major studios, and their careers in the film industry were all but ruined. The national fervor over communism continued to plague Hollywood well into the 1950s, and the wounds created then still linger today. In 1999, the Academy of the Motion Picture Arts and Sciences presented an honorary Oscar to Elia Kazan, a formidable director in the 1950s and 1960s (*A Streetcar Named Desire, On the Waterfront, East of Eden*) who testified before HUAC in 1952 and identified eight colleagues, along with himself, who at one time belonged to the American Communist Party. Many people, including actors like Rod Steiger, who starred in Kazan's movies, protested the Academy's decision to honor the filmmaker.

the paramount decision

Coinciding with the political investigations, the government increased its scrutiny of the industry's expanding practices. By the mid-1940s, the Justice Department demanded that the five major film companies—Paramount, Warner Brothers, Twentieth Century Fox, MGM, and RKO—end vertical integration. In 1948, after a series of court appeals, the Supreme Court ruled against the film industry in what is commonly known as "the Paramount decision," forcing the studios to gradually divest themselves of their theaters.

Although the government had hoped to increase competition, the Paramount case never really changed the oligopoly structure of the commercial film industry. Initially, the 1948 decision did create opportunities in the exhibition part of the industry. In addition to art houses showing documentaries or foreign films, thousands of new drive-in theaters sprang up in farmers' fields, welcoming new suburbanites who had left the city and embraced the automobile. Although drive-ins had been around since the 1930s, by the end of the 1950s more than four thousand existed. The Paramount decision encouraged other new indoor theater openings as well, but the major studios continued to dominate distribution. By producing the most polished and popular films, they still controlled consumer demand and orchestrated where the movies would play.

moving to the suburbs

Common sense might suggest that television alone precipitated the decline in post–World War II movie attendance, but the most dramatic drop actually occurred in the late 1940s—*before* most Americans even had TV sets.[15] In fact, with the FCC freeze on TV licenses between 1948 and 1952, most communities did not have TV stations up and running until 1954. By then, the theatergoing audience had already dropped by half.

The transformation of a wartime economy and an unprecedented surge in consumer production had a significant impact on moviegoing. With industries turning from armaments to appliances, Americans started cashing in their savings bonds for household goods and new cars. Discretionary income that formerly went to movie tickets now went to acquiring consumer products. And the biggest product of all was a new house in the suburbs, far from the downtown theaters where movies still premiered. Relying on government help through Veterans Administration loans, people left the cities in record numbers to buy affordable houses in suburban areas where tax bases were lower. Home ownership in the United States doubled between 1945 and 1950, while the moviegoing public decreased just as quickly. According to census data, new housing starts, which had held steady at about 100,000 a year since the late 1920s, leaped to more than 930,000 in 1946 and peaked at 1,700,000 in 1950.

After World War II, the average age for couples entering marriage dropped from twenty-four to nineteen. Unlike their parents, many postwar couples had their first children before they turned twenty-one. The combination of social and economic changes meant there were significantly fewer couples dating at the movies. The suburban move altered spending patterns and had a far more profound impact on movie attendance than did television in the early 1950s. In terms of income, there was little left over for movies after mortgage and car payments. When television exploded in the late 1950s, there was even less discretionary income—and less reason to go to the movies.

television changes hollywood

In the late 1940s, radio's popularity had a stronger impact than television on film's apparent decline. Not only were 1948 and 1949 high points in radio listenership but with the shift to the suburbs, radio entertainment (as it had in the 1930s) offered Americans an inexpensive alternative to the movies. As a result, many people stayed home and listened to radio programs until TV assumed this social function in the mid-1950s. Moviegoing was already in steep decline by the time television further eroded the annual number of movie tickets sold, which had peaked at four billion in 1946 but had declined and then leveled off at around one billion by 1963.

By the mid-1950s, television had displaced both radio and movies as the medium of national entertainment. With growing legions of people gathering around their living-room TV sets, movie content slowly shifted toward more serious subjects. While this may at first have been a response to the war and an acknowledgment of life's complexity, later movies started to focus on subject matter that television did not encourage. This shift in content began with the rise of film noir in the 1940s but continued into the 1950s as commercial movies, for the first time, explored larger social problems, such as alcoholism (*The Lost Weekend*, 1945), anti-Semitism (*Gentleman's Agreement*, 1947), mental illness (*The Snake Pit*, 1948), racism (*Pinky*, 1949), adult-teen relationships (*Rebel without a Cause*, 1955), and drug abuse (*The Man with the Golden Arm*, 1955).

Directors even explored sexual relationships that were formerly off-limits to film (in movies such as *Peyton Place*, 1957; *Butterfield 8*, 1960; and *Lolita*, 1962) and certainly off-limits to viewers of wholesome family television. Filmmakers also challenged the industry's own prohibitive Motion Picture Production Code (see Chapter 16), which had placed restrictions on film content to quiet public and political concerns about the movie business. Like sound recording executives in the early 1990s, movie administrators who worried about government regulation and public boycotts began planning a self-imposed ratings system. The explicit language and situations of *Who's Afraid of Virginia Woolf?* (1966), based on an Edward Albee play, led to the formation of the current ratings system in 1967. Nevertheless, filmmakers continued to make movies considered inappropriate for television as a way of holding on to under-thirty audiences, which had become the dominant group of theatergoers. By the 1980s and 1990s, however, with the baby-boom generation growing older and starting families, commercial opportunities emerged for popular feature-length cartoons and family movies, making Disney the most successful contemporary studio.

In terms of technology, Hollywood tried a number of approaches in an effort to appeal to the new TV generation. Technicolor, invented by an MIT scientist in 1917, had gradually improved, and offered images that far surpassed those on a fuzzy black-and-white TV. Color advancement, though, was not enough for studio chiefs, who were increasingly alarmed by the popularity of television. Just as radio in the 1950s worked to improve sound to maintain an advantage over television, the film industry introduced a host of gimmicks to draw attention to the superiority of movie narratives.

In the early to mid-1950s, Cinerama, CinemaScope, and VistaVision all arrived in movie theaters, featuring striking wide-screen images, multiple synchronized projectors, and stereophonic sound. Then 3-D (three-dimensional) movies appeared, including Warner Brothers' horror film *House of Wax*, wildly popular in its first few weeks in theaters. But, like other experiments, 3-D required a large investment in new projection technology plus special glasses distributed to all moviegoers. In addition, 3-D suffered from out-of-focus images; it wore off quickly as a novelty. Panavision, which used special Eastman color film and camera lenses that decreased the fuzziness of images, finally became the wide-screen standard throughout the industry. The new gimmicks, however, generally failed to address the movies' primary problem: the middle-class flight to the suburbs, away from downtown movie theaters.

While IMAX is chiefly known for its larger-than-life documentaries shown at science museums and theme parks, Sony has brought the big-screen format into downtown neighborhoods. Viewers can don special headgear and see 3-D dinosaurs leaping from the screen in *T-Rex*, or watch Val Kilmer in *Wings of Courage*, a short adventure film. Whether IMAX will go beyond gimmickry and turn into a viable storytelling form is uncertain, however. Production of IMAX film tends to be slow and cumbersome: It takes twenty minutes to load an IMAX camera, which weighs as much as a small refrigerator.

▌hollywood adapts to video

Just as nickelodeons, movie palaces, and drive-ins transformed movie exhibition in earlier times, the key marvel that has transformed contemporary movie exhibition is the videocassette. Despite the scope of Technicolor and wide-screen cinema, and despite theaters experimenting with five-story IMAX megascreens and surround sound, most people still prefer the convenience of watching movies at home. Aside from cassettes, pay-per-view and premium cable have also stolen parts of the theatergoing crowd, leaving box-office receipts accounting for just 24 percent of total film revenue by 1998. To keep their edge, TV manufacturers have introduced stereo sets and produced larger TV screens. New digital screens permit image projection the size of a living-room wall, more closely replicating a theater experience. As television monitors adopt the 16 x 9 aspect ratio of the film screen (wider than the standard 4 x 3 dimension of television screens), the home-video experience will feel even more like going to a movie theater.

> "So TV did not kill Hollywood. In **the great Hollywood whodunit** there is, after all, not even a corpse. The film industry never died. Only *where* we enjoy its latest products has changed, forever."
>
> —Douglas Gomery,
> *Wilson Quarterly*,
> 1991

Even though theater crowds have dwindled over the years, watching movies is a bigger business than ever. Film studios initially feared the coming of television in the 1950s—to the point of banning film actors from performing on the small screen—but television has, ironically, become a major second-run venue for many movies. In similar fashion, the movie industry tried to stall the arrival of the VCR in the 1970s—even filing suits to prohibit consumers from copying movies from television. But home-cassette rentals and purchases have turned into a bonanza for the movie business, extending the profitability of a movie product. For example, Disney's *Beauty and the Beast* was the third-highest-grossing film in 1991, with ticket revenues of $69 million. In video rentals and sales, though, the film earned quadruple that amount—$270 million—for Disney's video and distribution subsidiary Buena Vista. Buena Vista's total cassette revenues in 1992 surpassed $1.1 billion, making the subsidiary one of the most profitable business ventures in the entire film industry that year.

With VCRs in nearly 90 percent of U.S. homes by 1999, consumers spent $17 billion on prerecorded videos, about evenly split between purchases and rentals. Although growth in the video industry has leveled off, chains such as Blockbuster and Hollywood Video still maintain an edge over pay-per-view and premium cable channels by offering large libraries of titles. As movie titles began to be released on the DVD medium in 1997, and as prices for consumer DVD players dropped below $500, video stores began offering DVD versions of movies for sale and rental.

the economics of the movie business

Despite the development of made-for-TV movies as well as the rise of the network era, cable television, pay-per-view, and home video, the movie business has continued to thrive. In fact, since 1963 Americans have purchased roughly one billion movie tickets each year.[16] With average price of first-run movie tickets rising gradually to more than $6 by the late 1990s, gross revenues from box-office sales had climbed to $6.94 billion a year by 1998, up from $3.8 billion annually in the mid-1980s, as shown in Figure 7.2. In addition, video rentals and sales produced another $17 billion a year, more than doubling box-office receipts. To survive and flourish, the movie industry not only followed middle-class migration to the shopping malls but moved right into suburban homes. In other words, by the late 1990s more people watched commercial films on home-video players in one month than attended movie theaters for the entire year.

Figure 7.2
**Gross Revenues from
Box-Office Sales,
1982–98**
Source: Motion Picture Association of America, Inc.

production, distribution, and exhibition today

It took until the 1970s for the movie industry to determine where the moviegoers had gone and how to catch up with them. Among the major "stars" in this effort were multiscreen movie complexes, located either in shopping malls or at the crossroads of major highways. Throughout the 1970s, attendance by young moviegoers at the new multiplexes made megahits of *The Godfather* (1972), *The Exorcist* (1973), *Jaws* (1975), *Rocky* (1976), and *Star Wars* (1977). During this period, *Jaws* and *Star Wars* became the first movies to gross more than $100 million at the box office in a single year.

In trying to copy the success of these blockbuster hits, the major studios set in place economic strategies for the 1980s and 1990s. With 80 to 90 percent of newly released movies failing to make money at the box office, the studios hoped for at least one major hit each year to offset losses on other films. By the 1980s, though, studios were already recouping box-office losses through the lucrative video market, as well as through foreign markets. For example, while Kevin Costner's *Waterworld* (1995) earned only about $88 million in the United States (well short of its $175 million in production and marketing costs), it went on to earn an additional $167 million in foreign markets and recorded an overall profit.

Even with the rise of smaller-budget independent-style films, Hollywood movie costs continue to soar. By 1997, a major studio film, on average, cost nearly $54 million to produce, an increase of 34 percent over the previous year. Marketing, advertising, and print costs climbed 12 percent, to $22.2 million per film, bringing the total average cost for major studio motion pictures to more than $75 million by the late 1990s.[17] To recover these costs, a studio receives money from at least five sources. First, about 40 percent of the box-office revenues from a film go to the producing studio, with 60 percent going to the theaters. Second, movie-video sales and rentals account for more than half of all domestic-film income for major studios. Third, studios earn profits from distributing films in foreign markets. Fourth, studios make money by distributing the work of independent producers and filmmakers, who usually must hire the studios to gain wide circulation. Independents pay the studios between 30 and 50 percent of the box-office and video-rental money they make from movies. As distributors, the film studios bear no production costs and charge independents for advertising and promoting their movies. Independents also pay distributors for making copies of the films sent to theaters and video stores. Since producers make money only after all distribution costs are paid, distributors can earn revenue even when the producers don't.

Finally, major studios are increasingly gaining revenue from product placements in their movies. In the earlier days of television and film, characters generally used generic products, or product labels weren't highlighted in shots. For example, Bette Davis's and Humphrey Bogart's cigarette packs were rarely seen in their movies. But, with soaring film production costs, product placements are adding extra revenues while lending an element of authenticity to the staging. Famous product placements in movies include Reese's Pieces in *E.T.: The Extra-Terrestrial* (1982), Pepsi-Cola in *Back to the Future II* (1989), McDonald's (with a sign that says "over 19 dozen sold") in *The Flintstones* (1994), and BMW, briefly driven by James Bond in *GoldenEye* (1995). The high profile of America Online in *You've Got Mail* (1998) netted between $3 and $6 million for Warner Brothers—the largest product placement deal yet.

Sometimes product-placement deals go awry if changes in the movie story negatively affect the product placements. For example, in 1997 Reebok sued Tristar Pictures for breach of contract for portraying Reebok in a poor light in *Jerry McGuire*. Reebok had provided Tristar with more than $1.5 million in advertising, promotional support, and merchandise in exchange for an ending in which Tidwell, the ambitious football player, finally gets noticed with an expensive endorsement package from Reebok. Instead, after the original scene was cut for creative reasons, the movie ends on a sour note for Reebok, with Tidwell bitter about being ignored by the athletic footwear company. Such conflicts raise questions about how severely product placements should impact a movie's narrative.

Generally, major stars and directors receive separate fees and percentages totaling another $30 million over and above the production costs for a blockbuster-type movie. Lesser-known actors and directors, assistant producers, screenplay writers, costume and set designers, film editors, music composers, and the cinematographers who physically shoot the movie, however, are paid a flat fee for their work and do not usually share in the net profits from a movie (although Dreamworks, Disney, Warner Brothers, and Columbia Pictures now write contracts that give cartoon animators and screenwriters a share of a film's profits). With the *total* cost for producing and distributing many Hollywood movies amounting to as much as $130 million by 1997, the studios claim that little revenue remains to share once the bills are paid.[18]

Film exhibition, like distribution, is now controlled by a handful of theater chains. By the end of the 1990s, several major consolidations had left ten companies operating more than 60 percent of U.S. screens. The major chains include General Cinema, Regal Cinemas, Carmike Cinemas, Loews Cineplex Entertainment, and United Artists Theatres. All five chains own thousands of screens each in suburban malls and at highway crossroads, and have expanded into international markets as well. Since distributors require access to movie screens, they do business with these chains that control the most screens. In a multiplex, an exhibitor can project a potential hit on two or three screens at the same time; films that do not debut well are relegated to the smallest theaters or bumped quickly for a new release.

The strategy of the leading theater chains is to build more multiplexes, but with more luxurious screening rooms and upscale concession services to make moviegoing a special event. The strategy appears to be working—attracting 1.48 billion admissions in 1998, the most since 1959. Still, going out to the movies appeals to only a specific market of people: Frequent moviegoers make up only 28 percent of the population, but they account for 81 percent of ticket sales.[19]

Tapping into markets that are generally under-served, Earvin "Magic" Johnson (formerly of the NBA's Los Angeles Lakers) teamed up with Sony Theatres in the 1990s to build Magic Johnson Theatres in urban minority communities in Los Angeles,

Atlanta, Houston, and elsewhere. By building near existing shopping areas and hiring from the surrounding community, these state-of-the-art multiplexes provide employment opportunities and foster local economic growth as well as offer entertainment.

the major players

The American commercial film business and the classic Hollywood narrative remained dominant into the twenty-first century. Although MGM/UA (*Get Shorty*, *Tomorrow Never Dies*) was making a comeback after years of neglect and mismanagement, the industry was ruled primarily by six companies: Warner Brothers, Paramount, Twentieth Century Fox, Universal, Columbia Pictures, and Walt Disney. Except for Disney, all of these companies are owned by large parent conglomerates (see Table 7.4). One new studio, Dreamworks, created in 1994 by Steven Spielberg, former Disney executive Jeffrey Katzenberg, and sound recording tycoon David Geffen, began to rival the production capabilities of the majors with films like *The Peacemaker*, *Saving Private Ryan*, and *Antz*. Nevertheless, the six major studios accounted for more than 90 percent of the revenue generated by commercial films. They also controlled more than half the movie market in Europe and Asia, with nearly a third of the industry's annual box-office profits coming from overseas in the late 1990s.

In the 1980s, to offset losses resulting from box-office failures, the movie industry began to diversify, expanding into other product lines and other mass media. This expansion included television programming, print media, sound recordings, and home videos as well as cable and computers, electronic hardware and software, videocassettes, and theme parks such as Universal Studios. Indicative of the effectiveness of this strategy, in 1980 more than 80 percent of movie-studio revenue came from box-office receipts; by the late 1990s, less than 25 percent came from that source.

To maintain the industry's economic stability, management strategies today rely on both heavy advance promotion (which can double the cost of a commercial film) and the process of *synergy*—the promotion and sale of a product throughout the various subsidiaries of the media conglomerate. In other words, companies promote not only the new movie itself but its book form, sound track, calendars, T-shirts, Web site, toy action figures, and "the-making-of" story for distribution on television, cable, and home video. The Disney studio, in particular, has been successful with its multiple packaging of the company's movies, which includes comic books, toys, cable specials, fast-food tie-ins,

TABLE 7.4
The Major Players in the Movie Business

Studio	Parent Company	Other Subsidiaries
Warner Brothers	Time Warner (USA)	Turner Broadcasting, WB TV network, HBO, cable systems, magazines, records, D.C. Comics, books, Book-of-the-Month Club, theme parks
Walt Disney	Disney (USA)	ABC, theme parks, ESPN, broadcast stations, cable channels, books, magazines, newspapers, hockey team, baseball team
Columbia Pictures	Sony (Japan)	TV sets, VCRs, camcorders, CD-ROM drives, CD players, Walkman, videotapes, records, TV programs, Loews Cineplex (movie theaters)
Twentieth Century Fox	News Corp. (Australia)	Fox TV network, newspapers, broadcast stations, cable channels, books, satellite-delivery services, baseball team, rugby team
Paramount	Viacom (USA)	Blockbuster Video, UPN TV network, records, books, magazines, MTV, Nickelodeon, Showtime, movie theaters, broadcast stations
Universal	Seagram (Canada)	MCA Records, PolyGram Records, books, cable channels, beverages

and new theme-park attractions. Since the 1950s, this synergy has been the biggest change in the film industry, and a key element in the flood of corporate mergers.

The first company to change hands in the atmosphere of postwar business mergers was Paramount, which was sold to Gulf & Western Industries in 1966. (Paramount is now owned by Viacom, which originally made its mark by syndicating TV shows.) The next year Transamerica, an insurance and financial services company, bought United Artists (which merged with MGM in 1981). The biggest mergers, however, have involved the internationalization of the American film business. This began in 1985, when the Australian media conglomerate News Corp. paid nearly $1 billion for Twentieth Century Fox. Along with News Corp., the new players in Hollywood have been large Japanese electronics firms. First purchased by Coca-Cola in 1980, Columbia Pictures was absorbed by Sony for more than $4 billion in 1989. In the deal, Sony acquired a library of twenty-seven hundred films and twenty-three thousand TV episodes. In 1990, Matsushita paid $7 billion for MCA/Universal and in 1995 sold 80 percent of its Universal stock to Seagram, the Canadian beverage company.

Investment in American popular culture by the international electronics industry is particularly significant. This business strategy represents a new, high-tech kind of vertical integration—an attempt to control both the production of electronic equipment that consumers buy for their homes and the production/distribution of the content that runs on that equipment. Companies such as Sony or Philips in the Netherlands have sought to increase markets for their electronics hardware by buying "software," especially movies, recordings, and TV shows.

While foreign investment in the U.S. commercial film industry has increased, government policies in many nations have attempted to limit the influence of American films. Restrictions on importing U.S. films and TV programs are intended to encourage the domestic film/TV industries in various countries and blunt the impact of U.S. popular culture. In 1989, for example, twelve European countries began placing a 50 percent quota on the amount of time they would allocate for the exhibition of American films and TV shows. With the expansion of cable and satellite-delivered television and movies, however, many countries still depend on inexpensive and abundant U.S. products to fill up channels.

> "It is hard to mix **business and culture**. Business is going to **win**."
> —Jeremy Thomas, British Film Institute, 1996

alternative voices

The growing market and profitability of independent films in the 1990s has helped new voices bring a great breadth of American experiences to film screens. For example, Julie Dash's *Daughters of the Dust* (1992) was the first film to tell a story set in the African American Gullah culture that developed off the coast of South Carolina. *Eve's Bayou*, directed by young black female director Kasi Lemmons, became one of the most successful independent films of 1997, and is notable for resisting Hollywood's stereotypical "black" themes of poverty and gang violence, and instead telling the dramatic story of a middle-class black family in Louisiana in the early 1960s. *The Celluloid Closet* (1995) turned the movie camera on Hollywood itself, documenting the history of homosexual character portrayals in motion pictures. And, after decades of Hollywood films depicting Indians as bad guys, *Smoke Signals* (1998) offered tales of contemporary experiences as the first feature film written and directed by Native Americans.

Like the relationship between the major music corporations (many of which are owned by the same parent corporations that own the major movie studios) and the small labels, independent filmmakers usually want both wide distribution and creative control. The growing number of film festivals, the Sundance and Independent Film Channels on cable and DBS, and the proposed Sundance Cinema chain may provide more creative outlets for these artists.

Although alternative films may be hard to find, most other movies are readily available today—at the mall, on broadcast and cable television, in campus auditoriums, on videocassettes and DVDs, on pay-per-view, and in neighborhood theaters. However flawed, most of these are Hollywood films: the common currency in a global market.

At the cultural level, commercial U.S. films function as *consensus narratives*, a term that describes cultural products that become popular and command wide attention. For all their limitations, classic Hollywood movies, as consensus narratives, provide shared cultural experiences, operating across different times and cultures. In this sense, movies are part of a long narrative tradition, encompassing "the oral-formulaic of Homer's day, the theater of Sophocles, the Elizabethan theater, the English novel from Defoe to Dickens, . . . the silent film, the sound film, and television during the Network Era."[20] Consensus narratives—whether they are dramas, romances, westerns, or mysteries—speak to central myths and values in an accessible language that often bridges global boundaries.

At the international level, countries continue to struggle with questions about the influence of American films on local customs and culture. Like other media industries, the long reach of Hollywood movies is one of the key contradictions of contemporary life: Do such films contribute to a global village in which people throughout the world share a universal culture that breaks down barriers? Or does an American-based common culture stifle the development of local cultures worldwide and diversity in moviemaking? Clearly, the steady production of profitable action/adventure movies—whether they originate in the United States, Africa, France, or China—continues not only because these movies appeal to teens and young adults but because they translate easily into other languages.

With the rise of international media conglomerates, it has become more difficult to awaken public debate over issues of movie diversity and America's domination of the film business. In addition, technological innovations—whether they affect radio, television, film, cable, or the Internet—tend to outpace questions of legislation and regulation. Consequently, issues concerning greater competition and a better variety of movies sometimes fall by the wayside. As critical consumers, those of us who enjoy movies and recognize their cultural significance must raise these broader issues in public forums as well as in our personal conversations.

REVIEW QUESTIONS

Early Technology and the Evolution of Movies

1. How did film go from the novelty stage to the mass-medium stage?

2. Why were early silent films popular?

3. What contribution did nickelodeons make to film history?

The Power of the Studio System

4. Why did Hollywood end up as the center of film production?

5. Why did Thomas Edison and the patents Trust fail to shape and control the film industry, and why did Adolph Zukor of Paramount succeed?

6. How does vertical integration work in the film business?

The Triumph of Hollywood Storytelling

7. Why did a certain structure of film—called classic Hollywood narrative—become so dominant in moviemaking?

8. Why are genres and directors important to the film industry?

9. Why are documentaries an important alternative to traditional Hollywood filmmaking? What contributions have they made to the film industry?

The Transformation of the Hollywood System

10. What political and cultural forces changed the Hollywood system in the 1950s?

11. Explain how television changed the film industry.

12. How has the movie industry used television to its advantage?

The Economics of the Movie Business

13. How do a few large film studios manage to control more than 90 percent of the commercial industry?

14. Why do U.S. movies remain popular worldwide while other countries have had great difficulty getting their films into the United States?

15. Do films contribute to a global village in which people throughout the world share a universal culture? Or do U.S.-based films overwhelm the development of other cultures worldwide? Discuss.

QUESTIONING MEDIA

1. Describe your earliest memory of going to a movie. Do some research and compare this with a parent's or grandparent's earliest memory. Compare the different experiences.

2. Do you remember a movie you were not allowed to see? Discuss the experience.

3. How often do you go to movie theaters today? How often do you rent movies on video or DVD? Which experience do you prefer and why?

4. If you were a Hollywood film producer or executive, what kinds of films would you like to see made? What changes would you make in what we see at the movies?

5. Look at the international film box-office statistics in the latest issue of *Variety* magazine. Note which films are the most popular worldwide. What do you think about the significant role U.S. movies play in global culture? Should their role be less significant? Explain your answer.

SEARCHING THE INTERNET

http://www.hollywood.com
Hollywood Online includes film reviews, movie trailers and clips, sound-track files, TV movies, Hollywood headlines, film-release calendars, film festival reports, and an online store.

http://www.film.com
More film reviews, movie trailers and clips, movie sound-track files, film-release calendars, film-festival reports, and an online film store.

http://www.aint-it-cool-news.com
Movie reviews and humorous, critical industry-insider accounts written by Texas-based Harry Knowles.

http://us.imdb.com
The Internet Movie Database is a powerful, searchable movie database of more than 180,000 film titles.

http://movieweb.com
Movieweb contains listings of all motion-picture releases dating back to 1995, organized by year and by studio, as well as weekly box-office rankings.

http://www.indiewire.com
News about independent films and do-it-yourself moviemaking information.

http://www.sundance.org
Information on the Sundance Film Festival, and a searchable database of independent films.

In Brief

In class, make a tally of who prefers to attend movies in the theater and who prefers to watch movies at home on video or DVD. Discuss the advantages and disadvantages of both viewing habits. Discuss whether theatergoing will become obsolete in the next decade, given that increasingly more revenue is earned in video release than through box-office receipts.

What could be done to enhance moviegoing in theaters? Make a list. How might your ideas be reasonably financed? Would there be a payoff for theater owners?

In Depth

Pick a current popular film you have seen or one the class has seen together. Write a three- to four-page (750–1,000 word) movie critique either defending or attacking the movie as a form of popular culture (see Chapter 1). Include plenty of examples to fortify your argument, and focus on three or four significant points. Use the following plan to organize your critique:

1. Introduction. In your opening paragraph, identify the central argument (the critical stand you are taking) that will help focus and organize your essay.

2. Body. Support your argument by drawing on examples from the movie. Think about the first three critical stages: description, analysis, and interpretation. For example, in preparing to write your paper, describe important plot, theme, or character points that are relevant to your argument. (This is essentially the note-taking part of your paper; most of your paper should not merely describe plots and character details.) Then analyze the particular patterns (the three or four significant points) that you have chosen to examine. Finally, interpret what all of this information might mean based on the evidence you provide.

3. Conclusion. Discuss the limits of your critique and offer evaluations of the film industry based on your evidence and your interpretations. Evaluate the movie by judging whether it works as high art or as popular culture. As part of your evaluation, cite reviews from other publications to support your point of view.

CHAPTER 8

In 1887, a young reporter left her job at the *Pittsburgh Dispatch* to seek her fortune in New York City. Although only twenty-three years old, she had grown tired of merely replying to letters and writing for the society pages. She wanted to be on the front page. In those days, however, it was considered unladylike for women journalists to use their real names, so the *Dispatch* editors changed her name from Elizabeth "Pink" Cochrane to Nellie Bly, a name adapted from a Stephen Foster song about the servant daughter of former slaves.

After four months of persistent job-hunting and freelance writing, Nellie Bly earned a tryout at Joseph Pulitzer's *New York World*, the nation's biggest paper. Her assignment: investigate the deplorable conditions at the Women's Lunatic Asylum on Blackwell's Island. Her method: get herself declared mad and committed to the asylum. After practicing the look of a disheveled lunatic in front of mirrors, wandering city streets dazed and unwashed, and terrifying her fellow boarders in a New York rooming house by acting crazy, she succeeded in convincing doctors and officials to commit her. Other New York newspapers even reported her incarceration, speculating on the identity of this "mysterious waif," this "pretty crazy girl" with the "wild, hunted look in her eyes."[1]

Ten days later, an attorney from the *World* went in to get her out. Her two-part story appeared in October 1887 and caused a sensation in New York. She was the first reporter to have pulled off such a stunt. In the days before so-called objective journalism, Nellie Bly's dramatic first-person accounts documented harsh cold baths ("three buckets of water over my head—ice cold water—into my eyes, my ears, my nose and my mouth"); "cruel" attendants who abused and taunted patients; and newly arrived immigrant women, completely sane, who were committed to this "rat trap" simply because no one could understand them. After the series, Bly was famous. Pulitzer gave her a permanent job, and the city of New York committed $1 million toward upgrading the conditions of its asylums.

Within a year, Nellie Bly exposed a variety of shady scam artists, corrupt politicians and lobbyists, and unscrupulous business practices. Posing as an unwed mother with an unwanted child, she uncovered an outfit trafficking in newborn babies. Disguised as a sinner in need of reform, she revealed the appalling conditions at a home for "unfortunate women." And after stealing $50 from another woman's purse, she got herself arrested and reported on how women were treated in New York jails.

A lifetime champion of women and the poor, Nellie Bly also pioneered what was called at the time *detective* or *stunt* journalism. Her work would inspire the whole twentieth-century practice of investigative journalism—from Ida Tarbell's exposés of oil corporations in the early 1900s to the award-winning *Wall Street Journal* investigations of big tobacco companies in the mid-1990s. From the vantage point of both the press and the public, this investigative tradition remains one of journalism's most revered contributions to democracy.

Along with their watchdog role, newspapers play many parts in American culture. As chroniclers of daily life, newspapers both inform and entertain. They give assurances that communities are safe and nations are secure. Newspapers also help readers make choices about everything from the kind of food to eat to the kind of leaders to vote for. Comic strips and political cartoons find humor in everyday events. Opinion pages organize public debates and persuade readers to a particular point of view. Syndicated columnists offer everything from practical advice to political insight.

Despite the importance of newspapers in daily life, in today's digital age the industry is losing both papers and readers at an alarming rate. Newspapers still garner a substantial portion of the nation's advertising dollars, but the loss of papers and readers raises significant concerns in a nation where newspapers have historically functioned as a watchdog over democratic life. To provide some background for the current declines, we will trace the history of newspapers through a number of influential periods and styles. We will explore the eras of the early political-commercial press, the penny press, and yellow journalism. Turning to the modern era, we will examine the influence of the *New York Times* and twentieth-century journalism's embrace of objectivity. During this era, interpretive journalism emerged in the 1920s and 1930s to improve news practices; the revival of literary journalism followed in the 1960s. We will also look at the evolution of contemporary newspapers and examine different ways of categorizing them. Finally, we will review issues of chain ownership, new technology, and the role of newspapers in a democracy.

> "There's almost no media experience sweeter . . . than poring over a good newspaper. In the quiet morning, with a cup of coffee—so long as you haven't turned on the TV, listened to the radio, or checked in online—it's as comfortable and personal as information gets."
>
> —Jon Katz,
> *Wired* magazine,
> 1994

the evolution of american newspapers

The idea of news is as old as language itself. The earliest news was passed along orally from family to family, from tribe to tribe, by community leaders and oral historians. The first written news accounts, or *news sheets*, were probably posted items distributed by local rulers and governments. The earliest known news sheet, *Acta Diurna* (Latin for "daily events") was developed by Julius Caesar and posted in Rome in 59 B.C. Even in its oral and early written stages, news informed people on the state of their relations with neighboring tribes and towns. The development of the printing press in the fifteenth century greatly accelerated a society's ability to send and receive information. Throughout history, news has satisfied our need to know things we cannot experience personally. Newspapers today continue to document daily life and bear witness to ordinary and extraordinary events.

colonial newspapers and the partisan press

The first newspaper produced in North America was *Publick Occurrences, Both Foreign and Domestick*, published on September 25, 1690, by Boston printer Benjamin Harris. The colonial government objected to Harris's negative tone regarding British rule, and local ministers were offended by a report that the king of France had an affair with his son's wife. Consequently, the newspaper was banned after one issue.

In 1704, the first regularly published newspaper appeared in the American colonies—the *Boston News-Letter*, published by John Campbell. Considered dull, it reported on mundane events that had taken place in Europe months earlier. Because European news took weeks or months to travel by ship, these early colonial papers were not very timely. In their more spirited sections, however, the papers did report local illnesses, public floggings, and even suicides. In 1721, also in Boston, James Franklin, the older brother of Benjamin Franklin, started the *New England Courant*. The *Courant* established a tradition of running stories that interested ordinary readers rather than printing articles that appealed primarily to business and colonial leaders. In 1729, Benjamin Franklin, at age twenty-four, took over the *Pennsylvania Gazette*, which historians rate among the best of the colonial papers. Although a number of colonial papers operated solely on subsidies from political parties, the *Gazette* also made money by advertising products; with a few thousand readers, it had the highest circulation in its day.

Another important colonial paper was the *New York Weekly Journal*, which appeared in 1733. John Peter Zenger had been installed as the printer of the *Journal* by the Popular Party, a political group that opposed British rule and ran articles that criticized the royal governor of New York. After a Popular Party judge was dismissed from office, the *Journal* escalated its attack on the governor. When Zenger shielded the writers of the critical articles, he was arrested in 1734 for *seditious libel*—defaming a public official's character in print. Championed by famed Philadelphia lawyer

> "**Oral news systems** must have arrived early in the development of language, some tens or even hundreds of thousands of years ago. . . . And the dissemination of news accomplishes some of the basic purposes of language: informing others, entertaining others, **protecting the tribe**."
>
> —Mitchell Stephens, *A History of News*, 1988

The *New-England Courant* was founded in 1721 as Boston's fourth newspaper by James Franklin, older brother of Benjamin Franklin. At a time before photography, the elaborate biblical-style engraving used on this 1722 front page to surround the letter *H* helped enhance the dull grayness of printed copy.

Andrew Hamilton, Zenger ultimately won his case in 1735. A sympathetic jury, in revolt against the colonial government, ruled that newspapers had the right to criticize government leaders as long as the reports were true. After the Zenger case, the British never prosecuted another colonial printer. Although the case did not substantially change sedition laws at the time, the Zenger decision would later provide a key foundation for the First Amendment to the Constitution—the right of a democratic press to criticize public officials.

By 1765, about thirty newspapers operated in the American colonies. The first *daily* paper began in 1784. These papers were of two general types: political or commercial. The development of both types was shaped in large part by social, cultural, and political responses to British rule and by its eventual overthrow. The gradual rise of political parties and the spread of commerce also played a significant role in the development of these early papers. Although the political and commercial papers carried both party news and business news, they had different agendas. The political paper, or **partisan press**, generally argued one point of view or pushed the plan of the particular political group that subsidized the paper. The more commercial press, on the other hand, served the leaders of commerce, who were interested in economic issues. Both of these early developments in journalism left a legacy. The partisan press gave us the editorial pages, and the early commercial press was the forerunner of the business section in modern papers.

From the early 1700s to the early 1800s, even the largest of these papers rarely reached a circulation of fifteen hundred. Readership was confined primarily to educated or wealthy men who controlled local politics and commerce. During this time, though, a few pioneering women operated newspapers, including Elizabeth Timothy, the first American woman newspaper publisher. After her husband died of smallpox in 1738, Timothy took over the *South Carolina Gazette*, established in 1734 by Benjamin Franklin and the Timothy family, which included her eight children. Also during this period, Anna Maul Zenger ran the *New York Journal* throughout her husband's trial and after his death in 1746.[2] In general, though, the interests of women readers were not well addressed by either the political or commercial press. By the 1830s, however, the Industrial Revolution and the rise of the middle classes had spurred the growth of literacy and set the stage for a more popular and inclusive press.

the penny-press era

By the late 1820s, the average newspaper cost six cents a copy and was sold not through street sales but through annual subscriptions priced at $10 to $12. Because that price represented more than a week's salary for most skilled workers, newspaper readers were mostly affluent. The Industrial Revolution spawned the conversion from expensive handmade to inexpensive machine-made paper. And when cheaper paper combined with increased literacy, *penny papers* soon began competing with conventional six-cent papers. In the 1820s, breakthroughs in technology, particularly steam-powered presses replacing mechanical presses, permitted publishers to produce as many as four thousand newspapers an hour. Subscriptions remained the preferred sales tool of many penny papers, although they began relying increasingly on the daily sales of street vendors.

In 1833, printer Benjamin Day founded the *New York Sun.* After cutting the price to one penny, he also eliminated subscriptions. The *Sun* (whose slogan was "It shines for all") highlighted local events, scandals, and police reports. It also ran serialized stories, making legends of frontiersmen Davy Crockett and Daniel Boone and blazing the trail for the media's twentieth-century enthusiasm for celebrity news. In the tradition of today's tabloids, the *Sun* fabricated stories, including the famous moon hoax, which reported "scientific" evidence of life on the moon. Within six months, the *Sun's* lower price had generated a circulation of eight thousand, twice that of its nearest competitor.

The *Sun's* success initiated a wave of penny papers that favored **human-interest stories**: news accounts that focus on the trials and tribulations of the human condition, often featuring ordinary individuals facing extraordinary challenges. These kinds of stories show journalism's ties to literary traditions (which today can be found in the horror or gangster news-story genres of urban drug and crime coverage).

The penny-press era also featured James Gordon Bennett's *New York Morning Herald,* founded in 1835. Bennett, considered the first press baron, aimed to free his newspaper from political parties. He wanted to establish an independent paper serving middle- and working-class readers as well as his own business ambitions. The *Herald* concentrated on crime reports, human

Newsboys and newsgirls sold Hearst and Pulitzer papers on the streets of New York in the 1890s. With more than a dozen dailies competing, street tactics were ferocious, and publishers often made "newsies"—many of whom were under twelve—buy the papers they could not sell.

interest, moral reflections, political scandals, fashion notes, and colloquial tales and jokes. By 1860, it reached nearly eighty thousand readers, making it the world's largest daily paper at the time.

The penny papers were innovative. They were the first to assign reporters to cover crime. In New York, where the penny-press competition was fierce, readers enthusiastically embraced the reporting of local news and crime. Although the *Herald* carried political essays and business stories, it also included a letters section, religious news, play reviews, society news, sports stories, and later, reports from dozens of correspondents sent to cover the Civil War. In an era before modern "objective" journalism, Bennett's paper sponsored yacht and balloon races, financed safaris, and overplayed crime and sex stories. After his first visit to America in the early 1840s, British writer Charles Dickens used the *Herald* as a model for the sleazy *Rowdy Journal,* the fictional newspaper in his novel *Martin Chuzzlewit.*

By gradually separating daily front-page reporting from overt political viewpoints on an editorial page, New York's penny papers shifted their economic base from political-party subsidies to the market—to advertising revenue, classified ads, and street sales. Although many partisan papers took a moral stand against advertising certain questionable products, the penny press became more neutral toward advertisers and printed virtually any ad. In fact, many penny papers regarded ads as a kind of consumer news. The rise in ad revenues and circulation accelerated the growth of the newspaper industry. In 1830, 650 weekly and 65 daily papers operated in the United States, reaching 80,000 readers. By 1840, a total of 1,140 weeklies and 140 dailies attracted 300,000 readers.

In 1848, six New York newspapers in a cooperative arrangement founded the Associated Press (AP), the first major news wire service. **Wire services** began as commercial organizations that relayed news stories and information around the country and the world using telegraph lines (and eventually radio waves and digital transmissions). In the case of AP, the New York papers provided access to both their own stories and those from other newspapers. In the 1850s, papers started sending reporters to cover Washington, and in the early 1860s more than a hundred reporters from northern papers went south to cover the Civil War, relaying their reports back to their home papers via telegraph and wire services. The news-wire companies permitted news to travel rapidly from coast to coast and set the stage for modern journalism.

The combination of marketing news as a national and global product and using modern technology to dramatically cut costs gradually elevated newspapers to the status of a mass medium. By also adapting news content, penny papers captured the middle- and working-class readers who could now afford the paper and also had more leisure time to read it. As newspapers sought to sustain their mass appeal, news and "factual" reports about crimes and other items of human interest eventually superseded partisan articles about politics and commerce.

the age of yellow journalism

The rise of competitive dailies and the penny press spawned the next significant period in American journalism. Labeled the era of **yellow journalism**, this late 1800s development emphasized profitable papers that carried exciting human-interest stories, crime news, large headlines, and more readable copy. This period is generally regarded as the age of sensationalism, the direct forerunner of today's tabloid papers and TV magazine shows like *A Current Affair*. The era of yellow journalism featured two major characteristics. First were the overly dramatic stories about crimes, disasters, scandals, and intrigue. The second, and sometimes forgotten, legacy is that the yellow press provided the roots for investigative journalism: news reports that hunted out and exposed corruption, particularly in business and government. Reporting was viewed as a crusading force for common people, with the press assuming a watchdog role on behalf of the public.

> "There is room in this **great and growing city** for a journal that is not only cheap but bright, not only bright but large . . . that will expose all **fraud and sham**, fight all public evils and abuses—that will serve and battle for the people."
>
> —Joseph Pulitzer,
> publisher,
> *New York World*,
> 1883

During this period, a newspaper circulation war pitted William Randolph Hearst's *New York Journal* against Joseph Pulitzer's *New York World*. A key player in the war was the first popular cartoon strip, "The Yellow Kid," created by artist R. F. Outcault in 1895. The phrase *yellow journalism* has since become associated with the cartoon strip, which shuttled between the Hearst and Pulitzer papers during their furious battle for readers in the mid to late 1890s.

Pulitzer and the *New York World*. After a brief career in St. Louis politics, Joseph Pulitzer, a Jewish-Hungarian immigrant, became part owner of the *St. Louis Post* newspaper in the early 1870s. He then bought the bankrupt *St. Louis Dispatch* for $2,500 at an auction in 1878 and merged it with the *Post*. The *Post-Dispatch* became known for stories that highlighted "sex and sin" ("A Denver Maiden Taken from Disreputable House") and satires of the upper class ("St. Louis Swells"). Pulitzer also viewed the *Post-Dispatch* as a "national conscience" that promoted the public good. Pulitzer carried on the legacies of Bennett: making money and developing a "free and impartial" paper that would "serve no party but the people." Within five years, the *Post-Dispatch* had become one of the most influential newspapers in the Midwest.

THE BIG TYPE WAR OF THE YELLOW KIDS.

Generally considered America's first comic-strip character, the Yellow Kid was created in the mid-1890s by cartoonist Richard Outcault. The cartoon was so popular that newspaper barons Joseph Pulitzer and William Randolph Hearst fought over Outcault's services, giving yellow journalism its name. A New York street urchin, the Kid became a merchandising marvel, with his image plastered on everything from cracker tins to cigarette packs.

In 1883, Pulitzer bought the *New York World* for $346,000. He encouraged plain writing and the inclusion of maps and illustrations to help immigrant and working-class readers. In addition to running sensational stories on crime, sex, and cannibalism, Pulitzer instituted advice columns and women's pages. Like Bennett, Pulitzer treated advertising as a kind of news that displayed consumer products for readers. Department stores became a major advertising source during this period. The revenue from these stores contributed directly to the expansion of consumer culture and indirectly to the acknowledgment of women as newspaper readers and to their eventual employment as reporters.

The *World* reflected the contradictory spirit of the yellow press. It crusaded for improved urban housing, better conditions for women, and equitable labor laws. It campaigned against monopoly practices by AT&T, Standard Oil, and Equitable Insurance. Such popular crusades helped lay the groundwork for tightening federal antitrust laws in the early 1910s. At the same time, Pulitzer's paper manufactured news events and staged stunts, such as sending star reporter Nellie Bly around the world in seventy-two days to beat the fictional record in the popular 1873 Jules Verne novel, *Around the World in Eighty Days.* Reflecting the spirit of contradiction, Pulitzer was also a ruthless businessman who once tried to break a strike by the *World*'s newsboys and newsgirls (who believed they should not have to pay Pulitzer for papers they did not sell).

Pulitzer did manage to redeem his reputation by leaving $2 million to establish the graduate school of journalism at Columbia University in 1912. In 1917, part of Pulitzer's Columbia endowment launched the Pulitzer Prizes, the prestigious awards given each year for distinguished achievements in journalism, literature, drama, and music.

Hearst and the *New York Journal*. By 1887, the *World*'s Sunday circulation had soared to more than 250,000, the largest in the world. Eight years later, however, the paper faced its fiercest competition when William Randolph Hearst bought the *New York Journal.* Before moving to New York, Hearst had taken the reins of the *San Francisco Examiner* from his father, George Hearst, who had purchased the paper to further a political career. In 1887, when George was elected to the U.S. Senate, he turned the paper over to his twenty-four-year-old son, who had recently been expelled from Harvard for a practical joke he played on his professors. In 1895, with an inheritance from his father, the son bought the ailing *New York Journal* (a penny paper founded by Pulitzer's brother Albert) and then raided Joseph Pulitzer's paper for editors, writers, and cartoonists.

Taking his cue from Bennett and Pulitzer, Hearst focused on lurid, sensational stories and appealed (and pandered) to immigrant readers by using large headlines and bold layout designs. To boost circulation, the *Journal* invented interviews, faked pictures, and encouraged conflicts that might result in a story. One account of Hearst's tabloid legacy describes "tales about two-headed virgins" and "prehistoric creatures roaming the plains of Wyoming."[3] In promoting journalism as storytelling, Hearst reportedly said, "The modern editor of the popular journal does not care for facts. The editor wants novelty. The editor has no objection to facts if they are also novel. But he would prefer a novelty that is not a fact to a fact that is not a novelty."[4]

Hearst is remembered as an unscrupulous publisher who once hired gangsters to distribute his newspapers. He was also, however, considered a champion of the underdog, and his paper's readership soared among the working and middle classes. In 1896, the *Journal*'s daily circulation reached 450,000, and by 1897 the Sunday edition of the paper rivaled the 600,000 circulation of the *World*. By the 1930s, Hearst's holdings included more than forty daily and Sunday papers, thirteen magazines (including *Good Housekeeping* and *Cosmopolitan*), eight radio stations, and two film companies. In addition, he controlled King Feature Syndicate, which sold and distributed articles, comics, and features to many of the nation's twenty-five hundred dailies. Hearst, the model for Charles Foster Kane, the ruthless and lonely publisher in Orson Welles's classic 1940 film *Citizen Kane*, operated the largest media business in the world—the Time Warner of its day.

american print journalism in the modern period

Although objectivity is considered a modern journalistic idea, the early commercial and partisan press was, to some extent, covering important events impartially. These papers often carried verbatim reports of presidential addresses, murder trials, or the annual statements of the U.S. Treasury. In the late 1800s, this journalistic ideal was overshadowed as newspapers pushed for circulation and emphasized sensational news, especially in New York. By the late 1890s, two distinct types of journalism were competing for readers: a *story* model, advanced by the penny and the yellow press, which emphasized dramatizing important events, and an *information* model, advocated by the six-cent papers, which emphasized an approach that appeared more factual.[5]

the advent of modern journalism

As the consumer marketplace expanded during the Industrial Revolution, facts and news became marketable products that could be sold to consumers. Throughout the mid-1800s, the more a newspaper appeared not to take sides, the more its readership base could be extended (although editorial pages were often rabidly supportive of particular political candidates). In addition, wire-service organizations were serving a variety of newspaper clients in different regions of the country. To satisfy all their clients and the wide range of political views, newspapers began to at least look more impartial.

Ochs and the *New York Times*. The ideal of an impartial, or informational, news model was reinvented by Adolph Ochs, who bought the *New York Times* in 1896. The son of immigrant German Jews, Ochs grew up in Ohio and Tennessee, where at age twenty-one he took over the *Chattanooga Times* in 1878. Known more for his business and organizational ability than for his writing and editing skills, he transformed the Tennessee paper. Ochs then moved to New York and invested $75,000 in the struggling *Times*. Through wise hiring, Ochs's staff of editors rebuilt the paper around substantial news coverage and provocative editorial pages. To distance themselves from the yellow press, the editors also downplayed entertainment news and sensational features, favoring the documentation of major events or issues.

Such distancing was partly a marketing strategy to counter the large circulations of the Hearst and Pulitzer papers. Ochs offered a distinct contrast to the more sensational newspapers: an *informational* paper that offered stock and real-estate reports to businesses, court reports to legal professionals, treaty summaries to political leaders, and theater and book reviews to intellectuals. Ochs's promotional gimmicks took direct aim at yellow journalism, advertising the *Times* under the motto "It does not soil the breakfast cloth." The strategy of the *Times* was similar to many TV marketing plans today, which target upscale viewers who control a disproportionate share of consumer dollars.

With the Hearst and Pulitzer papers capturing the bulk of working- and middle-class readers, managers at the *Times* at first associated their straightforward reporting with people of higher social status. In 1898, however, Ochs lowered the paper's price to a penny. His thinking was that people bought the *World* and the *Journal* primarily because they were cheap, not because of their storytelling. As a result, the *Times* began attracting more middle-class readers who gravitated to the paper as a status marker for the educated and well informed. Between 1898 and 1899, its circulation rose from 25,000 to 75,000. By 1921, the *New York Times* had a daily circulation of 330,000 and 500,000 on Sunday. (For contemporary circulation figures, see Table 8.1.)

"**Just the facts, please**." At the dawn of the twentieth century, with reporters adopting a more scientific attitude to news- and fact-gathering, the ideal of objectivity began to anchor journalism. In **objective journalism**, which distinguishes factual reports from opinion columns, modern reporters strive to maintain a neutral attitude toward the issue or event they cover; they also search out competing points of view among the sources for a story. This kind of reporting is often distinguished by the **inverted-pyramid style**. (See Figure 8.1.) Civil War correspondents developed this style by imitating the terse, compact press releases that came from Lincoln's secretary of war, Edwin M. Stanton.[6] Often stripped of adverbs and adjectives, inverted-pyramid reports began with the most dramatic or newsworthy information. They answered *who, what, where, when* (and, less frequently, *why* or *how*) questions at the top of the story and then tailed off with less-significant details. If wars or natural disasters disrupted the telegraph transmissions of these dispatches, the information the reporter chose to lead the story often had the best chance of getting through.

TABLE 8.1
The Nation's Largest Daily Newspapers

Newspaper	1998 Circulation*	Newspaper	1998 Circulation*
Wall Street Journal	1,740,450	Newsday	572,444
USA Today[+]	1,653,428	Houston Chronicle	550,763
Los Angeles Times	1,067,540	Chicago Sun-Times	485,666
New York Times	1,066,658	Dallas Morning News[+]	479,863
Washington Post	759,122	San Francisco Chronicle	475,324
(New York) Daily News	723,143	Boston Globe	470,825
Chicago Tribune	673,508		

*Average weekday circulation at the nation's largest newspapers for the six months ending September 30, 1998.

[+]Fridays excluded.

Source: Audit Bureau of Circulations, Schaumburg, Il.; <www.mediainfo.com> (Web site for *Editor & Publisher*, trade publication for newspaper industry).

Figure 8.1
The Inverted-Pyramid Style of Reporting

Most important, newsworthy, or dramatic information—answer who, what, when, where, why, and how questions

Key quotes, supporting evidence, and details

Supporting facts and explanations—more quotes

Supporting quotes and alternative explanations

Least important details

For most of this century, the inverted-pyramid style has served as an efficient way to arrange a timely story. As one news critic points out, the wire services that used the inverted-pyramid style when distributing stories to newspapers nationwide "had to deal with large numbers of newspapers with widely different political and regional interests. The news had to be 'objective' . . . to be accepted by such a heterogeneous group."[7] Among other things, the importance of objectivity and the reliance on the inverted pyramid signaled journalism's break from the partisan tradition. Although difficult to achieve, the notion of objectivity nonetheless became (and in many ways remains) the guiding ideal of the modern press.

Despite the success of the *New York Times* and other informational papers, the more factual approach toward news has come under increasing scrutiny. As newswriting coach Roy Peter Clark has noted: "Some reporters let the pyramid control the content so that the news comes out homogenized. Traffic fatalities, three-alarm fires and new city ordinances all begin to look alike. In extreme cases, reporters have been known to keep files of story forms. Fill in the blanks. Stick it in the paper."[8] Although the inverted-pyramid style has for years solved deadline problems for reporters and allowed editors to cut a story from the bottom to fit available space, it has also discouraged many readers from continuing beyond the key details in the opening paragraphs. Research studies have demonstrated that the majority of readers do not follow a front-page story when it continues, or "jumps," inside the paper.

By the 1920s, the *New York Times* had established itself as the official *paper of record*, the standard that other newspapers emulated and that libraries throughout the country stocked to document important daily occurrences. Filled with the texts of treaties, court reports, political speeches, and other national documents, the *Times* became more than a powerful alternative to the storytelling of earlier papers; it became the official way to do journalism in the 1900s. The modern reporter evolved, ideally, as a detached observer who gathered information and adapted it to an informational or objective formula.

interpretive journalism

By the 1920s, the information model of reporting had become the standard for most mainstream journalism. There was still a sense, however, especially after the trauma of World War I, that the impartial approach to reporting was insufficient in explaining complex national and global conditions. Partly as a result of "drab, factual, objective reporting," one news scholar contended that "the American people were utterly amazed when war broke out in August 1914, as they had no understanding of the foreign scene to prepare them for it."[9]

The Limits of Objectivity. Modern journalism had undermined an early role of the partisan press—that of offering analysis and opinion. But with the world becoming more complex in the modern age, some papers began to reexplore the analytical function of news. The result was the rise of **interpretive journalism**, which tries to explain key issues or events and to place them in a broader historical or social context. According to one historian, this approach, especially in the 1930s and 1940s, was a viable way for journalism to address "the New Deal years, the rise of modern scientific technology, the increasing interdependence of economic groups at home, and the shrinking of the world into one vast arena for power politics."[10] In other words, journalism took an analytic turn in a world grown more interconnected and complicated.

248

Noting that objectivity and factuality *should* serve as the foundation for journalism, by the 1920s editor and columnist Walter Lippmann thought the press should do more. He ranked three press responsibilities: (1) "to make a current record," (2) "to make a running analysis of it," and (3) "on the basis of both, to suggest plans."[11] Reporters and readers alike have historically distinguished between informational reports and editorials, or interpretive pieces, that offer particular viewpoints or deeper analyses of the issues. The boundary between information and interpretation can be somewhat ambiguous. For this reason, American papers have traditionally placed news analysis in separate columns and opinion articles on certain pages so that readers do not confuse them with "straight news."

In the 1930s, the Depression and the Nazi threat to global stability helped news analysis take root in newsmagazines and radio commentary. First developed in the partisan era, editorial pages also made a strong comeback. More significant, however, was the growth of the political column. Although literary and humor columns existed prior to World War I, the political column was a new form. More than 150 syndicated columns developed between 1930 and 1934 alone. Moving beyond the informational and storytelling functions of news, journalists and newspapers began to extend their role as analysts.

The Press-Radio War. In the 1930s, with the rise of radio, the newspaper industry became increasingly annoyed by broadcasters who took their news directly from papers and wire services. As a result, a major battle developed between radio journalism and the established power of print. Although they would eventually lose most of these cases in court, mainstream newspapers attempted to copyright facts reported in the news and even sued radio stations, which routinely used newspapers as their main sources (a common practice today). Editors and newspaper lobbyists argued that radio should be permitted to do only commentary. By conceding this interpretive role to radio, the print press temporarily protected its dominion over "the facts." It was amid the press-radio war that radio analysis began to flourish as a form of interpretive news. Lowell Thomas delivered the first daily network analysis for CBS on September 29, 1930, attacking Hitler's rise to power in Germany. By 1941, twenty regular network commentators were explaining their version of the world to millions of listeners.

In the 1930s, many print journalists and some editors believed that interpretive stories, rather than objective reports, could better compete with radio. They realized that interpretation was a way to counter radio's (and later television's) superior ability to report breaking news quickly. In 1933, the American Society of Newspaper Editors (ASNE) supported the idea of interpretive journalism, resolving to "devote a larger amount of attention and space to analytical and interpretative news and to presenting a background of information which will enable the average reader more adequately to understand the movement and the significance of events."[12]

Newspapers, however, did not fill their front pages with probing analysis during the 1930s. Even Walter Lippmann believed that news commentary and interpretation were misdirected without the foundation of facts and a "current record." As he put it, "the really important thing is to try and make opinion increasingly responsible to the facts."[13] Still, by the early 1930s, the ideals of objectivity and impartiality had shifted.

In Europe, interpretive news and partisan papers have long been the norm, but in American dailies explicit interpretation remains relegated to the two editorial and opinion pages in most papers. After World War II, interpretive journalism diminished substantially. It wasn't until the 1950s—with the Korean War, the development of atomic power, tensions with the Soviet Union, and the anticommunist movement— that reporting as analysis resurfaced in a new form on television. Interpretive journalism in newspapers grew at the same time, especially in such areas as the environment, science, agriculture, sports, and business. Today, stories favoring analysis over description frequently find their way onto most front pages, but the interpretive approach has not gained equal footing with the information model.

literary forms of journalism

By the late 1960s, many people were criticizing America's major social institutions. Political assassinations, civil-rights protests, the Vietnam War, the drug culture, and the women's movement were not easily explained. Faced with so many unusual situations, many individuals began to lose faith in the ability of institutions to oversee and direct the social order. Members of protest movements as well as many Middle Americans began to suspect the privileges and power of traditional authority. As a result, key institutions—including journalism—lost much of the credibility they had previously commanded.

The Attack on Objectivity. Former *New York Times* columnist Tom Wicker has argued that in the early 1960s an objective approach to news remained the dominant model. According to Wicker, the "press had so wrapped itself in the paper chains of 'objective journalism' that it had little ability to report anything beyond the bare and undeniable facts."[14]

Throughout the 1960s, attacks on the detachment of reporters escalated. News critic Jack Newfield even indicted journalistic impartiality as "a figleaf for covert prejudice": "Objectivity is believing people with power and printing their press releases. Objectivity is not shouting 'liar' in a crowded country."[15] Consequently, the authority of experts and professionals in a variety of fields became suspect along with the ideal of objectivity.

A number of reporters in the late 1960s responded to the criticism by rethinking the framework of conventional journalism. To improve on the older approach, they adopted a variety of alternative techniques. One of these was *advocacy journalism*, an approach in which the reporter actively promotes a particular cause or viewpoint. Following this approach, some women reporters displayed feminist points of view in their writing; they argued that merely recording events in a neutral way failed to confront the unequal arrangements of jobs and power in many institutions. *Precision journalism*, another technique, attempted to push news more in the direction of science. Precision journalists argued that only by applying rigorous social-science methods, such as using poll surveys and questionnaires, could they achieve a valid portrait of social reality.

> "Stop them damn pictures! I don't care so much what papers write about me. My constituents can't read. But, damn it, they can see pictures!"
> —Boss Tweed

Journalism as Art. Throughout the modern period, the story dimension of news reports was downplayed to favor such conventions as the inverted pyramid and the separation of fact from opinion. Dissatisfied with these approaches, some reporters began reexploring journalism's ties to storytelling. This model of reporting, **literary journalism**—sometimes dubbed *new journalism*—adapted so-called fictional storytelling techniques to nonfictional material and in-depth reporting. In the United States, literary journalism's roots are evident in such novelists as Mark Twain, Stephen Crane, and Theodore Dreiser, all of whom started out as reporters in the nineteenth century. In the late 1930s and 1940s, new journalism surfaced in literary reports: Journalists began to demonstrate how writing about real events could achieve an artistry often associated only with good fiction.

A leading proponent and practitioner, Tom Wolfe, argued that literary journalism mixed the *content* of reporting with the *form* of fiction to create "both the kind of objective reality of journalism" and "the subjective reality" of the novel.[16] Writers such as Wolfe (*Electric Kool-Aid Acid Test*), Truman Capote (*In Cold Blood*), Joan Didion (*Slouching toward Bethlehem*), and Norman Mailer (*Miami and the Siege of Chicago*) turned to literary journalism in the 1960s in an attempt to overcome the weaknesses they perceived in routine reporting. Their often self-conscious treatment of social problems gave their writing a perspective that conventional journalism did not offer.

According to critics, the dilemmas of the sixties demanded a new journalistic form that could deal more effectively with social contradictions. After the tide of intense social upheaval ebbed, however, the new journalism subsided as well. In retrospect, literary reporting has often been criticized for being influenced by television or for blurring the lines between fact and fiction. Nevertheless, the legacy of literary journalism continues. Not only did it influence magazines like *Mother Jones* and *Rolling Stone*, but it affected the lifestyle and sports sections of most daily newspapers. In virtually every daily paper, we see longer feature stories on cultural trends and social issues. These reports reject the inverted-pyramid format by inviting readers into the stories through a more literary style that tries to set the scene using detailed description or dialogue. (See Table 8.2 for top works in American journalism.)

> "Critics [in the 1960s] claimed that urban planning created slums, that school made people stupid, that medicine caused disease, that psychiatry invented mental illness, and that the courts promoted injustice. . . . And objectivity in journalism, regarded as an antidote to bias, came to be looked upon as the most insidious bias of all. For 'objective' reporting reproduced a vision of social reality which refused to examine the basic structures of power and privilege."
>
> —Michael Schudson, *Discovering the News*, 1978

contemporary journalism

If the seeds of modern journalism were sown by Adolph Ochs and the *New York Times* in the late 1890s, a postmodern brand of journalism arose from two developments in the early 1980s. First was the electronic newspaper. In 1980, the *Columbus Dispatch* became the first paper to go online and transmit its pages via computers and cable channels. By the late 1990s, more than eight hundred American newspapers were offering some kind of computerized news service. Second, the arrival of the colorful *USA Today* in 1982 radically changed the look of most major U.S. dailies. This new paper incorporated features closely associated with the postmodern style, including an

TABLE 8.2
Exceptional Works of American Journalism in the Twentieth Century

Working under the aegis of New York University's journalism department, thirty-six judges compiled a list of the Top 100 works of American journalism in the twentieth century. Published in 1999, the list took into account not just the newsworthiness of the event but the craft of the writing and reporting. What do you think of the Top 10 works listed below? What are some problems associated with making a list like this? Do you think newswriting should be judged in the same way we judge novels or movies?

Journalists	Title or Subject	Publisher	Year
1. John Hersey	"Hiroshima"	New Yorker	1946
2. Rachel Carson	*Silent Spring*	Book	1962
3. Bob Woodward/Carl Bernstein	Watergate investigation	Washington Post	1972–73
4. Edward R. Murrow	Battle of Britain	CBS Radio	1940
5. Ida Tarbell	"The History of the Standard Oil Company"	McClure's	1902–04
6. Lincoln Steffens	"The Shame of the Cities"	McClure's	1902–04
7. John Reed	*Ten Days That Shook the World*	Book	1919
8. H. L. Mencken	Coverage of the Scopes "monkey" trial	Baltimore Sun	1925
9. Ernie Pyle	Reports from Europe and the Pacific during World War II	Scripps-Howard newspapers	1940–45
10. Edward R. Murrow/Fred Friendly	Investigation of Senator Joseph McCarthy	CBS	1954

Source: New York University department of journalism, New York, N.Y.

emphasis on surface slickness over substantive news and the use of brief news items that appealed to readers' short attention span. *USA Today* represents the only successful launch of a new major U.S. daily newspaper in the last several decades. A sign of its marketing savvy, *USA Today* was the first paper to pay tribute to network TV's central role in mass culture: The paper designed its vending boxes to look like color TV sets.

Writing for *Rolling Stone* in March 1992, media critic Jon Katz argued that the authority of modern newspapers was being usurped by a variety of "new news" forms that combined information, entertainment, persuasion, and analysis. Katz claimed that the news authority of most prominent daily papers, such as the *New York Times* and the *Washington Post*, was being challenged by "news" coming from talk shows, television sitcoms, popular films, and even rap music. In other words, we were passing from a society in which the transmission of knowledge depended mainly on books, newspapers, and magazines to a society dominated by a mix of print, visual, electronic, and digital information. In the process, the new forms of news have been taking over the roles of traditional journalism, setting the nation's cultural, social, and political agendas. For instance, Matt Drudge, conservative Internet news source and gossip behind *The Drudge Report*, hijacked the national agenda in January 1998 and launched the Clinton-Lewinsky scandal when he posted a story claiming that *Newsweek* had backed off, or "spiked," a story about President Clinton having an affair with a White House intern. While Drudge's report was indeed true, *Newsweek* delayed the story because its editors thought they needed more confirming sources before they could responsibly publish the allegations. Drudge effectively "outed" the *Newsweek* story prematurely, though critics debate whether his actions were legitimate or irresponsible.

Today, a fundamental tension exists between print and electronic conceptions of news. With news-reading habits among young people in decline, TV magazine programs, talk shows, sitcoms, movies, and popular music are sparking public conversation more often than are traditional newspapers. Add to this the speed at which personal computers can now transmit data. As Jon Katz wrote in *Wired*, "When in January 1994

With a daily circulation of 1.7 million (more than 2.2 million for the Friday edition), *USA Today* ranks second only to the *Wall Street Journal*. Appealing to a national rather than a local or regional audience, *USA Today* also gives away an additional 400,000 copies a day to hotel guests and airline passengers, targeting travelers who want a brief rundown of the day's news or the sports score from the team back home. *Source:* Copyright © 1999, USA Today. Reprinted with permission.

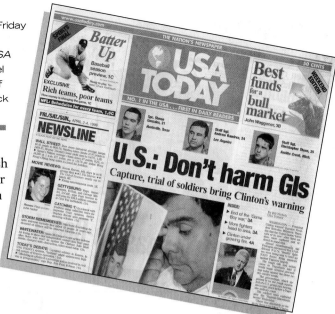

a RadioMail subscriber used his wireless modem to flash news of the LA earthquake to the Net well before CNN or the Associated Press could report it, a new news medium was born."[17] With radio, television, film, music, and the Internet all competing with newspapers, their traditional roles are being seriously challenged and changed. By the late 1990s, more and more readers were beginning their day by logging on to computers to scan a wide variety of the nation's online newspapers.

categorizing news and u.s. newspapers

The reason for newspapers' decline in the United States stems in part from the industry's slow response to the electronic and digital revolutions. Yet in spite of this, newspapers have not been abandoned. The nation's fifteen hundred daily papers still reach more than sixty-two million readers each day. But this is down from twenty-six hundred dailies in 1910, the high-water mark for daily newspapers in the United States.

In the news industry today, there are several kinds of papers. *National newspapers* (such as the *Wall Street Journal*, the *New York Times*, the *Christian Science Monitor*, and *USA Today*) serve a broad readership across the country. Other papers primarily serve specific geographic regions. Roughly 120 *metropolitan dailies* have a circulation of 100,000 or more. About 40 of these papers had a circulation of more than 250,000 by the mid-1990s. Most daily newspapers, however, are either medium dailies (50,000 to 100,000 in circulation) or small dailies (under 50,000 in circulation). While dailies serve urban and suburban centers, more than 8,000 nondaily and *weekly newspapers* (down from 14,000 in 1910) serve small towns and communities.

consensus vs. conflict

Smaller nondaily papers tend to play a consensus role in communities, promoting social and economic harmony. Besides providing community calendars and meeting notices, **consensus-oriented papers** carry articles on local schools, social events, town government, property crimes, and zoning issues. Recalling the partisan spirit of an earlier era, small newspapers are often owned by business leaders who occasionally serve in local politics. Because consensus-oriented papers have a small advertising base, they are generally careful not to offend local advertisers, who provide the financial underpinnings for many of these papers.

In contrast, national and metro dailies practice **conflict-oriented journalism** in which news is defined primarily as events, issues, or experiences that deviate from social norms. Under this news orientation, journalists see their role not merely as neutral fact-gatherers but as observers who monitor their city's institutions and problems.

253

They often maintain an adversarial relationship with local politicians and public officials. These papers offer competing perspectives on such issues as education, government, poverty, crime, and the economy. It would be considered unethical, a conflict of interest for publishers, editors, or reporters on these papers to play a major role in community politics. In theory, modern newspapers believe their role in large cities is to keep a wary eye fixed on local and state intrigue and events.

In telling stories about complex and controversial topics, journalists under the conflict model often turn such topics into two-dimensional stories, pitting one idea or person against another. This convention, often called "telling both sides of a story," allows a reporter to take the position of a detached observer. Although this practice offers the appearance of balance, it usually functions to generate conflict and sustain a good news story; and sometimes reporters ignore the idea that there may be *more* than two sides to a story. But faced with deadline pressures, reporters often do not have the time—or the space—to develop a multifaceted and complex report.

ethnic, minority, and oppositional newspapers

Historically, small-town weeklies and daily newspapers have served predominantly white, mainstream readers. Exceptions to this include the various minority, foreign-language, and alternative papers, which have played a prominent role for Mexican and Cuban immigrants, Korean Americans, disabled veterans, retired workers, gay and lesbian communities, and the homeless. Most of these weekly and monthly newspapers serve some of the same functions for their constituencies as the "majority" papers. Minority papers, however, are often published outside the social mainstream. Consequently, they provide viewpoints that are different from the mostly middle- and upper-class white attitudes that have shaped the media throughout much of America's history.

The Immigrant and Ethnic Press. Since Benjamin Franklin launched the short-lived German-language *Philadelphische Zeitung* in 1732, newspapers aimed at ethnic groups have played a major role in initiating immigrants into American society. During the nineteenth century, Swedish- and Norwegian-language papers informed various immigrant communities in the Midwest. The early twentieth century gave rise to papers written in German, Yiddish, Russian, and Polish, which assisted the massive influx of European immigrants. In the 1980s, hundreds of small papers developed to serve immigrants from Cuba, Haiti, Pakistan, Laos, Cambodia, and China. More than sixty small U.S. papers are now printed in Vietnamese. By the 1990s, several hundred foreign-language daily and nondaily presses existed in at least forty different languages. These papers help readers both adjust to foreign surroundings and retain ties to their traditional heritage. Many are financially healthy today, supported by classified ads, local businesses, and increased ad revenue from long-distance phone companies and online computer service, which see the ethnic press as an ideal place to reach those customers most likely to use international phone services or the Internet.[18]

African American Newspapers. Between 1827 and the end of the Civil War in 1865, forty newspapers directed at black readers and opposed to slavery struggled for survival. These papers faced not only higher rates of illiteracy among black slaves and citizens but also hostility from white society and the majority press of the day. The first black newspaper, *Freedom's Journal*, operated from 1827 to 1829 and opposed the racism of many New York newspapers. In addition, it offered a voice for a number of antislavery societies. Other notable papers included the *Alienated American*

(1852–56) and the *New Orleans Daily Creole*, which began a short life in 1856 as the first black-owned daily in the South. The most influential oppositional newspaper at the time was Frederick Douglass's *North Star*, a weekly antislavery newspaper in Rochester, New York, which began in 1847 and reached a circulation of three thousand. Besides writing essays on slavery, Douglass, a former slave, addressed a variety of national and international topics.

Since 1827, more than 3,000 newspapers have been edited and owned by blacks. These papers, with an average life span of nine years, took stands against race baiting, lynching, and the Ku Klux Klan. They promoted racial pride long before the civil-rights movement of the 1950s and 1960s. More than 150 such papers survive today and remain influential, including Baltimore's *Afro-American*, New York's *Amsterdam News*, and the *Chicago Defender*. The most widely circulated black-owned paper was Robert C. Vann's weekly *Pittsburgh Courier*, founded in 1910. Its circulation peaked at 350,000 in 1947—the year professional baseball was integrated by Jackie Robinson, thanks in part to relentless editorials in the *Courier* that denounced the color barrier in pro sports. As they have throughout their history, these papers offer oppositional viewpoints to the mainstream press and record the daily activities of black communities by listing weddings, births, deaths, graduations, meetings, and church functions.

The circulation rates of most black papers have dropped sharply, however, particularly since the 1960s. The local and national editions of the *Pittsburgh Courier*, for instance, had a combined circulation of only 20,000 by the early 1980s.[19] Several factors contributed to these declines. First, television and specialized black radio stations tapped into the limited pool of money businesses allocated for advertising. Second, some advertisers, to avoid controversy, withdrew their support when the black press started giving favorable coverage to the civil-rights movement in the 1960s. Third, the loss of industrial urban jobs in the 1970s and 1980s not only diminished readership but hurt small neighborhood businesses, which could no longer afford to advertise in both the mainstream and the black press. Finally, after the enactment of civil-rights and affirmative-action laws, black papers were raided by mainstream papers seeking to integrate their newsrooms with good black journalists. Black papers could seldom match the offers from large white-owned dailies.

As civil-rights legislation improved economic conditions for many working- and middle-class African Americans, the mainstream press began to court them as a consumer group, devoting weekly special sections to black issues and finding advertisers to support those sections. In siphoning off both ads and talent, a more integrated mainstream press diminished the status of many black papers—an ironic effect of the 1960s civil-rights laws. By the late 1990s, 11 to 12 percent of the newsroom staffs at the nation's fifteen hundred daily papers were African American, Hispanic, Asian American, and Native American.[20]

Spanish-Language Newspapers. Bilingual and Spanish-language newspapers have long served a variety of Cuban, Mexican, Puerto Rican, and other Latino readerships. New York's *El Diario–La Prensa* has been serving Spanish-language readers since 1914. Los Angeles boasts *La Opinión*, the nation's largest Spanish-language daily. Other prominent publications are in Miami (*La Voz* and *Diario de las Americas*), Houston (*La Información*), Chicago (*El Mañana Daily News* and *La Raza*), San Diego (*El Sol*), and New York (*El Noticias del Mundo*). By the late 1990s, some two hundred Hispanic newspapers reached more than ten million readers nationwide.

Until the late 1960s, Hispanic issues and culture were virtually ignored by mainstream newspapers. But with the influx of Mexican, Haitian, Puerto Rican, and Cuban immigrants over the past two decades, many mainstream papers began to feature weekly Spanish-language supplements. The first was the *Miami Herald*'s section, "El Nuevo Herald," introduced in 1976. Other mainstream papers also joined in, but

> "Too long have others spoken for us."
> —*Freedom's Journal*, 1827

Ethnic and foreign-language newspapers serve an important function, providing news and a sense of community to ethnic and native populations not targeted by mainstream papers. Pictured here are front pages from the *Indian Time* (Native American), *Al Hayat* (Arab American), *Ming Pao Daily News* (Chinese American), and the *National Herald* (Greek American).

many were folding their supplements by the mid-1990s. In 1995, the *Los Angeles Times* discontinued its supplement, "Nuestro Tiempo," and the *Miami Herald* trimmed budgets and staff for "El Nuevo Herald." Spanish-language radio and television had beaten the papers to these potential customers and to advertisers. While many of the nation's mainstream papers were cutting their Spanish-language sections, TV advertising aimed at Hispanic markets jumped 25 percent.[21] By 1998, Spanish-language radio formats were thriving in many urban areas and taking advertisers with them.

Native American Newspapers. An activist Native American press has also provided oppositional voices to mainstream American media since 1828, when the *Cherokee Phoenix* appeared in Georgia. Another prominent early paper was the *Cherokee Rose Bud*, founded in 1848 by tribal women in the Oklahoma territory. The Native American Press Association has documented more than 350 different Native American papers, most of them printed in English but a few in tribal languages. Two national papers include *Akwesasne Notes*, a radical paper from the Mohawk nation published a few times a year, and *Wassaja*, a bimonthly paper of the American Indian Historical Society that promotes tribal pride and education. In opposing the lack of coverage of their culture's viewpoints in the mainstream press, Native American newspapers have helped to educate various tribes about their heritage and build community solidarity. In addition, these papers provide a forum for debates on tribal conflicts, which are generally ignored in mainstream papers.

The Underground Press. Another important historical development in the mid to late 1960s involved the explosion of alternative newspapers. Labeled the *under-*

ground press at the time, these papers questioned mainstream political policies and conventional values. Generally running on shoestring budgets, they often voiced radical viewpoints and were erratic in meeting publication schedules. Springing up on college campuses and in major cities, underground papers were inspired by the writings of socialists and intellectuals from the 1930s and 1940s and, in their own time, by a new wave of thinkers and artists. Particularly inspirational were poets and writers (such as Allen Ginsberg, LeRoi Jones, Jack Kerouac, and Eldridge Cleaver) and "protest" musicians and performers (including Bob Dylan, Pete Seeger, Joan Baez, and Lenny Bruce). In criticizing social institutions, alternative papers questioned the official reports distributed by public-relations agents, government spokespeople, and the conventional press (see "Case Study: The Alternative Journalism of Dorothy Day and I. F. Stone" on page 260).

During the 1960s, underground papers played a unique role in documenting social tension by including the voices of students, women, blacks, gays, and others whose opinions were often excluded from the mainstream press. The first and most enduring underground paper, the *Village Voice*, was founded in Greenwich Village in 1955. Among campus underground papers, the *Berkeley Barb* was the most influential, developing amid the free-speech movement in the mid-1960s. Other significant underground papers of the 1960s included the *Los Angeles Free Press*, the *Boston Phoenix*, the *Fifth Estate* in Detroit, the *Washington Free Press*, the *Seed* in Chicago, *Kaleidoscope* in Milwaukee, and the *Distant Drummer* in Philadelphia.

Despite their irreverent and often vulgar tone, many underground papers turned a spotlight on racial and gender inequities and, on occasion, influenced mainstream journalism to examine social issues. Like the black press, though, most underground papers either lost circulation or folded after the 1960s. Given their radical outlooks, it was difficult for them to generate sponsors or keep advertisers. In addition, like the black press, the underground press was raided by mainstream papers, which began expanding their coverage of culture by hiring the underground's best editors and writers.

economic demands vs. editorial duties

Although a weekly paper may employ only two or three people and a major metro daily more than two thousand, most newspapers generally distinguish business operations from editorial or news functions. Although journalists' and readers' praise or criticism usually rests on the quality of a paper's news and editorial components, business and advertising decisions drive the industry.

Business Operations. Most major daily papers devote one-half to two-thirds of their pages to advertisements. Accounting for 20 to 25 percent of all ad dollars spent annually in the United States, newspapers carry everything from expensive full-page spreads for prominent department stores to classifieds, which consumers can purchase for a few dollars to advertise everything from old cars to used furniture. In most cases, ads are positioned in the paper first. The space left over after ads are placed is called the *newshole*, which accounts for the remaining 35 to 50 percent of daily newspapers—everything from front-page news reports to horoscopes and advice columns.

In addition to managing a paper's finances, business operations generally include departments of advertising, circulation, and promotion. Advertising staffs sell space to various companies and classified spots to individuals and small businesses. Circulation departments oversee distribution through street-corner boxes and newsstand sales, neighborhood paper routes, mail subscriptions, and, most recently, the Internet. Promotion departments try to attract new readers and advertisers, paying particular attention to younger, hard-to-reach readers. Mechanical departments, supervised by a production manager, generally run the technical and computerized processes of assembling the pages of the paper and operating the printing presses.

News Responsibilities. On the news and editorial side, the chain of command at most larger papers starts at the top, with the publisher and owner, and then moves to the editor in chief, the person in charge of the daily news-gathering and writing processes. Under this main editor, assistant editors and news managers run different news divisions, including features, sports, photos, local news, state news, and wire-service reports that contain much of the day's national and international news. In addition, copy editors check each story for accuracy, style, and grammar and write the headlines for each report.

Reporters work for editors and are generally grouped into two broad categories: *general assignment reporters*, who handle all sorts of stories that might emerge in a given day, and *specialty reporters*, who are assigned to particular beats (police, courts, city government) or topics (education, religion, technology, economy, health, environment). On large dailies, *bureau reporters* file reports every day from other major cities—such as Washington or their state's capital. Daily papers also feature columnists and critics; these reporters have usually worked their way up the hierarchy and may review or analyze everything from fashion to foreign policy. Increasingly, newspapers are employing a separate staff for their online operations.

Wire Services and Feature Syndication. Major daily papers might have between 100 and 150 local reporters and writers, but they still cannot cover the world or produce enough material to fill up the newshole each day. For this reason, newspapers rely on wire services and syndicated feature services to supplement local coverage. A few major dailies, such as the *New York Times*, run their own wire services, selling their reprinted stories to other papers. Other agencies, such as the Associated Press and United Press International (UPI), have hundreds of staffers stationed throughout major U.S. cities and the world capitals. They submit stories and photos each day for distribution to newspapers across the country. Some U.S. papers also subscribe to foreign wire services, such as Agence France-Presse in Paris or Reuters in London. Daily papers generally pay monthly fees for access to all wire stories, which are relayed by computer, satellite, or Teletype machines. Although they use only a fraction of what is available over the wires, editors carefully monitor wire services each day for important stories and ideas for local angles. Wire services have greatly expanded the national and international scope of news, but editors often must put their trust in a handful of powerful wire firms when they select a newsworthy issue or event for reprinting.

In addition, *feature syndicates*, such as United Features, King Features, and Tribune Media Services, are commercial outlets that contract with newspapers to provide work from the nation's best political writers, editorial cartoonists, comic-strip artists, and self-help

Foreign correspondents have one of the most interesting—and often dangerous—jobs in journalism. Covering everything from elections to revolutions, reporters in foreign countries provide a first-hand account of important international events. In this 1996 photo, a reporter covering unrest in Afghanistan taps into a car battery to power his computer so he can file a story with his editor.

columnists. These companies serve as brokers, distributing horoscopes and crossword puzzles as well as the columns and comic strips that appeal to a wide audience. When a paper bids on and acquires the rights to a cartoonist or columnist, it signs exclusivity agreements with a syndicate to ensure that it is the only paper in the region to carry Dilbert, Ellen Goodman, Clarence Page, George Will, or Dear Abby. Feature syndicates, like wire services, wield great influence in determining which writers and cartoonists gain national prominence.

issues of ownership, economics, and technology

A number of tough issues face the newspaper industry as it adapts to changes in economics and technology. For publishers and journalists, no issues are more worrisome than the decline in newspaper readership and the failure of many papers to attract younger readers. Other problems persist as well, including the inability of most cities to support competing newspapers and the capability of online computer services to vie with newspapers for lucrative classified advertising. Finally, the newspaper industry struggles to find its place on the information highway, trying to predict the future of printed and digital versions of the news.

circulation woes

Newspaper owners struggle daily with readership concerns. Since the mid-1960s, yearly circulation has flattened out at just over sixty million copies per day. Although the population has increased during that period, the percentage of adults who read the paper at least once a week dropped from 78 percent in 1970 to around 59 percent by 1997. This decline in readership actually began during the Depression and the rise of radio. Between 1931 and 1939, six hundred newspapers ceased operation. Between the early 1940s and the late 1990s, the number of daily papers in the United States dropped from nineteen hundred to fifteen hundred.

The biggest circulation crisis for newspapers occurred from the late 1960s through the 1970s. Both the rise in network television viewing and competition from suburban weeklies intensified the decline in daily readership. In addition, with an increasing number of women working full-time outside the home throughout the seventies, newspapers could no longer consistently count on one of their core readership groups. Circulation dropped by more than 20 percent in the nation's twenty largest cities (even though the population declined by only 6 percent in those areas).[22]

While some newspapers experienced circulation gains in the 1980s and early 1990s, especially in more affluent suburban communities, readership in the United States generally declined or flattened out during this period. Increases at many suburban weekly papers actually siphoned off readers of large city dailies. By comparison, many other countries did not experience readership declines. For example, for every one thousand people, Sweden sells five hundred papers per day. In the United States, which has more diverse populations, social classes, and cultural choices, that figure is only about 250 copies sold daily for every one thousand people. Countries such as Norway, Finland, Japan, South Korea, and Germany also have higher rates of readership. (See Table 8.3 for a list of the world's most widely circulated newspapers.)

"**Declining readership** is a symptom well understood by the leaders of our industry. Only recently, however, have newspaper people come to agree that content is first among the many reasons readership is in decline."

—Robert Giles,
editor and publisher,
Detroit News

The Alternative Journalism of Dorothy Day and I. F. Stone

Over the years, a number of unconventional reporters have struggled against the status quo to find a place for unheard voices and alternative ways to practice their craft. James Franklin stubbornly refused to get a news license during the early 1700s; Ida Wells fearlessly investigated violence against blacks for the *Memphis Free Speech* in the late 1800s; and the underground papers of the late 1960s made it possible for the voices of many groups to be heard. Newspaper lore offers a rich history of alternative journalists and their publications. Two such papers were Dorothy Day's *Catholic Worker* and *I. F. Stone's Weekly*.

In 1933, Dorothy Day (1897–1980) cofounded a radical religious organization with a monthly newspaper, *Catholic Worker*, that opposed war and supported social reforms. Like many young intellectual writers during World War I, Day was a pacifist; she also joined the Socialist Party. Quitting college at age eighteen to work as an activist reporter for socialist newspapers, Day participated in the ongoing suffrage movement, which in 1920 helped pass the Nineteenth Amendment, giving women the right to vote. Throughout the 1930s, her Catholic Worker organization invested in thirty hospices for the poor and homeless, providing food and shelter for five thousand people a day. This legacy would endure into the 1980s and 1990s, with the organization continuing to fund soup kitchens and homeless shelters throughout the country.

An advocate journalist, Day used the *Catholic Worker* to defend the rights of working people and to encourage nonviolent social change. For more than sixty years, the *Worker* has consistently advocated personal activism to further social justice, opposing anti-Semitism, Japanese American internment camps during World War II, nuclear weapons, the Korean War, military drafts, and the communist witch-hunts of the 1950s. During the Cold War, Day was jailed four times for opposing military-style civil-defense drills in public schools. In the early 1970s, at age seventy-five, Day was arrested for supporting migrant workers while she picketed with Cesar Chavez in California. She also used the paper to advocate religious change, urging Catholics to resist consumer culture and return the Church to its early radical teachings. Although the paper's circulation peaked in 1938 at 190,000, it fell dramatically during World War II, when Day's pacifism was at odds with much of America.

▪ joint operating agreements

Although the FCC once limited the number of TV stations a person or corporation could own, newspaper owners have historically faced few government limitations. Gannett, for instance, owns more than eighty daily papers (and forty more nondailies), ranging from small suburban papers to the Nashville *Tennessean* and *USA Today*. In the past, antimonopoly rules prevented a single owner from controlling all the newspapers in a city or town. Today, however, such rules have little impact because just a single paper has survived to serve most communities. In addition, prior to the 1996 Telecommunications Act, the FCC prohibited newspaper owners from purchasing broadcast or cable outlets in the same markets where they publish newspapers. Such restrictions once encouraged more voices in the media marketplace.

During the Vietnam War and the protest movements, however, it climbed again, to more than 100,000.

I. F. Stone (1907–1989) shared Dorothy Day's passion for social activism. He also started early, publishing his own monthly paper at the age of fourteen and becoming a full-time reporter by age twenty. He worked as a Washington political writer for the *Nation* in the early 1940s and later for the *New York Daily Compass* until the early 1950s. A lifelong socialist, Stone challenged the conventions and privileges of both politics and journalism. In 1941, for example, he resigned from the National Press Club when it refused to serve his guest, the nation's first African American federal judge. In the early 1950s, he actively opposed Joseph McCarthy's rabid search to rid government and the media of alleged communists.

When the *Daily Compass* failed in 1952, the radical Stone was unable to find a newspaper job and decided to create his own newsletter, *I. F. Stone's Weekly*, which he published for nineteen years. Practicing interpretive and investigative reporting, Stone became as adept as any major journalist at tracking down government records to discover contradictions, inaccuracies, and lies. Over the years, besides taking on McCarthy, Stone challenged the policies of J. Edgar Hoover's FBI, questioned decisions by the Supreme Court, investigated the substandard living conditions of many African Americans, and criticized political corruption on both the Right and the Left. Working only with his wife and an occasional researcher, Stone guided the *Weekly* to a circulation that reached seventy thousand during the 1960s, when he probed American investments of money and military might in Vietnam.

I. F. Stone and Dorothy Day embodied a spirit of independent reporting that has been threatened by the decline in newspaper readership and the rise of chain ownership. Stone, who believed that alternative ideas were crucial to maintaining a healthy democracy, once wrote that "there must be free play for so-called 'subversive' ideas—every idea 'subverts' the old to make way for the new. To shut off 'subversion' is to shut off peaceful progress and to invite revolution and war."[1]

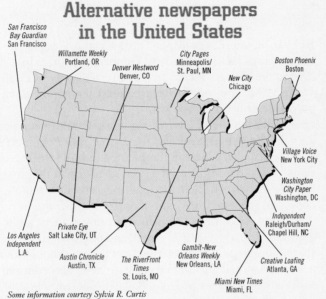

Alternative newspapers in the United States

San Francisco Bay Guardian — San Francisco
Willamette Weekly — Portland, OR
Denver Westword — Denver, CO
City Pages — Minneapolis/St. Paul, MN
New City — Chicago
Boston Phoenix — Boston
Village Voice — New York City
Washington City Paper — Washington, DC
Independent — Raleigh/Durham/Chapel Hill, NC
Los Angeles Independent — L.A.
Private Eye — Salt Lake City, UT
Austin Chronicle — Austin, TX
The RiverFront Times — St. Louis, MO
Gambit-New Orleans Weekly — New Orleans, LA
Creative Loafing — Atlanta, GA
Miami New Times — Miami, FL

Some information courtesy Sylvia R. Curtis

Although regulation has lessened, in general the government continues to monitor the declining number of newspapers in various American cities as well as mergers in cities where competition among papers might be endangered. The Justice Department has allowed a number of mergers over the years, but it was not until 1970 that Congress passed the Newspaper Preservation Act, which enabled failing papers to continue operating through a **joint operating agreement (JOA)**. Under a JOA, two competing papers keep separate news divisions while merging business and production operations for a period of years.

JOAs are now in place in fifteen cities, including Cincinnati, Seattle, and Tucson. Although JOAs and mergers encourage monopolistic tendencies, they have sometimes been the only way to maintain competition between newspapers in the Information Age. For instance, in the mid-1920s about five hundred American cities

Newspaper	Country	Circulation	Newspaper	Country	Circulation
Yomiuri Shimbun	Japan	14,532,694	Sankei Shimbun	Japan	2,890,835
Asahi Shimbun	Japan	12,601,375	Nihon Keizai Shimbun	Japan	2,705,877
Sichuan Ribao	China	8,000,000	Gongren Ribao	China	2,500,000
Mainichi Shimbun	Japan	5,845,857	Daily Mail	England	2,387,867
Bild	Germany	5,674,400	Daily Mirror	England	2,339,001
Chunichi Shimbun	Japan	4,323,144	Chosun Ilbo	South Korea	2,225,000
Sun	England	3,718,354	Dong-A Ilbo	South Korea	2,150,000
Renmin Ribao	China	3,000,000	Hokkaido Shimbun	Japan	1,962,666

Source: <www.mediainfo.com> (Web site for *Editor & Publisher*, the main trade organization for the newspaper industry).

had two or more newspapers with separate owners. By the late 1990s, fewer than twenty cities had independent, competing papers. In 1995, the *Houston Post* folded, leaving the nation's fourth-largest city with only one daily paper, the *Houston Chronicle*. In 1998, the *Nashville Banner* closed, leaving the Gannett-owned *Tennessean* as the only daily print game in town.

Until the 1990s, Detroit was one of the most competitive newspaper cities in the nation. The *Detroit News* and the *Detroit Free Press* both ranked among the ten most widely circulated papers in the country and sold their weekday editions for just fifteen cents a copy. But in the early 1990s, managers at the two papers began exploring joint ways to stabilize flat circulations and revenue declines. Claiming that in Detroit's depressed economy the death of one newspaper might result in substantial job losses, the papers asked for a JOA, which the government authorized. In the largest JOA to date, the *News*, owned by Gannett, and the *Free Press*, owned by Knight-Ridder, began sharing business and production operations, although the companies remained independently owned and staffed separate news and editorial departments. On Saturday and Sunday, the two papers circulated one edition, which featured special sections from both papers. Beginning in the summer of 1995, a prolonged and bitter strike by several unions sharply reduced circulation, especially at the *News*, which had become a home-delivered afternoon daily under the terms of the JOA. One of the unions' concerns involved reduced competition under the JOA, which had allowed managers at both papers to cut costs and jobs to sustain high profits for stockholders. Before the 1995 strike, Gannett and Knight-Ridder—later accused of trying to break the labor unions in Detroit—had both reported profit margins of well over 15 percent on their other newspaper holdings.[23] By 1999 *neither* of the Detroit papers was ranked among the nation's top fifteen papers, according to circulation figures.

newspaper chains

Another key economic change in the newspaper industry has been the rise of **newspaper chains**, companies that own several papers throughout the country. Edward Wyllis Scripps founded the first newspaper chain in the 1890s. By the 1920s, there were about 30 chains in the United States, each one owning an average of five papers. The emergence of chains parallels the major business trend during the twentieth century: the movement toward oligopolies in which fewer and fewer corporations control each industry. By the 1980s, more than 130 chains owned an average of nine papers each, with the 12 largest chains accounting for 40 percent of the total circulation in the United States. By the mid-1990s, chains controlled nearly 80 percent of all daily newspapers, and by 1999 the top 7 chains circulated more than one-third of all the nation's daily papers.

Similar to cable companies, newspapers operate as monopolies in most cities. Furthermore, many newspaper owners, instead of investing in investigative journalism or attracting new readers, have devoted their energies to buying radio and TV stations. Gannett, for instance, the nation's largest chain, owns more than twenty radio and TV stations. Rupert Murdoch's News Corp., among the world's largest chains, now owns twenty-two U.S. television stations, the most in history. Right after the passage of the 1996 Telecommunications Act, the Tribune Company in Chicago paid more than $1 billion to acquire six more TV stations, now reaching into a third of all U.S. households.[24]

A disturbing trend in the 1990s finds daily newspapers changing hands at a much faster rate than in previous years. For example, between 1993 and 1996, more than 250 of the nation's 1,500-plus daily papers were sold—usually to distant chains not headquartered in the community where the paper operates.[25] News critics fear that a few chain owners will make it more difficult for multiple viewpoints to be expressed in the news media. They are also concerned about whether out-of-town owners and newly installed editors will put the special needs of their communities above corporate interests and the bottom line. Increasingly, chains favor editors who are bottom-line-oriented business managers over independent or progressive editors who seek to increase the newshole and the number of reporters or investigative assignments.

changes in technology

Modern technology began radically revolutionizing newsrooms in the 1970s. VDTs (video display terminals), for instance, displaced typewriters, enabling reporters to easily change or share stories; editors could also measure headlines or design pages on their personal computer screens. As dramatic as this change was, however, it did not pose the challenges of the information highway and digital news, which brought a brand of competition that newspapers had never seen.

The 1996 Telecommunications Act spurred alliances among cable television and telephone companies in their quest to deliver digital data into homes via cable, copper, and fiber-optic wires. Hundreds of newspapers responded by developing online versions of their paper product. Most newspaper editors believe they can provide the best electronic versions of local community news and services, in contrast to the national services offered by cable or phone systems. Many newspapers now face competition with online computer services, cable companies, and phone services in the battle for lucrative local classified advertisements.

Because of their local monopoly status, many newspapers were slower than other media to confront the challenges of the electronic revolution. Into the late 1990s, however, newspapers were still the media leader in collecting advertising revenue. The nation's newspapers annually attract around 22 percent of all ad revenues spent in the United States, which is down from a 27 percent share in the late 1980s (see Figure 8.2). While newspaper managers expressed concern because nearly two-thirds of the nation's sixty largest metro dailies had reported circulation declines by the mid-1990s, in 1998 U.S. circulation figures rose slightly for the first time since 1986.

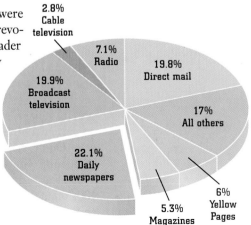

2.8% Cable television

7.1% Radio

19.8% Direct mail

19.9% Broadcast television

17% All others

22.1% Daily newspapers

5.3% Magazines

6% Yellow Pages

Figure 8.2
Newspapers' Slice of the Advertising Pie
Source: McCann Erickson Inc., Newspaper Association of America.

Although some observers think newspapers are on the verge of extinction as the digital age eclipses the print era, the industry is no dinosaur. In fact, the history of communication demonstrates that older mass media have always adapted. Actually, with more than eight hundred newspapers now online, newspapers are tackling one of the industry's major economic headaches: the cost of newsprint. After salaries, purchasing newsprint from paper manufacturers is the industry's largest expense, accounting for more than 20 percent of a newspaper's total cost.

In addition, online newspapers are truly taking advantage of the flexibility the Internet offers. Since space is not an issue, newspapers can post stories and reader letters online that they weren't able to print in the paper edition. They can also run longer stories with more in-depth coverage, as well as offer immediate updates to breaking news. For instance, during the Microsoft antitrust trial in the late 1990s, several newspapers devoted extra resources to their online coverage and reporters posted stories to their Web sites several times a day. Online newspapers are also making themselves an invaluable resource to readers by offering hyperlinks to Web sites related to stories and by linking news reports to an archive of related articles. Free of charge or for a modest fee, a reader can search the newspaper's database from home and investigate the entire sequence and history of an ongoing story, such as the outcome of a trial over the course of several months. Taking advantage of the multimedia capabilities of the Internet, online newspapers offer readers the ability to download audio and video files—everything from presidential news conferences to sports highlights. Today's online newspapers offer readers a living rather than a static resource—one that does more than line the bottom of a bird cage a day after publication.

alternative voices

With most news organizations moving toward the digital age and online editions, traditional printed newspapers found a new outlet in the 1980s with the development of street papers. Originally an idea for employing homeless people—both as street vendors and as news writers—the first such paper, *Street News*, emerged in New York in 1989. A number of urban imitators soon followed, including *Spare Change* in Boston and Toronto, *Street Sheet* in San Francisco, *Homeless Gazette News* in Dallas, and *Hard Times* in Los Angeles. These papers typically sell for twenty-five cents to $1, and the proceeds go to the homeless.

The appearance of street papers followed the emergence of homelessness as a major and mushrooming urban problem throughout the 1980s. Such papers frequently cover the political and economic factors that contribute to homelessness, including the appearance of inexpensive drugs like crack cocaine, the loss of urban manufacturing jobs, the downsizing of mental hospitals, and the gentrification of urban downtown areas. Featuring stories by and about the homeless, these papers serve as a voice for the disenfranchised.

By the late 1990s, more than fifty U.S. street papers were available, as well as another eighty worldwide. In addition to sporadic publishing schedules and financial woes, many street papers face bureaucratic obstacles that curtail distribution. For example, a New York Transit Authority regulation in the mid-1990s prohibited street vendors from selling papers on commuter trains, and in 1998 the Dallas public library system, a major gathering place for the homeless, declared a "temporary moratorium" on displaying free publications and street papers.

Oddly enough, in 1998 street papers in Los Angeles even found themselves competing with a glossy general-interest publication, the *Big Issue*. Started in London in 1991 as a simple street paper and currently boasting a weekly circulation of over 400,000 in England, the *Big Issue* launched an L.A. version in April 1998. With color photos, celebrity profiles, and plenty of advertisements, the *Big Issue* is now designed

EXAMINING ETHICS

Codes of Conduct for Online Journalism

by J. D. Lasica

In this age of public distrust of the media, one would think that enterprising executives would make every effort to draw distinctions between their brand of journalism and the questionable style of reporting practiced in some quarters of cyberspace.

Certainly, readers rightly judge a publication's credibility based on its track record. But buttressing that record with a declaration of principles would send a powerful message, especially at a time when a cynical public often lumps Matt Drudge, MSNBC and the *Dallas Morning News* into a single, ominous force.

How to regain the public's trust? Here's one way: Tell readers about your standards and values. If you have an ethics policy, post it online. Do you have a code of conduct for employees, or a set of guiding journalistic principles? A policy to prevent the intrusion of advertising influence in editorial content? A disclosure statement about your publication's corporate parentage? Let's see it. (And please, don't let the lawyers muck it up.)

A handful of publications online—but only a handful—have laid their principles on the line. Among the best:

- The *San Antonio Express-News* in April 1998 crafted a new ethics code, written in plain language, which covers such topics as conflicts of interest, plagiarism, freebies, anonymous sources, documentary photojournalism and (more controversially) political activism and membership on community boards. All employees are required to sign off on the code, which is posted on the paper's Web site at <www.expressnews.com>.

- The online financial publication *TheStreet.com* discloses its investors and business partners and posts its stringent conflict-of-interest policy on stock ownership by employees.

- International Data Group, the corporate parent of *Computerworld, Macworld, PC World,* and other print and Web magazines, has adopted an online ethics policy that sets down standards for separating editorial content from advertising based on new-media guidelines adopted by the American Society of Magazine Editors.

- CNET: The Computer Network discloses its investors and business partners and plans to post its in-house code of conduct. The model ethics code covers employee freebies and stock transactions, disclosure of the company's affiliations in news stories, evenhanded use of hyperlinks and how to forthrightly correct errors online.

Judyth Rigler, chairman of the *Express-News*' Ethics Committee, says the paper decided to make its code public because the editors wanted to make a statement.

"There's just a different climate for news today," she says. "It's coming at us from all directions. We wanted to tell the community, in an honest and candid way, 'Here are the rules we're following. Here is what we do and don't do.' "

The paper's editor, Robert Rivard, adds: "By affirming our values in our news columns and online, it's as if we're restating our vows to serve our readers, who feel a real ownership in their hometown newspapers."

Clair Whitmer, executive editor of *CNET.com* and one of the drafters of its ethics policy, says the guidelines are rooted in traditional journalism but also embrace the realities of cyberspace publishing. For instance, "When most publications make a mistake on their Web site, they cover their tracks and pretend it was never wrong," Whitmer says. "We felt that was disingenuous, so for any mistake of substance, we post a correction on our front page and keep it archived for several months."

Another ethical minefield involves separation of editorial and advertising. "Throughout the industry, there's a real emphasis on achieving profitability," says Whitmer. "We're seeing cross-promotional deals being struck and story pages with 'sponsored links' [to related products] that are paid for by advertisers. Our policy is that any advertising link has to be clearly labeled."

Chris Barr, CNET's top editor, agrees that disclosure is often the answer. As co-chairman of the Internet Content Coalition, a group of major online media companies, he's helping to craft guidelines that cover advertising links; advertorials; targeted ads (in which advertisers buy placement of their ad near a particular column or story); sponsored pages (in which advertisers pay to have their brand name on a page of editorial content); and other issues that directly affect a Web publication's credibility.

"It's a very rapidly changing field," Barr says, "but one constant is the need for greater user education."

Part of that education should involve publishing rules of conduct, in an open compact with readers. Who, after all, does an ethics policy serve?

Source: J. D. Lasica, "So If You've Got It, Flaunt It," *American Journalism Review*, October 1998.

to be sold by the homeless to middle-class youths. While some content is provided by the homeless and seventy-five cents of the $1 price goes to homeless vendors, the success of the *Big Issue* has left many street-paper publishers questioning the value of a large-circulation street paper that generates money for the homeless at the expense of empowering them. Still, by 1999 street papers had become a viable alternative voice to the mainstream press and TV networks, which had generally stopped reporting on homelessness by the mid-1990s.

newspapers and democracy

Despite their considerable achievements as investigators of corruption and chroniclers of daily life, newspapers and journalists today are often viewed in a negative light. Seen as jaded or cynical, reporters in the 1990s are sometimes perceived merely as invaders of people's privacy. Yet in some historical periods, newspapers and reporters were more highly regarded. Particularly noteworthy have been the courageous war correspondents, many of whom gave their lives to bear witness to major civil and world wars. Still, the last time that a significant number of Americans viewed the press heroically was in 1974, when newspapers played a key role in forcing Richard Nixon to resign the presidency in the wake of the Watergate scandal. The best example of this coverage was the daily reporting in the *Washington Post* by Bob Woodward and Carl Bernstein, who later recounted their Watergate investigations in the book *All the President's Men*.

Certainly, of all mass media, newspapers have played the longest and strongest role in sustaining democracy. As a venue for the expression of ideas and the distribution of information, newspapers keep readers abreast of issues and events in their community, their nation, and their world. Over the years, newspapers have fought heroic battles in places that had little tolerance for differing points of view. In the 1990s alone, hundreds of reporters from several countries died or disappeared while trying to report sensitive stories that threatened political leaders or military regimes. From 1995 through 1998, 128 reporters from around the world were killed, and during this same period another 300 were held in prisons for trying to do their jobs. In these settings, reporters and editors continue to articulate unpopular and oppositional ideas even when their right to publish has been threatened.

Although newspapers remain a strong medium of communication, critics have raised a number of concerns about their future. For instance, some charge that newspapers have become so formulaic in their design and reporting styles that they may actually discourage new approaches to telling stories and reporting news. In addition, given the rise of newspaper chains, the likelihood of including new opinions, ideas, and information in mainstream daily papers may be diminishing. Although wealthy and powerful chains may keep smaller struggling papers solvent, such chains sometimes have little commitment to local communities beyond profits. Chain journalism tends to discourage watchdog journalism and the crusading traditions of newspapers. Like other business managers, many news executives prefer not to offend investors or outrage potential advertisers by running too many investigative reports, especially business probes. Indeed, reporters have generally undercovered the business and ownership arrangements in their own industry.

Critics today have raised some important questions regarding the transformation from a modern print to a postmodern digital culture. For example, does such a transformation represent a cheapening of public discourse? Do "new news" forums and nonprint media offer opportunities to improve democracy by permitting public conversations that are not dependent on major newspapers? Also, what is the role of large corporations in this transformation? Do they allow enough different voices and

> "Journalism, and specifically the newspaper, ought to become a **support system** for public life." —Jay Rosen, news scholar, 1992

Regarded as one of the best online newspapers, the *Mercury Center* is the Web-based extension of the *San Jose Mercury News*. Offering in-depth news, analysis, and services, the *Mercury Center* is a substantial resource for both national and regional news, particularly concerning coverage of Silicon Valley and the titans of the computer industry.

viewpoints into the market? (We will return to these questions and the *public journalism* movement in Chapter 14.)

By the late 1990s, the social definition and role of a reporter seemed in question. In reporting the latest White House gossip, weekly supermarket tabloids had a readership three and four times larger than that of the *New York Times*, which itself had followed up on stories that first appeared in tabloids. Talk-show hosts were also performing news functions by bringing to light controversial issues. Giving third-party candidates like Ross Perot a platform, Larry King's talk show on CNN played a journalistic role in both the 1992 and the 1996 presidential elections. By 2000, the 24-hour cable news prime-time talk shows promised to be major venues for political discussion and national debate. The mid-1990s also saw furious competition for younger readers weaned on moving images in a highly visual culture. Since most major newspapers are now available via interactive computer services, the old battle lines between print and electronic culture need to be redrawn and remapped. For better or worse, journalism today encompasses a host of resources that perform news and entertainment functions. Newspapers are working to keep up as they compete in a world overloaded with information. The best of them continue to sustain journalism's democratic traditions: They make sense of important events and watch over our central institutions.

REVIEW QUESTIONS

The Evolution of American Newspapers

1. What are the limitations of a press that serves only partisan interests? Why did the earliest papers appeal mainly to more privileged readers?

2. How did newspapers emerge as a mass medium during the penny-press era? How did content changes make this happen?

3. What are the two main features of yellow journalism? How have Joseph Pulitzer and William Randolph Hearst contributed to newspaper history?

American Print Journalism in the Modern Period

4. Why did objective journalism develop? What are its characteristics? What are its strengths and limitations?

5. Why did interpretive forms of journalism develop in the modern era? What are the limits of objectivity?

6. How would you define literary journalism? Why did it emerge in such an intense way in the 1960s? How is literary journalism an attack on objective news?

Categorizing News and U.S. Newspapers

7. What is the difference between consensus- and conflict-oriented newspapers?

8. What role have ethnic, minority, and oppositional newspapers played in the United States?

9. Why have African American newspapers struggled to maintain their circulation figures over the past two decades?

Issues of Ownership, Economics, and Technology

10. What is the impact of a JOA (joint operating agreement) on the business and editorial divisions of competing newspapers?

11. Why did newspaper chains become an economic trend in the twentieth century?

12. What are the major reasons for the decline in newspaper circulation figures?

13. What major challenges does new technology pose to the newspaper industry?

Newspapers and Democracy

14. What is a newspaper's role in a democracy?

15. How has the definition of a reporter changed in the 1990s?

QUESTIONING THE MEDIA

1. What kinds of stories, topics, or issues are not being covered well by mainstream papers?

2. Why do you think people aren't reading daily newspapers as frequently as they once did? What can newspapers do to increase circulation?

3. Discuss whether newspaper chains are ultimately good or bad for the future of journalism.

4. Are Larry King, Oprah Winfrey, or Ricki Lake practicing a form of journalism on their talk shows? Explain your answer.

5. Do newspapers today play a vigorous role as watchdogs of our powerful institutions? Why or why not?

6. Will television news and online news services eventually replace newspapers? Explain your response.

SEARCHING THE INTERNET

http://www.mediainfo.com
The official Web site of *Editor & Publisher*, the newspaper industry's top trade journal. This site offers statistics on the industry, links to national and international newspaper sites, library and research services, and major stories on the newspaper business.

http://www.nytimes.com
The site for the nation's best newspaper, the *New York Times*, not only offers a Web version of its daily newspaper but also updates major stories throughout the day.

http://www.wsj.com
The site for the nation's most widely circulated daily newspaper, the *Wall Street Journal*. Although parts of the site are by paid subscription only, free services allow readers to access current articles on a range of topics including the economy, financial markets, and politics.

http://www.latimes.com
The site for the nation's leading West Coast paper, the *Los Angeles Times*, offers main sections and updates of its print version and similar services as other leading national papers.

http://www.usatoday.com
The colorful site for the Web version of the nation's newest national paper, *USA Today*, founded in 1982, offers online counterparts to its four main print sections as well as a version of its famous full-color weather map.

http://www.washingtonpost.com
The site for one of the nation's most influential papers, the *Washington Post*, whose publisher also owns *Newsweek* magazine.

In Brief

In class, make several lists on the board regarding what sections of the newspaper you and your classmates read first, second, and/or not at all. Why do you make these choices? What do you think draws you to these particular sections? In terms of the whole class, which sections were people more likely to read first? Can you make any generalizations about the newspaper-reading behavior of you and your classmates?

In Depth

The purpose of this project is to extend your critical approach to news. Work with a partner or in a small group. Over a period of three weekdays, study the *New York Times*, *USA Today*, and one local daily paper. Devise a chart and a descriptive scheme so that you can compare how each of the three papers covered *international* news. You should consider international news any news story that is *predominantly* about a country other than the United States. Exclude the sports section of the papers. Follow these steps as you work on your project:

1. *Description.* Count the total number of international news stories in each paper. Which foreign cities are covered? Which countries? What are the subjects of these stories (civil wars, anti-Americanism, natural disasters, travelogue profiles, etc.)? Prepare a descriptive chart to show the differences among the three papers.

2. *Analysis.* Using your chart as a guide, write two or three paragraphs discussing *patterns* that emerge. What locales seem to get the most attention? What kinds of stories seem to appear most frequently? In other words, what kind of issue or event makes another country newsworthy? Do not try to summarize your chart here. Instead, just write about three or four intriguing patterns that you noticed.

3. *Interpretation.* Write a two- or three-paragraph critical interpretation of your findings. What does your analysis mean? Why do some countries appear more frequently than others? Why do certain kinds of stories seem to get featured?

4. *Evaluation.* Discuss the limitations of your study. Which paper seemed to do the best job of covering the rest of the world? Why? Do you think newspapers give us enough information about other people's cultures?

CHAPTER 9

Gwyneth, Brad, Julia and Hollywood's hidden dress cod

JANE

MARCH

Hot new reason to have sex
(as if you needed one)

Cindy Crawford
Goofier than you've ever seen her

Spring fashions for $50!

How they look now
The Big Makeunder Reunion

Guard dogs and guns:
Behind the scenes at an abortion clinic

US $2.95 Canada $3.95

03>

Exclusive
Claire Danes
A movie sta

Jane Pratt knew she wanted to work at magazines when she was fifteen. Feeling disconnected and lonely at an elite New England boarding school, she sought—and found—comfort in teen magazines. After majoring in communication and dance at college, Pratt had internships at *McCall's* and *Rolling Stone,* and worked for a short time at a teen publication. At age twenty-four, she became editor in chief of *Sassy,* and shook up the world of teen-girl magazines by speaking to teens in their language, with frank talk about sexuality, criticism of fashion models who looked too good, and personal-care columns like "Zits and Stuff." From 1988 to 1994, Jane Pratt led *Sassy* to a peak of 800,000 in circulation, and changed the way teen magazines like *Seventeen, YM,* and *Teen* targeted young women. In just a few short years, Pratt also helped to launch *Dirt* magazine, *Sassy*'s male-oriented counterpart, and hosted television talk shows on Fox and Lifetime. She also wrote a book. She became famous. To her audience, she was a big sister, known simply as "Jane." She knew how to connect with teens.

In September 1997, Pratt started a new magazine for her grown-up *Sassy* readers. The tone is still irreverent, but "we didn't need to insert 'likes' and 'you knows,'" Pratt says. "It's not written for fifteen-year-olds." The new publication—entitled what else but *Jane*—hopes to attract the same female demographic niche (ages eighteen through thirty-four) currently served by magazines such as *Mademoiselle, Cosmopolitan, Marie Claire, Elle,* and *Glamour.* Pratt argues that her magazine's approach is different, though. "I didn't want to create a magazine that would make women feel bad after reading it. I didn't want it to be a manual for all your flaws and all the things you need to fix."[1] One of the magazine's most popular features is the Jane Makeunder, in which select readers are treated to a more natural, simple style. And just so readers know that all this success hasn't gone to Jane's head, she subtitles her editor's-note column with "Why I'm Not Quite the Biggest Egomaniac in the World Even Though the Name of This Magazine May Lead You to Believe Otherwise."

The start-up of *Jane* seems promising, especially with a $5 million promotional campaign and 300,000 free first issues sent out to previous *Sassy* subscribers. Still, there is no guarantee of success. *Jane* must be provocative enough to lure readers from competing magazines while avoiding being so radical that advertisers are scared away (a problem *Sassy* originally had). In 1996, two years after Pratt and her original staff left, the once-phenomenal *Sassy* folded when the new ownership instituted a more mainstream tone that left its readers disenchanted. By 1999, *Jane's* monthly circulation was over 600,000.

When television was on the rise in the early 1950s, many critics predicted the collapse of the magazine industry. But, like radio, the magazine industry showed remarkable resilience in adapting to a changing media landscape. In fact, by the late 1990s more than three hundred new consumer magazines, like *Jane*, were being launched annually.

Magazines adapted readily to the TV era. The introduction in 1953 of an inconspicuous publication—*TV Guide*—was a significant turning point in modern magazine history. That magazine capitalized instantly on TV's popularity. *TV Guide* was also an early example of media convergence: one medium devoting its content to another medium. It demonstrated one way the magazine industry could survive television, which would soon digest ever-larger portions of the national advertising pie.

Traditional national magazines discovered they would have to retool rapidly; television was snatching away sponsors and displacing general-circulation magazines as the dominant family medium. As a result, many magazines started developing market niches, appealing to advertisers who wanted to reach specific audiences defined by gender, age, race, class, or social interests.

Since the 1740s, magazines have played a key role in our social and cultural lives. More than newspapers, which have been mainly local and regional in scope, magazines became America's earliest national mass medium. They created some of the first spaces for discussing the large social issues of the age, including public education, the abolition of slavery, women's suffrage, literacy, and the Civil War. Early publications provided a political forum for debates among the colonial elite. In addition, many leading literary figures used magazines to gain public exposure for their essays and fiction.

In the nineteenth century, magazines became an important educational forum for women, who were barred from higher education and from active participation in the nation's political life. At the turn of the century, magazines contained probing reports that would influence a century of investigative print and broadcast journalism. From an economic perspective, magazines helped reorient households toward advertised products, hastening the rise of a consumer society. From a cultural perspective, magazines pioneered the use of engraving and photography, providing the earliest hints of the visual culture to come.

"The media—including *Jane*—is often accused of contributing to celebrity fixation and worship. It's always been our mission to take celebs off those pedestals and show them as the real people they are."
—Jane Pratt, editor in chief, *Jane*, 1999

Today—despite movies, radio, television, and cable—magazines still give us voices that are not readily heard in mainstream electronic culture. Certainly, newsmagazines such as *Time* and *Newsweek* play a pivotal role in determining what consumers think about. But outside the mainstream, numerous specialized magazines cover everything from radical politics to unusual hobbies. These publications bring information and viewpoints to readers who are not being served by the other major media channels.

More than twelve thousand commercial and alternative magazines, and an additional thirteen thousand noncommercial publications and newsletters, are published in the United States annually. Like newspapers and television, magazines continue to both reflect and construct portraits of American life. They are catalogues for daily events and experiences. They show us the latest products, putting our consumer culture on continuous display. Just as we delve into other forms of culture, we read and view our favorite magazines to learn something about our community, our nation, our world, and ourselves.

In this chapter, we will investigate the history and health of the magazine industry, highlighting the colonial and early American eras, the arrival of national magazines, and the development of engraving and photography. Turning to the modern American magazine, we will also focus on the age of muckraking and the rise of general-interest publications and consumer magazines. We will then look at the decline of mass-market magazines and TV's impact on the older print medium. We will see how magazines have specialized in order to survive in a fragmented market and adapt in the Information Age. Finally, we will investigate the organization and economics of magazines and their function in a democracy.

the early history of magazines

The first magazines probably developed in seventeenth-century France, originating from bookseller catalogues and notices that book publishers inserted into newspapers. The word *magazine* derives from the French term *magasin*, meaning storehouse. The earliest magazines were indeed storehouses of contemporary writing and reports taken mostly from newspapers. Today, the word **magazine** broadly refers to collections of articles, stories, and advertisements appearing in nondaily (such as weekly or monthly) periodicals that are published in tabloid style rather than newspaper style.

The first political magazine, called the *Review*, appeared in London in 1704. Edited by political activist and novelist Daniel Defoe (author of *Robinson Crusoe*), the *Review* was printed sporadically until 1713. Like the *Nation*, the *National Review*, and the *Progressive* in the United States today, early European magazines were channels for political commentary and persuasion. These periodicals looked like newspapers, but they appeared less frequently and were oriented more toward broad domestic and political issues than toward recent news.

In the eighteenth century, regularly published magazines or pamphlets, such as the *Tatler* and the *Spectator*, also appeared in England. They offered poetry, politics, and philosophy for London's elite, and they served readerships of a few thousand. The first publication to use the term *magazine* was *Gentleman's Magazine*, which appeared in London in 1731 and consisted of reprinted articles from newspapers, books, and political pamphlets. Later, the magazine began publishing original work by such writers as Defoe, Samuel Johnson, and Alexander Pope.

colonial magazines

With neither a substantial middle class nor advanced printing technology, magazines developed slowly in the United States. Like partisan newspapers, magazines served politicians, the educated, and the merchant classes, interpreting their political, commercial, and cultural world. Paid circulations were slight—between one hundred and fifteen hundred. In the late 1700s, reading magazines was not a habit among the working classes; most adults were illiterate. However, early magazines did document a new nation coming to terms with issues of taxation, state versus federal power, Indian treaties, public education, and the end of colonialism. George Washington, Alexander Hamilton, and John Hancock all wrote for magazines, and Paul Revere worked as a magazine illustrator for a time.

The first colonial magazines appeared in Philadelphia in 1741, about fifty years after the first newspapers. Andrew Bradford started it all with *American Magazine, or A Monthly View of the Political State of the British Colonies.* Three days later, Ben Franklin's *General Magazine and Historical Chronicle* appeared. Bradford's magazine lasted only three months and three issues. It faced circulation and postal obstacles that Franklin, who had replaced Bradford as Philadelphia's postmaster, put in its way. For instance, Franklin mailed his magazine without paying the high postal rates that he subsequently charged others. Franklin's magazine primarily duplicated what was already available in local papers. After six months, he, too, stopped publication.

Following the Philadelphia experiments, magazines emerged in other colonies as well. Boston produced several magazines beginning in the 1740s. The most successful publications simply reprinted articles from leading London periodicals, keeping readers abreast of European events. Magazines such as the *Independent Reflector* also sprang up in New York, featuring poetry as well as cultural and political essays. The *Pennsylvania Magazine*, edited by activist Thomas Paine, helped rally the colonies against British rule. While editing the magazine, Paine worked on his famous 1776 pamphlet *Common Sense*, which made the intellectual case for American independence. By 1776, about a hundred colonial magazines had appeared and disappeared. Although historians consider them dull and uninspired, these magazines did launch a new medium that would catch on after the Revolution.

the first u.s. magazines

The early growth of magazines in the United States was steady but slow. Delivery costs remained high, and some postal carriers even refused to carry magazines because they added so much weight to a load. Twelve magazines operated in 1800. By 1825, about a hundred magazines existed, although another five hundred or so had failed in the first twenty-five years of the nineteenth century. By the early 1800s, most communities had their own weekly magazines, but much of the material was still reprinted from other sources. These magazines featured essays on local issues, government activities, and political intrigue. They sold some advertising but were usually in precarious financial straits because of their small circulations.

The idea of specialized magazines devoted to certain categories of readers developed throughout the nineteenth century. Many early periodicals, for instance, were overtly religious. Published by various denominations, religious magazines boasted the largest readerships in their day. The Methodist *Christian Journal and Advocate*, for example, claimed 25,000 subscribers by 1826. Literary magazines also emerged. The *North American Review*, for example, established the work of important writers such as Ralph Waldo Emerson, Henry David Thoreau, and Mark Twain. Besides religion and literature, magazines addressed various professions, lifestyles, and topics, including agriculture (*American Farmer*), education (*American Journal of Education*), law (*American Law Journal*), medicine (*Medical Repository*), and science (*American Journal of Science*). Such specialization spawned the modern trend of reaching readers who share a profession, a set of beliefs, cultural tastes, or a social identity.

In 1821, two young Philadelphia printers, Charles Alexander and Samuel Coate Atkinson, launched the *Saturday Evening Post*, which became the longest-running magazine in U.S. history. The printers ran their venture from the same printing plant that once published Franklin's newspaper, the *Pennsylvania Gazette*. Like most magazines of the day, the early *Post* included a few original essays by its own editors but "borrowed" many pieces from other sources. Eventually, the *Post* developed into one of the leading magazines of the nineteenth century, featuring news, poetry, essays, and play reviews. Its editors published such prominent popular authors as Nathaniel Hawthorne and Harriet Beecher Stowe. It was the first major magazine to appeal directly to women, starting the "Lady's Friend," a column that addressed women's issues. During the 1800s, the weekly *Post* became the first important general-interest magazine aimed at a national audience.

the arrival of national magazines

With increases in literacy and public education and developments in faster printing technology in the mid-1980s, a market was created for more magazines like the *Post*. Improvements in rail transportation also made it possible to ship magazines and other consumer products easily from city to city. Whereas in 1825 a hundred magazines struggled for survival, by 1850 nearly six hundred magazines were being produced. During this twenty-five-year period, publishers launched as many as five thousand magazines, although most of them lasted less than a year.

Besides the *Saturday Evening Post*, the most influential general magazines of the day were targeted at women. In 1828, Sarah Josepha Hale started the first women's magazine, *Ladies' Magazine*. It advocated women's rights and schools to train women as teachers. (Hale did not believe men and women should be educated together.) After nine years and marginal success, Hale merged her magazine with its main rival, *Godey's Lady's Book* (1830–98), which she edited for the next forty years. By 1850, *Godey's*, known for its colored fashion illustrations, had a circulation of 40,000, at that time the biggest ever for a U.S. magazine. By 1860, circulation swelled to 150,000. Hale's magazine, a champion of women's property rights, played a central role in educating working- and middle-class women, who were denied access to higher education throughout the nineteenth century.

Other magazines also marked the shift to national periodicals. *Graham's Magazine*, published in Philadelphia from 1840 to 1858, was one of the most influential and entertaining magazines in the country. Also important at the time was the precursor of the *New Yorker, Knickerbocker* (1833–64), which drew from such New York literary talent as Washington Irving, James Fenimore Cooper, and Nathaniel Hawthorne. The magazine introduced the "Editor's Table," a breezy and often humorous column that discussed the topics of the day and would later be imitated by

Americanized versions of Paris fashion trends appeared in *Godey's Lady's Book*, one of the first American magazines for women and a pioneer in colorized illustrations. America's most popular magazine in the mid-nineteenth century, *Godey's* was run for forty years by writer-editor Sarah Josepha Hale, who also wrote the children's poem "Mary Had a Little Lamb."

the *New Yorker*. Also emerging during this period was the *Nation*, founded in 1865 by E. L. Godkin. The oldest surviving American political opinion magazine, the *Nation* continues to serve mostly an educated national readership whose politics are left of center. In addition, the weekly *Youth's Companion* (1826–1929) became one of the first successful magazines for younger readers. It, too, sought to extend the reach of magazines beyond local boundaries.

pictorial pioneers

Like the first newspapers, many early magazines were dull and gray in appearance, totally dependent on the printed word. Beginning in the 1850s, however, some newspapers and magazines started printing elaborate engravings and illustrations. Printing photographs took a bit longer. Mathew Brady and his employees, whose thirty-five hundred photos documented the Civil War, had popularized photography by the 1860s. But it took newspapers and magazines until the 1890s to figure out how to adapt photos to print media.

By the mid-1850s, drawings, engravings, woodcuts, and other forms of illustration had become major features of magazines. During this time, *Godey's Lady's Book* employed up to 150 women to color-tint its magazine illustrations and stencil drawings. *Harper's New Monthly Magazine*, founded in 1850, published top American and British writers but also offered extensive woodcut illustrations with each issue. During the Civil War, many readers relied on *Harper's* for its elaborate battlefield sketches. Publications like *Harper's* married visual language to the printed word, helping to transform magazines into a popular national mass medium.

the development of modern american magazines

In 1870, about twelve hundred magazines were produced in the United States. By 1890, the number of magazines reached forty-five hundred; by 1905, more than six thousand existed, most of them intended for local and regional audiences. The rate of failure, however, was still high. Although publishers launched approximately seventy-five hundred magazines between 1895 and 1905, more than half of them died or merged with other magazines.[2] Part of this surge in titles and readership had been facilitated by the Postal Act of 1879, which gave magazines cheaper rates and put them on an equal footing with newspapers delivered by mail.

While cheaper postal rates and better rail transportation were reducing magazines' distribution costs, advances in modern technology were lowering production costs. By the end of the nineteenth century, advances in mass-production printing, conveyor systems, assembly lines, and faster presses made large-circulation national magazines possible.[3] These technological improvements allowed magazine entrepreneurs to slash the price of magazines, which ran about thirty-five cents a copy in the late 1880s. As prices dropped to fifteen and then to ten cents, the working classes were gradually able to purchase national publications. By 1905, there were about twenty-five national magazines, available from coast to coast and serving millions of readers.[4]

> "They spring up as fast as mushrooms, in every corner, and like all rapid vegetation, bear the seeds of early decay within them . . . and then comes a 'frost, a killing frost,' in the form of bills due and debts unpaid. . . . The average age of periodicals in this country is found to be six months."
>
> —*New-York Mirror*, 1828

As magazine circulation started to skyrocket, publishers began deriving higher ad revenues from companies eager to sell their wares in this expanding market. Ad pages in national magazines soared. *Harper's,* for instance, devoted only seven pages to ads in the mid-1880s, nearly fifty pages by 1890, and more than ninety pages by 1900.[5] By the turn of the century, advertisers increasingly used national magazines to get consumers' attention and build a national marketplace. In addition, the dramatic growth of drugstores and dime stores, supermarkets, and department stores offered new venues and shelf space for selling consumer goods, including magazines. As jobs and the population began shifting from farms and small towns to urban areas, magazines helped readers to imagine themselves as part of a nation rather than as individuals with only local or regional identities.

One magazine that took advantage of these changes was *Ladies' Home Journal,* begun in 1883 by Cyrus Curtis. Prior to *LHJ,* many women's magazines had been called *cookie-and-pattern* publications because they narrowly confined women's concerns to baking and fashion. *LHJ* broadened the scope of magazines as its editors and advertisers realized that women consumers were a growing and lucrative market. Publishing popular fiction and sheet music as well as the latest consumer ads, *LHJ* had a circulation of half a million by the early 1890s—the highest of any magazine in the country. In 1903, it became the first magazine to reach a circulation of one million.

social reform and the muckrakers

The economics behind the rise of popular magazines was simple: A commercial publisher could dramatically expand circulation by dropping the price of an issue *below* the actual production cost for a single copy. The publisher recouped the loss through ad revenue, guaranteeing large readerships to advertisers who were willing to pay more to reach more readers. Throughout the twentieth century, many commercial magazines adopted this principle. However, simply lowering costs from twenty-five or thirty-five cents to a dime wasn't enough. Like the penny press, magazines had to change content as well.

Besides being attracted to the ten-cent price tag, readers were drawn to the issues that magazines addressed. While printing the fiction and essays of good writers of the day, magazines also engaged in one aspect of yellow journalism—crusading for social reform on behalf of the public good. In the early 1890s, for example, Curtis's *LHJ* and its editor, Edward Bok, led the fight against unregulated patent medicines (which often contained nearly 50 percent alcohol). Other magazines joined the fight against phony medicines, poor living and working conditions, and unsanitary practices in various food industries.

The rise in overall magazine circulation coincided with the search for better jobs. In the move from farms to factories, hundreds of thousands of Americans and new immigrants poured into cities. Thus the nation that journalists and magazines wrote about had grown increasingly complex by the turn of the century. Some reporters became dissatisfied with conventional journalism and turned from newspapers to magazines, where they were able to write in greater depth about broader issues. They wrote both factual and fictional accounts on such topics as big-business and government corruption, urban problems faced by immigrants, labor-management conflicts, and race relations. Angry with so much negative reporting, President Theodore Roosevelt in 1906 dubbed these reporters *muckrakers,* because they were willing to crawl around in society's muck to uncover a story. **Muckraking** was a label that Roosevelt used with disdain, but it was worn with pride by reporters such as Ray Stannard Baker, Frank Norris, Lincoln Steffens, and Ida Tarbell.

In 1902, *McClure's* magazine (1893–1933) touched off this investigative era in magazine reporting with a series of probing stories on business monopolies, life-insurance frauds, political dishonesty in city governments, and the problems of labor and working people. The muckrakers distrusted established institutions and undertook to protect ordinary citizens from corruption. First serialized in *McClure's*, Ida Tarbell's *The History of the Standard Oil Company* took on John D. Rockefeller's big oil monopoly. Lincoln Steffens's "Shame of the Cities" series for *McClure's* tackled urban problems. Steffens said of his own investigations, "When I set out to describe the corrupt systems of certain typical cities, I meant to show simply how the people were deceived and betrayed."[6]

In 1906, *Cosmopolitan* (1886–), recently purchased by William Randolph Hearst, joined the muckraking parade with a series called "The Treason of the Senate." *Collier's* (1888–1957) developed "The Great American Fraud" series, focusing on patent medicines (whose ads accounted for 30 percent of the profits made by the American press by the 1890s). Influenced by Upton Sinclair's novel *The Jungle*, a fictional account of Chicago's meatpacking industry, and *Collier's* and *LHJ's* muckraking reports, Congress passed the Pure Food and Drug Act in 1906.

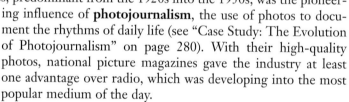

the rise of general-interest magazines

The heyday of the muckraking era lasted into the mid-1910s. Then national social crusades and reforms became less significant, as America and journalism were gradually drawn into the first major international war. After World War I, the prominent publications were **general-interest magazines**, which offered occasional investigative articles but covered a wide variety of topics aimed at a broad national audience. A key to these magazines, predominant from the 1920s into the 1950s, was the pioneering influence of **photojournalism**, the use of photos to document the rhythms of daily life (see "Case Study: The Evolution of Photojournalism" on page 280). With their high-quality photos, national picture magazines gave the industry at least one advantage over radio, which was developing into the most popular medium of the day.

Saturday Evening Post. As we have noted, the first widely popular general-interest magazine was the *Saturday Evening Post*. When Cyrus Curtis bought the *Post* in 1897 for $1,000, it had a circulation of approximately ten thousand. Curtis's strategy for reinvigorating the magazine included printing popular fiction and romanticizing American virtues through words and pictures (a *Post* tradition best depicted in the three hundred cover illustrations by Norman Rockwell). Curtis also

This 1935 Thanksgiving cover of the *Saturday Evening Post* was illustrated by Norman Rockwell (1894–1978). Rockwell created realistic, sentimental, and humorous scenes from small-town life, and over the years more than three hundred of his paintings graced the cover of the *Post*. His illustrations often invoked images of traditional American family values.

featured articles that celebrated the business boom of the 1920s. This reversed the journalistic direction of the muckraking era, in which business corruption was often the focus. By the 1920s, the *Post* had reached two million in circulation, the first magazine to hit that mark. By 1920, about fifty-five magazines fit the general-interest category; by 1946, more than a hundred such magazines competed with radio networks for the national audience.

Reader's Digest. The most widely circulated general-interest magazine during this period was *Reader's Digest*. Started in 1922 by Dewitt Wallace and Lila Acheson Wallace for $5,000 in a Greenwich Village basement, *Reader's Digest* championed one of the earliest functions of magazines: printing condensed versions of selected articles from other magazines. In the magazine's early years, the Wallaces refused to accept ads and sold the *Digest* only through subscriptions. The *Digest*'s circulation was just over 100,000 by the late 1920s, when it began to appear on newsstands. With its inexpensive production costs and low price, the magazine's circulation climbed to one million in 1935 during the heart of the Depression. By 1946, *Reader's Digest* was the nation's most popular magazine, with a circulation of nine million. Its pocket-size format made it popular both at home and for travel. By 1963, the *Digest* had a circulation of more than fourteen million, five million more than its nearest rival, *TV Guide*.

For years the *Digest* selected articles based on three criteria: "applicability" (articles relevant to readers' daily lives); "lasting interest" (articles that could still be read the next year); and "constructiveness" (articles that had an optimistic, upbeat outlook on life).[7] Although over the years *Reader's Digest* has been both chastised and praised for its conservative viewpoints and occasionally pious moral tone, by the mid-1980s it had become the most popular magazine in the world. At its peak, it reached a circulation of twenty million in America and another ten to twelve million in 160 other countries. (See Table 9.1 for the circulation figures of the Top 10 U.S. magazines.)

Time. During the general-interest era, national newsmagazines such as *Time* were also major commercial successes. Begun in 1923 by Henry Luce and Britton Hadden, *Time* developed a magazine brand of interpretive journalism, assigning reporter-

TABLE 9.1
The Top 10 Magazines
(ranked by paid U.S. circulation, 1972 vs. 1998)

1972		1998	
Rank/Publication	Circulation	Rank/Publication	Circulation
1 Reader's Digest	17,827,661	1 Modern Maturity	20,402,096
2 TV Guide	16,410,858	2 NRTA/AARP Bulletin	20,360,798
3 Woman's Day	8,191,731	3 Reader's Digest	14,675,541
4 Better Homes and Gardens	7,996,050	4 TV Guide	13,085,971
5 Family Circle	7,889,587	5 National Geographic	8,783,752
6 McCall's	7,516,960	6 Better Homes and Gardens	7,616,114
7 National Geographic	7,260,179	7 Family Circle	5,005,084
8 Ladies' Home Journal	7,014,251	8 Ladies' Home Journal	4,521,970
9 Playboy	6,400,573	9 Good Housekeeping	4,517,713
10 Good Housekeeping	5,801,446	10 McCall's	4,239,622

Source: Magazine Publishers of America.

The Evolution of Photojournalism

by Christopher R. Harris

From glossy magazines to content-rich Internet news sites, striking images of events from across the country and around the globe may seem commonplace today. These easily reproducible images have the power to convey vivid impressions of places we have never visited and events we have not witnessed. Yet before the mid-nineteenth century, readers had to rely primarily on the verbal descriptions provided by reporters, and events were always interpreted in words rather than depicted with images. Thus *photojournalism*, reporting in which photographs are as—or more—important than text, is a vital and relatively new component in the way we view world events.

What we now recognize as photojournalism started with the assignment of photographer Roger Fenton, of the *Sunday Times* of London, to document the Crimean War in 1856. Technical limitations did not allow *direct* reproduction of photodocumentary images in the publications of the day, however. Woodcut artists had to interpret the photographic images as black-and-white-toned woodblocks that could be reproduced by the presses of the period. Images interpreted by artists therefore lost the inherent qualities of photographic visual documentation: an on-site visual representation of facts for those who weren't present.

Woodcuts remained the basic method of press reproduction until 1880, when *New York Daily Graphic* photographer Stephen Horgan invented half-tone reproduction using a dot-pattern screen. This screen allowed metallic plates to directly represent photographic images in the printing process; now periodicals could bring exciting visual reportage to their pages.

Child laborer in an Alexandria, Va., glass factory. Lewis Hine, 1909.
Courtesy George Eastman House

In the mid-1890s, Jimmy Hare became the first photographer recognized as a photojournalist in the United States. Taken for *Collier's Weekly*, Hare's photoreportage on the sinking of the battleship *Maine* in 1898 near Havana, Cuba, established his reputation as a newsman traveling the world to bring back images of news events. Hare's images fed into growing popular support for Cuban independence from Spain and eventual U.S. involvement in the Spanish-American War.

In 1888, George Eastman opened photography to the working and middle classes when he introduced the first flexible-film camera from Kodak, his company in Rochester, New York. Gone was the bulky equipment and fragile photographic plates of the past. Now families and journalists could more easily and affordably document gatherings and events.

As photography became easier and more widespread, photojournalism began to take on an increasingly important social role. At the turn of the century, the documentary photography of Jacob Riis and Louis Hine captured the harsh working and living conditions of the nation's many child laborers, including crowded ghettos and unsafe mills and factories. Reaction to these shockingly honest photographs resulted in public outcry and new laws against the exploitation of children. Photographs also brought the horrors of World War I to people far from the battlefields.

In 1923, visionaries Henry Luce and Britton Hadden published *Time*, the first modern photographic newsweekly; *Life* and *Fortune* soon followed. From coverage of the Roaring Twenties to the Great Depression, these magazines used images that changed the way people viewed the world.

Life, with its spacious 10- by 13-inch format and large photographs, became one of the most influential magazines in America, printing what are now classic images from

World War II and the Korean War. Often, *Life* offered images that were unavailable anywhere else: Margaret Bourke-White's photographic proof of the unspeakable concentration camps; W. Eugene Smith's gentle portraits of the humanitarian Albert Schweitzer in Africa; David Duncan's gritty images of the faces of U.S. troops fighting in Korea.

Television photojournalism made its quantum leap into the public mind as it documented the assassination of President Kennedy in 1963. In televised images that were broadcast and rebroadcast, the public witnessed the actual assassination and the confusing aftermath, including the live coverage of the murder of alleged assassin Lee Harvey Oswald and of President Kennedy's funeral procession.

Photojournalism also provided visual documentation of the turbulent 1960s, including aggressive photographic coverage of the Vietnam War—its protesters and supporters. Pulitzer Prize–winning photographer Eddie Adams shook the emotions of the American public with his photographs of a South Vietnamese colonel's summary execution of a suspected Vietcong terrorist. Closer to home, shocking images of the civil-rights movement culminated in pictures of Birmingham police and police dogs attacking civil-rights protesters.

In the 1970s, new computer technologies emerged that were embraced by print and television media worldwide. By the late 1980s, computers could transform images into digital form, easily manipulated by sophisticated software programs. In addition, any photographer can now transmit images around the world almost instantaneously using digital transmission, and the Internet allows publication of virtually any image, without censorship. In 1999, a reporter in war-torn Kosovo could take a picture and within minutes send that picture to news offices in Tokyo, Berlin, and New York; moments later, the images could be posted on the Internet or used in a late-breaking TV story.

Digital technology is likely to revolutionize photojournalism, perhaps even more than the advent of roll film did in the late nineteenth century. Because of fast delivery times, competition among print publications, television networks, and online news providers is heightened, as each can run late-breaking images transmitted from anywhere in the world.

Nguyen Ngoc Loan, National Police Chief for South Vietnam, moments before shooting a suspected Viet Cong prisoner to death. Eddie Adams, 1968.

There is a dark side to digital technology. Because of the absence of physical film, there is a resulting loss of proof, or veracity, of the authenticity of images. Original film has qualities that make it easy to determine whether it has been tampered with. Digital images, by contrast, can be easily altered, but such alteration can be very difficult to detect. A relatively recent example of image-tampering involved mug shots taken of O.J. Simpson after his arrest in 1994. Both *Newsweek* and *Time* ran one of these shots on their covers; *Newsweek* ran the image as photographed, while *Time* artificially darkened the image so that Simpson appeared more menacing. Accusations of foul play from the public and the media forced *Time* to address the issue and apologize, but this event gives only a small indication of the dangers of altering photographs.

Photojournalists and news sources are now confronted with unprecedented concerns over truth-telling. In the past, trust in documentary photojournalism rested solely on the verifiability of images as they were used in the media. Just as we must evaluate the words we read, at the turn of a new century we must also view with a more critical eye these images that mean so much to so many.

Christopher R. Harris is an associate professor in the radio-TV-photography department at Middle Tennessee State University.

researcher teams to cover stories over a period of several weeks. A rewrite editor would then put the whole project together in narrative form and provide an interpretive point of view. Luce believed that journalistic objectivity was a myth and sought instead to be fair. Critics, however, charged that *Time* became increasingly conservative politically as the magazine grew more successful in the 1940s and 1950s. Time had a circulation of 200,000 by 1930, increasing to more than three million by the mid-1960s.

Time's success encouraged prominent imitators, including *Newsweek* (1933–) and *U.S. News & World Report* (1948–). When the major weekly general-interest magazines *Life* and *Look* failed in the early 1970s, newsmagazines took over photo-journalism's role in news reporting, visually documenting both national and international events. By the late 1990s, the three major newsmagazines had circulations ranging from *Time*'s 4.1 million to *Newsweek*'s 3.2 million and *U.S. News*'s 2.2 million.

Life. Despite the commercial success of *Reader's Digest* and *Time*, these two magazines did not come to symbolize general-interest publications during the 1920s and 1930s. That honor belongs to the oversized pictorial weeklies *Look* and, especially, *Life*. More than any other magazine of its day, *Life* developed an effective strategy for competing with popular radio by advancing photojournalism. Launched as a weekly by Henry Luce in 1936, *Life* combined the public's fascination with images (invigorated by the movie industry), radio journalism, and the popularity of advertising and fashion photography. By the end of the 1930s, *Life* had a *pass-along readership*—the total number of people who come into contact with a single copy of a magazine—of more than seventeen million, rivaling the ratings of popular national radio programs.

Life's first editor, Wilson Hicks, formerly a picture editor for the Associated Press, built a staff of renowned photographer-reporters who chronicled the world's ordinary and extraordinary events from the late 1930s through the 1960s. Among them were Margaret Bourke-White, the first woman war correspondent to fly combat missions during World War II, and Gordon Parks, who would become Hollywood's first African American director of major feature films. *Life*—child of the turn-of-the-century pictorial magazines and parent to *People*, *US*, and *Entertainment Weekly*—used an oversized format featuring ninety-six pages of pictures with a minimum of written text.

the fall of
general-interest magazines

In 1970, *Life*'s circulation peaked at 8.5 million, with an estimated pass-along readership of nearly 50 million. *Life*'s chief competitor, *Look*, founded by Gardner Cowles in 1937, reached 2 million in circulation by 1945 and 4 million by 1955. It climbed to almost 8 million in 1971. Dramatically, though, both magazines suspended publication. The demise of these popular periodicals at the peak of their circulations seems inexplicable, but their fall illustrates a key economic shift in media history as well as a crucial moment in the conversion to an electronically oriented culture.

TV Guide Is Born. While *Life* and *Look* were just beginning to make sense of the impact of television on their audiences, *TV Guide* appeared in 1953. Taking its cue from the pocket-size format of *Reader's Digest* and the supermarket sales strategy used by women's magazines, *TV Guide*, started by Walter Annenberg's Triangle Publications, soon rivaled the success of *Reader's Digest* by specializing in TV listings and addressing the nation's growing fascination with television. The first issue sold a

Founded in 1953, *TV Guide* has grown up alongside television and adjusted to changes in the industry. No longer just a compact magazine, the *TV Guide* franchise has expanded to include a cable channel (TV Guide Channel), a user interface for cable systems (TV Guide Interactive), and a Web site (TV Guide Online).

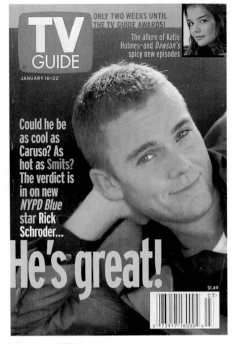

record 1.5 million copies in ten urban markets. The next year, *TV Guide* featured twenty-seven regional editions, tailoring its listings to TV channels in specific areas of the country. Since many newspapers were not yet listing TV programs, *TV Guide*'s circulation soared to 2.2 million in its second year. In 1962, the magazine became the first weekly to reach a circulation of 8 million with its seventy regional editions.

TV Guide would rank among the nation's most popular magazines from the late 1950s into the 1990s. However, with increased competition from newspaper TV supplements and thousands of new magazines, *TV Guide*'s prominence and circulation began flattening out in the 1980s. Then, in 1988, media baron Rupert Murdoch acquired Triangle Publications for $3 billion. Out of this magazine group (which included *Seventeen* and the *Daily Racing Form*), Murdoch kept only *TV Guide*. Murdoch's News Corp. already owned the new Fox network, and buying *TV Guide* ensured that the fledgling network would have its programs listed. Prior to this move, many predicted that no one would be able to start a new network because ABC, CBS, and NBC exercised so much control over television. By the mid-1990s, however, Fox was using *TV Guide* to promote the network's programming in the magazine's 115 regional editions. The other networks occasionally complained that their programs were not treated as well and even threatened to pull their ads.

The *TV Guide* story illustrates a number of key trends in the magazine business. First, in exploiting Americans' shared interest in television, *TV Guide* emerged as a wildly successful magazine just as general magazines like *Life* and *Look* began their economic decline. Second, *TV Guide* demonstrated the growing sales power of the nation's checkout lines, which also sustained the high circulation rates of women's magazines and supermarket tabloids. Third, News Corp.'s ownership of *TV Guide* underscored the fact that magazines were facing the same challenges as other mass media: Large media companies were strategically buying up smaller media outlets and applying the economic synergy of using one medium to promote another.

With the Fox network firmly established and with *TV Guide*'s circulation slowly falling, Murdoch's News Corp. sold *TV Guide* in 1998 to United Video Satellite Group for $2 billion. United Video—owned by cable giant TCI—operated cable television's Prevue Channel, which lists the time and channel for all programs. The *TV Guide* acquisition allowed United Video the synergy of offering both print and cable listings to potential advertisers, and of extending brand-name identity by relaunching the Prevue Channel as the TV Guide Channel in 1999. News Corp. hasn't relinquished complete control of *TV Guide*, however. As part of the deal, News Corp. received a nearly 50 percent share in United Video, giving News Corp. influence in the operation of *TV Guide* and the TV Guide Channel.

Throughout its history, *TV Guide* has been criticized by the networks for an anti-television bias and by TV critics for not being tough enough on the networks. The magazine has also been chastised for Annenberg's conservative viewpoints, which sometimes leaked into editorial copy, particularly when he used the magazine to endorse Ronald Reagan's candidacy for president in 1980. Nonetheless, *TV Guide* became widely circulated, even surpassing *Reader's Digest* for a time in the 1980s with a U.S. circulation of more than eighteen million.

The rise of *TV Guide* paralleled the decline of the weekly general-interest magazines that had dominated the industry for thirty years. In 1956, both *Collier's* (founded in 1888) and *Woman's Home Companion* (founded in 1873) folded. Each magazine had a national circulation of more than four million the year it died. No magazine with this kind of circulation had ever shut down before. Together, the two publications brought in advertising revenues of more than $26 million in 1956. Although some critics blamed poor management, both magazines were victims of changing consumer tastes, rising postal costs, falling ad revenues—and television, which began usurping the role of magazines as the family medium.

Life and *Look* Expire.

Although *Reader's Digest* and women's supermarket magazines were not greatly affected by television, other general-interest magazines were. The weekly *Saturday Evening Post* folded in 1969, *Look* in 1971, and *Life* in 1972. At the time, all three magazines were rated in the Top 10 in terms of paid circulation; each had a readership that exceeded six million per issue. To maintain these figures, however, their publishers were selling the magazines for far less than the cost of production. For example, by the early 1970s a subscription to *Life* cost a consumer twelve cents an issue, yet it cost the publisher more than forty cents per copy to make and mail a single issue.

Eventually, the national advertising revenue pie that helped make up the cost differences for *Life* and *Look* had to be shared with network television—and magazines' slices were getting smaller. *Life's* high pass-along readership meant that it had a larger audience than many prime-time TV shows. But it cost more in 1971 to reach that general audience with a single full-page ad in *Life* than it did to buy a minute of time during evening television. National advertisers were often forced to choose between the two, and in the late 1960s and early 1970s television seemed a slightly better buy to many general advertisers looking for the biggest audience.

The failure of prominent general magazines was complicated by other problems as well. Essentially, both distribution and production costs (especially paper) were rising, while national magazine ad sales had flattened out. Also, the *Saturday Evening Post*, *Life*, and *Look* still relied more on subscriptions than on supermarket and newsstand sales. Dramatic increases in postal rates, however, had a particularly negative effect on oversized publications (those larger than the 8- by 10.5-inch standard for most magazines). In the 1970s, postal rates increased by more than 400 percent for these magazines. The *Post* and *Life* cut their circulations drastically to save money. The *Post* went from producing

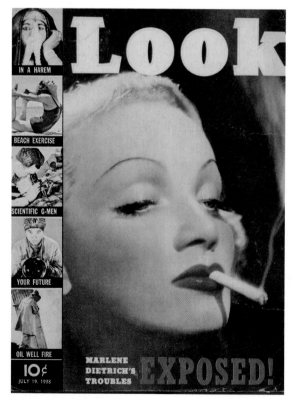

With large pages, beautiful photographs, and compelling stories on such celebrities as Marlene Dietrich, *Look* entertained millions of readers from 1937 to 1971, emphasizing photojournalism to compete with radio. By the late 1960s, however, TV hired away national advertisers, postal rates increased, and production costs rose, forcing *Look* to fold despite a readership of more than six million.

6.8 million to 3 million copies per issue; *Life*, which lost $30 million between 1968 and 1972, cut circulation from 8.5 million to 7 million. The economic rationale here was that limiting the number of copies would reduce production and postal costs, enabling the magazines to lower their ad rates to compete with network television. But, in fact, with decreased circulation, these magazines became less attractive than television for advertisers trying to reach the largest general audience.

The general magazines that survived the competition for national ad dollars tended to be women's magazines, such as *Good Housekeeping, Better Homes and Gardens, Redbook, Ladies' Home Journal*, and *Woman's Day*. These publications were in smaller formats and depended primarily on supermarket sales rather than on expensive mail-delivered subscriptions. However, the most popular magazines, *TV Guide* and *Reader's Digest*, benefited not only from supermarket sales but from their larger circulation (twice that of *Life*), their pocket size, and their small photo budget. Although the *Saturday Evening Post* and *Life* later returned as downsized monthlies, their failure as oversized weeklies ushered in a new era of specialization.

> "At $64,200 for a black-and-white [full] page ad, *Life* had the **highest rate of any magazine**, which probably accounts for its financial troubles. . . . If an **advertiser** also wants to be on television, he may not be able to afford the periodical."
>
> —John Tebbel, historian, 1969

People **Puts** *Life* **Back into Magazines.** In March 1974, Time Inc. launched *People*, the first successful mass-market magazine to appear in decades. With an abundance of celebrity profiles and human-interest stories, *People* showed a profit in two years and reached a circulation of more than two million within five years. By the early 1990s, *People* ranked second behind *TV Guide* in generating revenue from advertising and circulation sales—more than $700 million.

The success of *People* is instructive, particularly since only two years earlier television had helped kill *Life* by draining away national ad dollars. Instead of using a bulky oversized format and relying on subscriptions, *People* downsized and generated most of its circulation revenue from newsstand and supermarket sales. For content, it took its cue from our culture's fascination with celebrities. Supported by plenty of photos, its articles were short, with about one-third as many words as a typical newsmagazine.

Time Inc. used *People* as the model for reviving *Life* in 1978. As a standard-size supermarket monthly, *Life* maintained a steady circulation of around 1.5 million by the late 1990s. Although *People* never achieved the broad popularity that *Life* once commanded, it does seem to defy the contemporary trend of specialized magazines aimed at narrow but well-defined audiences, such as *Tennis World, Teen*, or *Hispanic Business*. One argument suggests that *People* is not, in fact, a mass-market magazine but a specialized publication targeting people with particular cultural interests: a fascination with music, TV, and movie stars. If *People* is viewed as a specialty magazine, its financial success makes much more sense in a world dominated by electronic mass media.

the domination of specialization

The general trend away from mass-market publications and toward specialized magazines coincided with radio's move to specialized formats in the 1950s. With the rise of television in that decade, magazines ultimately reacted the same way radio did: They adapted, trading the mass audience for smaller, discrete audiences that could be guaranteed to advertisers. Two major marketing innovations also helped ease the industry into a new era: the development of regional and demographic editions.

regional editions

As television advertising siphoned off national ad revenues, magazines began **regional editions**: national magazines whose content is tailored to the interests of different geographic areas. For example, *Reader's Digest* for years had been printing different language editions for international markets. Largely by necessity, *TV Guide* also developed special editions for each major TV market in the country. Produced on a cheaper grade of paper, different regional listings were inserted into a glossy national section that featured the same photos and articles across the country. *TV Guide* today has more than a hundred regional editions to suit various markets.

While magazine content shifted in these regional editions, ads generally remained the same. Other magazines, however, soon adapted this idea to advertising variations and inserts. Often called **split-run editions**, these national magazines tailor ads to different geographic areas. Most editions of *Time* and *Newsweek*, for example, contain a number of pages of regional ads. The editorial content remains the same, but the magazine includes a few pages of ads purchased by local or regional companies in various areas of the country. By the end of the 1960s, nearly 250 magazines featured split-run editions. This strategy has been enhanced by the growth of regional printing centers, which allow publishers to download national magazines from communication satellites for printing near their distribution points. The local ads are inserted at the various regional production sites.

Another recent innovation in computer technology, called **ink-jet imaging**, allows a magazine publisher or advertiser to print personalized messages to individual subscribers. In this technique, a national news story on political elections might contain the individual subscriber's own voting district in a special inset within the larger national story. In other words, the same technology that allows magazines to encode names and addresses on magazine covers makes it possible to print names inside the magazine as well. The technique is frequently used to personalize an ad. For more than a decade, Publishers Clearinghouse and other direct-mail advertisers have used this technology to identify consumers by name as potential sweepstakes winners.

demographic editions

Another variation of specialization includes **demographic editions**, which target particular groups of consumers. In this strategy, market researchers identify subscribers by occupation, class, and zip-code address. In an experiment conducted in 1963, *Time* pioneered demographic editions by carrying advertising from a drug company that was inserted into copies of its magazine. These editions were then sent to only sixty thousand doctors who had been chosen from *Time*'s subscription rolls. By the 1980s, aided by developments in computer technology, *Time* had also developed special editions for top management, high-income zip-code areas, and ultrahigh-income professional/managerial households. Certain high-zip-code editions, for instance, would include ads for more expensive consumer products. *Newsweek*, too, began to use demographic specialization. One annual edition, for example, targets college campuses with special inserts featuring articles on college life and ads aimed only at students.

The economic strategy behind regional and demographic editions was to guarantee clients a particular magazine audience at lower rates. Since these ads would run only in special editions, advertisers had to purchase only part of the total audience. Not only is this cheaper than buying access to a publication's entire readership but it also links a national magazine with local retailers. The magazine can then compete with advertising in regional television and newspaper supplements. Because of the

Calvin and Hobbes

flexibility of special editions, new sources of income opened up for national magazines. Ultimately, these marketing strategies permitted the massive growth of magazines in the face of predictions that television would cripple the magazine industry.

magazine categories and types

Although regional and demographic editions provided specific strategies for financial survival, the magazine industry ultimately prospered by fragmenting into a wide range of choices and categories. (See Table 9.2.) Given their current variety, magazines are not easily classified by type; but a number of strategies have been used. One method has been to label magazines according to two categories already discussed: general-interest magazines that reach diverse national audiences and specialized magazines that appeal to readers' common traits. A second approach is to divide periodicals between mainstream or mass-market magazines (such as *Time* or *Reader's Digest*), which appeal to a diverse readership, and alternative magazines (such as *In These Times* or *Against the Current*), which target distinct audiences and are generally critical of conventional culture. Because magazines are so varied, however, large two-category distinctions are not very helpful in cataloguing them.

Another industry strategy for grouping magazines has been to divide them by advertiser type, although this approach neglects magazines such as *Ms.*, *Mad*, and *Consumer Reports*, which rely solely on subscription and newsstand sales and accept no advertising. Nevertheless, given the influence of the ad industry, magazines are often categorized as *consumer magazines* (*Newsweek*, *Details*), which carry a host of general consumer-product ads; as *business* or *trade magazines* (*Advertising Age*, *Progressive Grocer*), which include ads for products and services for various occupational groups; or as *farm magazines* (*Dairy Herd Management*, *Dakota Farmer*), which contain ads for agricultural products and farming lifestyles. Grouping by advertisers further distinguishes commercial magazines from noncommercial magazine-like periodicals. The noncommercial category includes everything from activist newsletters and scholarly journals to business newsletters created by companies for distribution to employees.

As we have seen, during the 1950s radio, film, and magazines arrived at a crossroads as they encountered television. In their own ways, all three media shifted to specialization. Radio developed formats for older and younger audiences, for rock fans and classical fans. At the movies, filmmakers focused on more adult subject matter that

287

TABLE 9.2
Number of New Consumer Magazine Launches
by Interest Categories, 1998

Category	Number	Category	Number
Media personalities	39	Women's	6
Sex	34	Epicurean	5
Crafts/Games/Hobbies	33	Fashion/Beauty/Grooming	5
Computers	32	Fishing and hunting	5
Sports	32	Gay interest	5
Metro/Regional/State	31	Health	5
Special interest	29	Men's	5
Business and finance	27	Motorcycles	5
Music	16	Photography	5
Dogs/Pets	15	Boating and yachting	4
Automotive	14	Gardening	4
Arts and antiques	13	Literary/Reviews/Writing	4
Entertainment	12	Fitness	3
Black interest	10	Gaming	3
Pop culture	9	Military/Naval	3
Children's	8	Religious/Denominational	3
Home/Home service	8	TV/Radio/Communications	3
Mystery/Science fiction	7	Aviation	2
Science/Technology	7	Babies	2
Camping and outdoor	6	Bridal	2
Teen	6	Comics/Comic technique	2
Travel	6	Arts and humanities	1
		Total	476

Source: Magazine Publishers of America, <http://www.magazine.org>.

was off-limits to television's family medium image. The depiction of language, violence, and sexuality all changed as movies sought an identity apart from television.

Magazines also used such strategies as they searched for niche audiences that were not being served by the new medium. In the magazine industry, publications targeted older and younger readers, tennis buffs, and quilting enthusiasts. Magazine content changed, too. *Playboy*, started in 1953 by Hugh Hefner, undermined the conventional values of pre–World War II America and emphasized subject matter that was taboo on television in the 1950s. Scraping together $7,000, Hefner published his first issue, which contained a nude calendar reprint of actress Marilyn Monroe, together with a less famous attack on alimony payments and gold-digging women. With the financial success of that first issue, which sold more than fifty thousand copies, Hefner was in business.

Circulation gradually climbed, and Hefner introduced advertising in 1956. *Playboy*'s circulation peaked in the 1960s, at more than seven million, but fell gradually throughout the 1970s as the magazine faced competition from imitators and video, and criticism for "packaging" women for the enjoyment of men. Throughout the 1970s and 1980s, government commissions and religious groups succeeded in eliminating the sale of *Playboy* and similar magazines at military bases and many local retail chains.

the fragmented magazine marketplace

Playboy's early financial success demonstrated to the magazine industry that specialty magazines aimed at men could achieve large circulation figures. Women's publications sold in supermarkets had long demonstrated that gender-based magazines were highly marketable and that women wielded enormous economic clout. *Better Homes and Gardens, Good Housekeeping, Ladies' Home Journal, Family Circle, Woman's Day,* and *McCall's* have all ranked among the Top 12 for years, with circulations ranging from 4 to 7.6 million by the late 1990s. But these numbers are the exception rather than the norm. Of the twelve thousand or so consumer magazines published in the United States today, only about ninety have a circulation of more than 1 million. Most contemporary magazines and newsletters aim at smaller communities of readers who share values, interests, or social identity—from Asian Americans to disabled veterans and conservative students. Indeed, in the early 1990s, the Magazine Publishers of America trade organization listed more than forty special categories of consumer magazines, illustrating the fragmentation of the industry. These included magazines organized around sports and leisure activities, travel and geography, lifestyle and age, and race and ethnicity.

Leisure, Sports, and Music Magazines. The television age spawned not only *TV Guide* but a number of specialized leisure magazines. For example, *Soap Opera Digest* updates viewers on the latest plot twists and their favorite characters. By the mid-1990s, the four leading soap-opera magazines had a combined circulation of more than two million. In the age of specialization, magazine executives have developed multiple magazines for fans of soap operas, running, tennis, golf, hunting, quilting, antiquing, surfing, and video-game playing, to name only a few. Within categories, magazines specialize further, targeting older or younger runners, men or women golfers, duck hunters or bird-watchers, and midwestern or southern antique collectors.

The most popular sports and leisure magazine is *Sports Illustrated*, which took its name from a failed 1935 publication. Launched in 1954 by Henry Luce's Time Inc., *Sports Illustrated* was initially aimed at well-educated, middle-class men. It has become the most successful general sports magazine in history, covering everything from major-league sports and mountain climbing to fox hunts and snorkeling. Although frequently criticized for its popular but exploitative yearly swimsuit editions, *Sports Illustrated* over the years has done major investigative pieces on racketeering in boxing and on land conservation. Its circulation climbed from more than half a million in its first year to 2 million by 1980 and more than 3.2 million by 1998.

> "Every magazine has its own architecture. *National Geographic* is a Greek revival temple. *TV Guide* is a fruit stand. The *New Yorker* is a men's hat store. The *Atlantic* is a church (Congregational)."
>
> —Roger Rosenblatt, *New Republic*, 1989

Time Warner capitalized on the name recognition and profitability of *Sports Illustrated* in the 1990s by launching two more specialized versions of the magazine: *Sports Illustrated for Kids* and *Sports Illustrated for Women*. Written for children between the fifth and eighth grades and launched in 1989, *Sports Illustrated for Kids* is a successful monthly magazine that combines articles on sports, learning, and games. Spurred by the rise in women's sports participation at all levels—from recreational to professional—in the past two decades, *Sports Illustrated for Women* was launched to target an emerging, but not yet profitable, women's sports market. *Sports Illustrated for Women* released two issues in 1997, stopped publication in 1998 to conduct more market research, and then released four issues in 1999. Three other competitors appeared in 1997: Condé

Nast launched *Women's Sports and Fitness*, geared toward athletic women interested in staying in shape; women's sports advocate Amy Love launched *Real Sports*, which covers women's team sports; and Weider Publications released *Jump*, which targets the teenage-girl audience. In addition, *Outside* magazine released *Women Outside* in 1998, a magazine that targets women and rugged outdoor sports.

Another popular magazine type that fits loosely into the leisure category includes magazines devoted to music—everything from rap's the *Source* to country's *Country Weekly*. The all-time circulation champ in this category is *Rolling Stone*, started in 1967 as an irreverent, left-wing political and cultural magazine by twenty-one-year-old Jann Wenner. Once considered an alternative magazine, *Rolling Stone* by 1982 had paddled into the mainstream with a circulation approaching 800,000—half of its ninety-six-plus pages now devoted to high-gloss fashion and consumer ads. By the late 1990s, *Rolling Stone*, still famous for its personality profiles and occasionally featuring radical articles on economics or politics, had a circulation of more than 1.2 million. Many fans of the early *Rolling Stone*, however, disappointed with its move to increase circulation and reflect mainstream consumer values, turned to less high-gloss alternatives such as *Spin*.

Travel and Geography Magazines. In 1992 and 1993, capitalizing on the increasing longevity of the American population and retirees interested in travel, publishers introduced thirty new travel magazines. Periodicals such as *Discover, Smithsonian, AAA World, Travel & Leisure,* and *Condé Nast Traveler* have all ranked among the nation's top two hundred magazines. Some accompany subscriptions to museum organizations or travel clubs, like the American Automobile Association (AAA). Others are devoted to exploring distant cultures or planning trips to various locales.

The undisputed champion in this category is *National Geographic*. Boston lawyer Gardiner Green Hubbard and his famous son-in-law Alexander Graham Bell founded the magazine in 1888, along with the nonprofit National Geographic Society. From the outset, *National Geographic* relied for its content on a number of distinguished mapmakers, natural-

National Geographic is one of the few current magazines whose back issues are valued by used-book stores. Saved by faithful subscribers, the magazine is frequently passed along from generation to generation. A pioneer in color photography, the magazine was founded by the National Geographic Society in 1888.

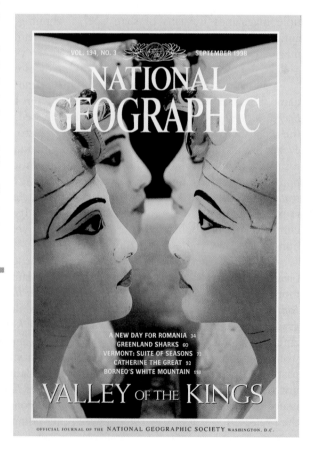

ists, explorers, geologists, and geographers. Bell, who became the society's director in 1889, referred to the magazine as "a vehicle for carrying the living, breathing human-interest truth about this great world of ours to the people."[8] Promoted as "humanized geography," *National Geographic* helped pioneer color photography in 1910. It was the first publication to publish both undersea and aerial color photographs. It remains one of the few magazines that subscribers save from year to year and also pass along from generation to generation. In addition, many of *National Geographic*'s nature and culture specials on television, which began in 1965, rank among the most popular programs in the history of public television. *National Geographic*'s popularity grew slowly and steadily throughout the twentieth century, reaching a million in circulation in 1935 and ten million in the 1970s. In the late 1990s, its circulation of paid subscriptions slipped to under nine million, prompting the staid National Geographic Society to diversify and lend its name to for-profit ventures such as CD-ROMs, television miniseries, and a line of road maps and atlases.

Magazines for the Ages. For years, magazines have targeted readers by economic class and lifestyle, usually distinguishing the mass appeal of *Life* and *Reader's Digest* from the more sophisticated appeal of the *New Yorker, Esquire,* or *Vogue.* In the age of specialization, however, magazines have further delineated readers along ever-narrowing age lines, appealing more and more to very young and to older readers, groups that have often been ignored by mainstream television.

The first children's magazines appeared in New England in the late 1700s. Ever since, magazines such as *Youth's Companion, Boy's Life* (the Boy Scouts' national publication since 1912), *Highlights,* and *Ranger Rick* have successfully targeted preschool and elementary-school children. *Boy's Life* led the top children's magazine category in the late 1990s, with a circulation of 1.3 million, followed by two magazines with TV connections—*Disney Adventures* and *Sesame Street Magazine,* both reaching about a million subscribers. The leading high-school education magazines included the *Scholastic* group (*Update, Scope, Voice,* and *Science World*), which totaled more than 2 million in circulation in the early 1990s. In the popular arena, humor magazines such as *Mad, Cracked,* and *National Lampoon* have had high readerships among male teens and young adults. Overall circulation for the leading female teen magazines showed substantial growth in the late 1990s; the top magazines for thirteen- to nineteen-year-olds included *Seventeen, YM,* and *Teen.* Their loyal fans demonstrated that many young people, in search of their own social and cultural identities, remain avid readers despite the competition from television and computer games.

In targeting audiences by age, the most dramatic success has come from magazines aimed at readers over fifty-five, America's fastest-growing age segment. These publications have tried to meet the cultural interests of older Americans, who historically have not been prominently featured in mainstream consumer culture. The American Association of Retired Persons (AARP) and its magazine, *Modern Maturity,* were founded in 1958 by retired California teacher Ethel Percy Andrus, who eleven years earlier had established the National Retired Teachers Association (NRTA). For years, both groups published newsletters—which they later merged into the *NRTA/AARP Bulletin*—keeping older citizens current on politics, health, and culture.

Subscriptions to six issues per year of *Modern Maturity* and the AARP newsletter have always come with a modest membership fee ($8 in 1999). By the early 1980s, *Modern Maturity*'s circulation approached seven million. However, with the AARP signing up thirty thousand new members each week by the late 1980s, both *Modern Maturity* and the joint newsletter overtook *TV Guide* and *Reader's Digest* as the top circulated magazines. By the mid-1990s, both had circulations of more than twenty mil-

"**Demographics** should be the province of marketers and advertisers, not magazine editors."
— Matt Goldberg, former editor of the defunct magazine *Swing,* 1998

lion. Not available at newsstands, *Modern Maturity* also did not carry advertising during its first ten years. The conventional wisdom in many ad agencies, dominated by staffers under age fifty, suggested that people over fifty were loyal to certain brand names and were difficult to influence through ads. Research demonstrated, however, that many in this group are more affluent than eighteen- to forty-nine-year-olds and have consumer interests increasingly in line with the thirty-nine to forty-nine age bracket. Today, *Modern Maturity* still carries few consumer ads, relying mostly on inexpensive subscriptions, the growth of the plus-fifty-five age group, and its readers' continuing interest in the printed word.

elite magazines and cultural minorities

In his important 1964 study, *Magazines in the Twentieth Century*, historian Theodore Peterson devoted a chapter to cultural minorities. In the mid-1960s, though, the term *cultural minorities* referred to elite readers who were served mainly by non-mass-market political and literary magazines such as *Atlantic Monthly, Kenyon Review*, the *Nation, National Review*, the *New Republic, Partisan Review*, and *Poetry*. In general, these political and literary magazines appealed to formally educated readers who shared political ideas, aesthetic concerns, or social values. To their credit, the editors and publishers of these magazines have often struggled financially to maintain the integrity of their magazines in an industry dominated by advertising and mass-market publications.

The *New Yorker*. The most widely circulated "elite" magazine in this century has been the *New Yorker*. Launched in 1925 by Harold Ross, the *New Yorker* became the first city magazine aimed at a national upscale audience. In some ways, the *New Yorker* was the magazine equivalent of the *New York Times*, cultivating an affluent and educated audience and excluding general readers. Snubbing the Midwest, Ross once claimed, "The *New Yorker* will be the magazine which is not edited for the old lady in Dubuque. It will not be concerned in what she is thinking about."[9] Over the years, the *New Yorker* has featured many of this century's most prominent biographers, writers,

Famous for its inventive cartoons, well-crafted prose, and whimsical covers, the *New Yorker* first appeared in 1925. Originally planned as a local publication, the *New Yorker* developed into one of the nation's most influential magazines over the years, shaping public opinion on everything from national politics to popular culture.

reporters, and humorists, including A. J. Liebling, Dorothy Parker, Lillian Ross, John Updike, E. B. White, and Garrison Keillor, as well as James Thurber's cartoons and Ogden Nash's poetry. It introduced some of the finest literary journalism of the twentieth century, devoting an entire issue to John Hersey's *Hiroshima* and serializing Truman Capote's *In Cold Blood*.

By the mid-1960s, the *New Yorker*'s circulation hovered around 500,000. Just as the *New York Times* became known as the nation's best newspaper, the *New Yorker* made promotional claims as the country's best magazine. By the 1960s, the magazine even had a hundred subscribers in Dubuque, Iowa, including a number of "old ladies." In 1985, the *New Yorker* was acquired for $168 million by Advance Publications, the Newhouse newspaper-publishing conglomerate. By the late 1990s, the magazine's circulation had reached 800,000, but the *New Yorker* had yet to experience a profitable year since Advance purchased it.

Redefining Cultural Minorities. By the 1980s and 1990s, the term *cultural minority* had taken on different connotations. It referred to distinctions regarding gender, age, race, ethnicity, and sexual orientation. Since the late 1960s, with attention drawn to many discriminatory practices, a number of magazines have developed to address concerns that were often ignored by mainstream magazines. Historically, one key magazine has been the *Advocate*, which began in 1967 as a twelve-page newsletter addressing issues about homosexuality. By the mid-1980s, the magazine had a circulation of nearly 100,000, and by the early 1990s more than fifteen new magazines aimed at gay men or lesbians had been launched. The *Advocate* has published some of the best journalism on AIDS, antigay violence, and policy issues affecting homosexual communities. In some instances, its reporting has led to increased coverage of important issues by the mainstream press.

In general, the term *cultural minority* has been more closely associated with racial and ethnic groups that have often been misrepresented or underrepresented in America's popular media. To counter white mainstream conceptions, African American magazines, for example, date to antislavery publications such as the *Emancipator, Liberator,* and *Reformer* during the pre–Civil War era. In the modern age, the major magazine publisher for African Americans has been John H. Johnson, a former Chicago insurance salesman who started *Negro Digest* in 1942 on $500 borrowed against his mother's furniture. By 1945, with a circulation of more than 100,000, the *Digest*'s profits allowed Johnson and a small group of editors to start *Ebony*, a picture-text magazine modeled on *Life* but serving chiefly black readers. The Johnson Publishing Company has since successfully introduced *Jet*, a pocket-size supermarket magazine that originally contained shorter pieces left over from *Ebony*. By the late 1990s, *Jet*'s circulation was near one million.

Johnson's publications were one of the first places where people could see black images on a weekly basis in American popular culture. Originally criticized for favoring light-skinned over dark-skinned black faces, *Ebony* has developed over the years into the leading popular magazine forum for black politics and social life in the United States. In fact, Johnson's publications were among the first forums to help clarify what it meant to be black and middle-class in America after World War II. By the late 1970s, *Ebony*'s circulation had reached 1.3 million; by the late 1990s, it had more than 1.8 million paid subscribers and an estimated pass-along readership of 11 million. In 1970, the first successful magazine aimed at black middle-class women, *Essence*, was started by Edward Lewis. It enjoyed a circulation of 1 million by 1998.

With increases in Hispanic populations and immigration, magazines appealing to Spanish-speaking readers have developed rapidly since the 1980s. In 1983, the De Armas Spanish Magazine Network began distributing Spanish-language versions of

Launched in 1996, *Latina* is the first bilingual lifestyle magazine to address the interests of Hispanic women in the United States. Stories written in both English and Spanish cover everything from cooking and relationships to career issues and personal finance.

mainstream American magazines, including *Cosmopolitan en Español*, *Harper's Bazaar en Español*, and *Ring*, the prominent boxing magazine. In 1989, Casiano Communications launched *Imagen*, a glossy upscale publication for middle- and upper-middle-class Hispanic readers. By the early 1990s, however, the best-selling Spanish-language magazine was *Selecciones del Reader's Digest*, with more than 150,000 paid subscriptions in the United States alone. In the late 1990s, a new wave of magazines was released, some in Spanish, some in English, and some in a combination of both languages to reflect the bilingual lives of many Americans of Hispanic descent. The involvement of major media corporations signaled that the Hispanic magazine audience had arrived for major advertisers: The bilingual *Latina* magazine was started with the help of Essence Communications in 1996, media giant Time Warner launched *People en Español* nationally in 1997, and Condé Nast and Ideas Publishing Group introduced *Glamour en Español* in 1998. Other recent start-ups included *Latina Bride*, *MiGente*, *Moderna*, *Latina Style*, and *Estylo*. The new magazines are targeted at the most upwardly mobile segments of the growing American Latino population, which reached about thirty million people—nearly 11 percent of the U.S. population—at the end of the 1990s.

supermarket tabloids

After TV star Carol Burnett won a $1.6 million libel judgment (reduced to $800,000 on appeal) against the *National Enquirer* in the 1980s, supermarket tabloids behaved for a time. Although tabloids have usually been protected by the First Amendment, celebrities have sued them frequently over the years for fallacious stories. Partly due to tabloids' bad reputation, neither the newspaper nor the magazine industry likes to claim them as part of its domain. But the Audit Bureau of Circulations, which checks newspaper and magazine circulation figures to determine advertising rates, counts weekly tabloids as magazines. Although tabloids trace their history to newspapers' use of graphics and pictorial layouts in the 1860s and 1870s, the modern U.S. tabloid dates from the founding of the *National Enquirer* by William Randolph Hearst in 1926. The *Enquirer* struggled until it was purchased in 1952 by Generoso Pope, who had worked in the cement business and for his father's New York–based Italian-language newspaper, *Il Progresso*. Also a former intelligence officer for the CIA's psychological warfare unit, Pope intended to use the paper to "fight for the rights of man" and "human decency and dignity."[10] In the interest of profit, though, he settled on the "gore formula" to transform the paper's anemic weekly circulation of seven thousand: "I noticed how auto accidents drew crowds and I decided that if it was blood that interested people, I'd give it to them."[11]

By the mid-1960s, Pope had built the *Enquirer*'s circulation to 1 million through the use of bizarre human-interest stories, gruesome murder tales, violent accident accounts, unexplained phenomena stories, and malicious celebrity gossip. Later, the *Enquirer* incorporated some of yellow journalism's crusading traditions, reporting government cover-ups and stories of bureaucratic waste. By 1974, the magazine's weekly circulation topped 4 million, where it remained for several years. In 1977, its edition covering the death of Elvis Presley included a controversial picture of Presley in his open coffin and sold more than 6.6 million copies, still a tabloid record.

In 1974, Rupert Murdoch's News Corp. launched the *Star*, built on the "circus-poster layout, garish headlines, and steamy prose" traditions of Great Britain's sleazy tabloid press. Among the *Star*'s announced objectives: to "not be politically committed, not be a killjoy, not be bullied, not be boring."[12] The *Star* and a third major tabloid player, the *Globe* (founded in 1954), cut into the *Enquirer*'s circulation and set the tone for current trends in tabloid content, including stories on medical cures, astrological predictions, celebrity gossip, and the occult.

Between 1990 and 1996, the three largest tabloids lost about 30 percent of their circulation. The *National Enquirer* fell from 4 to 2.7 million, the *Star* from 3.6 to 2.5 million, and the *Globe* from 1.3 million to less than 1 million. Not only did imitators like the *National Examiner*, the *Sun*, and the *Weekly World News* offer competition but *People, US*, new entertainment magazines, newsmagazines, and talk shows also began claiming part of the tabloid audience.[13] At the same time, occasional investigative and political stories started appearing in tabloids and influencing coverage by major newspapers and newsmagazines. Tabloid editors, however, have tried to avoid most political stories: Circulation apparently declines when political intrigue graces their front pages.[14] Ironically, one of the biggest "tabloid" stories of the late 1990s had to do with politics. The Clinton–Monica Lewinsky affair, which was covered by virtually all news media, left tabloids with the dilemma of finding other stories that would be more eye-catching. Although their popularity peaked in the 1980s, tabloids continue to specialize in reaching audiences not served by mainstream media.

> "It's wonderful. I love talking to witches and Satanists and vampire hunters, and people who have been kidnapped by UFOs—it sure beats covering zoning board meetings."
>
> —Cliff Linedecker,
> former associate editor,
> *National Examiner*

webzines and media convergence

The Internet's flexibility and vast, inexpensive distribution capabilities make it an attractive area of investment for companies and individuals looking to create a successful magazine. Most print magazines have a Web site that offers a few stories online while encouraging readers to subscribe or buy the magazine at the newsstand. Some publishers offer vast research capabilities, such as Time Warner's Pathfinder site, which allows users to search for articles in *Time, People, Money, Fortune,* and *Entertainment Weekly.*

The World Wide Web also offers a solution to some of the problems associated with magazines. With production costs much lower than glossy print publications, and with the potential for a graphic-rich (albeit computer-monitor-based) appearance and widespread distribution, the Web provides an alternate route to maintaining our culture's connection to words, analysis, and ideas. Webzines such as *Feed, Images, Salon,* and *Slate* have made the Web a legitimate site for breaking news and discussing culture and politics. Although some Webzines have big corporate backers, such as

Microsoft's *Slate*, most original Webzines have more modest beginnings and arise out of an interest in creating a cultural or political forum. For example, *Salon* magazine was founded in 1995 by five former reporters of the *San Francisco Examiner* who wanted to break from the traditions of newspaper publishing and build "a different kind of news-room" to create well-developed stories and commentary. With the help of positive word-of-mouth comments, *Salon* became the leading Webzine by 1998, claiming more than 600,000 readers and planning for growth with a new position on one of America Online's primary channels. So far, the World Wide Web isn't producing a lucrative new magazine industry segment (as *Slate* discovered, Web readers aren't likely to pay for subscriptions), but it is providing an accessible outlet for good magazine writing.

In the meantime, while many magazines were losing advertising revenues and subscribers to specialized cable TV channels and Internet sites that target similar audiences, many media companies viewed the magazine industry as an area of growth. In 1998, ESPN cable sports network launched *ESPN the Magazine*, and Yahoo!, one of the most popular Internet portals, partnered with hi-tech publisher Ziff-Davis to produce *Yahoo! Internet Life*. And, in true synergy fashion, Miramax Films and Hearst Magazines joined forces in 1999 to create Talk Media, a company responsible for publishing *Talk* (a celebrity-filled general-interest magazine to compete with *Vanity Fair*) as well as producing television programs and publishing books.

the organization and economics of magazines

Given the great diversity in magazine content and ownership, it is hard to offer a common profile of a successful magazine. Unlike a broadcast station or a daily newspaper, a small newsletter or magazine can begin cheaply via computer-driven **desktop publishing** technology, which allows one aspiring publisher-editor to write, design, lay out, and even print a modest publication. Such magazines—sometimes called **zines**—are also mushrooming on the World Wide Web and other sectors of the Internet. (See "Tracking Technology: The Personal Zine Explosion" on page 297.)

departments and duties

Most major magazines are now available through online computer services, some of which allow readers to interact electronically with writers and editors at various magazines. Other technological advances enable magazines to offer subscribers digital versions of both text and photos. Today, many magazines are also available on the information highway through telephone lines, satellite delivery, or CD-ROM. Not surprisingly, great debates persist over whether online and digital magazines, such as *Salon* or *Slate*, will eventually replace traditional printed versions. Throughout the 1990s, however, electronic alternatives had not slowed the growth of printed magazines. Despite the rise of zines and desktop publishing, most large commercial firms still operate several departments, which employ hundreds of people.

Production and Technology. The magazine unit most concerned with merging old and new ideas is the production and technology department, which maintains the computer and printing hardware necessary for mass-market production. Unlike daily newspapers, though, magazines do not face daily production deadlines and are therefore able to farm out the final printing to separate companies. Since magazines are usually printed weekly, monthly, or bimonthly, it is not economically practical for

One of the most dramatic developments in media history may be those personal, self-published magazines called *zines* (pronounced "zeens"). Riding the wave of personal computer programs for designing newsletters and magazines, zines are a grassroots publishing phenomenon. They usually appeal to younger readers and in recent years have found a home on the Internet.

Zines first emerged in the 1930s as part of cult groups who read and then wrote about science fiction. They produced single-copy zines on typewriters and passed them around to friends. In the late 1960s, zines emerged as part of the student protests against the Vietnam War. These zines were still produced on typewriters, but they could be inexpensively copied on Xerox machines, stapled together, and sold on street corners or given away to friends. In the 1970s, newsletter-style zines paid tribute to the alternative lifestyles of punk-rock culture. But zines really took off with the explosion of desktop publishing in the 1980s and Internet sites in the 1990s.

In print versions alone, more than fifty thousand zines celebrate rock performers, promote various religious views, confront the problems of substance abuse, expound on politics, or document an individual's emotional issues. Some are rambling autobiographies, some offer poetry or science fiction, and others sound like letters to close friends.

A few national chains—like Borders and Tower Records—now carry a variety of zines, especially those devoted to culture and music; for example, *Stay Free!* <http://metalab.unc.edu/stayfree> explores the ways in which advertising and celebrity shape culture. Nevertheless, zines rarely make money, even though more and more have begun to carry ads. A zine entitled *Factsheet Five* <www.factsheet5.com> emerged in the mid-

1980s for the purpose of reviewing other zines; it offers capsule summaries of zines such as *Thrift Score, MAXIMUMROCKNROLL, Dishwasher,* and *Pathetic Life.*

Desktop publishing can produce a decent-looking, four-page zine for a few hundred dollars. Zine sites on the World Wide Web cost only the fee of a monthly provider. Zines usually find their audiences by word of mouth, and most sell through direct mail. Some are distributed free over the Internet.

Personal zines operate at the extreme edge of magazine specialization; they are often distributed to just a few people besides the publisher and his or her family and friends. Many are intentionally designed to counter mainstream, mass-market publications. These zines sometimes focus on topics so narrow or obscure that only a handful of readers may be interested in them, yet they can also offer a sense of community as readers connect with one another through shared interests and letters pages.

Zines are sometimes a manifestation of loneliness and the desire to connect as well as venues for spreading information about subject matter ignored by mainstream media. Zine publishers and readers may be looking for solutions to larger problems, or they may just be looking for a sense of community outside of the conventional.

most magazine publishers to maintain expensive print facilities. As with *USA Today*, many national magazines are now able to digitally transport magazine copy via satellite to various regional printing sites for the insertion of local ads and for faster distribution.

To attract advertisers and audiences over the years, magazines have deployed other technological innovations: from *National Geographic's* pioneering 3-D color holograph cover to digitized full-color versions of magazines on the World Wide Web. Through reader questionnaires and electronic databases, magazines have further refined their demographic editions. Today they have developed special inserts, called *selective edits*, for specific customers. For example, in 1993 *Child* magazine began using data from the birth dates of its subscribers' children; it inserted customized monthly editorial and advertising sections on children at a specific age or developmental stage. In 1994, *Sports Illustrated* identified 400,000 serious golfers among its readers and began a "Golf Plus" insert for those copies sent to golfing enthusiasts.[15]

Editorial Content. The lifeblood of a magazine is the editorial department, which produces its content, excluding advertisements. Like newspapers, most magazines have a chain of command that begins with the publisher and extends to the editor in chief, the managing editor, and a variety of subeditors. These subeditors oversee such editorial functions as photography, illustrations, reporting and writing, copyediting, and layout and design. Writing staffs for magazines generally include *contributing writers*, who are specialists in certain fields. These writers may have recurring columns or may cover specific topics, such as medicine, law, or politics. Magazines also hire professional, nonstaff *freelance writers*, who are assigned to cover particular stories or a region of the country. Many magazines, especially those with small budgets, also rely on well-written unsolicited manuscripts to fill their pages. Most commercial magazines, however, reject more than 95 percent of unsolicited pieces.

Advertising and Sales. The advertising and sales department of a magazine secures clients, arranges promotions, and places ads. Industrywide, this unit has pioneered innovations such as the scent strip in perfume ads, pop-up ads, and ads on computer microchips that emit sounds when a page is turned. Besides stuffing magazines with the ever-present subscription-renewal postcards, this department also conducts market research to study trends and changes in magazine-reading habits. For instance, audience research from the mid-1990s suggested that the average male reader of *GQ* was twenty-nine years old and lived in a household with an annual income of around $42,000. *Esquire's* typical reader, on the other hand, was a thirty-seven-year-old male whose household income averaged $40,000 a year.

Magazines generate about half their annual revenue from selling ads, with the remaining money coming from single-copy and subscription sales (see Figure 9.1). (Another source of magazine revenue—but one that the magazine industry rarely

Figure 9.1
Changing Sources of Magazine Revenue
Source: Magazine Publishers of America.

wishes to discuss with the general public—is the sale of subscription lists to advertisers and marketers.) Like radio and TV stations, consumer magazines offer advertisers *rate cards*, which list what a magazine charges for an ad. For example, a top-rated consumer magazine might charge $64,000 for a full-page color ad and $20,000 for a one-third page, black-and-white ad. However, in today's competitive world, most rate cards are not very meaningful: Almost all magazines offer 25 to 50 percent rate discounts to advertisers.[16]

Although fashion and general-interest magazines carry a higher percentage of ads than do political-literary magazines, the average magazine contains about 45 percent of ad copy and 55 percent of editorial material. This figure has remained fairly constant over the past twenty-five years. Some dispute these categories, though, since many readers of fashion magazines consider the ads the main editorial content.

A few contemporary magazines, such as *Mad*, have decided not to carry ads and rely solely on subscriptions and newsstand sales. To protect the integrity of its various tests and product comparisons, for instance, *Consumer Reports* carries no advertising. To strengthen its editorial independence, *Ms.* magazine abandoned ads in 1990 after years of pressure from the food, cosmetic, and fashion industries to feature recipes and more *complementary copy:* positive, upbeat articles that support the ads carried in various consumer magazines and often blur the lines between editorial copy and advertising. Some advertisers and companies have canceled ads when a magazine featured an unflattering or critical article about a company or industry.[17] In some instances, this practice has put enormous pressure on editors not to offend advertisers. The cozy relationships between some advertisers and magazines have led to a dramatic decline in investigative reporting, once central to popular magazines during the muckraking era (see "Examining Ethics: Sex, Lies, and Advertising" on page 300).

> "Anyone who's in the magazine business thinks about advertisers when they write about something. And anyone who says they don't is a liar."
>
> —John F. Kennedy Jr., former editor in chief of *George*, 1998

Circulation and Distribution. The circulation and distribution department of a magazine monitors single-copy and subscription sales. Subscriptions, which dominated the industry's infancy, have made a strong comeback. For example, toward the end of the general-interest era in 1950, single-copy sales at supermarkets and newsstands accounted for about 43 percent of magazine sales, while subscriptions constituted 57 percent. By the 1990s, single-copy sales were just under 20 percent, while subscriptions had risen to more than 80 percent. One tactic used by circulation departments is to encourage consumers to renew well in advance of their actual renewal dates. Magazines can thus invest and earn interest on early renewal money as a hedge against consumers who drop their subscriptions each year.

Magazines circulate in two basic ways: paid or controlled. *Paid circulation* simply means that consumers either pay for a regular subscription to the magazine or they pay for individual copies at a newsstand or supermarket. Most consumer magazines depend on paid circulation as well as advertising. *Controlled circulation* provides readers with the magazine at no charge. This type of circulation generally targets captive audiences such as airline passengers or association members. Many business or technical magazines and newsletters, which depend on advertising or corporate sponsorship, are distributed free to members or loyal customers. Major magazine publishing company Hachette Filipacchi developed new titles in the 1990s by producing custom-controlled circulation magazines for specific organizations. For example, *Trump Style* was developed for guests of Donald Trump's casinos and properties, while other custom magazines were created for customers of Century 21, Ferrari, and Philip Morris.[18]

Sex, Lies, and Advertising

by Gloria Steinem

What could women's magazines be like if they were as free as books? as realistic as newspapers? as creative as films? as diverse as women's lives? We don't know.

But we'll find out only if we take women's magazines seriously. If readers were to act in a concerted way to change traditional practices of all women's magazines and the marketing of all women's products, we could do it. After all, they are operating on our consumer dollars; money that we now control. You and I could:

• write to editors and publishers (with copies to advertisers) that we're willing to pay more for magazines with editorial independence, but will not continue to pay for those that are just editorial extensions of ads;

• write to advertisers (with copies to editors and publishers) that we want fiction, political reporting, consumer reporting—whatever is, or is not, supported by their ads;

• put as much energy into breaking advertising's control over content as into changing the images in ads, or protesting ads for harmful products like cigarettes;

• support only those women's magazines and products that take us seriously as readers and consumers.

Those of us in the magazine world can also use the carrot-and-stick technique. For instance: pointing out that, if magazines were a regulated medium like television, the demands of advertisers would be against FCC rules. Payola and extortion could be punished. As it is, there are probably illegalities. A magazine's postal rates are determined by the ratio of ad to edit[orial] pages, and the former costs more than the latter. So much for the stick.

"put as much energy into breaking advertising's control over content as into changing the images in ads"

The carrot means appealing to enlightened self-interest. For instance: there are many studies showing that the greatest factor in determining an ad's effectiveness is the credibility of its surroundings. The "higher the rating of editorial believability," concluded a 1987 survey by the *Journal of Advertising Research*, "the higher the rating of the advertising." Thus, an impenetrable wall between edit and ads would also be in the best interest of advertisers.

Unfortunately, few agencies or clients hear such arguments. Editors often maintain the false purity of refusing to talk to them at all. Instead, they see ad sales people who know little about editorial, are trained in business as usual, and are usually paid by commission. Editors might also band together to take on controversy. That happened once when all the major women's magazines did articles in the same month on the Equal Rights Amendment. It could happen again. . . .

Even as I write this, I get a call from a writer for *Elle*, who is doing a whole article on where women part their hair. Why, she wants to know, do I part mine in the middle?

It's all so familiar. A writer trying to make something of a nothing assignment; an editor laboring to think of new ways to attract ads; readers assuming that other women must want this ridiculous stuff; more women suffering for lack of information, insight, creativity, and laughter that could be on these same pages.

I ask you: Can't we do better than this?

Sample pages are from the first issue of *Ms.* magazine, Spring 1972.
Source: Gloria Steinem, "Sex, Lies, and Advertising," *Ms.* (July–August 1990), 18–28.

Studies by the Magazine Publishers of America suggest that more than 80 percent of all American households either subscribe to a magazine or purchase one on a regular basis. The average household typically purchases at least six different titles during a given year. Although the magazine industry was generally regarded as economically healthy throughout the 1980s, some signs worry editors and publishers. For instance, in 1990, for the first time since the Depression, the number of consumer-magazine titles declined. In addition, a decline in operating pretax profit margins for magazines, which began in the early 1990s, plagued the industry. In part, the decline is attributed to the proliferation of specialized cable television channels and new personal-computer and Internet services that compete for the same advertisers. By 1998, though, the Magazine Publishers of America claimed that the magazine industry was healthy again, and riding a revenue boom that was expected to last into the next decade.

major magazine chains

In terms of ownership, the commercial magazine industry most closely resembles the cable television business, which actually patterned its specialized channels on the consumer-magazine market. About twelve thousand commercial magazine titles appear each year—many of them independently owned—just as roughly eleven thousand cable systems now operate in the United States. Also, like the cable industry, large companies or chains increasingly dominate the magazine business. This raises yet unanswered questions about the impact of a handful of powerful magazine owners on the ideas that circulate in the commercial marketplace.

Time Warner, the nation's second-largest cable operator, also runs a magazine subsidiary, Time Inc., a major player among magazine-chain operators with more than twenty titles. (See Table 9.3.) Other important commercial players include Mortimer Zuckerman, who owns the *Atlantic Monthly* and *U.S. News & World Report*, and the Meredith Publishing Company, which specializes in women's magazines. The Hearst Corporation, the leading magazine chain early in the twentieth century, still remains a formidable publisher. New York City–based PRIMEDIA (formerly K-III Communications, and owned by investment firm Kohlberg Kravis Roberts) publishes 205 magazine titles, ranging from *Low Rider* to *Modern Bride*, and also controls the school-based Channel One news.

Long a force in upscale consumer magazines, Condé Nast is now a division of Advance Publications, which operates the Newhouse newspaper chain. The Condé Nast group controls several key magazines, including *Vanity Fair*, *GQ*, and *Vogue*. Advance Publications also owns *Parade* magazine, the popular Sunday newspaper supplement that goes to 36 million homes each week. Since Sunday supplements come with newspaper subscriptions, they are not counted among most official magazine tallies. Nevertheless, *Parade* and its closest rival, *USA Weekend* (21.1 million weekly circulation), reached more readers than the leading popular magazines in the late 1990s.

International companies like Paris-based Hachette Filipacchi are also major players in the U.S. magazine industry. Hachette owns more than thirty consumer magazines, with a worldwide readership of more than fifty million. Its holdings include *Mirabella*, *Woman's Day*, and *Car and Driver*. In 1995, Hachette spent $20 million to launch *George*, the political-cultural magazine cofounded by John F. Kennedy Jr. Australia's News Corp. (which owns part of *TV Guide*) and Britain's Reed Elsevier (owner of *Variety*, the American trade magazine for show business) also play influential roles in American magazine publishing.

In addition, a number of American magazines have carved out market niches worldwide. *Reader's Digest*, *Cosmopolitan*, *Newsweek*, and *Time*, for example, all produce

TABLE 9.3
Major Magazine Chains
(selected holdings as of 1999)

Advance Publications
(Staten Island, N.Y.)
Condé Nast Group
   Allure
   Architectural Digest
   Bon Appetit
   Bride's
   Condé Nast Traveler
   Details
   Glamour
   Gourmet
   GQ
   Mademoiselle
   Self
   Vanity Fair
   Vogue
New Yorker
Parade

Bertelsmann
(Gütersloh, Germany)
Child
Family Circle
Fitness
McCall's
Parents
YM

Hachette Filipacchi, a subsidiary of
Lagardère Groupe (Paris)
Car and Driver
Cycle World
Elle
Elle Decor
Family Life
George
Metropolitan Home
Mirabella
Premiere

Road & Track
Video
Woman's Day

Hearst Corporation
(New York, N.Y.)
Cosmopolitan
Country Living
Esquire
Good Housekeeping
Harper's Bazaar
House Beautiful
Marie Claire
Popular Mechanics
Redbook
Town & Country

Meredith Corporation
(Des Moines, Ia.)
Better Homes and Gardens
Country Home
Golf for Women
Ladies' Home Journal
Motherhood
Successful Farming
Wood

New York Times Company
(New York, N.Y.)
Cruising World
Golf Digest
Golf World
Sailing World
Snow Country
Tennis

PRIMEDIA (New York, N.Y.)
American Baby
Chicago
Dog World

Modern Bride
New York
Sail
Seventeen
Soap Opera Digest
Soap Opera Weekly
Truckin'

Reed Elsevier (London)
Lexis-Nexis (online magazine/
   newspaper search service)
Publishers Weekly
Variety
Yachting World

Time Inc. (New York, N.Y.)
Asiaweek
Entertainment Weekly
FORTUNE
InStyle
Life
Money
Parenting
People
Progressive Farmer
SI for Kids
Sports Illustrated
Sunset
This Old House
Time
Vibe

Ziff-Davis (New York, N.Y.)
Computer Life
Computer Shopper
PC/Computing
PC Magazine
PC Week
Yahoo! Internet Life

Sources: Hoover's Guide to Media Companies (Austin, Tex.: Hoover's Business Press, 1996), 46, 90, 110, 129, 149, 165, 279; *Advertising Age*, Ad Age Dataplace, <adage.com/dataplace>, 1999.

international editions in several languages. In general, though, most American magazines are local, regional, or specialized and therefore less exportable than this country's movies and television. Of twelve thousand titles, only about two hundred magazines from the United States circulate routinely in the world market. Such magazines, however, like exported American TV shows and films, still play a key role in determining the look of global culture.

alternative voices

With fewer than 80 of 12,000 American magazines reaching circulations that top one million, the great bulk of alternative publications struggle to satisfy small but loyal groups of readers. Of these more modest periodicals, alternative magazines number more than 2,000 with many failing and others starting up from month to month.

Alternative magazines have historically defined themselves in terms of politics—published either by the Left (e.g., the *Progressive, In These Times*, the *Nation*) or the Right (e.g., *National Review, American Spectator, Insight*). However, what constitutes an alternative magazine has broadened far beyond politics to include just about any publication considered "outside the mainstream," ranging from politics to punkzines—the magazine answer to punk rock. The *Utne Reader*, widely regarded today as "the *Reader's Digest* of alternative magazines," has defined *alternative* as any sort of "thinking that doesn't reinvent the status quo, that broadens issues you might see on TV or in the daily paper."

Occasionally, alternative magazines have become marginally mainstream. For example, during the more conservative Reagan era in the 1980s, William F. Buckley's *National Review* saw its circulation swell to more than 100,000—enormous by alternative standards. In the late 1980s, the *Review* even ran slick TV ads featuring actors like Charlton Heston, Tom Selleck, and Ronald Reagan. On the Left, *Mother Jones* (named after labor organizer Mary Harris Jones), which continues to champion the muckraking tradition of investigative journalism, had reached a circulation of more than 200,000.

Most alternative magazines, however, are content to swim outside the mainstream. These are the small magazines that typically include diverse political, cultural, religious, international, environmental, and humorous alternative publications such as *Against the Current, Christianity and Crisis, Jewish Currents, Asia Book Club Review, Southern Africa Report, Whole Earth Review, Yellow Silk: Journal of Erotic Arts, Hysteria: Women, Humor and Social Change*, and the *Journal of Polymorphous Perversity* ("a social scientist's answer to *Mad* magazine").

magazines in a democratic society

Like other mass media whose product lines have proliferated, magazines are a major part of the cluttered media landscape. To keep pace, the magazine industry has become fast-paced and high-risk. Of the eight to nine hundred new magazines that start up each year, fewer than two hundred will survive longer than a year.

As an industry, magazine publishing—like advertising and public relations—has played a central role in transforming the United States from a producer to a consumer society. Since the 1950s, though, magazines have not been the powerful national voice they once were, uniting separate communities around important issues such as abolition and suffrage. Today, with so many specialized magazines appealing to distinct groups of consumers, magazines play a much-diminished role in creating a sense of national identity.

On the positive side, magazine ownership is more diversified than ownership in other mass media. More magazine voices circulate in the marketplace than do broadcast or cable television channels. Moreover, many new magazines still play an important role in uniting geographically dispersed groups of readers, often giving cultural minorities or newly arrived immigrants a sense of membership in a broader community.

A. *Magazine* is an example of the increasing diversity of American popular culture. Published since 1990, this bimonthly reviews Asian influences on mass media and covers prestigious Asian Americans in business, politics, law, entertainment, and sports. A. *Magazine* is now branching out by producing CDs and video documentaries, publishing books, and sponsoring rock concerts.

Contemporary commercial magazines provide essential information about politics, society, and culture, thus helping us think about ourselves as participants in a democracy. Unfortunately, however, they have often identified their readers as consumers first and as citizens only secondarily. With magazines' growing dependence on advertising, controversial content sometimes has difficulty finding its way into print. More and more, magazines define their readers merely as viewers of displayed products and purchasers of material goods.

At the same time, magazines arguably have had more freedom than other media to encourage and participate in democratic debates. In addition, because magazines are distributed weekly, monthly, or bimonthly, they are less restricted by the deadline pressures of daily newspapers or evening broadcasts. Released from this burden, good magazines can usually offer more analysis of and insight into society than other media outlets. In the midst of today's swirl of images, magazines and their advertisements certainly contribute to the commotion. But good magazines also maintain our connection to words, sustaining their vital role in an increasingly electronic and digital culture.

REVIEW QUESTIONS

The Early History of Magazines

1. Why did magazines develop later than newspapers in the American colonies?

2. Why did most of the earliest magazines have so much trouble staying financially solvent?

3. How did magazines become national in scope?

The Development of Modern American Magazines

4. What role did magazines play in social reform at the turn of the century?

5. When and why did general-interest magazines become so popular?

6. Why did some of the major general-interest magazines fail?

The Domination of Specialization

7. What triggered the move toward magazine specialization?

8. What are the differences between regional and demographic editions?

9. What are the most useful ways to categorize the magazine industry? Why?

The Organization and Economics of Magazines

10. What are the four main departments at a typical consumer magazine?

11. Which are the major magazine chains, and what is their impact on the mass-media industry in general?

12. In what ways do magazines serve a democratic society?

QUESTIONING THE MEDIA

1. What are your earliest recollections of magazines? Which magazines do you read regularly today? Why?

2. What role did magazines play in America's political and social shift from being colonies of Great Britain to becoming an independent nation?

3. Why is the muckraking spirit—so important in popular magazines at the turn of the century—generally missing from magazines today?

4. Imagine that you are the marketing director of your favorite magazine. What would you do to increase circulation?

5. Think of stories, ideas, and images (illustrations and photos) that do not appear in mainstream magazines. Why do you think this is so? (Use the Internet, NEXIS, or the library to compare your list with Project Censor, an annual list of the year's most underreported stories.)

6. Discuss whether your favorite magazines define you primarily as a consumer or as a citizen. Do you think magazines have a responsibility to educate their readers as both? What can they do to promote citizenship?

7. Do you think cable television, the World Wide Web, and other specialized computer technology will eventually displace magazines? Why or why not?

SEARCHING THE INTERNET

http://adage.com/dataplace/index.html
The *Advertising Age*-Ad Age Dataplace provides data on the advertising industry: information on the top-selling magazines, circulation rankings, the top U.S. advertisers, the top media companies, the top global advertising markets, and the top-selling brand products.

http://www.feedmag.com
A thought-generating Webzine, *Feed* describes itself as "a guide to all the news feeds, data feeds, and live feeds, a way of sorting signal from noise, wisdom from raw information."

http://www.janemag.com
The online version of *Jane* magazine includes many of the fashion, beauty, gossip, and "real life" segments of the print publication, as well as archives of former issues.

http://www.nationalgeographic.com
An extensive site that includes articles, discussion forums, a children's page, map resources, and links to other National Geographic Society publications and activities.

http://www.salonmagazine.com
Founded in 1995, *Salon* is an award-winning, daily original-content Internet magazine that covers books, politics, arts, and ideas.

http://www.utne.com
An online version of the *Utne Reader*, with in-depth reports in the following departments: Culture, Society, Spirit, Body, Media, and New Planet. The site also includes the popular Café Utne Web discussion forum.

In Brief

Using a few sample magazines in class, consider the following issues with magazine advertisements:

- Are ads placed in proximity to editorial content of a related topic (e.g., suntan lotion or sunglasses ads next to an article about beach vacations)?

- How aesthetically similar are the ads and editorial content (e.g., the style of a magazine's photo shoot and its fashion ads)?

- Are there ads that seem to be at odds with the editorial content (e.g., cigarette ads in a youth-oriented magazine)?

- Do ad pages outnumber editorial-content pages?

- Do ad pages make it hard to find the magazine's table of contents?

Discuss the following questions: Do advertisements add a positive experience to magazine reading? Do advertisements seem to influence magazine content? Can a magazine's credibility be damaged by too much adherence to advertiser values? Are there some magazines that are purchased largely for the advertisements?

In Depth

The purpose of this project is to offer a particular type of critical approach to magazines. Work with a partner or in small groups. (This project could also be converted into a formal argument paper.)

1. Take any recent issue of *Time* and *Newsweek*. (Other magazines may be substituted, or contemporary issues may be compared with issues from earlier decades.) Review all photos in the two magazines, counting the males and females represented. For each magazine, keep a separate count of the number of men and women depicted in the ads and the number shown in the news photos that accompany the stories.

   (*Option:* You might also break down your count by race and age. When these categories are difficult to determine, create a category called unknown.)

2. Devise a rough chart to organize your findings. Write a one- or two-paragraph critical interpretation of your findings based on the following questions:

   - What patterns emerge? Are men treated differently from women? If so, in what ways? (Document your evidence.)

   - Do the magazines differ in their treatment of men and women? Explain.

   - Do the content, photos, and ads in these magazines make you think of yourself as a consumer or as a citizen? Who do the magazines think their readers are? Based on your limited analysis, sketch a profile of the typical reader of each magazine.

     (*Option:* Now call the research department at various magazines and see if they will give you a profile sketch of their typical reader. Compare your profile with theirs.)

   - Explain the limits of simply counting gender depictions in ad and news photos. What issues cannot be addressed by such a method? How might we go about doing a fuller study of issues raised in this project?

CHAPTER 10

308

JANE HAMILTON
AUTHOR OF A MAP OF THE WORLD

OPRAH'S
Book
Club

THE BOOK OF
RUTH

• • •

"An American beauty this book... The narrator of Jane Hamilton's
sensational first novel is a holy lusty innocent."
—Vogue

Publishers call it "the Oprah effect." It happens when a certain talk-show host selects a book for discussion, asks viewers to read it, and hundreds of thousands do.

The talk-show host, of course, is Oprah Winfrey, and the event sending happy shock waves through the publishing industry is Oprah's Book Club. The idea behind the book club is a grassroots phenomenon of the past decade—the rise of reading groups. Across the United States and Canada, small groups of people join together to read selected books and then meet in places like living rooms, libraries, bookstores, churches, and community centers to debate and discuss them. Reading groups take an individualistic medium—the book—and use it as a launching pad for the shared experience of conversation and friendship.

"I want the biggest reading book club in the whole world," said Winfrey, a lifelong avid reader.[1] With thirty-three million television viewers a week in the United States, Winfrey had little difficulty realizing this goal. But the success of Oprah's Book Club has extended far beyond anyone's expectations. Each selection has become an immediate best-seller, generating tremendous excitement within the book industry.

Oprah's Book Club began in September 1996, when Oprah recommended that her viewers read *The Deep End of the Ocean* by Jacquelyn Mitchard. After viewers read the book, they were instructed to email or write Winfrey with their comments. From that group, four readers were invited to dinner and discussion with Winfrey and the author. Later, Winfrey invited Mitchard to the show for all her viewers to see.

Within weeks of the Oprah mention, the sales of Mitchard's book jumped from an impressive 100,000 copies to nearly a million. "We knew that being mentioned on the *Oprah Winfrey Show* would be good for sales. We had no idea that it would go through . . . the rafters," said Mitchard, a columnist for the *Milwaukee Journal-Sentinel*.[2] Bookstores were so overwhelmed with requests that Winfrey now secretly tells publishers in advance whether their titles will be selected. The chosen books—with a first printing of usually at least 750,000 copies—ship in plain packaging to bookstores, who are advised not to reveal Oprah's book selection until it's announced on her show. Online bookstores, such as Amazon.com, carry special Oprah lists, and users can be notified by email as soon as the monthly Oprah's Book Club selection is announced.

Since September 1996, more than twenty-five books have been featured on the now coveted Oprah's Book Club list, including Toni Morrison's *Song of Solomon* (which sold twice as many copies in a few months after making Oprah's list as it had in the previous nineteen years), Jane Hamilton's *The Book of Ruth*, and Wally Lamb's *She's Come Undone*.

A by-product of the Oprah effect is that, suddenly, talking about books on TV is cool. David Gergen now has a book-talk segment on PBS's *The News Hour with Jim Lehrer*. Cable's Black Entertainment Television features work by current African American authors each Sunday morning on *Buy the Book*. And in 1998 C-Span2 and its bookish founder and CEO, Brian Lamb, committed their entire weekend schedule to Book TV, a collection of programs that focus on discussions, interviews, book festivals, and readings.

Over the past two decades, the interdependence between print and visual forms of popular media has become commonplace. Apart from economics, however, a cultural gulf between the two genres remains. Public debate continues to pit the "superior" quality of print media—usually represented by serious books—against the "inferior" fluff of television. Even within print culture itself, a mini-version of the high-low cultural gulf is apparent. It pits high-quality literature against such popular forms as the newest legal thriller, a supermarket romance novel, or a superhero comic book.

As individuals and as a society, we continue to create cultural classifications that distinguish good from bad, organizing the world through simple black-and-white categories. We also make critical judgments about the

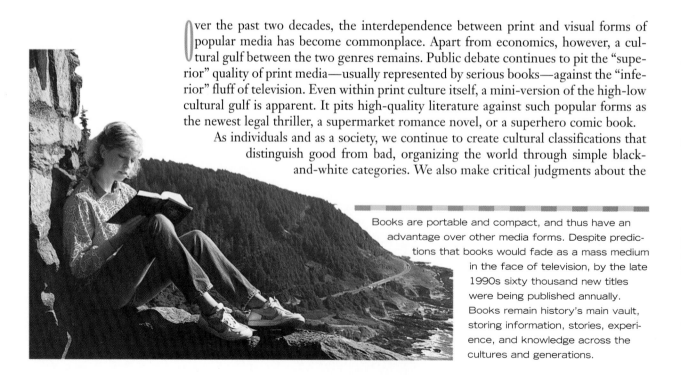

Books are portable and compact, and thus have an advantage over other media forms. Despite predictions that books would fade as a mass medium in the face of television, by the late 1990s sixty thousand new titles were being published annually. Books remain history's main vault, storing information, stories, experience, and knowledge across the cultures and generations.

kinds of culture that best entertain, inform, and serve a democracy. Because the lines between print and electronic culture have become blurred, we need to look at the developments that have made these media more interdependent. On the one hand, book publishers and video-stocked libraries use talk shows, TV advertising, and public-service announcements to promote reading. On the other hand, the networks follow made-for-TV movies, special miniseries, and even NBA basketball games with promotions for books and libraries.

In the 1950s and 1960s, cultural forecasters thought that the popularity of television might spell the demise of a healthy book industry. It did not happen. In 1950, more than eleven thousand new book titles were introduced, and by the late 1990s publishers were producing more than five times that number—more than sixty thousand titles per year (see Table 10.1). In the first half of the 1990s alone, consumer book sales increased 30 percent. Despite the trend toward the absorption of small publishing houses by big media corporations, more than twenty thousand different publishers—most of them small independents—issue at least one title a year. More than twelve thousand bookstores operate today—from gargantuan superstores to neighborhood used-book stores—an increase of 75 percent from the 1980s. Still, economic trends in the book industry are similar to those in other media industries: Several large publishing firms, distribution companies, and bookstore chains control the commercial end of the business and claim the bulk of the profits.

The bottom line is that the book industry has met the social and cultural challenges of television. Books have managed to maintain a distinct cultural identity, partly because of the book industry's willingness to capitalize on TV's reach. As one example, Joseph Campbell, who wrote about the similarity of mythologies across various cultures, published his influential *Hero with a Thousand Faces* back in 1949. By the mid-1980s, the book was still selling about one thousand copies a year. But after Bill Moyers interviewed Campbell in a six-part 1988 series on PBS, the forty-year-old book sold thirty-five thousand copies a month for a time.

> "All good books are alike in that they are truer than if they had really happened and after you are finished reading one you will feel that all that happened . . . belongs to you: the good and the bad, the ecstasy, the remorse and sorrow, the people and the places and how the weather was."
>
> — Ernest Hemingway,
> *Esquire magazine,*
> 1934

TABLE 10.1
Annual Numbers of New Book Titles Published, Selected Years

Year	Number of Titles	Year	Number of Titles
1778	461	1935	8,766 (drop during the Depression)
1798	1,808		
1880	2,076	1940	11,328
1890	4,559	1945	6,548 (drop during World War II)
1900	6,356		
1910	13,470 (peak until after World War II)	1950	11,022
		1960	15,012
1915	8,202	1970	36,071
1919	5,714 (low point as a result of World War I)	1980	42,377
		1990	46,473
1925	8,173	1996	68,175 (peak)
1930	10,027	1997	65,796

Sources: Figures through 1945 from John Tebbel, *A History of Book Publishing,* 4 vols. (New York: R. R. Bowker, 1978); figures after 1945 from various editions of *The Bowker Annual Library and Trade Book Almanac* (R. R. Bowker).

Our oldest mass medium is still our most influential and our most diverse. The very portability and compactness of books make them a preferred medium in many situations, including relaxing at the beach, passing the lunch hour in the park, resting in bed, and traveling to work on city buses or commuter trains. Most important, books and print culture enable individuals and nations to store knowledge from the past. In their key social role, books are still the main repository of human history and everyday experience, passing along stories, knowledge, and wisdom from generation to generation.

In this chapter, we will trace the history of the book from its earliest roots in Egyptian papyrus plants to its evolution as a paperback and as a CD-ROM. After examining the development of the printing press, we will investigate the rise of the book industry. We will look first at publishing in Europe and colonial America and later at the development of publishing houses in the nineteenth and twentieth centuries. As part of this discussion, we will review the various types of books and the economic issues facing the book industry, particularly the growth of book clubs, bookstore chains, and publishing conglomerates. Finally, we will consider trends in the industry, including books on tape, electronic books, and book preservation. Influencing everything from educational curriculums to popular movies, books continue to play a pivotal role in media culture and democratic life. They are still our central storehouse of personal stories and public knowledge.

the history of books
from papyrus to paperbacks

Since the ancient Babylonians and Egyptians first began experimenting with alphabets some five thousand years ago, people have found ways to preserve their written symbols. Initially, pictorial symbols and letters appeared on wood strips or clay tablets, tied or stacked together to form the first "books." As early as 2700 B.C., the Egyptians wrote on **papyrus** (from which the word *paper* is derived) made from plant reeds found along the Nile River. They rolled these writings in scrolls, much as builders do today with blueprints. This method was adopted by the Greeks in 500 B.C. and by the Romans (who imported the papyrus from Egypt) from 300 to 100 B.C. Plato's *Republic* remains the oldest surviving writing collected together in book form, although it was not originally compiled as a book in 400 B.C.

Around 1000 B.C., the Chinese made booklike objects from strips of wood and bamboo tied together in bundles. At about the time the Egyptians started using papyrus, the Babylonians began pressing symbols and marks into small tablets of clay. These stacked tablets recorded business transactions, government records, favorite stories, and local history. Gradually, **parchment**—treated animal skin—replaced papyrus. Parchment was stronger, smoother, more durable, and less expensive, since it did not have to be imported from Egypt.

Although the Chinese began making paper in 105 A.D., paper made by hand from cotton and linen did not replace parchment in Europe until the thirteenth century. Paper was not as strong as parchment, but it was cheaper. The first proto modern book was probably produced in the fourth century by the Romans, who created the **codex**, a type of book cut into sheets and sewed together along the edge, then bound with thin pieces of wood and covered with leather. Whereas scrolls had to be wound, unwound, and rewound, codices could be opened to any page, and their configuration allowed writing on both sides of a page.

manuscript culture

During the Middle Ages (400 to 1500 A.D.), the Christian clergy strongly influenced what has become known as *manuscript culture*. During this time, priests and monks advanced the art of bookmaking; in many ways, they may be considered the earliest professional editors. Known as *scribes*, they "wrote" most of the books of this period, making copies of existing philosophical tracts and religious books, especially versions of the Bible. Through tedious and painstaking work, scribes became the chief caretakers of recorded history and culture.

Many works from the Middle Ages were *illuminated manuscripts*. These books featured decorative, colorful designs and illustrations on each page. Their covers were made from leather, and some were inscribed with precious gems or gold and silver trim. During this period, scribes developed rules of punctuation and made distinctions between small and capital letters; they also put space between words, which made reading easier. Older Roman writing had used all capital letters, and words ran together on a page, making reading a tortuous experience.

The oldest *printed* book still in existence is China's *Diamond Sutra* by Wang Chieh, from 868 A.D. It consists of seven sheets pasted together and rolled up in a scroll. To make copies of pages, early Chinese printers developed *block printing*, a technique using sheets of paper applied to a block of inked wood with raised surfaces in hand-carved letters and sketches. This constituted the basic technique used in printing newspapers, magazines, and books through much of modern history. Although hand-carving each block, or "page," was time-consuming, this printing breakthrough enabled multiple copies to be produced and then bound together. In 1295, explorer Marco Polo introduced these techniques to Europe after his excursion to China. The first handmade printed books appeared in Europe during the 1400s, and demand for them began to grow among the literate middle-class populace emerging in large European cities.

the gutenberg revolution

The next step in printing was the radical development of movable type, first invented in China around the year 1000. Movable type featured letters in an alphabet made from reusable pieces of wood or metal. Printers arranged or moved letters into various word combinations, greatly speeding up the time it took to make a page. This process, also used in Korea as early as the thirteenth century, developed independently in Europe in the 1400s. Then, in Germany, between 1453 and 1456, Johannes Gutenberg used movable type to develop a *printing press*, which he adapted from a wine press. Gutenberg's staff of printers produced the first so-called modern books, including two hundred copies of a Latin Bible, twenty-one copies of which still exist. The Bible required six presses, many printers, and several months to produce. It was printed on fine handmade paper, a treated animal skin called *vellum*. The pages were hand-decorated, and the use of woodcuts made illustrations possible.

> "For books, issuing from those primal founts of heresy and rebellion, the printing presses have done more to shape the course of human affairs than any other product of the human mind because they are carriers of ideas and it is ideas that change the world." —John Tebbel, *A History of Book Publishing*, 1972

Essentially, Gutenberg and his printing assistants had not only found a way to carry knowledge across geographic borders but had also formed the prototype for mass production. Printing presses spread rapidly across Europe in the late 1400s and early 1500s. Chaucer's *Canterbury Tales* became the first English work to be printed in book form. Many early books were large, elaborate, and expensive, taking months to illustrate and publish. They were usually purchased by aristocrats, royal families, religious leaders, and ruling politicians. Printers, however, gradually reduced the size of books and developed less expensive grades of paper, making books cheaper so more people could afford them.

The social and cultural transformations ushered in by the spread of printing presses and books cannot be overestimated. As historian Elizabeth Eisenstein has noted, when people could learn for themselves by using maps, dictionaries, Bibles, and the writings of others, they could differentiate themselves as individuals; their social identities were no longer solely dependent on what their leaders told them or on the habits of their families, communities, or social class. The technology of printing presses permitted information and knowledge to spread outside local jurisdictions. Gradually, individuals had access to ideas far beyond their isolated experiences, and this permitted them to challenge the traditional wisdom and customs of their tribes and leaders.[3]

book production in the united states

In colonial America, English locksmith Stephen Daye set up a print shop in the late 1630s in Cambridge, Massachusetts. In 1640, Daye and his son Matthew printed the first colonial book, *The Whole Booke of Psalms* (known today as *The Bay Psalm Book*). This collection of biblical psalms sold out its printing of 1,750 copies even though fewer than 3,500 families lived in the colonies at the time. By the mid-1760s, all thirteen colonies had printing shops.

In 1744, Benjamin Franklin imported *Pamela; or, Virtue Rewarded*, the first novel reprinted and sold in colonial America. *Pamela* had been written four years earlier by Britain's Samuel Richardson, who helped pioneer the novel as a literary form. *Pamela* and Richardson's second novel, *Clarissa; or, The History of a Young Lady* (1747), connected with the newly emerging and literate middle classes, especially with women who were just starting to gain a social identity as individuals apart from the men they were married to or worked for. Still restricted from active participation in politics and professional education, women were drawn to these novels for their glimpses into new social worlds. Richardson's novels, overly long and sentimental by current standards, were among the earliest mass-media works to portray women in subordinate roles. Richardson also, however, depicted women triumphing over tragedy, so he is credited as one of the first popular writers to take the domestic life of women seriously.

By the early 1800s, the demand for books among both literate women and men was growing, but the printing process still took time. A page of metal type had to be arranged by hand. The introduction of **linotype** machines in the mid-1880s finally allowed printers to set type mechanically using a typewriter-style keyboard. The introduction of steam-powered machines and high-speed rotary presses also permitted the production of more books at lower costs. Another printing development in the 1800s, **offset lithography**, allowed books to be printed from photographic plates rather than metal casts. Reducing the cost of color and illustrations, offset printing accelerated production and eventually led to computerized typesetting.

In the 1830s, machine-made paper supplanted more expensive handmade varieties. Using cloth rather than leather covers also helped reduce book prices. By the mid-1800s, *paperback books* made with cheaper paper covers had been introduced in the United States from Europe. In 1860, Erastus and Irwin Beadle pioneered paperback

Paperback books, which originated in Europe, were first published in the United States in the early 1830s. In the 1860s, the Beadle brothers helped make paperback "dime novels" into a dominant form of popular culture. By 1870, dime novels had sold seven million copies, with the Beadle line alone producing some six hundred titles—including the *Hurricane Nell* series.

dime novels. Magazine editor-writer Ann Stephens authored the Beadles' first dime novel, *Malaeska: The Indian Wife of the White Hunter*, which was actually a reprint of a serialized magazine story she had written in 1839 for the *Ladies' Companion*.[4] By 1885, one-third of all books published in the United States were popular paperbacks and dime novels, sometimes identified as *pulp fiction*, a reference to the cheap, machine-made pulp paper they were printed on.

The early history of publishing demonstrated that books could widely disseminate and preserve culture and knowledge over time. Even if a paperback fell apart, another version usually existed in a public library or a personal book collection. Oral culture depended on information and values passed down through the wisdom and memories of a community's elders or tribal storytellers, and sometimes these rich traditions were lost. Print culture and the book, however, gave future generations different and often more enduring records of particular authors' words at particular periods in history.

modern publishing and the book industry

Throughout the 1800s, the rapid spread of knowledge and literacy as well as the Industrial Revolution spurred the emergence of the middle class. New professions developed in areas such as the social sciences, business management, and journalism. The demand for books also encouraged the development of a class of publishing professionals, who capitalized on increased middle-class literacy and widespread compulsory education. Many of these early publishers were less interested in skillful marketing strategies than in finding quality authors. But with the growth of advertising and the rise of a market economy in the latter half of the nineteenth century, publishing gradually became more competitive and more concerned with the sales value of titles and authors.

the formation of publishing houses

The modern book industry developed gradually throughout the nineteenth century with the formation of the early prestigious *publishing houses:* companies that tried to identify and produce the works of good writers.[5] These companies professionalized the book industry by dividing into discrete tasks the jobs of acquiring, publishing, and marketing books. Among the oldest American houses established in the 1800s (although most of them are now part of media conglomerates) were J. B. Lippincott

(1792); Harper & Bros. (1817), which became Harper & Row in 1962 and Harper-Collins in 1990; Houghton Mifflin (1832); Little, Brown (1837); G. P. Putnam (1838); Scribner's (1842); E. P. Dutton (1852); Rand McNally (1856); and Macmillan (1869). Out of this group, Scribner's—known more for its magazines in the late 1800s than for its books—became the most prestigious literary house of the 1920s and 1930s, publishing the first novels of F. Scott Fitzgerald (*This Side of Paradise*, 1920) and Ernest Hemingway (*The Sun Also Rises*, 1926).

Between 1880 and 1920, as the center of social and economic life shifted from rural farm production to an industrialized urban culture, the demand for books and bookstores grew. Helped by the influx of European immigrants, the book industry acclimated newcomers to the English language and to American culture. In fact, 1910 marked a peak year in the number of new titles produced—13,470—a record that would not be challenged until the 1950s.

The turn of the century also marked the next wave of prominent publishing houses, as entrepreneurs began to better understand the marketing potential of books. These houses included Doubleday (1897), McGraw-Hill (1909), Prentice-Hall (1913), Alfred A. Knopf (1914), Simon & Schuster (1924), and Random House (1925). After World War II, Doubleday became the world's largest publishing firm for a time. Unlike radio and magazines, however, book publishing sputtered from 1910 into the 1950s. Book-industry profits were adversely affected by the two world wars and the Great Depression. Radio and magazines fared better because they were generally less expensive and could more immediately cover topical issues during times of crisis.

> "He was a genius at devising ways to put **books** into the hands of the **unbookish**."
> —Edna Ferber, writer, commenting on Nelson Doubleday, publisher

types of books

The division of the modern book industry, a $23 billion business in the United States in 1998, comes from economic and structural categories developed by publishers and by trade organizations such as the Association of American Publishers (AAP) and the American Booksellers Association (ABA). The categories include trade books (both adult and juvenile); professional books; elementary, high-school, and college textbooks; mass-market paperbacks; religious books; reference works; and university press books. An additional category—comic books—also exists but is not acknowledged by most conventional publishers (see "Case Study: Comic Books: Alternative Themes, but Superheroes Prevail" on page 318).

Trade Books. By far the most lucrative part of the industry, *trade books* include hardbound and paperback books aimed at general readers and sold at various retail outlets (see Figure 10.1). The industry distinguishes between adult and juvenile trade divisions. Adult trade books include hardbound fiction; current nonfiction and biographies; literary classics; books on hobbies, art, and travel; popular science, technology, and computer publications; self-help books; and cookbooks. (*Betty Crocker's Cookbook*, first published in 1950, has sold more than twenty-two million copies in hardcover trade editions.) Like most of the book industry, fiction and nonfiction trade books have experienced healthy growth in the electronic age. Between 1985 and 1990, for example, trade sales doubled, and by the late 1990s Americans were spending an average of $75 to $80 a year on books, compared with $55 to $60 a year spent on recorded music.[6]

Juvenile book categories range from preschool picture books to young-adult or young-reader books, such as Bantam's *Sweet Valley* adventure series, Scholastic's *Goosebumps* books, and Pocket Books' *Fear Street* series (the latter two written by R. L. Stine). In the electronic age, juvenile book sales have climbed, although studies show that children's and teenagers' reading scores on national tests have slipped. Neverthe-

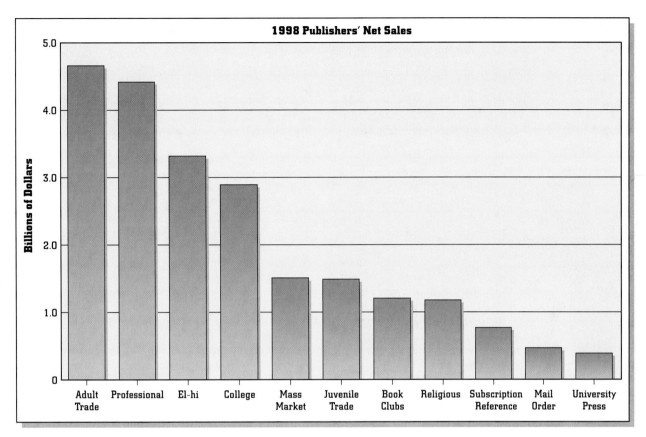

1998 Publishers' Net Sales

Billions of Dollars

Adult Trade · Professional · El-hi · College · Mass Market · Juvenile Trade · Book Clubs · Religious · Subscription Reference · Mail Order · University Press

less, according to one industry study, sales of juvenile books between the early 1970s and the early 1980s jumped more than 200 percent. Stine, for example, sells *Goosebumps* books to the under-age-twelve crowd at a rate of 1.25 million copies per month. In the 1980s and 1990s, library circulation of books for juveniles also increased sharply.

Professional Books. The counterpart to trade publications in the magazine industry, *professional books* target various occupational groups and are not intended for the general consumer market. This area of publishing mirrors the growth of professional and technical specialties that has characterized the job market, particularly since the 1960s. Traditionally, the industry has subdivided professional books into the areas of law, business, medicine, and technical-scientific works. These books are sold mostly through mail order or by sales representatives knowledgeable about various subject areas. This segment of the book industry has found profitable market niches by capitalizing on the expansion of job specialization.

Textbooks. In the mid-1800s, William H. McGuffey, Presbyterian minister and college professor, sold more than 100 million copies of his *Eclectic Reader*, which taught most nineteenth-century elementary-school children to read—and to respect their nation's political and economic systems. Ever since the McGuffey reader, *textbooks* have served a nation intent on improving literacy rates and public education. Elementary textbooks found a solid market niche in the nineteenth century, but college textbooks boomed in the 1950s, when the GI Bill enabled hundreds of thousands of working- and middle-class men, returning from World War II, to attend college. The demand for textbooks further accelerated in the 1960s, as opportunities for women and other minorities expanded.

Figure 10.1
A Sales Overview of the Book Publishing Industry
Source: American Association of Publishers, <http://www.publishers.org/home/stats/prelim.htm>, 6/17/99.

317

CASE STUDY

Comic Books: Alternative Themes, but Superheroes Prevail

by Mark C. Rogers

At the precarious edge of the book industry are comic books, which are sometimes called *graphic novels* or simply *comix*. A medium that neither conventional book nor magazine publishers will claim as their own, comics have long integrated print and visual culture. They remain a paradoxical medium, existing as both collectibles and consumables. They are perhaps the medium most open to independent producers—anyone with a pencil and access to a Xerox machine can produce mini-comics. Nevertheless, two companies—Marvel and DC— have dominated the commercial industry for more than thirty years, publishing the routine superhero stories that have been so marketable.

Comics are a relatively young mass medium, first appearing in their present format in the 1920s in Japan and in the 1930s in the United States. They began as simple reprints of newspaper comic strips, but by the mid-1930s most comic books featured original material. Comics have always been published in a variety of genres, but their signature contribution to American culture has been the superhero. In 1938, Jerry Siegel and Joe Shuster created Superman for DC comics. Bob Kane's Batman character arrived the following year. In 1941, Marvel comics introduced Captain America to fight Nazis, and, except for a brief period in the 1950s, the superhero genre has dominated the history of comics.

After World War II, comic books moved away from superheroes and began experimenting with other genres, most notably crime and horror. With the end of the war, the reading public was ready for more moral ambiguity than was possible in the simple good-versus-evil world of the superhero. Comics became increasingly graphic and lurid as they

tried to compete with other mass media, especially television and mass-market paperbacks.

In the early 1950s, the popularity of crime and horror comics led to a moral panic about their effects on society. Frederic Wertham, a prominent psychiatrist, campaigned against them, claiming they led to juvenile delinquency. Wertham was joined by many religious and parent groups, and Senate hearings were held on the issue in 1954. In October 1954, the Comics Magazine Association of America adopted a code of acceptable conduct for publishers of comic books. One of the most restrictive examples of industry self-censorship in mass-media history, the code kept the government from legislating its own code or restricting the sale of comic books to minors.

The code had both immediate and long-term effects on comics. In the short run, the number of comics sold in the United States declined sharply. Comic books lost many of their adult readers because the code confined comics' topics to those suitable for children. Consequently, comics have rarely been taken seriously as a mass medium or as an art form; they remain stigmatized as the lowest of low culture—a sort of literature for the subliterate.

In the 1960s, Marvel and DC led the way as superhero comics regained their dominance. This period also gave rise to underground comics, which featured more explicit sexual, violent, and drug themes. These alternative comics, like underground newspapers, originated in the 1960s counterculture and challenged the major institutions of the time. Instead of relying on newsstand sales, underground comics were sold through record stores, alternative bookstores, and in a growing number of comic-book specialty shops.

In the 1970s, responding in part to the challenge of the underground form, "legitimate" comics began to increase the political content and relevance of their story lines. In 1974, a new method of distributing comics—direct sales—developed, catering to the increasing number of comic-book stores. This direct-sales method involved selling comics on a nonreturnable basis but with a higher discount than was available to newsstand distributors, who bought comics only on the condition that they could return unsold copies. The percentage of comics sold through specialty shops increased gradually, and by the early 1990s more than 80 percent of all comics were sold through direct sales.

The shift from newsstand to direct sales allowed comics to once again approach adult themes and also created an explosion in the number of comics available and in the number of companies publishing comics. Spurred by direct sales and by a rise in speculation, the industry's sales reached historic highs in the early 1990s but had plummeted by the mid-1990s, falling to less than half of their peak. Although DC and Marvel still control the majority of this market, worth about $500 million annually, some smaller companies have made significant cuts into their shares. For example, Image and Dark Horse, together with Marvel and DC, controlled about 75 percent of the comic-book market in the late 1990s, leaving another 150 smaller firms to split the remaining quarter share. Despite recent sales declines, superheroes still sell the best. Comics continue to represent virtually every genre, including autobiography (*Self-Loathing Comics*), nonfiction journalism (*Palestine*), and historical fiction (*Berlin*). Mainstream comics

include traditional juvenile and superhero fare as well as more experimental material, such as DC's Vertigo line of horror and fantasy comics (*Sandman*) for "mature readers."

In the wake of the 1980s success of *Teenage Mutant Ninja Turtles* (who began life in an alternative comic book), many independent companies have been purchased by or have entered into alliances with larger media firms that want to exploit particular characters or superheroes. DC, for example, is owned by Time Warner, which has used the DC characters, especially Superman and Batman, to build successful film and television properties. Image, Dark Horse, and other small independents have licensed their properties for both animated cartoons (*The Tick*) and feature films (*Spawn*).

As print media face more competition from electronic media, comics seem well suited in the long run to adapt and survive, appearing frequently in electronic form, on CD-ROM and on the World Wide Web. In 1992, comics' flexibility was demonstrated in *Maus: A Survivor's Tale* by Art Spiegelman, cofounder and editor of *Raw* (an alternative magazine for comics and graphic art). The first comic-style book to win a Pulitzer Prize, Spiegelman's two-book fable merged print and visual styles to recount his complex relationship with his father, a Holocaust survivor. As other writers and artists continue to adapt the form to both fictional and nonfictional stories, comics endure as part of popular and alternative culture.

Mark C. Rogers teaches communication at Walsh University. He wrote his doctoral dissertation on the comic-book industry.

Textbooks are divided into elementary-high school, known as *el-hi*; vocational education; and college texts. In most states, local school districts determine which *el-hi* textbooks are appropriate for their students. Texas and California, however, use statewide adoption policies that control text selections. In such situations, only a small number of texts are mandated by the state. If individual schools choose to use books other than those mandated, they are not reimbursed by the state for their purchases. Some teachers and publishers have argued that such sweeping authority undermines the local autonomy of districts, which have varied educational needs and problems. The statewide system of adoptions also allows a few states, which are courted heavily by publishers, to virtually determine the content of the texts sold to every state in the nation. In addition, when publishers aim textbooks at a broad nationwide audience, they tend to water down the content by eliminating regional material or controversial ideas that might offend a group of adopters or a local selection committee.

Unlike el-hi texts, which are subsidized by various states and school districts, hardbound and softcover college texts are paid for by individual students (and parents). At some time during most students' experience, in fact, disputes erupt on campuses about the increasing cost of textbooks and the profit margins of local college bookstores, which in many cases face no on-campus competition. According to a 1998 survey, college students spend $275 on textbooks each term—$168 for new books and $107 for used—and buy an additional $50 of books each term that aren't textbooks.[7] Today, more than 3,600 college bookstores in the United States sell both texts and trade books. In the late 1990s, several new online booksellers, modeled on Amazon.com but specializing in college textbooks, promoted themselves as an alternative to local college bookstores.

Mass-Market Paperbacks. In terms of popular appeal, paperbacks represent the prime-time television of the book industry. In fact, about two out of every three books sold in the United States are **mass-market paperbacks**.[8] Unlike larger trade paperbacks, which are sold mostly in bookstores, mass-market paperbacks are sold off racks in drugstores, supermarkets, and airports as well as in bookstores. In 1998, for example, John Grisham's novel *The Partner* sold more than four million copies and ranked No. 1 in paperback sales, after high sales the year before as a hardcover fiction book. The revenue generated in this area of publishing is enormous. Assorted romance book publishers alone, for instance, offer sixty new titles each month.

Paperbacks did not hit it big until the 1870s, when they became popular among middle- and working-class readers. This phenomenon sparked fear and outrage among those in the professional and educated classes, many of whom thought that reading cheap westerns and crime novels might ruin civilization. Some of the earliest paperbacks ripped off foreign writers, who were unprotected by copyright law and did not receive royalties for the books they sold in the United States. This changed with the International Copyright Law of 1891, which mandated that all authors' works could be reproduced only with their permission.

The popularity of paperbacks hit a major peak in 1939 with the establishment of Pocket Books under the leadership of Robert de Graff. Revolutionizing the paperback industry, Pocket Books lowered the standard book price of fifty or seventy-five cents to twenty-five cents. To accomplish this, de Graff cut bookstore discounts from 30 to 20 percent. The book distributor's share was trimmed from 46 to 36 percent of the cover price, and author royalty rates went from 10 to 4 percent. In its first three weeks in business, the company sold 100,000 books in New York City alone. Among its first titles was *Wake Up and Live* by Dorothea Brande, a 1936 best-seller on self-improvement, which ignited an early wave of self-help books. In testing the market with both nonfiction and fiction, Pocket Books also published paperbacks of *The Mur-*

> "Universally priced at twenty-five cents in its early years, the paperback democratized reading in America."
>
> —Kenneth Davis, *Two-Bit Culture*, 1984

Calvin and Hobbes

by Bill Watterson

der of Roger Ackroyd by Agatha Christie; *Enough Rope*, a collection of poems by Dorothy Parker; *Five Great Tragedies* by Shakespeare; and *Bambi* by Felix Salten, which became a children's classic three years before Walt Disney released the film version. Pocket Books' success spawned a series of imitators, including Dell, Fawcett, and Bantam Books (see Table 10.2).

A major innovation of paperback publishers was the *instant book*, a marketing strategy that involves publishing a topical book quickly after a major event. Pocket Books produced the first instant book, *Franklin Delano Roosevelt: A Memorial*, six days after FDR's death in 1945. Similar to made-for-TV movies that capitalize on con-

TABLE 10.2
Mass-Market Paperback Best-Sellers: The First Twenty-Five Years
(Approximate Sales 1940–65)

Millions of Copies Sold	Title, Author, Year of Publication, Publisher
18.5	*Baby and Child Care*, Benjamin M. Spock, M.D. (1946), Pocket Books
15.5	*The Merriam-Webster Pocket Dictionary* (1947), Pocket Books
10.0	*Peyton Place*, Grace Metalious (1957), Pocket Books
8.0	*God's Little Acre*, Erskine Caldwell (1946), New American Library
6.5	*Webster's New World Dictionary of the American Language* (1958), Popular Library
6.0	*University of Chicago English-Spanish, Spanish-English Dictionary* (1950), University of Chicago
	In His Steps, Charles Sheldon (1960), Advance
5.5	*Exodus*, Leon Uris (1959), Bantam
	To Kill a Mockingbird, Harper Lee (1962), Popular Library
	Roget's Pocket Thesaurus (1946), New American Library
	The Carpetbaggers, Harold Robbins (1962), Pocket Books
5.0	*How to Win Friends and Influence People*, Dale Carnegie (1940), Pocket Books
	Return to Peyton Place, Grace Metalious (1960), Dell
4.5	*The Pocket Cook Book*, Elizabeth Woody (1942), Pocket Books
	Profiles in Courage, John F. Kennedy (1947), Pocket Books
	The Big Kill (1951), *I, The Jury* (1948), *My Gun Is Quick* (1950), Mickey Spillane, New American Library
	1984, George Orwell (1950), New American Library

Source: Kenneth Davis, *Two-Bit Culture: The Paperbacking of America* (Boston: Houghton Mifflin, 1984), 289.

temporary events, instant books allow the industry to better compete with journalism and magazines. Such books, however, like their TV counterparts, have been accused of exploiting tragedies for quick profits.

Bantam began dominating this field in 1964 with *The Report of the Warren Commission on the Assassination of President Kennedy*, the first Bantam "extra" edition. (*Extra* is a term borrowed from daily newspapers, which produced extra editions to tell important breaking news stories in the pre-TV era.) After receiving the 385,000-word report on a Friday afternoon, Bantam staffers began editing the Warren report on the way to the airport; the book was produced within a week. The publisher, in a joint venture with the *New York Times*, ultimately sold 1.6 million copies.

Today, instant books continue to capitalize on a variety of contemporary events, from the arrest of Unabomber suspect Theodore Kaczynski in 1996 to the death of Princess Diana in 1997. In the Unabomber case, within thirteen days of Kaczynski's arrest, Pocket Books produced a quickie book. But while it was being reviewed for clearance by the FBI (one coauthor was an ex-agent), Warner Books published *Mad Genius: The Odyssey, Pursuit, and Capture of the Unabomber Suspect* and won the race to market. In the case of Diana's death, on August 31, 1997, publishers such as Simon & Schuster, Pocket Books, and Archway Paperbacks responded by quickly issuing large print runs of existing Diana book titles. Warner Books also moved up the publishing date for Kitty Kelley's *The Royals*, which already had a planned September 1997 release date. Diana's death—in which many people had implicated the "tabloid" media—resulted in great caution in the race to turn out instant books, although at least one instant book appeared within twelve days. Most publishers instead took more time to craft commemorative books. Although instant books make fast money for their publishers, they often sacrifice the kind of in-depth analysis and historical perspective that the book medium has generally brought to important social events.

Still, even global distribution via the World Wide Web hasn't stopped instant books. In late 1998, independent counsel Kenneth Starr's report on the Clinton-Lewinsky sex scandal was released on the Web for free, and was quickly read by some six million people. The report was also published in full and abridged versions in hundreds of newspapers during the following days. Yet three publishers (Pocket, Prima, and Public Affairs) released paperback versions of the report for $5.99 to $10 within a few days, and hundreds of thousands of copies were sold, putting the book version on the *New York Times* best-seller list for five weeks. Industry analysts suggested that even though the Starr report was easily available on the Web and in newspapers, a paperback book copy is more portable and also serves as a commemorative medium for important documents like the report.[9]

Religious Books. The best-selling book of all time is the Bible, in all its diverse versions. Over the years, the success of Bible sales spawned a large *religious-book* industry, now divided into four categories: Bibles, hymnals, and other materials related to religious observances; spiritual or inspirational books aimed at lay readers; professional publications focusing on the work of clergy and theologians; and religious-education textbooks.

After World War II, sales of religious books soared. Historians attribute the sales boom to economic growth and a nation seeking peace and security while facing the threat of "godless communism" and the Soviet Union.[10] By the 1960s, though, the scene had changed dramatically. The impact of the civil-rights struggle, the Vietnam War, the sexual revolution, and the youth rebellion against authority led to declines in formal church membership. Not surprisingly, sales of some types of religious books dropped as well. To compete, many religious publishers extended their offerings to include serious secular titles on such topics as war and peace, race, poverty, gender, and civic responsibility.

Throughout this period of change, the publication of fundamentalist and evangelical literature remained steady. It then expanded rapidly during the 1980s, when the Republican Party began making political overtures to conservative groups and prominent TV evangelists. Among the religious right in the media, televangelists Jerry Falwell and Oral Roberts inspired a number of successful books. Another televangelist, Pat Robertson, owned the Christian Broadcast Network, TV's *700 Club*, and a college in Virginia dedicated to placing conservative Christians in the broadcast industry. Robertson grew increasingly influential in the Republican Party, although he failed in his bid for the party's presidential nomination in 1992. The popularity of conservative and tradition-bound publications stabilized religious publishing during turbulent social times. From 1994 to 1995, the total book industry grew 6 percent, but the sales of religious and spiritual books—a $1-billion-a-year industry—grew 20 percent. The religious-book industry continued to expand in the late 1990s, accounting for nearly 10 percent of all books purchased.

Reference Books. Another major division of the book industry includes all sorts of reference books, typically divided into three categories: reference works for home and office (accounting for roughly 80 percent of reference sales); those for schools and libraries (about 5 percent); and works distributed through mail-order marketing (about 15 percent). *Reference books* include dictionaries, encyclopedias, atlases, and a number of substantial volumes directly related to particular professions or trades, such as legal casebooks and medical manuals.

The idea of developing encyclopedic writings to document the extent of human knowledge is attributed to Aristotle. Pliny the Elder (23–79 A.D.) wrote the oldest reference work still in existence, *Historia Naturalis*, detailing in Latin thousands of facts about animals, minerals, and plants. But it wasn't until the early 1700s that the compilers of reference works began organizing articles in alphabetical order and relying on specialists to contribute essays in their areas of interest. Between 1751 and 1771, a group of French scholars produced a twenty-eight-volume set of encyclopedias. The circulation of these volumes, full of new and often radical ideas, encouraged support for the French Revolution against aristocratic rule later in that century.

The oldest English-language encyclopedia still in production, the *Encyclopaedia Britannica (EB)*, was first published in Scotland in 1768. Significant U.S. encyclopedias followed, including *Encyclopedia Americana* (1829), *The World Book Encyclopedia* (1917), and *Compton's Pictured Encyclopedia* (1922), bought by *EB* in 1961. *EB* produced its first U.S. edition in 1908. Purchased by Sears in 1920 and later by a U.S. ad agency, *EB* was eventually run as a nonprofit venture

In the 1990s, one of the best examples of media convergence was the proliferation of digitized encyclopedias and other reference works. The sheer volume and weight of these bulky print materials made them prime candidates for digital conversion and storage. A twenty-five-volume encyclopedia occupies far less space and uses far fewer natural resources in its computer hard drive or CD-ROM incarnations.

for the University of Chicago. *EB* contributed more than $125 million to the university over the years. However, its sales fell from 117,000 sets in 1990 to 51,000 in 1994. Eventually, the company was forced to reorganize and disband its famous door-to-door sales force. *EB* was much slower to adapt to the electronic environment than were other reference firms. In 1995, it finally issued a CD-ROM version that sold for $995 (a traditional bound set ran about $1,500), a price targeted at libraries and other institutional buyers. By this time, though, Microsoft was already selling a CD-ROM Funk & Wagnalls encyclopedia for $99, a price tailored to mass-market buyers. Many computer packages sold today feature encyclopedias preloaded in the hard drive, and by the mid-1990s digital encyclopedias were outselling print versions by a four-to-one margin. *EB*, Microsoft's *Encarta*, and the *World Book Multimedia Encyclopedia* are the leading CD-ROM encyclopedias today, and range in price from about $70 to $100.

Dictionaries have also accounted for a large portion of reference sales. Like encyclopedias, the earliest dictionaries were produced by Greek and Roman writers attempting to document specialized and rare words. During the manuscript period in the Middle Ages, however, European scribes and monks began creating glossaries and dictionaries to help people understand Latin. In 1604, a British schoolmaster prepared a three-thousand-word English dictionary. A sixty-thousand-word English dictionary was produced in 1721, followed by Samuel Johnson's *Dictionary of the English Language* in 1755. Describing rather than prescribing word usage, Johnson was among the first to understand that language changes—that words and usage cannot be fixed for all time. Johnson's dictionary served as the model and standard for English dictionaries into the mid-1800s. In the United States in 1828, Noah Webster, using Johnson's work as a model, published the seventy-thousand-word, two-volume *American Dictionary of the English Language*, differentiating between British and American usages and simplifying spelling (for example, *colour* became *color* and *musick* became *music*).

Other reference works include the atlases and almanacs that have become so popular in schools, homes, offices, and libraries. A number of specialty works, such as the *Readers' Guide to Periodical Literature*, are available in libraries. Since 1908, high-school and college students have used the *Guide* as a starting point to locate references to magazine articles on virtually any topic. In addition, media trade organizations publish their own reference works, such as *Editor & Publisher Yearbook* and *Broadcasting & Cable Yearbook*. Each year, R. R. Bowker publishes *Books in Print* and *Paperbound Books in Print*, which list all new and available book titles. *The Bowker Annual Library and Trade Book Almanac* reprints articles and compiles statistics on the book industry.

University-Press Books. The smallest unit in the book industry is the noncommercial *university press*, which publishes scholarly works for small groups of readers interested in specialized areas. Professors often try to secure book contracts from reputable university presses to increase their chances for tenure, a lifetime teaching contract. Some university presses are very small, producing as few as ten books a year. The largest, the University of Chicago Press, regularly publishes more than two hundred titles a year. Among the oldest and most prestigious of these presses are Yale University Press, established in 1908, and Harvard University Press, formally founded in 1913 but claiming roots that go back to 1639, when Stephen Daye published the first colonial book in a small shop behind the house of Harvard's president.

University presses traditionally have not faced pressure to produce commercially viable books, so they can encourage innovative writers and thinkers. Large commercial trade houses are often criticized for encouraging only blockbuster books, but university presses often suffer an opposite criticism—producing subsidized books that only a handful of scholars read. Many social-science and humanities professors are content to write for one another; they believe that university presses need to protect narrowly focused, specialized, noncommercial publications. Others argue that it is time to declare "an end to scholarly publications as a series of guarded conversations between professors."[11]

University-press books typically sell fewer than a thousand copies each, most of which are sold to libraries. Although they bring academic institutions a certain prestige, university presses routinely lose money. Even academic books written in accessible language rarely attract the interest of the general public because university presses have little money for marketing and promotion. Increasingly, administrators are reducing subsidies, requiring presses to show more profit. This has led to a decrease in the number of books university presses can publish. To offset costs and increase revenue, some presses are trying to form alliances with commercial houses to help promote and produce academic books that have wider appeal. Such ties led to increases in sales in 1997 and again in 1998.

the organization and ownership of the book industry

Compared with the revenues earned by other mass-media industries, the steady growth of book publishing has been relatively modest. From the mid-1980s to the late 1990s, total revenues went from $9 billion to more than $23 billion. Within the industry, the concept of who or what constitutes a publisher varies widely. A publisher may be a large company that is a subsidiary of a global media conglomerate and occupies an entire office building, or a publisher may be a one-person home-office operation using a desktop computer. Unlike commercial television and film, small book publishers can start up relatively easily because of advances in personal computer technology.

the structure of book publishing

Medium-size and large publishing houses employ hundreds of people and share certain similarities. Most of the thousands of small houses, however, have staffs of fewer than twenty. In the larger houses, divisions usually include acquisition and development; copyediting, design, and production; marketing and sales; and administration and business. Unlike newspapers but similar to magazines, most publishing houses contract independent printers to produce their books.

Most publishers employ acquisitions editors to seek out and sign authors to contracts. In the trade-fiction area, this might mean discovering talented writers by reading hundreds of unsolicited manuscripts. In nonfiction, editors might examine manuscripts and letters of inquiry or actively match a known writer to a particular topic or project (such as a celebrity biography). Acquisitions editors also handle **subsidiary rights** for an author—that is, selling the rights to a book for use in other media forms, such as a mass-market paperback or CD-ROM, or as the basis for a movie screenplay.

As part of their contracts, writers sometimes receive *advance* money, which is actually an early payment against royalties to be earned later. New authors may receive little or no advance from a publisher, but commercially successful authors can receive millions. For example, *Interview with a Vampire* author Anne Rice hauled in a $17 million advance from Knopf for three more vampire novels, and Simon & Schuster advanced Mary Higgins Clark (*I'll Be Seeing You, Remember Me*) more than $30 million for six new mysteries. First-time authors who are nationally recognized, such as political leaders, sports figures, or movie stars, can also command large advances from publishers who are banking on the well-known person's commercial potential.

"The [university] presses are meant to be one of the few **alternative sources** of scholarship and information available in the United States. . . . Does the bargain involved in publishing commercial titles compromise that role?"
—Andre Schiffren, *The Chronicle of Higher Education*, 1999

For example, retired general Colin Powell, who directed military operations during the Persian Gulf War and was the first African American to head the Joint Chiefs of Staff, received a $6.5 million advance from Random House for his autobiography. Typically, an author's royalty is between 5 and 15 percent of the net price of the book. But before a royalty check is paid, advance money is subtracted from royalties earned during the sale of the book (see Figure 10.2).

After a contract is signed, an author's manuscript is reviewed by the acquisitions editor. In educational publishing, a major text may also be turned over to a development editor, who provides the author with feedback, makes suggestions for improvements, and obtains advice from knowledgeable academics. If a book is illustrated, editors work closely with photo researchers to select appropriate photographs and pieces of art. After the development stage, copyediting, design, and production people enter the picture. While copy editors attend to specific writing or length problems, production and design managers work on the look of the book, making decisions about type style, paper, cover design, and layout.

Simultaneously, plans are under way to market and sell the book. Decisions generally need to be made concerning number of copies to print, how to best reach potential readers, and costs for promotion and advertising. For trade books and some scholarly books, publishing houses may send early or advance copies of a book to appropriate magazines and newspapers with the hope of receiving favorable reviews that can be used later in promotional material. Prominent trade writers typically sign autographs at selected bookstores and travel the radio and TV talk-show circuit to promote their new books. Unlike trade publishers, college-textbook firms rarely sell directly to bookstores. Instead, they contact instructors either through direct-mail brochures or sales representatives assigned to various geographic regions. As we noted earlier, el-hi salespeople may be dealing with local school districts or state adoption committees.

Large trade houses spend millions of dollars promoting new books. Viking Penguin routinely spends more than $750,000 to promote each of Stephen King's new books. In the early 1990s, Warner Books spent $600,000 to promote *Scarlett*, Alexandra Ripley's romance sequel to Margaret Mitchell's *Gone with the Wind*, the top-selling fiction trade book in both 1936 and 1937. To help create a best-seller, trade houses often distribute large cardboard bins, called *dumps*, to thousands of stores to display a book in bulk quantity. Like food merchants who buy eye-level shelf placement for their products in supermarkets, large trade houses buy shelf space from major chains

Figure 10.2
Book Economics
Source: Brill's Content, October 1998, p. 125.

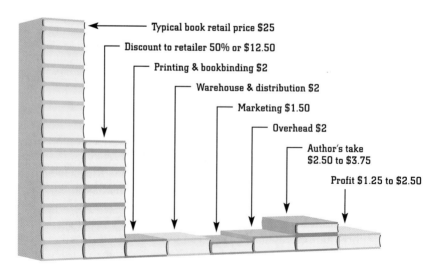

Typical book retail price $25

Discount to retailer 50% or $12.50

Printing & bookbinding $2

Warehouse & distribution $2

Marketing $1.50

Overhead $2

Author's take $2.50 to $3.75

Profit $1.25 to $2.50

to ensure prominent locations in bookstores. They also buy ad space on buses and billboards and in newspapers and magazines. Some trade houses now routinely purchase ads on television and radio. To promote *Scarlett*, for instance, Warner Books bought thirty-second spots during talk shows and soap operas shortly before the book was released. *Scarlett* became the top-selling fiction book in 1991.

The final part of the publishing process involves the business and order-fulfillment stages—getting books to market and shipping and invoicing orders to thousands of commercial outlets and college bookstores. Warehouse inventories are monitored to ensure that enough copies of a book will be available to meet demand. Anticipating such demand, though, is a tricky business. No publisher wants to get stuck with books it cannot sell or be caught short if a book becomes more popular than originally predicted. Today, most of these business procedures are managed by computer programs, and bookstores can usually tell customers instantly whether they have a particular book in stock or how long it will take to obtain the book.

book clubs and mail order

In terms of selling books, two alternative strategies have worked for a number of years—book clubs and mail order. In fact, these strategies have often sustained publishers during the changeover from a print-based to an electronically influenced culture. Both tactics also helped the industry in earlier times when bookstores were not as plentiful. Modeled on the turn-of-the-century catalogue sales techniques used by retailers such as Sears, direct-mail services brought books to rural and small-town areas that had no bookstores. Doubleday became the first publisher to introduce direct mail to readers during the early 1900s.

The Book-of-the-Month Club and the Literary Guild both started in 1926. Using popular writers and literary experts to recommend new books, the clubs were successful immediately. By the mid-1990s, more than 150 book clubs for adults were operating, ranging from the Arts and Crafts Book Society to the Civil Engineers Book Club.[12] Book clubs have long served as editors for their customers, screening thousands of titles and recommending key books in particular genres. Occasionally, though, important books have been overlooked by clubs, including Steinbeck's *The Grapes of Wrath* and Hemingway's *The Sun Also Rises*.

During the 1980s, as book clubs experienced declining sales, they became more susceptible to pressure from major publishers. Indeed, the outside experts for the clubs began complaining not only that their recommendations were frequently bypassed by club editors but that the clubs were stressing commercially viable authors without regard to literary merit. In 1994, the Book-of-the-Month Club eliminated outside judges altogether.[13]

Besides screening new books for consumers, clubs have offered incentives, such as free books and occasional price reductions, to compete with bookstores. Book clubs offer the same advantages as a cable home-shopping network: You can order from the comfort of your home and avoid "mall madness" or the congestion of downtown shopping. Although Time Warner operates the Book-of-the-Month Club (the largest single club, with more than one million members), Doubleday remains the most active publisher in the book-club business. In the late 1990s, Doubleday owned and operated both the Literary Guild and Doubleday Book Club, as well as several specialty clubs, including the Mystery Guild, the Military Book Club, the Science-Fiction Book Club, and the Audio Book Club. The total membership of the Doubleday clubs was estimated at around three million in 1995. Worldwide, German-based book giant Bertelsmann, corporate parent of Doubleday, carries more than thirty-five million book- and music-club members.[14]

Mail-order bookselling is used primarily by trade, professional, and university-press publishers. The mail-order strategy offers many of the benefits of book clubs in terms of immediately notifying readers about new book titles. Mail-order bookselling was pioneered in the 1950s by magazine publishers. They created special sets of books, such as Time-Life Books, focusing on science, nature, household maintenance, cooking, and so forth. These series usually offered one book at a time (unlike encyclopedias) and sustained sales through direct-mail flyers and newspaper, magazine, radio, and television advertising. To enhance their perceived value and uniqueness, most of these sets could be obtained only through the mail. Although such sets are more costly due to advertising and postal charges, mail-order books still appeal to customers who prefer the convenience of mail to the hassle of shopping. Others like the privacy of mail order (particularly if they are ordering sexually explicit books or magazines).

bookstores

Although the book industry remains the most diverse of all mass media, the same media trend toward large chain ownership prevails. In the late 1990s, more than twelve thousand bookstores in the United States made more than 50 percent of their revenue from the sale of books and magazines. Another fifteen thousand stores, such as department or drugstores, also sell books (see Table 10.3). By the late 1990s, book sales were dominated by two large chains: Borders-Walden and Barnes & Noble, which includes all

TABLE 10.3			
Bookstores in the United States, 1997			
Category	Number of Stores	Category	Number of Stores
Antiquarian general	1,497	Gift shop	375
Antiquarian mail order	606	Juvenile*	382
		Mail order general	405
Antiquarian specialized	283	Mail order specialized	860
Art-supply store	69	Metaphysics, New Age, and occult	304
College general	3,479	Museum store and art gallery	591
College specialized	145	Nature and natural history	162
Comics	302	Newsdealer	134
Computer software	270	Office supply	54
Cooking	183	Other§	2,362
Department store	2,206	Paperback‡	379
Educational*	281	Religious*	4,050
Federal sites†	289	Self-help/Development	63
Foreign language*	134	Stationer	23
General	6,861	Toy store	115
		Used*	827
		Total	**27,691**

*Includes mail-order shops for this topic, which are not counted elsewhere in this survey.

†National historic sites, national monuments, and national parks.

‡Includes mail order. Excludes used-paperback bookstores, stationers, drugstores, or wholesalers handling paperbacks.

§Stores specializing in subjects or services other than those covered in this survey.

Source: The Bowker Library and Trade Book Annual, 1998 (New Providence, N.J.: R. R. Bowker), 541.

One amazing aspect of the enduring popularity of books was the recent emergence of the superstore. By stocking 100,000 titles, providing coffee shops, and selling CDs and cassettes, Borders-Walden and Barnes & Noble made it increasingly difficult for thousands of small independent booksellers around the nation to remain competitive.

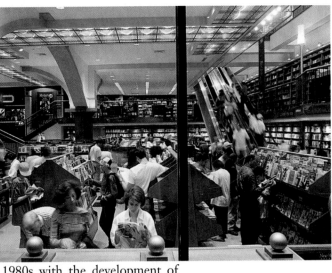

B. Dalton and Doubleday stores. These chains operate more than one thousand stores each and account for about 40 percent of all trade-book sales.[15] The two next-largest chains are Books-A-Million and Crown Books.

Shopping-mall bookstores have boosted book sales since the late 1960s. But the trend currently reinvigorating the business began in the 1980s with the development of **superstores**. The idea was to adapt to the book trade the large retail-store concept, such as Builders Square in home improvement or Wal-Mart in general retail. Following the success of a single Borders store in Ann Arbor, Michigan, a number of book chains began developing superstores that catered to suburban areas and avid readers. A typical superstore now stocks 100,000 titles, compared with the 20,000 or 40,000 titles found in older B. Dalton or Waldenbook stores. As superstores expanded, they also started to sell recorded music and to feature coffee shops, restaurants, and live performances. By 1999, Borders had grown from only 14 superstores in 1991 to more than 245 superstores in the United States and in Australia, Singapore, and the United Kingdom, while Barnes & Noble had surpassed the 500 superstore mark.

One benefit to booksellers in the electronic era has been the increased value of used and rare books. Many small cities, especially in college towns, now support a half-dozen small used-book stores. For example, Ann Arbor, a city of 110,000 with the University of Michigan at its center, supported twenty-five bookstores in the mid-1990s, and at least twelve of those specialized in used books. As the city where Borders originated, Ann Arbor had the nation's highest books-per-capita ratio: The average Ann Arborite adult spent more than $230 a year on books (Berkeley, California, and Madison, Wisconsin, also university cities, ranked second and third).

Despite the control that chains have over commercial trade books, the majority of bookstores today remain small and independent. For example, nearly one thousand used- and rare-book stores now operate nationwide. To oppose chains, many independents have formed regional or statewide groups to plan survival tactics. In 1992, for instance, independents in Madison, Wisconsin, countered the arrival of a new Borders superstore by redecorating, extending hours and services, creating newsletters, and offering musical and children's performances. In 1999 in Capitola, California, a small town near San Jose, many community residents fought a proposed "big box" Borders bookstore, fearing it would drive out several independent bookstores and change the character of the city. Many smaller stores also fear the rise of superstores, their ability to offer discount prices on best-sellers, and their relationship with large publishers who pay chains for quality shelf space. Chains pose a threat to the continued health of independent booksellers, whose overall sales slipped in the 1990s as the number of superstores expanded to more than 750 nationwide. The effect of the superstores on independent bookstores has been devastating. According to American Booksellers Association president Richard Howorth, "In 1991, when Barnes & Noble and Borders began to expand, there were 5,200 members of the ABA. Today [1998] there are 3,300."[16]

"There is a public interest at stake in the fate of bookstores that quickens the public's appetite for printed words."
—George Will, *Washington Post*, 1991

329

online bookstores

In just a few short years, online booksellers have created an entirely new book-distribution system on the Internet. The trailblazer is Amazon.com, established in 1995 by then-thirty-year-old Jeff Bezos, who left Wall Street to start a Web-based business. Bezos realized books were an untapped and ideal market for the Internet, with more than three million publications in print and plenty of distributors to fulfill orders. So he moved to Seattle and started Amazon.com, so named because Web search engines like Yahoo! list categories in alphabetical order, putting Amazon near the top of the list.

In 1997, Barnes & Noble, the leading terra-firma bookseller, launched its heavily invested and carefully researched Bn.com Web site (of which publishing giant Bertelsmann bought 50 percent in the following year when it canceled plans to start its own online store). Borders started Borders.com a year later. In 1999, the American Booksellers Association launched BookSense.com to help independent bookstores create an online presence. Although several online sites have laid claim to being the world's largest bookstore, their size is not based on their warehouse inventory but on the number of books they can access for customers via distributors. In the case of Amazon.com, for example, a book is usually not ordered from a supplier until an online order is placed by a customer.

By 1998, online booksellers controlled only about 3 percent of the retail book market, but their share of the market continues to grow, as Borders and other traditional booksellers enter the online business.[17] The strength of online sellers lies in their convenience, low prices, and especially their ability to offer backlist titles and less-famous authors that even 150,000-volume superstores don't carry on their shelves. Online customers are also drawn to the interactive nature of these sites, which allow them to post their own book reviews or read those of fellow customers. The chief business strategy of online booksellers is to buy exclusive listings with the most popular World Wide Web portals. For example, Bn.com signed a multimillion-dollar deal with Microsoft to be the "buy books" button on MSN.com, and is the exclusive bookseller on America Online. Similarly, Amazon.com has marketing agreements with the busy Yahoo! and Excite Web sites and is the exclusive music retailer on MSN.com.

Established in 1995, Amazon.com has quickly become the darling of Internet shoppers and Wall Street investors. Originally offering millions of books, Amazon.com swiftly expanded to sell CDs, DVDs, cassettes, videos, and computer games. Today, the company aggressively invests in promising companies and technologies, giving Amazon.com the ability to operate online auctions, sell prescription drugs, and send electronic greeting cards.

ownership patterns

Like most mass media, commercial publishing is dominated by a handful of major corporations with ties to international media conglomerates such as Viacom/Paramount (which now owns Simon & Schuster), Time Warner, Newhouse's Advance Publications, and Bertelsmann, which began by publishing German Bibles in the 1700s. Since the 1960s and 1970s—when CBS acquired Holt, Rinehart & Winston, Popular Library, and Fawcett—mergers and consolidations have driven the book industry. Germany's Bertelsmann purchased Dell in the late 1970s for $35 million and in the 1980s bought Doubleday for $475 million. In 1998, Bertelsmann shook up the book industry by adding Random House, the largest U.S. book publisher, to its fold. With the $1.4 billion purchase of Random House from Advance Publications, Bertelsmann gained control of about one-third of the U.S. trade-book market, about 10 percent of the total U.S. book market, and became the world's largest publisher of English-language books.[18] Bertelsmann's book companies include Bantam Doubleday Dell, Random House, and the Random House imprints of Knopf, Vintage, Ballantine-Fawcett, Modern Library, and Fodor's Travel Publications, among others (see Table 10.4).

A number of concerns have surfaced regarding conglomerates' control over the publishing industry. The distinctive styles of older houses and their associations with certain literary figures and book types no longer characterize the industry. Of special concern has been the financial struggle of independent publishers and booksellers, who are often undercut in price and promotion by large corporations and bookstore chains. Large houses also tend to favor blockbusters or best-sellers and do not aggressively pursue more modest or unconventional books.

From the corporate point of view, book-industry executives argue that large companies can financially support a number of smaller struggling firms and that the editorial ideas of these firms can remain independent from the parent corporation. Executives also tout the advantages of *synergy:* the involvement of several media subsidiaries under one corporate umbrella, all working to develop different versions of a similar product. One writer commented on these synergistic possibilities when Time and Warner merged in 1990: "Theoretically, this unprecedented corporate fusion makes it possible for a title to be published in hardcover by Little, Brown (a division of Time Inc.), featured as a Book-of-the-Month Club main selection, reviewed by *Time* magazine, issued in paperback by Warner Books, made into a major motion pic-

TABLE 10.4
Top 10 U.S. Trade Book Publishers

Rank	Publisher	Parent Company	1997 Revenues ($ mil.)
1	Random House	Bertelsmann	1,245.0
2	Reader's Digest	Reader's Digest Assoc. Inc.	1,190.0
3	Time Warner	Time Warner Inc.	1,140.0
4	Penguin Putnam	Pearson Inc.	865.9
5	HarperCollins	News Corp.	737.0
6	Scholastic Inc.	Scholastic Corp.	721.8
7	Bantam Doubleday Dell	Bertelsmann	680.0
8	Simon & Schuster	Viacom	560.0
9	Grolier Inc.	Lagadere SCA	480.0
10	Encyclopaedia Britannica	Jacob Safra	450.0

Source: Peterson's Media Companies 2000 (Princeton, NJ: Peterson's, 1999), 46.

ture, and turned into a TV series by Warner television."[19] Still, authors and critics worry that book ideas that lack such multimedia potential may be rejected in the trend toward large corporate control.

On one level, the industry appears healthy, with thousands of independent presses still able to make books using inexpensive production techniques and desktop computer publishing. Many independents, however, struggle against the few large conglomerates that define the direction of much of the industry. Between 1990 and 1998, the number of independent bookstores in the United States declined by a third, and for the first time more trade books were being sold by chains than by independents.

trends in book publishing

A number of technological changes in the publishing industry demonstrate the blurring of print and electronic cultures. The book industry has adapted successfully in the digital age by using computer technology to effectively lower costs. Today, everything from an author's word-processing program to printing and distribution is computerized.[20] In 1992, the first multimedia books appeared, including electronic versions of Michael Crichton's *Jurassic Park* and Lewis Carroll's *Alice's Adventures in Wonderland* (first published in 1865). These paperless books were produced using Apple Computer software that integrated printed text with animated cartoons and sound effects. Much skepticism remains, however, regarding whether enough consumers will give up the printed page to read a book from a computer screen, even with futuristic visual and audio accompaniment. Reference books have become a primary target for multimedia adaptations on computer hard drives and CD-ROMs. A digitized CD-ROM reference book can easily store more than 100,000 pages of text, avoiding the high cost of paper and book production.

In studying various mergers of print and electronic forms, most forecasters suggest that electronic and digital publications are best suited to reference works, some children's literature, and educational materials. Most media observers do not believe that electronic technology will seriously undermine the traditional printed book (see "Tracking Technology: E-books and the Future of Reading" on page 333). Some evidence exists, however, that because of the computerization of best-seller lists and the quicker tracking of inventories, stores may get rid of books before the gradual word of mouth has a chance to build up. This slower oral tradition once held much more clout in popularizing book titles. One new company, Lightning Print—a division of leading book distributor Ingram Book Company—uses digital technology and on-demand printing to revive books that would otherwise go out of print. Because Lightning Print holds books in digital form, and prints copies only when orders are received, publishers need not worry about getting stuck with unsold books, or being unable to respond to limited demand for a book.

> "Electronic text processing marks the next major shift in **information technology** after the development of the printed book. It promises (or threatens) to produce effects on our culture, particularly on our literature, education, criticism, and scholarship, just as radical as those produced by **Gutenberg's moveable type**."
>
> —George Landow, 1992

influences of television and film

Through their vast television exposure, books by TV anchors and actors such as Tom Brokaw, Peter Jennings, Ellen DeGeneres, or Jerry Seinfeld have sold millions of copies—enormous sales in a business where 100,000 in sales constitutes remarkable success. In national polls conducted in the 1980s and 1990s, nearly 30 percent of

For people who associate books with curling up on a comfortable couch for an afternoon of reading, the idea of experiencing the latest best-seller through a computer screen may seem distasteful. Fans of books argue that the bound medium is portable and intimate. You can read a book in any posture, take it to bed or to the beach, and enjoy the simple pleasures of the texture of the paper and the high resolution of the ink on the page. Not so, they say, with the computer.

Since 1998, however, a new wave of portable reading devices has been attempting to approximate every aspect of the printed book, with a few extra conveniences as well. NuvoMedia, the same company that created the PalmPilot, developed Rocket eBook, a lightweight (twenty-ounce) tablet designed to feel as if you're holding a paperback with rolled-back pages. Virtual Press released SoftBook, a three-pound, leatherbound model (another way to capture the *feel* of a book) that turns on when users flip it open and displays text on a single screen. Everybook Inc. launched three versions of its EB Dedicated Reader, ranging from a low-end one-pound model to a high-end seven-pounder. EveryBook says that their devices are "true" electronic books, displaying text on opposing screens and offering color formatting that replicates book layouts.

All of the latest devices are battery-operated and offer numerous features: flat, back-lit screens; simple control buttons to turn pages; functions for bookmarks, electronic dog-ears, and keyword searches; and enough memory to hold from four thousand color to half a million black-and-white pages. Depending on the reading device, users can also write (and later erase) margin notes with a touch-screen pen, highlight text with their fingers, listen to sound files through a speaker, enlarge the text, or click on any word to get an instant dictionary definition.

In the future, content delivery may determine which e-book controls the market. Rocket eBook users must first access an online bookstore from their personal computer and download the text onto their hard drive (in an encrypted format that prevents duplication). Then they dock their e-books into a cradle that's attached to their computer to transfer the material. Both the SoftBook and the EB Dedicated Reader have built-in modems that directly connect to any standard phone jack or cable connection, allowing users to access the companies' own virtual bookstores.

The prices for various e-books differ as well. In 1999, the Rocket eBook sold for $499. The SoftBook was priced at a much cheaper $299, but users were required to pay a monthly $19.95 subscription fee for two years. The EB Dedicated Readers ranged from $500 to $2,000.

Since much of today's publishing process is already digitally based, e-book companies forecast that any book available in a bookstore will also be released electronically. While fifty thousand printed texts go out of print each year because of high printing, distribution, and storage costs, e-book users could potentially download books that would otherwise be unavailable in print. E-book manufacturers hope people will eventually download best-sellers from authors like Stephen King, but they are also marketing their products to students and "information-intensive professionals" who have to carry loads of journals and business-related books on business trips.

Yet, with all these features, it remains to be seen whether people will surrender their current book-reading practices to the glowing screen and the electronic bookmark. As Peter Lewis of the *New York Times* put it, "Of course, paper books don't crash, run out of battery power over Nebraska, spew error messages, demand periodic upgrades, require technical support, attract professional thieves, entice the purchase of expensive upgrades or go to the repair shop for days at a time."

respondents said they had read a book because they had seen the story or a promotion on television.

In fact, Brokaw's book, *The Greatest Generation*, and Jennings's elaborately illustrated *The Century* both ranked as best-sellers throughout much of 1998 and early 1999. Interest in these books was enormously enhanced by network/publisher cross-promotions and cross-media ventures. A special on NBC's *Dateline* and a profile of Brokaw's project on *NBC Nightly News* both promoted his book (NBC owns nearly a 25 percent interest in the book). Jennings's book grew out of a twelve-part ABC documentary project on the twentieth century. Its publisher, Doubleday (a subsidiary of Random House, which also published Brokaw's book), developed a Web site linking ABC to the publisher and sponsored a fifteen-hour History Channel series for cable based on the book. While some critics frowned at network anchors using network time to promote their own books, Thomas Rosenstiel, former *Los Angeles Times* media critic and director of the Project for Excellence in Journalism, disagreed: "If you're able to communicate things of substance to people and that dribbles into *Dateline* instead of the newest celebrity book on one-liners or 'How I Got to Be a Sitcom Star,' then I think the culture is better off."[21]

Even before the development of her book club, Oprah Winfrey's afternoon talk show had become a major power broker in selling books. In 1993, for example, Holocaust survivor and Nobel Prize recipient Elie Wiesel appeared on *Oprah*. Afterward, his 1960 memoir, *Night*, which came out as a Bantam paperback in 1982, returned to the best-seller lists. In 1996, novelist Toni Morrison's nineteen-year-old book *Song of Solomon* became a paperback best-seller after Morrison appeared on *Oprah*. In 1998, Winfrey, as actor and producer, brought another of Morrison's novels—the Pulitzer Prize–winning *Beloved*—to movie screens. The film version inspired new interest in the book, putting *Beloved* on the best-seller lists.

Television and film continue to get many of their story ideas from books. Michael Crichton's *Jurassic Park* and Michael Ondaatje's *The English Patient* became blockbuster movies. *A Civil Action*, Jonathan Harr's critically acclaimed 1996 account of the true story of a lawyer who fought two industrial corporations for poisoning the drinking water of families in Woburn, Massachusetts, inspired the 1999 film of the same name, starring John Travolta. Even nineteenth-century novels still translate to the screen. For example, the popular 1994 film version of *Little Women*, written in 1868 by Louisa May Alcott, sent the Random House reissue of the novel to the top of the juvenile best-seller list. In another example from the juvenile book business, the summer of 1995 featured eight of Scholastic's *Goosebumps* books among the Top 10 best-sellers for young readers. Scholastic, the leading publisher of educational magazines, then cut a deal with Fox to produce a TV series based on the books. By 1996, the series had become the most popular children's show on television. Even in children's literature, inspiration for books can come from television, too. For example, in 1998 Scholastic transformed *Teletubbies*, the popular British-import children's television program, into the latest top-selling children's book series.

▮blockbusters and licenses

Since Harriet Beecher Stowe's abolitionist novel, *Uncle Tom's Cabin*, sold fifteen thousand copies in fifteen days back in 1852 (and three million total copies prior to the Civil War), many American publishers have stalked the best-seller. As in the movie business, large publishers are always searching for the blockbuster. To ensure popular success, publishers often pay rights to license popular film and television programs, especially in the juvenile book trade. Books developed from licenses now account for 5 percent of trade industry sales. For instance, the Disney company's resurgence in animated films since the 1980s generated a wave of successful book titles based on its movies. In addition, the popularity of the syndicated TV series *Mighty Morphin Power Rangers* in the 1990s produced millions of dollars in book reincarnations. Despite phenomena such as *Goosebumps*, many critics and publishers believe that it is no longer possible for a book to become popular without television and film support. Consequently, major publishers are often hesitant to develop popular books or series that do not come with a built-in TV or movie audience.

The drive to create blockbusters in the book industry also led to a number of overpriced book advances to media figures without much writing talent. Although Tim Allen, Ellen DeGeneres, and Jerry Seinfeld had best-selling books, readers apparently do not find the written work of all comedians to be compelling reading. Whoopi Goldberg received a whopping $6 million advance for a book that sold poorly, while Paul Reiser nearly matched that with $5.6 million for an underperforming second book. Jay Leno's publisher took a beating after Leno's $4 million advance resulted in 400,000 returned unsold copies of his book. The O.J. Simpson trial created the biggest bidding frenzy as publishers tried to find books with juicy insider information but ended up with duds like Paula Barbieri's memoir of boyfriend O.J., a book that failed to recoup its $3 million advance.

talking books

Another major development in publishing has been the merger of sound recording with publishing. Audio books, or *books on tape*, generally feature actors or authors reading abridged versions of popular fiction and nonfiction trade books. Indispensable to many sightless readers and older readers whose vision has weakened, talking books are also popular among regular readers who do a lot of commuter driving. A study in 1993 by the Audio Publishers Association reported that nearly 50 percent of all audiobook use took place in cars. Among 1999's audio best-sellers were Tom Wolfe's *A Man in Full* (read by actor David Ogden Stiers) and Fannie Flagg's *Welcome to the World, Baby Girl* (read by the author) in fiction, and Suze Orman's *9 Steps to Financial Freedom* (read by the author) and A. Scott Berg's *Lindbergh* (read by actor Eric Stolz) in nonfiction. Classics such as Charles Dickens's *A Christmas Carol* have also done well in audio form. The number of books on tape borrowed from libraries soared in the 1990s, and small bookstore chains such as Talking Book World, Earful of Books, and Bookears developed to cater to the audio-book niche. Audio books also began to be released on CDs in the late 1990s, as compact-disk players became more commonplace in automobile sound systems.

book preservation

Another recent trend in the book industry involves the preservation of older books, especially those from the nineteenth century printed on acid-based paper. Ever since the conversion to machine-made publishing materials during the Industrial Revolution, paper had been produced using chemicals that gradually deteriorate over time. At the turn of the century, research provided evidence that acid-based paper would eventually turn brittle and self-destruct. This research, which had been initiated by libraries concerned with losing valuable older collections, was confirmed by further studies in the 1940s and 1950s. The paper industry, however, did not respond. In the 1970s, leading libraries began developing techniques to de-acidify book pages in an attempt to halt any further deterioration (although this process could not restore books to their original state). Meanwhile, more and more books were removed from circulation and were

Charles Frazier's debut novel, *Cold Mountain*, was buoyed by excellent reviews and word-of-mouth from independent bookstores before landing on the best-seller list for much of 1997 and 1998. Set during the Civil War, *Cold Mountain* won a 1997 National Book Award and became a runaway success for a medium-size U.S. publishing house.

available to the public only on microfilm and microfiche, which were difficult to read.

Despite evidence that alkaline-based paper was easier on machinery, produced a whiter paper, and caused less pollution, the paper industry did not change. By the early 1990s, motivated almost entirely by economics rather than by the cultural value of books, the industry finally began producing paper that was acid-free. Libraries and book conservationists, however, still had to focus attention on older, at-risk books. While clumsy, hard-to-read microfilm remained an option, some institutions began photocopying original books onto acid-free paper to make copies available to the public. Libraries then stored the originals, which had been treated to halt further wear.

More recently, pioneering projects in digital technology by Xerox and Cornell University have produced electronic copies of books through computer scanning. This process allows a computer to safely "read" a book that is deteriorating and reproduce it in a digitized version. Once transferred to a digital format, the book can be reproduced at any time and stored on a CD-ROM or other digital formats.

alternative voices

Even though the book industry is increasingly dominated by large book conglomerates, smaller publishers and specialty publishing houses can still thrive. For example, the winner of a 1997 National Book Award was Charles Frazier's *Cold Mountain*, a million-volume seller for Atlantic Monthly Press, a medium-size independent publishing house. Frazier's book edged out other, more heavily promoted books from huge publishing houses like Simon & Schuster. Independents are also finding success in such subject areas as women's issues, spirituality, self-help, alternative healing, and ecology—topics not well served by larger publishing houses.

books and the future of democracy

As we tentatively enter the digital age, the book-reading habits of children and adults are a social concern. After all, books have played an important role not only in spreading the idea of democracy but in connecting us to new ideas beyond our local experience. In surveys taken in the 1990s, however, only about 27 percent of middle-school students indicated that they read for pleasure each day (although they reported watching about three hours of television per day). Adults also reported sporadic reading habits. For instance, only about 50 percent of U.S. adults said that they read at least one book a year. Likewise, 40 percent of young adults between ages nineteen and twenty-one reported that they did not read books. Yet studies also suggest that reading habits are generally more evident among the young than among older people; 60 percent of all avid or regular book readers, for example, are under the age of forty. Overall, the share of regular book readers in the population is about 25 percent, a figure that has remained steady since the 1930s.

Although our society is being dramatically influenced by electronic and digital culture, the impact of our oldest mass medium—the book—remains immense. Without the development of printing presses and books, the idea of democracy would be hard to imagine. From the impact of Stowe's *Uncle Tom's Cabin*, which helped end slavery in the 1860s, to Rachel Carson's *Silent Spring*, which led to reforms in the pesticide industry in the 1960s, books have made a difference. They have told us things that we wanted—and needed—to know.

Over time, the wide circulation of books gave many ordinary people the same opportunities to learn that were once available to only a privileged few. However, as societies discovered the power associated with knowledge and the printed word, books were subjected to a variety of censors (see "Examining Ethics: Censorship Issues in Book Publishing" on page 338). Imposed by various rulers and groups intent on maintaining their authority, the censorship of books often prevented people from learning about the rituals and moral standards of other cultures. Political censors sought to banish "dangerous" books that promoted radical ideas or challenged conventional authority. Some versions of the Bible, Karl Marx's *Das Kapital* (1867), *The Autobiography of Malcolm X* (1965), and Salman Rushdie's *Satanic Verses* (1989) have all been banned at one time or another. In fact, one of the triumphs of the Internet is that it allows the digital passage of banned books into nations where printed versions have been outlawed.

Beyond censorship issues, other concerns have surfaced regarding the limits that democratic societies place on books. For example, the economic clout of publishing houses run by large multinational corporations has made it more difficult for new authors and new ideas to gain a foothold in commercial publishing. Often, editors and executives prefer to invest in commercially successful writers or authors who have a built-in television, sports, or movie audience.

> "Most **would-be censors** object to the obvious 's' words—sex, suicide, Satanism and swearing. The novels of J. D. Salinger and John Steinbeck, which deal with self-conscious teenagers and **the rough edge of life**, respectively, are perennial targets."
> —Mary B. W. Taylor, *New York Times*, 1995

Another issue is whether the contemporary book industry, in its own way, has contributed to entertainment and information overload. For example, in his book *The Death of Literature*, Alvin Kernan argues that serious literary work has been increasingly overwhelmed by the triumph of consumerism. In other words, people accumulate craftily marketed celebrity biographies and popular fiction but seldom read serious work. Kernan's critique reflects the long-standing view that "superior" cultural taste is associated with reading literature. He contends that cultural standards have been undermined by marketing ploys that divert attention from serious books and toward mass-produced works that are more easily read.[22]

Since democracies generally depend on literate populations to sift through cultural products and arrive at informed decisions, the abundance of media products raises other important questions. Of particular concern is the apparent decline in juvenile reading levels as measured by standardized tests over the past few decades. Indeed, the increase in published book titles since the 1950s does not mean that we have become a more literate society. The adult illiteracy rate has remained fairly constant at about 10 percent over the years. And today children have multiple electronic and digital distractions and options competing for their leisure time.

Over the years, small communities and large nations have successfully kept certain books out of the hands of their citizens. In 1929, for instance, Edgar Rice Burroughs's *Tarzan* series was pulled from the Los Angeles public library system because Tarzan and Jane lived together but were not married. In 1989, the Ayatollah Khomeini of Iran not only banned Salman Rushdie's novel *Satanic Verses* for blaspheming the Islamic religion but also ordered Rushdie killed, forcing the author into hiding for several years. In 1998, censorship of a different kind revolved around *East and West*, a book critical of the Chinese government written by former Hong Kong governor Chris Patten. Chinese officials expressed deep opposition to the book, and the book's publisher, HarperCollins, was directed by parent company News Corp. and its chairman Rupert Murdoch to cancel

Banned in Boston, Boise, and Butte? A Selection of Controversial Books

The Scarlet Letter—Nathaniel Hawthorne
Leaves of Grass—Walt Whitman
The Adventures of Huckleberry Finn— Mark Twain
Tarzan—Edgar Rice Burroughs
Ulysses—James Joyce
Lady Chatterley's Lover—D. H. Lawrence
Tropic of Cancer—Henry Miller
As I Lay Dying—William Faulkner
Of Mice and Men—John Steinbeck
The Diary of a Young Girl—Anne Frank
The Catcher in the Rye—J. D. Salinger
Lolita—Vladimir Nabokov
Naked Lunch—William S. Burroughs
To Kill a Mockingbird—Harper Lee
I Know Why the Caged Bird Sings— Maya Angelou
Are You There God? It's Me, Margaret— Judy Blume
In the Night Kitchen—Maurice Sendak
The Color Purple—Alice Walker
The Satanic Verses—Salman Rushdie
Nappy Hair—Carolivia Herron

publication because the book threatened the corporate giant's considerable business interests in China.

Books have faced innumerable cultural and social challenges. Censorship campaigns have often attempted to remove certain books from libraries and classrooms. The American Library Association (ALA), which represents more than thirty thousand libraries nationwide, documents more than six hundred censorship attempts annually.[1]

One of the most celebrated censorship cases involved Walt Whitman's *Leaves of Grass*. The book became the center of a legal battle in the early 1880s and was eventually banned in Boston. Because of their provocative sexual themes and language, the full versions of D. H. Lawrence's *Lady Chatterley's Lover* (1928) and Henry Miller's *Tropic of Cancer* (1934) were banned in the United States until the early 1960s.

During the 1980s and 1990s, the books most frequently challenged in school libraries and curriculums have included either controversial language or sexual themes. In New York City in 1998, parents targeted the book *Nappy Hair*—a children's text written by an African American woman which celebrates kinky, nappy hair—as racially

insensitive. As a result, the teacher who chose the book for her classroom was transferred and a nationwide discussion in the media on the purpose of books in education was revived. Censorship campaigns—initiated by both liberal and conservative groups—have sometimes tried to "protect" preteens and teenagers from significant works of literature. Often these books use common street language or introduce adolescents to complex personal and social themes that some adults believe are inappropriate for young people.

Censorship campaigns have targeted everything from John Steinbeck's *Of Mice and Men* to Judy Blume's *Are You There God? It's Me, Margaret*. But the most censored book has been Mark Twain's *Adventures of Huckleberry Finn*, an 1884 classic that still sells tens of thousands of copies a year in paperback. The novel routinely uses the word *nigger* the way it was used in everyday language in nineteenth-century America. Most high-school teachers are taught how to handle the sensitive racial issues raised in the book. Occasionally, though, parent groups and some civil-rights organizations have argued that the frequent appearance of the offensive word gives the book racist overtones.

Yet books and reading have survived the challenge of visual and digital culture. Developments such as word processing, books on tape, children's pictorial literature, and online computer services have integrated aspects of print and electronic culture into our daily lives. Most of these new forms carry on the original legacy of books—transcending geographic borders to provide personal stories, world history, and general knowledge to all who can read.

Despite a commercial book industry that has increasingly developed its own star system of authors, approximately a thousand new publishers enter the business each year. Tensions persist, however, between businesspeople who publish books as a moneymaking enterprise and authors trying to write well and advance knowledge—or between authors who seek fame and fortune and editor-publishers interested in wisdom and the written word. Some argue that the industry balanced these conflicts better before corporate takeovers tipped the scales heavily toward profit motives. As our oldest media institution, the book industry bears the weight of these economic and cultural battles perhaps more than any other medium.

Given our increasing channels of specialized media, people are able to zero in on their own interests. Books, however, are one medium that takes us in other directions. Since the early days of the printing press, books have helped us to understand ideas and customs outside our own experiences. For democracy to work well, we must read. When we examine other cultures through books, we discover not only who we are and what we value but who others are and what our common ties might be.

REVIEW QUESTIONS

The History of Books from Papyrus to Paperbacks

1. What distinguishes the manuscript culture of the Middle Ages from both the oral and print eras in communication?

2. Why was the printing press such an important and revolutionary invention?

3. Why were books considered so dangerous to colonial rulers and other leaders during the early periods of American history?

Modern Publishing and the Book Industry

4. Why did publishing houses develop?

5. Why have instant books become important to the paperback market?

6. What are the major issues that affect textbook publishing?

7. Why have religious books been so successful historically?

8. What has hampered the sales of subscription reference encyclopedias?

The Organization and Ownership of the Book Industry

9. What are the general divisions of a typical publishing house?

10. Why have book clubs and mail-order strategies continued to flourish despite the rapid growth of mall stores and superstores?

11. Why have book superstores been so successful over the past few years?

12. What are the strengths of the emerging online bookstore industry?

13. What are the current ownership patterns in the book industry? How have these trends affected independent stores?

Trends in Book Publishing

14. What role has licensing played in the trade-book industry over the past few years?

15. Why did paper manufacturers convert to acid-free paper in the late 1980s and early 1990s?

Books and the Future of Democracy

16. What have book publishers and sellers done to keep pace with changes in technology and society?

17. What have been the major contributions of books to democratic life?

QUESTIONING THE MEDIA

1. What are your earliest recollections of books? Do you read for pleasure? If yes, what kind of books do you enjoy? Why?

2. What can the book industry do better to ensure that we are not overwhelmed by a visual and electronic culture?

3. If you were opening an independent bookstore in a town with a chain, such as a Borders or Barnes & Noble, how would you compete?

4. If you were running a college bookstore, what would you do differently from your local store to improve relations with students?

5. Imagine that you are on a committee that oversees book choices for a high-school library in your town. What policies do you think should guide the committee's selection of controversial books?

6. Why do you think television and cable haven't substantially decreased the number of new book titles available each year? What do books offer that television doesn't? Will cable television and specialized computer technology eventually displace books? Why or why not?

SEARCHING THE INTERNET

http://www.bookwire.com/pw/pw.html
The online version of *Publishers Weekly*, the book industry's trade magazine.

http://www.publishers.org/2.htm
Home site for the Association of American Publishers, the principal trade association of the book-publishing industry.

http://www.gutenberg.net
Founded in 1971, Project Gutenberg is a nonprofit database that makes hundreds of public-domain literature (from Jane Austen to Tolstoy) available to Internet users for free.

http://www.bookbuzz.com
A Web site for lovers of books and people interested in the publishing industry, bookselling, book marketing, and book publicity.

http://www.amazon.com
Established in 1995, the online bookseller claims to be the world's largest bookstore. Competing online bookstores include Bn.com (Barnes & Noble) and Borders.com.

http://www.nytimes.com/books/home
This Web site features the *New York Times*'s book reviews, best-seller lists, first chapters, art news, and book forums. (It's a free site, but registration is required.)

http://www.ala.org/bbooks
Part of the American Library Association's Web site, this page provides information about censorship and banned books.

In Brief

This "think-pair-share" exercise focuses on the publishing and sales of college and university textbooks.

Think: On your own, spend two to three minutes writing down:

- how much money you spent this semester on textbooks

- which books cost the most money

- if you returned any books last semester, how much money you got back

- what choices are available at your university or college for purchasing textbooks

Pair: Turn to your neighbor and discuss your observations for a few minutes and consider these questions: Which types of books seem to be most expensive? Why do you think these books cost so much? What do you typically do with textbooks at the end of a semester—keep them or sell them back—and why? Who do you think is responsible for pricing the books? Who do you think reaps the most profit from textbook sales? Do you buy books that are supplemental or aren't required?

Share: As a class, consider the college-textbook publishing business. Who in the class spent the most money? If a book is more expensive, are you more or less likely to buy it? Should professors tie lectures closely to the texts, or should the required reading be done independently by the student? If you didn't spend your money on textbooks, what do you think you would do with the money? What are some of the factors in the production and distribution of textbooks that account for their cost? Are there media that might deliver the same information as a textbook, but at a lower cost?

In Depth

In groups of just a few students, investigate a small independent publisher or bookseller in your area. In addition to answering questions, a local company might allow you to observe the publishing or selling process. In your investigation, try to address the following questions:

1. What kinds of books does the firm specialize in? Profile a typical reader.

2. How does the firm identify writers and/or get a book to the customer? List the steps the firm goes through.

3. What kinds of commercial obstacles does this independent firm face?

4. According to the people who own or work at the firm, what are the major problems facing the publishing industry?

5. What strategies does the firm use in marketing or selling a book? Do the large corporate houses or chains impede this process? If so, in what ways?

6. According to the people at this firm, how easy or difficult is it to enter the industry? Are student internships a possibility at this firm or at other independent houses or sellers?

Add other questions and information as you go along.

Depending on the time allotted by your group and by the instructor, meet to discuss your findings. As a group, prepare a chart or provide information on the firm you investigated so that your findings can be shared with the rest of the class.

Advertising
and Commercial Culture

In his recent novel *Infinite Jest*, David Foster Wallace writes of a time in the not-so-distant future when entire calendar years will be sponsored by corporations. So a letter dated 17 November Y.D.A.U. means it was written in the Year of the Depend Adult Undergarment. Subsequent twelve-month periods are renamed the Year of Dairy Products from the American Heartland, the Year of the Trial-Size Dove Bar, the Year of the Whopper, and the Year of the Tucks Medicated Pad.

Wallace's jesting is not far from today's reality. College-football bowl games are rarely named after regional flowers and agricultural goods these days. Instead, we have the Nokia Sugar Bowl, the FedEx Orange Bowl, the Tostitos Fiesta Bowl, the Micron PC Bowl, the Insight.com Bowl, and the Chick-fil-A Peach Bowl, among others. The sites for sporting events, too, are largely past the days when they would be named for an esteemed coach or player, or the host city. Instead, naming goes to the highest bidder. Today, major-league baseball and NBA games can be found in places like Coors Field, the United Center, the Bank One Ballpark, the Fleet Center, and Qualcomm Stadium.

The trend is catching on at colleges and universities, too. Syracuse has the Carrier Dome, Louisville has the Papa John's Cardinal Stadium, and Ohio State has the Value City Arena (with an athletics hall of fame sponsored by Kroger grocery stores and a special Huntington Bank club for luxury box-seat holders). College

343

athletes are billboards for products as well, with the ubiquitous Nike swoosh logo on the uniforms of nearly every NCAA Division I sports powerhouse. The commercial battle for students' eyes and minds even extends to secondary and elementary schools, particularly as Coke and Pepsi sign exclusive agreements with school districts that allow the beverage companies to cover schools with vending machines and advertisements.

Some people wonder if the commercialization of everyday life has gone too far. At the Barcelona Olympics in 1992, some pro basketball team members for the gold-winning U.S. Dream Team who had private endorsement contracts with Nike refused to publicly wear the logo of Reebok, the U.S. Olympic Committee's own corporate sponsor for the Games. In 1998, a high-school student in Georgia was suspended not for violent behavior or drug use but for wearing a Pepsi shirt on his school's official "Coke Day."

You could try to get away from all of the sponsorships, but a trip to Ocean City, Maryland, would only get you a Coke, which has been the official beverage of Ocean City since 1997. (No word yet on what happens to Ocean City residents wearing Pepsi shirts.) Or, you could really try to get away from it all—like taking a trip to one of Club Med's international resorts. But you'd still be drinking beverages from Coca-Cola, which signed a five-year exclusive worldwide partnership with the tropical vacation company.

Yet the relationship with advertising and its symbols around the world is more complicated than sponsorship agreements and corporate sellouts. Millions of people happily purchase and don clothing decorated with Nike swooshes, soft-drink logos, NFL-sports team symbols, college and university names, Disney characters, or the clothing's designer name. Others delight in a McDonald's jingle or Budweiser's talking frogs, admire the daring design of Calvin Klein print ads, and feel comforted by the homespun familiarity of Saturn's commercials. Advertising can be an annoying, even oppressive, invasion into our lives, but it is also a seemingly natural and indelible part of our popular culture.

"You can tell the ideals of a nation by its advertisements."
—Norman Douglas, *South Wind*, 1917

Today, ads are scattered everywhere—and they are multiplying. Chameleon-like, advertising adapts to many media forms. At local theaters, advertisements now precede the latest Hollywood movies. Corporate sponsors spend millions for *product placement:* buying spaces for their particular goods to appear on a TV or movie set or in the background as supporting props. Ads are also part of every deejay's morning patter, and they routinely interrupt our favorite television and cable programs. By 1996, network television carried more than six thousand ads each week, double the count from the early 1980s. During the 1996 summer Olympics in Atlanta, NBC devoted 170 hours to covering events and 26 hours to airing advertisements. During the 1999 Super Bowl, the Fox network sold 58 minutes of ad time at an average of $1.6 million for each 30-second spot, generating about $93 million in revenue in just one football game.

Ads take up more than half the space in most daily newspapers and consumer magazines. They are inserted into trade books and textbooks. They clutter Web sites on the Internet. They fill our mailboxes and wallpaper our buses. Dotting the nation's landscape, billboards promote fast-food and hotel chains, while neon signs announce the names of stores along major streets and strip malls. In 1999, the Food Marketing Institute reported that the typical supermarket's shelves are filled with 30,000 to 50,000 different brand-name packages, each functioning like miniature billboards. Most recently, consumers have been able to order products displayed on cable home-shopping networks and on the World Wide Web twenty-four hours a day. In sum, each day American consumers come into contact with thousands of different kinds of advertising urging him or her to purchase something.

Advertising comes in many forms, everything from classified ads to business-to-business ads that provide detailed information on specific products. In this chapter, however, we will concentrate on the more conspicuous advertisements that shape product images and brand-name identities. Because so much consumer advertising intrudes into daily life, ads are often viewed in a negative light. Although business managers agree that advertising is the foundation of a healthy media economy—far preferable to government-controlled media—citizens routinely complain about how many ads they are forced to endure. Accordingly, the national cynicism about advertising has forced advertisers to become more competitive. And ad agencies, in turn, create ads that not only seem natural but also stand out in some way. To get noticed, ads routinely employ celebrities, humor, computer animation, and music-video devices. Ad agencies, in fact, often develop ads that are superior in their execution to the print or electronic content they interrupt.

Given the public's increasing sophistication regarding visual culture, companies have to work especially hard to get our attention. The ad industry's annual CLIO awards recognize the best TV commercials as forms of contemporary art. But consumers have found a variety of ways to dodge ads they dislike: remote controls, mute buttons, and VCRs programmed to erase advertising that runs longer than thirty seconds. Advertisers try to counter the new technology with computer tricks and technological wizardry of their own, such as creating a talking Chihuahua to promote a Mexican fast-food chain. To ensure that we pay attention, advertisers also spend enormous sums to associate their products with celebrities. For example, in 1998, his second full year as a golf professional, twenty-two-year-old Tiger Woods was the leading golf spokesperson, providing endorsements for American Express, Asahi Cobra, Electronic Arts, *Golf Digest*, Nike, All Star Cafe, Rolex, Titleist, Wheaties® and Sports line. The king of celebrity endorsers, though, is Michael Jordan, who continued to earn more than $45 million annually from various product endorsements even when he retired from professional basketball in 1999.

The cultural and social impact of advertising has been extensive. By the early 1900s, advertising had helped to transform American society from agrarian, small-town customs to urban, consumer-driven lifestyles. The same kind of social transformations occurred with the fall of the communist governments in Europe in the 1980s and 1990s. When Poland escaped Soviet influence in the late 1980s, TV ads and billboards proliferated—announcing Poland's leap into a market-driven economy. For generations, advertisers have informed society about "new and improved" products, both satisfying consumers' desires and creating needs we never knew we had. Advertising has enabled many of us to have a wide choice among consumer products, even though we may have little input into what those products are. Advertising, finally, has taught us to imagine ourselves as consumers before thinking of ourselves as citizens.

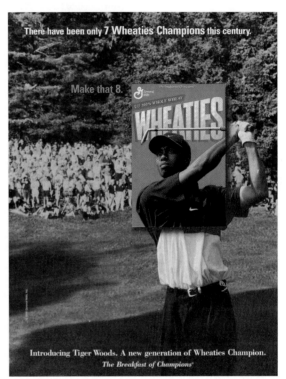

Golf phenom Tiger Woods is a champion on the golf course and on Madison Avenue. Multimillion-dollar endorsement deals with such products as Wheaties®, Nike, and American Express keep Tiger's image routinely on television and in magazines. Advertisers count on his ability to appeal to young consumers and to symbolize global diversity.

Without consumer advertisements, mass-communication industries would cease to function in their present forms. Ads are the economic glue that holds the media together. Yet, despite advertising's importance to the economy, many of us remain skeptical about its impact on American life. In this chapter, we will examine the historical development and role of advertising—an industry that helped transform a number of nations into consumer societies. We will look at the first U.S. ad agencies, early advertisements, and the emergence of packaging, trademarks, and brand-name recognition. Then, we will consider the growth of advertising in the twentieth century, scrutinizing the increasing influence of ad agencies and the shift to a more visually oriented culture. In keeping with our goal of developing critical skills, we will outline the key persuasive techniques used in consumer advertising. In addition, we will investigate ads as a form of commercial speech and discuss the measures aimed at regulating advertising. Finally, we will look at political advertising and its impact on democracy.

early developments in american advertising

Advertising has existed since 3000 B.C., when shop owners in ancient Babylon first began hanging outdoor signs carved in stone and wood so that customers could spot their stores. Merchants in early Egyptian society hired town criers to walk through the streets, announcing the arrival of ships and listing the goods on board. When archaeologists were searching for Pompeii, the ancient Italian city destroyed when Mount Vesuvius erupted in 79 A.D., they turned up advertising messages painted on walls. By 900 A.D., many European cities featured town criers who not only called out the news of the day but directed customers to various stores.

"In a mobile society, commercial products with familiar [brand] names provide people with some **sense of identity** and continuity in their lives."
—Michael Schudson,
Advertising, the Uneasy Persuasion,
1984

The earliest media ads were in the form of handbills, posters, and *broadsides* (long newsprint-quality posters). English booksellers printed brochures and bills announcing new books as early as the 1470s, when posters advertising religious books were tacked on church doors. In 1622, print ads imitating the oral style of criers began appearing in the first English newspapers. Announcing land deals and ship cargoes, the first newspaper advertisements in colonial America ran in the *Boston News-Letter* in 1704.

To distinguish themselves from the commercialism of newspapers, early magazines refused to carry advertisements. By the mid-1800s, though, most magazines contained ads and most publishers started magazines hoping to earn advertising dollars. About 80 percent of early advertisements covered three subjects: land sales, transportation announcements (stagecoach and ship schedules), and runaways (ads placed by farm and plantation owners whose slaves had fled). Other ads told about goods available from merchants or described new books for sale at local print shops.[1]

the first advertising agencies

Until the 1830s, little need existed for elaborate advertising. Prior to the full impact of manufacturing plants and the Industrial Revolution, few goods and products were even available for sale. Demand was also low, since 90 percent of Americans lived in isolated areas and produced most of their own tools, clothes, and food. The minimal advertising that did exist usually featured local merchants selling goods and services in their own communities. National advertising, which initially focused on patent medicines, didn't start in earnest until the 1850s. At that point, railroads first linked towns from the East Coast to the Mississippi River and began carrying newspapers, handbills, and broadsides—as well as national consumer goods—across the country.

The first American advertising agencies were really newspaper space brokers, individuals who purchased space in newspapers and sold it to various merchants. Newspapers, accustomed to a 25 percent nonpayment rate from advertisers, welcomed the space brokers, who paid up front. In return, brokers usually received discounts of 15 to 30 percent and would sell the space to advertisers at the going rate. The discounts from the newspapers represented a broker's profit. In 1841, Volney Palmer opened the first ad agency in Boston; he had been retained by newspaper publishers to sell space to advertisers for a 25 percent commission.

advertising in the 1800s

The first so-called modern ad agency, N. W. Ayer, worked primarily for advertisers and product companies rather than for publishers. Opening in 1875 in Philadelphia, the agency helped to create, write, produce, and place ads in selected newspapers and magazines. To this day, under a payment structure that began in the nineteenth century, the typical agency collects a fee from its advertising client, keeps 15 percent of this fee for itself, and passes the rest on to the appropriate mass media. The more ads an agency places, the larger the agency's revenue. Thus agencies have little incentive to buy fewer ads on behalf of their clients. Since the beginning of space brokerage in the 1840s, few have seriously challenged this odd relationship, which drives up costs, adds clutter to the media landscape, and does not always represent the best interests of the client.

Trademarks and Packaging. Some historians contend that the Industrial Revolution generated so many new products that national advertising was necessary to sell these goods quickly and keep factories humming. Now, though, other historians point to a more fundamental reason for advertising's development on a national scale: "the need to get control of the price the manufacturer charged for his goods."[2] During the mid-1800s, most manufacturers served retail-store owners, who usually set their own prices by purchasing goods in large quantities. Over time, however, manufacturers came to realize that if their products were distinctive and became associated with quality, customers would ask for them by name; manufacturers would then be able to dictate prices without worrying about being undersold by generic products or bulk items. To achieve this end, manufacturers began to use advertising, establishing the special identity of their products and separating themselves from competitors. Like many ads today, nineteenth-century advertisements for patent medicines and cereals often created the impression of significant differences among products when very few actually existed. But when consumers began demanding certain products—either because of quality or because of advertising—manufacturers seized control of pricing. With ads creating and maintaining brand-name recognition, retail stores had to stock the desired brands.

One of the first brand names, Smith Brothers, has been advertising cough drops since the early 1850s. Quaker Oats, the

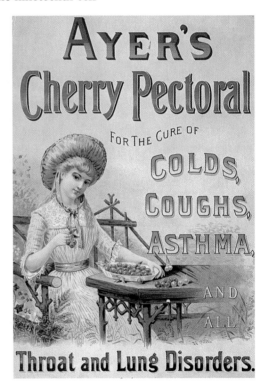

Unregulated patent medicines represented a bonanza for nineteenth-century print media in search of advertising revenue. The problem was, most of these medicines were full of alcohol and other addictive drugs. This innocent-looking ad for Ayer's Cherry Pectoral did not mention that the product's active ingredient was heroin. After a vigorous reporting campaign against patent medicines by magazines like *Ladies' Home Journal,* Congress created the Federal Drug Administration in 1906.

first cereal company to register a trademark, has used William Penn, a Quaker who founded Pennsylvania in 1681, to project a company image of honesty, decency, and hard work since 1877. The Campbell Soup brand came along in 1869, followed by Levi Strauss overalls in 1873, Ivory Soap in 1879, Chase & Sanborn coffee in 1886, and Eastman Kodak film in 1888. Many of these companies packaged their products in small quantities, thus distinguishing them from the generic products sold in large barrels and bins (not unlike the generic products sold in bulk in many stores today).

Packaging also allowed manufacturers to add preservatives and to claim less contamination and more freshness than might be found in loose food barrels at the local general store. Quaker Oats developed the *folding carton*, which could be printed with color displays and recipes before it was filled with cereal. This marketing strategy represented "the beginning of the end of selling cereal to retailers in bulk."[3] Product differentiation associated with brand-name packaged goods represents the single biggest triumph of advertising. Studies suggest that although most ads are not very effective in the short run, over a period of time they create demand by leading consumers to associate particular brands with quality.

Not surprisingly, building or sustaining brand-name recognition is the focus of many product-marketing campaigns. But the costs that packaging and advertising add to products generate many consumer complaints. The high price of many contemporary products results from advertising costs. For example, designer jeans that cost $40 or $50 (or more) today are made from the same inexpensive denim that has outfitted farmworkers since the 1800s. The difference now is that more than 90 percent of the jeans' costs go toward advertising and profit. For years, critics have decried both the price markups by clothing retailers and the overpackaging that creates environmental problems.

Other product lines tell a similar story. For example, in the early 1990s, the grain in a $4 box of Frosted Mini-Wheats or Cinnamon Toast Crunch cost the manufacturer only a few cents; packaging added another sixty to seventy-five cents; and the remaining costs went to advertising and profit margins. A dramatic rise in cereal prices in 1995, in fact, led to a congressional investigation, and manufacturers such as Kellogg's and General Mills reduced prices to fend off consumer criticism. Meanwhile, generic cereals and less expensive store brands benefited; without the added cost of advertising, these "unknown" cereals have usually sold for half the price of brand-name items.

Patent Medicines and Department Stores. By the end of the 1800s, patent medicines and department stores dominated advertising copy, accounting for half of the revenues taken in by ad agencies. During this period, one-sixth of all print ads came from patent-medicine and drug companies. Such ads ensured the financial survival of numerous magazines, as "the role of the publisher changed from being a seller of a product to consumers to being a gatherer of consumers for the advertisers."[4] Bearing names like Lydia Pinkham's Vegetable Compound, Dr. Lin's Chinese Blood Pills, and William Radam's Microbe Killer, patent medicines were often made with water and 15 to 40 percent concentrations of ethyl alcohol. One patent medicine—Mrs. Winslow's Soothing Syrup—actually contained morphine. The alcohol and other powerful drugs in these medicines went a long way toward explaining why people felt "better" after taking them; at the same time, they triggered lifelong addiction problems for many customers.

Many contemporary products, in fact, originated as medicines. Coca-Cola, for instance, was initially sold as a

> "The department store did less to provide quality in consumption than to encourage a democracy of aspirations and desires. They contributed to the democratization of envy."
>
> —Michael Schudson, *Advertising, the Uneasy Persuasion,* 1984

medicinal tonic and even contained traces of cocaine until 1903, when that drug was replaced by caffeine. A Methodist congregation developed Welch's Grape Juice as a substitute for wine. Early Post and Kellogg's cereal ads promised to cure stomach and digestive problems. Many patent medicines made outrageous claims about what they could cure, leading ultimately to increasing public cynicism. As a result, advertisers began to police their ranks and develop industry codes to repair customer confidence. Partly to monitor patent-medicine claims, the Food and Drug Act was passed in 1906.

Along with patent medicines, department-store ads were also becoming prominent in newspapers and magazines. By the early 1890s, more than 20 percent of ad space was devoted to department stores and the product lines they carried. At the time, these stores were frequently reviled for undermining small shops and businesses, which depended on shopkeepers to direct people to store items. The more impersonal department stores allowed shoppers to browse and find brand-name goods themselves. Because these stores purchased merchandise in large quantities, they could generally sell the same products for less. With increased volume and less money spent on individualized service, department-store chains, like Kmart and Wal-Mart today, undercut small local stores and put more of their profits into advertising.

With the advent of the Industrial Revolution, "continuous-process machinery" kept company factories operating at peak efficiency, helping to produce an abundance of inexpensive packaged consumer goods.[5] The companies that produced those goods were some of the first to advertise, and they remain major advertisers today (although many of these brand names have been absorbed by larger conglomerates). They include Procter & Gamble, Colgate-Palmolive, Heinz, Borden, Pillsbury, Eastman Kodak, Carnation, and American Tobacco (see Table 11.1). A few firms, such as Hershey's Chocolate, chose not to advertise initially yet still rose to national prominence

TABLE 11.1
The Top 20 National Advertisers

Rank	Advertiser	1997 Advertising Expenditures (in millions)
1	General Motors	$3,087.4
2	Procter & Gamble	2,743.2
3	Philip Morris	2,137.8
4	Chrysler	1,532.4
5	Ford Motor	1,281.8
6	Sears Roebuck & Co.	1,262.0
7	Walt Disney	1,249.7
8	PepsiCo	1,244.7
9	Diageo	1,206.6
10	McDonald's	1,041.7
11	Time Warner	1,013.2
12	IBM	924.9
13	Johnson & Johnson	920.2
14	Unilever	908.9
15	J. C. Penney	906.2
16	Bristol-Myers Squibb	885.2
17	Toyota Motor	851.9
18	Tricon Global Restaurants	851.2
19	AT&T	781.1
20	Sony	777.5

Source: *Advertising Age*, Ad Age Dataplace, <http://adage.com/dataplace/archives/dp268.html>, 5/1/99.

through word-of-mouth reputations. By the 1880s, however, the demand for newspaper advertising by product companies and retail stores had significantly changed the ratio of copy at most newspapers. Whereas in the mid-1880s papers featured 70 to 75 percent of news and editorial material and only 25 to 30 percent of advertisements, by the early 1900s more than half of the space in daily papers was devoted to advertising. This trend continues today, with about 60 percent of the space in large daily newspapers generally consumed by ads.

promoting social change and dictating values

As American advertising became more pervasive, it contributed to major social changes in the twentieth century. First, it significantly influenced the switch from a producer-directed to a consumer-driven society. By stimulating demand for new products, advertising helped manufacturers to create new markets and to recover product start-up costs more quickly. From farms to cities, advertising spread the word—first in newspapers and magazines and later on radio and television. Second, advertising promoted technological advances by showing how new machines, such as vacuum cleaners, washing machines, and cars, improved daily life. Third, advertising encouraged economic growth by increasing sales. To meet the demand generated by ads, manufacturers produced greater quantities, which reduced their costs per unit, although they did not always pass these savings along to consumers.

By the early 1900s, advertisers and ad agencies believed that women, who constituted 70 to 80 percent of newspaper and magazine readers, controlled most household purchasing decisions. (This is still a fundamental principle of advertising today.) Ironically, more than 99 percent of the copywriters and ad executives at this time were men, primarily from Chicago and New York. They emphasized stereotyped appeals to women, believing that simple ads with emotional and even irrational content worked best. Thus early ad copy featured personal tales of "heroic" cleaning products and household appliances. The intention was to help consumers feel good about defeating life's problems—an advertising strategy that endured for much of the twentieth century.

Although ad revenues fell during the 1930s, World War II marked a rejuvenation for advertising. For the first time, the federal government bought large quantities of advertising space to promote America's involvement in a war. These purchases helped offset a decline in traditional advertising, as many industries had turned their attention and production facilities to the war effort. Also during the 1940s, the industry began to actively deflect criticism that advertising created consumer needs that ordinary citizens never knew they had. To promote a more positive image,

TODAY, HER
ASTHMA
CAN BE AS
EASY AS...
BREATHING.

For 15 million people with asthma, breathing doesn't always come easy. An asthma attack begins with a tightening of the chest and difficulty inhaling, and can leave sufferers gasping for breath with the overwhelming feeling of suffocation. Severe attacks can require an emergency trip to the hospital. But in recent years, pharmaceutical company researchers have discovered and developed new breakthrough medicines that allow patients more effective control over their asthma—and even help prevent an attack before it happens. So, for the millions of people with asthma, an attack isn't as frightening as it used to be. Today, asthma is more controllable, but we won't rest until it's cured. Then we'll all breathe easier.

America's Pharmaceutical Companies

Leading the way in the search for cures

Most advertising companies devote some of their time to creating public-service announcements like this one, which informs consumers about asthma and the kind of research pharmaceutical companies are doing to curb its effects.

the industry developed the War Advertising Council—a voluntary group of agencies and advertisers that organized war-bond sales, blood-donor drives, and the rationing of scarce goods.

The postwar extension of advertising's voluntary efforts became known as the Ad Council, praised over the years for its Smokey the Bear campaign ("Only you can prevent forest fires"), its fund-raising campaign for the United Negro College Fund ("A mind is a terrible thing to waste"), and its "crash dummy" spots for the Department of Transportation, which substantially increased seat-belt use. Choosing a dozen worthy causes annually, the Ad Council continues to produce pro bono *public-service announcements* (PSAs) on a wide range of topics, including literacy, homelessness, drug addiction, antismoking, and AIDS education. Independently of the Ad Council, many agencies throughout the nation perform pro bono services in their communities.

After the Depression and World War II, television dramatically altered advertising. With this new visual medium, ads increasingly intruded on daily life. Criticism of advertising grew as the industry appeared to be dictating American values as well as driving the economy. Critics discovered that some agencies used **subliminal advertising**. This term, coined in the 1950s, refers to hidden or disguised print and visual messages that allegedly register on the unconscious and fool people into buying products. Only a few examples of subliminal ads actually exist (for example, a "Drink Coca-Cola" ad embedded into a few frames of a movie, or hidden sexual activity drawn into liquor ads), and research has suggested that such ads are no more effective than regular ads.

early ad regulation

During the early 1900s, the emerging clout of ad agencies and revelations of fraudulent advertising practices led to the formation of several watchdog organizations. Partly to keep tabs on deceptive advertising, in 1913 advocates in the business community created the nonprofit Better Business Bureau, which by the 1990s had more than two hundred branch offices in the United States, Canada, and Israel. At the same time, advertisers wanted a formal service that tracked newspaper readership, guaranteed accurate audience measures, and ensured that papers would not overcharge agencies and their clients. As a result, publishers formed the Audit Bureau of Circulation (ABC) in 1914. That same year, the government created the Federal Trade Commission (FTC), in part to help monitor advertising abuses. Thereafter, the industry urged self-regulatory measures in order to keep government interference at bay. The American Association of Advertising Agencies (AAAA), for example, established in 1917, tried to minimize government oversight by imploring ad agencies to refrain from making misleading product claims.

the shape of american advertising today

Most of the history of modern advertising has been influenced by the print media and the facility of copywriters, who create the words in advertisements. Until the 1960s, the shape and pitch of most U.S. ads were determined by a *slogan:* the phrase that attempts to sell a product by capturing its essence in words. With slogans such as Clairol's "Does she or doesn't she?" and "Only her hairdresser knows for sure," the visual dimension of ads was merely a complement. Eventually, however, through the influence of movies, television, and European design, images asserted themselves and visual style began to dictate printed substance in American advertising.

the influence of visual design

Just as a postmodern design phase developed in art and architecture during the 1960s and 1970s, an era of stunning image fragments began to affect advertising at the same time. Part of this visual revolution was imported from non-American schools of design; ad-rich magazines such as *Vogue* and *Vanity Fair* increasingly hired European designers as art directors. These directors tended to be less tied to America's word-driven radio advertising, since most European countries had government-sponsored radio systems with no ads.

By the early 1970s, agencies had developed teams of writers and artists: Images and words were granted equal status in the creative process. By the mid-1980s, the visual techniques of MTV, which initially modeled its videos on advertising, influenced many ads and most agencies. MTV promoted a particular visual aesthetic—rapid edits, creative camera angles, compressed narratives, and staged performances. Video-style ads soon saturated television and featured such prominent performers as Paula Abdul, Ray Charles, Michael Jackson, and Elton John. The popularity of MTV's visual style also started a trend in the 1980s to license hit songs for commercial tie-ins. Warner Music, for example, aggressively pitched its music catalogue for use by advertisers. By the 1990s, a wide range of short polished musical performances and familiar songs were routinely used in TV ads to encourage consumers not to click the remote control.

the mega-agency

During the twentieth century, large full-service advertising agencies emerged, and many of those early companies remain major players today (see Table 11.2). Although more than thirteen thousand ad agencies currently operate in the United States, the recent tendency is toward **mega-agencies**: large ad firms that are formed by merging several individual agencies that maintain worldwide regional offices. In addition to

TABLE 11.2
The World's Largest Advertising Agencies, 1998

Rank	Company	Headquarters	1998 Income (in $ millions)
1	Omnicom Group (includes BBDO, DDB Needham)	New York	$4,812.0
2	Interpublic Group (includes McCann-Erickson, Campbell-Ewald)	New York	4,304.5
3	WPP Group (includes J. Walter Thompson, Ogilvy & Mather)	London	4,156.8
4	Dentsu (includes DCA)	Tokyo	1,786.0
5	Young & Rubicam (owns Burson-Marsteller; has thirty-year partnership with Dentsu)	New York	1,659.9
6	Havas Advertising	Paris	1,297.9
7	True North Communications	Chicago	1,242.3
8	Grey Advertising	New York	1,240.4
9	Leo Burnett	Chicago	949.8
10	Publicis	New York	930.0
11	Snyder Communications	Bethesda, Md.	904.2
12	MacManus Group	New York	859.2

Source: Advertising Age, Ad Age Dataplace, <http://adage.com/dataplace/archives/dp318.html>, 5/1/99.

providing both advertising and public-relations services, many of these agencies operate their own in-house radio and TV production studios. In the early 1990s, the two largest agencies were British-based firms, the WPP Group and Saatchi & Saatchi. WPP, which had its beginnings as a British company named Wire & Plastic Products, grew quickly in the 1980s, with the 1987 purchase of J. Walter Thompson, the largest U.S. firm at the time, and Hill and Knowlton, one of the largest public-relations agencies, and the 1989 acquisition of Ogilvy & Mather Worldwide, another significant U.S. agency. WPP remains one of the world's largest communication/marketing groups, with more than twenty-two thousand employees in over eight hundred offices in ninety countries. WPP Group's top competitors, the New York–based Omnicom Group and the Interpublic Group, are also huge international holding companies, each with dozens of advertising and marketing firms operating around the globe.

The mega-agency trend has stirred debate among consumer and media watchdog groups. Some consider large agencies a threat to the independence of smaller firms, which are slowly being bought out. An additional concern is that a few firms now control the distribution of advertising dollars globally. As a result, the cultural values represented by American and European ads may undermine or overwhelm the values and products of developing countries, which are still trying to establish their own markets and economic systems.

the boutique agency

The visual revolutions in advertising during the 1960s elevated the standing of designers and graphic artists, who became closely identified with the look of particular ads. Breaking away from bigger agencies, many of these creative individuals formed small **boutique agencies** to devote their talents to a handful of select clients. Offering more personal services, the boutiques prospered, bolstered by innovative ad campaigns and increasing profits from TV accounts. By the 1980s, large agencies had bought up many of the boutiques. Nevertheless, they continued to operate as fairly independent subsidiaries within multinational corporate structures.

One boutique agency in Portland, Oregon, Weiden & Kennedy, made its name by winning the Nike sneaker account in the 1980s and developing the slogan "Just do it" (see "Examining Ethics: Fighting over Sneakers" on page 354). Like other boutique agencies at the time, the firm experimented with merging television imagery and popular music to appeal to the baby-boom generation. Weiden & Kennedy gained notoriety in 1987 with a Nike ad driven by the beat of the 1968 Beatles protest song "Revolution." Nike had bought permission to use the song from Michael Jackson, who owns the copyright to many early Beatles recordings. But Apple Records, the Beatles' old label, objected to commercializing the song and filed a $15 million lawsuit (which it later dropped). Weiden & Kennedy went on to develop the "Bo knows" campaign, using former pro-football and baseball star Bo Jackson; the Michael Jordan spots directed for Nike by Spike Lee; and a 1998 campaign of fourteen dialogue-free commercials that emphasized the comical extremes athletes take to train for competition (including the Denver Broncos' offensive line abruptly halting the running of the bulls in Spain), which won Adweek's Best Campaign of the Year award.

the structure of ad agencies

The nation's agencies, regardless of their size, generally divide the labor of creating and maintaining advertising campaigns among four departments: market research, creative development, media selection, and account services. A separate administrative unit, besides paying employee salaries, pays each media outlet that runs ads and col-

Fighting over Sneakers

During the 1950s and 1960s, most serious basketball players wore simple canvas sneakers—usually Converse or Keds. Encouraged by increasing TV coverage, interest in sports exploded in the late 1960s and 1970s, as did a wildly competitive international sneaker industry. First Adidas dominated the industry, then Nike and Reebok. The Great Sneaker Wars have since continued unabated, although they may have peaked at the 1992 Olympics when pro-basketball stars Michael Jordan and Charles Barkley—Nike endorsers—refused to display the Reebok logo on their team jackets at the awards ceremony. Reebok had paid dearly to sponsor the Olympics and wanted the athletes to fall in line. A compromise was eventually worked out in which the two players wore the jackets but hid the Reebok name.

Although the Olympic incident seems petty, battles over brand-name sneakers and jackets in the 1980s were a more dangerous "game." Advertisers found themselves embroiled in a controversy that, for a time, threw a bright and uncomfortable spotlight on the advertising industry. In many poor and urban areas throughout the United States, kids and rival gangs were fighting over and stealing brand-name sportswear from one another. Particularly coveted and targeted were $100-plus top-of-the-line basketball shoes, especially the Nike and Reebok brands heavily advertised on television. A few incidents resulted in shootings and killings. Articles in major newspapers and magazines, including *Sports Illustrated* ("Your Sneakers or Your Life") took advertisers to task. Especially hard hit was Nike, which by the early 1990s controlled nearly 30 percent of the $5.5 billion world sneaker market. Nike's slogan—"Just do it"—became a rallying cry for critics who argued that while for most middle-class people, the command simply meant get in shape, work hard, and perform, for kids from poorer neighborhoods, "Just do it" was a call to arms: "Do what you have to do to survive."

The problem was exacerbated during the 1980s by under-lying economic conditions. As the gap between rich and poor grew, advertisements suggested that our identity came from the products that we own. It is not surprising, then, that the possession of a particular brand-name product became increasingly significant for kids who felt they did not own much. Having the "right" sneaker or jacket came to represent a large part of their identity. For some groups and gangs, such possession became a requirement for membership.

The controversy over brand-name products has raised serious concerns about the moral responsibilities of agencies and advertisers. On one hand, Nike and other advertisers have become a lightning rod for the problems of a consumer culture that promises the good life to everyone who "just does it." On the other hand, criticisms of advertising have often stopped with the ads and have not examined whether they *cause* the violence or are simply *symptoms* of the inequities in contemporary America. Although many critics vilified Nike at the time, few were willing to discuss the drawbacks of capitalism and consumerism in general.

Fights over sneakers and jackets generate significant questions at the heart of our consumer culture. Does brand-name advertising unrealistically raise hopes about attaining the consumer "dreams" that some ads promise? Who should share the ultimate responsibility for violence that takes place in the name of a coveted shoe or jacket? As a society, should we mandate noncommercial messages and public-service announcements that offer alternative visions? While we need to debate these issues vigorously as individuals and as a society, in some communities kids and adults have already acted. Although brand-name products continue to sell well, an alternative attitude rejects such labeling and opts for cheaper generic products and used rummage-sale clothing. Posing a challenge to the advertising industry, this attitude undermines the view that brand-name identification is a requirement of our times.

lects an agency's fees. For instance, a series of full-page, color advertisements in a national magazine may cost an advertiser $100,000. After an agency creates and places the ads on behalf of its advertiser/client, the magazine bills the agency, whose administrative unit then collects the payment from the advertiser. The agency sends $85,000 to the magazine and pockets the standard 15 percent commission—$15,000. Expenses incurred for producing the ads are part of a separate negotiation between the agency and the advertiser. As a result of this commission arrangement, it generally costs most large-volume advertisers no more to use an agency than it does to use their own staff.

Market Research and VALS. Before an agency can pay bills or collect commissions, however, a great deal of planning and research takes place. Since computer technology now allows companies to gather intimate data about consumers, the **market research** department plays a significant role in any agency. This department assesses the behaviors and attitudes of consumers toward particular products long before any ads are created. It may study everything from possible names for a new product to the size of the copy for a print ad. Research is conducted not only on toothpastes and cereals but on books, television comedies, and Hollywood action films. In trying to predict customers' buying habits, researchers also test new ideas and products on groups of consumers to get feedback before developing final ad strategies. In addition, some researchers contract with outside polling firms, who are better equipped to conduct regional and national studies of consumer preferences.

As the economic stakes in advertising have grown, agencies have employed scientific methods to study consumer behavior. In 1932, Young & Rubicam first used statistical techniques developed by pollster George Gallup. By the 1980s, most large agencies retained psychologists and anthropologists to advise them on human nature and buying habits. The earliest type of market research, **demographics**, mainly documented an audience's age, gender, occupation, ethnicity, education, and income. Early demographic analyses provided advertisers with data on people's behavior and social status but revealed less about feelings and attitudes. Today, demographic data are much more specific. They allow advertisers to locate consumers in particular geographic regions—usually by zip code. This enables advertisers to target ethnic neighborhoods or affluent suburbs for direct mail, point-of-purchase store displays, or specialized magazines and newspaper inserts.

By the 1960s and 1970s, television had greatly increased advertising revenues, allowing agencies to expand their research activities. Advertisers and agencies began using **psychographics**, a research approach that attempts to categorize consumers by their attitudes, beliefs, interests, and motivations. Psychographic analysis often uses the **focus group**: a small-group interview technique in which a moderator leads a discussion about a product or an issue, usually with six to twelve people. Because focus groups are small and less scientific than most demographic research, the findings from such groups are often controversial. Many critics wonder whether focus groups can accurately predict future success in the larger marketplace.

In 1978, the Stanford Research Institute (SRI), now called SRI International, instituted its **Values and Lifestyles**, or **VALS** strategy, which divides consumers into types. Using questionnaires, VALS researchers parceled the public into clusters and measured psychological factors, including how consumers think and feel about products. VALS classified people according to three broad categories: inner-directed, outer-directed, and need-driven. Each of these groups also had several subclassifications, such as achievers, experiencers, societally conscious, belongers, and survivors. Many advertisers adopted VALS to help focus their sales pitch, trying to get the most appropriate target audience for their dollars. VALS research assumed that not every product suited every consumer, encouraging advertisers to vary their sales slants to find their specific market niches.

In the late 1980s, VALS 2 was launched; it not only classified people by values and lifestyles but also considered the ways consumers achieve (or do not achieve) the lifestyles to which they aspire (see Figure 11.1 on facing page). VALS 2 distinguished principle-oriented, status-oriented, and action-oriented consumer types. The principle-oriented group, for instance, includes *fulfilleds*—"mature, satisfied, comfortable, reflective people who value order, knowledge, and responsibility." These consumers apparently like products that are functional, fairly priced, and durable. Also in this group, *believers* have "modest but sufficient" income and education; they are generally considered "conservative, conventional people with concrete beliefs based on traditional, established codes." VALS and similar research techniques ultimately provide advertisers with microscopic details about which consumers are most likely to buy which products.

> "The best advertising artist of all time was Raphael. He had the best client—the papacy; the best art director—the College of Cardinals; and the best product—salvation. And we never disparage Raphael for working for a client or selling an idea."
>
> —Creative Director Mark Fenske,
> N. W. Ayer,
> 1996

Agencies and clients—particularly auto manufacturers—have relied heavily on VALS to determine the best placement for TV and magazine ads. VALS data suggest, for example, that *achievers* and *experiencers* watch more sports and news programs; these groups prefer luxury cars or sport-utility vehicles like the Jeep Grand Cherokee and the Ford Explorer. *Fulfilleds*, on the other hand, favor TV dramas and documentaries. In cars, they like the functionality of minivans or the gas efficiency of Hondas. VALS researchers do not claim that most people fit neatly into a category. But many agencies believe that VALS research can give them an edge in markets where few differences in quality may actually exist among top-selling brands, whether they are headache medicines or designer jeans. Consumer groups, wary of such research, argue that too many ads promote only an image and provide little information about a product's price, its content, or the work conditions under which it was produced.

Creative Development. The creative aspects of the advertising business—teams of writers and artists—make up its nerve center. Many of these individuals regard ads as a commercial art form. For print ads, the creative department outlines the rough sketches for newspaper, magazine, and direct-mail advertisements, developing the words and graphics. For radio, the creative side prepares a working script, generating ideas for everything from narration to sound effects. For television, the creative department develops a **storyboard**: a sort of blueprint or roughly drawn comic-strip version of the potential ad.

Just as tension has always existed between network executives and the creative people who develop TV programs, advertising has its own version of this battle. Often the creative side of the business (the copywriters who create jingles and the graphic artists who design the look of an ad) finds itself in conflict with the research side (the marketers who collect the consumer data to target an ad campaign). In most cases, however, both sides share the responsibility for successful or failed ad campaigns. In the 1960s, for example, both Doyle Dane Bernbach (now DDB Needham) and Ogilvy & Mather downplayed research; they championed the art of persuasion and what "felt right." Yet DDB's simple ads for Volkswagen Beetles in the 1960s were based on weeks of intensive interviews with VW workers as well as on creative instincts. The campaign was remarkably successful in establishing the first niche for a foreign-car manufacturer in the United States. Although sales of the VW "bug" had been growing before the ad campaign started, the successful ads helped Volkswagen preempt the Detroit auto industry's entry into the small-car field.

Figure 11.1
(facing page)
VALS 2 Types and Characteristics
Source: SRI International, 1999, <http://future.sri.com/vals/vals home.html>.

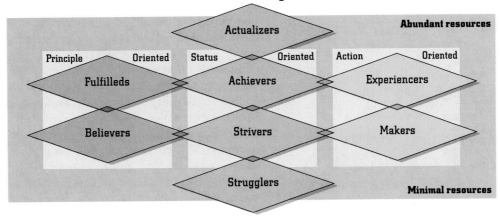

The VALS 2 Categories

VALS Types and Characteristics

Actualizers Actualizers are successful, sophisticated, active, "take-charge" people with high self-esteem and abundant resources. They are interested in growth and seek to develop, explore, and express themselves in a variety of ways—sometimes guided by principle, and sometimes by a desire to have an effect, to make a change.

Fulfilleds Fulfilleds are mature, satisfied, comfortable, reflective people who value order, knowledge, and responsibility. Most are well educated and in (or recently retired from) professional occupations. They are well informed about world and national events and are alert to opportunities to broaden their knowledge. Content with their career, families, and station in life, their leisure activities tend to center around the home.

Achievers Achievers are successful career and work-oriented people who like to—and generally do—feel in control of their lives. They value consensus, predictability, and stability over risk, intimacy, and self-discovery. They are deeply committed to work and family. Work provides them with a sense of duty, material rewards, and prestige. Their social lives reflect this focus and are structured around family, church, and career.

Experiencers Experiencers are young, vital, enthusiastic, impulsive, and rebellious. They seek variety and excitement, savoring the new, the offbeat, and the risky. Still in the process of formulating life values and patterns of behavior, they quickly become enthusiastic about new possibilities but are equally quick to cool. At this stage in their lives, they are politically uncommitted, uninformed, and highly ambivalent about what they believe.

Believers Believers are conservative, conventional people with concrete beliefs based on traditional, established codes: family, church, community, and the nation. Many Believers express moral codes that are deeply rooted and literally interpreted. They follow established routines, organized in large part around home, family, and social or religious organizations to which they belong.

Strivers Strivers seek motivation, self-definition, and approval from the world around them. They are striving to find a secure place in life. Unsure of themselves and low on economic, social, and psychological resources, Strivers are concerned about the opinions and approval of others.

Makers Makers are practical people who have constructive skills and value self-sufficiency. They live within a traditional context of family, practical work, and physical recreation and have little interest in what lies outside that context. Makers experience the world by working on it—building a house, raising children, fixing a car, or canning vegetables—and have enough skill, income, and energy to carry out their projects successfully.

Strugglers Struggler lives are constricted. Chronically poor, ill-educated, low-skilled, without strong social bonds, elderly, and concerned about their health, they are often resigned and passive. Because they are limited by the need to meet the urgent needs of the present moment, they do not show a strong self-orientation. Their chief concerns are for security and safety.

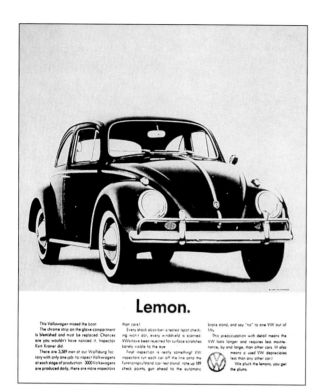

Lemon.

This Volkswagen missed the boat.
The chrome strip on the glove compartment is blemished and must be replaced. Chances are you wouldn't have noticed it. Inspector Kurt Kroner did.

There are 3,389 men at our Wolfsburg factory with only one job: to inspect Volkswagens at each stage of production. 3000 Volkswagens are produced daily; there are more inspectors than cars.)

Every shock absorber is tested (spot checking won't do!), every windshield is scanned. VWs have been rejected for surface scratches barely visible to the eye.

Final inspection is really something! VW inspectors run each car off the line onto the Funktionsprüfstand (car test stand), tote up 189 check points, gun ahead to the automatic brake stand, and say "no" to one VW out of fifty.

This preoccupation with detail means the VW lasts longer and requires less maintenance, by and large, than other cars. (It also means a used VW depreciates less than any other car.)

We pluck the lemons; you get the plums.

The 1960s initiated an era of "creative advertising," in which campaigns combined a single-point sales emphasis with bold layouts, humor, and honesty. Bill Bernbach's famous Volkswagen ads, which began in 1959, not only sold many cars but were also among the most widely read ads ever.

A different story resulted from a well-researched and carefully produced Oldsmobile campaign, hatched by Leo Burnett in the 1980s, which attempted to transform the image of the "Olds" into a hip, stylish car for younger people. The clever slogan, "This is not your father's Oldsmobile," was repeated in a series of seemingly persuasive, musically powerful, artistic commercials. Nevertheless, the ad campaign failed. Not only did the ad fail to attract young buyers—difficult to do when the car your father drives is nicknamed Olds—but it alienated older customers, who felt abandoned by the campaign's emphasis on youth.

The cost of advertising, especially on network television, grows higher and higher. The average cost of a thirty-second national TV spot for the 1998–99 television season was $153,000, but the most popular shows are far more expensive. For example, television's No. 1 show, *ER*, charged $565,000 for thirty seconds, while the same amount of time cost $425,000 on *Friends* and $330,000 on *The X-Files*. And, even with their greater emphasis on market research, agencies and advertisers are still not sure which ad pitches will work and which will not. In most cases, both the creative and research sides of the business acknowledge that they cannot predict with any certainty which campaigns will succeed. They say ads work best by slowly creating brand-name identities—by associating certain products over time with quality and reliability in the minds of consumers. Some economists, however, believe that much of the money spent on advertising is ultimately wasted because it simply leads consumers to change from one brand name to another. Such switching may increase profits for a particular manufacturer, but it has little positive impact on the overall economy.

Media Selection. Another integral department in an ad agency, media selection, is staffed by **media buyers**: people who choose and purchase the types of media that are best suited to carry a client's ads and reach the targeted audience. For instance, a company like Procter & Gamble, the world's leading advertiser, displays its fifty-five major brands, most of them household products, on TV shows viewed primarily by women. To reach male viewers, however, media buyers encourage beer advertisers to spend their ad budgets on cable and network sports programming, evening talk radio, sports magazines, or the sports pages in local newspapers. Media buyers pay particular attention to the relative strengths and weaknesses of print and electronic forms of advertising. For example, ad campaigns aimed at supermarket shoppers effectively use newspapers, direct mail, and magazine inserts, all of which encourage the tradition of coupon clipping; local news programs, which do not have many teenage viewers, might not be a good buy for a client selling rap music or junk food.

As noted earlier, ad agencies have traditionally received 15 percent of what media outlets charge advertisers. Today, though, this fee is more negotiable, usually ranging from 10 to 15 percent. Another approach, taken by some ad agencies, is to simply charge clients a preset flat fee for every ad they place. Advertisers often add *incentive clauses* to their contracts with agencies, raising the fee if sales goals are met and lowering it if goals are missed. With incentive clauses, it is in the agencies' best interests to conduct repetitive **saturation advertising**, in which a variety of media are inundated with ads aimed at target audiences. The initial Miller Lite beer campaign

("Tastes great, less filling"), which used humor and retired athletes to reach its male audience, became one of the most successful saturation campaigns in media history. It ran from 1973 to 1991 and included television and radio spots, magazine and newspaper ads, and billboards and point-of-purchase store displays. The excessive repetition of the campaign helped light beer overcome a potential image problem, that of being viewed as watered-down beer, unworthy of "real" men.

Account and Client Management. Ad agencies also include a department composed of client liaisons, or **account executives**: individuals responsible for bringing in new business and managing the accounts of established clients. Generally, this department oversees new ad campaigns in which several agencies bid for the business of a client. Account managers coordinate the presentation of a proposed campaign and various aspects of the bidding process, such as what a series of ads will cost a client. Account executives function as liaisons between the advertiser and the creative team that produces an ad. Since most major companies maintain their own ad departments to handle everyday details, account executives also coordinate activities between their agency and a client's in-house personnel.

> "Ads seem to work on the very advanced principle that a small pellet or pattern in a noisy, redundant barrage of repetition will gradually assert itself."
> —Marshall McLuhan, *Understanding Media*, 1964

The advertising business tends to be volatile, and account departments are especially vulnerable to upheavals. For instance, when Ogilvy & Mather lost its $60 million American Express account ("Don't leave home without it") in the early 1990s, more than fifty people were fired, many from account services. Clients routinely conduct **account reviews**: the process of evaluating and reinvigorating a product's image by reviewing an existing ad agency's campaign or by inviting several new agencies to submit new campaign strategies, which may result in the product company's switching agencies.[6] One industry study conducted in the mid-1980s indicated that client accounts stayed with the same agency for about seven years, but by the late 1980s clients were changing agencies much more quickly. D'Arcy Masius Benton & Bowles, for example, won the $80 million Maxwell House coffee account in 1989 from Ogilvy & Mather, which then won it back the following year. There are a few exceptions, however: Campbell-Ewald has held GM's Chevrolet account since 1922—more than seventy-five years— and Leo Burnett has managed the Green Giant (now a subsidiary of Pillsbury) account since 1935, when it was one of Burnett's original clients.

persuasive techniques in contemporary advertising

Ad agencies and product companies often argue that the main purpose of advertising is to inform consumers straightforwardly of available products. In fact, many types of advertisements, like classified ads in newspapers, are devoted primarily to delivering price information. Most consumer ads, however, merely tell stories about products without revealing much about prices. Since national advertisers generally choose to buy a one-page magazine ad or a thirty-second TV spot to deliver their pitch, consumers get little information about how a product was made or how it compares with similar brands. In managing space and time constraints, advertising agencies engage in a variety of persuasive techniques. We will look briefly at some specific techniques and then focus on the *association principle* and *myth analysis*, which serve as strategies for critiquing advertising as well as for explaining how advertisers try to persuade consumers.

conventional persuasive strategies

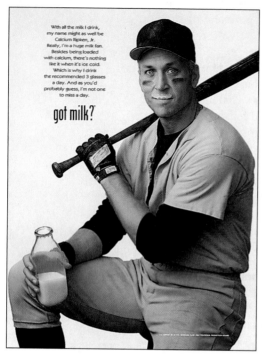

With all the milk I drink,
my name might as well be
Calcium Ripken, Jr.
Really, I'm a huge milk fan.
Besides being loaded
with calcium, there's nothing
like it when it's ice cold.
Which is why I drink
the recommended 3 glasses
a day. And as you'd
probably guess, I'm not one
to miss a day.

got milk?

Athletes, supermodels, movie and TV actors, music stars, and even politicians have donned the now famous milk mustache for the wildly successful "got milk?" ads. Famous-person testimonials from public figures like Cal Ripken have helped revive milk sales, spawned numerous parodies, and even led to the publication of a book containing all the print ads and the history of the ad campaign.

One of the most frequently used advertising approaches is the **famous-person testimonial**, whereby a product is endorsed by a well-known person, such as former senator and presidential candidate Bob Dole touting the benefits of the drug Viagra. Another technique, the **plain-folks pitch**, associates a product with simplicity. Over the years, Volkswagen ("Think small"), General Electric ("We bring good things to life"), and Microsoft ("Where do you want to go today?") have each used slogans that stress how new technologies fit into the lives of ordinary people. By contrast, the **snob-appeal** approach attempts to persuade consumers that using a product will maintain or elevate their social station. Advertisers selling jewelry, perfume, clothing, and luxury automobiles often use snob appeal. For example, Infiniti cars, associated with elegance, are frequently advertised against a backdrop of high-society parties; ads for Mitsubishi sedans use phrases like "a new level of luxury," "superb road manners," "full-size refinement," and "an upscale attitude."

Another approach, the **bandwagon effect**, points out in exaggerated claims that everyone is using a particular product. Brands that refer to themselves as "America's favorite" or "the best" imply that consumers will be left out—or that they are not hip—if they ignore these products. A different technique, the **hidden-fear appeal**, plays on consumers' sense of insecurity. Deodorant, mouthwash, and dandruff-shampoo ads frequently invoke anxiety, pointing out that only a specific product could possibly relieve embarrassing personal-hygiene problems.

A final ad strategy, used more in local TV and radio campaigns than in national ones, has been labeled **irritation advertising**: creating product-name recognition by being annoying or obnoxious. Although both research and common sense suggest that irritating ads do not work very well, there have been exceptions. In the 1950s and 1960s, for instance, an aspirin company ran a TV ad showing a hammer pounding inside a person's brain. Critics and the product's own agency suggested that people bought the product, which sold well, to get relief from the ad as well as from their headaches. For years, Charmin tissue used the annoying Mr. Whipple, a fussy store clerk who commanded customers, "Please don't squeeze the Charmin." One study found that people hated the ad but bought the product anyway. On the regional level, irritation ads are often used by appliance discount stores or local car dealers, who yell at the camera or dress in outrageous costumes. Some consumers may purposely avoid companies that engage in irritating ads. A few agencies, however, contend that consumers become so annoyed by the ads that they actually go to the store or dealership to complain—and end up buying a TV set or used car.

the association principle

Historically, American car advertisements have displayed automobiles in natural settings: on winding back roads that cut through rugged mountain passes or across shimmering wheat fields. These ads rarely contain images of cars on congested city streets or in other urban settings where most driving really occurs. Instead, the car—an example of advanced technology—merges effortlessly with the natural world.

This type of advertising exemplifies the **association principle**, a persuasive technique used in many consumer ads. Employing this principle, an ad associates a product with some cultural value or image that has a positive connotation but may have little connection to the actual product. For example, Chevrolet's slogan in the 1980s—"the heartbeat of America"—associated the car with nationalism. In trying "to convince us that there's an innate relationship between a brand name and an attitude,"[7] agencies and advertisers associate products with happy families, success at school or work, natural scenery, and humor. (Some ad agencies contend, however, that viewers do not always remember products associated with funny or quirky situations.) Over the years, the most controversial use of the association principle has been the linkage of products to stereotyped caricatures of women. In numerous instances, women have been portrayed either as sex objects or as clueless housewives who, during many a daytime TV commercial, needed the powerful offscreen voice of a male narrator to instruct them in their own kitchens (see "Case Study: Women, Ads, and Stereotypes" on page 362).

Another strong association used in advertising is nature. In one of the most striking and enduring magazine ad campaigns, Kool cigarettes have been associated with cool mountain waterfalls and tranquil beaches, neither of which has a logical connection to cigarettes. These settings, however, conjure up positive images and link the product to nature. Philip Morris's Marlboro brand also used the association principle to completely transform the product's initial image. In the 1920s, Marlboro began as a fashionable woman's cigarette. Back then, the company's ads equated smoking with emancipation and a sense of freedom, attempting to appeal to women who had just won the right to vote. Marlboro, though, did poorly as a women's product, and new campaigns in the 1950s and 1960s transformed the brand into a man's cigarette. In these campaigns, powerful images of active, rugged men were the central characters. Often, Marlboro associated its product with the image of a lone cowboy roping a calf, building a fence, or riding through a pristine natural landscape. Ironically, over the years two of the Marlboro Man models died of lung cancer associated with smoking. Yet in 1993 *Financial World* magazine called Marlboro the world's "most valuable brand name," having an estimated worth of $39 billion.

As a response to corporate merger mania and public skepticism toward large impersonal companies, the *disassociation corollary* has emerged as a recent trend in advertising. The nation's largest winery, Gallo, pioneered the idea in the 1980s by establishing a dummy corporation, Bartles & Jaymes, to sell jug wine and wine coolers, thus avoiding the Gallo corporate image in ads and on its bottles. The Gallo ads featured Frank and Ed, two low-key, grandfatherly types as "co-owners" and ad spokesmen. This ad concept revealed that simulated entrepreneurship was "a way to connect with younger consumers who yearn for products that are handmade, quirky, and authentic."[8] In contrast, Gallo pitched another

These billboards along Sunset Boulevard in Los Angeles are symbolic of the pervasiveness of advertising. From towering billboards to people's T-shirts, sales pitches and product messages constantly bombard us. Leo Burnett's successful Marlboro Man images, which associate the cigarette with stoic masculinity and rugged individualism, are considered part of the most successful ad campaign in history.

Circa early 1900s

In advertising, the stereotypical portrayal of women has generated considerable controversy. This is not surprising, given that women have been the chief audience for advertising throughout most of the twentieth century, although men have produced most of the ads. Ads have often stereotyped women as brainless or helpless or offered them as a man's reward for drinking a particular beer, wearing cool jeans, or smoking the right cigarette. Influenced by the women's movement and critiques of advertising culture, such as Betty Friedan's *The Feminine Mystique*, ads depicting women have changed. Although many sexist stereotypes still persist in advertising, women today are often portrayed in a variety of social roles.

Over the years, critics and consumers alike have complained about the *stereotyping* in mainstream advertising. Invisible stereotyping occurs when whole segments of the population are ignored—particularly African, Arab, Asian, Latin, and Native Americans. Visible stereotyping occurs in many ads, as when men are portrayed as stupid, inferior to the heroic products that "save" their lives. Stereotyping robs people of their individuality by assigning them to groups. Members of a group are falsely assumed to act as a single entity and to display certain characteristics, which are usually negative.

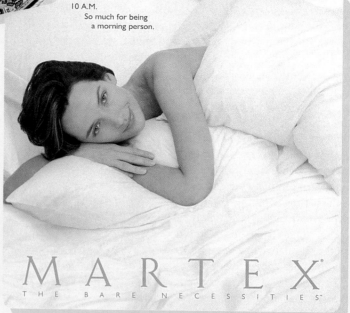

WestPoint Services Inc.

Circa mid-1990s

While the feminist movement and the rise of women's sports have helped change the representation of women in advertising, women are still more likely than men to be depicted in passive or horizontal physical positions.

label, Turning Leaf, to upscale consumers who wouldn't be caught dead purchasing wine in jugs or twist-cap bottles.

In the 1990s, the disassociation strategy was used by Miller Brewing Company's Red Dog beer, sold under the quaint Plank Road Brewery logo, and by R. J. Reynolds's Moonlight Tobacco Company, which sells local brand cigarettes such as City and North Star. In addition, General Motors, still reeling from the failed Oldsmobile campaign and a declining corporate reputation, "disassociate[d] itself from its innovative offspring, the Saturn"; GM ads have packaged the Saturn as "a small-town enterprise, run by folks not terribly unlike Frank and Ed," who provide caring, personal service.[9] As an advertising strategy, disassociation links new brands in a product line to eccentric or simple regional places rather than to the image conjured up by giant conglomerates.

myth analysis

Another way of looking at ads, **myth analysis** provides insights into how ads work at a general cultural level. According to myth analysis, most ads are narratives with stories to tell and social conflicts to resolve. The term *myth* is not used here in a pejorative sense, referring to an untrue story or outright falsehood. Rather, myths help us to define people, organizations, and social norms. Myths are the stories a society constructs to bring order to the conflicts and contradictions of everyday life.

Three common mythical elements are found in many types of ads:

1. Ads incorporate myths in mini-story form, featuring characters, settings, and plots.

2. Most stories in ads involve conflicts, pitting one set of characters or social values against another.

3. Such conflicts are negotiated or resolved by the end of the ad, usually by applying or purchasing a product. In advertising, the product and those who use it often emerge as the heroes of the story.

Even though the stories ads tell are usually compressed into thirty seconds or onto a single page, they still include the traditional elements of narrative. For instance, Marlboro ads often tell the mini-story of a lone and tough cowboy and his horse, dwarfed by towering pines and snow-covered mountains. The ads ask us to imagine his adventure, as he returns home after an autumn cattle drive, perhaps. The cowboy's ability to survive amid the forces of nature is a tribute to rugged individualism, probably America's most powerful cultural value. The conflict is generated by the audience's implicit understanding of what is not in the ads—a fast-paced, technology-driven urban world where most smoking actually takes place. This implied conflict between the natural world and the manufactured world is apparently resolved by invoking the image of Marlboro. Although Marlboros are an addictive, manufactured product and advertisers are mandated by the FTC and the Surgeon General to warn us about the lethal dangers of cigarettes, the ads attempt to downplay those facts. Instead, they offer an alternative story about the wonders of nature. The natural is substituted for the manufactured, and the "spirit of Marlboro" becomes the soothing negotiator between these competing worlds.

In an increasingly technology-dependent environment, modern societies have come to value products that claim affiliation with the *real* and the *natural*. Coke sells itself as "the real thing," and the cosmetics industry offers synthetic products that make us look "natural." These twin adjectives, which saturate American ads, almost always describe processed goods.

Most advertisers do not expect consumers to accept without question the stories they tell or the associations they make in their ads; they do not "make the mistake of asking for belief."[10] Instead, ads are most effective when they create attitudes and reinforce values. Then they operate like popular fiction, encouraging us to suspend our disbelief. Although most of us realize that ads create a fictional world, we often get caught up in their stories and myths. Indeed, ads often work because the stories offer comfort about our deepest desires and conflicts—between men and women, nature and technology, tradition and change, the real and the artificial. Most contemporary consumer advertising does not provide much useful information about products. Instead, it tries to reassure us that through the use of familiar brand names everyday tensions and problems can be managed.

commercial speech and regulating advertising

In 1791, Congress passed the First Amendment to the U.S. Constitution, promising, among other guarantees, to "make no law . . . abridging the freedom of speech, or of the press." Over the years, we have developed a shorthand label for the First Amendment, misnaming it the free-speech clause. The amendment ensures that citizens and reporters can generally say and write what they want, but it says nothing directly about speech that is not free. What, then, about **commercial speech**—any print or broadcast expression for which a fee is charged to organizations and individuals buying time or space in the mass media? Whereas freedom of speech refers to the right to express thoughts, beliefs, and opinions in a marketplace of ideas, commercial speech supports the right to circulate goods, services, and images in the marketplace of products. Although most people can buy some commercial speech inexpensively, such as a classified newspaper ad, only wealthy citizens and companies can routinely afford speech that reaches millions.

New forms of commercial speech and advertising continue to crowd the media landscape. Cable television offers several home-shopping networks, with nonstop banter about must-have goods. Late-night television is also filled with long-form commercials advertising "talk romance" and "talk sex" to the lonely, the young, and the curious via 900 telephone numbers that charge exorbitant per-minute rates and often result in unrequested extra charges on telephone bills.

Infomercials represent another substantial growth area in cable and broadcast television. These thirty-minute late-night and daytime programs usually feature fading TV and music celebrities, who advertise a product or service in a format that looks like a laid-back talk show. Even on regular talk shows, guests generally appear when they have a book to sell or a movie to promote. Paid a fee by the program to boost ratings, such guests use their celebrity status and allotted time as a commercial forum to promote themselves.

Although the mass media have often not hesitated to carry product- and service-selling advertisements in publications, and have embraced the concept of program-length infomercials and even 24-hour cable shopping channels, they have also refused certain issue-based advertising that might upset their traditional advertisers. For example, although corporations have great ease in placing ads, many labor unions have had their print and broadcast ads rejected as "controversial." The nonprofit Media Foundation, based in Vancouver, Canada, has also had difficulty getting networks to air their "uncommercials." One of their spots promotes the Friday after Thanksgiving (traditionally, the beginning of the huge holiday buying season) as "Buy Nothing Day." CNN did air the uncommercial in November 1998, but "continued attempts to buy airtime on the NBC, CBS and ABC have been rejected."[11]

In his 1957 book *The Hidden Persuaders*, Vance Packard expressed concern that advertising was manipulating helpless consumers, attacking our dignity, and invading "the privacy of our minds."[12] According to this view, the advertising industry was considered to be all-powerful. Although consumers have historically been regarded as dupes, research reveals that the consumer mind is not as easy to predict as some advertisers once thought. In the 1950s, for example, Ford failed to successfully sell its new mid-size car, the Edsel, which was aimed at newly prosperous Ford customers looking to move up to the latest in push-button window wipers and antennas. After a splashy and expensive ad campaign, Ford sold only sixty-three thousand Edsels in 1958 and just two thousand in 1960, when the model was discontinued. In the 1960s, the Scott paper company predicted that its disposable-clothing line would challenge traditional apparel, but, despite heavy advertising, this never happened. Today, more than ever, most people are not easily persuaded by advertising. Over the years, studies have suggested that between 75 and 90 percent of new consumer products typically fail because they are not embraced by the buying public.[13]

Despite public resistance to many new products and the cynical eye we cast toward advertising, the ad industry has made contributions, including raising the American standard of living and supporting most media industries. Yet serious concerns over the impact of advertising remain. In the mid-1990s, as Congress slashed the budgets of public broadcast stations, these non-commercial stations tried to persuade Congress to approve more commercial advertising for public and educational broadcasting. Watchdog groups worried about expanding advertising's reach, however, and critics continued to condemn ads that associate products with sex appeal, youth, and narrow definitions of female beauty. Some of the most serious concerns involve children, teens, and health.

> "The **American apparatus of advertising** is something unique in history. . . . It is like a grotesque, smirking gargoyle set at the very top of America's skyscraping adventure in acquisition *ad infinitum*."
>
> —James Rorty,
> *Our Master's Voice*,
> 1934

Children and Advertising. Children and teenagers, living in a culture dominated by TV ads, are often viewed as consumer trainees. For years, groups such as Action for Children's Television (ACT) worked to limit advertising aimed at children. In the 1980s, ACT fought particularly hard to curb *program-length commercials:* thirty-minute cartoon programs (such as *G.I. Joe, My Little Pony and Friends, The Care Bear Family*, and *He-Man and the Masters of the Universe*) developed for television syndication primarily to promote a line of toys.

In addition, parent groups have worried about the heavy promotion of sugar-coated cereals during children's programs. Pointing to European countries, where children's advertising is banned, these groups have pushed to limit advertising directed at children. Congress, faced with the protection that the First Amendment offers commercial speech, has responded weakly. The Children's Television Act of 1990 mandated that networks provide some educational and informational children's programming, but the Act has been difficult to enforce and did little to restrict advertising aimed at kids. Most studies on the impact of advertising on children reveal that young children are vulnerable to commercialism, particularly in the way ads can pressure children to want products they either do not need or their parents cannot afford.

Advertising in Schools. Among the most controversial developments in recent years was the introduction of Channel One into thousands of schools during the 1989–90 school year. The brainchild of Whittle Communications, Channel One offered "free" video and satellite equipment (tuned exclusively to Channel One) in exchange for a ten-minute package of current-events programming that included two minutes of commercials. If school districts decided to curtail or limit the program, Whittle could reclaim its "free" equipment. In 1994, Channel One was acquired by K-III Communications (now known as PRIMEDIA, and publisher of *Weekly Reader, Seventeen,* and *Soap Opera Digest*). By the late 1990s, Channel One, available in more than twelve thousand of the nation's junior-high and high schools and reaching a captive audience of eight million students, grossed more than $800,000 each school day.

Over the years, the National Dairy Council and other organizations have also used schools to promote products, providing free filmstrips, posters, magazines, folders, and study guides adorned with corporate logos. Teachers, especially in underfunded districts, have usually been grateful for the support. Channel One, however, has been viewed as a more intrusive threat, violating the implicit cultural border between an entertainment situation (watching commercial television) and a learning situation (going to school). One study showed that schools with a high concentration of low-income students were more than twice as likely as affluent schools to receive Channel One.[14] Some individual school districts have banned Channel One, as has the state of New York. These school systems have argued that Channel One provides students with only slight additional knowledge about current affairs; but students find the products advertised—sneakers, cereal, and soda, among others—more worthy of purchase because they are advertised in educational environments.[15]

Health and Advertising. We are well aware that advertising has a powerful impact on the standards of youthful beauty in our culture. A long-standing trend in advertising is the association of certain products with ultrathin female models, promoting a style of "attractiveness" that girls and women are invited to emulate. Some forms of fashion and cosmetics advertising actually pander to individuals' insecurities and low self-esteem. Such advertising suggests standards of style and behavior that may be not only unattainable but also harmful, encouraging eating disorders such as anorexia and bulimia. In fact, some female models became so skinny that critics began referring to the style of their ads as "heroin chic" because the models looked like victims of prolonged drug use. To their credit, many ad agencies refused to do this type of advertising, which was then usually produced by the fashion industry's own in-house staff. Throughout history, however, many companies have capitalized on unhappiness and insecurity by promising relief or the kind of body that is currently fashionable.

Along with criticism of promoting skeleton-like beauty, probably the most sustained criticism of advertising is its promotion of alcohol and tobacco consumption. Opponents of such advertising have become more vocal in the face of grim statistics. Each year, 400,000 Americans die from diseases related to nicotine addiction and poisoning, 100,000 die from alcohol-related diseases, and another 15,000 to 18,000 die in car crashes involving drunk drivers.

Tobacco ads disappeared from television in 1971, under pressure from Congress and the FCC, and the hard-liquor industry voluntarily banned TV and radio ads for many decades. Still, enormous amounts of money are spent each year to encourage these habits. In the mid-1990s, tobacco companies alone spent nearly $5 billion annually on advertising—about $13 million a day, according to the Federal Trade Commission (FTC)—even though no money went to television.

Over the years, numerous ad campaigns have appealed to teenage cigarette consumers. In 1988, for example, R. J. Reynolds, a subdivision of RJR Nabisco, revived its Joe Camel cartoon character from an earlier campaign, outfitting him with hipper clothes and sunglasses. Spending $75 million annually, the company put the new Joe on billboards and store posters and in sports stadiums and magazines. One study revealed that before the 1988 campaign less than 1 percent of teens under eighteen smoked Camels. After the ad blitz, however, 33 percent of this age group preferred Camels. In response, the ad industry's trade journal, *Advertising Age*, raised some seri-

By 1999, the status of tobacco companies and their advertising in the United States had hit a low point. A $206 billion settlement between tobacco companies and state attorney generals ended tobacco advertising on billboards and severely limited the ways in which cigarette companies can promote their products in the United States. Advertising bans and antismoking public-service announcements contributed to a growing disfavor about tobacco in America, with smoking rates dropping from a high of 42.5 percent in 1965 to 24.7 percent thirty years later.

As Western cultural attitudes have turned against tobacco, the large tobacco multinationals have shifted their global-marketing focus, targeting Asia in particular. Underfunded government health programs and populations that generally admire American and European cultural products make Asian nations ill-equipped to deal with cigarette marketing efforts. For example, even though Vietnam strengthened its ban on print, broadcast, and billboard ads in 1994, nearly three-fourths of Vietnamese men smoke, the highest male smoking rate in the world.

Advertising bans have actually forced tobacco companies to find alternative and, as it turned out, better ways to promote smoking. Philip Morris, the largest private tobacco company, and its global rival, British American Tobacco (BAT), practice "brand stretching," linking their logos to race-car events, soccer leagues, youth festivals, disco parties, rock concerts, TV shows, and popular cafés. The higher prices for Western cigarettes in Asia has the effect of only increasing their prestige, and makes packs of Marlboro symbols of middle-class aspirations.

The unmistakable silhouette of the Marlboro Man is ubiquitous throughout developing countries, but particularly in Asia. In Hanoi, Vietnam, almost every corner boasts a street vendor with a trolley cart, the bottom half of which carries the Marlboro logo or one of the other premium foreign brands. Vietnam's Ho Chi Minh City has two thousand such trolleys. Children in Malaysia are especially keen on Marlboro clothing, which, along with watches, binoculars, radios, knives, and backpacks, they can win by collecting a certain number of empty Marlboro packages. (Tobacco-brand clothing and merchandise is now illegal in the United States.)

Smoker near a streetside cigarette vendor in Hanoi, Vietnam

Sporting-event sponsorship has proved to be an especially successful brand-stretching technique with men, who smoke the majority of cigarettes in Asia. Philip Morris pumps close to $80 million a year in Formula One race-car sponsorship, which is now broadcast to 130 countries, and many argue that much of the popularity of Marlboro cigarettes in China derives from Philip Morris's sponsorship of the Marlboro soccer league. Throughout Asia, attractive young women wearing tight red Marlboro outfits cruise cities in red Marlboro minivans, frequently stopping to distribute free cigarettes, even to minors.

Some suggest that these same marketing strategies will make their way into America and other Western countries, but that's unlikely. Tobacco companies are mainly interested in developing regions like Asia for two reasons. First, China alone smokes 30 percent of the world's cigarettes, consuming 1.8 trillion cigarettes a year. Because only one in ten cigarettes now sold in China is a foreign brand, the potential market is staggering. Second, the majority of smokers in countries like China are unaware that smoking causes diseases like lung cancer. Ignorance, for tobacco companies like Philip Morris, is bliss.

A 1998 agreement between the tobacco industry and the U.S. government prohibits cigarette makers from targeting youths with advertisements, such as the popular cartoon figure Joe Camel. Many critics, including some in the advertising industry, feel the commercial-speech rights of the tobacco industry must be balanced with a sense of social responsibility for impressionable youths.

ous questions. For example, shouldn't cigarette advertisers' profit interests be balanced against their "unique social responsibility" in light of the health risks of smoking? Although Canada has long banned cigarette advertising in both print and broadcast forms, the FTC remained reluctant to lead a battle pitting the government against the commercial-speech rights of the tobacco industry.

In addition to young smokers, the tobacco industry has targeted other groups. In the 1960s, for instance, the advertising campaigns for Eve and Virginia Slims cigarettes (reminiscent of the ads during the suffrage movement in the early 1900s) associated their products with liberation, equality, and slim fashion models. And in 1989, Reynolds introduced a cigarette called Uptown, targeting African American consumers. The ad campaign fizzled, however, due to public protests by black leaders and government officials. When these leaders pointed to the high concentration of cigarette billboards in poor urban areas and the high mortality rates among black male smokers, the tobacco company withdrew the brand from the market.

The government's position regarding the tobacco industry began to change in the mid-1990s, when new reports revealed that some tobacco companies knew that nicotine was addictive as early as the 1950s and withheld that information from the public. In 1998, after four states had won settlements against the tobacco industry and the remaining states threatened to bring more expensive lawsuits against the companies, the tobacco industry agreed to an unprecedented settlement that carried significant limits on advertising and marketing tobacco products. The agreement's provisions included banning cartoon characters in advertising, thus ending the use of the Joe Camel character; prohibiting the industry from targeting youths in ads and marketing, including free samples, tobacco-brand clothing, and other merchandise; and ending outdoor billboard and transit advertising. The agreement also bans tobacco-company sponsorship of concerts and athletic events, and strictly limits other corporate sponsorships by tobacco companies.

Many of the complaints regarding tobacco advertising are also being directed at alcohol ads. For example, one of the most popular beer ad campaigns of the late 1990s, featuring the trio of Budweiser frogs (who croak *Bud - weis - errrr*) and two envious lizards, has been accused of using cartoonish animal characters to appeal to young viewers. In fact, the Budweiser ads would be banned under the standards of the tobacco settlement, which prohibits the attribution of human characteristics to animals, plants, or other objects.

"Alcohol marketers appear to believe that the prototypical college student is (1) male; (2) a nitwit; and (3) interested in nothing but booze and 'babes.'"
—Michael F. Jacobson and Laurie Ann Mazur, *Marketing Madness*, 1995

Alcohol ads have also targeted minority populations. Malt liquors, which contain higher concentrations of alcohol, have appeared in high-profile television ads for products like Colt 45, PowerMaster, and Magnum. Featuring actors like Billy Dee Williams, these ads have usually been shown during programs that appeal to a high percentage of black viewers.

A nonprofit organization based in Canada, the Media Foundation says its spoof ads are designed to "put out a better product and beat the corporations at their own game." Ads satirizing Joe Camel, Nike, and Absolut Vodka (*right*) are ways to "de-market" the products and draw attention to the myriad social problems linked to advertising, including smoking, global working conditions, and alcoholism.

College students, too, have been heavily targeted by alcohol ads, particularly by the beer industry. By the mid-1990s, college students were buying more than $4 billion in alcoholic drinks annually. Although colleges and universities have outlawed "beer bashes" hosted and supplied directly by major brewers, both Coors and Miller, a unit of Philip Morris, still employ student representatives to help "create brand awareness." These students notify brewers of special events that might be sponsored by and linked to a specific beer label. The images and slogans in alcohol ads often associate the products with power, romance, sexual prowess, athletic skill, or guns. In reality, though, alcohol is a chemical depressant; it diminishes athletic ability and sexual performance, triggers addiction in roughly 10 percent of the U.S. population, and is a factor in many spousal-abuse cases.

watching over advertisers

In 1996, Seagram, the Canadian liquor company and media conglomerate, defied the sixty-year voluntary ban by the American liquor industry on hard-liquor advertising in broadcasting. (Such ads had been banned from radio since 1936 and from television since 1948.) Faced with declining sales, the company argued that wine and beer, which have long advertised on television and radio, had an unfair market advantage over the hard-liquor industry. To promote its Crown Royal whiskey, Seagram began testing regional TV ads in Texas. Executives at Seagram called the old ban "obsolete." They pointed to other countries that featured liquor ads on television and noted the escalating World Wide Web sites devoted to marketing liquor. In 1996, following Seagram's lead, the Distilled Spirits Council of the United States, the liquor industry's trade association, voted to lift its voluntary ban on broadcast ads. At the time, ABC, CBS, Fox, and NBC executives refused to carry the ads nationally, citing both their efforts to promote responsible drinking and the threat that liquor advertising posed to their beer and wine ad revenues.[16]

Advertisers and agencies have generally had their commercial-speech rights protected by the First Amendment. But the Seagram move touched off renewed activity at both state and federal levels to pass legislation restricting alcohol advertising. In addition to legislation aimed at controversial products, oversight agencies—such as the Better Business Bureau, the National Fraud Information Center, and the FTC—have long monitored deceptive and false ads. During the Reagan administration in the 1980s, however, the FTC underwent sizable staff cuts, going from more than seventeen hundred employees to fewer than nine hundred. With these reductions and a relatively small budget, the FTC has become a less effective watchdog agency over the past fifteen years.

In addition to oversight groups, professions like medicine and law have long had uneasy relationships with advertising and often try to limit ads through their professional organizations. For example, bar associations actually prohibited lawyers from advertising until 1978, when the Supreme Court ruled that lawyers have a First Amendment right to promote their services. (The Supreme Court has since outlined some limits, ruling in 1995 that states may prevent lawyers from sending direct-mail ads within thirty days of an accident for the purpose of soliciting victims or survivors as clients.) Nonetheless, although prestigious law and medical practices have traditionally shunned advertising, many firms advertise to jump-start a new business or to reinvigorate a sagging practice.

Comparative Advertising. For years it was considered taboo for one advertiser to mention a competitor by name in its ads. Industry guidelines discouraged such advertising, and TV networks prohibited it. The government and networks feared that comparative ads would degenerate into unseemly name-calling, and advertisers believed they should not give free time or space to competitors. This led to the development of so-called Brand X products, which identified a competing brand without using a real name. The FTC, however, began encouraging comparative advertising in 1971. The agency thought such ads would help consumers by providing more product information. Subsequently, various food industries started taste-test wars specifically targeting each other in their ads. Burger King took on McDonald's, and Pepsi challenged Coke. As comparative ads became the norm, Japanese and American auto manufacturers even began to compare prices, gas mileage, safety records, and repair and recall rates in their ads.

Puffery and Deceptive Ads. Since the days when Lydia Pinkham's Vegetable Compound promised "a sure cure for all female weakness," false and misleading claims have haunted advertising. Over the years, the FTC has played an investigative role in substantiating the claims of various advertisers. A certain amount of puffery—ads featuring hyperbole and exaggeration—has usually been permitted, particularly when a product says it is "new and improved." However, when a product claims to be "the best," "the greatest," or "preferred by four out of five doctors," the FTC has often asked for supportive evidence.

Typical of deceptive advertising over the years were the Campbell Soup ads that used marbles in the bottom of a soup bowl to push more ingredients—and less water—to the surface. In another instance, a 1990 Volvo commercial featured a monster truck driving over a line of cars and crushing all but the Volvo; the company later admitted that the Volvo had been specially reinforced and the other cars' support columns had been weakened. Finally, a more subtle form of deception featured the Klondike Lite ice-cream bar—"the 93 percent fat-free dessert with chocolate-flavored coating." The bars were indeed 93 percent fat-free, but only after the chocolate coating was removed.[17] In 1996, the FTC asked five automakers to stop ads for "no-money down" or "one penny down" car leases because the fine print—virtually impossible for consumers to read on television—required more than $1,000 in various fees and taxes before a car could actually be driven off the lot. When the FTC discovers deceptive ads, it usually requires advertisers to change their ads or remove them from circulation. Although the FTC does not have the power to assess financial penalties, it occasionally requires an advertiser to run corrective ads to offset deceptive ones.

advertising's threat to journalism

Much of the power advertising wields is subtle and difficult to monitor. One problem, particularly troubling for newspapers during economic recessions, occurs when reporters cover news issues that reflect poorly on a newspaper's major advertisers. Local real-estate firms or car dealers, for instance, are no longer so dependent on newspapers as their main advertising channel. Companies can now take their ad business to direct mail, cable, and the Internet if they are unhappy with negative stories in the local newspaper. With many dailies facing financial difficulties in the 1990s, some editors have turned their investigative eyes away from controversial business stories in order to keep advertisers happy.

In 1992, a report by the nonprofit Center for the Study of Commercialism investigated fifty news stories that were allegedly "killed or downplayed by news media to appease advertisers."[18] The *Portland Oregonian*, for example, Oregon's largest daily paper, destroyed thousands of copies of a Sunday edition in 1989 after a sales-person in the advertising department complained to editors about a real-estate story. The story advised readers on how to sell a home without the help of a real-estate agent. The editor responsible for publishing the article was later demoted. In 1990, car dealers in Hartford, Connecticut, withdrew advertising from the *Hartford Courant* over an article that urged consumers to be wary of shady dealers. After the *Courant's* publisher apologized to the dealers, they ended their boycott, but many readers in the community were upset that the paper backed down. Two years later, one dealer in sub-urban Hartford reported that he had seen no more negative articles about dealers: "Consumer reporting is virtually nonexistent now."

Occasionally, newspapers stand up to their advertisers. Nordstrom, a large department-store retailer, reduced its advertising in the *Seattle Times* in the early 1990s after the paper criticized the company's labor difficulties. In this case, the newspaper did not back down. Michael Fancher, then the executive editor of the *Times*, told the *Wall Street Journal*, "You can't just sell your soul in little bits and pieces and expect that readers will understand it. A lot of newspapers don't understand that."[19] Although the coverage of business at many papers has improved over the years, papers in small com-munities with fewer advertisers remain more vulnerable to this problem. Large dailies are better able to withstand lost ad revenue from a few disgruntled advertisers.

advertising and the internet

Although the Internet accounted for only about $1 billion of the $200 billion Ameri-can advertising market in 1998, it is slowly gaining support in the industry as a medium that can both target and track potential consumers. By 1999, five years after the Web became a site for commerce, many of the nation's traditional top advertis-ers—including DaimlerChrysler, Johnson & Johnson, and Xerox—had finally begun to spend part of their ad budgets on the Net, joining companies like Procter & Gam-ble and Toyota, who had established a Web presence years earlier.

The most common style of Web advertising, accounting for more than 50 per-cent of the market, is the banner ad—typically a rectangular ad that loads at the top of the Web page. Although popular, banner ads pose a dilemma for Internet advertis-ers. On one hand, effective ads need to be eye-catching, with some kind of animation, to motivate the user to click on the ad. On the other hand, banner ads with animation and other complex graphics often aggravate users by prolonging the time it takes for the Web page to load.

Other forms of Web advertising aren't as obvious as banners and have blurred the lines between advertising and the editorial content of Web sites, leaving readers to wonder how much content is sponsored or ad-related. For example, in 1999, news reports revealed that Amazon.com's reviews for recommended books were often paid for by book publishers. Similarly, search engines often give top billing in search-result lists to companies that pay for prominence.

Another form of Web advertising is through affiliate referrals on the Web. A Web site becomes an affiliate when it carries a hot button for an Internet business on its page; the affiliate then earns a commission—typically 10 to 20 percent—for any sales that it creates for the Web business. Amazon.com and CDNow, both of which actively seek affiliates on their Web sites, have more than 200,000 affiliate Web pages that carry their hot-button logos to refer customers to buy books, music, and other offerings.

"Web surfers are becoming increas-ingly immune to **the shriek of banner ads**, the online equiva-lent of freeway billboards dotting the cyber landscape."
—Jonathan Gaw, *Los Angeles Times*, 1999

Finally, the Internet is also being used to track millions of consumers by developing information profiles that help Web sites direct targeted advertisements to visitors. Internet user information is often gained through online surveys—for example, an ESPN.com contest required users to fill out a survey to be eligible to win sports tickets—or through sites such as Nytimes.com, which requires users to provide demographic information for free access to the newspaper's site. By 1999, many privacy advocates and some lawmakers in Congress were calling for legislation to limit the ability of Web sites to collect personal data, to notify people how the information will be used, and to allow people to disallow the collection of their personal information.

advertising and democracy

As advertising has become more pervasive and consumers more discriminating, ad practitioners have searched for ways to weave their work more seamlessly into the social and cultural fabric. Products now blend in as props or even as "characters" in TV shows and movies. In addition, almost every national consumer product now has its own site on the World Wide Web, displaying advertising on computers around the globe. With today's video technology and computer graphics, producers can even generate a TV advertising image on a wall or a flat surface when in reality no image exists.

Among the most intriguing efforts to become enmeshed in the culture are the ads that exploit, distort, or transform the political and cultural meanings of popular music. In the 1990s, for instance, a number of once radical or progressive rock songs made their way into TV ads, muddying the boundary between art and commerce. Not only did "Revolution" (1968) promote Nike shoes but Bob Dylan's "The Times They Are a-Changin'" (1964) advertised both an accounting firm and the Bank of Montreal. Buffalo Springfield's "For What It's Worth" (1967) sold Miller beer—with the commercial stopping just short of the band's Vietnam War protest lyric, "There's a man with a gun over there." David Bowie's "Heroes" (1977) peddled Microsoft software, and Sly and the Family Stone's "Everyday People" (1969) sold Toyota cars.

A much more straightforward form of cultural blending is **political advertising**: the use of ad techniques to promote a candidate's image and persuade the public to adopt a particular viewpoint. Since the 1950s, political consultants have been imitating market-research and advertising techniques to sell their candidates. In the early days of television, politicians running for major offices either bought or were offered half-hour blocks of time to discuss their views and the significant issues of the day. As advertising time became more valuable, however, local stations and the networks became reluctant to give away time in large chunks. Gradually, TV managers began selling thirty-second spots to political campaigns just as they sold time to product advertisers.

In the late 1980s, a research team at the University of Pennsylvania's Annenberg School of Communication began critiquing political advertisements that reduce a candidate's ideas to a thirty-second advertising pitch. Using powerful visual images, these ads often attack other candidates and distract viewers from misleading verbal messages. In the early 1990s, the major networks began using the school's techniques in a news segment called Ad Watch. After critiquing a political ad, a commentator labeled it "true," "correct but . . . ," "misleading," or "false." As a result of Ad Watch, media consultants began paying more attention to the veracity of their ads. Ad Watch pieces, however, usually ran only once, so they were viewed mainly by people who regularly watch the evening news.[20]

During the 1992 and 1996 presidential campaigns, third-party candidate Ross Perot restored the use of the half-hour time block when he ran political infomercials on cable and the networks. However, only very wealthy candidates can afford such promotional strategies because television does not usually provide free airtime to politicians. Questions about political ads continue to be asked. Can serious information on political issues be conveyed in thirty-second spots that many candidates can barely afford? Do repeated attack ads, which assault another candidate's character, so undermine citizens' confidence in the electoral process that they stop voting?[21] How does a society ensure that alternative political voices, which are not so well financed or commercially viable, still receive a hearing in a democratic society?

During the 1996 presidential campaign, a bipartisan group of politicians, broadcasters, critics, and activists—the Free TV for Straight Talk Coalition—persuaded the major networks to restore a few minutes of free time for candidates every night during the last month of the presidential campaign. The coalition promised, "No tricky images. No unseen narrators. No journalists. No surrogates. Just candidates making their best case to the biggest audience America assembles every night."[22] Critics protested that the process still ignored alternative and third-party candidates, and journalists raised another concern: By taking a probing adversarial reporter out of the loop, the strategy turned the free time into an opportunity for free political advertising.

> "The press enjoys special constitutional protection for being an **instrument of self-rule**, an educational tool of democracy, not simply to protect the profits of advertisers and the media. But if the citizenry is only told what suits advertisers, the democratic ideal is **left in tatters**."
>
> —Michael F. Jacobson and Laurie Ann Mazur, *Marketing Madness*, 1995

Although advertising—for both products and politicians—has generated a culture that is often critical of advertising's pervasiveness, the growth of the industry has not diminished. Ads continue to fascinate. Many consumers buy magazines or watch the Super Bowl just for the advertisements. Adolescents decorate their rooms with their favorite ads and associate with the images certain products convey. By 1999, more than $435 billion worldwide ($212 billion of that in the United States) was being spent on advertising each year—enough money to finance the operation of several small countries. A number of factors have allowed advertising's largely unchecked growth. Many Americans tolerate advertising as a necessary "evil" for maintaining the economy, but many others dismiss advertising as not believable and even trivial. Thus, because we are willing to downplay its centrality to global culture, many citizens do not think advertising is significant enough to monitor or reform. Such attitudes have ensured advertising's pervasiveness and suggest the need to escalate critical vigilance.

As individuals and as a society, we have developed an uneasy relationship with advertising. Favorite ads and commercial jingles remain part of our cultural world for a lifetime. But we detest irritating and repetitive commercials, using the remote control to mute the offenders on television. We realize that without ads many mass media would need to reinvent themselves. At the same time, we remain critical of what advertising has come to represent: the overemphasis on commercial acquisitions and cultural images, and the disparity between those who can afford new products and those who cannot.

REVIEW QUESTIONS

Early Developments in American Advertising

1. Whom did the first ad agents serve?

2. How did packaging and trademarks influence advertising?

3. Explain why patent medicines and department stores figured so prominently in advertising in the late 1800s.

4. What role did advertising play in transforming America into a consumer society?

The Shape of American Advertising Today

5. What influences did visual culture exert on advertising?

6. What are the differences between boutique and mega ad agencies?

7. What are the major divisions at most ad agencies? What is the function of each department?

8. What causes the occasional tension between the research and creative departments at some agencies?

Persuasive Techniques in Contemporary Advertising

9. How do the common persuasive techniques used in advertising work?

10. How does the association principle work, and why is it an effective way to analyze advertising?

11. What is the disassociation corollary?

12. How can myth analysis be used to critique an ad?

Commercial Speech and Regulating Advertising

13. What is commercial speech?

14. What are three serious contemporary issues regarding health and advertising? Why is each issue controversial?

15. What is comparative advertising?

Advertising and Democracy

16. What are some of the major issues involving political advertising?

17. What role does advertising play in a democratic society?

QUESTIONING THE MEDIA

1. What is your earliest recollection of watching a television commercial? Do you have a favorite ad? A most-despised ad? What is it about these ads that you particularly like or dislike?

2. Why are so many people critical of advertising?

3. If you were (or are) a parent, what strategies would you use to explain an objectionable ad to your child or teenager? Use an example.

4. Should advertising aimed at children be regulated? Support your response.

5. Should tobacco (or alcohol) advertising be prohibited? Why or why not? How would you deal with First Amendment issues regarding controversial ads?

6. Would you be in favor of regular advertising on public television and radio as a means of financial support for these media? Explain your answer.

7. Is advertising at odds with the ideals of democracy? Why or why not?

SEARCHING THE INTERNET

http://www.adcouncil.org
The site of the nonprofit Ad Council, which uses the pro bono work of top ad agencies to create public-service announcements on topics like education and preventive health.

http://www.adbusters.org
Satire with a sharp anticonsumerist critique is the style of the Vancouver-based Media Foundation, publisher of *Adbusters* magazine.

http://adage.com
Ad Age is the leading advertising trade journal, with a large data portfolio of agency and brand rankings.

http://www.adweek.com
The online version of *Adweek*, a top advertising, marketing, and media publication.

http://www.clioawards.com
The official site for the advertising industry's major awards competition.

http://future.sri.com/vals/valshome.html
The site for the online VALS questionnaire, which categorizes adult consumers based on their psychology and several key demographics.

http://www.naag.org/tob2.htm
Excellent coverage of 1998's historic settlement between tobacco corporations and state attorneys general, which had significant impact on the marketing of tobacco products in the United States.

In Brief

As a class, consider the impact of advertising on your college campus. Are any buildings or sports facilities named after advertisers? Are any on-campus dining facilities run by fast-food franchises? Who has the soda franchise on your campus? (Can you find out how much Coke or Pepsi pays for this franchise?) What are the dominant kinds of companies that advertise on your campus (such as on signs and billboards, beverage containers, banners in dining halls, etc.)? Why do you think these specific advertisers and sponsors target college students? Should college campuses be one of the few environments in society that are free of advertisements? Why or why not? Are there any places in society that are totally free of ads and corporate sponsorship?

In Depth

From a business perspective, magazine ads function to promote advertisers' goods or services over competing brands and to place these goods or services before consumers so that they can make informed buying decisions. We know, however, that ads mean more than what advertisers intend, since readers form their own opinions. We know, too, that ads function as popular culture. Ads operate on a symbolic level to affirm cultural values.

In a three- or four-page analysis, compare and critique three magazine ads. The ads should all feature the same type of product but should be taken from contrasting magazines (for example, three alcohol ads from women's and men's magazines, or three clothing ads from various kinds of publications). In your critique, use the association principle or myth analysis to deal with the ads' cultural meanings. Your analysis should go beyond the issue of whether the ads successfully market their products.

Now think about these questions in regard to the ads you have chosen: What different sets of values are being sold (for example, ideas about patriotism, family, ethnicity, sex, beauty, femininity, masculinity, age, nature, technology, tradition)? Are the ads selling a particular vision (or stereotype) of what it means to be male or female? Of what it means to be young, old, or middle-class? Of what it means to be a member of a particular race or ethnic group?

Your paper should have a central thesis, drawing on evidence from your ads. To this end, organize your paper around an argument that is worth proving. For example, pointing out that your ads "sell their products in different ways" is not an argument. But if you state that an ad sells "the American dream as equal opportunity for all," or that it is racist or sexist, these arguments are worth proving.

In the mid-1950s, the blue-jeans industry was in deep trouble. After hitting a postwar peak in 1953, jeans sales began to slide. The durable one-hundred-year-old denim product had become associated with rock and roll and teenage troublemakers. Popular movies, especially *The Wild One* and *Blackboard Jungle,* featured emotionally disturbed, blue-jeans-wearing "young toughs" terrorizing adult authority figures. A Broadway play about juvenile delinquency was even entitled *Blue Denim*. The worst was yet to come, however. In 1957, the public school system in Buffalo, New York, banned the wearing of blue jeans for all high-school students. Formerly associated with farmers, factory workers, and an adult work ethic, jeans had become a reverse fashion statement for teenagers—something many adults could not abide.

In response to the crisis, the denim industry waged a public relations (PR) campaign to eradicate the delinquency label and rejuvenate denim's image. In 1956, the nation's top blue-jeans manufacturers formed the national Denim Council "to put schoolchildren back in blue jeans through a concerted national public relations, advertising, and promotional effort."[1] First the council targeted teens, but its promotional efforts were unsuccessful. The manufacturers soon realized that the problem was not with the teens but with the parents, administrators, teachers, and school boards. It was the adults who felt threatened by a fashion trend that seemed to promote disrespect through casualness. In response, the council hired a public relations firm to turn the image of blue jeans around. Over the next five years, the firm did just that.

The denim public relations team determined that mothers were refusing to outfit their children in jeans because of the product's association with delinquency. To change this perception among women, the team encouraged fashion designers to update denim's image by producing new women's sportswear styles made from the fabric. Media outlets and fashion editors were soon inundated with news releases about the "new look" of durable denim.

The denim PR team next enlisted sportswear designers to provide new designs for both men's and women's work and utility clothes, long the backbone of denim sales. Targeting business reporters as well as fashion editors, the team transformed the redesign effort into a story that appealed to writers in both areas. They also planned retail-store promotions nationwide, including "jean queen" beauty contests, and advanced positive denim stories in men's publications.

The team's major PR coup, however, involved an association with the newly formed national Peace Corps. The brainchild of the Kennedy administration, the Peace Corps encouraged young people to serve their country by working with people from poorer nations. Envisioning the Peace Corps as the flip side of delinquency, the Denim Council saw its opening. In 1961, it agreed to outfit the first group of two hundred corps volunteers in denim. As a result of all these PR efforts, by 1963 manufacturers were flooded with orders, and sales of jeans and other denim goods were way up. The delinquency tag disappeared, and jeans gradually became associated with a more casual, though not antisocial, dress ethic.

The blue-jeans story illustrates a major difference between advertising and public relations: Advertising is controlled publicity that a company or an individual buys; public relations attempts to secure favorable media publicity (which is more difficult to control) to promote a company or client. In advertising, clients buy space or time for their products or services, and consumers know who paid for the messages. But with public relations the process is more subtle, requiring news media to accept the premise or legitimacy of a PR campaign and to use it as news. The transformation of denim in the public's eye was achieved primarily without buying advertising. The PR team restyled denim's image mainly by cultivating friendly relations with reporters who subsequently wrote stories associating the fabric with a casual, dedicated, youthful America.

Publicity refers to one type of PR communication: messages that spread information about a person, corporation, issue, or policy in various media. Public relations today, however, uses many communication strategies besides publicity. In fact, much of what PR specialists do involves dealing with negative or unplanned publicity. For example, when documents and audiotapes surfaced in the fall of 1996 revealing that top executives at Texaco had made racist remarks, an intense PR campaign began. It employed a range of tactics, including paid TV advertising, major news conferences, and meetings with regional Texaco distributors. To counter national protests by African American groups and plunging stock-market values, Texaco's CEO apologized quickly and initiated broad strategies for improving race relations throughout the company.

Because it involves multiple forms of communication, **public relations** is difficult to define precisely. It covers a wide array of actions, such as managing complicated issues, shaping the image of a politician or celebrity, repairing the image of a major corporation, establishing two-way communication between consumers and companies, and molding wartime propaganda. Broadly defined, *public relations* refers to the entire range of efforts by an individual, an agency, or any organization attempting to reach or persuade audiences.[2]

The social and cultural impact of public relations, like that of advertising, has been immense. In its infancy, PR helped convince many American businesses of the value of nurturing the public, who had been redefined as purchasers rather than as producers of their own goods. PR also set the tone for the corporate image-building that characterized the economic environment of the twentieth century. Not only did modern PR pave the way for the public's tacit approval of phone and utility monopolies but it transformed the profession of journalism by complicating the way "facts" could be interpreted. Perhaps PR's most significant effect, however, has been on the political process in which individuals and organizations—on both the Right and the Left—hire *spin doctors* to shape their media images.

Without public relations, the news profession would be hard-pressed to keep up with every upcoming event or complex issue. Although reporters and editors do not like to admit it, PR departments and agencies are a major source of story ideas and information. In this chapter, we will examine the impact of public relations and the historical conditions that affected its development as a modern profession—how it helped to transform America into a more image-conscious society. We will begin by looking at nineteenth-century press agents and the role that railroads and utility companies played in developing corporate PR. We will then consider the rise of modern PR, particularly the influences of ex-reporters Ivy Lee and Edward Bernays. In addition, we will explore the major practices and specialties of public relations, the reasons for the long-standing antagonism between journalists and the PR profession, and the social responsibilities of PR in a democracy.

> "An image . . . is not simply a trademark, a design, a slogan or an easily remembered picture. It is a studiously crafted personality profile of an individual, institution, corporation, product or service."
>
> —Daniel Boorstin, *The Image*, 1961

early developments in public relations

At the beginning of the twentieth century, the United States slowly shifted to a consumer-oriented, industrial society, which fostered the rapid spread of advertising and publicity for new products and services. During this gradual transformation from farm to factory, PR emerged as a profession, partly because businesses needed to fend off increased scrutiny from muckraking journalists and emerging labor unions.[3]

Prior to this time, the first PR practitioners were simply theatrical **press agents**: those who sought to advance a client's image through media exposure, primarily via stunts staged for newspapers. The potential of these early PR techniques soon became obvious to business executives who wanted to boost their companies and to politicians who needed a positive public image to win votes. For instance, press agents were used by people like Daniel Boone, who engineered various land-grab and real-estate ventures, and Davy Crockett, who in addition to his heroic exploits was also involved in the massacre of Native Americans. Such individuals often wanted to repair and shape their reputation as cherished frontier legends or as respectable candidates for public office.

p. t. barnum, buffalo bill, and the railroads

The most notorious theatrical agent of the 1800s was Phineas Taylor (P. T.) Barnum, who used gross exaggeration, fraudulent stories, and staged events to secure newspaper coverage for his clients, his American Museum, and later, his circus. Barnum's best-known acts included the "midget" General Tom Thumb, Swedish soprano Jenny Lind, Jumbo the Elephant, and Joice Heth, who Barnum claimed was the 161-year-old nurse of George Washington (although she was actually 80 when she died). These performers became some of the earliest nationally known celebrities because of Barnum's skill in using the media for promotion. Decrying outright fraud and cheating, Barnum understood that his audiences liked to be tricked. In newspapers and on handbills, he later often revealed the strategies behind his more elaborate hoaxes.

From 1883 to 1916, former army scout William F. Cody, who once killed buffalo for the railroads, promoted himself in his "Buffalo Bill's Wild West and Congress of Rough Riders" traveling show. Cody's troupe—which featured bedouins, cossacks, and gauchos as well as "cowboys and Indians"—re-created dramatic gunfights, the Civil War, and battles of the Old West. The show employed sharpshooter Annie Oakley and Lakota medicine man Sitting Bull, whose own legends were partially shaped by Cody's nine publicity agents. These agents were led by John Burke, who promoted the show for its thirty-four-year run. Burke was one of the first PR agents to use a variety of media channels: promotional newspaper stories, magazine articles and ads, dime novels, theater marquees, poster art, and early films. Burke's efforts successfully elevated Cody's show, which was seen by more than fifty million people in a thousand cities in twelve different countries.[4] Burke and Buffalo Bill shaped many of the lasting myths that developed about rugged American individualism and frontier expansion. Along with Barnum, they were among the first to use publicity to elevate entertainment-centered culture to an international level.

One of the first publicity agents, P. T. Barnum (1810–1891) started his famous circus in 1871. Using poster art, print-media ads, and publicity stunts, Barnum made his name synonymous with the circus. In 1881, he merged his traveling show with Joseph Bailey's. Barnum & Bailey called their product the "greatest show on earth." The five Ringling brothers from Baraboo, Wisconsin, bought out Barnum & Bailey in 1907.

During the 1800s, America's largest industrial companies, particularly the railroads, also employed press agents to win favor in the court of public opinion. Initially, government involvement in railroad development was minimal; local businesses raised funds to finance the spread of rail service. Around 1850, however, the railroads began pushing for federal subsidies, complaining that local fund-raising efforts took too long. In its drive for government support, for example, Illinois Central promoted the following public strategy: "The railroad line would be expensive to construct; it would open up new land for economic development; without subsidy, the line might not be built; with subsidy the public interest would be served."[5] Illinois Central was one of the first companies to use government lobbyists to argue that railroads between the North and the South would ease tensions, unite the two regions, and prevent a war.

The railroads successfully campaigned for government support by developing some of the earliest publicity tactics. Their first strategy was simply to buy favorable news stories through direct bribes. By the late 1880s, this practice was so common that a Chicago news reporter published his tongue-in-cheek rates: "For setting forth of virtues (actual or alleged) of presidents, general managers, or directors, $2 per line. . . . For complimentary notices of the wives and children of railroad officials, we demand $1.50 per line. . . . Epic poems, containing descriptions of scenery, dining cars, etc., will be published at special rates."[6] In addition to planting favorable articles in the press, the railroads engaged in *deadheading:* the practice of giving reporters free rail passes with the tacit understanding that they would write glowing reports about rail travel. Occasionally, railroads also hired academics to write articles supporting their rationale for subsidies. This was a particularly good way to influence legislators and intellectual readers. Eventually, wealthy railroads received federal subsidies and increased their profits, while the public shouldered much of the financial burden for rail expansion.

In terms of power and influence, companies like Illinois Central and the Pennsylvania Railroad in the late 1800s were comparable to American automakers in the 1950s. Having obtained construction subsidies, the larger rail companies turned their attention to bigger game—lobbying the government to control rates and reduce competition, especially from smaller, aggressive regional lines. Any PR strategy used for this purpose would have faced an uphill battle, however, since the entrepreneurial spirit of the times encouraged competition. Consequently, the campaign for regulation tried to convince people that competitive lower rates did not benefit the average citizen and that competition actually encouraged unfair business practices.

Railroad lobbyists argued that federal support would improve service and guarantee quality, since the government would be keeping a close watch. These lobbying efforts, accompanied by favorable publicity, led to passage of the Interstate Commerce Act in 1881, authorizing railroads "to revamp their freight classification, raise rates, and eliminate fare reduction."[7] Historians have argued that the PR campaign's success actually led to the decline of railroads; artificially maintained higher rates and burdensome government regulations forced smaller firms out of business and eventually drove many customers to other modes of transportation.

> "Public relations developed in the early part of the twentieth century as a profession which responded to, and helped shape, the public, newly defined as irrational, not reasoning; spectatorial, not participant; consuming, not productive."
> —Michael Schudson,
> *Discovering the News,*
> 1978

the modern public relations agent

Along with the railroads, utility companies such as Chicago Edison and AT&T also used PR strategies in the late 1800s to derail competition and eventually attain monopoly status. In fact, although both local and regional competitors existed at the time, AT&T's PR and lobbying efforts were so effective that they eliminated all telephone competition—with the government's blessing—until the 1980s.

The tactics of the 1880s and 1890s, however, would haunt public relations as it struggled to become a respected profession. In addition to buying the votes of key lawmakers, the utilities used a number of shady practices. These included third-party editorial services, which would send favorable articles about utilities to newspapers; assigning company managers to become leaders in community groups; producing ghostwritten articles (often using the names of prominent leaders and members of women's social groups, who were flattered to see their names in print); and influencing textbook authors to write histories favorable to utilities.[8]

As the promotional agendas of many companies escalated in the late 1800s, a number of reporters and muckraking journalists began investigating these practices.

By the early 1900s, with an informed citizenry paying more attention, it became more difficult for large firms to fool the press and mislead the public. With the rise of the middle class, increasing literacy among the working classes, and the spread of information through print media, democratic ideals began to threaten the established order of business and politics—and the elite groups who managed them.

"Poison Ivy" Lee. Most nineteenth-century corporations and manufacturers cared little about public sentiment. By the early 1900s, though, executives realized that their companies could sell more products if they were associated with positive public images and values. Into this public space stepped Ivy Ledbetter Lee, considered one of the founders of modern public relations. Lee understood the undercurrents of social change. He counseled clients that honesty and directness were better PR devices than the deceptive practices that had prevailed in the 1800s, which had fostered a climate of suspicion and anti-big-business sentiment.

A minister's son and once a Princeton economics student, Lee, a former reporter, opened one of the first New York PR firms with a colleague in the early 1900s. Lee quit the firm in 1906 to work for the Penn Railroad, which, following a rail accident, wanted him to help downplay bad publicity. Lee's advice, however, was that Penn admit its mistake, vow to do better, and let newspapers in on the story. These suggestions ran counter to what the utilities and railroads had been doing. Nevertheless, Lee, who believed in open, frank relationships between the press and business, argued that such a policy would lead to a more favorable public image in an era when companies could no longer afford to alienate customers. In the end, Penn adopted Lee's strategies.

In 1914, Lee went to work for John D. Rockefeller, who by the 1880s controlled 90 percent of the nation's oil industry (Rockefeller once said, "It is my duty to make money and still more money").[9] Rockefeller suffered from periodic image problems, particularly after Ida Tarbell's powerful muckraking series in *McClure's* magazine on Rockefeller's Standard Oil trust. Despite his philanthropic work, Rockefeller was often depicted in the press as a tyrant, as were other corporate bosses. The Rockefeller and Standard Oil reputations reached a low point in April 1914, when tactics to stop union organizing erupted in tragedy at a fuel and iron company in Ludlow, Colorado. During a violent strike, fifty-three workers and family members, including thirteen women and children, died.

Ivy Lee was hired to contain the damaging publicity fallout. He immediately distributed a series of "fact" sheets to the press, telling the corporate side of the story and discrediting the United Mine Workers, which had been trying to organize the Ludlow workers. As he had done for Penn, Lee brought in the press and staged photo opportunities. John D. Rockefeller Jr., who by then ran his father's company, donned overalls and a miner's helmet and posed with the families of workers and union leaders. While Lee helped the company improve conditions for workers, the publicity campaign also kept the union out of the Ludlow coal mines. This was probably the first use of a PR campaign in a labor-management dispute. Over the years, Lee completely transformed the family's image, urging the discreet Rockefellers to publicize their charitable work. To improve his image, the senior Rockefeller took to handing out dimes to children wherever he went—a strategic ritual that historians attribute to Lee.

Called "Poison Ivy" by newspaper critics and corporate foes, Lee had a complex understanding of facts. He realized, better than most journalists of his day, that facts were open to various interpretations. For Lee, facts were elusive and malleable, begging to be forged and shaped. Interpreting facts so as to shine the best light on a client was not viewed as a particularly honorable practice, however. In the Ludlow case, for instance, Lee noted that the women and children who died while retreating from the charging

"Since crowds do not reason, they can only be organized and stimulated through symbols and phrases."

—Ivy Lee, 1917

company-backed militia had overturned a stove, which caught fire and killed them. His PR fact sheet implied that they had, in part, been victims of their own carelessness.

In the 1930s, Ivy Lee was investigated by Congress for counseling German industries during the Nazi regime and for fraternizing with the Soviet Union under Joseph Stalin. Some critics thought that Lee's interest in a communist nation represented a curious contradiction for an avowed capitalist. In Lee's earlier work for railroads and utilities, however, he had advocated an anticompetition, pro-consolidation theme that he believed was in the best interests of his clients. Lee had argued for corporate-controlled monopolies, which benefited from protective government regulation. Thus Lee did share some common ground with foreign governments that ran state-controlled, anticompetitive business monopolies.

Edward Bernays. The nephew of Sigmund Freud, former reporter Edward Bernays inherited the public relations mantle from Ivy Lee and dressed it up with modern social science. Bernays, who died in 1995 at age 103, was the first person to apply the findings of psychology and sociology to the business of public relations. He also referred to himself as a "public relations counselor" rather than as just a publicity agent. Over the years, Bernays's client list included General Electric, the American Tobacco Company, General Motors, *Good Housekeeping* and *Time* magazines, Procter & Gamble, RCA, the government of India, and the city of Vienna. In addition, he served as an adviser to President Coolidge in the 1920s, helping the president revamp his stiff, formal image.

Bernays made key contributions to public relations education.[10] He taught the first class called *public relations*—at New York University in 1923—and wrote the field's first textbook, *Crystallizing Public Opinion*. For many years, his definition of PR was a standard: "Public relations is the attempt, by information, persuasion, and adjustment, to engineer public support for an activity, cause, movement, or institution." Bernays worked for the Committee on Public Information (CPI) during World War I, developing propaganda that supported America's entry into that struggle. Later, CPI helped create the image of President Woodrow Wilson as a peacemaker, among the first full-scale governmental attempts to mobilize public opinion.

Hired by the American Tobacco Company after World War I, Bernays was asked to develop a campaign that would make smoking more publicly acceptable for newly liberated women who had recently won the right to vote. Among other strategies, Bernays staged an event: placing women smokers in New York's 1929 Easter parade. He labeled cigarettes "torches of freedom" and encouraged women to smoke as a symbol of their newly acquired suffrage and independence from men. He also asked the women he used in the parade to contact newspaper and newsreel companies in advance— to announce their symbolic protest. The campaign received plenty of free publicity from newspapers and magazines. Within five weeks of the parade, men-only smoking rooms in New York theaters began opening up to women.

Through much of his writing, Bernays suggested that emerging forms of social democracy threatened the established hierarchical order. He thought it was important for experts and leaders to keep business and society pointed in the right directions: "The duty of the higher strata of society—the cultivated, the learned, the expert, the intellectual—is therefore clear. They must inject moral and spiritual motives into public opinion."[11] Bernays saw a typical public relations campaign giving shape to public opinion—what he termed the "engineering of consent." Bernays believed that for any PR campaign to work, securing the consent of the people was the crucial ingredient.

> "It was the **astounding success of propaganda** during the war which opened the eyes of the intelligent few in all departments of life to the possibilities of regimenting the public mind."
>
> —Edward Bernays, *Propaganda*, 1928

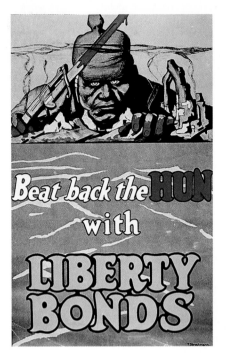

During World War I, PR pioneer Edward Bernays (1891–1995) worked for the federal Committee on Public Information (CPI). One of the main functions of the CPI was to create the poster art and print ads that would persuade reluctant or isolationist Americans to support the war effort against Germany.

Ivy Lee believed that public opinion was based on people's self-interests. Both Lee and Bernays thought that such opinion was pliant and not always rational: In the hands of the right experts, leaders, and PR counselors, public opinion was ready for shaping in forms that people could rally behind.[12] Walter Lippmann, the newspaper columnist who wrote *Public Opinion* in 1922, also believed in the importance of an expert class to direct the more irrational twists and turns of public opinion. But he saw the development of public relations as "a clear sign that the facts of modern life [did] not spontaneously take a shape in which they can be known."[13] Lippmann lamented that too often PR professionals with hidden agendas, rather than detached reporters, were giving only their meaning to the facts.

Throughout Bernays's most active years, his business partner and later his wife, Doris Fleischman, worked on many joint projects as a researcher and coauthor. Beginning in the 1920s, she was one of the first women to work in advertising and public relations. She edited a pamphlet called *Contact*, which explained the emerging profession of public relations to America's most powerful leaders. Because it was a new quasi-profession, not claimed entirely by men, PR was one of the few professions—apart from teaching and nursing—that were accessible to women who chose to work outside the home. By the mid-1990s, women made up more than half of the sixteen thousand members of the Public Relations Society of America (PRSA), the professional organization that was founded in 1948.

pseudo-events and manufacturing news

Armed with its new understanding of public psychology, modern public relations changed not only the relationship between corporations and the public but among corporations, politics, and journalism. In his influential book *The Image*, historian Daniel Boorstin coined the term **pseudo-event** to refer to one of the key contributions of PR and advertising in the twentieth century. Basically, a pseudo-event is any circumstance created for the purpose of gaining coverage in the media. In other words, if no news media show up, there is no event. Boorstin extended this idea to argue that any advertisement is a classic example of a pseudo-event, since an ad would not exist without collusion between advertisers and various media outlets.[14]

More typical pseudo-events are interviews, press conferences, TV and radio talk shows, the Super Bowl pregame show, or any other staged activity aimed at drawing public attention and media coverage. Such events depend on the participation of clients and performers and on the media's recording the performances. In regard to national politics, Theodore Roosevelt's administration set up the first White House pressroom and held the first presidential press conferences in the early 1900s. In the 1990s, Vice President Al Gore championed White House Internet sites, making it possible for larger public audiences to interact with reporters and leaders in electronic press conferences.

As powerful companies, savvy politicians, and activist groups became aware of the media's susceptibility to pseudo-events, these activities proliferated. For example, to get free publicity, companies began staging press conferences to announce new product lines. During the 1960s, antiwar and civil-rights protesters began their events only when the news media were assembled. One anecdote from that era aptly illustrates the principle of a pseudo-event: A reporter asked a student leader about the starting time for a particular protest; the student responded, "When can you get here?"

Politicians running for national office have become particularly adept at scheduling press conferences and interviews around 5 or 6 P.M. They realize that local TV news is live during these times, so they stage pseudo-events to take advantage of TV's appetite for live remote feeds and breaking news.

the practice of public relations

By the late 1990s, more than 150,000 practitioners as well as 5,000 companies offered various types of PR services in the United States. In addition, the formal study of public relations, especially since the 1980s, experienced significant growth in colleges and universities. As certified PR programs expanded (often featuring journalism as a minor), the profession relied less and less on the ranks of reporters for its workforce. At the same time, new courses in professional ethics and issues management trained future practitioners to be more responsible.

The growth of formal PR education has been fairly dramatic. In the 1970s, the majority of students in communications and journalism programs indicated in surveys that they intended to pursue careers in news or magazine writing. By the late 1980s, however, similar surveys indicated that the majority of students wanted to enter public relations or advertising. Throughout the 1990s, entry-level salaries and opportunities were greater in these latter areas. By the late 1990s, the Public Relations Student Society of America (PRSSA) had more than 5,500 members and chapters in 200 colleges and universities. Such growth parallels the general rise of business schools and majors throughout the 1970s and 1980s.

approaches to organized pr

In 1988, the PRSA offered this useful definition of PR: "Public relations helps an organization and its publics adapt mutually to each other." To carry out this mutual communication process, the PR industry has two major approaches. First, many agencies function as independent companies whose sole job is to provide various clients with PR services. (During the 1980s and 1990s, though, many large ad agencies acquired independent PR firms as subsidiaries.) Second, most companies, which may or may not buy the services of independent PR firms, maintain their own in-house staffs to handle routine PR tasks, such as writing press releases, managing various media requests, staging special events, and dealing with the public.

Independent Agencies. About sixteen hundred American companies identify themselves exclusively as public relations counseling firms. Two of the biggest, Burson-Marsteller and Hill and Knowlton, are now subsidiaries of global ad agencies (see Table 12.1). Young & Rubicam, an advertising giant, operates Burson-Marsteller, founded in 1953. With billings of $200 million or more annually, Burson-Marsteller

		% Change	Number
TABLE 12.1			
The Top 15 Public Relations Firms, 1998			
(by Net Fees)			
Firm	1998 Net Fees	vs. 1997	of Employees
Burson-Marsteller	$258,417,000	+4.2	1,765
Hill and Knowlton	206,000,000	+8.9	1,570
Porter Novelli International	183,050,000	+23.6	1,822
Shandwick	170,300,000	+7.3	1,731
Fleishman-Hillard	160,692,000	+19.1	1,231
Edelman Public Relations Worldwide	157,840,530	+18.1	1,636
Ketchum	125,248,000	+29.6	1,032
BSMG Worldwide	118,963,000	+93.0	913
Weber Public Relations Worldwide	83,166,000	+36.2	648
GCI/APCO	79,667,957	+28.4	763
Ogilvy Public Relations Worldwide	77,927,000	+40.8	700
Manning, Selvage & Lee	76,037,050	+19.6	520
Golin/Harris International	52,973,267	+11.9	430
Ruder Finn	51,199,000	+10.1	458
Waggener Edstrom	40,900,000	+20.3	409

Source: The J. R. O'Dwyer Company, 1999, <www.odwyerpr.com>.

was one of PR's top-ranking firms in the 1990s. It has about sixty offices operating in more than twenty-five countries and nearly eighteen hundred employees worldwide. Among its major clients have been Coca-Cola and General Electric.

Hill and Knowlton claimed the title "counsel of choice" in the mid-1990s for "more than one quarter of the world's largest corporations."[15] A unit of the world's largest ad agency, the WPP Group, Hill and Knowlton employs more than twelve hundred people in twenty-five offices in sixty countries. Its clients have included IBM, Kodak, Nintendo, Pepsi, Procter & Gamble, Xerox, former president Richard Nixon, and the royal family of Kuwait. By the late 1990s, most of the largest PR firms were owned by or affiliated with ad agencies, which had long provided PR as a part of their full-service operations.

In-House Services. In contrast to independent agencies, the most common type of public relations is done in-house by individual companies and organizations. Although about a third of America's largest companies retain an external PR firm, almost every company involved in a manufacturing or service industry has an in-house department. Such departments are also a vital part of many professional organizations, such as the American Medical Association, the AFL-CIO, and the National Association of Broadcasters, as well as large nonprofit organizations, such as the American Cancer Society, the Arthritis Foundation, and most universities and colleges.

performing public relations

Public relations, like advertising, pays careful attention to the various audiences and clients that it interacts with or serves. These groups include not only consumers and the general public but company employees, shareholders, media organizations, government agencies, and community and industry leaders. Among potential clients, which constitute another public, are politicians, educational institutions, small businesses, industries, and nonprofit organizations (including some hospitals, museums, religious groups, and various charities).

Public relations involves a multitude of practices and techniques. The PRSA identifies a number of general activities associated with PR: publicity, communication, public affairs, issues management, government relations, financial PR, community relations, industry relations, minority relations, advertising, press agentry, promotion, media relations, and propaganda. This last activity, **propaganda**, is communication strategically placed, either as advertising or publicity, to gain public support for a special issue, program, or policy, such as a nation's war effort. All of these activities are typical of public relations, whether they are carried out by a large PR firm or by the in-house department of a product company, a nonprofit organization, or a politician.

The practice of public relations encompasses a wide range of activities. PR personnel produce employee newsletters, manage client trade shows and conferences, conduct historical tours, appear on news programs, organize damage control after negative publicity, and analyze complex issues and trends that may affect a client's future. Basic among these activities, however, are writing and editing, media relations, special events, research, and community and government relations. PR practice is generally divided into two roles: PR technicians, who handle daily short-term activities, and PR managers, who counsel clients and manage activities over the long term.

Writing and Editing. One of the chief day-to-day technical functions in public relations is composing news or **press releases**: announcements, written in the style of news reports, that give new information about an individual, company, or organization and pitch a story idea to the news media (see Figure 12.1). In issuing press releases, often called *handouts* by the news media, PR agents hope that their client information will be picked up and transformed into news. Through press releases, PR firms manage the flow of information; they often control which media get what material in which order. (Sometimes a PR agent will target TV over newspapers or reward a cooperative reporter through the strategic release of information.)

News editors and broadcasters sort through hundreds of releases daily to determine which ones contain the most original ideas or the most currency for their readers and viewers. The majority of large media institutions rewrite and double-check the information in news releases, but small media companies and small-town newspapers often use them verbatim, especially if their own editorial resources are limited or if they are under deadline constraints. Usually, the more closely a press release resembles actual news copy, the more likely it is to be used, which is why newspaper work is a good training ground for PR.

Since the 1970s and the introduction of portable video equipment, agencies and departments have been using **video news releases (VNRs)**, which are thirty- to ninety-second visual PR stories packaged to mimic the style of a broadcast news report. Many large companies now operate their own TV studios, which enable them to produce training videos for their employees and to create VNRs for their clients. Broadcast news stations in small TV markets regularly use video material from VNRs. Although large stations with more resources may get story ideas from VNRs, their news directors do not like to use video material obtained directly from PR sources; they prefer to assemble their own reports in order to maintain their independence. On occasion, news stations have been criticized for using bits of video footage from a VNR without acknowledging the source. *TV Guide* sharply criticized VNRs as "false news" in 1992 after Hill and Knowlton distributed a pro-Kuwaiti VNR to promote American support for the Desert Storm military offensive in 1991.

In addition to issuing press releases, nonprofit groups also produce **public-service announcements (PSAs)**: fifteen- to sixty-second reports or announcements

Figure 12.1
Differences between a Press Release and a News Story

News reporters—especially in medicine, science, and technology—are heavily dependent on public relations for story ideas. Here are excerpts from a medical PR release, written by the in-house PR staff at a suburban Detroit hospital, and a *Detroit News* story, written by a medical reporter, based partly on information in the release.

Source: Courtesy Jim Tobin and Yvette Monet.

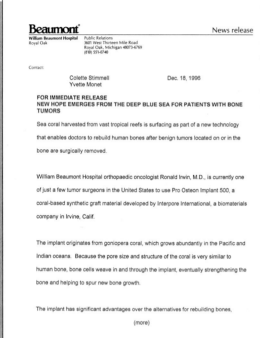

Coral for bone

The coral used in Christian Groth's femur (thighbone) has a maze of interconnected channels, virtually identical to the architecture of human bones themselves. Bone cells and blood vessels grow through the channels, gradually becoming one with the coral.

Bone
Coral
Osteocytes
Blood vessels and new bone cell (Osteocytes) grow in coral

Human bone   Sea coral
(Magnified)

Source: Interpore International

Chris Willis / The Detroit News

Beaumont®

William Beaumont Hospital
Royal Oak

Public Relations
3601 West Thirteen Mile Road
Royal Oak, Michigan 48073-6769
(810) 551-0740

News release

Contact:

Colette Stimmell   Dec. 18, 1996
Yvette Monet

FOR IMMEDIATE RELEASE
NEW HOPE EMERGES FROM THE DEEP BLUE SEA FOR PATIENTS WITH BONE TUMORS

Sea coral harvested from vast tropical reefs is surfacing as part of a new technology that enables doctors to rebuild human bones after benign tumors located on or in the bone are surgically removed.

William Beaumont Hospital orthopaedic oncologist Ronald Irwin, M.D., is currently one of just a few tumor surgeons in the United States to use Pro Osteon Implant 500, a coral-based synthetic graft material developed by Interpore International, a biomaterials company in Irvine, Calif.

The implant originates from goniopera coral, which grows abundantly in the Pacific and Indian oceans. Because the pore size and structure of the coral is very similar to human bone, bone cells weave in and through the implant, eventually strengthening the bone and helping to spur new bone growth.

The implant has significant advantages over the alternatives for rebuilding bones,

(more)

Sea coral bone graft gives teen chance at being a kid again

An amazing coincidence of nature helps put implant patients back on their feet.

By James Tobin
The Detroit News

Because of a gift from the sea — tropical coral harvested in the south Pacific — Christian Groth is swimming again.

The coral rests snugly inside the femur (thigh bone) of his right leg, just above the knee. It fills a hole the size of a large marble, replacing a benign tumor that was making it harder and harder for Chris, 14, to play the sports he loves.

If you used a powerful magnifying glass to compare the coral to Chris' bone, you couldn't tell the difference. The two materials are almost exactly the same.

Groth

Thanks to this remarkable coincidence of nature, Chris — one of the first people in Metro Detroit to have a bone repaired with sea coral — is "doing everything," said his doctor, Ronald Irwin, an orthopedic oncologist affiliated with Beaumont Hospital, Royal Oak. "It looks good," Irwin said. "He'll ski this year."

The material won't work for every bone problem, but for Chris, an eighth-grader from Birmingham, and others, it means less pain and a quicker recovery than with other bone-graft materials, including his own bone.

The new process begins in the Pacific and Indian oceans, where a California company called Interpore International, the only provider so far, harvests a couple tons of coral annually — a yield so small that environmentalists aren't upset.

At Interpore, the coral is blasted with heat and chemicals to convert it to a substance called coralline hydroxyapatite, the strength-giving mineral in bone. Then it's cut into small blocks or crumbled into granules.

The key advantage: It retains the coral's structure — an intricate, three-dimensional maze of tiny channels.

Bone doctors sculpt the blocks to fit the problem — a tumor site, like Chris', or a fracture or shattered bone that needs extra material. Irwin used the granules, since he couldn't get a sculpted block into the cavity inside Chris' femur. The surgery was performed Aug. 20.

Once the coral was in place, bone cells and blood vessels began to creep into the coral's tiny channels, like vines through a trellis. Chris' immune system didn't reject the coral because its structure and substance is so similar to human bone.

Gradually, the coral and bone become one.

Traditionally, doctors have used bone from the patient's own pelvis for such repairs. But that demands two surgeries instead of one, and the pelvic surgery means a lot of pain and difficult recoveries.

Using grafts from cadavers carries a slight risk of infection, and using grafts from living donors sometimes provokes the immune system.

Irwin uses the coral only for benign tumors, not malignancies or fractures. But other doctors are looking to coral for those repairs, too, and it may be useful for some bone breaks in people with osteoporosis.

---

for radio and television that promote government programs, educational projects, voluntary agencies, or social reform. As part of their requirement to serve the public interest, broadcasters historically have been encouraged to carry free PSAs. Since the deregulation of broadcasting began in the 1980s, however, there has been less pressure and no minimum obligation for TV and radio stations to air PSAs. When PSAs do run, they are frequently scheduled between midnight and 6 A.M., a less commercially valuable time slot with relatively few viewers or listeners.

The writing and editing part of PR also involves creating brochures and catalogues as well as company newsletters and annual reports for shareholders. It may include writing and editing speeches that aim to boost a politician's image or a company's stature. Major politicians and business leaders today seldom write their own speeches. Instead, they hire speechwriters or PR specialists.

Media Relations. Through publicity, PR managers specializing in media relations promote a client or organization by securing favorable coverage in the news media. Media specialization often requires an in-house PR person to speak on behalf of an organization or to direct reporters to experts who can provide the best, or at least official, sources of information.

Media-relations specialists also perform *damage control* or *crisis management* when negative publicity occurs (see "Case Study: GM Trucks and NBC's *Dateline* Disaster" on page 391). Occasionally, in times of crisis—such as a virus outbreak at a hospital, a scandal at a university, or a safety recall by a car manufacturer—a PR spokesperson might be designated as the only source of information available to news media. Although journalists often resent being cut off from higher administrative levels and leaders, the institution or company wants to ensure that rumors and inaccurate stories do not circulate easily in the media. In these situations, a game often develops in which reporters attempt to circumvent the company spokesperson and induce a knowledgeable insider to talk *off the record*, providing background details without being named directly as a source.

PR agents who specialize in media relations also recommend advertising to their clients when it seems appropriate. Unlike publicity, which is sometimes outside a PR agency's control, paid advertising may help to focus a complex issue or a client's image. Publicity, however, carries the aura of legitimate news and thus has more credibility than advertising. In addition, media specialists cultivate associations with editors, reporters, freelance writers, and broadcast news directors to ensure that press releases or VNRs are favorably received. Since the majority of this material goes unused, a PR specialist who can get information accepted as news is especially valuable.

Special Events. Another public relations specialty involves coordinating special events. Since the late 1960s, for instance, the city of Milwaukee has run Summerfest, a ten-day music and food festival that attracts nearly a million people each year. As the festival's popularity grew, various companies sought to become sponsors of the event. Local manufacturers and the beer industry, for example, signed up to support different musical venues. The Miller Brewing Company sponsored a festival stage devoted to jazz. In exchange for sponsorship, the stage carried the Miller name, which also accompanied many items connected with Summerfest. In this way, Miller received favorable publicity by showing a commitment to the city that serves as the company's corporate headquarters.[16]

Many business executives score points with the public by associating their company with special community events. For example, the city of Milwaukee runs Summerfest, one of the world's largest food and music festivals. Since the late 1960s, the festival has been prominently supported by the region's beer industry.

More typical of special-events publicity is the corporate sponsor that aligns its company image with a cause, or an organization that has positive stature among the general public. For example, for more than twenty-five years, Mobil Oil has underwritten special programming such as *Masterpiece Theater* on PBS. At the local level, companies often sponsor a community parade or a charitable fund-raising activity. When a new professional sports team arrives in a community, a host of local companies may compete to associate themselves with the new franchise. In this kind of situation, a team's PR specialist attempts to identify those companies that will provide the most favorable publicity for the client.

Research. Just as advertising is driven today by demographic and psychographic research, PR uses similar strategies to project a client's image to the appropriate audience. The research area is PR's fastest-growing segment as the profession attempts to bring new social-science techniques to its audience studies and image campaigns. Since historically it has been difficult to determine why particular campaigns succeed or fail, research has become the key ingredient in PR forecasting. Like advertising studies, PR research targets specific audiences. It uses mail and telephone surveys to get a fix on an audience's perceptions of a client's reputation.

As in advertising research, focus groups have become prominent in public relations campaigns. Although such groups are often unreliable because of small sample size, they are fairly easy to set up and do not require elaborate statistical designs. In 1990, for example, Gemstar Development Corporation introduced a remote-control technology that helps people program television codes into their VCRs more easily. This device, which employs a one-step recording technique using number codes printed in *TV Guide* and most newspaper TV supplements, was the end product of research initiated by a California PR firm, Rogers and Associates. The firm used three focus groups totaling forty-eight participants to learn that the majority of the nation's then seventy million VCR owners did not know how to tape movies or TV programs because the steps seemed too complicated. The research project concluded that users were most interested in "high-fidelity picture quality," one-step recording, and "a VCR that quickly locates a segment on your recorded tape for playback or editing." Not only did the participants help pick the name of the product—VCR Plus+—but 77 percent of them bought or ordered the device after their experience in the focus group.[17]

Community and Consumer Relations. Two other PR activities involve building relationships between companies and their communities. Companies have learned that sustaining close ties with their neighbors not only enhances their image but promotes the idea that the companies are good citizens. Such ties expose a business to potential customers through activities such as plant tours, town parades and open houses, and special events such as a company's anniversary. Many companies also operate museums—with attached gift shops—that point up their historical importance to the community.

Socially conscientious PR firms encourage their employees and their clients to get involved in community projects, donating work and time that pays off by strengthening a firm's image. For example, the efforts of Habitat for Humanity—building low-income housing using volunteers and donated material—are often supported by progressive public relations companies.

Besides encouraging client employees to get involved in community activities, many PR firms like their clients to make charitable donations that build local bonds. Some companies offer their work sites to local groups for meetings and help in fund-raising efforts. More progressive companies get involved in unemployment and job-retraining programs, and others donate equipment and workers to urban revitalization projects such as Habitat for Humanity.

In terms of customer relations, PR has become much more sophisticated since the 1960s, when Ralph Nader's *Unsafe at Any Speed* revealed safety problems concerning the Chevrolet Corvair. Nader's book gave General Motors a corporate migraine that resulted in the discontinuance of the Corvair line. More important, however, Nader's book lit the fuse that ignited a vibrant consumerism movement. During the 1960s, consumers became more sophisticated and, consequently, unwilling to readily accept the claims of those in power—including corporate leaders. Contributing to this movement was the trend toward large multinational corporate mergers and the rise of impersonal chain stores, both of which signaled a decreasing accountability to consumers.

For a while, the consumerism movement drew media attention. Many newspapers and TV stations hired consumer reporters, who tracked down the sources of customer complaints and often embarrassed companies by putting them in the media spotlight. Firms that were PR savvy responded by paying more attention to customers, establishing product and service guarantees, and ensuring that all calls and mail from customers were answered promptly. The smartest companies produced consumer-education literature about specific products and developed close ties with local consumer groups.

GM Trucks and NBC's *Dateline* Disaster

On November 17, 1992, NBC's new *Dateline* program aired a report that showed two different full-size Chevy pickup trucks bursting into flames after being hit broadside by small cars. Along with the demonstration, *Dateline* implied that the trucks' side-mounted fuel tanks were extremely dangerous.

There was only one problem: The report was phony. For dramatic impact, *Dateline* had rigged the trucks with special igniters. With careful editing, the effect in each case was a big explosion and leaping flames, suggesting that drivers and passengers were at risk. In response, a General Motors crisis-management team fought back. During a thorough investigation, GM got a tip from an area news reporter who had found a witness to the enhanced presentation—a firefighter who had made his own video recording of each crash. GM investigators also located the rigged trucks in an Indiana junkyard.

A GM public relations team wrote a series of letters asking NBC to acknowledge the deception. When NBC executives continued to stand by the report, GM filed a lawsuit in February 1993. The defamation suit was announced at a press conference conducted by Harry Pearce, GM's general counsel. More than 150 reporters, photographers, and TV camera crews attended Pearce's own two-hour exposé of *Dateline*. Systematically critiquing the sixteen-minute report, Pearce convincingly showed that the only fires in both rigged sequences were brief grass fires ignited mainly by gasoline spurting from ill-fitting gas caps that came loose on impact. At the end of the conference, Pearce called on the assembled members of the news media to monitor the episodes of abuse in their own profession.

The day after the conference, NBC and GM entered negotiations, with GM demanding public repentance. On February 9, 1993, *Dateline* coanchors Jane Pauley and Stone Philips read a four-minute retraction and apology. Eventually, three *Dateline* producers were fired and an on-air reporter demoted. Michael Gartner, NBC News president, resigned in disgrace. Up until the press conference, Gartner had claimed that NBC's report was accurate and responsible. NBC reimbursed GM $2 million for the costs of the company's investigation. In turn, GM dropped its defamation suit.

During its battle, GM's PR team also had to confront charges from national safety experts, many of whom were on NBC's payroll. GM was able to discredit these officials and also fend off a recall effort by the National Highway Traffic Safety Administration (NHTSA), which raised its own questions about truck safety. The NHTSA asked GM to recall the trucks in question even before the organization had finished its own investigation. GM refused and made convincing public arguments in two additional press conferences about the flawed conclusions of the NHTSA concerning the proficiency of its older trucks.

The NBC deception is a story that might not have been told had GM decided not to challenge the network. After all, it is very difficult for public individuals and companies to win damages in suits against the mainstream news media, which citizens count on to watch for abuses in politics and business. The strategy used by GM now serves as a crisis-management model for handling complicated cases that have both legal and ethical implications. Although GM is one of the world's largest companies and had the resources (and evidence) to fight back in this case, its PR strategy demonstrated that all citizens have a responsibility to watch over the watchdog.

Today, the impact of the consumer movement is especially evident in the resources devoted to carefully training employees in good customer relations. Many product and service companies have also developed customer-satisfaction questionnaires and "consumer creeds." For example, many restaurants and department stores go beyond asking consumers for advice, outlining what treatment customers should expect and what they should do when those expectations are not met. PR professionals routinely advise clients that satisfied customers mean not only repeat business but new business, based on a strong word-of-mouth reputation about a company's behavior and image.

Government Relations and Lobbying. Public relations also entails maintaining connections with government agencies that have some say in how companies operate in a particular community, state, or nation. The PR divisions of major firms are especially interested in making sure that government regulation neither becomes burdensome nor reduces their control over their businesses. Specialists in this area often develop self-regulatory practices, which either keep governments at some distance or draw on them for subsidies, as the railroads and utilities did in the nineteenth century. Such specialists also monitor new and existing legislation, create opportunities to ensure favorable publicity, and write press releases and direct-mail letters to educate the public on the pros and cons of new regulations.

In many firms, government relations has developed into **lobbying**: the process of attempting to influence the voting of lawmakers to support a client's or an organization's best interests. In seeking favorable legislation, some PR agents lobby government officials on a daily basis. Since lobbyists have generally developed a negative reputation for aggressively hawking special interests, many in public relations are wary of counting lobbying among their activities. Nevertheless, most major firms provide lobbying services. In Washington, D.C., alone, nearly seven thousand registered lobbyists write speeches, articles, and position papers in addition to designing direct-mail campaigns, buying ads, and befriending editors.

Today, most major corporations, trade associations, labor unions, consumer groups, professional organizations, religious groups, and even foreign governments employ lobbyists. For instance, prior to the Persian Gulf War, lobbyists representing both the U.S. oil industry and the government of Kuwait had to work extremely hard to deflect that country's image as a privileged, oil-rich state. Lobbyists tried to change Kuwait's image in order to justify U.S. and UN military action against Iraq, which had invaded Kuwait in 1990. To that end, the Kuwaiti royal family (who went into exile before Iraq invaded Kuwait) hired Hill and Knowlton to help rally public support for U.S. military intervention. The firm developed the idea of a "congressional human rights caucus," which in October 1990 reported acts of barbarism perpetrated by Iraqis on Kuwaitis. Later it was discovered that one witness, a fifteen-year-old Kuwaiti girl who testified at the caucus to seeing acts of cruelty, was the daughter of the Kuwaiti ambassador to the United States and "had been witness to no such events." In January 1991, the United States invaded Iraq, with the majority of Americans, according to opinion polls, supporting the intervention.[18]

tensions between pr and the press

In 1932, Stanley Walker, an editor at the *New York Herald Tribune*, compared public relations agents and publicity advisers to "mass-mind molders, fronts, mouthpieces, chiselers, moochers, and special assistants to the president."[19] Walker added that newspapers and public relations agencies would always remain enemies, even if PR professionals adopted a code of ethics (which they did in the 1950s) to "take them out of the red-light district of human relations."[20] Walker's tone captures the spirit of one of the most mutually dependent—and antagonistic—relationships across mass media.

Much of this antagonism, directed at public relations from the journalism profession, is historical. Reporters have long considered themselves part of an older public-service profession, whereas many regard PR as a pseudo-profession created to distort the facts that reporters work so hard to gather. Over time, reporters and editors developed a nationwide derogatory term for a PR agent—**flack**—which continues in usage to this day. The term derives from the military word *flak*, meaning the antiaircraft artillery shells fired to deflect aerial attack, and from the related *flak jacket*, the protective military attire worn to ward off enemy fire. For journalists, the word *flacks* has come to mean PR people who insert themselves between their business or political employers and the "enemy"—members of the press.

In the 1960s, an Associated Press manual for editors defined a flack as "a person who makes all or part of his income by obtaining space in newspapers without cost to himself or his clients." The AP depiction continued: "A flack is a flack. His job is to say kind things about his client. He will not lie very often, but much of the time he tells less than the whole story. You do not owe the PR man anything. The owner of the newspaper, not the flack, pays your salary. Your immediate job is to serve the readers, not the man who would raid your columns." This description, however, belies journalism's dependence on public relations. Many editors, for instance, admit that more than half of their story ideas each day originate with PR people. Since reporting staffs are limited, they are not privy to all the potential news ideas in a community. For this reason, they rely heavily on PR professionals for suggestions. Throughout the twentieth century, this growing interdependent relationship came to shape both professions.

elements of professional friction

The relationship between journalism and PR is an important and complex one. Although journalism lays claim to independent traditions, the news media have become increasingly reliant on public relations because of the increasing amount of information now available. Staff cutbacks at many papers and television's need for local newscast events have also increased the news media's need for PR story ideas.

Further depleting journalism, PR firms routinely raid the ranks of reporting for new talent. Since most press releases are written in a style that imitates news reports, the PR profession has always sought good writers who are well connected to sources and savvy about the news business. For instance, the fashion industry likes to hire former style or fashion news writers for its PR staff, and university information offices seek reporters who once covered higher education. It is interesting to note that although reporters frequently move into PR, public relations practitioners seldom move into journalism. Furthermore, the news profession rarely accepts prodigal sons or daughters back into the fold once they have left reporting for public relations. According to many reporters and editors, any profession that shapes images is considered manipulative or self-serving—and its practitioners may not be redeemable. Nevertheless, the professions remain co-dependent: PR needs journalists for publicity, and journalism needs PR for story ideas. Several historical explanations shed light on the discord and on the ways in which different media professions interact.

"Tabloid journalists, no matter how pleasant, are not your friends. They are often there to trick or trap your client."
—Fran Matera, *Public Relations Journal*, 1990

Undermining Facts and Blocking Access. Modern public relations rede-fined and complicated the notion of facts. PR professionals demonstrated that the same set of facts can be spun in a variety of ways, depending on what information is emphasized and what is downplayed. As Ivy Lee noted in 1925, "The effort to state an absolute fact is simply an attempt to achieve what is humanly impossible; all I can do is to give you *my interpretation of the facts.*"[21] With practitioners like Lee showing the emerging PR profession how facts and news could be manipulated, the journalist's role as a custodian of accurate information became much more difficult.

Journalists have also objected to PR flacks who block press access to key leaders. At one time, reporters could talk to such leaders directly and obtain quotable infor-mation for their news stories. Now, however, PR people insert themselves between the press and the powerful, thus disrupting the old ritual in which reporters would vie for interviews with top government and business leaders. With the rise of PR, the news media began to receive more carefully controlled information, much of it sent out simultaneously to all media outlets. If PR agents today want to manipulate or use reporters, they may give information to journalists who are likely to cast a story in a favorable light in return for getting the information first. On rarer occasions, a reporter's access to key sources might be cut off altogether if that journalist has writ-ten unfavorably about a client.

Promoting Publicity and Business as News. Another explanation for the professional friction between the press and PR involves simple economics. The trade journal *Edi-tor & Publisher* once called public relations agents "space grab-bers"; what editors and publishers feared actually became a reality: PR agents helped companies "promote as news what otherwise would have been purchased in advertising."[22]

As Ivy Lee wrote to John D. Rockefeller after the oil mag-nate gave money to Johns Hopkins University: "In view of the fact that this was not really news, and that the newspapers gave so much attention to it, it would seem that this was wholly due to the manner in which the material was 'dressed up' for newspaper consumption. It seems to suggest very considerable possibilities along this line."[23] Many newspeople react strongly to this sort of manipulation. And while editors can certainly choose whether to run PR-inspired news stories, by the late 1990s the news profession had become more and more susceptible, given news-staff cutbacks (especially in monopoly newspaper towns trying to maintain or increase their profit margins). Increasingly, newspapers rely on PR professionals for ideas. Yet critics worry that public relations is taking media space and time away from other voices, especially from those who do not have the financial resources or the sophistication to become readily visible in the public eye. Beyond this lies another issue: If public relations can secure publicity for clients in the news, the added credibility of a journalistic context gives clients a status that the purchase of advertising cannot confer.

Today, however, something more subtle underlies journalism's contempt for public relations: Much of journalism actually functions the same way. For instance, politicians, celebrities, and PR firms with abundant resources are clearly afforded more coverage by the news media than are their lesser-known counterparts. For example, workers and union leaders have long argued that the money that corporations allocate to PR leads to more favorable coverage for management positions in labor disputes. Standard news reports may feature subtle language choices, with "rational, cool-headed management making *offers*" and "hot-headed workers making *demands.*" Walter Lippmann saw such differences in 1922 when he wrote: "If you study the way many a strike is reported in the press, you will find very often that [labor] issues are rarely in the headlines, barely in the leading paragraph, and sometimes not even mentioned anywhere."[24] Most newspapers now have business sections that focus on the work of various managers, but few have a labor, worker, or employee section. In fact, most large metro papers have eliminated the specialty beat of labor reporting.[25]

Business, economic, and stock "news" reports generated by corporate PR agents inundate newspapers and the evening news. A single business reporter at a large metro daily sometimes receives as many as a hundred press releases a day—far outnumbering the fraction of handouts generated by organized labor or grassroots organizations. This imbalance is particularly significant in that the great majority of workers are neither managers nor CEOs, and yet these workers receive little if any media coverage on a regular basis. Essentially, as a number of critics have pointed out, mainstream journalism best serves managers and the status quo.

managing the press

Public relations, by making reporters' jobs easier, has often helped reporters become lazy. PR firms now supply what reporters used to work hard to gather for themselves. Instead of going out to beat the competition, many journalists have become content to wait for a PR handout or a good tip before following up on a story. Small community groups, social activists, and nonprofit organizations often cannot afford elaborate publicity. These groups argue that because of PR, large corporations and connected politicians enjoy easier access to reporters and receive more frequent news coverage. Occasionally, also because of PR, powerful firms and individuals receive less critical scrutiny. Some members of the news media—grateful for the reduced workload that occurs when they are provided with handouts—may be hesitant to criticize a particular PR firm's clients.

Dealing with both a tainted past and journalism's hostility have often preoccupied the public relations profession, leading to the development of several image-enhancing strategies. Over the years, for example, as public relations has subdivided itself into specialized areas, it has used more positive descriptive terms, such as "institutional relations," "corporate communications," and "news and information services." With the development of its own professional organization, PRSA, the PR industry has also increased its standing among the public and even the news media.[26] PRSA functions as an internal watchdog group that accredits individuals, maintains a code of ethics, and publishes newsletters and trade publications. Most PRSA local chapters and national conventions also routinely invite reporters and editors to speak to PR practitioners about what the news media expect from their rival professionals. In addition, independent agencies, devoted to uncovering shady or unethical public relations activities, publish their findings in publications like *PR Tactics, PR Week,* or *PR Watch* (see Table 12.2). Ethical issues have become a major focus of the PR profession, with self-examination of these issues routinely appearing in PR textbooks as well as in various professional newsletters.

Public relations' best press strategy, however, may be the limitations of the journalism profession itself. For most of the twentieth century, many reporters and edi-

TABLE 12.2
PRSA Ethics Code

The public relations profession first established an ethics code more than forty-five years ago, yet less than 10 percent of individual practitioners and firms formally subscribe to today's PRSA code. Listed here are the first ten points of the current code.

Public Relations Society of America Code of Professional Standards for the Practice of Public Relations

These articles have been adopted by the Public Relations Society of America to promote and maintain high standards of public service and ethical conduct among its members.

1. A member shall conduct his or her professional life in accord with the **public interest**.
2. A member shall exemplify high standards of **honesty and integrity** while carrying out dual obligations to a client or employer and to the democratic process.
3. A member shall **deal fairly** with the public, with past or present clients or employers, and with fellow practitioners, giving due respect to the idea of free inquiry and to the opinions of others.
4. A member shall adhere to the highest standards of **accuracy and truth**, avoiding extravagant claims or unfair comparisons and giving credit for ideas and words borrowed from others.
5. A member shall not knowingly disseminate **false or misleading information** and shall act promptly to correct erroneous communications for which he or she is responsible.
6. A member shall not engage in any practice which has the purpose of **corrupting** the integrity of channels of communications or the processes of government.
7. A member shall be prepared to **identify publicly** the name of the client or employer on whose behalf any public communication is made.
8. A member shall not use any individual or organization professing to serve or represent an announced cause, or professing to be independent or unbiased, but actually serving another or **undisclosed interest**.
9. A member shall **not guarantee the achievement** of specified results beyond the member's direct control.
10. A member shall **not represent conflicting** or competing interests without the express consent of those concerned, given after a full disclosure of the facts.

Source: PRSA.

tors clung to the ideal that journalism is, at its best, an objective institution that gathers information on behalf of the public. Reporters have only occasionally turned their pens, computers, and cameras on themselves to examine their own practices or their vulnerability to manipulation. Thus, by not challenging PR's more subtle strategies, many journalists have allowed PR professionals to interpret "facts" to their clients' advantage.

Limited by its reluctance or failure to identify and evade savvy public relations tactics, conventional journalism remains vulnerable. Take this hypothetical situation: A wealthy and powerful development corporation decides to raze a homeless shelter to build a condo. The firm uses public relations resources that overwhelm the protests of a few homeless activists. The major newspaper in town attempts to remain neutral on the issue. However, the strength of the corporation's PR unit has already tipped the balance via an abundance of PR handouts. To recenter the scales, the newspaper in this case would have to take an advocacy position on behalf of the activists. But in conventional journalism, detachment prohibits this, and thus the corporate point of view triumphs—or, at least, gains most of the space and time in the news. Although many alternative newspapers and advocacy reporters do a fine job of critiquing the limits of some questionable public relations activities, conventional journalism has few mechanisms for rebalancing the scales tipped by PR embellishment, whether advanced by government or business leaders. Journalists have rarely challenged "the routines of government news management and the creation of pseudo-events."[27]

public relations, social responsibility, and democracy

Although the image of public relations professionals may not be as negative as that of advertisers, a cynical view of the profession nonetheless exists beyond the field of journalism. Given the history of corporate public relations, many concerned citizens believe that when a company or an individual makes a mistake or misleads the public, too often a PR counsel is hired to alter the image rather than to admit the misdeed and correct the problem. An anecdote about a lawn-service/weed-control company illustrates this scenario: "A PR manager for a company named ChemLawn complained that the entire city of Columbus, Ohio, its headquarters, hated the company because it makes . . . chemicals. 'But what can you do?' she asked a couple of colleagues. They replied immediately—and in unison—'Change the name.'"[28] Although ChemLawn did not change its name, a company's decision to simply alter an image rather than deal with a problem highlights a dilemma for many PR agencies and their clients.

Let's look at a more familiar PR dilemma. In the aftermath of one of the largest natural disasters of this century—the Exxon *Valdez* oil spill along the Alaskan coast in 1989—the multinational corporation eventually changed the name of the tanker *Valdez* to the *Mediterranean* in the 1990s. The name change was just a small tactic in a series of damage-control strategies that Exxon enacted to cope with the oil spill. Such disaster management may reveal the worst—or best—attributes of the profession. How to enhance a company's image and, at the same time, encourage the company to be a socially responsible corporate citizen remains a major challenge for public relations.

The Exxon *Valdez* case was a corporate as well as a natural disaster, despite the company's outlay of $2 billion to clean up both its image and the spill. When eleven million gallons of crude oil were dumped into Prince William Sound, contaminating fifteen hundred miles of Alaskan coastline and killing countless birds, otters, seals, and fish, Exxon was slow to react to the crisis and even slower to accept responsibility. Although its PR advisers had encouraged a quicker response, the corporation failed to send any of its chief officers immediately to the site to express concern. Many believed that Exxon was trying to duck responsibility by laying the burden of the crisis on the shoulders of the tanker's captain. A former president of NBC News, William Small, maintained that Exxon "lost the battle of public relations" and suffered "one of the worst tarnishings of its corporate image in American history."[29]

A decidedly different approach was taken in the 1982 tragedy involving Tylenol pain-relief capsules. Seven people died in the Chicago area after someone tampered with several bottles and laced them with poison. Like the oil spill, the case was a major news story. Discussions between the parent company, Johnson & Johnson, and its PR and advertising representatives focused on whether withdrawing all Tylenol capsules might send a signal that corporations could be intimidated by a deranged person. Nevertheless, Johnson & Johnson's chairman, James E. Burke, and the company's PR agency, Burson-Marsteller, opted for full disclosure to the media and the immediate recall of the capsules nationally, costing the company an estimated $100 million. Before the incident, Tylenol had a market share of 37 percent, making it the leading pain-relief medicine. After the capsule withdrawal, Tylenol's share was cut nearly in half.

"The **Exxon** *Valdez* Story: How to Spend a Billion or Two and Still Get a Black Eye in Public."
—Business school conference title, Fordham University, 1990

In the late 1990s, a growing tide of Americans focused on the problems of *outsourcing:* using the production, manufacturing, and labor resources of foreign companies to produce American brand-name products, sometimes under deplorable working conditions. In 1999, students at several universities—including Duke, Georgetown, the University of Wisconsin, and some Ivy League schools—staged rallies encouraging administrators to take a hard line against companies that use overseas sweatshops to make apparel bearing university logos. At many of these schools, administrators complied by instating tougher guidelines for overseas licensing.

In 1996, outsourcing was pushed into the public eye when major media attention focused on morning talk-show host Kathie Lee Gifford when she discovered that part of her clothing line, made and distributed by Wal-Mart, came from sweatshops in New York and Honduras. The sweatshops paid less than minimum wages, and some employed child laborers. Human-rights activists claimed that in the overseas sweatshops in particular, children were being exploited in violation of international child-labor laws.

Levi Strauss & Co. pioneered a program to guard against sweatshop practices.

Many global companies now conform to international guidelines that protect children and pay workers living wages. Many countries, however, including the United States, still tolerate sweatshop conditions in which workers take home minimal pay, sometimes as little as a dollar an hour for working ten- to twelve-hour shifts six days a week.

As labor unions, the national media, and human-rights groups began tracking the problem of sweatshops, stories about worker exploitation were exposed. One U.S. firm, Levi Strauss & Company, pioneered an institutional public relations program to guard against sweatshop practices. With more than seven hundred sewing contractors making jeans and other clothing in fifty countries, Levi Strauss developed the first set of international, anti-sweatshop guidelines for its contractors. The guidelines were the company's response to early criticism about its moving some of its manufacturing overseas in search of low-cost labor markets.

The Levi Strauss plan focused on balancing "the company's merchandising and production needs with corporate social responsibility." Managers at Levi Strauss studied var-

As part of its PR strategy to overcome the negative publicity and to restore Tylenol's market share, Burson-Marsteller tracked public opinion nightly through telephone surveys and organized satellite press conferences to debrief the news media. In addition, emergency phone lines were set up to take calls from consumers and health-care providers, who altogether sent two million messages to Johnson & Johnson. When the company reintroduced Tylenol three months after the tragedy began, it did so with tamper-resistant bottles that were soon copied by almost every major drug manufacturer. Burson-Marsteller, which received PRSA awards for its handling of the crisis, found that the public thought Johnson & Johnson had responded responsibly to the crisis and did not hold Tylenol responsible for the deaths. In less than three years, Tylenol had recaptured its former share of the market.

The Exxon and Tylenol incidents demonstrate both dim and bright aspects of public relations, a profession that continues to provoke concern (see "Examining ious ways of dealing with the cultural values and differences in the countries where they had manufacturing interests.[1]

To execute the plan, Levi Strauss instituted a training program involving more than a hundred "in-country" managers who understood the language, culture, and values of their workforces. The company met with apparel workers' unions to get input and support; the trained managers then regularly monitored and audited their plants. The Levi Strauss media plan succeeded in positioning the company as a leader in global business practices, while "distinguishing itself from other companies as the 'bright spot' in otherwise negative sourcing stories."[2]

By 1993, all of Levi Strauss's worldwide contractors had been audited. About 70 percent met the anti-sweatshop standards set by company policy. About 25 percent of the contractors promised to make mandated improvements in the treatment

Stanford University students and faculty protest a visit by Nike CEO Phil Knight.

of their workers. Five percent of the contractors were dropped for violating anti-sweatshop agreements. The company withdrew outsourcing from both Burma and China after human-rights violations persisted. It also suspended its contract with Peruvian plants because of employee safety concerns. In 1993, *Fortune* magazine ranked Levi Strauss as "America's most admired apparel company," and *Business Ethics* magazine honored the jeans company with its Award for Excellence in Ethics.

A number of companies have used Levi's outsourcing policies as a model. In 1996, J. C. Penney declared that it would sever ties with any of its sixty-six hundred worldwide suppliers who were found to be operating sweatshops. Wal-Mart executives, still smarting from the Kathie Lee Gifford incident, started special training programs for buyers and contractors based on the Levi Strauss public relations model.

Ethics: Levi Strauss and Anti-Sweatshop Public Relations," above). The bulk of the criticism leveled at public relations argues that the crush of information produced by PR professionals overwhelms traditional journalism—a profession that needs to take more responsibility for the ways it sometimes lets PR control the news agenda. In one example, former president Richard Nixon, who resigned from office in 1974 to avoid impeachment hearings regarding his role in the Watergate scandal, hired Hill and Knowlton to restore his post-presidency image. Through the firm's guidance, Nixon's writings, mostly on international politics, began appearing in Sunday op-ed pages. He started showing up on *Nightline* and spoke frequently before groups such as the American Newspaper Publishers Association and the Economic Club of New York. In 1984, after a media blitz by Nixon's PR handlers, the *New York Times* announced, "After a decade, Nixon is gaining favor," and *USA Today* trumpeted, "Richard Nixon is back." Before his death in 1994, Nixon, who never publicly apologized for his role in Watergate, saw a large portion of his public image shift from that of an arrogant, disgraced politician to that of a revered elder statesman.[30] Many media critics have charged that the press did not balance the scales and treated Nixon too reverently after the successful PR campaign.

In terms of its immediate impact on democracy, the information crush delivered by public relations is at its height during national election campaigns. In fact, PR's most significant impact may be on the political process, especially when organizations hire spin doctors to favorably shape or reshape a candidate's media image. During the 1998 governor's race in Minnesota, former pro wrestler and navy SEAL Jesse "the Body" Ventura successfully combined a third-party PR and ad campaign to defeat the leading Democratic and Republican candidates. Ventura's strategy—which targeted independent voters and young adults—transformed his image as an evil, cross-dressing, "dumb rassler" into that of a patriotic, rugged individualist. Minnesota's registered-voter turnout—more than 60 percent—was the highest in the nation in 1998. And during the 1996 presidential campaign Republican candidate Bob Dole, drawing on advice from his PR handlers, decided to resign from the Senate to distance himself from his negative image as a dull but capable government bureaucrat. After Dole left Washington, his PR strategists were able to remind voters of his small-town roots and his contributions as a war hero during World War II, in which he was seriously injured. To put a counterspin on Dole's campaign strategy, the PR tacticians serving President Clinton's reelection effort sent out the word that Dole was "abandoning" his civic duties and extensive Washington experience at a time when the nation needed them most.

Though public relations often provides political information and story ideas during an election, the PR profession probably bears only part of the responsibility for manipulating the news media; after all, it is the job of an agency to spin the news favor-

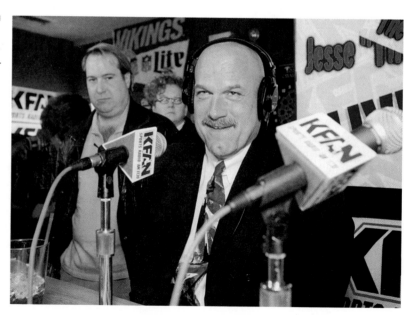

With a slick PR and advertising campaign and an abundance of charisma, third-party candidate and former professional wrestler Jesse "the Body" Ventura transformed himself into Jesse "the Mind" Ventura, scoring the political shocker of 1998 by winning the governorship of Minnesota in a fiercely contested election.

ably for its candidate. PR professionals should certainly police their own ranks (and usually do) for unethical or irresponsible practices, but the news media should also monitor the public relations industry, as they do other government and business activities. This media vigilance should be on behalf of citizens, who are entitled to robust debates on important social and political issues. When these debates are overwhelmed by public relations blitzes, journalism is discredited and citizens are poorly served.

In a democracy, journalism and public relations need to retain their guarded posture toward each other. But journalism itself may need to make changes that will make it less dependent on PR and more conscious of how its own practices play into the hands of spin strategies. Especially during local and national elections, journalists need to become more vigilant in monitoring questionable PR tactics. A positive example of change on this front is that many major newspapers and news networks now offer regular critiques of the facts and falsehoods contained in political advertising.

Like advertising and other forms of commercial speech, publicity campaigns that result in free media exposure raise a number of questions regarding democracy and the expression of ideas. Large PR agencies and product companies, like well-financed politicians, have money to invest to figure out how to obtain favorable publicity. The question is not how to prevent that but how to ensure that other voices, less well financed and less commercial, receive an adequate hearing. To that end, journalists need to become less-willing conduits in the distribution of publicity. PR agencies, for their part, need to show clients that participating in the democratic process as responsible citizens can serve them well and enhance their image.

> "In politics, image [has] replaced action."
> —Randall Rothenberg, *Where the Suckers Moon,* 1994

REVIEW QUESTIONS

Early Developments in Public Relations

1. What did people like P. T. Barnum and Buffalo Bill Cody contribute to the development of modern public relations in the twentieth century?

2. How did railroads and utility companies give the early forms of corporate public relations a bad name?

3. What contributions did Ivy Lee make toward the development of modern PR?

4. How did Edward Bernays affect public relations?

5. What is a pseudo-event? How does it relate to the manufacturing of news?

The Practice of Public Relations

6. What are two approaches to organizing a PR firm?

7. What are press releases, and why are they important to reporters?

8. What is the difference between a VNR and a PSA?

9. What special events might a PR firm sponsor to build stronger ties to its community?

10. Why have research and lobbying become increasingly important to the practice of PR?

Tensions between PR and the Press

11. Explain the historical background of the antagonism between journalism and public relations.

12. How did PR change old relationships between journalists and their sources?

13. In what ways is conventional news like public relations?

14. How does journalism as a profession contribute to its own manipulation at the hands of competent PR practitioners?

Public Relations, Social Responsibility, and the Press

15. What are some socially responsible strategies that a PR specialist can use during a crisis to help a client manage bad publicity?

16. In what ways does the profession of public relations serve democracy? In what ways can it impede democracy?

1. What do you think of when you hear the term *public relations?* What images come to mind? Where did these impressions come from?

2. What might a college or university do to improve public relations with homeowners on the edge of a campus who have to deal with noisy weekend student parties and a shortage of parking spaces?

3. What steps can reporters and editors take to monitor PR agents who manipulate the news media?

4. Can and should the often hostile relationship between the journalism and PR professions be mended? Why or why not?

5. Besides the Exxon *Valdez* and Tylenol cases cited in this chapter, investigate and research an international PR crisis (such as the Union Carbide disaster in India, the Perrier contamination story in France, or the Coke contamination in Belgium). How was the crisis handled?

http://www.prsa.org
The official site of the Public Relations Society of America, the leading U.S. professional PR organization. Provides information on membership, awards, conferences, PR publications, and links to other PR-related sites.

http://www.prssa.org
This site of the Public Relations Student Society of America gives information on local student chapters around the United States.

http://www.careeropps.com
This twice-monthly job newsletter lists information on PR-related employment opportunities.

http://www.online-pr.com
An online catalogue of PR, media, and marketing resources.

http://www.odwyerpr.com
This site, linked to an influential and independent publisher of PR news and directories of PR firms, includes information on the field and statistics on numerous firms.

http://silveranvil.org
A resource center and archive for case studies of award-winning PR campaigns.

http://www.prwatch.org
This site is the online presence of the Center for Media and Democracy, a nonprofit, public interest organization dedicated to investigative reporting on the PR industry.

In Brief

Imagine that you work for a high-powered PR firm and a controversial client (e.g., a tobacco company, President Bill Clinton, Dr. Jack Kevorkian, etc.) hires your firm to reshape the client's image. To perform this job, what are the strategies you would employ and why? (Before you begin, your class may want to discuss clients you would refuse to work for.)

In Depth

Split the class into groups of three or four for a bit of investigative work to be done over a three- to four-week period. Each group should try to identify one or two press releases that were converted into a *substantial* news story by a local paper. In the newspaper, look for articles that highlight a particular organization or profile a prominent business or government leader. The business section of most papers is a particularly good source for PR-influenced stories.

The goal is to get a copy of the original press release and compare it with the article that appears in the paper (see example on page 388). Here are some strategies your group might use:

- Call a local reporter (ideally, the person who wrote the story), explain the assignment, and see if he or she will provide your group with the original release to compare against the news story.

- Call a public relations department at a local company, explain your assignment, and see if someone will provide your group with a copy of the original release.

Another part of this assignment is to interview both a PR agent and a reporter about the use and success of news releases. Your group should devise a questionnaire for each professional. The questions listed here may be helpful.

To the reporter:

1. What determines whether a PR release will be used?

2. How does a reporter go about rewriting press releases? What information should be kept? Eliminated?

3. What is the newspaper's policy on rewriting press releases? Does the paper ever print releases verbatim? Why or why not?

To the PR agent:

1. What determines whether a PR release will be used? What are some writing tips for composing a good release?

2. Do newspapers ever print releases verbatim? Should they?

Feel free to develop other questions. After the releases and news stories have been gathered and the subjects interviewed, your group should address the following:

- What changes, if any, were made between each public relations release and the corresponding news story? Why do you think these changes were made?

- Which version represented the best story—the press release or the news story? Why? (Keep in mind that each story has a different purpose and audience.)

    Each group should report its findings to the entire class.

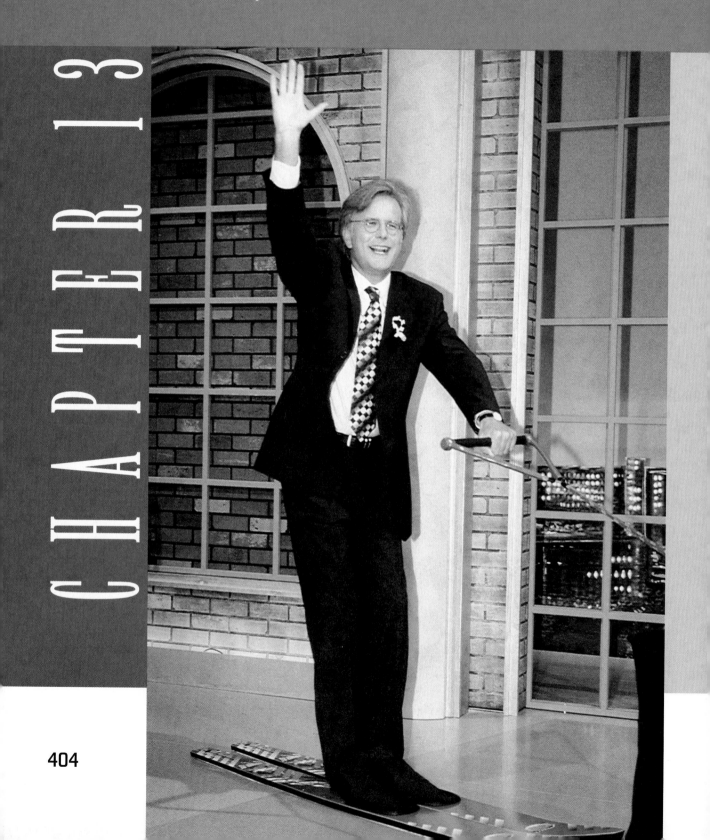

It is a familiar sight on late-night television: the tall host in jacket and tie, with wire-frame glasses and expressions alternating between silly and serious. He walks onto the stage to the beat of the house band, jokes about topics like Monica Lewinsky's impact on the presidency and Viagra's role in slowing down (or speeding up) the aging process. He sits down at a desk—a fake nighttime cityscape behind him—occasionally sipping his favorite beverage as he banters with the show's bandleader and guests like Dennis Rodman and Tony Bennett. Later, he introduces musical performers like Natalie Imbruglia.

It is a familiar sight, except the bandleader's name is Helmut, not Paul, the backdrop for this show is Cologne, Germany, not New York, and the host is a German guy, not David Letterman. The familiar-sounding television personality is Harald Schmidt, whom *Entertainment Weekly* calls "the Teutonic version of America's gap-toothed King of Late Night." Schmidt's show began in 1996, and plays four nights a week on SAT 1 in Germany and several other European countries. *Die Harald Schmidt Show* is just one of many Letterman-inspired late-night programs. Other Letterman clones have surfaced in Russia, Argentina, Norway, and the Netherlands, illustrating once again the influence of American popular culture around the globe.

Imitation is just one measure of America's influence on the world's cultural scene. In many regions, American media exports dominate markets. According to the Motion Picture Association of America, U.S. films are shown in more than 150 countries, and American television programs are broadcast in more than 125 markets worldwide, with shows like *The X-Files* and *Buffy the Vampire Slayer* leading the list of popular internationally distributed programs. If they are not exported in their original form, American media products are adapted to fit regional cultures, putting old ideas in new packages. For example, *Guess the Price,* a favorite game show in Poland, is a repackaging of the longtime syndicated U.S. game show *The Price Is Right.* By the end of 1998, MTV had created fourteen different 24-hour feeds to fit regional preferences. As MTV debuted in Russia in late 1998, the music was programmed to limit foreign videos to about 50 percent of the airplay to give new Russian bands opportunities for stardom.

Aided by the new markets that emerged with the collapse of the Soviet bloc in 1991, software and entertainment products from the United States topped $60 billion in international sales by the late 1990s, outstripping the food and aerospace industries as America's most successfully exported global products. Ironically, the prestige of U.S. cultural software, especially movies and music, has risen in inverse proportion to the decline of the United States as a manufacturer of electronic hardware. In 1995, for instance, the LG (Lucky-Goldstar) group, a South Korean conglomerate, paid more than $350 million to acquire Zenith, the last American-owned firm to make TV sets (though most of those were actually being produced in Mexico). A few U.S. manufacturers continue to make televisions and VCRs, but these firms are no longer American-owned. Globally, since the 1980s, electronic hardware firms such as Sony and Matsushita in Japan, Philips in the Netherlands, and Thomson in France have been acquiring American companies and such prestigious historical brand names as Zenith and RCA.

More significantly, however, these companies have been buying up American cultural software. Today, American television, music, and films are among the world's most marketable products, bringing in billions of dollars a year. To enter this market, Sony of Japan paid $2 billion for CBS Records in 1988 and $4.9 billion for Columbia Pictures in 1989. Australia's News Corp. paid $2.8 billion in 1988 for three American magazines, including *TV Guide.* And in 1995—for $5.7 billion—the Canadian beverage giant Seagram acquired 80 percent of music and movie conglomerate MCA/Universal (a U.S. company that had been acquired by Matsushita, the Japanese electronic megafirm, for $6.13 billion in 1990). Among the five largest sound recording companies, only Time Warner remained a U.S.-based firm by the late 1990s.

The influence of American popular culture has created considerable debate in international circles. On the one hand, the notion of freedom that is associated with innovation and rebellion in American culture has been embraced internationally. The global spread of media software and electronic hardware has made it harder for political leaders to secretly repress dissident groups since so much police and state activity, such as the 1989 student uprising and massacre in China, can now be documented on video and dispatched by satellite around the world. On the other hand, American media are shaping the cultures and identities of other nations. American styles in fashion and food, as well as media fare, dominate the global market—what many critics have identified as *cultural imperialism.*

The rash of global media mergers over the last two decades has made our world—at least in economic terms—very distinct from earlier generations. In this chapter, we will explore the issues and tensions that have contributed to current economic conditions. We will look at the rise of the Information Age, distinguished by its flexible, global, and specialized markets. We will discuss the breakdown of economic borders, focusing on media consolidation, corporate mergers, synergy, deregulation, and the emergence of an economic global village. We will also take up ethical and social issues in media economics, investigating the limits of antitrust laws, the concept of consumer control, and the threat of cultural imperialism. Finally, after examining the role of journalism in monitoring media economics, we will consider the impact of media consolidation on democracy and on the diversity of the marketplace.

analyzing the media economy

Given the sprawling scope of the mass media, the study of their economic conditions poses a number of complicated questions. For example, does the government need to play a stronger role in determining who owns what mass media and what kinds of media products should be manufactured? Should the government step back and let competition and market forces dictate what happens to mass-media industries? Should citizen groups play a larger part in demanding that media organizations help maintain the quality of social and cultural life? Does the rapid spread of American culture smother or encourage the growth of democracy and local cultures? Does the increasing concentration of economic power in the hands of several international corporations restrict or expand the number of players and voices in media markets? Answers to such questions roam the economic spectrum. On the one hand, critics express concerns about the increasing power and reach of large media conglomerates. On the other hand, many free-market advocates maintain that as long as these structures ensure efficient operation and generous profits, they measure up as quality media organizations. In order to probe economic issues from different perspectives, we need to understand key economic concepts in two broad areas: media structure and media performance.[1]

> "Unlike American automobiles, television sets, and machine tools, American cultural products—movies, TV programs, videos, records, cassettes, and CDs—are sweeping the globe."
> —Richard J. Barnet and John Cavanagh, *Global Dreams*, 1994

the structure of media organizations

In economic terms, three common organizational structures characterize the media business: monopoly, oligopoly, and limited competition. First, a **monopoly** occurs when a single firm dominates production and distribution in a particular industry, either nationally or locally. At the national level, for example, until the mid-1980s, AT&T ran a rare government-approved-and-regulated monopoly—the telephone business. Software giant Microsoft, accused of monopolistic business practices throughout much of the 1990s, faced charges in federal court in 1998 and 1999. On the local level, monopoly situations are more plentiful, occurring in any city that has only one newspaper or one cable company. Until the 1996 Telecommunications Act, the government had historically encouraged owner diversity by prohibiting a newspaper from operating a broadcast or cable company in the same city. Many individual local media monopolies, though, have been purchased by large national and international firms. For instance, TCI and Time Warner—for years the nation's largest cable operators—own hundreds of small local cable monopolies. And in 1999 AT&T swallowed TCI, a multibillion-dollar deal that married the world's largest phone company and the world's largest cable TV operation. Likewise, in the newspaper business, chain operators like Gannett own more than a hundred daily and weekly papers, most of which constitute a monopoly in their communities.

Second, an **oligopoly** describes an economic situation in which just a few firms dominate an industry. The commercial sound-recording and feature-film businesses are both oligopolies. Each has five or six major players that control the production and distribution of more than 90 percent of that industry. Since 1999, three multinational firms—Seagram of Canada, Sony of Japan, and Time Warner of the United States—have been major players in *both* the movie and the music oligopolies. Usually conducting business only in response to each other, such companies face little economic competition from small independent firms. Oligopolies often add new ideas and product lines by purchasing successful independents.

Third, **limited competition**, sometimes called *monopolistic competition*, characterizes a media market with many producers and sellers but only a few differentiable products within a particular category.[2] For instance, although the 1996 Telecommunications Act encouraged consolidation by lifting ownership restrictions on radio, hundreds of independently owned stations still operate in the United States. (CBS, which recently bought Infinity Broadcasting, now owns more than two hundred stations and dominates radio advertising nationwide.) Most of these commercial stations, however, feature a limited number of formats—such as country, classic rock, and contemporary hits—from which listeners may choose. Since commercial broadcast radio is now a difficult market to enter, requiring an FCC license and major capital investment, most station managers play the few formats that attract sizable audiences. Under these circumstances, fans of blues or classical music may not be able to find the radio product that matches their interests. Given the high start-up costs of launching a commercial media business, diverse players offering alternative products are becoming more rare as we enter the twenty-first century.

the performance of media organizations

A second important area in media economics is analyzing the behavior and performance of media companies. Economists pay particular attention to the two ways the media collect revenues, through direct and indirect methods. **Direct payment** involves media products supported primarily by consumers, who pay directly for a book, a music CD, a movie, an online computer service, or a cable TV subscription. **Indirect payment** involves media products supported primarily by advertisers, who pay for the quantity or quality of audience members that a particular medium delivers. Over-the-air radio and TV broadcasting, daily newspapers, and consumer magazines rely on indirect payments for the majority of their revenue. Through direct payments, consumers communicate their preferences immediately. Through indirect payments of advertiser-supported media, "the client is the advertiser, not the viewer or listener or reader."[3] Advertisers, in turn, seek media that persuade customers with discretionary income to acquire new products or switch brand loyalty. Many forms of mass media, of course, generate revenue both directly and indirectly, including newspapers, magazines, World Wide Web services, and cable systems, which charge subscription fees in addition to selling commercial time to advertisers (see Table 13.1).

In reviewing other behaviors of the media, economists look at many elements of the commercial process, including program or product costs, price setting, marketing

TABLE 13.1
Average Annual Individual Consumer Spending on Selected Media, 1990–97

Year	Cable Television and Other Subscription Services	Recorded Music	Daily Newspapers	Consumer Books	Consumer Magazines	Home Video	Movies in Theaters	Consumer Online Internet-Access Services
1990	$87.90	$36.64	$47.55	$63.90	$33.14	$56.35	$24.40	$2.93
1991	94.44	37.73	46.56	68.18	33.45	58.69	23.13	3.61
1992	102.56	43.05	48.54	68.95	34.26	59.25	23.24	4.39
1993	110.12	47.42	48.25	72.25	35.27	64.17	24.33	5.35
1994	111.87	56.35	49.12	77.62	36.36	68.96	25.20	6.20
1995	125.06	56.92	50.08	79.23	36.10	71.38	25.38	11.33
1996	138.38	57.34	50.90	80.95	36.80	76.88	27.05	17.13
1997	154.70	55.42	50.90	78.03	37.61	76.25	28.82	25.52

Source: Hoover's Guide to Media Companies (Austin, Tex.: Hoover's Business Press, 1996), 8. Veronis, Suhler & Associates industry report, <www.veronissuhler.com>, 1998. *Peterson's Media Companies 2000* (Princeton, NJ: Peterson's, 1999), 24–25.

strategies, and regulatory practices. For instance, marketers and media economists determine how high a local newspaper can raise its weekly price before enough disgruntled readers drop their subscriptions and offset the profits made from the price increase. Let's look at another example. In 1996, critics and government agencies began reviewing the artificially inflated price of CDs. They demonstrated that the **economies of scale** principle, which refers to the practice of increasing production levels so as to reduce the overall cost per unit, should have driven down the price of a CD in the same way that the price of blank videotapes and movie videos dropped in the 1980s. By 1999, however, CD prices remained inflated, largely as a result of the oligopoly formed by the five major recording conglomerates.

In a final example, in the 1980s, when citizen groups and the FCC determined that the TV networks were not meeting the needs of children, the government began placing regulatory limits on the minutes per hour of commercial time during Saturday-morning programs. By 1996, the FCC had also mandated that local broadcast TV stations and networks carry three hours of children's educational programs each week. This regulation was unusual in that major media have a history of instituting self-regulatory measures (like ratings systems) to keep the government out of their business. In most cases, media companies try to respond to citizen pressure. Businesses, after all, want to maintain good public images that encourage sales and limit government regulation.

Over the years, economists, media critics, and consumer organizations have asked the mass media to meet certain performance criteria. Following are some of the key expectations of media organizations: introducing new technologies to the marketplace; making media products and services available to all economic classes; facilitating free expression and robust political discussion; acting as public watchdogs over wrongdoing; monitoring times of crisis; playing a positive role in education; and maintaining the quality of culture.[4] Although media industries live up to some of these expectations better than others, economic analyses permit consumers and citizens to examine the instances when the mass media fall short. For example, when corporate executives at the networks trimmed TV news budgets in the early 1990s to make their businesses leaner and increase profit margins, their decision jeopardized the networks' role as watchdog on the rest of society.

the transition to an information economy

During the last half of the twentieth century, a number of key economic changes affected the media. The 1950s, for instance, marked a transition period in which the machines that drove the modern Industrial Age changed gear in the new Information Age. With offices displacing factories as major work sites, centralized mass production gave way to decentralized and often temporary service work. Indeed, by the early 1990s, the temporary-employment agency Manpower had surpassed General Motors as the largest U.S. private employer.

> "Had anyone in 1975 predicted that the two oldest and most famous corporate producers and marketers of American recorded music **[the RCA and CBS labels]** would end up in the hands of German printers and publishers [Bertelsmann] and Japanese physicists and electronic engineers [Sony], the reaction in the industry would have been **astonishment**."
>
> —Barnet and Cavanagh,
> *Global Dreams*, 1994

A major global change, which continues to unfold, accompanied this transformation. Bolstered by the passage of NAFTA (North American Free Trade Agreement) and GATT (General Agreement on Tariffs and Trade) in the mid-1990s, global cooperation fostered the breakdown of economic borders. Transnational media corporations executed business deals across international terrain. Global companies took over high-profile brand-name industries, particularly the electronic equipment once associated with the United States. In 1995, for example, Matsushita, the world's seventeenth-largest company according to *Fortune* magazine, produced VCRs under the General Electric, Magnavox, Sylvania, and J. C. Penney labels.

The first half of the twentieth century emphasized mass production, the rise of manufacturing plants, and the intense rivalry of one country's products against another. The contemporary era, however, emphasizes information distribution and retrieval as well as transnational economic cooperation. The major shift to an information-based economy began in the 1950s as various mass-media industries were able to market music, movies, television programs, and computer software on a global level. During this time, the emphasis on *mass* production shifted to the cultivation of specialized *niche* markets. In the 1960s, the first waves of national media consolidation began, escalating into the global media mergers of the 1980s and 1990s.

deregulation trumps regulation

During the rise of industry in the nineteenth century, entrepreneurs such as John D. Rockefeller in oil, Cornelius Vanderbilt in shipping and railroads, and Andrew Carnegie in steel created giant companies that monopolized their respective industries. In 1890, Congress passed the Sherman Antitrust Act, thus outlawing the monopoly practices and corporate trusts that often fixed prices to force competitors out of business. In 1911, the government used the act to break up both the American Tobacco Company and Rockefeller's Standard Oil Company, which was divided into thirty smaller competing firms. In 1914, Congress passed the Clayton Antitrust Act, prohibiting manufacturers from selling only to dealers and contractors who agreed to reject the products of business rivals. The Celler-Kefauver Act of 1950 further strengthened antitrust rules by limiting any corporate mergers and joint ventures that reduced competition. Today, these laws are enforced by the Federal Trade Commission and the antitrust division of the Department of Justice.

In recent decades, government regulation has often been denounced as a barrier to the more flexible flow of capital. Although the Carter administration (1976–80)

Screens for high-definition television (HDTV) sets are inspected along an assembly line in Rome, Italy. Beginning in the fall of 1998, the major broadcast networks were required by Congress to begin airing programs with digital signals to help foster the market for HDTV technology.

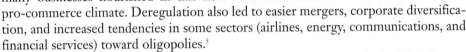

actually initiated deregulation, under President Reagan (1980–88) most controls on business were drastically weakened. Sometimes the deregulation had severe consequences—such as the savings and loan industry scandal, which cost consumers billions of dollars—but many businesses flourished in this new pro-commerce climate. Deregulation also led to easier mergers, corporate diversification, and increased tendencies in some sectors (airlines, energy, communications, and financial services) toward oligopolies.[5]

In the broadcast industry, the Telecommunications Act of 1996 lifted most restrictions on how many radio and television stations one corporation could own. The act further welcomed the seven powerful regional telephone companies, known as the Baby Bells, into the cable TV business. In addition, cable operators not only regained the right to raise cable rates with less government oversight but were also authorized to compete in the local telephone business (although high entry costs keep most cable companies out of the phone business). Economists thought the new competition would bring down consumer prices for a time but would also encourage more mergers and eventually a powerful oligopoly controlling *both* the telephone and the cable industries. In fact, AT&T's 1999 purchase of cable giant TCI foreshadows a time when one megacorporation will control most of the wires entering a home and dictate both phone and cable TV pricing.

Since the 1980s, a spirit of deregulation and special exemptions has guided communication legislation. For example, in 1995, despite complaints from NBC, Rupert Murdoch's Australian company News Corp. received a special dispensation from the FCC and Congress, allowing the firm to continue owning and operating the Fox network and a number of local TV stations. The Murdoch decision ran counter to the government decisions made in the early days of Marconi and RCA, right after World War I. At that time, the government feared outside owners and limited foreign investment in U.S. broadcast operations to 20 percent. However, in today's global business climate, special exemptions for foreign media owners have become acceptable.

Deregulation has also returned media economics to nineteenth-century principles, which suggest that markets can take care of themselves with little government interference. In this context, one of the ironies in broadcast history is that seventy years ago commercial radio broadcasters demanded government regulation to control technical interference and amateur competition. By the mid-1990s, however, the original impetus for regulation had reversed course. With new cable channels and Internet sites, broadcasting was no longer regarded as a scarce resource—once a major rationale for regulation as well as government funding of noncommercial and educational stations. Roughly ten thousand U.S. commercial AM and FM stations and twelve hundred commercial VHF and UHF television stations now operate in U.S. cities.

411

consolidation and mergermania

In spite of the strong antitrust laws of the twentieth century, these rules have been unevenly and curiously applied, especially in terms of the media. When International Telephone & Telegraph (ITT) tried to acquire ABC in the 1960s, loud protests and government investigations sank the deal. But when General Electric purchased RCA/NBC in the 1980s, the FTC, the FCC, and the Justice Department found few problems. Other actions have been even more significant. Even though the Justice Department broke up AT&T's century-old monopoly in the mid-1980s—creating telephone competition—at the same time the government was also authorizing a number of mass-media mergers that consolidated power in the hands of a few large companies.

Although the original Big Three TV networks—ABC, CBS, and NBC—constituted a prime-time oligopoly from the 1950s into the 1980s, competition from cable and VCRs changed the economic terrain. Eventually, the government allowed GE to buy back RCA for its NBC network in 1985. Then, in 1996, the software giant Microsoft joined with NBC to create a CNN alternative, MSNBC: a 24-hour interactive news channel available on both cable and the World Wide Web.

Among the world's biggest media deals, Disney in 1995 acquired ABC. Disney paid $19 billion. Shortly thereafter, Westinghouse, another global electronics firm, purchased the last remaining independent network, CBS, for $5.4 billion (subsequently, Viacom purchased CBS for $37 billion in 1999). To ensure its rank as the world's largest media conglomerate, Time Warner made an offer for Turner Broadcasting in 1995 for $7.5 billion. Although this merger was questioned by FTC officials, who raised concerns about the concentration of too much power over cable in too few hands, the deal went through in 1996.

Until the 1980s, antitrust rules had historically attempted to ensure diversity of ownership among competing businesses. Sometimes this happened, as in the breakup of AT&T, and sometimes it did not, as in the cases of local newspaper and cable monopolies. What has occurred consistently, though, is that media competition has been usurped by media consolidation. Today, the same anticompetitive spirit exists that once allowed a few utility and railroad companies to control their industries—in the days before antitrust laws.

> "Big is bad if it **stifles competition** . . . but big is good if it produces quality programs."
>
> —Michael Eisner, CEO, Disney, 1995

> "It's a small world, after all."
>
> —theme song, Disney theme parks

Most media companies have skirted monopoly charges by purchasing diverse types of mass media rather than trying to control just one medium. For example, Disney, rather than trying to dominate one area, provides programming to a TV network, a cable channel, and movie theaters. The company evades charges of monopoly by scattering products across many media ventures. In 1995, Disney CEO Michael Eisner defended the ABC takeover on a number of ABC News shows. According to Eisner, as long as large companies remain dedicated to quality—and as long as Disney did not try to buy the phone lines and TV cables running into homes—such mergers benefit America. But Eisner's position raises questions: If companies cannot make money on quality products, what happens? If ABC News cannot make a substantial profit, should Disney's managers lay off their national or international news staff? How should the government and citizens respond?

flexible markets

In addition to the trend toward consolidation, today's information culture is also characterized by flexibility. It emphasizes "the new, the fleeting . . . and the contingent in modern life, rather than the more solid values implanted" during Henry Ford's day, when relatively stable mass production drove mass consumption.[6] The new elastic

One entrepreneur who has thrived in the flexible economy of the 1990s is Richard Branson, the flamboyant owner of the Virgin Group, a collection of over one hundred companies focused on media, travel, and leisure businesses. Based in London, his holdings include Virgin Atlantic Airways, Virgin Cola, V2 Records, and Virgin Megastores, which sell music, movies, books, games, and software.

economy features the expansion of the service sector (most notably in health care, banking, real estate, fast food, video rental, and computer software) and the search for products to serve individual consumer preferences. This type of economy relies on cheap labor, often exploiting poor workers in sweatshop conditions, and on quick high-volume sales to offset the costs of making so many niche products for specialized markets.

Given that 80 to 90 percent of most new consumer and media products fail, a flexible economy demands fast product development and market research. Companies need to score a few hits to offset investments in their failed products. For instance, during the peak summer movie season, studios premiere dozens of new feature films. A few are hits but many more miss, and studios hope to recoup their losses via video rentals. Similarly, the networks introduce scores of new programs in the fall and then quickly replace those that fail to attract high numbers or the "right" kind of affluent viewers. At the same time, new music recordings are released daily on radio and in stores, while magazines vie for attention on supermarket shelves and through direct-mail solicitation. This flexible media system, of course, heavily favors large companies with greater access to capital over small businesses that cannot so easily absorb the losses incurred from failed products.

global markets and specialization

Labor unions made strong gains on behalf of workers after World War II and throughout the 1950s. In response, manufacturers and other large industries began to look for ways to cut the rising cost of labor. With the shift to an information economy, many jobs, such as making CD players, TV sets, and VCRs, were exported to avoid the higher price of U.S. unionized labor. As large companies bought up small companies across national boundaries, commerce developed rapidly at the international level.

By the mid-1990s, as global firms sought greater profits, they looked to less economically developed countries that were short on jobs. But in many cases global expansion by U.S. companies ran counter to America's early-twentieth-century vision. Henry Ford, for example, followed his wife's suggestion to lower prices so workers could afford Ford cars. (In fact, with assembly-line production, Ford managed to drop the price of the average Model T from $850 in 1908 to $260 by 1925.) In many countries today, however, most workers cannot afford the stereo equipment and TV sets they are making.

The new globalism has coincided with the rise of specialization. The magazine, radio, and cable industries sought specialized markets both in the United States and overseas, in part to counter television's mass appeal at the national level. By the 1980s,

413

Consumer Ratings and TV Economics

Whether network TV shows live or die has usually depended on whether advertisers are satisfied that enough young, affluent viewers are watching. Indeed, television has often been defined as an industry in which networks, producers, and distributors target and "sell" viewers in guaranteed blocks to advertisers.

Since 1950, the major organization tracking prime-time viewers has been the A. C. Nielsen Market Research Company. Nielsen provides overnight viewing estimates on the programs that viewers watched the night before in forty-four major TV markets. Each month, broadcast stations across the nation pay thousands of dollars for such ratings data, which ultimately determine the fate of most television programs.

Nielsen surveys national and local audiences both through written weekly diaries kept by viewers (used in 150 smaller markets), through phone surveys, and through computerized boxes, called *people meters*, hooked up to five thousand households in the United States. Measurements are most important during *sweeps:* month-long measurement periods conducted four times a year (six times in larger markets). Sweeps statistics determine both local and national ad rates for the next two to three months. During sweeps, the networks pack their schedules with special events and Hollywood movies—a distortion of their regular listings during non-sweeps periods.

Friends

Viewers typically question the power of ratings. After all, how can a few thousand Nielsen families represent the tastes and desires of 280 million Americans? In theory, however, statistical samples are fairly accurate estimates. To use a medical analogy, a doctor does not have to draw all the blood from a body to get a fix on a person's health. Similarly, to get a representative idea, statisticians do not have to ask *everyone* what they have been watching.

Theoretically, a "perfect" representative random sample gives each TV household an equal chance to be chosen. In reality, this rarely occurs. In broadcast ratings, researchers have trouble getting adequate representation of people with lower incomes and less formal education, of homes in rural areas and central cities, and of non–English speaking communities. As a result, ratings services offer small cash bonuses to entice viewers to complete diaries. When this fails, statisticians have to juggle the numbers through *weighting*—assigning more weight to a particular respondent to correct the under-represented group in the original sample.

Ratings suffer from other problems as well. Prior to the installation of people meters in 1987, Nielsen's original rating method could not determine if people were actually sitting in front of their TV sets. In fact, research in the 1980s suggested that about 13 percent of the time the TV set was on but no one was watching. In addition, written weekly diaries are not always filled out or are filled out inaccurately. A *halo effect* can occur in which diary keepers write down not what they actually watched, but what they think they *should* have watched.

The people meter has its own limitations. One problem with early models was *button fatigue*, brought on by weary viewers who quit punching in. All household members and guests were assigned a number and asked to log on or off the meter whenever they watched TV, but weary viewers sometimes stopped punching in.

When the people meter system was instituted in 1987, early data suggested a dramatic drop in network prime-time viewership. This meant losses in ad revenue to networks. After the 1988 season, the networks had to return $200 million in ad money to make up for the apparent audience decline. Upset network executives authorized a detailed, independent study completed in 1989 which severely criticized Nielsen. The study found that the initial rate of cooperation for the Nielsen families selected for people-meter hook-up was under 50 percent. In 1998, the networks and some major advertisers, again upset with plunging ratings, tried to start their own ratings service, but the expensive project collapsed in 1999.

Over the years, researchers have toyed with improved ratings systems. One study led to a passive people meter.

With this system, computerized surveillance equipment "sensed" who was watching TV. These infrared sensing machines, though, sometimes mistook wind-blown curtains, thrown balls, and family pets for people watching television.

Ratings are mainly used as guidelines for advertisers in negotiating prices with local stations and networks. The cost of advertising to sponsors has soared dramatically. In the mid-1960s, buying a thirty-second spot on national television during a high-rated series cost between $20,000 and $25,000. Today, by contrast, the most expensive spot on the national level is the annual Super Bowl, which many advertisers now use as a forum for introducing new ad campaigns. In 1999, a thirty-second spot during the Super Bowl cost $1.3 million. In regular prime-time TV, a thirty-second spot was much less expensive, ranging from $75,000 for a new program to $750,000 for NBC's top-rated *ER*.

Many TV and ad executives argue that the ratings system, though admittedly imperfect, is nevertheless a democratic measure that represents "the people" who "vote" for their favorite TV show by tuning in. Yet it is clear that the votes of some segments of the population count much more than others. In fact, some programs, such as WB's *Buffy the Vampire Slayer* and *Felicity*, never rate among top 30 shows. They stay on the air, though, because they attract young, affluent viewers. In the mid-1990s, NBC ran *Lois & Clark* on Sunday evening opposite CBS's *Murder, She Wrote*. This top-rated network show at the time had an audience nearly twice as large as *Lois & Clark*, which ranked among the least-watched prime-time shows. Yet NBC was able to charge sponsors about $130,000 for a thirty-second com-mercial while *Murder, She Wrote* commanded about $115,000 per half-minute.

Why? *Lois & Clark* reached more viewers between the ages of eighteen and thirty-five; *Murder, She Wrote* drew viewers whose median age was well over fifty. Although people over 50 are usually more affluent than younger viewers, research suggested they were harder to influence in their buying habits—and quicker to mute the remote control during commercials.

In 1994, CBS actually lost a number of affiliates to Fox partly because Fox's prime-time schedule was more appealing to younger, urban viewers. Two decades earlier, this same reasoning led to "the great rural series purge," a group of popular programs tossed off the air by CBS in the early 1970s, including *Hee Haw* (ranked No. 16 in 1970–71) and *Green Acres* (No. 19 in 1968–69). These programs were apparently enjoyed by too many people under twelve and over fifty.

As we enter the new century, the Nielsen company is experimenting with a digital ratings system that more accurately measures the exploding number of cable as well as network programs. This could be a crucial development, since one of the major concerns for some cable channels with very small audiences is that ad rates can fluctuate wildly if just one of those five thousand metered households forgets to report that it viewed the channel. The major problem remains: too often good shows or channels with the "wrong" viewers (too young, too old, or too poor) get axed and less popular shows and channels with the "right" numbers are renewed.

Nielsen TV Ratings

May 14, 1997		May 12, 1999	
1. **ER** (NBC)	23.6	1. **ER** (NBC)	18.4
2. **Seinfeld** (NBC)	20.9	2. **NBC Monday Night Movie** (NBC)	17.1
3. ***Mario Puzo's The Last Don, Pt. 1*** (CBS)	17.8	3. **Friends** (NBC)	14.3
4. **Fired Up** (NBC)	15.6	4. **CBS Sunday Movie** (CBS)	13.8
* **Friends** (NBC)		* **Frasier** (NBC)	
6. **Suddenly Susan** (NBC)	14.8	6. **Law and Order** (NBC)	13.4
7. **Touched by an Angel** (CBS)	13.8	7. **Will & Grace** (NBC)	12.0
8. **20/20** (ABC)	13.0	8. **Veronica's Closet** (NBC)	11.9
9. **Home Improvement** (ABC)	13.0	9. **Touched by an Angel** (CBS)	11.7
10. **Ellen** (ABC)	12.7	10. **Dateline NBC-Tuesday** (NBC)	11.2

A ratings point represents 970,000 TV households

A ratings point represents 994,000 TV households

➤ One ratings point represents approximately 1% of U.S. TV households.

➤ (*) indicates a Nielsen ratings tie.

➤ Ratings information from the A. C. Nielsen Company.

With increasing competition from cable and other electronic media, network TV ratings continue to decline. Yet networks can charge increasingly higher advertising rates as TV remains the only medium whereby advertisers can consistently reach ten to twenty million potential consumers.

however, even television—confronted with the growing popularity of home video and cable—began niche marketing, targeting eighteen- to thirty-five-year-old viewers, who controlled the bulk of consumer spending (see "Case Study: Consumer Ratings and TV Economics" on page 414). Younger and older audiences were increasingly abandoned by the networks but were sought by other media outlets and advertisers. Magazines such as *Seventeen* and *Modern Maturity* flourished. Cable channels such as Nickelodeon served the under-eighteen market, while Lifetime addressed the over-fifty viewer.

Beyond specialization and national mergers, though, what really distinguishes current media economics is the extension of synergy to international levels. In Henry Ford's day, national companies competed against one another, and national pride was at stake. "Made in Japan," for instance, went from being a label of inferiority in the 1950s to a mark of superiority in the 1980s, especially in the automobile and electronics industries. Major foreign electronics firms began purchasing American popular culture by the boatload—to guarantee content for their TV, VCR, and CD-ROM (and now Internet) technologies.

The global extension of America's vast popular media output occurred for a couple of key reasons. First, media technologies became cheaper and more portable, allowing proliferation both inside and outside national boundaries. Audiocassettes and CDs became compact enough to fit into a Sony Walkman, transportable to every room in the house and beyond. Thus, even when U.S. radio stations were not heard outside national borders, American music went everywhere. Furthermore, the transmission of visual images via satellite made North American and European TV available at the global level. Cable services such as CNN and MTV quickly took their national acts to the international stage, and by 1999, CNN and MTV were available in more than 170 countries.

Second, as we have noted, VCR, CD, and TV manufacturers lowered costs by moving plants outside the country. In addition, global manufacturing permitted companies that lost money on products at home to profit in the international market. About 70 to 80 percent of American movies, for instance, do not earn back their costs in the United States and depend on foreign circulation to recoup early losses.

In the global television market, consider these examples of programs that were not particularly successful in the United States but became hits internationally. When MGM/United Artists produced *Fame*, a TV drama about talented students from a New York performing-arts high school, NBC canceled it after one year. However, the program continued to be produced for national and international syndication from 1983 through 1987. In fact, at one point in the mid-1980s, *Fame* was the most popular program in Great Britain. More amazing is the phenomenon of *Baywatch*, which went into first-run syndication in 1991, also after being canceled by NBC. The program's producers claimed that by the late 1990s, *Baywatch*, a show about the adventures of underdressed lifeguards who make the beach safer for everyone, was the most-watched program in the world, with more than a billion viewers. The dialogue in the series, like that of action movies, was limited and fairly simple, making it easy and inexpensive to translate into other languages.

disney: a postmodern media conglomerate

To understand the story of media economics in the twentieth century, we need only examine the transformation of Disney from a struggling cartoon producer to one of the world's largest media conglomerates (see Table 13.2). Walt Disney's first cartoon company, Laugh-O-Gram, went bankrupt in 1922, when he was twenty-one years old. But when Disney moved to Hollywood, he found his niche. After inventing Mickey Mouse

TABLE 13.2
The Fifteen Largest U.S. Media Companies

Rank	Company	Headquarters	1998 Revenue ($ mil.)
1	Time Warner	New York	14,288
2	AT&T	New York	9,872
3	CBS	New York	7,685
4	Walt Disney	New York/Burbank, Calif.	7,541
5	NBC TV (General Electric Co.)	Fairfield, Conn.	5,269
6	News Corp.	Sydney	4,972
7	Gannett	Arlington, Va.	4,910
8	America Online	Dulles, Va.	4,800
9	Cox Enterprises	Atlanta	3,884
10	Advance Publications	Newark, N.J.	3,859
11	DirecTV (General Motors Corp.)	El Segundo, Calif.	3,655
12	Hearst	New York	3,292
13	Viacom	New York	3,035
14	Knight Ridder	San Jose, Calif.	2,950
15	New York Times Co.	New York	2,937

Source: *Advertising Age*, Ad Age Dataplace, <http://adage.com/dataplace/archives/dp362.html>, 8/16/99.

(originally named Mortimer) in the first sound cartoons in the late twenties, Disney developed the first feature-length cartoon, *Snow White*, completed in 1937.

The first economic period for Disney—roughly from the late 1920s to the late 1940s—set the standard for popular cartoons and children's culture for much of the twentieth century. The *Silly Symphonies* series (1929–39), which featured classic cartoon shorts like "The Three Little Pigs," established the studio's production reputation for quality cartoons. The series ran before feature movies throughout the Great Depression, providing escape, humor, and morality tales. Although the Disney company remained a minor studio during this period, *Fantasia* and *Pinocchio*—the two top-grossing films of 1940—each made more than $40 million. Nonetheless, the studio barely broke even because cartoon projects took time and commanded the company's entire attention. *Snow White*, for example, took four years to produce.

The second Disney period, encompassing the 1950s and early 1960s, was marked by corporate diversification. With the demise of the cartoon film short, Disney expanded into other areas. In 1949, for example, the studio made its first nature documentary short, *Seal Island*, and in 1953 its first feature documentary, *The Living Desert*. In 1950, Disney also produced its first live-action feature, *Treasure Island*.

Disney was also among the first film studios to embrace television. In 1954, the company launched a long-running prime-time show, an even more popular venue than theaters for displaying its products. Then, in 1955, Disneyland opened in Southern California. Eventually, the theme parks would produce the bulk of the studio's revenues (Walt Disney World in Orlando began operation in 1971).

In 1953, Disney started Buena Vista, its own distribution company. This was the first step in making the studio into a major player. In addition, the company began fully exploiting the box-office power of its early cartoon features. *Snow White*, for example, was successfully rereleased in theaters to many new generations of children before finally going to videocassette. Throughout the 1960s, successes came with *101 Dalmatians* (1961), *Mary Poppins* (1964), and *The Jungle Book* (1967). *Swiss Family Robinson*, a live-action adventure, even beat out Alfred Hitchcock's *Psycho* as the No. 1 box-office hit in 1960.

"In the States, going to Disneyland is a secular rite of passage, like visiting Mecca."
—Simon Hoggart, *The Guardian*, 1999

In 1966, the death of Walt Disney triggered a period of decline for the studio. But in 1984 a new management team, led by Michael Eisner, initiated the third Disney era. Eisner inherited Disney's newly created Touchstone division, and *Splash* (1984), starring Tom Hanks, became the first of many hits. However, it was *Who Framed Roger Rabbit?* (1988) that reinvented the live-action cartoon for adults as well as children. A string of animated hits followed, including *The Little Mermaid* (1989), *Beauty and the Beast* (1991), *The Lion King* (1994), and *Mulan* (1998). Along with opening a chain of merchandise mall outlets, the studio began releasing its classic cartoons on video. Disney movies have dominated videocassette sales since 1988.

Although some critics regard synergy as a monopolistic practice, Disney epitomizes the synergistic possibilities of media consolidation. By the late 1990s, Disney could produce an animated feature for both theatrical release and home-video distribution. With its ABC network, it could spin off a cartoon version of the movie and place it on ABC's Saturday-morning schedule. A book version could be released through Disney's publishing arm, Hyperion, and "the-making-of" versions could appear on cable's Disney Channel as well as in *Disney Adventures,* the company's popular children's magazine. Characters from the movie could eventually become attractions at Disney's theme parks or incentives for buying a Happy Meal at McDonald's. With the 1996 release of the live-action remake of *101 Dalmatians,* Disney licensed or sanctioned seventeen thousand different products, including clothing, candy, dinnerware, shoes, CD-ROM games, dolls, rugs, stuffed toys, and lamp shades.

Throughout the 1990s, Disney continued to find new sources of revenue in both entertainment and distribution. Through its purchase of ABC, Disney also became the owner of the cable sports channels ESPN and ESPN2. Building on its sports interests, Disney bought the NHL's Mighty Ducks and major-league baseball's Angels, both located in Anaheim, near Disneyland. Across the country in New York, Disney renovated several theaters and launched theater versions of *Beauty and the Beast* and *The Lion King* as successful Broadway musicals. In cyberspace, Disney purchased Infoseek, a Web browser, and used it as the basis to create the Internet portal Go, a powerful search engine that links all the Disney properties together.

Building on the international appeal of its cartoon features, in 1983 Disney extended its global reach by opening a successful theme park in Japan. In 1992, the studio also signed a ten-year deal with Russian television, which began showing six hours of Disney programming each week. In exchange, Disney received exclusive rights to sell ads during those programs. In 1986, the company started marketing cartoons to Chinese television, attracting an estimated 300 million viewers per week. This stopped in 1990 because of the rampant counterfeiting of popular Disney-trademark products, but the studio resumed the deal in 1992, eventually starting a Disney magazine in Chinese and opening several Disney·merchandise boutiques.

In the early 1990s, EuroDisney (now called Disneyland Paris) opened outside Paris. The French, though, did not eagerly embrace the theme park. It lost millions each month, well into the mid-1990s, before finally making money. Many Europeans continued to criticize the company for pushing out and vulgarizing classical culture. On the home front, a proposed historical park in Virginia, Disney's America, suffered defeat at the hands of citizens, historians, and politicians who raised concerns about Disney sanitizing, misinterpreting, or vulgarizing American history. Meanwhile, in 1995, shortly after the company purchased ABC, Disney suffered criticism for running a flattering company profile one evening on ABC's evening news program.

Despite criticism, little has slowed Disney's global expansion. Indeed, in 1997 Orbit—a Saudi-owned satellite relay station based in Rome—introduced Disney's 24-hour premium cable channel to twenty-three countries in the Middle East and North Africa. In the book *Global Dreams*, the authors set forth a formula for becoming a "great media conglomerate," a formula Disney exemplifies: "Companies able to use visuals to sell sound, movies to sell books, or software to sell hardware would become the winners in the new global commercial order."[7]

social issues in media economics

In recent years, we have witnessed billion-dollar takeovers and mergers between Time Inc. and Warner Communication, Viacom and Paramount, MCA/Universal and Polygram, Disney and ABC, Westinghouse and CBS, Time Warner and Turner, and AT&T and TCI. This mergermania accompanied stripped-down regulation, which has virtually suspended most ownership limits on media industries. As a result, a number of consumer advocates and citizen groups have raised questions about deregulation and ownership consolidation.

One longtime critic of media economics, Ben Bagdikian, questions ownership structure in his book, *The Media Monopoly*. Bagdikian worries that although there are abundant products in the market—"1,700 daily papers, more than 8,000 weeklies, 10,000 radio and television stations, 11,000 magazines, 2,500 book publishers"—only a limited number of companies are in charge of those products.[8] Bagdikian and others fear that this represents a dangerous antidemocratic tendency in which a handful of media moguls wield a disproportionate amount of economic control.

the limits of antitrust laws

The current consolidation of media owners has limited the number of independent voices and owners. Although meant to ensure multiple voices, American antitrust laws have been easily subverted since the 1980s. As we have noted, most media companies diversify among different product lines, never completely dominating a particular media industry. Time Warner, for example, spreads its holdings among television programming, cable, film, music, and publishing.

Such diversification strategies, of course, encourage oligopolies in which a few behemoth companies control media production and distribution. This kind of economic arrangement makes it difficult for many products—especially those offered

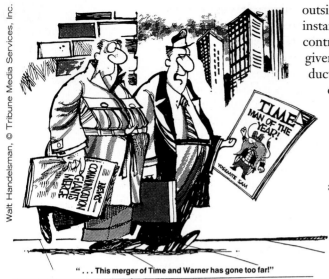

" . . . This merger of Time and Warner has gone too far!"

outside an oligopoly—to compete in the marketplace. For instance, in broadcast programming, the few networks that control prime time offer several competing programs at any given time. These programs are selected from known production companies that the networks either contract with on a regular basis or own outright. Thus even with a very good program or series idea, an independent production company, especially outside Los Angeles or New York, has a very difficult time entering the national TV market.

Occasionally, independent voices raise issues that aid the Justice Department and the FTC in their antitrust cases. For example, when the nation's largest book retailer, Barnes & Noble, was set to acquire the nation's largest book wholesaler and distributor, Ingram Book Group, for $600 million in late 1998, independent booksellers rose up in opposition to the monopoly implications of such a merger. They flooded federal offices with so many emails, petitions, faxes, and telephone protests that the FTC set up a special phone line. In 1999, Barnes & Noble withdrew its takeover offer.

Since antitrust laws aim to curb national monopolies, most media monopolies today operate locally. For instance, although Gannett owns seventy-five or so daily newspapers, it controls less than 10 percent of daily U.S. newspaper circulation. Nonetheless, almost all Gannett papers are monopolies: the only papers in their various towns. Virtually every cable company has been granted monopoly status in its local community; these firms alone often decide which channels are made available and what rates are charged. Furthermore, antitrust laws have no teeth globally. Although in late 1996 representatives from 160 countries met to discuss enforcing international copyright laws to protect the work of musicians and writers, no international antitrust rules exist to prohibit transnational companies from buying up as many media companies as they can afford.

consumer choice vs. consumer control

During the wave of mergers in the 1980s and 1990s, a number of consumer critics pointed to the lack of public debate surrounding the tightening oligopoly structure of international media. This lack of public involvement dates from the 1920s and 1930s. In that era, commercial radio executives, many who befriended FCC members, succeeded in portraying themselves as operating in the public interest, while labeling their noncommercial counterparts in education, labor, or religion as mere voices of propaganda. In these early debates, the political ideas of democracy became closely allied with the economic structures of capitalism. As one media historian has noted of this period, "By implicitly defining 'democracy' in terms of equal access to consumer products," political and business leaders created the appearance of running a fair society in which everyone had equal access to products and services.[9]

Throughout the Cold War period in the 1950s and 1960s, it became increasingly difficult to even criticize capitalism, which had become a synonym for democracy in many circles. In this context, any criticism of capitalism became an attack on the free marketplace. This, in turn, appeared to be a criticism of free speech, since the business community often sees its right to operate in a free marketplace as an extension of its right to commercial speech. As longtime CBS chief William Paley told a group of educators in 1937, "He who attacks the fundamentals of the American system" of commercial broadcasting "attacks democracy itself."[10] Broadcast historian Robert McChesney, discussing the rise of commercial radio in the 1930s, has noted that leaders like Paley "equated capitalism with the free and equal marketplace, the free and equal marketplace with democracy, and democracy with 'Americanism.'"[11] The collapse of the former Soviet Union's communist economy in the 1990s is often portrayed as a triumph for democracy. It was more accurately a victory for capitalism and free-market economies.

As many economists point out, capitalism is arranged vertically, with powerful corporate leaders at the top and hourly-wage workers at the bottom. But democracy, in principle, represents a more horizontal model in which each individual has an opportunity to have his or her voice heard and vote counted. In discussing free markets, economists also distinguish between *consumer control* over marketplace goods and freedom of *consumer choice:* "The former requires that consumers participate in deciding what is to be offered; the latter is satisfied if [consumers are] free to select among the options chosen for them by producers."[12] Most Americans and the citizens of other economically developed nations clearly have options among a range of media products. Yet consumers and even employees have limited power in deciding what kinds of media get created and circulated.

cultural imperialism

When Disney bought ABC in 1995, Yale literary scholar Harold Bloom called the deal a cultural "disaster" and told one newspaper, "At the end of this road lies cultural homogenization of the most ghastly kind." Bloom was not alone in his criticism. Today, numerous international observers contend that the idea of consumer control or input is even more remote in countries inundated by American fashion, food, movies, music, and television. Even mainstream U.S. newspapers report with skepticism on the 470,000 Brazilian Avon "beauty consultants," many of whom travel the backwaters of the Amazon jungle selling American cosmetics to women who can barely afford shoes.

Although many indigenous forms of media culture—such as Brazil's *telenovela* (a TV soap opera) and Ireland's Riverdance—are extremely popular, U.S. dominance in producing and distributing mass media puts a severe burden on countries attempting to produce their own cultural products. For example, American TV producers have generally recouped the costs of production in national syndication by the time their TV shows are exported. This allows American distributors to offer these programs to other countries at bargain rates, thus undercutting local production companies trying to create original programs in their own language. In Poland, for instance, the national TV station began producing a soap opera set in 1990 Warsaw. Although the program was extremely popular, it was far cheaper for station managers to buy *Dynasty* and *Santa Barbara* reruns from the United States than to develop more new series of their own. In the late 1990s, Polish TV was paying less than $1,000 to air one half hour of U.S. programming.

Defenders of American popular culture argue that because some of our culture challenges authority, national boundaries, and outmoded traditions, this creates an arena in which citizens can raise questions. Supporters also argue that a universal popular culture creates a global village and fosters communication across national boundaries. Critics, however, believe that although American popular culture often contains protests against social wrongs, such protests "can be turned into consumer products

"The perfect world of **Disney** has replaced the biblical **Garden of Eden** as the American vision of paradise."
—Judith Adams, *The American Amusement Park Industry,* 1991

and lose their bite. Protest itself becomes something to sell."[13] The harshest critics have labeled American culture in the international arena a form of cultural imperialism, which both hampers the development of native cultures and negatively influences teenagers, who abandon their own rituals to adopt the tastes of their American counterparts. The exportation of U.S. entertainment media is sometimes viewed as "cultural dumping," because it discourages the development of original local products.

The opening up of markets in Asia, Africa, and Eastern Europe, particularly after the failure of various totalitarian regimes in the 1980s, spurred the growth of global popular culture. At the same time, an economic form of piracy developed worldwide with the unlicensed pilfering and duplicating of cassettes, CDs, videos, movies, and software. According to one estimate, 85 percent of the thirty thousand video stores in South Korea alone stocked bootlegged tapes by the early 1990s. Although heavy fines and jail sentences are on the books to stop pirating, many governments have been reluctant to act against their own bootleggers, especially since pirating remains a source of jobs. In certain situations, U.S.-based companies have withdrawn distribution deals to put pressure on governments to end pirating and enforce copyright laws.

Perhaps the greatest concern regarding a global economic village is elevating expectations among people whose standards of living are not routinely portrayed in contemporary media. By the late 1990s, about two-thirds of the world's population could not afford most of the products advertised on American, Japanese, and European television. Yet more and more of the world's populations were able to glimpse consumer abundance and middle-class values through satellite technology and magazine distribution. Media managers as early as the 1950s feared political fallout—"the revolution of rising expectations"—in that ads and products would raise the hopes of poor people but not keep pace with their actual living conditions.[14] Furthermore, the conspicuousness of consumer culture makes it difficult for many of us to even imagine other ways of living that are not heavily dependent on the mass media and brand-name products.

the media marketplace and democracy

We have been and will continue to be involved in major global transformations of economies, cultures, and societies. The best way to monitor the impact of transnational economies is through vigorous news attention and lively public discussions on fundamental issues. Clearly, however, this process is hampered. In the 1990s, for example, news organizations, concerned about the bottom line, severely cut back the number of reporters assigned to cover international developments. This occurred just as global news became critical to an informed citizenry. We live in a society in which consumer concerns and profit aspirations, rather than broader citizen issues, increasingly dominate the media agenda. In response, critics have posed some key questions. As consumers, do we care who owns the media so long as most of us continue to have a broad selection of products? Do we care who owns the media so long as multiple voices *appear* to exist in the market?

Merged and multinational media corporations will continue to control more aspects of production and distribution. Of pressing concern is the impact of mergers on news operations, particularly the influences of General Electric, Westinghouse, Disney, Time Warner, and News Corp. on their news subsidiaries—NBC, CBS, ABC, CNN, and Fox, respectively. These companies have the capacity to use major news resources not only to promote their products but to determine the kind of

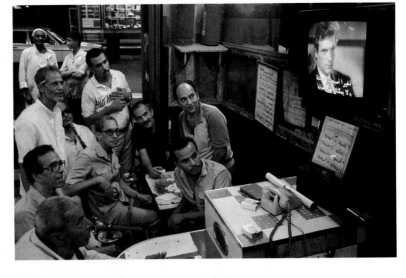

In Cairo, a group of Egyptian men watch a rerun of the CBS program *Falcon Crest* (1981–90). Research suggests that many international viewers enjoy programs portraying decadence and shallowness in American life.

national coverage that many issues will receive in the future.

In spite of (and perhaps because of) the growth in channels of communication, it has become increasingly difficult to sustain a public debate on economic and ownership issues. The promises of multichannel cable systems and the Internet, which would potentially give voices to the voiceless, may be in jeopardy because these systems are being bought at a rapid pace by large conglomerates. Whether these companies will open up their systems to alternative points of view and to people who cannot afford access is yet to be determined.

One promising spot in the current economic atmosphere concerns the role of independent and alternative producers, artists, writers, and publishers. Despite the movement toward economic consolidation, there remains in the media a diversity of opinions and ideas. In fact, when independent views become even marginally popular, they are often pursued by large media companies that seek to make them subsidiaries or to capitalize on their innovations. Alternative voices in the mass media often tap into social concerns that are not normally discussed in corporate boardrooms. In fact, business leaders depend on independent ideas in order to generate new product lines. A number of transnational corporations encourage the development of local artists— talented individuals who might have the capacity to transcend the regional or national level and become the next global phenomenon.

One key paradox of the Information Age is that for economic discussions to be meaningful and democratic, they must be carried out in the popular media as well as in educational settings. Yet public debates about the structure and ownership of the media are often not in the best economic interests of media owners. Nonetheless, in some places, local groups and consumer movements are addressing media issues that affect individual and community life. Such movements may be united by geographic ties, by common ethnic background, or by shared concerns about politics or technology. The Internet has made it possible for such groups to form globally, uniting around such issues as contesting censorship or monitoring the activities of large multinational corporations.

Another hopeful sign is similar to what took place around radio in the early 1930s. Given the collapse of so many anticapitalist totalitarian states, no "natural" economic enemy now exists to challenge American, Japanese, and European capitalism. However, because capitalism and democracy became fused in political discussions in the twentieth century, sometimes our economic systems have remained unexamined. Perhaps we are ready to question some of these hierarchical and undemocratic arrangements. Even in the face of so many media mergers, the public arena today seems open to such examinations, which might improve the global economy and also serve the public good. By understanding media economics, we can make a contribution to critiquing media organizations and evaluating their impact on democracy.

REVIEW QUESTIONS

Analyzing the Media Economy

1. How are the three basic structures of mass-media organizations—monopoly, oligopoly, and limited competition—different from one another?

2. What are the differences between direct and indirect payments for media products?

3. What are some of society's key expectations of its media organizations?

The Transition to an Information Economy

4. Why has the federal government emphasized deregulation at a time when so many media companies are growing so large?

5. How have media mergers changed the economics of mass media?

6. How do global and specialized markets factor into the new media economy?

7. Using Disney as an example, what is the role of synergy in the current climate of media mergers?

Social Issues in Media Economics

8. What are the differences between freedom of consumer choice and consumer control?

9. What is cultural imperialism, and what does it have to do with the United States?

The Media Marketplace and Democracy

10. What do critics and activists fear most about the concentration of media ownership? How do media managers and executives respond to these fears?

11. What are some promising signs regarding the relationship between media economics and democracy?

QUESTIONING THE MEDIA

1. Are you exposed to popular culture from other countries? Why or why not? Give some examples.

2. Do you read international news? Why or why not?

3. What steps can reporters and editors take to cover media ownership issues better?

4. How does the concentration of media ownership limit the number of voices in the marketplace? Do we need rules limiting media ownership?

5. Is there such a thing as a global village? What does this concept mean to you?

SEARCHING THE INTERNET

http://www.veronissuhler.com
Site for Veronis, Suhler & Associates Inc., a leading media-research and investment company devoted to communication, publishing, broadcasting, cable, and new media industries.

http://www.hoovers.com
Site for Hoover's Inc., a Texas-based company devoted to tracking the nation's largest industries, including media; features links to related sites.

http://www.mediainfo.com
Site for *Editor & Publisher*, the trade publication for the newspaper industry; provides statistics and links to other companies.

http://www.pathfinder.com/fortune/fortune500
This site provides overviews and summaries of revenues, assets, and other data on *Fortune* 500 companies.

http://www.aflcio.org/paywatch/index.htm
Part of the AFL-CIO labor-union site, PayWatch keeps track of the top U.S. CEOs' salaries.

http://stats.bls.gov
This site offers access to the top major data bank for the U.S. Bureau of Labor Statistics.

In Brief

Imagine that you are either a small independent record label or a book publisher. You have produced a high-quality product, but it has limited appeal. Without relying on signing distribution agreements with giant companies, how might you go about creating a market for your product and reaching the audience that might be interested in your product? Be specific.

In Depth

Split the class into three groups and stage a mock public forum on the issue of media mergers. Specifically, groups should examine whether it would be beneficial for a media corporation (for example, Sony, Seagram, Viacom, or Bertelsmann) to buy a television network. Students may volunteer for one of the following groups:

- *Group 1:* the pro-business team, which supports the globalization of media and mergers as healthy steps for the American and world economy

- *Group 2:* the pro-consumer or citizens' activist group, which worries about the increasing concentration of media ownership

- *Group 3:* journalists who cover the forum and ask key questions

The class should check *Hoover's Handbook* or *Peterson's Media Companies 2000* for a list of what the takeover company already owns. Then each group should meet and prepare for the forum. Groups 1 and 2 should appoint two or three spokespeople as "specialists" on various issues. Groups 1 and 2 should also anticipate the questions that reporters might ask and prepare answers. Group 3 should brainstorm and devise a list of questions to be asked.

After the groups plan their strategies, the class should reconvene. Groups 1 and 2 should then briefly state their positions before opening the forum up to questions from reporters.

After the forum and toward the end of class, *each group* should gather and write the first *two* sentences of a news story that reports on the forum. The news reports should highlight the key moments or findings of the forum. The groups should then share their abbreviated news stories, tell why they chose their particular story openings, and comment on one another's story. How do the stories of Groups 1 and 2 differ from those of Group 3? What are the agendas of each group? Can compromises be achieved that satisfy both business and democracy?

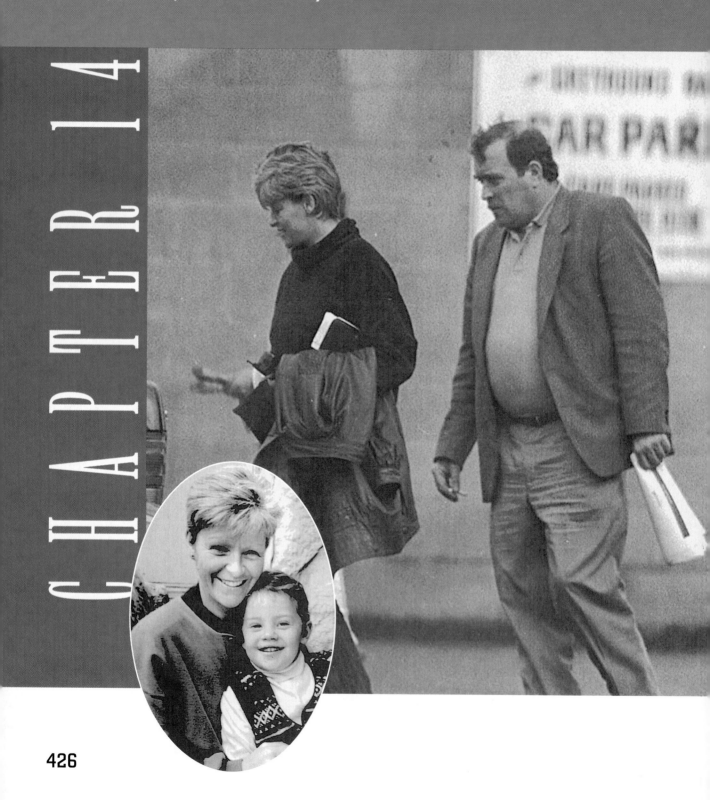

In 1994, someone fired bullets into the Dublin home of an Irish investigative reporter as she put her five-year-old son to bed. In 1995, a man forced his way into the reporter's home, held a gun to her head, lowered his aim, and shot her in the thigh. For Veronica Guerin, journalism had become a dangerous business.

Guerin was the first reporter to cover Ireland's escalating organized-crime and drug problem. She worked for Dublin's *Sunday Independent*. A few days after the 1995 assault, she wrote about the incident, vowing to continue her reporting despite her fears about safety. Later that year, she was punched in the face by the suspected head of Ireland's gang scene. He threatened to hurt Guerin's son and kill her if she wrote about him. She kept writing. In December 1995, she flew to New York to receive the International Press Freedom Award from the Committee to Protect Journalists.

When Guerin returned to Dublin, she continued her investigations, which went into greater and greater depth. She began naming names of gang members suspected of masterminding drug-related crimes and a string of eleven unsolved contract murders. Then, in June 1996, while waiting in her car at a suburban Dublin intersection, she was shot five times by two hired killers on a motorcycle. Veronica Guerin had become contract murder victim number twelve. Ireland mourned Guerin's death for three days. After her funeral, which was held at the church where she had gone to Mass each Sunday, the government invoked her name and passed a series of laws. The legislation allowed judges to deny bail to dangerous suspects and created a special bureau to confiscate money and property from suspected drug criminals and gang members.

In an *Independent* article after a 1995 incident, Guerin had discussed the danger she faced: "I have already said, and I will continue to say it again now, that I have no intention of stopping my work. I shall continue as an investigative reporter, the job I believe I do best. My employers have offered alternatives—any area I wish to write about seems to be open to me—but somehow I cannot see myself reporting from the fashion catwalks or preparing a gardening column."[1]

In contrast to modern American journalism, there is something unusual about the openness and directness of Guerin's writing. After all, for much of the twentieth century U.S. journalism operated on the premise that reporters should be detached from the turmoil they reported about. Guerin, however, became centrally involved in Ireland's crime and drug world. Her tough reports and tragic death connected her to her readers. Her powerful first-person stories were very different from the neutral third-person accounts that dominate most American news coverage.

"A journalist is the lookout on the bridge of the ship of state. He peers through the fog and storm to give warnings of dangers ahead. . . . He is there to watch over the safety and the welfare of the people who trust him."

—Joseph Pulitzer, 1904

News-related issues receive special attention in this chapter because journalism is the only media enterprise that democracy absolutely requires—and it is the only media practice that is specifically protected by the U.S. Constitution. However, with the gradual decline in news audiences and the growing criticism of an elite corps of East Coast journalists, the news media are searching for ways to reconnect with citizens. In this chapter, we will examine the changing definition of news. We will look at the implicit values underlying news practice and the ethical dilemmas confronting journalists. Next, we will study the legacy of print-news conventions and rituals. We will then turn to the impact of television and images on news. Finally, we will take up recent controversial developments in journalism and democracy, specifically examining the rise and the role of public journalism.

modern journalism in the information age

In modern America, the reporter's main job has been to provide information that enables citizens to make intelligent decisions. Today, this guiding principle has been derailed. First, in a world engulfed in media outlets and computer highways, we may be producing too much information. According to social critic Neil Postman, as a result of developments in media technology by the mid-1990s, society had developed an "information glut," transforming news and information into "a form of garbage."[2] Postman believes that scientists, technicians, managers, and journalists have merely piled up mountains of new data, which add to the problems of everyday life. As a result, too much unchecked data and too little thoughtful debate radiate from too many channels of communication.

A second, related problem suggests that the wealth of information the media now provide has made little impact on improving public and political life. In fact, many people feel cut off from our major institutions, including journalism. Many citizens, however, are looking for ways to take part in public conversations and civic debates—to renew a democracy in which many voices participate. We will look at both of these issues—information overload and public alienation—as we explore the culture of news in this chapter.

what is news?

In a 1963 NBC staff memo, news president Reuven Frank outlined the narrative strategies integral to all news: "Every news story should . . . display the attributes of fiction, of drama. It should have structure and conflict, problem and denouement, rising and falling action, a beginning, a middle, and an end."[3] Despite Frank's candid insights, most journalists today are not comfortable thinking of themselves as storytellers. Instead, they view themselves mainly as information-gatherers.

Over time, most journalists and journalism textbooks have come to choose and define news by a set of criteria for determining *newsworthiness*—information most worthy of transformation into news stories. Although other elements could be added to the list, news criteria generally include timeliness, proximity, conflict, prominence, human interest, consequence, usefulness, novelty, and deviance.[4] Journalists select and develop news stories based on different combinations of these criteria.

Most issues and events that journalists select as news are *timely* or new. Reporters, for example, cover speeches, meetings, crimes, or court cases that have just happened. In order to rate as news, most of these events also have to occur close by, or in *proximity* to, readers and viewers. Although local papers usually offer some national and international news, readers and viewers expect to find the bulk of news devoted to their own towns and communities. In addition to being new and near, most news stories are narratives and thus contain a healthy dose of *conflict*—a key ingredient in narrative writing. In fact, in developing news narratives, reporters are encouraged to seek contentious quotes from those with opposing views. For example, a story on a local tax hike might feature Republican and Democratic positions; it might also include a tax expert and a homeowner who espouse competing viewpoints.

Though timeliness, proximity, and conflict are the most common criteria for determining news topics, *prominence* and *human interest* play a role as well. Reader and viewer surveys indicate that most people identify more closely with a person than with an abstract issue. Therefore, the news media tend to report stories on powerful or influential people. Since these individuals often play a role in shaping the rules and values of a community, journalists have traditionally been responsible for keeping a watchful eye on them. Prominent celebrities, politicians, business leaders, and journalists themselves often dominate news. But reporters also

> "The 'information' the **modern media** provide leaves people feeling useless not because it's so bleak but because it's so trivial. It doesn't inform at all; it only **bombards with random data bits**, faux trends and surveys that reinforce preconceptions."
> —Susan Faludi, the *Nation*, 1996

Newsworthy events draw an abundance of public interest. Here, residents of East Jerusalem, Israel, gather at a newsstand to read about Jordan's ailing King Hussein shortly before his death in 1999.

look for human interest: extraordinary incidents that happen to "ordinary" people. In fact, good reporters can often relate a story about a complicated issue (such as unemployment or homelessness) by illustrating its impact on one person or family.

Two other news criteria, found less often in news stories, are *consequence* and *usefulness*. Stories about isolated or bizarre crimes, while they might be new, near, and notorious, often have little impact on our daily lives. To balance these kinds of stories, many editors and reporters believe that some news must also be of consequence to a majority of readers or viewers. For example, stories that affect a family's income or change a community's laws have consequence. Likewise, many people look for stories with a practical use: hints on buying a used car or choosing a college, advice on a political candidate or the stock market, strategies for training a pet or removing a troublesome stain.

Finally, news is often about the *novel* and the *deviant*. When events happen that are outside the routine of daily life, such as a spectacular warehouse fire or a seven-year-old girl trying to pilot a plane across the country, the news media are there. Reporters also cover events that appear to deviate from social norms, including murders, rapes, fatal car crashes, political scandals, and gang activities. Part of the allure of these occurrences is not only their deviation from norms but the fact that they meet other newsworthiness criteria—especially conflict.

> "In recent years, when resources were diverted to cover the O.J. Simpson story and Tonya Harding, there was a major story in Haiti, but we didn't cover it as extensively as we should have because all those resources were diverted to O.J. That was wrong."
>
> —Connie Chung,
> coanchor,
> *20/20*, 1998

Although newsworthiness criteria are a useful way to define news, they do not reveal much about the cultural aspects of news. As culture, news is both a product and a process. It is both the morning paper or evening newscast *and* a set of subtle values and rituals that have been adapted to historical and social circumstances, such as the partisan-press ideals of the 1700s and the informational standards of the 1900s. As culture, then, **news** in the twentieth century became the process of gathering information and making narrative reports—edited by individuals in a news organization—which offer selected frames of reference; within those frames, news helps the public make sense of prominent people, important events, and unusual happenings in everyday life.

neutrality and other values in american journalism

In 1841, Horace Greeley described the newly founded *New York Tribune* as "a journal removed alike from servile partisanship on the one hand and from gagged, mincing neutrality on the other."[5] Greeley feared that too much neutrality would make reporters look like wimps, who stood for nothing. Yet the neutrality Greeley warned against is today a major value of conventional journalism. Such a value, ironically, is in the spirit of value-free science, with reporters behaving as detached and all-seeing observers of social experience. Reporting, however, is seldom scientific; it remains essentially a literary or writing activity. As former reporter and journalism professor David Eason notes, "Reporters . . . have no special method for determining the truth of a situation nor a special language for reporting their findings. They make sense of events by telling stories about them."[6]

Even though journalists transform events into stories, they generally believe that they are—or should be—neutral observers who present facts without passing judgment on them. Conventions such as the inverted-pyramid news lead, the careful attribution of sources, the miserly use of adverbs and adjectives, and a detached third-person point of view all help reporters perform their work in a supposedly neutral way.

Like lawyers, therapists, and other professionals, modern journalists believe that their credibility derives from personal detachment. Yet the roots of this view reside in less noble territory. Jon Katz, media critic and former CBS News producer, discusses the history of the neutral pose:

> The idea of respectable detachment wasn't conceived as a moral principle so much as a marketing device. Once newspapers began to mass market themselves in the mid-1880s, after steam- and rotary-powered presses made it possible to print lots of papers and make lots of money, publishers ceased being working, opinionated journalists. They mutated instead into businessmen eager to reach the broadest number of readers and antagonize the fewest. . . .
>
> Objectivity works well for publishers, protecting the status quo and keeping journalism's voice militantly moderate.[7]

To reach as many people as possible across a wide spectrum, publishers and editors realized as early as the 1840s that abandoning partisanship might boost sales.

Neutral journalism remains a selective process. Reporters and editors turn some happenings into reports and discard many others. This process is governed by a deeper set of subjective beliefs that are not neutral. Sociologist Herbert Gans, who studied the newsroom cultures of CBS, NBC, *Newsweek*, and *Time* in the 1970s, has generalized that several basic "enduring values" are shared by most American reporters and editors. The most prominent of these values are ethnocentrism, responsible capitalism, small-town pastoralism, and individualism.[8] By **ethnocentrism** Gans means that in most news reporting, especially foreign coverage, reporters automatically judge other countries and cultures based on how "they live up to or imitate American practices and values." Critics outside the United States, for

> "Ads are *news*. What is wrong with them is that they are good news. In order to balance off the effect and to sell good news, it is necessary to have a lot of bad news."
>
> "Real news is bad news—bad news *about* somebody, or bad news *for* somebody."
> —Marshall McLuhan,
> *Understanding Media*,
> 1964

The major symbol of twentieth-century investigative journalism, Bob Woodward and Carl Bernstein's coverage of the Watergate scandal for the *Washington Post* helped topple the Nixon White House. In *All the President's Men*, the newsmen's book about their investigation, Woodward and Bernstein portrayed reporters as tenacious individuals locked in a bitter battle with corrupt and heartless institutions.

instance, point out that CNN's international news channels see world events and cultures primarily from an American point of view rather than through a more expansive global lens.

Gans also identified **responsible capitalism** as an underlying value, contending that journalists sometimes naively assume that businesspeople compete with one another not primarily to maximize profits but "to create increased prosperity for all." Gans points out that although most reporters and editors condemn monopolies, "there is little implicit or explicit criticism of the oligopolistic nature of much of today's economy."[9] In fact, by the late 1990s, many journalists worked in monopoly newspaper towns or for oligopoly parent companies. Thus writing about the limitations of such economic structures constituted biting the hand that feeds you.

Another value that Gans found was the romanticization of **small-town pastoralism**: favoring the small over the large and the rural over the urban. Reporters and editors, like most Americans, tend to prefer natural settings to their municipal counterparts. Many journalists equate small-town life with innocence and harbor deep suspicions of cities, their governments, and daily urban experience. Consequently, stories about rustic communities with drug or crime problems are usually framed as if the purity of country life had been contaminated by brutish city values.

> "There's a fine line between show biz and news biz. The trick is to walk up to that line and touch it with your toe but don't cross it. And some people stay so far away from the line that nobody wants to watch what they do. And other people keep crossing the line. . . . But there has to be a line because the line is called truth. And the difference between what we do is, we tell true stories and other people tell make believe stories."
>
> —Don Hewitt,
> executive producer,
> 60 Minutes

Finally, **individualism**, according to Gans, remains the single biggest value underpinning daily journalism. Many idealistic reporters are attracted to this profession because it rewards the rugged tenacity needed to confront and expose corruption. Beyond this, individuals who overcome personal adversity are the subjects of many investigative news stories. Often, however, journalism that focuses on personal triumphs fails to explain how large institutions work or fail. Conventional journalism lacks a larger framework for understanding complex institutions. Many reporters and editors, for instance, are unwilling or unsure of how to tackle the problems raised by institutional decay. In addition, since they are accustomed to working alone, many journalists distrust working on team projects or participating in citizen forums in which community members discuss their own interests.[10]

Traditionally, reporters have aligned *facts* with an objective position and *values* with subjective feelings.[11] Within this context, news reports offer readers and viewers details, data, and description. It then becomes the citizen's responsibility to judge and take a stand about the social problems represented by the news. Given these assumptions, reporters are responsible only for adhering to the traditions of the trade— "getting the facts." As a result, many reporters view themselves as neutral "channels" of information rather than as citizens themselves actively involved in public life.

ethics and the news media

In late April 1992, a not-guilty verdict was returned in a suburban Simi Valley courtroom, acquitting four Los Angeles police officers who had been charged with excessive force against Rodney King, an ex-con who had led police on a three-mile, high-speed chase through Los Angeles in 1991. According to police reports, King first refused to get out of his car and then resisted arrest; officers used batons and stun guns to subdue him. Without police knowledge, however, the incident was captured by a bystander on a home video. Played over and over on news programs, the video showed King on the ground offering little resistance as several officers kicked and beat him. The subsequent not-guilty verdict against the officers triggered fighting, looting, and arson fires in South Central Los Angeles. Fifty-eight people died. Officials estimated more than $1 billion in property damages. After the tragedy, the federal government filed a civil case against the four officers, charging them with deliberately depriving Rodney King of his civil rights. In 1993, two of the officers were found guilty and sentenced to thirty months in prison.

In the spring of 1992, between Rodney King's criminal and civil cases, Ted Koppel abandoned his command desk at ABC's *Nightline* and relocated to a church in South Central L.A. for a special *Nightline* show. Featuring interviews with gang members, church leaders, community activists, and neighbors, this *Nightline* looked a lot like Oprah and her talk program when she has visited urban housing projects. On the program, one older minister challenged Koppel's authority by accusing *Nightline* of pitting gang members against religious leaders to generate conflict for a more dramatic news story. Koppel, used to the more detached stance of the contemporary news reporter, was visibly uncomfortable and quickly changed the subject.

ethical predicaments

Ted Koppel's dilemma raises an ethical question: What is the moral and social responsibility of journalists, not only for the stories they report but for the actual events or issues they are shaping for millions of people? Wrestling with such *media ethics* involves determining the moral response to a situation through critical reasoning. Koppel's ethical jam was more subtle than many situations faced by journalists on a daily basis. He "solved" it by avoiding it, but media professionals respond in other ways to a variety of ethical problems. The most frequent ethical dilemmas involve intentional deception, privacy invasions, and conflicts of interest.

Deploying Deception. In 1996, ABC News lost a series of court cases in which the network was charged with misrepresentation and using false credentials to infiltrate private businesses (see "Examining Ethics: Why Those Hidden Cameras Hurt Journalism" on page 434). The verdicts sent a chill through the TV newsmagazine business. After all, ever since Nellie Bly faked insanity to get inside an 1880s asylum, investigative journalists have used deception to get stories. Today, journalists continue to use disguises and assume false identities to gather information on social transgressions. Beyond legal considerations, though, a key ethical question comes into play: Does the end justify the means? For example, can a newspaper or TV newsmagazine go undercover to expose a suspected fraudulent clinic that promises miracle cures at a high cost? By posing as clients desperate for a cure, are news professionals justified in using deception?

In terms of ethics, there are at least two major positions and multiple variations. First, *absolutist ethics* suggest that a moral society has laws and codes, including honesty, that everyone must live by. This means citizens, including members of the news media, should tell the truth at all times and in all cases. In other words, the ends (exposing a phony clinic) never justify the means (using deception to get the story). At the other end of the spectrum are *situational ethics*, which promote ethical decisions on a case-by-case basis. If a greater public good is served by using deceit, many journalists would sanction deception as a practice. Absolutists, however, would shun deceptive measures. Instead, they might cover this story by finding victims who have been ripped off by the clinic and telling the story through their eyes.

Should a journalist withhold information about his or her professional identity to get a quote or a story from an interview subject? Many sources and witnesses are

Why Those Hidden Cameras Hurt Journalism

by Paul Starobin

When a North Carolina jury took a swipe at hidden-camera television exposés [in January 1997], the press mostly circled the wagons and declared it a travesty. But what the Fourth Estate is defending is shoddy journalism, unworthy of the best tradition of investigative reporting.

The jury found ABC liable for $5.5 million in punitive damages for using deceptive research tactics, amounting to fraud, in a 1992 *Primetime Live* broadcast that accused the Food Lion supermarket chain of selling spoiled food. The show's producers faked résumés to get jobs at Food Lion stores and then used hidden cameras to catch workers prettying up tainted meat.

ABC's lawyer, Bill Jeffries, says the *Primetime* crew was punished "for being journalists." Nonsense. It was punished for trickery and deception.

Hidden cameras? That's the easiest call. Their growing use by TV news-magazine shows, including *Primetime Live* and NBC's *Dateline*, is part of a ratings-driven descent by the major networks into the swamp of tabloid journalism. Teaser promos for the programs hype concealed-camera feats to snag viewers who like to watch people who don't know they're being watched. But good journalism is not about sensationalizing how the story was obtained.

The more difficult case is the use of undercover practices to get a story that might otherwise be difficult to report. So what if a few producers falsified their résumés to land jobs at Food Lion: Isn't this part and parcel of muckraking journalism?

Subterfuge does have a long tradition in investigative reporting, but it is a dubious one. The pioneer was Nellie Bly, who in 1887 feigned insanity to gain admission to the New York City Lunatic Asylum.

Bly's report in the *New York World* on her ten days in the asylum exposed horrors that spurred needed reforms. But was that the only way to get the story? Probably not. The flamboyant Bly was an artful practitioner of what was known back then as "stunt journalism." She also posed as a prostitute and a thief and was regarded by some peers as a self-promoting sensationalizer and an embarrassment to the craft.

Broadsheet newspapers hyped derring-do disguise feats just as the TV newsmagazine shows now tout hidden-camera tricks. The headline for a front-page story on Bly's asylum exploit in the rival *New York Sun* blared "Playing Mad Woman," and the subhead declared, "Nellie Bly Too Sharp for the Island Doctors."

The greatest muckrakers shunned such ruses. Ida Tarbell brought down John D. Rockefeller's Standard Oil monopoly by the tireless bird-dogging of court records and other documents—a righteous tradition later upheld by I. F. Stone and honored these days by the crusaders who are following the money to expose the fund-raising practices of Newt Gingrich and Bill Clinton. And *Fortune* magazine didn't need to go undercover for its 1993 report on the exploitation of child labor in garment-industry sweatshops in New York City and Los Angeles.

Indeed, ABC could have done a devastating story on Food Lion without the tricks. Diane Sawyer, the *Primetime Live* anchor, said seventy current and former employees of the chain had attested to unhealthful food-handling practices in on-the-record interviews with the show's researchers. But that wasn't sexy enough, so ABC went undercover to dramatize the tale. A commercial imperative, not a journalistic one, drove this piece.

ABC points out that Food Lion sued for fraud, not libel, and so did not challenge the substance of the story. But news organizations should not be untruthful in their search for the truth. The North Carolina jury has fired a well-deserved warning shot. Stunt journalism saps the credibility of the press and makes life tougher for honest snoops.

Source: Paul Starobin, "Why Those Hidden Cameras Hurt Journalism," *New York Times*, January 28, 1997, p. A13.

reluctant to talk with journalists, especially about a sensitive subject that might jeopardize a job or hurt another person's reputation. Journalists know they can sometimes obtain information by posing as someone other than a journalist, such as a curious student or a licensed therapist. Most newsrooms frown on such deception. In particular situations, though, such a practice might be condoned if reporters and their editors believed that the public needed the information. The ethics code adopted by the Society of Professional Journalists is fairly silent on issues of deception. The code "requires journalists to perform with intelligence, objectivity, accuracy, and fairness," but it also says that "truth is our ultimate goal."[12] Furthermore, it does not offer much specific guidance on the ethical means necessary for arriving at the truth.

Invading Privacy. To achieve the truth, journalists routinely straddle a line between the public's right to know and a person's right to privacy. For example, journalists are often sent to hospitals to gather quotes from victims or from relatives of individuals who have suffered some injury. In many of these cases, there is very little the public might gain from such a quote, but journalists worry that if they don't get the quote, a competitor might. In these instances, have the news media responsibly weighed the protection of individual privacy against the public's right to know? Although the latter is not constitutionally guaranteed, journalists invoke the public's right to know as justification for many types of stories.

Privacy issues also affect corporations and institutions. For example, in 1998 a *Cincinnati Enquirer* reporter got into trouble for illegally gaining access to the voice-mail system at Chiquita, a company best known for selling bananas. The reporter used information attained from voice mail to report on the company's business practices. While a few journalists applauded the enterprising savvy of the reporter in obtaining this information, many critics said such a technique represented a violation of the company's privacy rights. At the very least, in our digital age, when reporters can gain access to private email messages as well as voice mail, such reporting practices raise serious questions about how far a reporter should go to get information.

In regard to both individual and institutional privacy, do the news media always ask the ethical questions: What public good is being served here? What significant public knowledge will be gained through the exploitation of a tragic private moment? Although journalism's code of ethics says, "The news media must guard against invading a person's right to privacy," this clashes with another part of the code: "The public's right to know of events of public importance and interest is the overriding mission of the mass media."[13] In general, when these two ethical standards collide, journalists usually err on the side of the public's right to know.

Conflict of Interest. Journalism's code of ethics also warns reporters and editors not to place themselves in positions that produce a **conflict of interest**—that is, any situation in which journalists may stand to benefit personally from stories they produce. "Gifts, favors, free travel, special treatment or privileges," the code states, "can compromise the integrity of journalists and their employers. Nothing of value should be accepted."[14] For instance, at large mainstream news media that subscribe to the code, newspapers or broadcast stations pay for the game tickets of their sports writers and for the meals of their restaurant critics. Small newspapers, however, with limited resources and poorly paid reporters, might accept such *freebies* from a local business or interview subject. This practice may be an economic necessity, but it is one that can increase the likelihood of conflict of interest.

On a broader level, ethical guidelines at many news outlets attempt to protect journalists from compromising positions. For instance, in most cities journalists do not actively participate in politics or support social causes. Some journalists will not reveal their political affiliations and occasionally will even refuse to vote. For these journalists, the rationale behind their decisions is straightforward: Journalists should not place themselves in a situation in which they might have to report on the misdeeds of an organization or political party to which they belong. If a journalist has a tie to any group, and that group is later discovered to be involved in shady practices or criminal activity, the reporter's ability to report on that group would be compromised—along with the credibility of the news outlet for which he or she works. Conversely, other journalists believe that *not* actively participating in politics or social causes is abandoning one's civic obligations.

resolving ethical problems

When a journalist is criticized for ethical indiscretions or questionable reporting tactics, a typical response might be "I'm just doing my job" or "I was just getting the facts." In retrospect, such explanations are troubling because reporters are transferring personal responsibility for the story to a set of institutional rituals. Journalists who disclaim personal or ethical responsibility can become mere extensions of a business enterprise.

> "We should have the **public interest** and not the bottom line at heart or else all we can do is wait for a time when **sex doesn't sell.**"
> —Susan Ungaro, editor, *Family Circle*, on media coverage of the Clinton-Lewinsky scandal, 1998

There are, of course, ethical alternatives to comments like "I'm just doing my job" that force journalists to think through complex issues. Broad ethical horizons used throughout history establish common ground and offer perspectives beyond narrow frames of reference. With the crush of deadlines and daily duties, most media professionals deal with ethical situations only on a case-by-case basis as dilemmas arise. However, examining major ethical models and theories provides a common strategy for addressing ethics on a general rather than a situational basis. Ethical and philosophical guidelines also offer universal measures for testing individual values and codes.

Although we cannot address all major moral codes here, a few key precepts can guide us. One principle entails the "categorical imperative," developed by German philosopher Immanuel Kant (1724–1804). A moral imperative or command argues that a society must adhere to moral codes that are universal and unconditional, applicable in all situations at all times. For example, the Golden Rule—Do unto others as you would have them do unto you—operates as such an absolutist moral principle. The First Amendment, which prevents Congress from abridging free speech, has likewise served as a national unconditional law.

Another ethical principle, derived from British philosophers Jeremy Bentham (1748–1832) and John Stuart Mill (1806–1873), promotes "the greatest good for the greatest number," directing us "to distribute a good consequence to more people rather than to fewer, whenever we have a choice."[15] The most well-known ethical standard, the Judeo-Christian command to "love your neighbor as yourself," also provides the basis for constructing ethical guidelines.

Arriving at ethical decisions involves several stages. These include laying out the case; pinpointing the key issues; identifying involved parties, their intent, and their competing values; studying ethical models; presenting strategies and options; and formulating a decision. In terms of privacy issues, for instance, the goal would be to develop an ethical policy that the news media might implement in covering the private lives of people who have become prominent in the news. (See Figure 14.1 on facing page for the SPJ Code of Ethics.)

Consider Richard Jewell, the Atlanta security guard who, for eighty-eight days, was the FBI's prime suspect in the park bombing at the 1996 Olympics. The FBI never charged Jewell with a crime, and he later sued several news organizations for libel. Putting legal issues aside, the Jewell story involved a rivalry among various news

**Figure 14.1
(facing page)
SPJ Code of Ethics**
Source: Society of Professional Journalists.

Code Of Ethics

Preamble

Members of the Society of Professional Journalists believe that public enlightenment is the forerunner of justice and the foundation of democracy. The duty of the journalist is to further those ends by seeking truth and providing a fair and comprehensive account of events and issues. Conscientious journalists from all media and specialties strive to serve the public with thoroughness and honesty. Professional integrity is the cornerstone of a journalist's credibility.

Members of the Society share a dedication to ethical behavior and adopt this code to declare the Society's principles and standards of practice.

Seek Truth and Report It

Journalists should be honest, fair and courageous in gathering, reporting and interpreting information.

Journalists should:

- Test the accuracy of information from all sources and exercise care to avoid inadvertent error. Deliberate distortion is never permissible.
- Diligently seek out subjects of news stories to give them the opportunity to respond to allegations of wrongdoing.
- Identify sources whenever feasible. The public is entitled to as much information as possible on sources' reliability.
- Always questions sources' motives before promising anonymity. Clarify conditions attached to any promise made in exchange for information. Keep promises.
- Make certain that headlines, news teases and promotional material, photos, video, audio, graphics, sound bites and quotations do not misrepresent. They should not oversimplify or highlight incidents out of context.
- Never distort the content of news photos or video. Image enhancement for technical clarity is always permissible. Label montages and photo illustrations.
- Avoid misleading re-enactments or staged news events. If re-enactment is necessary to tell a story, label it.
- Avoid undercover or other surreptitious methods of gathering information except when traditional open methods will not yield information vital to the public. Use of such methods should be explained as part of the story.
- Never plagiarize.
- Tell the story of the diversity and magnitude of the human experience boldly, even when it is unpopular to do so.
- Examine their own cultural values and avoid imposing those values on others.
- Avoid stereotyping by race, gender, age, religion, ethnicity, geography, sexual orientation, disability, physical appearance or social status.
- Support the open exchange of views, even views they find repugnant.
- Give voice to the voiceless; official and unofficial sources of information can be equally valid.
- Distinguish between advocacy and news reporting. Analysis and commentary should be labeled and not misrepresent fact or context.
- Distinguish news from advertising and shun hybrids that blur the lines between the two.
- Recognize a special obligation to ensure that the public's business is conducted in the open and that government records are open to inspection.

Minimize Harm

Ethical journalists treat sources, subjects and colleagues as human beings deserving of respect.

Journalists should:

- Show compassion for those who may be affected adversely by news coverage. Use special sensitivity when dealing with children and inexperienced sources or subjects.
- Be sensitive when seeking or using interviews or photographs of those affected by tragedy or grief.
- Recognize that gathering and reporting information may cause harm or discomfort. Pursuit of the news is not a license for arrogance.
- Recognize that private people have a greater right to control information about themselves than do public officials and others who seek power, influence or attention. Only an overriding public need can justify intrusion into anyone's privacy.
- Show good taste. Avoid pandering to lurid curiosity.
- Be cautious about identifying juvenile suspects or victims of sex crimes.
- Be judicious about naming criminal suspects before the formal filing of charges.
- Balance a criminal suspect's fair trial rights with the public's right to be informed.

Act Independently

Journalists should be free of obligation to any interest other than the public's right to know.

Journalists should:

- Avoid conflicts of interest, real or perceived.
- Remain free of associations and activities that may compromise integrity or damage credibility.
- Refuse gifts, favors, free travel and special treatment, and shun secondary employment, political involvement, public office and service in community organizations if they compromise journalistic integrity.
- Disclose unavoidable conflicts.
- Be vigilant and courageous about holding those with power accountable.
- Deny favored treatment to advertisers and special interests and resist their pressure to influence news coverage.
- Be wary of sources offering information for favors or money; avoid bidding for news.

Be Accountable

Journalists are accountable to their readers, listeners, viewers and each other.

Journalists should:

- Clarify and explain news coverage and invite dialogue with the public over journalistic conduct.
- Encourage the public to voice grievances against the news media.
- Admit mistakes and correct them promptly.
- Expose unethical practices of journalists and the news media.
- Abide by the same high standards to which they hold others.

Atlanta Journal EXTRA

TUESDAY, JULY 30, 1996

50 CENTS

FBI suspects 'hero' guard may have planted bomb

OCT. 27, 1996

Jewell is cleared in bomb case

For almost three months, security guard Richard Jewell was the FBI's main suspect in the July 1996 Olympic Park bombing that killed one person. When the FBI finally exonerated Jewell, he filed a libel suit against the *Atlanta Journal-Constitution* and NBC.

media to report unusual or important developments before the competition could do so. The battle for newspaper circulation and broadcast ratings added a complex dimension. As has occurred in other instances, editors were reluctant to back away from the story once it had begun circulating in the major media.

At least two key ethical questions emerged from the Jewell story: Should the news media have named Jewell as a suspect even though he was never charged with a crime? Should they have camped out daily in front of his mother's house in an attempt to interview him and his mother? The incidents surrounding the Richard Jewell case pit the media's right to tell stories and earn profits against a citizen's right to be left alone.

Journalists' livelihoods partly depend on using stories that attract audiences and keep up with their competition. To defend their behavior toward the Jewells, for example, the news media might invoke their constitutional right to free expression or argue that their intent was to serve the public's right to know. Similar justifications were employed by the photographers who hounded Princess Diana in 1997, creating an atmosphere that contributed partially to events leading to her death. To criticize such media behavior, however, we might ask whether any significant public knowledge is gained by stalking a potential interview subject. The news media need to balance principles and profit motives against an individual's right to privacy.

As journalists formally work through various ethical stages, they eventually formulate policies and ground them in an overarching moral principle, such as the commandment to "love your neighbor as yourself."[16] Would reporters, for instance, be willing to treat themselves, their families, or their friends the way they treated the Jewells? Ethical reporters could also invoke Aristotle's *golden mean:* seeking moral virtue between extreme positions. In Richard Jewell's situation, this might have entailed developing guidelines that would attempt to balance the interests of the suspect and the news media. For example, during his eighty-eight-day ordeal, in reparation for using Jewell's name in early accounts, reporters might have called off their stakeout and allowed him to set interview times at a neutral site. At such a location, he might have talked with a small pool of journalists designated to relay information to other media outlets.

438

reporting rituals and the legacy of print journalism

Unfamiliar with being questioned themselves, many reporters are uncomfortable discussing their personal values or their strategies for getting stories. Nevertheless, a stock of rituals, derived from basic American values, underlie the practice of reporting. These include focusing on the present, relying on experts, balancing story conflict, and acting as adversaries toward leaders and institutions.

focusing on the present

Historians mark the 1830s as the beginning of the transition between the partisan and modern press eras. Though American journalism began as a venue for partisan politics (encouraging debate over issues such as constitutional amendments, slavery, and states' rights), in the nineteenth century publishers figured out how to sell news as a product. They used modern technology to substantially cut their costs; they also began to change news content to appeal to emerging middle- and working-class people, who could now afford a paper and had the leisure time to read it. Publishers realized that they needed more practical content because many readers were not particularly interested in the intricacies of partisan politics.

When the telegraph enabled news to instantly crisscross America, modern journalism was born. To complement the new technical advances, modern editors called for a dogged focus on the present. Modern print journalism de-emphasized political discussions and historical context, accenting instead the new and the now.

As members of an emerging modern profession, many journalists and newspapers ignored Joseph Pulitzer's call for news that maintained a continuity with the past. As a result, the profession began drawing criticism for failing to offer historical analyses of important phenomena. In news stories about drugs, for example, individual characters—dealers, addicts, abusers, police, medical experts—pass through the frame of news, but only up to a point. Once these characters are no longer timely, they no longer meet the narrative requirements of daily news. Urban drug stories heavily dominated print and network news during the 1986 and 1988 election years. Such stories, however, virtually disappeared from the news in 1992 and 1994, although the nation's serious drug and addiction problems had not diminished.[17] Drug stories simply became "yesterday's news." Modern news tends to reject "old news" for whatever new event or idea disrupts today's routines. In the mid-1990s, when new statistics revealed that drug use among middle-class high-school students was rising, reporters again latched onto new versions of the drug story during the 1996 elections, but their reports made only limited references to the 1980s. Given the space and time constraints of current news practices, reporters infrequently link stories to the past or to the ebb and flow of history.

Getting a Good Story. Early in the 1980s, the Janet Cooke–Pulitzer Prize hoax demonstrated the difference between a reporter merely telling a good story and her social responsibility for the actual experience.[18] The major criticism against the former *Washington Post* reporter focused on her fabrication of an investigative report (for which she won a Pulitzer that was later revoked). She had created a cast of characters featuring a mother who contributed to the heroin addiction of her eight-year-old son. At the time the hoax was exposed, Chicago columnist Mike Royko criticized conventional journalism for allowing narrative conventions—getting a good story—to replace journalism's responsibility to the daily lives it documents: "There's something more important than a story here. This eight-year-old kid is being murdered. The editors should have said forget the story, find the kid. . . . People in any other profession would have gone right to the police."[19] Had editors at the *Post* demanded such help, Cooke's hoax would never have gone as far as it did.

In the pursuit of such dramatic and timely accounts, reporters act out two rituals: getting a good story and getting a story first. These rituals, which motivated reporters during the nineteenth century's yellow journalism phase, still inspire reporters today. According to Don Hewitt, the creator and executive producer of *60 Minutes*, "There's a very simple formula if you're in Hollywood, Broadway, opera, publishing, broadcasting, newspapering. It's four very simple words—tell me a story."[20] For most journalists, the bottom line *is* getting a story—an edict that overrides most other concerns. Getting a timely story fills up a journalist's day and meets routine deadline demands. It is the standard against which reporters measure one another and their profession (see "Case Study: The Case of *60 Minutes*" on page 442).

Getting a Story First. In a discussion on public television about the press coverage of a 1980s fatal plane crash in Milwaukee, a news photographer was asked to discuss his role in covering the tragedy. Rather than take up the poignant aspects of witnessing the aftermath of such an event, the excited photographer launched into a dramatic recounting of how he had slipped behind police barricades to snap the first grim photos, which later appeared in the *Milwaukee Journal*. Typically, reporters enjoy recounting how they evaded a PR flack or an authority figure to secure a story ahead of the competition.

The photojournalist's retelling points up the important role journalism plays in calling public attention to serious events and issues. Yet he also talked about the news-gathering process as a game that journalists play. Indeed, it has become routine for local television stations and newspapers today to run self-promotions about how they beat competitors to a story. In addition, during political elections local television stations and networks project winners in particular races and often hype their projections when they are able to forecast results before the competition does.

Such journalistic *scoops* and exclusive stories often portray reporters in a heroic light: They have won a race for facts, which they have gathered and presented ahead of their rivals. It is not always clear, though, how the public is better served by a journalist's claim to have gotten a story first. Certainly, enterprising journalists can get a story started by calling attention to an important problem or issue. But on occasion, as with the O.J. Simpson trials or the July 1999 plane crash that killed John F. Kennedy Jr., his wife, and his sister-in-law, scoop behavior has led to *herd journalism*, which occurs when reporters stake out a house or follow a story in

The public's distrust of journalism today is partly due to the news media's tendency to chase a story in packs and invade the privacy of individuals. Particularly annoying are photographers and broadcast news crews who often seem to be stalking their subjects.

such large groups that the entire profession comes under attack for invading people's privacy and exploiting their personal tragedies. Although readers and viewers might value the tenacity of adventurous reporters, the earliest reports are not necessarily better than stories written days later with more hindsight and perspective.

relying on experts

Another ritual of modern print journalism—relying on outside sources—has made reporters heavily dependent on experts. Reporters, though often experts themselves in certain areas by virtue of having covered them over time, are not typically allowed to display their expertise. Instead, they must seek outside authorities to give credibility to their neutral reports. What daily reporters know is generally subordinate to knowing whom to consult.

During the early 1900s, progressive politicians and leaders such as Theodore Roosevelt, William Jennings Bryan, Woodrow Wilson, and Walter Lippmann believed in cultivating strong ties among national reporters, government officials, natural scientists, business managers, and academic researchers. They wanted journalists supplied with expertise across a variety of areas. Today, a widening gap exists between citizens with expertise and those without it, creating a need for public mediators. Reporters have assumed this role, becoming surrogate citizens who represent both leaders' and readers' interests. Unlike experts, however, most reporters are generalists, lacking specialized knowledge in any particular field. But with their access to experts, reporters are able to act as agents for citizens, taking specialized knowledge and transforming it into the everyday language of news stories.

> "[M]arathon mourning is now a hit show biz formula for generating ratings and newsstand sales. . . .: The treacly theme music, the cheesy greeting-card art graphics, the New Age vocabulary of 'closure,' the ritualistically repeated slo-mo video clips." —Frank Rich, *New York Times* columnist, criticizing the excessive coverage of the 1999 plane crash that killed JFK Jr., Carolyn Bessette Kennedy, and Lauren Bessette

In the quest for facts, reporters frequently use experts to create narrative conflict by pitting a series of quotes against one another. On occasion, reporters also use experts to support a particular position (which, because of neutrality requirements, reporters are not allowed to state overtly). In addition, the use of experts allows journalists to distance themselves from daily experience; they are able to attribute the responsibility for the events or issues reported in a story to those who are quoted.

In the ritual use of experts, journalists are required to make direct contact with a source—by phone or email or in person. Journalists do not, however, heavily cite the work of other writers; that would violate the reporters' obligation to not only get a story first but to get it on their own. Telephone calls and face-to-face interviews are the stuff of daily journalism. More carefully researched interpretation is often assumed to rest in the hands of academics or magazine writers. News reporters are trained to believe that their credibility springs from their ability to track down sources and obtain in-person, fresh—though not necessarily more illuminating—quotes.

Of expert sources in general, *Newsweek*'s Jonathan Alter calls them the "usual suspects." Alter contends that "the impression conveyed is of a world that contains only a handful of knowledgeable people. . . . Their public exposure is a result not only of their own abilities, but of deadlines and a failure of imagination on the part of the press."[21] In addition, expert sources have historically been predominantly white and male. For example, based on a forty-month analysis of guests on ABC's *Nightline* between 1985 and 1988, Fairness and Accuracy in Media (FAIR) found that "89 percent of the U.S. guests were men, 92 percent were white, and 80 percent were professionals, government officials, or corporate representatives."[22] Beginning in 1995, coverage of the O.J. Simpson trials helped change this profile somewhat. Legal

In late 1998, when *60 Minutes* aired the videotape of an assisted suicide victim's actual death, some critics charged it was another callous attempt by a TV news program to boost ratings. However controversial the infamous death scene, *60 Minutes* probably did not really need a ratings boost. Even in early 1999, it was still a Top 10 program in terms of viewer ratings.

In fact, in the fifty-year history of television, *60 Minutes* remains the only program rated No. 1 in three different decades. It is the most popular (and profitable) TV program in history, finishing among the Nielsen Top 10 for more than twenty consecutive years—another record. From the mid-1970s to the late 1990s, a typical episode of *60 Minutes* reached a bigger audience than any other single news form in U.S. journalism.

Over the years, critics have tried to explain *60 Minutes'* standing as America's first popular news program. Early on, Don Hewitt, the program's creator and executive producer, pointed to storytelling as the key to the program's popularity: "I said to myself, 'I'll bet if we made it multisubject and we made it personal journalism—instead of dealing with issues we told stories; if we packaged reality as well as Hollywood packages fiction, I'll bet we could double the rating.'"[1] Hewitt rightly predicted that personal journalism, starring reporters in mini–news dramas, would dislodge institutional news documentaries in which the network point of view—what Hewitt called "the voice of the corporation"—seemed distant and aloof.

The secret of *60 Minutes* involves adapting a familiar story form long associated with fiction—the detective mystery.[2] Through this well-known frame, the reporters of *60 Minutes* perform not as detached journalists but as dramatic characters. Their mission: to make sense of the world through stories.

"*60 Minutes* is the adventures of five reporters," Hewitt has said, "more fascinating to the American public being themselves than Robert Redford and Dustin Hoffman were playing Woodward and Bernstein."[3] Cast as detectives, *60 Minutes'* reporters each week champion American indi-

vidualism in the face of insensitive corporations and heartless bureaucracy.

On any given Sunday, at least one episode features the detective news frame. In these stories, the reporters introduce the alleged injustices, which may range from political intrigue to murder. After identifying the major characters, the setting, and the crime, the reporters rely on their rational instincts and ability to expose other characters to solve the mystery. Like tidy Columbos, they look like detectives, often wearing trench coats when searching for clues. And like Sherlock Holmes, *60 Minutes* often succeeds where traditional, and sometimes inept, investigative agencies fail. In the end, the program fits together the puzzle as the reporter poses in front of the program's trademark storybook frame, explaining to us—armchair Dr. Watsons—the missing evidence, the fate of the villains, and any leftover disparities.

As in most conventional journalism, social reform is not the stated goal of the program. However, Mike Wallace has written that viewers regard the show as an "unofficial ombudsman," mediating between the people and the powerful. He reveals his own perceptions of the detective role he has performed since 1968: "By the late 1970s . . . I kept bumping into people who jumped at the chance to alert me to some scandal or outrage. . . . They would give me vivid accounts of foul deeds and the culprits perpetrating them, and urge me to take appropriate action: 'You really should look into this, Mike.'"[4] Certainly many powerful segments over the years have concluded with *60 Minutes* serving explicitly as mediating ombudsman—reporters calling for congressional investigations, redressing government oversights or wrongly accused prisoners, and championing individual rights in the face of bureaucratic ineptitude. These stories portray a heroic news medium monitoring abuses of power and breakdowns in basic values.

The legacy of *60 Minutes* is full of controversies, such as the death tape Mike Wallace received from assisted-suicide advocate Dr. Jack Kevorkian in 1998. Other controversies include a trail of alleged wrongly accused "villains." The Illinois Power Company, the apple industry, and the Audi automobile company have all launched campaigns against what these organizations regarded as unfair and misleading stories by *60 Minutes*. Nevertheless, throughout the late 1990s, the program had never lost a libel case (although at least one suit was settled out of court).

Critics of *60 Minutes* argue that most experiences appropriated for news are not generally well served by their representation in simplified detective stories. Such journalism often turns experience into melodrama, making the world simpler and more understandable. Detective stories celebrate individual heroes and condemn cruel villains. But, as in conventional journalism, stories about the inner workings of mundane and complex institutions are not well suited to *60 Minutes*.

Even the production techniques used on the program contribute to the image of the reporters as detectives. For instance, they typically receive more visual or frame space: They are almost always shown at a greater distance than the characters they interview. Frequently, in reaction shots, interview subjects appear in extreme close-ups—usually with

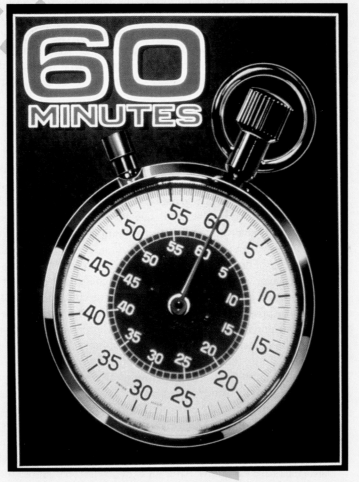

the top of the head cut from the frame. This is in contrast to the medium shots of the reporter, who is usually shown from mid-waist, with space revealed overhead. On one level, the greater space granted to the reporters may be read as the TV counterpart to print's neutrality. But on another level the greater distance endows the *60 Minutes* reporters not only with more space within which to operate but with more authority. They are, after all, detectives—and detectives search for truth. The *60 Minutes* reporters appear in greater control, whereas victims and villains often seem to be in less control—or out of control.

Over the years, *60 Minutes* has penetrated deeply into American consciousness. The reporter-detectives have tapped into our desires for truth, honesty, and intrigue. Each week *60 Minutes* locates us in a world of identifiable characters. The program's stories inform and affirm individualism and common sense. These are powerful attractions that, like church, draw viewers back to this same place Sunday after Sunday.

sources, especially on CNN and CNBC, featured a far more diverse array of expert participants. Nevertheless, as journalists have increased their reliance on experts over the years, they have inadvertently alienated many readers, who feel they no longer have a stake in day-to-day social and political life. After all, authoritative experts and knowledgeable journalists seem to be handling things.

By the late 1990s, many journalists were being criticized for blurring the line between being "objective" and being an expert. While shows like NBC's *The McLaughlin Group* and CNN's *Crossfire* have pitted opinionated columnists and reporters against one another since the 1980s, the boom in 24-hour cable news programs in the 1990s has led to a tremendous news vacuum that is filled with talk shows and interviews with journalists willing to give their views on the hot story of the day. During events with intense media coverage, such as the Clinton-Lewinsky scandal, many print journalists appear several times a day on various cable programs acting as experts on the story, not only offering the facts they have gathered but providing opinion and speculation as well. Some editors even encourage their reporters to go on these shows in the hope of selling more magazines and newspapers. Many critics contend that these practices erode the credibility of journalists and the profession by blending journalism with celebrity culture and commercialism.

> "Cable news is full of **spin doctors** shouting at each other. . . . **Jerry Springer** without the hair pulling."
>
> —Tom Rawlins, editor, *St. Petersburg Times*, 1998

▇balancing story conflict

Embedded deep within journalism is a belief in the two-dimensionality of news. A reporter sent to cover property-tax increases might be given this editorial advice: "Interview Republican and Democratic leaders from the district and have them fight it out in the story." Such "balance" is a narrative device that helps generate story conflict. For most journalists, balance means presenting all sides of an issue without appearing to favor any one position. Unfortunately, since time and space constraints do not always permit representing *all* sides, in practice this value has often been reduced to "telling *both* sides of a story." In recounting news stories as two-sided dramas, however, reporting often misrepresents social issues of multifaceted complexity. The abortion controversy, for example, is often treated as a story that pits two extreme positions (pro-life vs. pro-choice) against each other. Yet people whose views do not fall at one end of the spectrum are seldom represented; they are too far inside the outermost boundaries of a two-dimensional narrative conflict.

Although journalists often claim to be detached, they actually stake out a moderate or middle-of-the-road position between the two sides represented in a story. In claiming neutrality and inviting readers to share in their detached point of view, journalists circumvent their own values. The authority of their distant, third-person, all-knowing point of view (a narrative device that many novelists use as well) enhances the impression of neutrality by making the reporter appear value-free (or value*less*).

The claim for balanced stories, like the claim for neutrality, disguises journalism's narrative functions. After all, when reporters choose quotes for a story, these are usually the most dramatic or conflict-oriented words that emerge from an interview, press conference, or public meeting. Choosing quotes often has more to do with enhancing drama than with establishing neutrality. The balance claim also speaks to mainstream journalism's economic agenda; it is in the financial interest of modern news organizations to stake out the middle ground. William Greider, a former *Washington Post* editor, makes the connection between good business and balanced journalism: "If you're going to be a mass circulation journal, that means you're going to be talking simultaneously to lots of groups that have opposing views. So you've got to modulate your voice and pretend to be talking to all of them."[23]

acting as adversaries

Complementing the search for conflict, the value that journalists take the most pride in is their adversarial relationship with the prominent leaders and major institutions they cover. The prime narrative frame for portraying this relationship is sometimes called a *gotcha story*, which refers to the moment when the reporter nabs an evildoer. This narrative strategy—also known as the *tough-question style*—is frequently used in political reporting. Many journalists assume that leaders are hiding something and that the reporter's main job is to ferret out the truth through tenacious fact-gathering and gotcha questions. An extension of the search for balance, this stance locates the reporter in the middle, between "them" and "us," between political leaders and the people they represent.

Critics of the tough-question style of reporting argue that it fosters a cynicism among journalists that actually harms the democratic process. Although journalists need to guard against becoming too cozy with their political sources, they sometimes go to opposite extremes. By constantly searching for what politicians may be hiding, reporters may miss other issues and ideas that are important to readers and viewers.

News scholar Jay Rosen argues that "the essential problem is that the journalist's method of being critical is not disciplined by any political vision."[24] In other words, the bottom line for neutral or conventional journalists, who claim to have no political agenda, is maintaining an adversarial stance rather than improving the quality of political discussions. When journalists employ the gotcha model to cover news, being tough often becomes an end in itself. Thus reporters believe they have done their job just by roughing up an interview subject or by answering the limited "What is going on here?" question. Yet the Pulitzer Prize, the highest award honoring journalism, often goes to the reporter who asks the ethically charged and open-ended questions, such as "Why is this going on?" and "What ought to be?"

THE FAR SIDE   By GARY LARSON

Mike Wallace interviews the Devil

journalism in the age of television

The rules and rituals governing American journalism began shifting in the 1950s. At the time, former radio reporter John Daly hosted the CBS game show *What's My Line?* When he began moonlighting as the evening TV news anchor on ABC, the fledgling network blurred the entertainment and information border, foreshadowing what in the 1990s became a central criticism of journalism.

In those early days, the most influential and respected television news program was CBS's *See It Now*. Coproduced by Fred Friendly and Edward R. Murrow, *See It Now* practiced a kind of TV journalism lodged somewhere between the neutral and narrative traditions. Serving as the conscience of TV news in its early days, Murrow also worked as the program's anchor and main reporter, introducing the investigative model of journalism to television—a model that programs like *60 Minutes*, *20/20*, and *Dateline NBC* would later imitate.

Probably the most revered figure in television news history, CBS newsman Edward R. Murrow *(center)* is pictured here on a 1950s *See It Now* program, interviewing the U.S. ambassadors to Nationalist China and the Philippines. Murrow and *See It Now* set a standard for TV journalism that has been eroded by the increased blending of news and sensationalism found in most of today's news-magazine shows.

Generally regarded as "the first and definitive" news documentary on American television, *See It Now* sought "to report in depth—to tell and show the American audience what was happening in the world using film as a narrative tool."[25] In the early 1960s, *CBS Reports* carried on the traditions of *See It Now*, and as that decade unfolded, the literary model of reporting played a more significant role in the program. Friendly hinted at the importance of the narrative tradition to *CBS Reports:* "Though based on truth, the programs still have to have stories of their own, with the basic outline of beginning, middle and end."[26]

differences between print and television news

Although TV news reporters share many values, beliefs, and conventions with their print counterparts, television has transformed journalism in a number of significant ways. First, broadcast news is often driven by its technology. If a camera crew and microwave-relay van (which bounces a broadcast signal back to the station) are dispatched to a remote location for a live broadcast, reporters are expected to justify the expense by developing a story, even though one may not exist. This happens, for instance, when a national political candidate does not arrive at the local airport in time for an interview on the evening news, leaving the reporter and crew standing on an empty tarmac to report live on a flight delay. Print reporters, however, slide their notebooks or laptop computers back into their bags and report on the story when it actually occurs.

Second, although print editors must cut stories to fit a physical space around the slots allocated for ads, TV news directors have to time stories to fit news in between commercials. They are under pressure to condense the day's main events into a visual show. Despite the fact that a much higher percentage of space is devoted to print ads (more than 60 percent at most dailies), TV ads (which take up less than 25 percent of the time in a typical thirty-minute news program) generally seem more intrusive to viewers, perhaps because TV ads take up time rather than space.

Third, whereas print journalists are expected to behave as detached reporters, TV news derives its credibility from live, on-the-spot reporting, believable imagery,

446

and viewers' trust in the reporters and anchors who read the news. In fact, since the early 1970s, the annual Roper polls have indicated that the majority of viewers find television news a more credible resource than print news. Viewers tend to feel a personal regard for the local anchors who appear each evening on sets in their homes. Many print journalists have even come to resent operating in the relative anonymity of newspaper work while their TV counterparts become mini-celebrities.

By the mid-1970s, the public's fascination with the Watergate scandal and the improved quality of television journalism helped local news departments realize profits. In an effort to retain high ratings, stations began hiring consultants, who advised news directors to invest in one of the national packaged formats, such as Action News or Eyewitness News. Traveling the country, viewers noticed that similar theme music and opening visuals were available from market to market. Consultants also suggested that stations lead their newscasts with *crime blocks:* a group of stories that recount the worst criminal transgressions of the day. A cynical slogan soon developed in the industry: "If it bleeds, it leads."

A few stations around the country have responded to viewers and critics who complain about the overemphasizing of crime news—especially given that in the 1990s FBI statistics show that crime and murder rates fell in most major urban areas. In 1996, the news director at KVUE-TV in Austin, Texas, concerned about crime coverage, launched a new set of criteria that had to be met for news reports to qualify as responsible crime stories. The news director asked that her reporters answer the following questions: Do citizens or officials need to take action? Is there an immediate threat to safety? Is there a threat to children? Does the crime have significant community impact? Does the story lend itself to a crime-prevention effort? With KVUE's new standards, the station eliminated many routine crime stories. Instead, the station provided a context for understanding crime rather than a mindless running tally of what crimes were being committed each day.[27]

Sound Bitten. Beginning in the 1980s, the term **sound bite** became part of the public lexicon. The TV equivalent of a quote in print news, a sound bite is the part of a news report in which an expert, celebrity, victim, or person-on-the-street responds in an interview to some aspect of an event or issue. With the 1988 national elections, sound bites became the focus of intense criticism. Various studies revealed that during political campaigns the typical sound bite from candidates had shrunk from an average duration of forty seconds in the 1950s and 1960s to less than eight seconds by the late 1990s. With shorter comments from interview subjects, TV news sometimes seemed like dueling sound bites, with reporters creating dramatic tension by editing competing viewpoints together as if the individuals had actually been in the same location speaking to one another. Of course, print news also pits one quote against another in a story, even though the actual interview subjects may never have met. Once again, these reporting techniques are evidence of the profession's reliance on storytelling devices to replicate or create conflict.

Pretty-Face and Happy-Talk Culture. In the early 1970s, at a Milwaukee TV station, consultants advised the station's news director that the evening anchor looked too old. Showing a bit of gray, the anchor was replaced and went on to serve as the station's editorial director. He was thirty-two years old at the time. In the late 1970s, a woman reporter at the same station was fired because of a weight problem, although that was not given as the official reason. Earlier that year, she had given birth to her first child. In 1983, Christine Craft, formerly a Kansas City television news anchor, initially won $500,000 in damages in a sex-discrimination suit against station KMBC (she eventually lost the monetary award when the station appealed). She had

Managers of television news departments have often over-emphasized the visual nature of their medium, placing more weight upon the physical attractiveness of anchors than on their skills as reporters. In the early 1980s, news anchor Christine Craft was fired because consultants believed she was no longer youthful and attractive enough to draw a large audience.

been fired because consultants believed she was too old, too unattractive, and not deferential enough to men.

Such stories are rampant in the annals of TV news. They have helped create a stereotype of the half-witted but attractive news anchor, reinforced by popular-culture images (such as Ted Baxter on the *Mary Tyler Moore Show*, Corky Sherwood and Miller Redfield on *Murphy Brown*, and the William Hurt character in the 1987 movie *Broadcast News*). Although the situation has improved slightly, a generation of national news consultants set the agenda for what local reporters should cover—lots of local crime—as well as how they should look—young, attractive, pleasant, and usually white, with little or no regional accent. Essentially, news consultants (also known as *news doctors*) tried to replicate in local TV news the predominant advertising images of the 1960s and 1970s.

Another news strategy favored by news consultants has been *happy talk:* the ad-libbed or scripted banter that goes on among local news anchors, reporters, meteorologists, and sports reporters before and after news reports. During the 1970s, consultants often recommended such chatter to create a more relaxed feeling on the news set and to foster conversational intimacy with viewers. Some news doctors also believed that happy talk would counter much of that era's "bad news," which included coverage of urban riots and the Vietnam War. A strategy still used today, happy talk often appears forced and occasionally creates awkward transitions, especially when anchors must report on events that are sad or tragic.

visual language and critical limits

The brevity of a televised report is often compared unfavorably with the length of print news. However, newspaper reviewers and other TV critics seldom discuss the visual language of TV news and the ways in which images may capture events more powerfully than words.

In contemporary America, the shift from a print-dominated culture to an electronic-digital culture requires thoughtful scrutiny. Instead, the complexity of this shift is often reduced to a two-dimensional debate about information vs. entertainment. Yet over the past forty-five years television news has dramatized America's key events and provided a clearinghouse for shared information—a function that CNN is now performing on a global level. Civil-rights activists, for instance, acknowledge that the movement benefited enormously from televised pictures that documented the plight of southern blacks in the 1960s. Other enduring TV images, unfurled as a part of history to each new generation, are embedded in our collective memory: the

Kennedy-King assassinations in the 1960s; the turmoil of Watergate in the 1970s; the space-shuttle disaster and the Chinese student uprisings in the 1980s; the Persian Gulf War, the bombing of the Oklahoma City federal building, the Centennial Olympics, and the Clinton impeachment hearings in the 1990s. During these critical events, TV news has been a cultural reference point marking the strengths and weaknesses of a nation.

In contrast, many print critics overlooked a disturbing TV news strategy that developed in the mid to late 1980s. In their coverage of crack cocaine, news operations formulated a visual shot in which news photographers, or *shooters* (using shaky, handheld cameras), leaped from the back of police vans and followed gun-wielding authorities as they broke down the doors of various crack houses. At the time, few critics mentioned that in such a shot TV news actually represented the police or state's point of view. A profession that prides itself on neutrality and on watching over the police on society's behalf apparently did not question whether it was appropriate for reporters to implicitly tell these stories from the police's viewpoint. Many critics, untrained in analyzing and interpreting visual language, failed to comment.

conventional news, public journalism, and democracy

In 1990, Poland was experiencing growing pains as it shifted from a state-controlled economic system to a more open market economy. The country's leading newspaper, *Gazeta Wyborcza*, the first noncommunist newspaper to appear in Eastern Europe since the 1940s, was also undergoing challenges. Based in Warsaw with a circulation of about 350,000 at the time, *Gazeta Wyborcza* had to report on and explain the new economy and the new crime wave that accompanied it. Especially troubling to the news staff and to Polish citizens were gangs that preyed on American and Western European tourists at railway stations. Apparently, an inner circle of thieves snatched purses, wallets, and luggage, sometimes assaulting tourists in the process. The stolen goods would then pass to an outer circle whose members transferred the goods to still another outer ring of thieves. Even if the police caught the original inner-circle members, the loot disappeared.

These developments triggered heated discussions in the newsroom. A small group of young reporters, some of whom had worked in the United States, argued that the best way to cover the story was to describe the new crime wave and relay the facts to readers in a neutral manner. Another group, many of whom were older and more experienced, felt that the paper should take an advocacy stance and condemn the criminals through interpretive columns on the front page. The older guard won this particular debate, and more interpretive pieces appeared.[28]

the future of news

The Polish newsroom story illustrates the two competing models that have influenced American and European journalism since the early 1900s. The first—the *informational* or *modern model*—emphasizes describing events and issues from a neutral point of view. The second—a more *partisan* and *European model*—stresses analyzing occurrences and advocating remedies from an acknowledged point of view. In most American newspapers today, the informational model dominates the front page, while the partisan model remains confined to the editorial pages and an occasional front-page piece. Supplementing both models, photographs in newspapers and images on television tell parts of a story not easily captured in words. An alternative model—often labeled "public journalism"—has recently emerged to challenge modern journalistic ideals.

What Is Public Journalism? Since the late 1980s, a number of newspapers have been experimenting with ways to more actively involve readers in the news process. These experiments have surfaced primarily at midsize daily papers, including the *Charlotte Observer,* the *Wichita Eagle,* the *Virginian-Pilot,* the *Minneapolis Star Tribune,* and the *St. Louis Post-Dispatch.* Davis "Buzz" Merritt, editor and vice president of the *Wichita Eagle,* has defined key aspects of civic or **public journalism**:

- It moves beyond the limited mission of "telling the news" to a broader mission of helping public life go well, and acts out that imperative. . . .

- It moves from detachment to being a fair-minded participant in public life. . . .

- It moves beyond only describing what is "going wrong" to also imagining what "going right" would be like. . . .

- It moves from seeing people as consumers—as readers or nonreaders, as bystanders to be informed—to seeing them as a public, as potential actors in arriving at democratic solutions to public problems.[29]

Public journalism might best be imagined as a conversational map for journalistic practice. Modern journalism draws a distinct line between reporter detachment and community involvement; public journalism—driven by citizen forums, community conversations, and even talk shows—redraws this line.

> "We need to see people not as readers, nonreaders, endangered readers, not as customers to be wooed or an audience to be entertained, but as a public, citizens capable of action."
> —Davis "Buzz" Merritt, *Wichita Eagle,* 1995

The impetus behind public journalism is the realization that many citizens feel alienated from politics, from decision making, and from participating in public life in a meaningful way. This alienation arises, in part, from watching passively as the political process plays out in the news media. The process stars the politicians who run for office, the spin doctors who manage the campaigns, and the reporters who dig into every nook and cranny. Meanwhile, readers and viewers serve as spectators, watching a play that does not seem to involve them.

Despite criticism of the bland uniformity of most local news programs and their overemphasis on crime, they are particularly effective covering stories that concern local citizens, such as breaking weather news and community events like this rally to protect Native American fishing rights.

The public-journalism movement has drawn both criticism and praise as it has attempted to be taken seriously as another approach to journalism. Though not a substitute for investigative reporting or the routine coverage of daily events, public journalism is a way to involve both the public and journalists more centrally in civic and political life. Editors and reporters interested in addressing citizen alienation—and reporter cynicism—began devising ways to engage people as conversational partners in determining the news. In an effort to draw the public into discussions about community priorities, these journalists began sponsoring reader and citizen forums as one part of the news process. Through such forums, readers are supposed to have a voice in shaping aspects of the news that directly affect them.

Although isolated citizen projects and reader forums are sprinkled throughout the history of journalism, the current public-journalism movement began in earnest in the late 1980s. In 1987 and 1988, as Columbus, Georgia, suffered from a depressed economy, an alienated citizenry, and unresponsive leadership, a team of reporters from the *Columbus Ledger-Enquirer*, part of the Knight-Ridder chain, surveyed and talked with community leaders and other citizens about the future of the city. Based on the findings, the paper published an eight-part series.

When the provocative series evoked little public response, the paper's leadership realized there was no mechanism or forum for continuing the public discussions about the issues raised in the series. Consequently, the paper created such a forum by organizing a town meeting. Three hundred citizens showed up. The editor of the paper, Jack Swift, organized a follow-up cookout at his own home at which seventy-five concerned citizens created a new civic organization called United Beyond 2000, led by a steering committee with Swift as a leading member. Staffed by community volunteers, task forces formed around recreation, child care, racial tension, and teenage behavior. The committees spurred the city's managers and other political leaders into action. The Columbus project had generated public discussion, involved more people in the news process, and eased race and class tensions by bringing various groups together in public conversations. In the newsroom, the *Ledger-Enquirer* reimagined the place of journalists in politics: "Instead of standing outside the political community and reporting on its pathologies, they took up residence within its borders."[30]

Another important public-journalism project began in Wichita, Kansas, after the 1988 elections. Davis Merritt was so discouraged by the paper's typical and conventional political coverage that he led a campaign to use public journalism as a catalyst for reinventing political news. The *Eagle*'s first voter project during the 1990 governor's election used reader surveys and public forums to refocus the paper around a citizens' agenda. This involved dropping the tired horse-race metaphor—who's winning, who's losing—that usually frames political coverage. Merritt argues that "public life cannot regain its vitality on a diet of information alone." He believes that a new direction for journalism must "reengage citizens in public life" through two steps: "(1) Add to the definition of our job the additional objective of helping public life go well, and then (2) Develop the journalistic tools and reflexes necessary to reach that objective."[31] The *Eagle*'s project partially revitalized regional politics in Kansas in the early 1990s. It influenced other papers as well, including the *Charlotte Observer*, which created a citizens' agenda to determine key issues for its election coverage throughout the 1990s.

A final example involves editors at Norfolk's *Virginian-Pilot*, which has been on a mission to change the culture of the newsroom since the early 1990s (see Figure 14.2). Defying the long-standing tradition of lone reporters covering beats and topics on their own, the paper reorganized reporters into teams. The editors also began using deliberative citizen forums, called *community conversations*, to discover not what people want to read but how "to name and frame issues" central to the community. These issues then

Figure 14.2
Changing the Culture of the Newsroom:
Two Models at the *Virginian-Pilot*

In 1995, in the spirit of public journalism, the editors at the *Virginian-Pilot* attempted to transform the "belief system" of their newsroom, imagining themselves primarily as citizens helping to improve public life.
Source: Used by permission of the *Virginian-Pilot*.

became the driving force behind some of the paper's coverage. According to the leading theorist of public journalism, New York University's Jay Rosen, "The idea is to frame stories from the citizen's view, rather than inserting man-in-the-street quotes into a frame dominated by professionals."[32]

Criticizing Public Journalism. By the late 1990s, more than a hundred newspapers, many teamed with local television and public radio stations, had practiced a form of public journalism. Yet many critics and journalists remain skeptical of the experiment, which they often compare to a passing fad or a religious movement.[33] They are primarily concerned about civic journalism projects that undermine reporters' long-standing role as neutral watchdogs.

Critics of public journalism have raised a number of other issues. First, some editors and reporters argue that such journalism merely panders to what readers want and takes editorial control away from the newsrooms. They believe that very small focus-group samples and poll research—tools of the marketing department—blur the boundary between the editorial and business functions of a paper. Journalists have traditionally viewed their work as a public service and rarely think of the news as a product or a commodity. Some fear that as they become more active in the community they may be perceived as community boosters rather than as community watchdogs. These journalists raise legitimate concerns that their work may be compromised if later they are required to report on the wrongdoings of other civic organizations.

Second, some critics worry that public journalism might compromise the profession's credibility, which today derives from detachment. They argue that public journalism turns reporters into participants rather than observers. However, as Merritt points out, professionals who have credibility are regarded as "honest, intelligent, well-intentioned, trustworthy" and "share some basic values about life, some common ground about common good." Yet conventional journalists insist they "don't share values, with anyone; that [they] are value-neutral."[34] Merritt argues that modern journalism, as a result, actually has little credibility with the public. This view is buoyed by polls and studies that reveal the public's basic distrust of most major news media. Research studies in 1988, for instance, indicated that 50 percent of surveyed respondents said they had "a great deal of confidence in newspapers"; by 1993, similar polls showed that the confidence factor had dropped to 20 percent.[35] Still, many journalists believe that neutrality is a worthy ideal and the main source of a journalist's credibility.

Third, some reporters and editors argue that public-journalism projects remove their control over both stories and the writing process. They are concerned that conversational models of reporting may undermine their narrative voices as well as their independence, especially if they are placed in reporting teams. Defenders of public journalism, however, respond that its goal is merely to create more frames and narrative models—not to eliminate reporters' control over stories or to eradicate traditional

Experiments in public journalism are now going on at newspapers around the country. In rethinking the role of American journalism, many editors and publishers have tried to address the public cynicism directed at both politics and the press. Public journalism asks reporters to become more involved with—rather than detached from—the communities they serve.

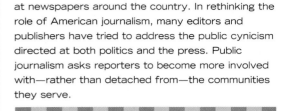

investigative forms of journalism. Public journalists say that their critics mistakenly believe that they merely give readers what they want, when in fact public journalists want to place more citizens at the table to help determine a more inclusive news agenda.

Fourth, critics contend that public journalism undermines the both-sides-of-a-story convention by constantly seeking common ground and community consensus. Public journalists counter that they are trying to set aside more room for centrist positions. Such positions are often representative of many in the community but are missing in the mainstream news, which is more interested in the extremist views that make for a gripping news story. Many journalists, who seek to portray conflict by means of extreme viewpoints, worry that such views will become muted in public journalism. They charge that in seeking a middle ground, public journalism runs the risk of dulling the rough and robust edges of democratic speech.

Fifth, considered by many traditional reporters as merely a tool of marketers and news managers, public journalism has not addressed the changing economic structure of the news business. With more and more newspapers (and broadcast stations) in the hands of fewer and fewer owners, both public journalists and traditional reporters need to raise tough questions about the disappearance of competing daily papers and the large profit margins generated by local monopoly newspapers. Facing little competition, will newspapers continue the 1990s trend of cutting reporting staffs and reducing the space for news? Such a trend may increase profits and satisfy stockholders, but it also limits the voices and views in a community.

public journalism reimagines reporting's role

Conventional journalism will fight ferociously for the overt principles that underpin its basic tenets—freedom of the press, the public's right to know, and two sides to every story—though it generally does not acknowledge any moral or ethical duty to improve the quality of daily life. Rather, journalism values its news-gathering capabilities and the well-constructed news narrative, leaving the improvement of civic life to political groups, nonprofit organizations, business philanthropists, and individual citizens.

Social Responsibility. Although reporters have traditionally thought of themselves first and foremost as observers and recorders, some journalists have occasionally acknowledged social responsibility. Among them was James Agee in the 1930s. In his book *Let Us Now Praise Famous Men*, which was accompanied by the Depression-era photography of Walker Evans, Agee regarded conventional journalism as dishonest, partly because the act of observing intruded on people and turned them into story characters, whom newspapers and magazines exploited for profit.

Agee also worried that readers would retreat into the comfort of his writing—his narrative—instead of confronting what for many families was the horror of the Great Depression. For Agee, the question of responsibility extended not only to journalism and himself but to the readers of his stories as well: "The reader is no less centrally involved than the authors and those of whom they tell." Agee's self-conscious analysis provides insights into journalism's hidden agendas and larger social duties. Foreshadowing public journalism, Agee spoke to the responsibility of all citizens for making public life go better.

In *Let Us Now Praise Famous Men*, which begins with haunting photos taken by Walker Evans, author James Agee questioned the basic honesty of daily journalism in the late 1930s. He thought that professional journalists could too easily exploit interview subjects simply as news stories that serve a business enterprise without actively engaging in changing the conditions of social life.

Deliberative Democracy. According to advocates of public journalism, when reporters are chiefly concerned with maintaining their antagonistic relationship to politics, and are less willing to improve political discourse, news and democracy suffer. *Washington Post* columnist David Broder thinks that national journalists—through rising salaries, prestige, and formal education—have distanced themselves "from the people that we are writing for and have become much, much closer to people we are writing about."[36] Broder believes that journalists need to become activists, not for a particular party but for the political process and in the interest of reenergizing public life. For the news media, this might involve spearheading voter-registration drives or setting up pressrooms in public libraries or even in shopping malls, where people converge in large numbers.

By advocating a more active role for reporters and the news media, public journalism intends to reinvigorate both reporting and politics. Most of all, it offers people models for how to deliberate in forums, and then it covers those deliberations. Public journalism aims to improve our standard *representative democracy*, in which most of us sit back and watch elected officials act on our behalf, by reinvigorating *deliberative democracy*, in which citizen groups, local government, and the news media together take a more active stand in shaping social and political agendas. In a more deliberative democracy, a large segment of the community discusses public life and social policy before advising or electing officials who represent the community's interests.

In 1989, the historian Christopher Lasch argued that "the job of the press is to encourage debate, not to supply the public with information."[37] Although he overstated his case—journalism does both and more—Lasch made a cogent point about how conventional journalism has lost its bearings. Adrift in data, mainstream journalism has lost touch with its partisan roots. The early mission of journalism—to advocate opinions and encourage public debate—has been relegated to alternative magazines, the editorial pages, an occasional TV documentary, cable news channels, and Sunday-morning news programs, starring Washington's elite reporters and prominent politicians. Ironically, Lasch connected the gradual decline in voter participation, which began in the 1920s, to more responsible conduct on the part of professional journalists. With a modern "objective" press, he contended, the public increasingly began to defer to the "more professional" news media to watch over civic life on its behalf.

As the advocates of public journalism acknowledge, people have grown used to letting their representatives think and act for them. Public journalism and other civic projects offer citizens an opportunity to deliberate and to influence their leaders. Public journalism asks the mainstream press to reconsider its role in deliberative democracy. For journalists, this may include broadening the story frames they use to recount experiences; paying more attention to the historical context of these stories; doing more reports that analyze both news conventions and social issues; taking more responsibility for their news narratives; and participating more fully in the public life of their communities. It should also include investigations into the impact of economics on news media.

Arguing that for too long journalism has defined its role only in negative terms, news scholar Jay Rosen notes, "To be adversarial, critical, to ask tough questions, to expose scandal and wrongdoing . . . these are necessary tasks, even noble tasks, but they are negative tasks." In addition, he suggests, journalism should assert itself as a positive force, not merely as a watchdog or as a neutral information conduit to readers but as "a support system for public life."[38]

> "Neither journalism nor public life will move forward until we actually rethink, redescribe, and **reinterpret what journalism is**; not the science or information of our culture but its poetry and conversation."
> —James Carey,
> *Kettering Review*,
> 1992

REVIEW QUESTIONS

Modern Journalism in the Information Age

1. What are the drawbacks of the informational model of journalism?

2. What is news?

3. What are some of the key values that underlie modern journalism?

Ethics and the News Media

4. How do issues such as deception and privacy present ethical problems for journalists?

5. Why is getting a story first important to reporters?

6. What are the connections between so-called neutral journalism and economics?

Reporting Rituals and the Legacy of Print Journalism

7. Why have reporters become so dependent on experts?

8. Why do many conventional journalists (and citizens) believe firmly in the idea that there are two sides to every story?

Journalism in the Age of Television

9. How is credibility established in TV news as compared to print journalism?

10. With regard to TV news, what are sound bites and happy talk?

Conventional News, Public Journalism, and Democracy

11. What is public journalism? How does it propose to make journalism better?

12. What are the major criticisms of the public-journalism movement, and why do the mainstream national media have concerns about public journalism?

13. How do public and conventional journalists differ when it comes to maintaining credibility with their audience?

14. What is deliberative democracy, and what does it have to do with public journalism?

QUESTIONING THE MEDIA

1. What are your main criticisms of the state of news today? In your opinion, what are the news media doing well?

2. As a reporter or editor, should you quit voting to demonstrate your ability to be neutral? Why or why not?

3. How would you go about formulating an ethical policy with regard to using deceptive means to get a story?

4. For a reporter, what are the dangers of both detachment from and involvement in public life?

5. What steps would you take to make journalism work better in a democracy?

SEARCHING THE INTERNET

http://www.cjr.org
The Web site for the *Columbia Journalism Review*, one of the nation's premier critics of contemporary journalism. Run by the Columbia Graduate School of Journalism, the site not only contains current CJR magazine articles on national and international news coverage, but also offers a valuable updated listed of "who owns what" in the media.

http://ajr.newslink.org
The site for the *American Journalism Review*, another top national magazine that takes a critical look at contemporary journalism. Run by the School of Journalism at the University of Maryland, the site features current articles from the magazine and a "joblink" service.

http://www.aim.org
The Web site for the conservative media watchdog group Accuracy in Media (AIM). Among other issues, the site showcases articles from its national newsletter and tracks what AIM regards as anti-business bias in national news reporting.

http://www.fair.org
The Web site for the progressive and left-leaning media watchdog group, Fairness and Accuracy in Reporting (FAIR). The site contains articles from its national magazine *EXTRA!*, and a feature called "economic reporting review" that examines news coverage of money-related issues.

In Brief

Make a short list of questionable or illegal methods that a reporter might use to get a story (e.g., withholding her identity as a reporter). Discuss the circumstances under which these methods might be justified.

In Depth

The purpose of this project is to extend your critical approach to the news. With a partner, choose for reading and viewing one local daily paper, the *New York Times*, and one network or CNN newscast—*all from the same weekday*.

Devise a series of charts and a descriptive scheme that will allow you to compare who gets quoted as expert sources in the stories for that particular day. For example, devise one chart that compares the occupations of the sources. Are they from academic, business, or government sectors? Or are they "ordinary" people? Throughout this project, *limit your focus to local, national, or international news*.

1. *Description.* Count the total number of sources used by each newspaper or network program. Look for quotes in news articles and for sound bites on television. Are all sources identified? How are they identified? Can you tell which area of the country these sources are from? What kinds of experts are quoted in the news? What jobs do they seem to hold? What gender are the news sources?

2. *Analysis.* After completing your charts, write one or two paragraphs discussing patterns that emerge. Who seems to get quoted most frequently? Among those quoted, what kinds of occupations generally appear? Do male or female sources dominate?

3. *Interpretation.* Write a one- or two-paragraph critical interpretation of your findings. How are the sources used? Why do you think certain sources appear in this day's news more frequently than others? Why do reporters seek out certain types of sources rather than others? Does the gender of sources mean anything?

4. *Evaluation.* Discuss the limitations of your study and whether you think print or television handles sources best. Did circumstances on the particular day you chose suggest why one type of expert appears more often than other types?

(*Note:* This assignment works either as an in-class presentation or as a written project. Either way, it should include charts that help organize the material.)

Media Effects
and Cultural Approaches to Research

In 1966, NBC showed the Rod Serling made-for-television thriller *The Dooms-day Flight*, the first movie to depict an airplane hijacking. In the story, a man plants a bomb and tries to extract ransom money from an airline. In the days following the telecast, the nation's major airlines reported a dramatic rise in anonymous bomb threats, some of them classified as teenage pranks. The network agreed not to run the film again.

In 1985, the popular heavy-metal band Judas Priest made headlines when two Nevada teenagers shot themselves after listening to the group's allegedly subliminal suicidal message on their 1978 *Stained Class* album. One teen died instantly; the other lived for three more years, in constant pain from severe facial injuries. The teenagers' parents lost a civil product-liability suit against the British metal band and CBS Records.

In 1993, the Walt Disney Company released a movie called *The Program*. The film included a controversial scene in which a troubled college quarterback believes he has to place his life in danger to test his "courage" and maintain his status among his peers. The test required him to lie down on the dividing line of a busy highway as cars zoomed past on either side. Shortly after the film's release, a rash of real-life copycat incidents occurred. After one teenager died, Disney recalled the film and cut the scene from the movie.

In 1995, an eighteen-year-old woman and her boyfriend went on a killing spree in Louisiana after reportedly watching Oliver Stone's 1994 film *Natural Born Killers* more than twenty times. The family of one of the victims filed a lawsuit against Stone and Time Warner, charging that the film—starring Juliette Lewis and Woody Harrelson as a demented celebrity-craving young couple on a murderous rampage—irresponsibly incited real-life violence. Part of their case is based on a 1996 interview in which Stone said, "The most pacifist people in the world said they came out of this movie and wanted to kill somebody." Stone and Time Warner later argued that the lawsuit should be dismissed on the grounds of free speech, but in 1999 the U.S. Supreme Court allowed the suit to continue.

Each of these incidents renewed long-standing cultural debates over the suggestive power of music, visual imagery, and screen violence. Since the emergence of popular music, movies, and television as influential mass media, the relationship between make-believe stories and real-life imitation has drawn a great deal of attention. Concerns have been raised not only by parents, teachers, and politicians but by several generations of mass-communication researchers as well.

When it comes to government- or university-sponsored mass-media research, no social groups have been pondered and probed more than children and teens. The dominant strain of this research—known in shorthand as *media effects*—has focused on a particular area: the connection between aggressive behavior and violent media stories. In the late 1960s, government leaders—reacting to the social upheavals of that decade—first set aside $1 million to examine this connection. Since that time, thousands of studies have told us what most kindergarten teachers believe instinctively: Violent scenes on television and in movies stimulate aggressive behavior in children—especially young boys. Over the years, children have imitated fight scenes from *Zorro*, the *Mighty Mouse Playhouse*, *Batman*, *Teenage Mutant Ninja Turtles*, and the *Mighty Morphin Power Rangers*, leading generations of adults to suspect the effects of mass media.

In this chapter, we will examine the evolution of media research over time. After looking at some early research efforts, we will focus on two major directions in media research: effects research and cultural studies. We will investigate the strengths and limitations of these two approaches. Finally, we will consider how media research interacts with democratic ideals.

early developments in media research

In the early days of the United States, philosophical and historical writings tried to explain the nature of news and print media. For instance, Frenchman Alexis de Tocqueville, author of *Democracy in America*, noted differences between French and American newspapers in the early 1830s:

> In France the space allotted to commercial advertisements is very limited, and . . . the essential part of the journal is the discussion of the politics of the day. In America three quarters of the enormous sheet are filled with advertisements and the remainder is frequently occupied by political intelligence or trivial anecdotes; it is only from time to time that one finds a corner devoted to the passionate discussions like those which the journalists of France every day give to their readers.[1]

During the mid to late nineteenth century, the major models of media analysis were based on moral and political arguments, as suggested in de Tocqueville's writings.[2] More scientific approaches to mass-media research did not begin to develop until the late 1920s and 1930s.

It was in 1920 that Walter Lippmann, in his book *Liberty and the News*, called on journalists to operate more like scientific researchers in gathering and analyzing factual material. Lippmann's next book, *Public Opinion*, published in 1922, applied psychology to journalism. It is considered by many academics to be "the founding book in American media studies."[3]

In America, the emphasis on applied research led to an expanded analysis of the effects of the media, emphasizing data collection and numerical measurement. According to media historian Daniel Czitrom, by the 1930s "an aggressively empirical spirit, stressing new and increasingly sophisticated research techniques, characterized the study of modern communication in America."[4] Czitrom traces four early trends between 1930 and 1960 that contributed to the rise of modern media research: propaganda analysis, public-opinion research, social-psychology studies, and marketing research.

One of the earliest forms of U.S. mass communication research—propaganda analysis—was prominent during the twentieth century's two world wars. Researchers studied the impact of war posters and other government information campaigns to determine how audiences could be persuaded to a position through stirring media messages about patriotism and duty.

Propaganda Analysis. After World War I, some media researchers became interested in the ways in which propaganda had been used to advance the American war effort. They found that during the war governments routinely relied on propaganda divisions as part of their "information" apparatus. Though propaganda was considered a positive force for mobilizing public opinion during the war, researchers after the war labeled propaganda as "partisan appeal based on half-truths and devious manipulation of communication channels."[5] Harold Lasswell's important 1927 study, *Propaganda Techniques in the World War*, focused on media representations, defining propaganda as "the control of opinion by significant symbols, . . . by stories, rumors, reports, pictures and other forms of social communication."[6] *Propaganda analysis* became a major early feature of mass-media research.

Public-Opinion Research. Researchers soon extended the study of war propaganda to include general concerns about how the mass media filtered information and shaped public attitudes. In the face of growing media influence, Walter Lippmann distrusted the public's ability to function as knowledgeable citizens as well as journalism's ability to help the public separate truth from lies. In promoting the place of the expert in modern life, Lippmann celebrated the social scientist as part of a new expert class that could best make "unseen facts intelligible to those who have to make decisions."[7]

Today, Lippmann's expert class conducts citizen surveys in the form of *public-opinion research*, which has become especially influential during political elections. On the upside, research on diverse populations has provided insights into citizen behavior and social differences, especially during election periods or following major national events. For example, election polls demonstrated that Bill Clinton's 1996 victory over Bob Dole was partly the result of the president's heavy support among women voters. In another example, polls conducted after the first O.J. Simpson verdict convincingly documented a wide disparity among white and black citizens regarding their relative trust or suspicion of police officers. A number of research studies—

461

informally copied by such network newsmagazines as ABC's *Primetime Live* (now known as *20/20*)—also demonstrated that a car with a group of young white males cruising a city's main thoroughfare was far less likely to be routinely stopped by police than was a similar car occupied by young black males driving along the same route.

On the downside, the journalism profession has become increasingly dependent on political polls. Some critics ask whether this heavy reliance on measured public opinion has begun to adversely affect active political involvement. For example, there are numerous stories and studies about citizens who decide not to vote because they have already seen poll projections on television and decided that their votes would not make a difference in the outcome. Furthermore, since the public does not design a CBS News or Gallup poll, it is just passively responding to surveys that mainly measure what interests business, government, academics, and the mainstream news media. As one critic notes, "Rather than offer governments the opinions that citizens want them to learn, polls tell governments—or other sponsors—what they would like to learn about citizens' opinions."[8]

Social-Psychology Studies. Whereas opinion polls measure public attitudes, *social-psychology studies* measure individual behavior and cognition. The most influential of these early investigations, the Payne Fund Studies, were a series of thirteen research projects conducted by social psychologists between 1929 and 1932. Named after the private philanthropic organization that provided financial support for the research, the Payne Fund Studies emerged from a growing national concern about the effects of motion pictures, which had become a particularly popular pastime for young people in the 1920s. These beginning studies, which were later used by politicians to attack the movie industry, linked frequent movie attendance to juvenile delinquency, promiscuity, and other antisocial behaviors, arguing that movies took "emotional possession" of young filmgoers.[9]

In one of the Payne studies, for example, children were taken to a movie house and wired with electrodes to galvanometers, mechanisms that detect any heightened response via the subject's skin. The researchers interpreted any galvanic changes in the skin as evidence of emotional arousal. In retrospect, the findings hardly seem surprising: The youngest children in the group (nine-year-olds) had the strongest reaction to violent or tragic movie scenes, while the teenage subjects reacted most strongly to scenes with romantic and sexual content. The researchers concluded that films could be dangerous for young children and might foster sexual promiscuity among teenagers. The conclusions of this and other Payne Fund Studies contributed to the establishment of the film industry's production code, which tamed movie content from the 1930s through the 1950s. As forerunners of today's TV violence and aggression research, the Payne Fund Studies became the model for media research beginning in the late 1960s. (See Figure 15.1 for one example of a contemporary policy that has developed from media research.)

Marketing Research. A fourth influential area of media research, primarily private, developed through the efforts of advertisers, book publishers, and product companies. They began conducting surveys on consumer buying habits, known as *marketing research*. Specialized researchers, using improved audience sampling and statistical techniques, began selling their services to advertisers and media firms in the 1920s. The emergence of commercial radio led to the first ratings systems that measured how many people were listening on a given night. By the 1930s, radio networks, advertisers, large stations, and advertising agencies all subscribed to ratings services. However, compared with print media, whose circulation departments kept careful track of customers' names and addresses, radio listeners were more difficult to trace.

"Research is formalized **curiosity**. It is poking and prying with a purpose."
—Zora Neale Hurston, writer

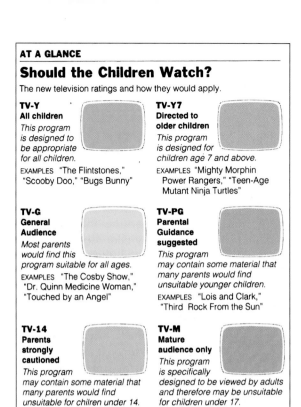

AT A GLANCE

Should the Children Watch?

The new television ratings and how they would apply.

TV-Y
All children
This program is designed to be appropriate for all children.
EXAMPLES "The Flintstones," "Scooby Doo," "Bugs Bunny"

TV-Y7
Directed to older children
This program is designed for children age 7 and above.
EXAMPLES "Mighty Morphin Power Rangers," "Teen-Age Mutant Ninja Turtles"

TV-G
General Audience
Most parents would find this program suitable for all ages.
EXAMPLES "The Cosby Show," "Dr. Quinn Medicine Woman," "Touched by an Angel"

TV-PG
Parental Guidance suggested
This program may contain some material that many parents would find unsuitable younger children.
EXAMPLES "Lois and Clark," "Third Rock From the Sun"

TV-14
Parents strongly cautioned
This program may contain some material that many parents would find unsuitable for chilren under 14.
EXAMPLES "NYPD Blue," "Cybill," "Walker Texas Ranger"

TV-M
Mature audience only
This program is specifically designed to be viewed by adults and therefore may be unsuitable for children under 17.
EXAMPLES "Dream On", "Red Shoe Diaries"

Figure 15.1
TV Rating Labels and the Impact of Media Research
Parents and politicians harshly criticized the new 1997 television rating labels for revealing too little about a particular program's actual content. The TV industry continues to study its self-imposed system, promising to fine-tune it to ensure that the government keeps its distance. However flawed, these standards are one example of a policy that was shaped in part by media research. Since the 1960s, a stockpile of accumulated evidence has pointed to links between violent TV images and increased levels of aggression among children and adolescents.
Source: The New York Times, December 20, 1996, p. A12.

This problem precipitated the development of increasingly sophisticated direct-mail diaries, television meters, phone surveys, the telemarketing industry, and eventually Internet tracking in trying to determine consumer preferences and measure media use worldwide.

research on media effects

As concern about public opinion, propaganda, and the impact of the media merged with the growth of journalism and mass-communication departments, media researchers looked more and more to behavioral science as a model. Between 1930 and 1960, "who says what to whom with what effect" became the key question "defining the scope and problems of American communications research."[10] Answering this question activated the major direction in media research, usually identified as **media effects**: research that attempts to understand, explain, and predict the impact—or effects—of mass media on individuals and society. For example, if children watch a lot of TV cartoons (stimulus or cause), will this repeated act influence their behavior toward their peers (response or effect)?

For most of the twentieth century, both media researchers and news reporters used different methods to answer similar sets of questions—who, what, when, and where—about our daily experiences. In practicing their professions, researchers and reporters have typically remained suspicious of concepts such as interpretation, subjectivity, and personal values, seeing them as problems to be avoided or even as dangerous contaminators of their work. A major difference exists between the two fields, however. Whereas daily news reporters *describe* what happens when teenagers watch

Rob Rogers
Pittsburgh Post-Gazette
United Feature Syndicate

violent movies, media researchers not only describe but try to *explain* what happened and often *predict* whether it will happen again.

Media research generally comes from the private or public sectors—each type with distinguishing features. *Private research*, sometimes called *proprietary research*, is generally conducted for a business, corporation, or even a political campaign. It is usually applied research in the sense that the information it uncovers typically addresses some real-life problem or need, such as determining consumer buying habits or market trends, trying to discover the hot-button issues for a political race, or measuring test-audience responses to variations of a movie ending. *Public research*, on the other hand, usually takes place in academic and government settings. It involves information that is often more *theoretical* than applied; it tries to clarify, explain, or predict the effects of mass media rather than to address a consumer problem. Most public research is subject to examination and refutation by other academics. In contrast, private research is seldom shared, although the results of some private opinion polls or broadcast ratings may be released to the public with the owners' permission.

By the 1960s, media studies had become synonymous with effects research and with the statistical measurement of audiences. Funding for this type of research was also easier to obtain, since it coincided with the interests of both the government and the media: Federal agencies were interested in monitoring various populations, and media industries were interested in the psychology and behavior of consumers.

key phases in research approaches

A major goal of scientific research is to develop theories or laws that can consistently explain or predict human behavior. The varied impacts of the mass media and the diverse ways in which people make popular culture, however, tend to defy predictable rules. Historical, economic, and political factors influence media industries, making it difficult to develop systematic theories that explain communication. What has developed instead are a number of small theories, or models, that help explain individual behavior rather than the impact of the media on large populations. But before these small theories began to emerge in the 1970s, mass-media research used several other models. Developing between the 1930s and the 1970s, these major models included the hypodermic needle, minimal effects, and uses and gratifications.

Hypodermic-Needle Model. One of the earliest and least persuasive media theories attributed powerful effects to the mass media. A number of intellectuals and academics were particularly fearful of the popularity of film and radio, which had become influential cultural forces in the 1920s and 1930s. Some of these observations were made by social psychologists and sociologists who arrived in this country after fleeing Hitler and Nazism in the 1930s. Having watched Hitler use radio, film, and print media as propaganda tools for Nazism, they worried that the popular media in America also had a strong hold over vulnerable audiences. This concept of powerful media affecting weak audiences has been labeled the **hypodermic-needle model**, sometimes also called the *magic-bullet theory* or the *direct-effects model*. It suggests that the media shoot their potent effects directly into unsuspecting victims.

One of the earliest challenges to the hypodermic-needle model of effects involved a study of Orson Welles's legendary October 30, 1938, broadcast of *The War of the Worlds*, which presented a fictional news report of Martian invaders (see Chapter 4, page 116). Welles's radio program frightened millions of listeners who didn't realize that the show was an adaptation of the H. G. Wells science-fiction novel. In a 1940 book-length study, *The Invasion from Mars: A Study in the Psychology of Panic*, radio researcher Hadley Cantril argued that contrary to the hypodermic-needle model, not all listeners thought the radio program was a real news report. Instead, Cantril noted—after conducting personal interviews and a nationwide survey of listeners, and analyzing newspaper reports and listener mail to CBS Radio and the FCC—that some people were more likely than others to believe in the Martian-invasion report. Factors like the listening situation were important, especially for people who tuned in late and missed the initial disclaimers for the program. Personal characteristics, too, were linked to the gullibility of certain audience members. For example, listeners with strong fundamentalist religious beliefs were more likely to think the invasion was an act of God and that the end of the world had indeed arrived.

> "Theories abound, examples multiply, but convincing facts that specific media content is reliably associated with particular effects have proved quite elusive."
> —Guy Cumberbatch, *A Measure of Uncertainty*, 1989

Cantril's research helped to lay the groundwork for the minimal-effects model, which would become more popular in the following decades. Although the hypodermic-needle model has been disregarded or disproved by social scientists, many people still attribute such direct effects to the mass media, particularly in the case of children.

Minimal-Effects Model. With the rise of empirical research techniques, social scientists began demonstrating that the media alone do not cause people to change their attitudes and behaviors. At this point, the limited or **minimal-effects model** emerged. Based on tightly controlled experiments and surveys, researchers generally argued that people engage in **selective exposure** and **selective retention** with regard to the media. That is, we selectively expose ourselves to media messages that are most familiar to us, and we retain messages that confirm values and attitudes we already hold. In other words, minimal-effects researchers argued that in most cases the mass-media reinforce existing behaviors and attitudes rather than change them.

The findings from the first comprehensive study of children and television, by Wilbur Schramm, Jack Lyle, and Edwin Parker in the late 1950s, best captures the minimal-effects tradition:

> For *some* children, under *some* conditions, *some* television is harmful. For *other* children under the same conditions, or for the same children under *other* conditions, it may be beneficial. For *most* children, under *most* conditions, *most* television is probably neither particularly harmful nor particularly beneficial.[11]

Joseph Klapper's important 1960 research review, *The Effects of Mass Communication*, found that the mass media influenced individuals who did not already hold strong views on an issue and that the media also had a greater impact on poor and uneducated heavy users. Solidifying the minimal-effects argument, Klapper concluded that strong media effects occur largely at an individual level and do not appear to have large-scale, measurable, and direct effects on society as a whole.[12]

Uses and Gratifications Model. Aside from difficulties in proving direct cause-effect relationships, the effects tradition usually assumed that audiences were passive and were acted upon by the media. As early as the late 1950s, Schramm, Lyle, and Parker suggested that there were problems with this position:

> In a sense the term "effect" is misleading because it suggests that television "does something" to children. The connotation is that television is the actor, the children are acted upon. Children are thus made to seem relatively inert; television, relatively active. Children are sitting victims; television bites them. Nothing can be further from the fact. It is the children who are most active in this relationship. It is they who use television, rather than television that uses them.[13]

Indeed, as the authors observed, numerous studies have concluded that viewers—especially young children—are often *actively* engaged in the media, using various forms to guide their play.

A response to the minimal-effects theory, the **uses and gratifications model** began developing in the 1940s to contest the notion of audience passivity. Under this model, researchers—usually using in-depth interviews to supplement survey questionnaires—studied the ways in which people used the media to satisfy various emotional or intellectual needs. The uses and gratifications model represented a middle position between the hypodermic-needle and the minimal-effects models. This research focused on audience use and the functions of the media. Instead of asking "What effects do the media have on us?" researchers asked "Why do we use the media?" Using this approach, one study found, for instance, that a majority of people said they read newspapers primarily for entertainment and that getting information was a less important function of news reading.[14]

Asking the *why* question allowed media researchers to develop inventories cataloguing how people employed the media. For example, individuals used the media to see authority figures elevated or toppled, to seek a sense of community and connectedness, to fulfill a need for drama and stories, and to confirm moral or spiritual values.[15] Though the uses and gratifications model addressed the *functions* of the mass media for individuals, it did not address the important questions related to the *impact* of the media on society. Once researchers had accumulated substantial lists of uses and functions, they often did not move in new directions. Consequently, the uses and gratifications model never became a dominant strain in media research.

approaches to media effects

Most media research today, whether conducted in universities or in public-policy institutes, has focused on the effects of the media on such issues as learning, attitudes, aggression, and voting habits. This research employs the **scientific method**, a blueprint long used by scientists and scholars to study phenomena in systematic stages. These steps include:

1. identifying the research problem

2. reviewing existing research and theories related to the problem

3. developing working hypotheses or predictions about what the study might find

4. determining an appropriate method or research design

5. collecting information or relevant data

6. analyzing results to see if the hypotheses have been verified

7. interpreting the implications of the study to determine whether they explain or predict patterns in human behavior

The scientific method relies on *objectivity* (eliminating bias and judgments on the part of researchers); *reliability* (getting the same answers or outcomes from a study or measure during repeated testing); and *validity* (demonstrating that a study actually measures what it claims to measure).

In scientific studies, researchers pose one or more **hypotheses**: tentative general statements that predict a relationship between a *dependent variable* that is influenced by an *independent variable*. For example, a researcher might hypothesize that a person's level of formal education (independent variable) influences higher instances of reading print media (dependent variable). That is, the more formal education acquired, the more print material consumed. Or, a researcher might predict that heavy levels of TV viewing among adolescents (independent variable) cause poor performance (dependent variable) in traditional school settings. Broadly speaking, the methods for studying media effects on audiences have taken two forms—experiments and survey research. To supplement these approaches, researchers also use content analysis as a technique for counting and documenting specific messages in mass media. We will look at all three.

Experiments. Like all studies that use the scientific method, **experiments** in media research isolate some aspect of content, suggest a hypothesis, and manipulate variables to discover a particular medium's impact on attitude, emotion, or behavior. To test whether a hypothesis is true, researchers expose an *experiment group*—the group under study—to a selected media program or text. To ensure valid results, researchers use a *control group*, which serves as a basis for comparison; this group is *not* exposed to the selected media content. Subjects are picked for each group through **random assignment**, which simply means that every subject has an equal chance of being placed in either group. Random assignment generally ensures that the variables researchers want to control are distributed to each group in the same way.

For instance, researchers might take a group of ten-year-old boys and randomly assign them to two groups. They expose the experimental group to a violent action movie that the control group does not see. Later, both groups are exposed to a staged fight between two other boys so that the researchers can observe how each group responds to an actual physical confrontation. Researchers then determine whether there is a statistically measurable difference between the two groups' responses to the fight. For example, perhaps the control subjects tried to break up the fight but the experimental subjects did not. Since the groups were randomly selected and since the only measurable difference between them was the introduction of the movie, researchers may conclude that under these conditions the violent film caused a different behavior.

When experiments carefully account for variables through random assignment, they generally work well in substantiating direct cause-effect links. Such research takes place both in laboratory settings and in field settings, where people can be observed using the media in their everyday environments. In field experiments, however, it is more difficult for researchers to control variables. In lab settings, researchers have more control, but other prob-

Experimental research demonstrating the link between aggressive behavior and fictional violence has inspired a variety of projects that show the media's impact in more practical terms. *Media Mayhem,* a visual literacy project developed by the University of Wisconsin–Green Bay, looks at how visual images glamorize violence.

lems may occur. For example, when subjects are removed from the environments in which they regularly use the media, they may act differently—often with fewer inhibitions—than they would in their everyday surroundings.

Experiments have other limitations as well. For instance, they are not generalizable to a larger population; they cannot tell us whether cause-effect results can be duplicated outside the laboratory. In addition, most academic experiments today are performed on college students, who are convenient subjects for research but are not representative of the general public. Although experiments are fairly good at predicting short-term media effects under controlled conditions, they do not predict how subjects will behave months or years later in the real world.

Surveys. For long-term studies of the media, surveys usually work best. In its simplest terms, **survey research** is a method of collecting and measuring data taken from a group of respondents. Using random sampling techniques that give each potential subject an equal chance to be included in the survey, this research method draws on much larger populations than those used in experimental studies. Surveys are simply measuring instruments and do *not* control variables through randomly assigned groups. Survey investigators cannot account for all the variables that might affect media use; therefore, they cannot show cause-effect relationships. Survey research can, however, reveal *correlations*—or associations—between two variables. For example, a random questionnaire survey of ten-year-old boys might demonstrate that a correlation exists between aggressive behavior and watching violent TV programs, but it does not explain which causes which. Unlike experimental research, however, surveys are usually generalizable to the larger society; they can approximate what percentage of a population exhibits certain media-induced behaviors.

> "Writing survey questions and gathering data are easy; writing good questions and collecting useful data are not."
> —Michael Singletary,
> *Mass Communication Research,* 1994

Surveys are also useful measures for comparing voting behavior and levels of media use. To aid survey research, subjects are sometimes assigned to panel studies in which smaller groups of people are interviewed in-depth on several occasions. In addition, surveys allow researchers to investigate various populations in long-term studies. For example, survey research might measure subjects when they are ten, twenty, and thirty years old to track changes in how frequently they watch television and what kinds of programs they prefer at different ages.

It is important to note, though, that surveys are only as good as the wording of their questions. The validity of survey questions—measuring the effect that the study claims to measure—is a chronic problem for survey practitioners. For example, in 1992 Americans were shocked to hear that a national survey had found that about 20 percent of Americans doubted the Holocaust ever happened. However, the results were later attributed to a confusing question, which asked, "Does it seem possible or does it seem impossible to you that the Nazi extermination of the Jews never happened?" A 1994 poll asked a more clearly stated version of the question: "Does it seem possible to you that the Nazi extermination of the Jews never happened, or do you feel certain that it happened?" The updated question found that only 2 percent of the respondents consistently denied the Holocaust.

Survey researchers usually locate their subjects by using direct mail, personal interviews, telephone calls, and—increasingly—email and Web sites. They can also accumulate large amounts of information by surveying diverse cross sections of people. These data allow researchers to examine demographic factors such as educational background, income levels, race, gender, age, lifestyle profiles, political affiliations, and attitudes. Large government and academic survey databases are now widely available to researchers for doing analyses and comparisons worldwide. This may lead to the development of more long-range—or longitudinal—studies, which allow social scientists to compare new studies with those conducted years earlier. In general, however, it is cheaper and easier to do short-term experimental and survey research, analyzing the effects of the media on particular individuals. Effects research focused on a large community or on societal responses to the media over time is much more difficult to conduct and sustain.

Content Analysis. Over the years, researchers recognized that traditional media-effects studies generally ignored specific media messages. As a corrective, researchers developed a method known as **content analysis** to study the messages of print and visual media. Such analysis is a systematic method of coding and measuring media content.

Although content analyses were first used during World War II, more recent studies have focused on television, tracking the number of male and female, black and white, and blue- and white-collar characters in daytime and prime-time programming. Probably the most influential content analyses have been conducted by George Gerbner and his colleagues at the University of Pennsylvania; since the late 1960s, they have coded and counted acts of violence on network television. Combined with survey methods, these annual "violence profiles" have shown that heavy watchers of television, including both children and retired Americans, tend to overestimate the amount of violence that exists in the actual world.[16]

The limits of content analysis have been well documented. This technique does not measure the effects of the media or explain why a particular media message gets produced in the first place. Because content analysis is basically descriptive, it is often used in combination with other research techniques. This allows researchers to analyze and interpret the figures produced by content counts. For example, a 1999 content analysis by the Kaiser Family Foundation of more than 1,300 television shows found that 56 percent of television shows had sexual content. Content analysis alone, however, cannot tell us exactly what this means to viewers who regularly watch television.

Throughout the 1990s, the syndicated afternoon children's program *Mighty Morphin Power Rangers* attracted the attention of millions of young viewers and the anger of many adults. Acknowledging the positive verbal messages in the shows, parent and teacher groups nevertheless complained that children mostly remembered and imitated the violent action scenes. The program's producers defended their morphing rangers, arguing that TV programs help children wrestle with the aggressive feelings that everyone has.

Problems of definition also occur. For instance, researchers in the Kaiser Foundation study defined sexual content as flirting, kissing, talking about sex, intimate touching, depictions of sexual intercourse, or the strong suggestion of it. But would most television viewers define sexual content in the same way?[17] Or, in the case of coding and counting acts of violence, how do researchers distinguish slapstick cartoon aggression from the violent murders or rapes in an evening police drama? Critics point out that such varied depictions may have diverse and subtle effects on viewers that are difficult to measure or quantify.

As content analysis grew as a primary tool in media research, it sometimes pushed to the sidelines other ways of thinking about television and media content. Broad questions concerning the media as a popular art form, as a democratic influence, or as a force for social control are difficult to address through strict measurement techniques. Critics of content analysis, in fact, have objected to the kind of social science that reduces culture to acts of counting. Such criticism has addressed the tendency by some researchers to favor measurement accuracy over intellectual discipline.[18] In response, many social scientists have come to regard content analysis as simply one of many techniques that can be used to understand the complex issues that abound in the mass media.

explaining media effects

By the 1960s, the first departments of mass communication began graduating Ph.D.-level researchers schooled in experimental or survey techniques and content analysis. These researchers began documenting consistent patterns found in mass communication. Two of the most influential contemporary frameworks that help explain media effects have been agenda-setting and the cultivation effect.

Agenda-Setting. A key phenomenon posited by media-effects researchers has been **agenda-setting**: the idea that when the mass media pay attention to particular events or issues, they determine—set the agenda for—the major topics of discussion for individuals and society. Like uses and gratifications, agenda-setting research has tried to strike a balance between the views of the mass media as all-powerful and as barely powerful. Essentially, agenda-setting researchers have argued that the mass media do not so much tell us what to think as *what to think about.* Traceable to Walter Lippmann's notion in the early 1920s that the media "create pictures in our heads," the first social-science investigations of agenda-setting began in the 1970s.[19]

Over the years, agenda-setting research has demonstrated that the more stories the news media do on a particular subject, the more importance audiences attach to that subject. For instance, when the media seriously began to cover ecology issues after the first Earth Day in 1970, a much higher percentage of the population began listing the environment as a primary social concern in surveys. When *Jaws* became the top box-office movie in 1975, the news media started featuring more shark-attack stories; even landlocked people in the Midwest began ranking sharks as a problem, despite the rarity of such incidents worldwide.

During the 1986 elections, local and national candidates often spoke about the problems of crime and illegal drugs. At the time, researchers documented a big leap in the media's attention to drugs, especially to crack cocaine; they found more than four hundred news stories over a forty-week period dealing with cocaine in America's major papers, newsmagazines, and newscasts.[20] Not surprisingly, the big jump in drug stories was accompanied by a parallel rise in public-opinion polls. In April 1986, only 2 percent of the respondents to a *New York Times*/CBS News poll picked drugs as the nation's most important problem. By early September 1986, however, a survey found that drugs topped the list, with 13 percent of 1,210 adults interviewed identifying drugs as the nation's most serious problem. This shift occurred even though government statisticians showed that illicit drug use—despite rises in the use of crack cocaine—had generally dipped and leveled off since peaking in 1979–80.[21] Although many people's attitudes toward drugs were not affected by the increase in news stories, the marked shift in public opinion is a good example of the agenda-setting effect of the news media.

The Cultivation Effect. Another mass-media phenomenon—the **cultivation effect**—suggests that heavy viewing of television leads individuals to perceive reality in ways that are consistent with the portrayals they see on television. In essence, this area of effects research attempts to push researchers past the focus on individual behavior and toward larger ideas about the media's impact on society. The major research in this area grew from the TV-violence profiles of George Gerbner and his colleagues, who attempted to make larger generalizations about the impact of televised violence on real life. The basic idea suggests that the more time an audience spends viewing television and absorbing its viewpoints, the more likely it is that the audience's own views of social reality will be "cultivated" by the images and portrayals they have seen on television.[22] For example, although less than 1 percent of Americans are victims of violent crime in any single year, people who watch a lot of television tend to overestimate this percentage. Such exaggerated perceptions, Gerbner and his colleagues argue, are part of a "mean world" syndrome, in which viewers with heavy, long-term exposure to television are more likely to believe that the external world is a mean and dangerous place.

According to the cultivation effect, media messages interact in complicated ways with personal, social, political, and cultural factors; they are one of a number of important factors in determining individual behavior and defining social values. Some critics have charged that cultivation research has provided limited evidence to support these findings. The cultivation framework, however, deserves close attention, especially with regard to findings about heavy television viewers who believe that the world is a meaner place than it actually is.

evaluating research on media effects

The mainstream models of media research have made valuable contributions to our understanding of the mass media, submitting content and audiences to rigorous testing. This wealth of research exists partly because funding for studies regarding the effects of the media on young people remains popular among politicians and draws ready government support. Because scientific methods are systematic and cumulative, we have substantial data—more than fifteen hundred studies—that clearly link aggression in children to violent images in the media.

Although the potential for government funding restricts the scope of some media research, other limits also face researchers, including the inability to address how the media affect communities and social institutions. Since most media research operates best in examining media and individual behavior, fewer research studies exist on media's impact on community and social life. Research has begun to address these limits and to turn more attention to the increasing impact of media technology on national life and international communication.

"Many studies currently published in mainstream communication journals seem filled with **sophisticated treatments of trivial data**, which, while showing effects . . . make slight contributions to what we really know about human mass-mediated communication."

—Willard Rowland and Bruce Watkins, *Interpreting Television*, 1984

cultural approaches to media research

During the rise of modern media research, approaches with a stronger historical and interpretive edge developed as well, often in direct opposition to the scientific models. In the late 1930s, some social scientists began to warn about the limits of "gathering data and charting trends," particularly when research served advertisers and media organizations. Such private market research tended to be narrowly focused on individual behavior, ignoring questions like "Where are institutions taking us?" and "Where do we want them to take us?"[23]

It is important here to distinguish directions in American media studies from British-European traditions. In Europe, media studies have favored interpretive rather than scientific approaches; in other words, researchers there approached media questions and problems as if they were literary or cultural critics rather than experimental or survey researchers. Such approaches built on the writings of political philosophers such as Karl Marx and Antonio Gramsci; researchers investigated how the mass media have been used to maintain existing hierarchies in society. They examined, for example, the ways in which popular culture or sports distracted people from redressing social injustices. They also studied the subordinate status of some social groups in attempting to address some of the deficiencies of emerging social-science research.

In the United States, early criticism of modern media research came from the Frankfurt School, a group of European researchers who were transplanted from Germany to America after they fled Nazi persecution in the 1930s. Under the leadership of Max Horkheimer, T. W. Adorno, and Leo Lowenthal, the school pointed to at least three inadequacies of traditional scientific approaches, arguing that they (1) reduced large "cultural questions" to measurable and "verifiable categories"; (2) depended on "an atmosphere of rigidly enforced neutrality"; and (3) refused to place "the phenomena of modern life" in a "historical and moral context."[24] The researchers at the Frankfurt School did not reject outright the usefulness of measuring and counting data. They contended, however, that historical and cultural approaches would focus critical attention on the long-range processes of the mass media and their complex relations with audiences.

Early media researchers were concerned about Hitler's use of national radio to control information and indoctrinate the German people throughout the 1930s. Germany's wartime international broadcasts, however, were considered failures. Trying to undermine morale in broadcasts aimed at Allied soldiers and British citizens, Germany hired British defector William Joyce ("Lord Haw Haw") and Ohioan Mildred Gillars ("Axis Sally"). Because so many media messages competed with Nazi propaganda in democratic countries, these radio traitors had little impact.

Since the Frankfurt School, criticisms of the effects tradition and its methods have continued, with calls for more interpretive studies of the rituals of mass communication. Academics who have embraced a cultural approach try to understand how media and culture are tied to the actual patterns of communication in daily life. An important body of research—loosely labeled **cultural studies**—began challenging the mainstream media-effects models in the 1960s. These studies have generally focused on how people make meaning, apprehend reality, and order experience through their use of cultural symbols in print and visual media. This research has attempted to make everyday culture the centerpiece of media studies, focusing on the subtle ways in which mass communication shapes and is shaped by history, politics, and economics. For example, in the 1970s Stuart Hall and his colleagues studied the British print media and the police as forms of urban surveillance. In *Policing the Crisis*, the authors revealed how political, economic, and cultural constraints aided the news media's success in mobilizing public opinion about crime.[25]

Cultural research focuses on the investigation of daily experience, especially on issues of race, gender, class, and sexuality, and the unequal arrangements of power and status in contemporary society. Such research highlights the nature of cultural differences, emphasizing how some social groups have been marginalized and ignored throughout history. Consequently, cultural studies have attempted to recover lost or silenced voices, particularly among African American, Native American, Asian and Asian American, Arabic, Latino, gay, and women's cultures. The major analytical approaches to cultural research are textual analysis, audience studies, and political economy.

> "I take culture . . . and the analysis of it to be therefore not an experimental science in search of law but an interpretive one in search of meaning."
>
> — Clifford Geertz, cultural anthropologist, 1973

Textual Analysis. In cultural research, the equivalent to measurement methods and content analysis has been labeled **textual analysis**: the close reading and interpretation of the meanings of culture, including the study of books, movies, and TV programs. Whereas content analysis approaches media messages with the tools of modern social science—replicability, objectivity, and data—textual analysis looks at rituals, narratives, and meanings.

Although textual analysis has a long and rich history in film and literary studies, a significant shift came in 1974 with Horace Newcomb's *TV: The Most Popular Art*, considered the first serious academic analysis of television stories. Newcomb analyzed and interpreted why certain TV programs became predominant, especially comedies, westerns, mysteries, soap operas, news, and sports. Newcomb took television programs seriously, examining patterns in the most popular programs, such as the *Beverly Hillbillies*, *Bewitched*, and *Dragnet*, which

In *TV: The Most Popular Art* (1974), a groundbreaking textual analysis of prime-time television, scholar Horace Newcomb critiqued programs like the *Beverly Hillbillies*, the No. 1 TV show in America from 1962 to 1964. Newcomb argued that the program—"complete with mountain folk values and barnyard menagerie"—actually reflected "the values of rural America as conceived by middle-class Americans."

traditional researchers had usually snubbed or ignored. Trained as a literary scholar, Newcomb argued that content analysis and other social-science approaches often ignored artistic traditions and social context. For Newcomb, "the task for the student of the popular arts is to find a technique through which many different qualities of the work—aesthetic, social, psychological—may be explored" and to discover "why certain formulas . . . are popular in American television."[26]

Prior to Newcomb's work, textual analysis had generally focused on "important" debates, films, poems, and books—either significant examples of democratic information or highly regarded works of art. But by the end of the 1970s a new generation of media-studies scholars, who had grown up on television and rock and roll, had become interested in less elite forms of culture. They extended the notion of what a "text" is to architecture, fashion, tabloid magazines, Madonna, rock music, soap operas, movies, cockfights, shopping malls, TV drug news, rap, Martha Stewart, and professional wrestling, trying to make sense of the most taken-for-granted aspects of everyday culture.

Oftentimes these seemingly minor elements of popular culture provide insight into bigger meanings within our society. For example, a 1998 textual analysis examined the sexual etiquette endorsed for teenage women in popular magazines such as *YM, Teen, Seventeen, Glamour,* and *Mademoiselle.* The researchers looked at advice columns and features from a sample of magazines between 1974 and 1994. They concluded that the stories of sexual etiquette changed very little during those twenty years, and that the magazines encouraged young women "to subordinate self for others and to be contained."[27] The study, then, sheds light on influences in the system of gender conditioning in American culture.

Audience Studies. Cultural research often analyzes the important role of culture as a link between individuals and society—as a force in organizing daily life and in maintaining social norms. Cultural-studies research that focuses on how people use and interpret cultural content is called audience or reader-response research.

For example, in *Reading the Romance: Women, Patriarchy and Popular Literature,* Janice Radway studied a group of midwestern women who were fans of the romance novel. Using her training in literary criticism but also employing interviews and questionnaires, Radway investigated the meaning of romance reading. She argued that this cultural activity functioned as personal time for some women, whose complex family and work lives provided very little time for themselves. The study also suggested that these particular romance-novel fans identified with the active, independent qualities of the romantic heroines they most admired. As a cultural study, Radway's work did not claim to be scientific, and her findings are not generalizable to a large group of women. Rather, Radway was interested in investigating and interpreting the relationship between reading popular fiction and ordinary life.[28]

As Radway's study demonstrated, cultural research uses a variety of interpretive methods and displays some common features. Most important, these studies define *culture* in broad terms, made up of both the *products* a society fashions and the *processes* that forge those products. As we discussed in Chapter 1, culture consists of the symbols of expression that individuals, groups, and societies use to make sense of daily life and articulate their values. Within this context, culture is viewed in part as a struggle over who controls symbols and meaning in society. For example, the battles over the meaning of rock and roll in the 1950s or of rap in the 1980s were important cultural wars that addressed issues of race, class, region, and religion, as well as generational differences.

Political Economy. The focus on the production of popular culture and the forces behind it are the topic of political-economy studies. The greatest concern political-economy studies have about the media is the increasing conglomeration of ownership, as noted in Chapter 13. This concentration of ownership means that the production of media content is being controlled by fewer and fewer organizations, investing those companies with more power. Moreover, the domination of public discourse by for-profit corporations may mean that the bottom line for all public communication and popular culture is money, not democratic expression.

Political-economy studies work best when combined with the textual-analysis and audience-studies approaches, which provide a well-rounded context for understanding the cultural content, the production of the content, and the audience's reception of it. For example, a major media corporation may, for commercial reasons, create a film and market it relentlessly through a number of venues (political economy), but the film's existence makes sense only within the historical and narrative contexts of the culture (textual analysis), and it may be interpreted by various audiences in ways both anticipated and unexpected (audience studies).

evaluating cultural approaches

In opposition to media-effects research, textual analysis and cultural studies involve reading written texts and visual programs as a sequence of spoken or written symbols that contain interpretation. As James Carey has put it, a more cultural approach "does not seek to explain human behavior, but to understand it. . . . It does not attempt to predict human behavior, but to diagnose human meanings."[29] In other words, a cultural approach does not provide explanations for the laws that govern the mass media. Rather, it offers interpretations of the stories, messages, and meanings that circulate throughout our culture.

One of the major strengths of a cultural approach is the freedom it affords to broadly interpret the impact of the mass media. Since cultural work is not bound by the precise control of variables, researchers can more easily examine the ties between media messages and the broader social, economic, and political scene. For example, effects research on politics has generally concentrated on election polls and voting patterns, whereas cultural research has broadened the meaning of politics to include class and income differences and the various uses of power by individuals and institutions in authority. Following Horace Newcomb, cultural investigators have also expanded the study of media content beyond "serious" works. They have studied many popular forms, including music, movies, and prime-time television.

Just as social-science measurement has limits, so do cultural studies. Sometimes such studies have focused too heavily on the meanings of media programs or "texts," ignoring their effect on audiences. More recent cultural studies, however, have tried to address this deficiency. For example, Elizabeth Bird's *For Enquiring Minds: A Cultural Study of Supermarket Tabloids* set up a three-part analysis that included (1) interviews with the writers and editors of popular tabloids, (2) in-depth discussions with tabloid readers, and (3) an analysis of the form and content of tabloids. Bird's research demonstrated how individuals derive their own diverse meanings

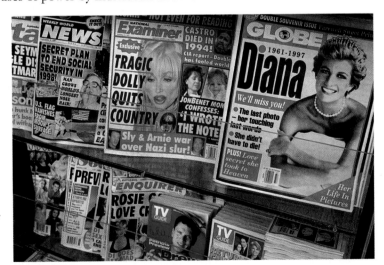

Supermarket tabloids have declined in popularity during the 1990s, but they continue to stir controversy. Although most media researchers steer away from "lower" forms of popular culture, some cultural scholars specialize in their study.

Television Promotes Literacy and Mutes Class Divisions in Brazil

by Laurie Fenlason

Television in the United States has been blamed for numerous social ills, including low literacy levels, social isolation, reduced attention spans, increased violence, and a general decline in culture. Using both scientific and cultural approaches, a study of Brazilian television in the 1980s countered many of these claims. The study also documented a number of television's beneficial effects in that country, such as softening class barriers and improving attitudes toward reading.

Anthropologist Conrad Kottak, author of *Prime Time Society: An Anthropological Analysis of Television and Culture*, spent three years in Brazil, interviewing Brazilian network executives, actors, censors, and politicians, and watching Brazilian programming.

Kottak combined research in rural Brazilian communities with investigations of national and local programming. His study revealed high correlations between long-term exposure to television and reduced corporal punishment of children; reduced stereotyping of jobs on the basis of sex; less sexist views on social issues; increased reading; and greater use of print media. As Kottak explained, "In Brazil, a much more illiterate society than America and one in which literacy is not as trusted or valued, television makes literacy respectable. Brazilians even in rural, undeveloped areas now see literate people who come into their homes every evening, on a regular basis."

In addition, Kottak found that television reduced divisions between social classes by familiarizing rural people with urban life and reducing "obsequious and fearful behavior." In the last twenty years, for example, Brazilians' use of the formal "you" when addressing elders or those of a higher social class—on television and in real life—has declined substantially.

According to Kottak, Brazil was a unique laboratory for television research:

I was able to do something in Brazil that you can't do in the United States any more, because almost any American under forty has been exposed to television since birth. Because Brazilians have been exposed to television in their homes for widely different lengths of time, I could separate the cumulative effect of watching television from the effects of normal life experiences—getting older, maturing, acquiring more education.

Beginning in January 1985, Kottak and a team of researchers interviewed Brazilians in four communities. After determining basic information such as age, sex, race, years of television exposure, and hours watched each day, they asked questions such as "Is your community safe?" "Do you trust the government?" "Is it okay for women to go to bars?" In each case, length of exposure to television was one of the strongest predictors of the citizen's response.

"The only stronger indicator of a Brazilian's views on most of the social issues we examined was education," Kottak noted. "Television exposure and gender were the next best predictors, and each explained more than income, social class, religiosity, age or race."

Kottak was cautious about generalizing his findings to include cultures other than Brazil, especially when discussing television's impact on literacy. Kottak speculated that the widely held belief in the United States that television reduces literacy—not supported by any study—arises partly from the importance that Americans place on reading. Television is seen as supplanting solitary, industrious pursuits such as reading.

"The stigma that Americans place on television is almost matched by the Brazilians' traditional disdain of reading," Kottak explained. "In Brazil, reading is held suspect because it is seen as a solitary pursuit. Watching television, on the other hand, is seen as an opportunity to spend more time with friends and family."

Source: Adapted from Laurie Fenlason, *News & Information Services,* University of Michigan, November 9, 1989.

BRAZIL

from this one ordinary form of popular culture, and how a researcher can combine textual analysis, audience studies, and political-economy approaches.

Both media-effects and cultural researchers today have begun to look at the limitations of their work more closely, borrowing ideas from each other to better assess the complexity of the media's impact. For instance, in *Democracy without Citizens*, political scientist Robert Entman employed both perspectives to examine journalism and politics. He used cultural theories about economics and politics to reveal how journalists slant the news and oversimplify complex issues. He supplemented his cultural inquiry with surveys that measured the impact of slanted reports on public opinion. By combining both approaches, Entman strengthened his argument, which called for substantial journalistic reform. (For another example of research that combines scientific and cultural approaches, see "The Global Village: Television Promotes Literacy and Mutes Class Divisions in Brazil" on page 476.)

media research, ivory towers, and democracy

One charge frequently leveled at academic studies is that they fail to address the everyday problems of life; they often seem to have little practical application. With the growth of mass-media departments in universities has come an increase in special terminology and jargon, which tend to intimidate nonacademics. Although media research has built a growing knowledge base and dramatically advanced what we know about individuals and societies, the academic world has paid a price. That is, the larger public has often been excluded from access to the research process. Researchers themselves have even found it difficult to speak to one another across disciplines because of the obscure language used to analyze and report findings.

The acceleration of jargon arrived with the splintering of academic life into narrow areas of specialization in the 1970s. We understand why chemistry, physics, math, and engineering require special symbols and languages. It is not as clear, however, why this practice extends to so many social-science and humanities disciplines. Although cultural research has affected academics in English, history, sociology, anthropology, and communication, they do not talk easily to one another about their work. Most social-science research is intended only for other social scientists with similar training and experience. For example, understanding the elaborate statistical analyses used to document media effects requires special training. This kind of research advances knowledge, but it does not generally engage a larger public.

Even in cultural research, the language used is often incomprehensible to students and to other audiences who use the mass media. Cultural research tends to identify with marginalized groups, yet this scholarship can be self-defeating if its complexity is too removed from the daily experience of the groups it addresses and the students it is designed to educate. Although it may be necessary for academics to construct special languages to dissect popular culture, the language that explains the research should be accessible to an informed general public.

A now famous hoax in 1996 pointed out just how inaccessible some academic jargon can be. Alan Sokal, a New York University physics professor, submitted an impenetrable article, "Transgressing the Boundaries: Toward a Transformative Hermeneutics of Quantum Gravity," to a special issue of the academic journal *Social Text* about science and postmodernism. As he unfortunately expected, the article—a hoax designed to point out how dense academic jargon can sometimes mask sloppy thinking—was published. According to the journal's editor, about six reviewers had

Violence Study Shows Television's Mental Block

by Ellen Goodman

Santa Barbara, California—Ed Donnerstein is not a cultural coroner. He doesn't believe that you can understand the problem of violence on television by merely doing a body count. Or a bullet count.

As one of the lead researchers on a study done at this oceanside campus of the University of California, he wants to make it perfectly clear that not all the violence on television is equally harmful nor are all young viewers equally harmed.

No, he would not oppose televising "Romeo and Juliet" despite the bodies in the last act. And no, he does not believe that violence on television is the sole or primary cause of violence in America.

But he says, "We can no longer deny that violence on television contributes to the problem." He offers this message slowly and distinctly, as if trying to be heard over the din.

The National Television Violence Study that he and his colleagues labored over for three years was released [in 1996] into the middle of heated political debate. It made page one just as the Telecommunications Act became law with its controversial provision for a V-chip, a device to help parents block out programs rated too violent. It hit the evening news just as broadcasters were pondering the president's invitation for a February 29 trip to the White House woodshed.

Rep. Ed Markey, the man with the V-chip on his mind, immediately praised the study as a Perry Mason Moment, the perfect evidence against an industry in the throes of denial. An NBC executive called the research "ridiculous." *Variety* suggested a lobotomy.

What the analysis of 2,693 television programs from twenty-three channels showed is that a majority of programs contain what the researchers call "harmful violence." These were programs that posed three distinct threats to public health: "learning to behave violently, becoming more desensitized to the harmful consequences of violence and becoming fearful of being attacked."

"The issue for us," Donnerstein says, "is not just that there was violence but how it was presented." In analyzing the plots, images and programs, the team asked, What makes violence a public health problem? What contexts should we worry about?

For one thing, violence turns out to do a lot of harm when it looks harmless. One of the lessons children learn watching television is that there are few consequences to the person who commits violence, or to the victim.

In 73 percent of the scenes, the violence went unpunished. In nearly half of the programs with slugfests and shoot-outs, the victims miraculously never appeared harmed. In 58 percent they showed no pain. In fact, only 16 percent of the programs showed any long-term problems— physical, emotional, or financial.

Add to this "positive" portrayal of negative behavior the fact that children's programs were least likely to show the bad effects of violence and most likely to make it funny. As Donnerstein says, "We're showing children violence that goes unpunished, is unrealistic and humorous."

As for other messages? Only a minuscule 4 percent of violent programs had an anti-violent theme. Or showed any alternative to the gym, the fist, the fight.

It's not surprising that this study is being touted in Washington as a sound basis for rating television violence. After all, if the V-chip is to become what Clinton called the "parents' power chip," we need a ratings system that's more sophisticated than one that counts dead bodies.

Indeed, selling the V-chip to an audience of Virginia parents, Clinton not only quoted the dark facts of the violence research, he promised that "new technologies can put you back in the driver's seat in your life...." It's an appeal to parents who want to regain some modest control over the messages coming into their houses and to their children.

But the same National Television Violence Study also hints at the limits of a technological fix to what is not really a technological problem.

The portrait that emerges from this analysis, after all, is not just of the television environment. It's a profile of an industry that narrowly equates entertainment with violence. It's a profile of a galaxy of broadcasters, producers, and programmers who have shown more imagination in claiming their programs are harmless than in changing the destructive plots.

The V-chip is a violence block. But the real problem in the television industry is a creative block. Soon we'll have the V-chip. Does anyone know how to get rid of the C-chip?

Source: Ellen Goodman, "Violence Study Shows TV's Mental Block," reprinted in *Ann Arbor News* (February 16, 1996), p. A9.

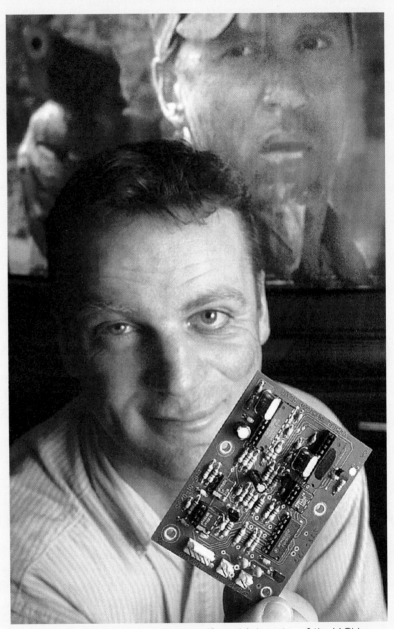

Tim Collins of Simon Fraser University (Canada), inventor of the V-Chip

"In quantum gravity, as we shall see, the space-time manifold ceases to exist as an objective reality; geometry becomes relational and contextual; and the foundational conceptual categories of prior science—among them, existence itself—become problematized and relativized. This conceptual revolution, I will argue, has profound implications for the content of a future postmodern and liberatory science."
— from Alan Sokal's published jargon-riddled hoax, 1996

read the article but didn't suspect that it was phony. A public debate ensued after Sokal revealed his hoax. Sokal said he worries that jargon and intellectual fads cause academics to lose contact with the real world and "undermine the prospect for progressive social critique."[30]

In addition to the issue of specialized language, other problems have arisen involving media research and democracy. By the mid-1990s, lawmakers and the public had become increasingly concerned about the emphasis on research over teaching at most major universities. Throughout the early 1990s, as the government slashed support for student loans and university research, universities escalated their campaigns to raise money and become affiliated with corporations. The late historian Christopher Lasch, however, warned of the dangers "of corporate control of the universities" and the potential for "corruption" in higher education: "It is corporate control that has diverted social resources from the humanities into military and technological research, fostered an obsession with quantification that has destroyed the social sciences, replaced the English language with bureaucratic jargon, and created a top-heavy administrative apparatus whose educational vision begins and ends with the bottom line."[31]

By the mid-1990s, it was also becoming more difficult for middle- and working-class students to attend college, which seemed to contradict the democratic progress that had been going on in higher education since the 1950s. After World War II, many students gained access to college through the government GI loans to war veterans. By the 1960s, spurred on by the women's and civil-rights movements, universities opened up further, allowing far greater access to students who were formerly excluded. These democratic movements also ushered in the study of popular culture and the mass media. The news media's coverage of the Watergate scandal alone sparked interest in journalism as an undergraduate major throughout the country.

Ironically, while campuses were becoming more democratic, increasing specialization in the 1970s began isolating many researchers from life outside the university. Academics were once again locked away in their ivory towers. As a remedy, education critics began reemphasizing the role and responsibility of teachers and researchers in public life. By the 1990s, in fact, the *Chronicle of Higher Education* reported renewed interest in the idea of public intellectuals: "Bruised after years of attack, professors in the humanities and related fields are working to answer their critics and to speak and write in a public voice. Their work marks a turn away from high literary theory toward autobiography, journalism, and the essay form, styles that in recent years were seen as popularizing and old-fashioned."[32] Early in the twentieth century, it was common for academics to operate as public intellectuals. But the proliferation of specialized fields widened the gap between the public and the university. Fortunately, a few researchers, such as paleontologist Stephen Jay Gould and the late astronomer Carl Sagan, made their academic work more accessible to a broader public.

An unprecedented television study at UCLA in 1994 pointed up the increasing effort to connect media research and public life. Funded by ABC, CBS, Fox, and NBC, the UCLA study tracked the depiction of violence in prime-time TV series through the 1994–95 TV season. Faced with the possibility of government-imposed restrictions on content, the networks authorized the study to respond to concerns about violent TV images. Finding high levels of violence in Hollywood films shown on cable channels and relatively low levels in prime-time television, the researchers worked hard to make their analyses and interpretations accessible. In fact, a CBS executive at the time praised the independent report for being "written in English" and "for presenting qualitative rather than quantitative analysis," suggesting that the study had set up a "legitimate debate" on the subject of TV violence (see "Case Study: Violence Study Shows Television's Mental Block" on page 478).[33]

Facing a number of critical problems in higher education, more academics in the 1980s and 1990s began stepping forward to broaden their ideas of research and to become active in political and cultural life. For example, literary scholar Henry Louis Gates Jr. began writing essays for *Time* and the *New Yorker* magazines. Cultural critic Mike Davis created heated discussions about the future of Los Angeles in his popular books *City of Quartz* and *Ecology of Fear.* Linguist Noam Chomsky, who tirelessly writes and speaks about excessive government and media power, was even the subject of an award-winning 1992 documentary, *Manufacturing Consent: Noam Chomsky and the Media.* And feminist critic Camille Paglia, whose hefty cultural history *Sexual Personae* became a best-selling paperback in 1991, has voiced her often controversial commentary in *Esquire,* the *Los Angeles Times,* the *New York Times,* and in a regular column for the online magazine *Salon.* Popular academic books ranging from conservative accounts (Allan Bloom's *Closing of the American Mind*) to progressive accounts (Cornel West's *Race Matters*) extended academic ideas beyond the boundaries of the university.

In the early 1990s, the TV coverage of the Persian Gulf War included many political scientists, military historians, and religion professors, who interpreted the war in the larger context of ongoing Middle Eastern struggles. In 1992 and 1996, Kathleen Hall Jamieson, dean of the communication college at the University of Pennsylvania, made regular appearances on PBS—and guest appearances on the *Tonight Show*—to analyze the presidential elections and perform textual analyses of political advertising. The biggest surge among academics, however, came during the O.J. Simpson trials from 1994 to 1997. During this period, scores of law professors made regular TV appearances and tried to place the trial in a larger historical and legal context. Many of those same academics—including law professors Greta Van Susteren and Roger Cossack, whose work as legal analysts for CNN during the Simpson trial led to the daily legal talk program *Burden of Proof*—continued their public discussions during media coverage of the Clinton-Lewinsky scandal and the impeachment process.

Other popular voices from the academic world have tried to help the public see university research as both less distant and less corporate. Like public journalists, public intellectuals based on campuses help to carry on the conversations of society and culture, actively circulating the most important new ideas of the day and serving as models for how to participate in public life.

> "In many ways the modern university has replaced its function as a **creative/ subversive institution** with a fondness for structure and organization among its parts, and the rigid compartmentalization of knowledge within these structures."
>
> —David Scholle and Stan Denski, *Media Education,* 1994

As model contemporary public intellectuals, Cornel West *(center)* and Henry Louis Gates Jr. *(right)* have dedicated much of their careers to communicating ideas to both academic communities and the larger public. Pictured here with exiled Nigerian author Wole Soyinka *(left),* West and Gates write academic texts, mass-market books, and also make appearances on radio and TV news and talk programs.

REVIEW QUESTIONS

Early Developments in Media Research

1. What were the earliest types of media studies, and why weren't they more scientific?

2. What were the major influences that led to scientific media research?

Research on Media Effects

3. What are the differences between experiments and surveys as media-research strategies?

4. What is content analysis and why is it significant?

5. What are the differences between the hypodermic-needle model and the minimal-effects model in the history of media research?

6. What are agenda-setting and the cultivation effect?

7. What are some strengths and limitations of modern media research?

Cultural Approaches to Media Research

8. Why did cultural approaches to media studies develop in opposition to media-effects research?

9. What are the features of cultural studies?

10. How is textual analysis different from content analysis?

11. What are some of the strengths and limitations of cultural research?

Media Research, Ivory Towers, and Democracy

12. How has specialization in academic research influenced universities?

13. How can public intellectuals and academics improve the relationships between campuses and the general public?

QUESTIONING THE MEDIA

1. What are your main concerns or criticisms about the state of media studies at your college or university?

2. One charge that has been leveled against a lot of media research—both the effects and the cultural models—is that it has very little impact on changing our media institutions. Do you agree or disagree and why?

3. Can you think of an issue that a media industry and academic researchers could study together? Explain.

4. In looking at media courses in a college curriculum, what do you think is the relationship between theory and practice? Do hands-on, practical skills courses such as news reporting, advertising copywriting, or TV production belong in a liberal-arts college or in a separate mass-communication college? Explain your answer.

SEARCHING THE INTERNET

http://www.cemnet.org
The Cultural Environment Movement, founded by media researcher George Gerbner, bills itself as "an international coalition of over 250 organizations and 6,300 individuals united in working for gender equity and general diversity in mass-media employment, ownership, and representation."

http://www.imagesjournal.com
Images is an online journal of media criticism that publishes accessible articles about movies, television, videos, and other popular visual arts.

http://www.igc.apc.org/mediascope/ntvs1.htm
This site contains the project overview and summary of findings and recommendations of the first year (1994–95) of the National Television Violence Study, the largest study of its kind ever undertaken

http://www2.localaccess.com/hardebeck
The Kill Your TV Web Site is an informative and entertaining collection of facts about television viewing, as well as a link to many articles, essays, TV-related Web pages, and cartoons.

In Brief

Consider the incidents outlined in the chapter's preview story, as well as any other recent violent media stories, and discuss the following questions in class: Does media-effects research support the charge that mass media should be responsible for the tragic instances of copycat behavior? How would you balance the First Amendment free-expression rights of the mass media with issues of social and moral responsibility?

In Depth

The purpose of this project is to extend your critical approach to media research and to the academic culture that has developed over the years. Here are three assignments that can work either as group projects in class or as individual writing assignments.

1. Create your own hypothesis with regard to the media or test one of the following arguments:

   • College students are less informed about current news events than their parents are.

   • Watching late-night TV talk-show monologues makes us more cynical about issues in the news.

   Come up with two or three different plans for testing either your own hypothesis or one of the hypotheses listed above. What types of research would you use? Why?

2. Choose an issue from two contemporary media-research journals—one devoted mostly to mainstream research (such as *Journalism & Mass Communication Quarterly*) and one devoted to cultural research (such as *Critical Studies in Mass Communication*). Make a list or chart of the topics that each particular issue covers. Pick one article from each issue, and write a paragraph critiquing how well you think the researchers made and supported their arguments. How accessible was the language in each article, and how important was the research? As a journalist, what would you report about these media-research projects?

3. Choose one well-established media-research journal—*Journalism & Mass Communication Quarterly*, *Public Opinion Quarterly*, or *Film Quarterly*—and read an issue of the journal for each decade from the 1930s or 1940s to the present. In your group or in an essay, document the subject matter and explain how the journal has changed over the years. Which issues did you find to be the best and why?

Legal Controls
and Freedom of Expression

CHAPTER 16

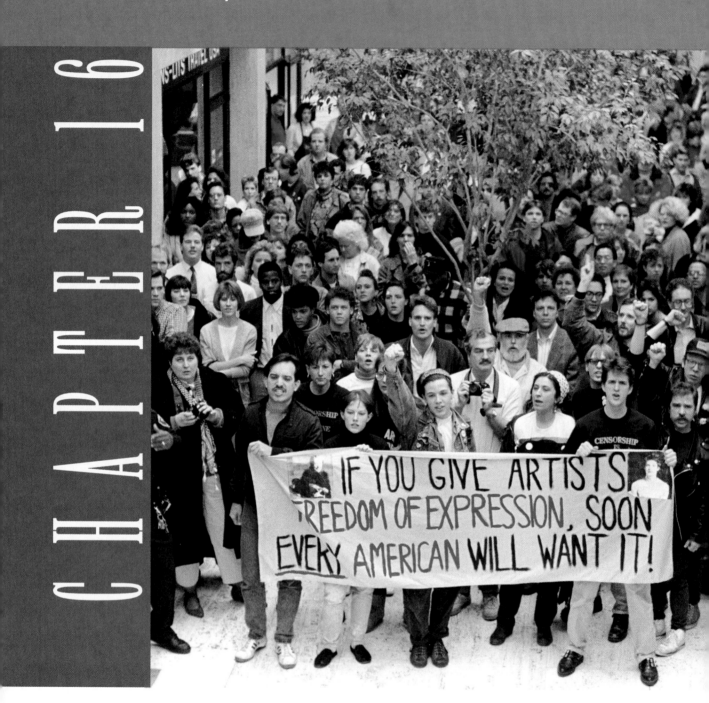

IF YOU GIVE ARTISTS FREEDOM OF EXPRESSION, SOON EVERY AMERICAN WILL WANT IT!

I n the fall of 1990, a record-store owner in Florida was convicted on obscenity charges for selling a 2 Live Crew rap album to minors. Responding to citizen complaints earlier that year, a court in Florida's Broward County said the recording, *As Nasty as They Wanna Be*, met the test for obscenity. The store owner had apparently ignored county sheriffs who had warned local retailers about selling the controversial album. The conviction was the first of its kind in U.S. legal history.

The 2 Live Crew ruling was also the first time a U.S. court had declared a musical recording obscene. The record contained references to oral sex, group sex, sadomasochism, and violence against women. Two years later, after 2 Live Crew appealed, a federal appellate court reversed the decision. The appeals court determined that the sheriff's office had the burden of proof to demonstrate that the recording was obscene. The court also decided that the sheriff's office had submitted no evidence to counter the band's claim that the work had merit as satire and comedic art. Under obscenity law, a work that demonstrates socially redeeming merit does not meet the obscenity test. The earlier conviction of the record-store owner was eventually overturned.

Meanwhile, during the same week in 1990 that the Florida store owner was convicted, an Ohio jury acquitted Dennis Barrie, then the head of Cincinnati's Contemporary Art Center. Barrie and his museum had been charged with obscenity for exhibiting sexually explicit photographs. This was the first such criminal trial involving the director of an art museum. In the spring of 1990, the Cincinnati museum had shown 175 photographs by the late artist Robert Mapplethorpe. The case focused on seven of the photos: two featuring nude minors and five with adult men in sadomasochistic poses. During the controversy, city officials discussed closing the exhibit. Defense lawyers for the museum claimed the pictures had serious artistic merit, which meant they did not violate obscenity standards. After art experts defended the pictures, eight jurors found Barrie and the museum not guilty.

As the 1990s began, the Florida and Ohio cases ignited legal and cultural fireworks. They raised important questions about the role of art, popular culture, legal limits, and free expression in a democracy. Should every kind of artistic or musical expression be protected by the First Amendment? How do we protect children from controversial works? Should we punish certain kinds of expression or art that offend or demean adults? Who decides?

With the battle over expression and pornography escalating in the 1990s, conservatives in the U.S. Congress protested the federal funding of sexually explicit art projects. Legal activists Andrea Dworkin and Catharine MacKinnon aided the conservative cause; their legal writings influenced local ordinances and a new Canadian law against pornography, which redefined obscenity to include any "materials that subordinate, degrade or dehumanize women." In affecting Canada's highest court, the Dworkin-MacKinnon strategy involved dodging the long history of protecting even repulsive or pornographic material. The attorneys argued that pornography itself was an act of violence and a violation of women's civil rights.

Although Dworkin and MacKinnon's efforts have many supporters, among their opposition are a number of feminist groups, including some leaders in the National Organization for Women (NOW). These groups argue that they do not need the police or state governments to intervene for them—that women are strong enough to fight the battles over pornography with other kinds of free speech. This position grudgingly defends pornographers' speech rights and is closely associated with an absolutist position on free-expression issues, which reaffirms the First Amendment: "Congress shall make *no* law . . . abridging the freedom of speech." To protect *all*

> "Congress shall make no law respecting an establishment of religion, or prohibiting the free exercise thereof; or **abridging the freedom of speech**, or of the press; or the right of the people to peaceably assemble, and to petition the government for a redress of grievances."
>
> —First Amendment, U.S. Constitution, 1791

forms of expression, this argument contends that even hateful, demeaning, and pornographic speech have to be tolerated—and fought against by using speech rather than censorship. Former Supreme Court Justice Hugo Black supported this absolutist view. Often taking a minority position on speech issues, he contended that even current libel and obscenity laws were unconstitutional.

The cultural and social struggles over free speech and press freedom have defined the nature of American democracy. In 1989, when Supreme Court Justice William Brennan Jr. was asked to comment on his "favorite part of the Constitution," he replied, "The First Amendment, I expect. Its enforcement gives us this society. The other provisions of the Constitution really only embellish it." Of all the issues that involve the mass media and popular culture, none are more central, or explosive, than freedom of expression and the First Amendment. Our fundamental development as a nation can often be traced to how much or how little speech we tolerated during particular historical periods.

As the 1990s end, we live in a volatile time for free-speech issues. As a society, we have debated hate-speech codes on campuses, explicit lyrics in music, and violent

In 1985, rock musicians like the late Frank Zappa (right) appeared before the Senate to protest warning labels on CDs and tapes as a First Amendment violation. By the late 1980s, though, to ward off government regulation, the music industry voluntarily agreed to place parental-advisory stickers on controversial recordings.

images in film. In this chapter, we will examine expression issues, focusing primarily on the implications of the First Amendment for a variety of mass media. We will investigate the origins of *free* expression and the standard models that underlie press freedoms. We will look at the definition of censorship and corresponding legal cases. Next, we will study the types of expression that are not always protected as speech. Focusing on the impact of cameras in the courtroom, we will examine some of the clashes between the First and Sixth Amendments. With regard to film, we will review the social and political pressures that gave rise to early censorship boards and the current film ratings system. We will turn to issues in broadcasting and examine why it has been treated differently from print media. Among other topics, we will inspect the idea of *indecency* in broadcasting and the demise of the Fairness Doctrine. Finally, we will explore the newest frontier in speech—expression in cyberspace and concerns about speech on the Internet.

the origins of free expression and a free press

When students from other cultures attend school in the United States, many are astounded by the number of books, news articles, editorials, cartoons, films, and TV shows that make fun of U.S. presidents. When writer-director Hugh Wilson toured Spain after his comedy film *Police Academy* (1984) had appeared there, he was astonished to discover that many Spanish citizens regarded him as a hero for "criticizing" the police. Many countries throughout history have jailed, even killed, their citizens for such speech "violations." In the 1990s, more than fifty journalists a year were still dying in the line of duty.[1] In the United States, however, we have generally taken for granted our right to criticize and poke fun at elected officials, politicians, and the police. Many of us are unaware of the ideas that underpin the freedoms we have. Indeed, when reporters have surveyed unwitting Americans about the First Amendment to the U.S. Constitution, the majority of respondents, unfamiliar with the amendment's wording, have usually indicated that its freedoms are far too generous.

To understand the development of free expression in the United States, we must understand a key idea underlying the First Amendment. In Europe throughout the 1600s, in order to monitor—and punish if necessary—the speech of editors and writers, governments controlled ideas by requiring printers to obtain licenses. In 1644, English poet John Milton, author of *Paradise Lost*, published his essay *Areopagitica*, which opposed government licenses for printers and defended a free press. Milton argued that all sorts of ideas, even false ones, should circulate freely in a democratic society and that truth would eventually emerge. In 1695, England stopped licensing newspapers, and most of Europe followed. In many democracies today, publishing a newspaper, magazine, or newsletter remains one of the few public or service enterprises that requires no license.

models for expression and speech

In 1996, an international survey of the news media in 187 countries, conducted by Freedom House, reported that although more than half the world's population lived under some form of democratic government, fewer than 45 countries offered a relatively free press. The survey related that 58 nations had virtually no press freedom; those governments exercised tight control over the news media, and this included jailing, intimidating, and even executing journalists. Championing the Internet as a way to bypass restrictive governments, the survey looked to new technologies to help improve the free flow of information worldwide.[2]

"Consider what would happen if—during this 200th anniversary of the Bill of Rights—the First Amendment were placed on the ballot in every town, city, and state. The choices: affirm, reject, or amend.

"I would bet there is no place in the United States where the First Amendment would survive intact."

—Nat Hentoff,
writer,
1991

Since the mid-1950s, four models for speech and journalism have been used to categorize the widely differing ideas underlying free expression.[3] These models include the authoritarian, communist, libertarian, and social-responsibility concepts. They are distinguished by the levels of freedom they each allow and by the attitudes of the ruling and political classes toward the freedoms granted to the average citizen. Given the diversity among nations, the experimentation of journalists, and the collapse of many communist press systems, these categories no longer hold up as well. Nevertheless, they offer a good point of departure for discussing the press and democracy.

The **authoritarian model** developed about the time the printing press arrived in sixteenth-century England. Its advocates held that the general public, largely illiterate in those days, needed guidance from an elite and educated ruling class. Government criticism and public dissent were not tolerated, especially if such speech undermined "the common good"—an ideal that ruling elites and leaders defined and controlled. Censorship was frequent, and the government issued printing licenses primarily to publishers who were sympathetic to government and ruling-class agendas.

Today, many authoritarian systems operate in developing countries throughout Asia, Latin America, and Africa, where journalism often joins with government and business to foster economic growth, minimize political dissent, and encourage social stability. The leaders in these systems generally believe that too much outspoken speech and press freedom would undermine the delicate stability of their social and political infrastructures. In these societies, criticizing government programs may be viewed as an obstacle to keeping the peace, and both reporters and citizens may be punished if they question leaders and the status quo too fiercely.

Under most authoritarian models, the news is still controlled by private enterprise. But under the **communist** or **state model**, press control sits in the lap of government. Speaking for ordinary citizens and workers, state leaders believe they are enlightened and that the press should serve the common goals of the state. Although some state systems encourage media and government cooperation, political and military leaders still dictate the agendas for newspapers and the broadcast media. Some government criticism is tolerated, but ideas that challenge the basic premises of state authority are not. Although state media systems were in decline throughout the 1990s, they were still operating in China, Cuba, Iran, Iraq, and North Korea, among other countries.

The **libertarian model**, the flip side of state and authoritarian systems, encourages vigorous government criticism and supports the highest degree of freedom for individual speech and news operations. In a strict libertarian model, no restrictions are placed on the mass media or on individual speech. Libertarians tolerate the expression of everything from publishing pornography to advocating anarchy. In North America and Europe, many political and alternative newspapers and magazines operate on such a model. Placing a great deal of trust in citizens' ability to sort truth from fabrication, libertarians maintain that the best way to fight outrageous lies or repulsive speech is not to suppress them but to speak out and write against them.

Along with the libertarian model, a **social-responsibility model** characterizes the main ideals of mainstream journalism in the United States. The concepts and assumptions behind this model coalesced in the controversial 1947 Hutchins Commission, which was formed to examine the increasing influence of the press. Henry Luce, then head of the Time-Life magazine empire, funded the commission with a large grant to his friend Robert Maynard Hutchins, chancellor of the University of Chicago. Hutchins used the grant to assemble a committee to study the press. Luce hoped the commission would endorse free-press ideals and keep outsiders from watching over the press. But to Luce's dismay, the commission's report called for the development of press-watchdog groups. The report argued that the mass media had grown too powerful and needed to become more socially responsible. Key recommendations encouraged comprehensive news reports that put issues and events in context, more news forums for the exchange of ideas, better coverage of society's range of economic classes and social groups, and stronger overviews of our nation's social values, ideals, and goals. Given the state of news media and the proliferation of information by the late 1990s, a number of academics, politicians, and media critics began calling for another Hutchins-type commission to examine the future of news media in the new millennium.

A socially responsible press is usually privately owned (although the government technically operates the broadcast media in most European and Scandinavian democracies). In this model, the press functions as a **Fourth Estate**—that is, as an unofficial branch of government that monitors the legislative, judicial, and executive branches for abuses of power. In theory, private ownership keeps the news media independent of government. Thus they are better able to watch over the system on behalf of citizens. Under this model, which is heavily influenced by the libertarian view, the press supplies information to citizens so they can make wise decisions regarding political and social issues; the press also operates without excessive government meddling in matters of content.

censorship as prior restraint

In the United States, the First Amendment has theoretically prohibited censorship. Over time, Supreme Court decisions have defined censorship as **prior restraint**. This means that courts and governments cannot block any publication or speech before it actually occurs, on the principle that a law has not been broken until an illegal act has been committed. In 1931, for example, the Supreme Court determined in *Near v. Minnesota* that a Minneapolis newspaper could not be stopped from publishing "scandalous and defamatory" material about police and law officials who were negligent in arresting and punishing local gangsters.[4] However, the Court left open the idea that the news media could be ordered to halt publication in exceptional cases. During a declared war, for instance, if a U.S. court judged that the publication of an article threatened national security, such expression could be restrained prior to its printing. In fact, during World War I, the U.S. Navy seized all wireless radio transmitters. This was done to ensure control over critical information about weather conditions and troop movements that might inadvertently aid the enemy. In the 1970s, though, the *Pentagon Papers* decision and the *Progressive* magazine case tested important concepts underlying prior restraint.

The Pentagon Papers Case. In 1971, with the Vietnam War still in progress, Daniel Ellsberg, a former Defense Department employee, stole a copy of a forty-seven-volume document, "History of U.S. Decision-Making Process on Vietnam Policy." A thorough study of U.S. involvement in Vietnam since World War II, the papers were classified by the government as top secret. Ellsberg and a friend leaked the study—nicknamed the Pentagon Papers—to the *New York Times* and the *Washington Post*. In June 1971, the *Times* began publishing articles based on the study. To block

In 1971, Daniel Ellsberg surrendered to government prosecutors in Boston. Ellsberg was a former Pentagon researcher who turned against America's military policy in Vietnam and leaked information to the press. He was charged with unauthorized possession of top-secret federal documents. Later called the Pentagon Papers, the documents contained evidence on the military's bungled handling of the Vietnam War. In 1973, an exasperated federal judge dismissed the case when illegal government-sponsored wiretaps of Ellsberg's psychoanalyst came to light during the Watergate scandal.

any further publication, the Nixon administration received a temporary restraining order to prepare its case, arguing that publishing the documents posed "a clear and present danger" to national security. The Nixon government had five national-security experts testify that publicizing the Pentagon Papers would impede the war effort.

A lower U.S. district court supported the newspaper's right to publish, but the government's appeal placed the case in the Supreme Court less than three weeks after the first articles were published. In a 6–3 vote, the Court sided with the newspapers. Justice Hugo Black, speaking for the majority, attacked the government's attempt to suppress publication: "Both the history and language of the First Amendment support the view that the press must be left free to publish news, whatever the source, without censorship, injunctions, or prior restraints."[5]

The *Progressive* Magazine Case. The issue of prior restraint ominously surfaced again in 1979, when an injunction was issued to block publication of the *Progressive*, a national left-wing magazine; the editors had announced that they were running an article entitled "The H-Bomb Secret: How We Got It, Why We're Telling It." The dispute began when the editor of the magazine sent a draft to the Department of Energy to verify technical portions of the article. Believing that the article contained sensitive data that might damage U.S. efforts to halt the proliferation of nuclear weapons, the Energy Department asked the magazine not to publish it. When the magazine said it would proceed anyway, the government sued the *Progressive* and asked a federal district court to block publication.

Judge Robert Warren sought to balance the *Progressive*'s First Amendment rights against the government's claim that the article would spread dangerous information and undermine national security. In an unprecedented action, Warren sided with the government, deciding that "a mistake in ruling against the United States could pave the way for thermonuclear annihilation for us all. In that event, our right to life is extinguished and the right to publish becomes moot."[6] During appeals and further litigation, several other publications, including the *Milwaukee Sentinel* and *Scientific American*, published articles related to the H-bomb, getting much of their information from publications already in circulation. None of these articles, including the one published in the *Progressive*, contained the precise technical details needed to actually design a nuclear weapon; nor did they provide information on where to obtain the sensitive ingredients necessary. Although the government dropped the case, Warren's injunction stands as the first time in American history that a prior restraint order imposed in the name of national security actually stopped the *initial* publication of a controversial news report.

unprotected forms of expression

Early in our nation's history, the Federalist Party, which controlled Congress, enacted the Sedition Act to silence opposition to an anticipated war against France. The act tried to curb criticism by the opposition Democratic-Republican Party. Many anti-Federalists supported France and America's newly arrived French immigrants. Led by President John Adams, the Federalists believed that defamatory articles could stir up discontent against the elected government and undermine its authority. Adams signed the act in 1798. Over the next three years, twenty-five individuals were arrested and ten convicted under the act, which was also used to prosecute anti-Federalist newspapers. After failing to curb opposition, the Sedition Act expired in 1801 during Thomas Jefferson's presidency. Jefferson, a Democratic-Republican who had challenged the act's constitutionality, pardoned all defendants convicted under the Sedition Act.[7]

Despite the First Amendment's order that "Congress shall make no law" restricting speech and press freedoms, the federal government has made other laws like the Sedition Act, especially during times of war. For instance, the Espionage Acts of 1917 and 1918, which were enforced during World Wars I and II, made it a federal crime to disrupt the nation's war effort. These acts also authorized severe punishment for seditious statements. Beyond the federal government, state laws and local ordinances have on occasion curbed expression, and over the years the court system has determined that some kinds of expression do not merit protection as speech under the Constitution. Today, for example, false or misleading advertising is not protected by law; nor are expressions that intentionally threaten public safety.

In the landmark *Schenck v. United States* appeal case during World War I, the Supreme Court upheld the conviction of a Socialist Party leader, Charles T. Schenck, for distributing leaflets urging American men to protest the draft, a violation of the newly passed Espionage Act. In upholding the act, Justice Oliver Wendell Holmes wrote two of the more famous interpretations and phrases in the First Amendment's legal history:

> But the character of every act depends upon the circumstances in which it is done. The most stringent protection of free speech would not protect a man in falsely shouting fire in a theater and causing a panic.

> The question in every case is whether the words used are used in such circumstances and are of such a nature as to create a clear and present danger that they will bring about the substantive evils that Congress has a right to prevent.

In supporting Schenck's sentence—a ten-year prison term—Holmes noted that the Socialist leaflets were entitled to First Amendment protection, but only during times of peace.

"Pretty Woman," Rap, and Copyright Law

by Michael M. Epstein

The protection of copyright has long helped writers, artists and filmmakers control where, when, and how their creative works are used by others. Under U.S. copyright law, the original creators can sue people who imitate or adapt their works commercially without permission. In most cases, the rule is as follows: If you make money off someone else's creative material, that money belongs to the person who owns the copyright to the material unless you have obtained his or her prior approval. One exception to copyright protection, known as *fair use*, allows journalists, critics, scholars, and students to excerpt limited portions of other peoples' creations for a variety of purposes.

2 Live Crew members Luther R. Campbell, Christopher Wong Won, Mark Ross, and David Hobbs

Until recently, parody was usually considered to be covered by copyright's fair-use exception, yet the Supreme Court did not rule on the issue until March 7, 1994. The Court unanimously found that the rap group 2 Live Crew did not violate U.S. copyright law when it released its 1989 song "Pretty Woman." A subversive, cynical, and controversial parody of Roy Orbison's 1964 anthem of hope and fulfillment, "Oh, Pretty Woman," the 2 Live Crew version developed a huge and profitable following among hip-hop audiences. Although the rap group had sought permission to use the song's signature first line for its parody, the owner of the song's copyright, Acuff-Rose Music, decided not to let the group use the famous ballad. When 2 Live Crew went ahead and used the song anyway, Acuff-Rose filed suit in federal court.

2 Live Crew members argued that their version of "Oh, Pretty Woman" was intended to be a parody of Orbison's song. As author Luther R. Campbell explained in a letter to Acuff-Rose, the group's purpose was "through comical lyrics, to satirize the original work." These lyrics, considered offensive and sexist by many, transformed Orbison's pretty woman into a "big hairy woman," "a bald-

In establishing the "clear and present danger" criterion for expression, the Supreme Court demonstrated the limits of the First Amendment. Appropriating a writer's or artist's words or music without consent or payment is another form of expression that is not protected as speech. Rap performers, in fact, have faced a number of court battles for copyright infringement; they have been accused of stealing other musicians' work by sampling their music, a technique fundamental to rap (see "Case Study: 'Pretty Woman,' Rap, and Copyright Law," above). A **copyright** legally protects the rights of authors and producers for their published or unpublished writing, music and lyrics, TV programs and movies, or graphic art designs. Beyond copyright protections, several kinds of controversial expression have historically had a great impact on print and other forms of mass media. These include libel, invasion of privacy, and obscenity.

headed woman," and a "two-timin' woman." Although 2 Live Crew gave credit for "Oh, Pretty Woman" to Roy Orbison and his coauthor William Dees on their album *Clean as They Wanna Be*, Acuff-Rose argued that Campbell's creation was nothing more than a commercial rip-off that made money for the rap group at the copyright owner's expense. Lawyers for the rappers argued, however, that "Pretty Woman" was a legitimate parody and thus exempt from copyright claims.

Although the federal district court in Nashville decided in favor of 2 Live Crew, a U.S. court of appeals later reversed the lower court's ruling, causing a furor in the creative community. The appellate court concluded that by "taking the heart of the original and making it the heart of a new work," the band had borrowed too much of the original song. The court also ruled that "Pretty Woman" could not be protected as fair use under copyright law because the rappers had recorded their version for "blatantly commercial purposes."

Justice David Souter, writing for a unanimous Supreme Court, rejected the ruling of the appellate court. Souter suggested that the rap version could be understood "as a comment on the naivete of the original of an earlier day, as a rejection of its sentiment that ignores the ugliness of street life and the debasement it signifies." Stating that parody's "art lies in the tension between a known original and its parodic twin," the Supreme Court ruled that works that adapt or transform an original creation "lie at the heart of the fair-use doctrine's guarantee of breathing space within the confines of copyright." Souter noted that Campbell's parody deserved credit for both "shedding light on an earlier work and . . . creating a new one."

In a media-saturated world that has seen the sampling by rap artists of previous recordings and the composite imaging of archival photos and films by computer, it is no wonder that the "Pretty Woman" case attracted wide attention. Satirists as diverse as *Mad Magazine* and political humorist Mark Russell filed friend-of-the-court briefs on behalf of 2 Live Crew. On the other hand, many songwriters and composers filed briefs in support of the music company.

It is still too early to tell whether the composers have lost the copyright-protection war. Indeed, since the ruling in *Campbell v. Acuff-Rose Music*, instances of copyright infringement are still decided on a case-by-case basis. Whether or not a parodist, or anyone else, is granted protection under copyright law is still subject to the general rules governing fair use. For example, if a parody is likely to damage the market for the original work, then the creator may be able to collect damages from the parodist. As the courts see it, imitation is still the sincerest form of flattery—but only up to a point.

Michael M. Epstein is a professor at Southwestern University School of Law and an attorney with a Ph.D. in American studies.

Libel. The biggest single legal worry that haunts editors and publishers is the issue of libel, another form of expression that is not protected as speech under the First Amendment. Whereas **slander** constitutes spoken language that defames a person's character, **libel** refers to defamation of character in written expression. Inherited from British common law, libel is generally defined as a false statement—either printed or broadcast—that holds a person up to public ridicule, contempt, or hatred, or injures a person's business or occupation. Examples of potentially libelous statements include falsely accusing someone of professional dishonesty or incompetence (such as medical malpractice); falsely accusing a person of a crime (such as drug dealing); falsely charging a person with mental illness or unacceptable behavior (such as public drunkenness); or falsely accusing a person of associating with a disreputable organization or cause (such as the Mafia or a neo-Nazi military group).

To protect the news media's right to aggressively pursue wrongdoing and stories, courts since the mid-1960s have tried to make it more difficult for public officials to win libel suits. This has not, however, deterred some individuals and organizations from intimidating the news media by either threatening to file or actually filing libel suits. Such legal actions in civil law can prove costly, particularly to a small newspaper or magazine, even when the defendant wins the case. As a result, over the years many small news organizations have avoided tough, probing stories, and large organizations have hired more lawyers to advise them on the libel implications of their more controversial investigative stories.

Juries, too, have traditionally been hostile to the media, often siding with plaintiffs and granting generous mental-anguish awards. Prior to the 1960s, libel awards rarely exceeded $25,000, but initial awards averaged nearly $500,000 by 1987–88 and $8 million by 1991. As a result of legal reform movements in the 1990s, the complexity of libel law, and the fact that some juries overlooked the letter of the law to sympathize with a wronged celebrity, many libel awards have been reduced in size or dismissed on appeal. Nevertheless, plaintiffs have won the majority of libel cases. In the 1980s, for example, of the twenty-five libel cases tried in U.S. civil courts against newspapers, the news media lost sixteen times.[8]

Since 1964, the *New York Times v. Sullivan* case has served as the standard for libel law. The case stems from a 1960 full-page advertisement placed in the *New York Times* by the Committee to Defend Martin Luther King Jr. and the Struggle for Freedom in the South. Without naming names, the ad criticized the general law-enforcement tactics of southern cities, including Montgomery, Alabama, for the methods used to break up civil-rights demonstrations. The ad condemned "southern violators of the Constitution" bent on destroying King and the movement. Taking exception, the city commissioner of Montgomery, L. B. Sullivan, sued the *Times* for libel, claiming the ad had defamed him indirectly. Although Alabama civil courts awarded Sullivan $500,000, the newspaper's lawyers appealed to the Supreme Court, which unanimously reversed the ruling, holding that Alabama libel law violated the *Times's* First Amendment rights.[9]

This is the 1960 *New York Times* advertisement that triggered one of the most influential and important libel cases in U.S. history.

In the *Sullivan* decision, the Supreme Court asked future civil courts to distinguish whether plaintiffs are *public officials* or private individuals. (In later cases, *public figures* such as entertainment or sports celebrities were also added to this mix.) Within this framework, to successfully argue a libel case, *private* individuals have to prove three things:

1. that the public statement about them was false

2. that damages or actual injury occurred, such as the loss of a job, harm to reputation, public humiliation, or mental anguish

3. that the publisher or broadcaster was negligent

But if a court determines that a plaintiff is a *public* official or figure, that person has to prove falsehood, damages, negligence, *and* **actual malice** on the part of the news medium. This latter test means that the reporter or editor knew the statement was false and printed or broadcast it anyway, or acted with a reckless disregard for the truth. Again, since actual malice is hard to prove, it remains difficult for public figures to win libel suits. The Court's rationale for the principle of actual malice not only protects the First Amendment rights of the media but, in theory, allows news operations to aggressively pursue legitimate news stories without fear of continuous litigation. In practice, however, the mere threat of a libel suit still scares off many in the news media.

Under current libel law, civil courts determine, on a case-by-case basis, whether plaintiffs are public or private persons. In general, public officials must have substantial responsibilities in conducting government affairs; therefore presidents, senators, mayors, police detectives, and city managers count as examples of public officials. Citizens with more "ordinary" jobs, such as city sanitation employees, undercover police informants, nurses, or unknown actors, are normally classified as private individuals.

Judges often have a tough time deciding who is a public figure. Many fuzzy categories exist, such as public high-school teachers, police officers, and court-appointed attorneys. Individuals from these professions have ended up in either category depending on a particular court's ruling. The Supreme Court has distinguished two categories of public figures: (1) public celebrities or people who "occupy positions of such pervasive power and influence that they are deemed public figures for all purposes," and (2) individuals who have thrown themselves—usually voluntarily but sometimes involuntarily—into the middle of "a significant public controversy," such as a lawyer defending a prominent client, an advocate for an antismoking ordinance, a labor-union activist, or a security guard like Richard Jewell. Made famous by the news media, Jewell was initially suspected of setting off the pipe bomb that killed a woman at the 1996 Olympics in Atlanta. (After he was cleared by the FBI, NBC News and CNN settled libel cases with Jewell. His lawyers had charged that after news media reports named him as the only suspect, he could not find work, even though he was never charged with the crime.)

Defenses against Libel Charges. Since the 1730s, the best defense against libel in U.S. civil court has been the truth. In most cases, if libel defendants can demonstrate that they printed or broadcast statements that were essentially true, such evidence usually bars plaintiffs from recovering any damages—even if their reputations were harmed. To this end, the news media are particularly careful about using any direct quotes in which a source may have lied, employing legal staffs to check the veracity of controversial stories before publication. If a source, for instance, libels a private person in a news report, the paper may also be held accountable. Even if the reporter did not know the quote was false, he or she might be considered negligent for not checking the truthfulness of the statement more carefully.

Beyond the truth, there are other defenses against libel. Prosecutors, for example, receive *absolute privilege* in a court of law when they make potentially damaging statements about a defendant's reputation. When prosecutor Marcia Clark (who became an NBC cable news host after the trial) accused O.J. Simpson of being a murderer and he was later acquitted, she was protected from libel on the legal theory that in public courtrooms the interests of an individual are overridden by the larger common good of the legal process. The reporters who printed or broadcast her statement were also protected against libel. Entitled to conditional or **qualified privilege**, journalists are allowed to report judicial or legislative proceedings even though the public statements being reported may be libelous.

When police detectives, judges, or prosecutors make unsubstantiated claims about a defendant, or when legislators verbally attack each other during a session, reporters are allowed to report those incidents—even when potentially libelous statements are relayed secondhand by the reporter. As a condition for qualified privilege, the reporting of these public events must be fair and accurate. If a reporter, for instance, has prior knowledge that a public statement is untrue and still reports it as the truth, a judge may suspend qualified privilege and hold the reporter accountable for libel.

Another defense against libel concerns the area of *opinion and fair comment*. For example, after O.J. Simpson was acquitted of murder in October 1995, many legal commentators and talk-show hosts continued to suggest that, in their *opinion*, he was guilty of killing his ex-wife, Nicole Brown, and her friend, Ron Goldman. Generally, however, libel applies only to misstatements of factual information rather than opinion, although the line between fact and opinion is often hazy. Some libel cases turn on a plaintiff's ability to persuade a judge or jury that a defendant's statement was a factual error and not merely opinion or fair comment. For this reason, lawyers advise journalists to first set forth the facts on which a viewpoint is based and then to state their opinion based on those facts. In other words, journalists should make it clear that a statement is a criticism and *not* an allegation of fact. Libel laws protect satire, comedy, and opinions expressed in reviews of books, plays, movies, or restaurants. Such laws may not, however, protect malicious statements in which plaintiffs can prove that defendants used their free-speech rights to mount a damaging personal attack.

One of the most famous tests of opinion and fair comment came in a case pitting conservative minister and political activist Jerry Falwell against Larry Flynt, publisher of *Hustler* magazine. The case became the subject of a major Hollywood movie, *The People vs. Larry Flynt* (1996). The actual *Falwell v. Flynt* case developed after a November 1983 issue of *Hustler* made an outrageous reference to Falwell. In a spoof of a Campari vermouth ad, the magazine asked readers to recall the "first time" they drank Campari. The parody stated that Falwell needed to be drunk before he could preach; it also described his "first time" as an incestuous encounter with his own mother. In fine print at the bottom of the page, a disclaimer read: "Ad parody—not to be taken seriously."

Often a target of Flynt's irreverence and questionable taste, Falwell sued for libel, asking for $45 million in damages. In the verdict, the jury rejected the libel suit but found that Flynt had intentionally caused Falwell emotional distress, awarding

On Larry King's cable talk show in 1997, Moral Majority leader Rev. Jerry Falwell *(right)* discusses pornography and forgiveness with *Hustler* magazine publisher Larry Flynt *(center)*—their first face-to-face meeting since their 1984 libel trial.

him $200,000. It was an unprecedented verdict in American legal history. Flynt's lawyers appealed, and in 1988 the Supreme Court unanimously overturned the verdict. Although the Court did not condone the *Hustler* spoof, the justices did say that it was entitled to constitutional protection. The case drew enormous media attention and raised concerns about the erosion of the media's right to free speech. In affirming *Hustler*'s speech rights, the Court suggested that while parodies and insults of public figures might indeed cause emotional pain, denying the right to publish them would undermine a key democratic principle and violate the spirit of the First Amendment.[10] (In 1998 and 1999, Larry Flynt would use his resources and magazine to expose the sexual affairs of conservative congressmen who were involved in the Clinton impeachment proceedings.)

The Right of Privacy. Whereas libel laws safeguard a person's character and reputation, the right of privacy protects an individual's peace of mind and personal feelings. Any public figure who has ever been subjected to intense scrutiny by the media has experienced an invasion of privacy. When British actor Hugh Grant and a prostitute were arrested for public indecency in California in 1995, tabloid photographers and TV cameras kept constant vigil over the actor's every move until the event gradually lost its immediacy and allure. In general, the news media have been granted wide protections under the First Amendment to subject public figures to the spotlight. Local municipalities and states, however, have passed laws that protect most individuals from unwarranted surveillance. During her lifetime, for instance, Jacqueline Kennedy Onassis successfully sought court orders to keep photographers at a minimum distance, although the technology of powerful zoom lenses often overcame this obstacle.

Public figures have received some legal relief, but every year brings a few stories of a Hollywood actor or sports figure punching a tabloid photographer or TV cameraman who got too close. In 1998, a Santa Monica, California, court found two photographers guilty of false imprisonment for badgering NBC reporter Maria Shriver and her celebrity husband, actor Arnold Schwarzenegger. The photographers blocked the couple's car as they tried to drive their young son to school. Such cases, as well as Princess Diana's death in 1997—partly attributed to harassment by paparazzi—have spawned a flurry of legislation attempting to protect celebrities and public figures from invasions of privacy. Such anti-paparazzi laws include prohibition of trespassing or using electronic devices (such as zoom lenses on cameras), which can capture audio or video images of a celebrity or crime victim engaged in personal or family activity on private property or outside public forums. In some states, the American Civil Liberties Union (ACLU) has challenged these laws as an infringement of the First Amendment

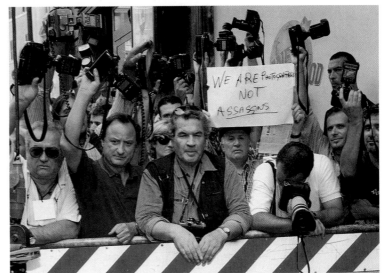

In the wake of Princess Diana's fatal car crash in 1997, paparazzi photographers were heavily criticized for their aggressive, often invasive tactics of capturing celebrity images. Although the direct cause of the accident was attributed to the drunk driver of Diana's car, critics agreed that the paparazzi contributed to the accident by recklessly chasing the car through Paris at high speeds.

rights of photographers and the news media. In 1999, the Supreme Court ruled that photographers and video news crews could not accompany police *inside* private property on authorized crime raids, such as a drug search, unless they received prior approval to enter the home or place of business from the occupants.

In the simplest terms, **invasion of privacy** addresses a person's right to be left alone, without his or her name, image, or daily activities becoming public property. Invasions of privacy occur in different situations, the most common of which are listed here.

1. intrusion, in which unauthorized tape recorders, wiretaps, microphones, or other surveillance equipment are used to secretly record a person's private affairs

2. the publication of private matters, such as the unauthorized disclosure of private statements about an individual's health, sexual activities, or economic status

3. the unauthorized appropriation of a person's name or image for advertising or other commercial benefit

As we have noted, the courts have generally given the news media a lot of leeway under the First Amendment. For instance, the names and pictures of both private individuals and public figures can usually be used without their consent in most news stories. If private citizens become part of public controversies and subsequent news stories, the courts have usually allowed the news media to record their quotes and use their images without the individuals' permission. In regard to these situations, the courts have generally argued that the greater public good served by news coverage outweighs the individuals' right to privacy. The courts have even ruled that accurate reports of criminal and court records, including the identification of rape victims, do not normally constitute privacy invasions. Nevertheless, most newspapers and broadcast outlets use their own internal guidelines and ethical codes to protect the privacy of victims and defendants, especially in cases involving rape and abused children.

Obscenity. Privacy and libel issues are part of civil or private law: individuals filing personal lawsuits against another individual or a media organization. Obscenity issues, though, are often guided by federal law and can be prosecuted as criminal offenses: a prosecutor making a case against a purveyor of obscene material on behalf of "the people."

For most of this nation's history, it has generally been argued that obscenity does not constitute a legitimate form of expression. The problem, however, is that little agreement has existed on how to define an obscene work. In the 1860s, a court could judge an entire book obscene if it contained a single passage believed capable of corrupting a person. In fact, throughout the 1800s certain government authorities outside the courts—especially U.S. post office and customs officials—held the power to censor or destroy written material they deemed obscene.

This began to change in the 1930s during the trial involving the celebrated novel *Ulysses* by Irish writer James Joyce. Portions of *Ulysses* had been serialized in the early 1920s in an American magazine, which was later seized and burned by postal officials. The publishers of the magazine, *Little Review*, were fined $50 and nearly sent to prison. Because of the four-letter words contained in the novel and the book-burning incident, British and American publishing houses backed away from the book, which was eventually published in Paris in 1922. In 1928, the U.S. Customs Office officially banned *Ulysses* as an obscene work. Ultimately, Random House agreed to publish the work in America only if it was declared "legal." Finally, in 1933, a U.S. judge ruled that *Ulysses* was an important literary work and removed it from unprotected status.

Battles over obscenity continued. In a key landmark case, *Roth v. United States,* the Supreme Court in 1957 offered this test of obscenity: whether to an "average person," applying "contemporary standards," the major thrust or theme of the material, "taken as a whole," appealed to "prurient interest" (in other words, was intended to "incite

> "I shall not today attempt to define [obscenity]. . . . And perhaps I never could succeed in intelligibly doing so. But I know it when I see it."
>
> —Supreme Court Justice Potter Stewart, 1964

lust"). By the 1960s, based on *Roth*, expression no longer constituted obscenity if only a small part of the work lacked "redeeming social value." Refining *Roth*, the current legal definition of **obscenity** derives from the 1973 *Miller v. California* case, which involved sanctions for using the mail to promote or send pornographic materials. After a series of appeals, the Supreme Court argued that an obscene work had to meet three criteria:

1. The average person, applying contemporary community standards, would find that the material as a whole appeals to prurient interest.

2. The material depicts or describes sexual conduct in a patently offensive way.

3. The material, as a whole, lacks serious literary, artistic, political, or scientific value.

Since this decision, courts have granted great latitude to printed and visual pornography. By the 1980s and 1990s, major cases prosecuting obscenity had become rare in the United States, as the legal system advanced the concept that a free society must tolerate even repulsive kinds of speech for democracy to work.

The *Miller* refinement of the *Roth* precedent contained two important ideas. First, it acknowledged that different communities and regions of the country have different values and standards; what is considered obscene in Fargo, North Dakota, for example, may not be judged obscene in Miami. The ruling sent various municipalities and states scrambling to develop lists of obscene acts and language that violated their communities' standards. (Some of these lists, when tested, were declared unconstitutional and had to undergo numerous revisions.) Second, the *Miller* decision also required that a work be judged *as a whole*. This removed a loophole in which some publishers would insert a political essay or literary poem to demonstrate in court that their publications contained redeeming features.

■first amendment vs. sixth amendment

Over the years, First Amendment protections of speech and the press have often clashed with the Sixth Amendment, which guarantees an accused individual in "all criminal prosecutions . . . the right to a speedy and public trial, by an impartial jury." In 1954, for example, the Sam Sheppard case, loosely the inspiration for the TV series *The Fugitive* and the subsequent 1994 film, involved enormous publicity. Featuring lurid details about the murder of Sheppard's wife, the Cleveland press editorialized in favor of Sheppard's quick arrest; some papers even pronounced him guilty. A prominent and wealthy osteopath, Sheppard was convicted of the murder. Twelve years later, though, Sheppard's new lawyer, F. Lee Bailey, argued before the Supreme Court that his client had not received a fair trial because of prejudicial publicity. The Court overturned the conviction and freed Sheppard.

Gag Orders and Shield Laws. One of the major criticisms of the O.J. Simpson criminal case in 1994–95 concerned the ways in which defense lawyers used the news media to comment publicly on court matters outside the presence of a sequestered jury. After the Sheppard reversal in the 1960s, the Supreme Court had suggested safeguards—some used in the Simpson case—that judges could employ to ensure a fair trial in a heavily publicized case. These included sequestering juries (Sheppard's jury was not sequestered), moving cases to other jurisdictions, limiting the number of reporters, seating reporters in a particular place in courtrooms, and placing restrictions, or **gag orders**, on lawyers and witnesses. Historically, gag orders have been issued to prohibit the press from releasing preliminary information that might prejudice jury selection. In most instances, however, especially since a Supreme Court review in 1976, gag rules have been struck down as a prior-restraint violation of the First Amendment.

In opposition to gag rules, **shield laws** have favored the First Amendment rights of reporters, protecting them from having to reveal their sources for controversial information used in news stories. The news media have argued that protecting the confidentiality of key sources maintains a reporter's credibility, protects a source from possible retaliation, and serves the public interest in that a source gives readers or viewers information they might not otherwise receive. In the 1960s and early 1970s, when the First Amendment rights of reporters clashed with Sixth Amendment fair-trial concerns, judges usually favored the Sixth Amendment arguments. In 1972, a New Jersey journalist became the first reporter jailed for contempt of court for refusing to identify sources in an investigative probe of the Newark housing authority. After this case, a number of legal measures were developed to protect the news media. By the 1990s, twenty-eight states had enacted some type of shield law, and many other states recognized the reporter's First Amendment rights not to divulge sources. In a few states, however, shield laws do not protect reporters who have been subpoenaed in grand-jury investigations. In the mid-1990s, for instance, a reporter from Warren, Ohio, was jailed for contempt of court after she refused to testify before a grand jury investigating a public official whom she had recently interviewed.

Cameras in the Courtroom. When Sam Sheppard was originally convicted in the 1950s, television news was in its infancy and did not play a major role in that trial. But by the mid-1990s, particularly during the Simpson criminal trial, TV cameras in the courtroom had become central to public discussions of our legal system. More and more judges and lawyers had come to believe that cameras made the judicial system more accountable and helped the public learn how U.S. law operated.

This view, however, took a long time to evolve. The debates over intrusive electronic broadcast equipment and photographers actually date to the sensationalized coverage of the Bruno Hauptmann trial in the mid-1930s. Convicted and executed for the kidnap-murder of the nineteen-month-old son of Anne and Charles Lindbergh (the aviation hero who made the first solo flight across the Atlantic Ocean in 1927), Hauptmann and his attorney had complained that the circus atmosphere fueled by the presence of radio and flash cameras prejudiced the jury and turned the public against him.

In 1935, the news media created a circus atmosphere at the trial of Bruno Hauptmann, the man eventually tried and executed for the kidnap-murder of the infant son of Anne and Charles Lindbergh. The behavior of radio reporters and photographers with flash cameras led to bans on electronic equipment in most courtrooms throughout much of the twentieth century.

After the trial, the American Bar Association amended a professional-ethics code, Canon 35, stating that electronic equipment in the courtroom detracted "from the essential dignity of the proceedings." Calling for a ban on photographers and radio equipment, the association believed that lawyers would begin playing to audiences and negatively alter the judicial process. For years after the Hauptmann trial, almost every state banned photographic, radio, and TV equipment from courtrooms.

As broadcast equipment became more portable and less obtrusive, however, and as television became the major news source for most Americans, courts gradually reevaluated their bans on broadcast equipment. In fact, in the early 1980s the Supreme Court ruled that the presence of TV equipment did not make it impossible for a fair trial to occur, leaving it up to each state to implement its own system. Today, most states allow television coverage of trials, leaving it up to the discretion of the judge. By 1999, only two states still banned coverage outright; others allowed the televising of civil but not criminal trials. In 1991, U.S. federal courts began allowing limited coverage of trials, although in 1999 the Supreme Court still banned TV and radio from its proceedings.

The judicial system got its very own national cable service when the Courtroom Television Network—Court TV—debuted in 1991. By the late 1990s, the channel was available in nearly thirty million homes, carrying both live and taped coverage of trials from around the United States. Anchored by experienced legal reporters, a prime-time lineup of programs developed on Court TV, including *Pros & Cons*, a daily wrap-up of key law-related news and court testimony from around the country. Similar to daytime talk shows, the channel focused intense public scrutiny on private family issues. In the trials of the Menendez brothers, for instance, juries had to decide whether children who had been physically and emotionally harmed by their parents could use such abuse as justification for murder. Although the first trial ended in a hung jury, the brothers were eventually convicted of murdering their parents during a second trial in 1996.

The Simpson criminal trial—the most publicized case in history—gave Court TV its greatest boost in 1994. The channel was picked to provide the one "pool" camera allowed at the trial, supplying all local news channels and the networks with the only footage from inside the courtroom. Before and during the criminal trial, a number of national discussions took place regarding the impact of the courtroom camera. Judge Lance Ito threatened to pull the plug on at least two occasions—once when the camera briefly panned across an alternate juror, and another time when he thought the camera had zoomed in too tightly on the defendant taking notes. (In Simpson's civil trial, which ended in 1997, the judge banned TV coverage.)

Critical analysis of the first Simpson trial continued long after the outcome. In retrospect, many legal analysts thought that the nine-month duration of the trial—the longest in California history—resulted from too many lawyers overacting for a national audience. Certainly, such intense focus on the case took attention away from other issues that the news media might have covered more fully had the trial not occurred. Still, televising the criminal trial contributed to the democratic process in at least two important ways. First, the Simpson criminal

> "Has TV done irreparable damage to the criminal justice system by laying claim to a **camera in the courtroom**? I doubt it. Has it made itself look foolish and unfeeling by turning a murder trial into TV's longest running entertainment special? I think so."
>
> —Don Hewitt,
> executive producer of
> *60 Minutes,* commenting
> on the first Simpson trial,
> 1995

Los Angeles defense attorney Johnnie Cochran, who led the legal team that got O.J. Simpson acquitted in his 1995–96 criminal case, became a national celebrity during the trial. He eventually got his own talk show on cable television.

trial gave many people their first sustained glimpse into the strengths and weaknesses of the U.S. legal system. Second, the TV trial focused national attention on the problems of spousal abuse, judicial reform, and racial tension, creating national debates on these issues that went on for months after the trial ended. To capitalize on these and other issues, Geraldo Rivera's program on CNBC focused on the successful civil suit later filed against Simpson by Ron Goldman's and Nicole Brown's families. To compete with Geraldo and Court TV, CNN also spun off a new legal show, *Burden of Proof*, starring two of its analysts from the criminal trial. In addition, Simpson's main criminal defense lawyer, Johnnie Cochran, began hosting a legal-political talk show—*Johnnie Cochran Tonight* (originally called *Cochran & Company*)—which premiered on Court TV in 1997.

The star-making allure of cable surfaced again during the Clinton impeachment hearings and subsequent trial. Covered round-the-clock by Court TV, MSNBC, CNBC, and Fox News, as well as by two C-Span channels, the Clinton affair gave many members of Congress, formerly unknown outside their own regions, a national platform. Throughout the hearings, there just didn't seem to be enough legislators—or law professors—to fill all the talk time on these cable channels. During the 1999 Senate trial, U.S. senators often started their day with TV appearances, conducted their business in the Senate, then spent their evenings once more making the cable rounds to discuss Clinton and the trial. As critics noted, one advantage of extending the trial was the free national TV publicity it afforded senators. But a few senators rejected the spotlight. Presidential candidate John McCain, a Republican from Arizona, said that as a sitting impeachment juror during the Clinton trial, it was irresponsible for him to discuss the trial on television.

Curbing the Law's Chilling Effect. As libel law and the growing acceptance of courtroom cameras indicate, the legal process has generally, though not always, tried to ensure that print and other news media are able to cover public issues broadly without fear of reprisals. Since the 1960s especially, legislators have sculpted laws that would not have a chilling effect on the news media, that would not curb their ability to actively pursue and report stories that are in the public interest. In a democracy, we expect journalists to act as watchdogs on public issues of vital importance. Such an expectation necessitates broad speech and press freedom. Because of this First Amendment freedom, as a society we occasionally tolerate pornography, hate speech, and other forms of expression that we may not support personally. We can, however, exercise our own free-speech rights and speak out against—or even boycott—language and expression that we find offensive, demeaning, or hateful.

film and the first amendment

When the First Amendment was ratified in 1791, even the most enlightened leaders of our nation could not have predicted the coming of visual media such as film and television. Consequently, new communication technologies have not always received the same kinds of protection granted to speech, pamphlets, newspapers, magazines, and books. For example, movies, in existence since the late 1890s, earned speech protection under the law only after a 1952 Supreme Court decision. In addition, broadcast stations, unlike newspapers or magazines, are licensed by the federal government and are subject to legislation that does not affect print media.

social and political pressure on the movies

During the early part of the twentieth century, movies rose in popularity among European immigrants and others from modest socioeconomic groups. This, in turn, spurred the formation of censorship groups, which believed that the popular new medium would threaten children, incite violence, and undermine morality. The number of nickelodeon theaters—often housed in ramshackle buildings—surged in 1905 and drew attention from public-health inspectors and city social workers. During this time, according to media historian Douglas Gomery, criticism of movies converged on four areas: "the effects on children, the potential health problems, the negative influences on morals and manners, and the lack of a proper role for educational and religious institutions in the development of movies."[11]

Film-Review Boards. Public pressure on movies came both from conservatives, who saw them as a potential threat to the authority of traditional institutions, and from progressives, who worried that children and adults were more attracted to movie houses than to social organizations and urban education centers. Afraid that movies created an illusory dreamworld, civic leaders publicly escalated their pressure, organizing local review boards that screened movies for their communities. In 1907, the Chicago City Council created an ordinance that gave the police authority to issue permits for a movie's exhibition. By 1920, more than ninety cities in the United States had some type of movie-censorship board made up of vice-squad officers, politicians, or citizen groups. By 1923, twenty-two states had established such boards.

Pressure began to translate into law as politicians, wanting to please their constituencies, began to legislate against films. Support mounted for a federal censorship bill. When Jack Johnson won the heavyweight championship in 1908, boxing films became the target of the first federal law aimed at the motion-picture industry. In 1912, the government outlawed the transportation of boxing movies across state lines. The laws against boxing films, however, had more to do with Johnson's race than with concern over violence in movies. The first black heavyweight champion, he was perceived as a threat to the white community.

Calvin and Hobbes   by Bill Watterson

The first Supreme Court decision regarding film's protection under the First Amendment was handed down in 1915 and went against the movie industry. In *Mutual v. Ohio*, the Mutual Film Company of Detroit sued the state of Ohio, whose review board had censored a number of the Michigan distributor's films. On appeal, the case arrived at the Supreme Court, which unanimously ruled that film was not a form of speech but "a business pure and simple" and, like a circus, merely a "spectacle" for entertainment with "a special capacity for evil." This ruling would stand for thirty-seven years. Although the U.S. movement to create a national censorship board failed, legislation to monitor and control movies, especially those from America, has passed in many other countries.

Industry Self-Regulation. As the film industry expanded after World War I, the impact of public pressure and review boards began to affect movie studios and executives who wanted to ensure control over their economic well-being. In the early 1920s, a series of scandals rocked Hollywood: actress Mary Pickford's divorce and quick marriage to actor Douglas Fairbanks; director William Desmond Taylor's unsolved murder; and actor Wallace Reid's death from a drug overdose. The most sensational scandal involved aspiring actress Virginia Rappe, who died a few days after a wild San Francisco hotel party hosted by popular silent-film comedian Fatty Arbuckle. After Rappe's death, the comedian was indicted for rape and manslaughter. After two hung juries, Arbuckle's career was ruined. Censorship boards across the country banned his films, even though he was acquitted at his third trial in 1922. Despite his exoneration, the movie industry tried to send a signal about the kind of values and lifestyles it would tolerate: Arbuckle was banned from acting in Hollywood. He later directed several films under the name Will B. Goode.

In response to the scandals, particularly the first Arbuckle trial, the movie industry formed the Motion Picture Producers and Distributors of America (MPPDA) and hired as its president Will Hays, former Postmaster General and Republican National Committee chair. Hays was paid $100,000 annually to clean up "sin city." Known as the Hays Office, the MPPDA attempted to smooth out problems between the public and the industry. Hays blacklisted promising actors or movie extras with even minor police records. Later, he developed an MPPDA public-relations division, which successfully lobbied against a movie censorship rule in Massachusetts and stopped a national movement for a federal law censoring movies.

the motion-picture
production code

During the 1930s, the movie business faced a new round of challenges. First, various conservative and religious groups—including the influential Catholic Legion of Decency—increased their scrutiny of the industry. Second, deteriorating economic conditions during the Depression forced the industry to tighten self-regulation to keep harmful public pressure at bay. In response, the Hays Office developed a list of "Don'ts and Be Carefuls" in 1927 to steer producers and directors away from questionable sexual, moral, and social themes. Nevertheless, pressure for a more formal and sweeping code mounted. In the early 1930s, the Hays Office established the Motion Picture Production Code, whose overseers officially stamped almost every Hollywood film with a moral seal of approval.

The code laid out its mission in its first general principle: "No picture shall be produced which will lower the moral standards of those who see it. Hence the sympathy of the audience shall never be thrown to the side of crime, wrong-doing, evil or sin." The self-regulatory code dictated how producers and directors should handle "methods of crime," "repellent subjects," "illegal drug traffic," and "sex hygiene." A section on profanity outlawed a long list of phrases and topics, including "toilet gags" and "traveling salesmen and farmer's daughter jokes." In the late 1930s, the producers of *Gone with the Wind* had to seek a special dispensation so that actor Clark Gable could say "damn." Under "scenes of passion," the code dictated that "excessive and lustful kissing, lustful embraces, suggestive postures and gestures are not to be shown," and the code

> "No approval by the Production Code Administration shall be given to **the use of . . . *damn* [or] *hell*** (excepting when the use of said last two words shall be essential and required for portrayal, in proper historical context, of any scene or dialogue based upon historical fact or folklore, or for the presentation in proper literary context of a Biblical, or other religious quotation, or a quotation from a literary work provided that no such use shall be permitted which is intrinsically objectionable or **offends good taste**)."
> —Motion Picture Production Code, 1934

required that "passion should be treated in such a manner as not to stimulate the lower and baser emotions." The section on religion revealed the influences of Jesuit priest Daniel Lord and Catholic publisher Martin Quigley, who helped write the code: "No film or episode may throw ridicule on any religious faith" and "ministers of religion . . . should not be used as comic characters or as villains."

Adopted by 95 percent of the industry, the code influenced nearly every commercial movie made between the mid-1930s and the early 1950s. It also gave the industry a relative degree of freedom, allowing the major studios to remain independent of outside regulation. When television arrived, however, competition from the new family medium forced movie producers to explore more adult subjects.

In 1952, the Supreme Court heard the *Miracle* case—officially *Burstyn v. Wilson*—named for the movie distributor who sued the head of the New York Film Licensing Board for banning Roberto Rossellini's film *Il Miracolo (The Miracle)*. A few New York City religious and political leaders considered the 1948 Italian film sacrilegious and pressured the film board for the ban. In the film, an unmarried peasant girl is impregnated by a scheming vagrant (played by Federico Fellini, who also wrote the story). In simple faith, she believes the tramp's story: He is St. Joseph and she has conceived the baby Jesus. The importers of the film argued that censoring it constituted illegal prior restraint; since such an action could not be imposed on a print version of the story, the same freedom should attach to the film. The Supreme Court eventually agreed, declaring movies "a significant medium for the communication of ideas." The decision granted films the same protections as the print media and other forms of speech. Even more important, the decision rendered most activities of film-review boards unconstitutional, since they had generally been engaged in prior restraint. Although a few local boards survived into the 1990s to handle complaints about movies that were considered obscene, most of them had disbanded by the 1970s.

rating movie content

The current voluntary movie rating system—the model for the advisory labels the music business and television now use—developed in the late 1960s after another round of pressure over movie content. *The Pawnbroker* in 1965, for instance, contained brief female nudity, and in 1966 *Who's Afraid of Virginia Woolf?* featured a level of profanity that had not been heard before in a major studio film. In 1966, the movie industry hired Jack Valenti to run the MPAA (Motion Picture Association of America, formerly the MPPDA), and in 1968 he established an industry board to rate movies.

Figure 16.1
The Voluntary Movie Rating System
Source: © 1996 Motion Picture Association of America, Inc.

What Everyone Should Know About The Movie Rating System.

GENERAL AUDIENCES
G G GENERAL AUDIENCES
Nothing that would offend parents for viewing by children.

PARENTAL GUIDANCE SUGGESTED
PG PG PARENTAL GUIDANCE SUGGESTED
Parents urged to give parental guidance. May contain some material parents might not like for their young children.

PARENTS STRONGLY CAUTIONED
PG-13 PG-13 PARENTS STRONGLY CAUTIONED
Parents are urged to be cautious. Some material may be inappropriate for pre-teenagers.

RESTRICTED
R R RESTRICTED
Contains some adult material. Parents are urged to learn more about the film before taking their young children with them.

NO ONE 17 AND UNDER ADMITTED
NC-17 NC-17 NO ONE 17 AND UNDER ADMITTED
Patently adult. Children are not admitted.

Eventually, G, PG, R, and X ratings emerged as guideposts for the suitability of films for various age groups. In 1984, PG–13 was added and sandwiched between PG and R to distinguish slightly higher levels of violence or adult themes in movies that might otherwise qualify as PG (see Figure 16.1).

The MPAA copyrighted all ratings designations as trademarks, except for the X rating, which was gradually appropriated as a promotional tool by the pornographic film industry. In fact, between 1972 and 1989, the MPAA stopped issuing the X rating. In 1990, however, based on protests from filmmakers over movies with adult sexual themes that they did not consider pornographic, the industry copyrighted the NC–17 rating—no children under age seventeen—and awarded the first NC–17 to *Henry & June*. In 1995, *Showgirls* became the first movie to intentionally seek an NC–17 to demonstrate that the rating was commercially viable. However, many theater chains in the mid-1990s refused to carry NC–17 movies, fearing economic sanctions and boycotts by their customers, religious groups, and other concerned citizens. Many newspapers also refused to carry ads for NC–17 films. Panned by the critics, *Showgirls* flopped at the box office. So far, the NC-17 rating has not proved commercially viable and distributors avoid releasing films with the rating. In 1999, director Stanley Kubrick reluctantly agreed to digitally alter graphic sexual scenes in *Eyes Wide Shut* to secure an R rating.

expression over the airwaves

During the Cold War, a vigorous campaign led by Joseph McCarthy, the ultraconservative senator from Wisconsin, tried to rid both government and the media of communist subversives who were allegedly challenging the American way of life. In 1950, a publication called *Red Channels: The Report of Communist Influence in Radio and Television* aimed "to show how the Communists have been able to carry out their plan of infiltration of the radio and television industry." *Red Channels*, inspired by McCarthy and produced by a group of former FBI agents, named 151 performers, writers, and musicians who were "sympathetic" to communist or "left-wing" causes. Among those named were Leonard Bernstein, Will Geer (who later played the grandfather on *The*

Waltons), Dashiell Hammett, Lillian Hellman, Lena Horne, Burgess Meredith, Arthur Miller, Dorothy Parker, Pete Seeger (the labor folksinger who in 1994 received a Kennedy Center Honors Award from President Clinton), Irwin Shaw, and Orson Welles. For a time, all were banned from working in television and radio even though no one on the list was ever charged with a crime.[12]

Although the First Amendment protects an individual's right to hold controversial political views, network executives either sympathized with the anticommunist movement or feared losing ad revenue. At any rate, the networks did not stand up to the communist witch-hunters. In order to work, a blacklisted or "suspected" performer required the support of the program's sponsor. Though *I Love Lucy*'s Lucille Ball, who in sympathy with her father once registered to vote as a communist in the 1930s, retained Philip Morris's sponsorship of her popular program, other performers were not as fortunate. Philip Loeb, who played the father on *The Goldbergs*, an early 1950s TV sitcom that came over from radio, found his name listed in *Red Channels.* Gertrude Berg, who owned and starred in the series, supported him. Nevertheless, boycott pressure on the program's sponsor, Sanka coffee, a General Foods brand, forced the company to abandon the program, which was dropped from CBS in 1951. After several months, it resurfaced on NBC, but Loeb had been replaced. Four years later, depressed and unable to find work, he committed suicide. Although no evidence was ever introduced to show how entertainment programs circulated communist propaganda, by the early 1950s the TV networks were asking actors and other workers to sign loyalty oaths denouncing communism—a low point for the First Amendment.

The communist witch-hunts demonstrated key differences between print and broadcast protection under the First Amendment—differences that are perhaps best illustrated in legal history. On the one hand, licenses for printers and publishers have been outlawed since the eighteenth century. On the other hand, in the late 1920s commercial broadcasters themselves asked the federal government to step in and regulate the airwaves. At that time, they wanted the government to clear up technical problems, channel noise, noncommercial competition, and amateur interference. Ever since, most broadcasters have been trying to free themselves from the government intrusion they once demanded.

fcc rules, broadcasting, and indecency

Drawing on the scarcity argument (that limited broadcast signals constitute a scarce national resource), the Communications Act of 1934 mandated in Section 309 that broadcasters operate in "the public interest, convenience, and/or necessity." Since the 1980s, however, with cable increasing channel capacity, station managers have lobbied for "ownership" of their airwave assignments. Although the 1996 Telecommunications Act did not grant such ownership, stations continue to challenge the "public interest" statute. They argue that since the government is not allowed to dictate content in newspapers, it should not be allowed to control licenses or mandate any broadcast programming.

Print vs. Broadcast Rules. Two cases—*Red Lion Broadcasting Co. v. FCC* (1969) and the *Miami Herald Publishing Co. v. Tornillo* (1974)—demonstrate the historic legal differences between broadcast and print. In the *Red Lion* decision, the operators of the small-town station in Red Lion, Pennsylvania, refused to give airtime to Fred Cook, author of a book that criticized Barry Goldwater, the Republican Party's presidential candidate in 1964. Cook had been criticized by a conservative radio preacher, the Reverend Billy James Hargis, and asked for response time from the two hundred stations that carried the Hargis attack. Most stations complied, granting Cook free reply time. But WGCB, the Red Lion station, offered only to sell Cook time. He appealed to the FCC, which ordered the station to give Cook free time. The station refused, claiming that its First Amendment rights granted it control over its program content. On appeal, the Supreme Court sided with the FCC, deciding that whenever a broadcaster's rights conflict with the public interest, it is the public interest that is paramount. In 1969, interpreting broadcasting as different from print, the Supreme Court upheld the constitutionality of the 1934 Communications Act by reaffirming that broadcasters' responsibilities to program in the public interest can outweigh their rights to program whatever they want.

In contrast, five years later, in *Miami Herald Publishing Co. v. Tornillo*, the Supreme Court sided with the newspaper in a case in which a political candidate, Pat Tornillo Jr., requested space to reply to an editorial opposing his candidacy. Previously, Florida had enacted a right-to-reply law, which permitted a candidate to respond, in print, to editorial criticisms from newspapers. Counter to the *Red Lion* decision, the Court in this case struck down the Florida state law as unconstitutional. The Court argued that mandating that a newspaper give a candidate space to reply violated the paper's First Amendment rights to publish what it chose to publish. The two decisions demonstrate that for most of the twentieth century the unlicensed print media received protections under the First Amendment that have not always been available to licensed broadcast media.

> **June 9, 1969** It is the right of the viewers and listeners, not the right of the broadcasters, which is paramount. . . .
> —Supreme Court decision in *Red Lion Broadcasting Co. v. FCC*, 395 U.S. 367

> **June 25, 1974** A responsible press is an undoubtedly desirable goal, but press responsibility is not mandated by the Constitution and like many other virtues it cannot be legislated.
> —Supreme Court decision in *Miami Herald Publishing Co. v. Tornillo*, 418 U.S. 241

Dirty Words and Indecent Speech. Although considered tame in a culture that now includes "shock jock" Howard Stern's lurid sexual programming, *topless radio* in the 1960s featured deejays and callers discussing intimate sexual subjects in the middle of the afternoon. The government curbed the practice in 1973, when the chairman of the FCC denounced topless radio as "a new breed of air pollution . . . with the suggestive, coaxing, pear-shaped tones of the smut-hustling host."[13] After an FCC investigation, a couple of stations lost their licenses, some were fined, and topless radio was checked temporarily. It reemerged in the 1980s, only with modern doctors and therapists—instead of deejays—offering intimate counsel over the airwaves.

In theory, communication law prevents the government from censoring broadcast content. Accordingly, the government may not interfere with programs or engage in prior restraint, although it may punish broadcasters after the fact. Over the years, a handful of radio stations have had their licenses suspended or denied after an unfavorable FCC review of past programming records. Concerns over indecent broadcast programming probably date from 1937. That year NBC was scolded by the FCC after

In the summer of 1972, comedian George Carlin was arrested by Milwaukee police after performing a routine about the seven words that could not be said on radio or television. The subject of a comedy monologue called "Filthy Words," Carlin's routine was later the centerpiece in a 1978 Supreme Court decision regarding a radio broadcast of the twelve-minute monologue. The Court upheld the FCC's authority to regulate indecent speech on the nation's airwaves.

running a sketch featuring comedian-actress Mae West on ventriloquist Edgar Bergen's network program. West had the following conversation with Bergen's famous wooden dummy, Charley McCarthy:

WEST: That's all right. I like a man that takes his time. Why don't you come home with me? I'll let you play in my woodpile . . . you're all wood and a yard long. . . .

CHARLEY: Oh, Mae, don't, don't . . . don't be so rough. To me love is peace and quiet.

WEST: That ain't love—that's sleep.[14]

After the sketch, West did not appear on radio for years. Ever since, the FCC has periodically fined or reprimanded stations for indecent programming, especially during times when children might be listening.

The current precedent for regulating radio indecency stems from one complaint to the FCC in 1973. In the middle of the afternoon, Pacifica's WBAI in New York aired George Carlin's famous comedy album about the seven dirty words that could not be uttered by broadcasters. A father, riding in a car with his fifteen-year-old son, heard the program and complained to the FCC, which sent WBAI a simple letter of reprimand. Although no fine was involved, the station appealed on principle and won its case in court. The FCC persisted, however, appealing all the way to the Supreme Court. Although no court has legally defined indecency, the Supreme Court's unexpected ruling in 1979 sided with the FCC and upheld the agency's authority to require broadcasters to air adult programming at later times. The Court ruled that so-called indecent programming, though not in violation of federal obscenity laws, was a nuisance (like a pig in a parlor, the Court said) and could be restricted to late-evening hours to protect children. The commission intended to ban indecent programs from most stations between 6 A.M. and 10 P.M. In 1990, the FCC tried to ban such programs entirely. Although a federal court ruled this move unconstitutional, it still upheld the time restrictions intended to protect children. This ruling lies at the heart of the indecency fines—totaling more than $1 million—that the FCC has leveled over the last several years against Howard Stern's syndicated morning program.

political broadcasts and equal opportunity

In addition to indecency rules, another law that the print media do not encounter is **Section 315** of the 1934 Communications Act, which mandates that during elections broadcast stations must provide equal opportunities and response time for qualified political candidates. In other words, if broadcasters give or sell time to one candidate, they must give or sell the same opportunity to others. Local broadcasters and networks have fought this law for years, since it has often required them to include poorly funded third-party candidates in political discussions. Broadcasters claim that since no Section

315–type rule applies to newspapers or magazines, the law violates their First Amendment right to control content. In fact, because of this rule, many stations have avoided all political programming. Ironically in these cases, a rule meant to serve the public interest by increasing communication backfired as stations decided to skirt the law.

The TV networks managed to get the law amended in 1959 to exempt newscasts, press conferences, and other events—such as political debates—that qualify as news. For instance, if a senator running for office appears in a news story, candidates running against him or her cannot invoke Section 315 and demand free time. Because of this provision, many stations from the late 1960s through the 1980s pulled TV movies starring Ronald Reagan. Since his film appearances did not count as bona fide news stories, candidates opposing Reagan could demand free time in markets that ran old Reagan movies. Supporters of the equal-opportunity law argue that it has provided forums for lesser-known candidates representing views counter to those of the Democratic and Republican parties. They further note that one of the few ways for alternative candidates to circulate their messages widely is to buy political ads, thus limiting serious outside contenders to wealthy candidates, such as Ross Perot, Steve Forbes, or members of the Bush or Kennedy families.

the demise of the fairness doctrine

Considered an important corollary to Section 315, the **Fairness Doctrine** was to controversial issues what Section 315 is to political speech. Initiated in 1949, this FCC rule required stations to air and engage in controversial-issue programs that affected their communities and, when offering such programming, to provide competing points of view. Antismoking activist John Banzhaf ingeniously invoked the Fairness Doctrine to force cigarette advertising off television in 1971. When the FCC mandated antismoking public-service announcements to counter "controversial" smoking commercials, tobacco companies decided to accept an outright ban rather than tolerate a flood of antismoking spots authorized by the Fairness Doctrine.

"There is no doubt about the unique impact of radio and television. But this fact alone does not justify government regulation. In fact, quite the contrary. We should recall that the printed press was the *only* medium of mass communication in the early days of the republic—and yet this did not deter our predecessors from passing the First Amendment to prohibit abridgement of its freedoms."

—Chief Judge David Bazelon, U.S. court of appeals, 1972

With little public debate, the Fairness Doctrine ended in 1987 after a federal court ruled that it was merely a regulation rather than an extension of Section 315 law. Over the years, broadcasters had argued that the doctrine forced many of them to play down controversial issues; they claimed that mandating opposing views every time a program covered a controversial issue was a burden not required of the print media. Since 1987, there has been periodic interest in reviving the Fairness Doctrine. Its supporters argue that broadcasting is fundamentally different from—and more pervasive than—the print media, requiring greater accountability to the public. Although many broadcasters disagree, supporters of fairness rules insist that as long as broadcasters are licensed as public trustees of the airwaves—unlike newspaper or magazine publishers—legal precedent permits the courts and the FCC to demand responsible content and behavior from radio and TV stations.

By the mid-1990s, broadcast and cable operators were increasingly demanding the same First Amendment rights as the print media. This pressure, combined with a growing belief that a free market can solve most economic problems, allowed a relaxation of the rules governing broadcasting and cable. Still, public concerns about visual violence and children's programming kept regulatory issues prominent during the presidential campaigns of 1992 and 1996. But questions about the negative impact of concentrated media ownership rarely surfaced. In fact, in mainstream media they were raised most frequently by fringe conservative candidate and TV pundit Pat Buchanan.

Should deregulation accelerate, however, the remaining public and noncommercial broadcast outlets are at risk. For example, Jesse Ventura, newly elected Reform Party governor of Minnesota, made eliminating government funding of public radio and television a priority for his state in 1999. Public broadcasting already faced severe revenue cutbacks in the mid-1990s, so more deregulation of the communications industry might cause a recurrence of the problems of the late 1920s and early 1930s. As we noted in Chapter 4, the Depression crippled noncommercial broadcasters because many of them were forced to sell or transfer their licenses to commercial interests. Although Congress in 1996 mandated that the broadcast networks carry three hours of educational programs a week, public radio and television still offer the bulk of programming that is not commercially viable.

cyberspace, expression, and democracy

Although the United States has tolerated a wide variety of speech and expression, critics charge that such tolerance has generally favored corporate interests and media industries. For example, it is far easier for large corporations and advertisers like Disney or General Motors to buy commercial speech than it is for small grassroots organizations that have important messages but limited finances. As a result, messages that counter mainstream culture might appear only in alternative magazines or on cable-access channels, where entry is cheap but audience reach is limited.

communication policy in cyberspace

Another arena that increases the voices—and noise—circulating in culture is the Internet. Its current global expansion is comparable to the early days of broadcasting, when economic and technological growth outstripped law and regulation. At that time, noncommercial experiments by amateurs and engineering students provided a testing ground that commercial interests later exploited for profit. Indeed, before the Radio Act of 1927, many noncommercial groups experimented extensively with the possibilities of the new broadcast medium.

In much the same way, "amateurs," students, and various interest groups have explored and extended the communication possibilities of the Internet. They have experimented so successfully that commercial vendors are now racing to buy up pieces of the information highway. Like radio in the 1920s, the Internet's noncommercial developers in the 1990s have been selling off services to commercial entrepreneurs. This is especially true of university consortiums, which had been running most of the regional Internet services. Like radio, experimenting and risk-taking took place at the noncommercial level before

"One of the most striking paradoxes of Internet culture is that children are the most computer literate among us, but their vulnerability to on-line predators prevents their being able to enjoy or explore freely what is likely to be the defining medium of their lives."
—Denise Caruso, *New York Times,* 1998

commercial adventurers stepped in to explore and exploit the profit possibilities.

The last serious widespread public debate on mass-media ownership occurred in the early 1930s and ended with the passage of the 1934 Communications Act and the defeat of the Wagner-Hatfield Amendment (which would have reserved 25 percent of the broadcast spectrum for noncommercial radio). In recent years, public conversations about the Internet have not typically been about ownership questions. Instead, the debates—often triggered by the news media—have focused on First Amendment issues such as civility and pornography in cyberspace. Reporters, in fact, tend to view Internet issues as entrepreneurial business stories ("What company is marketing the next software breakthrough?") with free-speech implications ("Who is using the high-way for pornographic purposes?"). Not unlike the public's concern over television's sexual and violent images, the scrutiny of the Internet is mainly about harmful images and information in cyberspace, not about who controls it and for what purposes.

In 1995, for example, a male University of Michigan student was arrested and dismissed from school for creating a violent pornographic cyberspace story in which he named and fantasized about a female student. This incident received widespread news coverage. As the federal court case against the student evolved, it became clear that few existing laws applied to speech in cyberspace. Federal attorneys eventually dropped the case against the student as Congress frantically hurried to extend existing obscenity and speech prohibitions to the Internet in the Telecommunications Act of 1996. However, this part of the new act was quickly judged unconstitutional. During this time, little public discussion has taken place over ownership of the Internet, even though control over its hub sites gradually began to pass from the public domain to private entrepreneurs.

As we watch the rapid expansion of the Internet worldwide, an important question confronts us: Will the Internet continue to develop democratically rather than hierarchically, evading government or corporate plans to contain it, change it, and closely monitor who has access? In the early days of broadcasting, commercial inter-

Since 1982, the Canadian Committee to Protect Journalists has operated IFEX, the International Freedom of Expression Exchange, which is based in Toronto. With more than twenty member organizations worldwide, IFEX has documented in print and on its Web site an average of two thousand attacks on free expression each year.

ests became dominant partly because the companies running radio (like the Hearst Corporation, which also owned chains of newspapers and magazines) did not report on ownership questions as serious news stories. It was not in their economic interest to do so. Today, once again, it has not been in the news media's economic interest to organize or lead the ownership debate; the major print and broadcast owners, after all, are heavily invested in the Internet.

Critics and observers hope that a vigorous debate develops on new communication technologies—a debate that goes beyond First Amendment issues. The promise of the Internet as a democratic forum—adding millions of new users each month—encourages the formation of all sorts of regional, national, and global interest groups. Whether such cyber communities could eventually help to frame and solve society-level problems remains at issue.

A positive sign is that global movements abound that use the Internet to fight political forms of censorship. The Digital Freedom Network, for example, circulates material that has been banned in certain countries, including excerpts from dissident Chinese writer Wei Jingsheng and Indonesian novelist Pramoedya Ananta Toer. In another instance, the International Freedom of Expression Exchange (IFEX)—a Toronto-based clearinghouse that documents nearly two thousand international press-freedom violations each year—relayed the 1994 story of a journalist from the former Yugoslavia who had been jailed in Serbia. IFEX (www.ifex.org) sent notices to its members by email; within days, Serbian officials, inundated with faxes and calls, released the reporter. In this example, the digital highway works as a global freeway—a democratic communication "weapon," bypassing both government bans and political restrictions. By 1999, more than twenty organizations around the world had joined the IFEX network, which has been operated since 1992 by Canadian Journalists for Free Expression (formerly the Canadian Committee to Protect Journalists). Just as fax machines, satellites, and home videos helped to document and expedite the fall of totalitarian regimes in Eastern Europe in the late 1980s, Internet services help to spread the word and activate social change today.

▮watchdog citizens

For most of our nation's history, citizens have counted on journalism to monitor abuses in government and business. During the muckraking period in the early part of the twentieth century, writers like Ida Tarbell, Upton Sinclair, and Sinclair Lewis made strong contributions in reporting corporate expansion and social change. Unfortunately, however, stories on business issues today have usually been reduced to consumer-affairs reporting. In other words, when a labor strike or a factory recall is covered, the story mainly tries to answer the question "How do these events affect consumers?" Although this is an important news angle, other questions remain: "How does the strike affect the families and future of workers and managers?" and "What is the role of unions and manufacturing industries as we move into the twenty-first century?" At this point, citizen discussions about media ownership or labor-management ethics are not part of the news frame that journalists typically use. When companies announce mergers, reporters do not routinely question the economic wisdom or social impact of such changes. Instead, they tend to tell stories about how individual consumers will be affected.

At one level, journalists have been compromised by the frenzy of media mergers involving newspapers and TV stations (see "Examining Ethics: How ABC News Covers Disney" on page 514). As Bill Kovach, curator of Harvard's Nieman Foundation for Journalism, pointed out

"For the past decade and a half, journalism has been slowly squeezed into a smaller and smaller corner of the expanding corporations that make up the communications industry."
—Bill Kovach, Nieman Foundation, 1995

In an NPR interview late in 1998, Disney CEO Michael Eisner told the radio interviewer, "I would prefer ABC not to cover Disney. I think it's inappropriate for Disney to be covered by Disney." Since Disney bought one of the world's leading news organizations in the mid-1990s, ABC News has faced the challenge of covering a prominent global power that is also its employer. Less than a week after it joined the Disney stable, ABC's evening-news broadcast, anchored by Peter Jennings, featured a flattering profile of its new owner. Then, late in 1998, the new national media criticism magazine, *Brill's Content*, charged that Disney executives may have helped kill an ABC news story that was critical of its boss.

The Disney story was not unlike the challenge *Time* magazine faces when it has to do stories on its corporate owner, Time Warner, yet another global media powerhouse. In June 1995, shortly after former senator Bob Dole criticized Hollywood and Time Warner, *Time* magazine itself criticized its parent company in a fourteen-page cover story entitled "Are Music and Movies Killing America's Soul?" Three months later, Time Warner decided to sell its share of a major gangsta-rap label. This incident contrasted sharply with another *Time* decision under a different editor in 1989. When Time Inc. and Warner Communication announced their plan to join forces—the largest media merger in history at the time—the editor of *Time* decided not to cover the story.

A troubling aspect of the *Brill's Content* story was the silence and "no comments" the magazine elicited when its editors asked this speculative question of twenty-one ABC reporters, editors, and producers: "Would you be comfortable continuing to work at ABC News if [a reporter's story] about Disney was killed because of Disney's connection with the story?" Hugh Downs, the *20/20* coanchor, said, "There's nothing I know at this point that cuts across the integrity of ABC news, which Disney promised not to interfere with. . . ." And ABC commentator Cokie Roberts added, "I'd have to know a lot more about it. One of the things about being

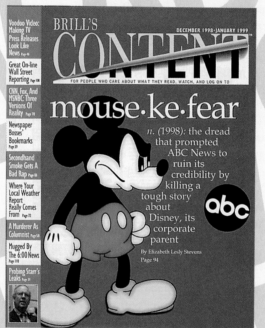

fifty-four is that very seldom are things black and white." Other prominent ABC journalists—including Barbara Walters, Diane Sawyer, Peter Jennings, Chris Wallace, Ted Koppel, and Sam Donaldson—refused to be interviewed.

So why are some of the nation's leading journalistic authorities, who have so much to say on their evening appearances on cable news and on the Sunday-morning network programs, wary of the *Brill's* question? In today's world, where increasingly a handful of large companies dominate the production and distribution of the world's media fare, these incidents raise serious concerns about the relationship of national news media to their behemoth parent companies. Media business stories have always made the news media nervous. Modern journalism has taught reporters and editors to focus on facts "out there" in the world. So when the story becomes the business of journalism's "inside" world, some news media and their editors balk. The rules of a neutral, detached press do not prepare most journalists well when they have to turn the lens on themselves. Many look away—and Disney's Eisner encourages such behavior.

The Disney dilemma and its employees' chilling silence raise important questions for our democracy. Do we have the right to know the inner workings of our large media conglomerates? With media companies becoming increasingly larger, how should CBS News cover its parent company, Westinghouse? How will NBC News continue to cover its owner, General Electric? And should the staff of ABC News seriously heed their boss and look the other way when the Disney media juggernaut makes a mistake?

In such a media world, we are at the mercy of news media that may determine it is not in their best interest to reveal the inside workings of their parent companies—although such revelations may be in the nation's best interest. The relationship between national news media and their multinational owners raises this key question: Who's watching the watchdog?

after the Disney-ABC and Westinghouse-CBS mergers, "This rush to merge mainly entertainment organizations that have news operations with companies deeply involved in doing business with the government raises ominous questions about the future of watchdog journalism."[15] In other words, how can journalists adequately cover and lead discussions on issues of media ownership when the very companies they work for are the prime buyers and sellers of major news-media outlets?

With the news media increasingly compromised by their complex relations to their corporations, it becomes important that the civic role of watchdog be shared by citizens as well as journalists. After all, the First Amendment protects not only the news media's free-speech rights but the rights of all of us to speak out. Mounting concerns over who can afford access to the media go to the heart of *free* expression.

As we struggle to determine the future of converging print, electronic, and digital media and to broaden the democratic spirit underlying media technology, we need to stay engaged in spirited public debates about media ownership and control, about the differences between commercial speech and free expression. As citizens, we need to pay attention to who is included and excluded from the opportunities not only to buy products but to speak out and shape the cultural landscape. To accomplish this, we need to challenge our journalists and our leaders. More important, we need to challenge ourselves to become watchdogs—critical consumers and engaged citizens— who learn from the past, care about the present, and map mass media's future.

REVIEW QUESTIONS

The Origins of Free Expression and a Free Press

1. What is the basic philosophical concept that underlies America's notion of free expression?

2. Explain the various models of the news media that exist under different political systems.

3. How has censorship been defined historically?

4. What is the significance of the Pentagon Papers and the *Progressive* magazine cases?

5. Why is the case of *New York Times v. Sullivan* so significant in First Amendment history?

6. What does a public figure have to do to win a libel case? What are the main defenses that a newspaper can use to thwart a charge of libel?

7. What is the legal significance of the *Falwell v. Flynt* case?

8. How does a court determine, in a legal sense, whether a magazine article constitutes obscenity?

Film and the First Amendment

9. Why were films not constitutionally protected as a form of speech until 1952?

10. Why did film-review boards develop, and why did they eventually disband?

11. How did both the Motion Picture Production Code and the current movie rating system come into being?

Expression over the Airwaves

12. The government and the courts view print and broadcasting as different forms of expression. What are the major differences?

13. What is the significance of Section 315 of the Communications Act of 1934?

14. Why didn't broadcasters like the Fairness Doctrine?

Cyberspace, Expression, and Democracy

15. What are the similarities and differences between the debates over broadcast ownership in the 1920s and Internet ownership in the 1990s?

16. Why is the Internet a potentially more democratic form than broadcasting?

1. Have you ever had an experience in which you thought personal or public expression went too far and should be curbed? Explain. How might you remedy this situation?

2. If you owned a community newspaper and had to formulate a policy for your editors about which letters from readers appear in a limited space on your editorial page, what kinds of letters would you eliminate and why? Are you acting as a censor in this situation? Why or why not?

3. The writer A. J. Liebling once said that freedom of the press belonged only to those who owned one. Explain why you agree or disagree.

4. What do you think of the movie rating system the industry now uses? Should it be changed? Why or why not?

5. Should the Fairness Doctrine be revived? Why or why not?

http://www.freedomforum.org
The Freedom Forum deals with all First Amendment issues, including religion, free press, free speech, assembly, and technology. It also includes original articles as well as stories from the Associated Press.

http://www.oneworld.org
The Index on Censorship produces a bimonthly magazine, much of which is available online. It contains articles, reports, and interviews from all over the world, showing how free speech affects political issues.

http://www.freeexpression.org
The Free Expression Network is a national coalition of organizations and individuals united in the belief that free expression is the indispensable precondition of liberty.

http://www.humanrights.dk
The Danish Center for Human Rights conducts research and provides information, education, and documentation relating to Danish, European, and international human-rights conditions.

http://www.ericnuzum.com/banned
Eric Nuzum maintains this site, which documents banned and censored (or otherwise altered) music beginning in the 1940s and keeps track of current music-censorship issues.

In Brief

As the owner of a community newspaper, what would be your policy on accepting advertising for pornographic movie theaters and movies rated NC–17? Justify whatever policy you develop.

In Depth

The purpose of this exercise is to examine free-speech and press issues. These two assignments can be developed either as group projects in class or as individual writing projects—or both.

1. Do some research on a major obscenity case that is not discussed in the chapter. Ask your instructor for some suggestions, or consult the Internet or computer database services such as LEXIS (legal cases) or NEXIS (news stories) for ideas. Write a summary of the case and be prepared to discuss it in class.

   As part of your project, obtain a copy of a local or state obscenity ordinance. Do you think the ordinance would be considered constitutional in a Supreme Court test? Why or why not?

2. Do some research on a major libel case involving the news media, other than *New York Times v. Sullivan*. Ask your instructor for suggestions or consult the Internet or computer database services such as those listed in the preceding assignment. Write a summary of the case and be ready to talk about what you learned.

   Discuss whether you think libel laws give too much or too little protection to the news media. Do you think public figures, especially Hollywood celebrities, deserve more protection than libel laws currently allow? Why or why not?

NOTES

CHAPTER 1

1. Neil Postman, *Amusing Ourselves to Death: Public Discourse in the Age of Show Business* (New York: Penguin Books, 1984), 19.
2. James W. Carey, *Communication as Culture: Essays on Media and Society* (Boston: Unwin Hyman, 1989), 203.
3. Postman, *Amusing Ourselves to Death*, 65. See also Elizabeth Eisenstein, *The Printing Press as an Agent of Change*, 2 vols. (Cambridge, England: Cambridge University Press, 1979).
4. See Plato, *The Republic*, Book II, 377B.
5. For a historical discussion of culture, see Lawrence Levine, *Highbrow/Lowbrow: The Emergence of Cultural Hierarchy in America* (Cambridge: Harvard University Press, 1988).
6. For an example of this critical position, see Allan Bloom, *The Closing of the American Mind: How Higher Education Has Failed Democracy and Impoverished the Souls of Today's Students* (New York: Simon & Schuster, 1987).
7. For overviews of this position, see Postman, *Amusing Ourselves to Death*; and Stuart Ewen, *Captains of Consciousness: Advertising and the Social Roots of the Consumer Culture* (New York: McGraw-Hill, 1976).
8. See Carey, *Communication as Culture*.
9. For more on this idea, see Cecelia Tichi, *Electronic Hearth: Creating an American Television Culture* (New York: Oxford University Press, 1991), 187–188.
10. See Jon Katz, "Rock, Rap and Movies Bring You the News," *Rolling Stone*, March 5, 1992, 33.

Examining Ethics: Trash, Teens, and TV Talk Shows, pp. 14–15

1. For reference and guidance on media ethics, see Clifford Christians, Mark Fackler, and Kim Rotzoll, *Media Ethics: Cases & Moral Reasoning*, 4th ed. (White Plains, NY: Longman, 1995); and Thomas H. Bivins, "A Worksheet for Ethics Instruction and Exercises in Reason," *Journalism Educator* (summer 1993): 4–16.

Case Study: The Material Girl as Postmodern Icon, pp. 24–25

1. Luc Sante, "Unlike a Virgin," *The New Republic* (August 20 and 27, 1990), 25–29.
2. Camille Paglia, quoted in Joseph Sobran, "Sign of the Crotch: Sex and the Single Girl," *National Review* (August 12, 1991), 32.
3. Michael McWilliams, "Why the Rock World Hates Madonna," *Detroit News* (April 21, 1990), p. C1.
4. Bell Hooks, "Madonna: Plantation Mistress or Soul Sister?" in *Black Looks: Race and Representation* (Boston: South End Press, 1992), 157–58.

Global Village: Bedouins, Camels, Transistors, and Coke, p. 30

1. Vaclav Havel, "A Time for Transcendence," *Utne Reader* (January/February 1995), 53.
2. Dan Rather, "The Threat to Foreign News," *Newsweek* (July 17, 1989), 9.

CHAPTER 2

1. Daniel Burstein and David Kline, *Road Warriors: Dreams and Nightmares along the Information Highway* (New York: Dutton, 1995), 8.
2. Ibid., 105.
3. Cheri Paquet, "Report Counts 147 Million Global Net Users," February 12, 1999.
4. Burstein and Kline, *Road Warriors*, 101–130.
5. Nicholas Negroponte, *Being Digital* (New York: Alfred A. Knopf, 1995), 23.
6. Hobbes's Internet Timeline. <www.isoc.org/guest/zakon/Internet/History/HIT.html>, (October 4, 1998).
7. Noah Robinson, "Browser Beware," *Brill's Content*, July/August 1998, 40–44.
8. Amy Harmon, "Researchers Find Sad, Lonely World in Cyberspace," *New York Times*, August 30, 1998, sec. 1, p. 1.
9. Denise Caruso, "Technology: Critics Are Picking Apart a Professor's Study That Linked Internet Use to Loneliness and Depression," *New York Times*, September 14, 1998, p. C5.
10. Burstein and Kline, *Road Warriors*, 104.
11. Amy Harmon, "'Hacktivists' of All Persuasions Take Their Struggle to the Web," *New York Times*, October 31, 1998, p. A1.
12. Amy Harmon, "The Rebel Code," *New York Times Magazine*, February 21, 1999, pp. 34–37.
13. William Raspberry, "Rumornet," *Washington Post*, February 5, 1999, p. A33.
14. See Urban Legends and Folklore, <http://urbanlegends.about.com/>.
15. Burstein and Kline, *Road Warriors*, 106–107.
16. Marc Gunther, "What's Your Stake in It All: Information Highway Looks Like a Rough Road," *Detroit Free Press*, November 18, 1993, p. D1.
17. Douglas Gomery, "In Search of the Cybermarket," *Wilson Quarterly* (summer 1994): 10.
18. Burstein and Kline, *Road Warriors*, 20.
19. See the *New York Times*'s seven-part series "The Downsizing of America," March 3–10, 1996. These articles and related discussion forums are available on both the *Times*'s

World Wide Web site <http://www.nytimes.com/downsize> and the AOL commercial service <@times>.

20. See "Cable Television over the Net," 1995 Fall Supplement to *Cable Television Developments* (Washington, D.C.: NCTA, 1995).

21. Matt Richtel and Declan McCullagh, "Yes, It Really Is a World Wide Web," *Yahoo! Internet Life*, September 1998, 94–96.

22. Howard W. French, "In Africa, Reality of Technology Falls Short," *New York Times*, January 26, 1998, pp. 1, 10.

23. Associated Press, "Study Says 70 Million American Adults Use the Internet," *New York Times*, August 26, 1998.

Case Study: E-commerce: Sale of the Century?, pp. 42–43

1. Tina Kelley, "Internet Shopping: A Mixed Bag," *New York Times*, July 30, 1998, pp. D1, D5.

Tracking Technology: WebCams: The Whole World Is Watching, p. 51

1. Brett Lieberman, "Truman, Meet JenniCam: Millions Check Out Web Site to See Round-the-Clock Photos of Her Life," *Cleveland Plain Dealer*, June 11, 1998, p. 6E.

CHAPTER 3

1. See Fred Schruers, "Sheryl: She Only Wants to Be with You," *Rolling Stone*, November 14, 1996, 64–71.

2. Thomas Edison, quoted in Marshall McLuhan, *Understanding Media* (New York: McGraw-Hill, 1964), 276.

3. See Bruce Tucker, "'Tell Tchaikovsky the News': Postmodernism, Popular Culture and the Emergence of Rock-'n'Roll," *Black Music Research Journal* 9, no. 2 (fall 1989): 280.

4. LeRoi Jones, *Blues People* (New York: Morrow Quill, 1963), 168.

5. See Mike Jagger, quoted in Jann S. Wenner, "Jagger Remembers," *Rolling Stone*, December 14, 1995, 66.

6. See Mac Rebennack (Dr. John) with Jack Rummel, *Under a Hoodoo Moon* (New York: St. Martin's Press, 1994), 58.

7. Little Richard, quoted in Charles White, *The Life and Times of Little Richard: The Quasar of Rock* (New York: Harmony Books, 1984), 65–66.

8. Quoted in Dave Marsh and James Bernard, *The New Book of Rock Lists* (New York: Fireside, 1994), 15.

9. B. Tucker, "'Tell Tchaikovsky the News,'" 287.

10. Ed Ward, in Ward, Geoffrey Stokes, and Ken Tucker, *Rock of Ages: The Rolling Stone History of Rock & Roll* (New York: Rolling Stone Press, 1986), 89.

11. Stuart Goldman, "That Old Devil Music," *National Review*, February 24, 1989, 29.

12. See Gerri Hershey, *Nowhere to Run: The Story of Soul Music* (New York: Penguin Books, 1984).

13. See Robert Palmer, *Deep Blues* (New York: Penguin Books, 1981), 8.

14. See Karen Schoemer, "Rockers, Models and the New Allure of Heroin," *Newsweek*, August 26, 1996, 50–54.

15. K. Tucker, in Ward, Stokes, and Tucker, *Rock of Ages*, 521.

16. Ibid., 560.

17. Stephen Thomas Erlewine, "Nirvana," in *All Music Guide: The Best CDs, Albums, & Tapes*, 2nd ed., Michael Erlewine, ed. (San Francisco: Miller Freeman Books, 1994), 233.

18. See Mikal Gilmore, "Puff Daddy," *Rolling Stone*, August 7, 1997, 50–56, 70–72.

19. Ronin Ro, *The Spectacular Rise and Violent Fall of Death Row Records* (New York: Doubleday, 1998).

20. Sonia Murray, "RAP'S B.I.G. CHANGE." *The Atlanta Journal and Constitution*, March 8, 1998, Arts, p. 1.

21. See Anita M. Samuels and Diana B. Henriques, "Going Broke and Cutting Loose," *New York Times*, February 5, 1996, pp. C1, C6.

22. See Richie Unterberger, "Bootleg Overview," in M. Erlewine, ed., *All Music Guide*, 1381.

23. Nat Hentoff, "Many Dreams Fueled Long Development of U.S. Music," *Milwaukee Journal*/United Press International, February 26, 1978, p. 2.

CHAPTER 4

1. Tom Lewis, *Empire of the Air: The Men Who Made Radio* (New York: HarperCollins, 1991), 181.

2. Ibid., 32.

3. Ibid., 73.

4. For a full discussion of early broadcast history and the formation of RCA, see Eric Barnouw, *Tube of Plenty* (New York: Oxford University Press, 1982); Susan Douglas, *Inventing American Broadcasting 1899–1922* (Baltimore: Johns Hopkins University Press, 1987); and Christopher Sterling and John Kitross, *Stay Tuned: A Concise History of American Broadcasting* (Belmont, CA: Wadsworth, 1990).

5. Harry P. Davis, quoted in Mitchell Stephens, *History of the News: From the Drum to the Satellite* (New York: Viking, 1988), 276.

6. Lowell Thomas, quoted in Lawrence Lichty and Malachi Topping, *American Broadcasting: A Source Book on the History of Radio and Television* (New York: Hastings House, 1975), 229.

7. Neil Strauss, "Play-for-Play on the Air but This Rendition Is Legal," *New York Times*, March 31, 1998, pp. A1, A21.

8. Neil Strauss, "Birth and Rebirth on the Airwaves," *New York Times*, July 21, 1996, pp. 26–27.

9. See Ed Ward, Geoffrey Stokes, and Ken Tucker, *Rock of Ages: The Rolling Stone History of Rock & Roll* (New York: Rolling Stone Press, 1986), 484.

10. See Gustav Nierburh, "Number of Religious Broadcasters Continues to Grow," *New York Times*, February 12, 1996, p. C7.

11. Dara Colwell, "Dunifer Vows to Continue His Fight," *Radio World*, September 2, 1998. See also Paul Davidson, "Radio Pirates Urge FCC to End Crackdown," *USA Today*, October 5, 1998, p. 2B.

12. Ed Shane, "The State of the Industry: Radio's Shifting Paradigm," *Journal of Radio Studies* 5 (2): 1–7 (1998).

13. Anthony DeBarrow, "Amid Consolidation, Fear of Less Diversity, Choice," *USA Today*, July 7, 1998, pp. A1, A2.

14. Christopher Parkes, "Mixed-Media Companies Fill the Space," *Financial Times*, (London) October 9, 1998, p. 24.

Examining Ethics: NPR and Support for Noncommercial Radio, p. 113

1. See the foreword in Linda Wertheimer, ed., *Listening to America: Twenty-Five Years in the Life of a Nation, as heard on National Public Radio* (Boston: Houghton Mifflin, 1995).

2. For a detailed discussion, see Robert McChesney, *Telecommunications, Mass Media & Democracy: The Battle for Control of U.S. Broadcasting, 1928–1935* (New York: Oxford University Press, 1993).

CHAPTER 5

1. Charles McGrath, "It Just Looks Paranoid," *New York Times Magazine*, June 14, 1998, p. 56.

2. See Elizabeth Kolbert, "Americans Despair of Popular Culture," *New York Times*, August 20, 1995, sec. 2, pp. 1, 23.

3. J. Fred MacDonald, *One Nation under Television: The Rise and Decline of Network TV* (Chicago: Nelson-Hall Publishers, 1994), 132.

4. Ibid., 70.

5. Edgar Bergen, quoted in MacDonald, *One Nation under Television*, 78.

6. See Horace Newcomb, *TV: The Most Popular Art* (Garden City, NY: Anchor Books, 1974), 31, 39.

7. Ibid., 35.

8. Paddy Cheyevsky, quoted in Eric Barnouw, *Tube of Plenty: The Evolution of American Television*, rev. ed. (New York: Oxford University Press, 1982), 163.

9. Barnouw, *Tube of Plenty*, 163.

10. Ibid., 163.

11. MacDonald, *One Nation under Television*, 181.

12. See Bill Carter, "Cadillac-Sized Hits by the VW of Producers," *New York Times*, January 22, 1996, p. C1.

13. See Richard Campbell, "Don Hewitt's Durable Hour," *Columbia Journalism Review* (September–October 1993): 25.

14. "Who Is Paper Tiger Anyway?" <www.papertiger.org>

15. B. J. Bullert, "Public Television: Safe Programming and Faustian Bargains," *Chronicle of Higher Education* (September 19, 1998): B7.

Tracking Technology: DTV: The Digital Revolution, p. 140

1. See Joel Brinkley, "F.C.C. Clears New Standard for Digital TV," *New York Times*, December 25, 1996, pp. C1, C15.

Case Study: Anatomy of a TV "Failure," p. 165

1. All Tim Reid and Hugh Wilson quotes from Jimmie L. Reeves and Richard Campbell, "Misplacing Frank's Place: Do You Know What It Means to Miss New Orleans?" *Television Quarterly* 24 (1989): 45–57.

CHAPTER 6

1. *Midwest Video Corp. v. FCC*, 571 F. 2d 1025 (8th Cir. 1978).

2. David Lieberman, "Cable's Cash Cow Operators Pad Channel List to Pad Bills," *USA Today*, March 16, 1998, p. 1B.

3. Pierre Brunel-Lantena, quoted in "Top of the News," *Economist*, May 9, 1992, 89.

4. T. Seideman, "Four Labels Ink Vidclip Deals with MTV," *Billboard*, June 23, 1984, 1, 67. See other issues of *Billboard* and *Variety* throughout this time period.

5. "Tom Freston: The Pied Piper of Television," *Broadcasting & Cable*, September 19, 1994, 40.

6. Wilson Dizard Jr., *Old Media New Media: Mass Communication in the Information Age* (White Plains, NY: Longman, 1994), 124.

7. Chip Crews, "Small Screen, Big Dream: Harry Evans Puts His Hopes into a Cable-Access Show," *Washington Post*, December 2, 1997, p. B01.

CHAPTER 7

1. John Cawelti, *Adventure, Mystery, and Romance: Formula Stories as Art and Popular Culture* (Chicago: University of Chicago Press, 1976), 35.

2. See Charles Musser, *The Emergence of Cinema: The American Screen to 1907* (New York: Scribner's, 1991).

3. Douglas Gomery, *Shared Pleasures: A History of Movie Presentation in the United States* (Madison: University of Wisconsin Press, 1992), 18.

4. Richard Schickel, *Movies: The History of an Art and an Institution* (New York: Basic Books, 1964), 44.

5. Douglas Gomery, *Movie History: A Survey* (Belmont, Calif.: Wadsworth, 1991), 53.

6. Ibid., 167.

7. See David Bordwell and Kristin Thompson, *Film Art: An Introduction*, 5th ed. (New York: McGraw-Hill, 1996); and David Bordwell, Janet Staiger, and Kristin Thompson, *The Classic Hollywood Cinema: Film Style & Mode of Production to 1960* (New York: Columbia University Press, 1985).

8. Bordwell and Thompson, *Film Art*, 70.

9. See Cawelti, *Adventure, Mystery, and Romance*, 80–98.

10. See Barbara Koenig Quart, *Women Directors: The Emergence of a New Cinema* (New York: Praeger, 1988).

11. Ismail Merchant, "Kitschy as Ever, Hollywood Is Branching Out," *New York Times*, November 22, 1998, sec. 2, pp. 15, 30.

12. See Gomery, *Shared Pleasures*, 171–180.

13. Jonathan Curiel, "Lost in the Translation: Foreign Films Face a Tougher Time Breaking into U.S. Market," *San Francisco Chronicle*, October 4, 1998, p. 53.

14. See Eric Barnouw, *Tube of Plenty: The Evolution of American Television*, rev. ed. (New York: Oxford University Press, 1975, 1982), 108–109.

15. See Douglas Gomery, "Who Killed Hollywood?" *Wilson Quarterly* (summer 1991): 106–112.

16. Gomery, *Movie History*, 429.

17. Jack Valenti, "Attendance and Box Office Reach All-Time High in 1997," March 10, 1998, <www.mpaa.org/jack/98/98_3_10a.htm>.

18. See Reed Abelson, "The Shell Game of Hollywood 'Net Profits,'" *New York Times*, March 4, 1996, pp. C1, C4.

19. Valenti, 1998.

20. David Thorburn, "Television as an Aesthetic Medium," *Critical Studies in Mass Communication* (June 1987): 168.

Case Study: Breaking through Hollywood's Race Barrier, pp. 214–21

1. Douglas Gomery, *Shared Pleasures: A History of Movie Presentation in the United States* (Madison: University of Wisconsin Press, 1992), 155–170.

CHAPTER 8

1. See Brooke Kroeger, *Nellie Bly: Daredevil, Reporter, Feminist* (New York: Times Books/Random House, 1994).
2. See Kay Mills, *A Place in the News: From the Women's Pages to the Front Page* (New York: Dodd, Mead, 1988).
3. Piers Brendon, *The Life and Death of the Press Barons* (New York: Atheneum, 1983), 136.
4. William Randolph Hearst, quoted in Brendon, *The Life and Death of the Press Barons*, 134.
5. Michael Schudson, *Discovering the News: A Social History of the American Newspapers* (New York: Basic Books, 1978), 23.
6. See David T. Z. Mindich, "Edwin M. Stanton, the Inverted Pyramid, and Information Control," *Journalism Monographs*, no. 140 (August 1993).
7. John C. Merrill, "Objectivity: An Attitude," in Merrill and Ralph L. Lowenstein, eds., *Media, Messages and Men* (New York: David McKay, 1971), 240.
8. Roy Peter Clark, "A New Shape for the News," *Washington Journalism Review* (March 1984): 47.
9. Ibid., 143, 189.
10. See Edwin Emery, *The Press and America: An Interpretative History of the Mass Media*, 3rd ed. (Englewood Cliffs, N.J.: Prentice-Hall, 1972), 562.
11. Walter Lippmann, *Liberty and the News* (New York: Harcourt, Brace and Howe, 1920), 92.
12. American Society of Newspaper Editors, *Problems of Journalism* (Washington, D.C.: ASNE, 1933), 74.
13. Lippmann, *Liberty and the News*, 64.
14. Tom Wicker, *On Press* (New York: Viking, 1978), 3–5.
15. Jack Newfield, "The 'Truth' about Objectivity and the New Journalism," in Charles C. Flippen, ed., *Liberating the Media* (Washington, D.C.: Acropolis Books, 1973), 63–64.
16. Tom Wolfe, quoted in Leonard W. Robinson, "The New Journalism: A Panel Discussion . . . ," in Ronald Weber, ed., *The Reporter as Artist: A Look at the New Journalism Controversy* (New York: Hastings House, 1974), 67. See also Tom Wolfe and E. E. Johnson, eds., *The New Journalism* (New York: Harper & Row, 1973).
17. Jon Katz, "Online or Not, Newspapers Suck," *Wired*, September 1994, 5.
18. See Sreenath Sreenivasan, "As Mainstream Papers Struggle, the Ethnic Press Is Thriving," *New York Times*, July 22, 1996, p. C7.
19. See Phyl Garland, "The Black Press: Down but Not Out," *Columbia Journalism Review* (September–October 1982): 43–50.
20. See Iver Peterson, "Hiring of Minorities Again Rises in Newsrooms, but Barely," *New York Times*, April 17, 1996, p. A12.

21. See Allen R. Myerson, "Newspapers Cut Spanish-Language Publications," *New York Times*, October 16, 1995, p. C7.
22. Michael Emery and Edwin Emery, *The Press and America: An Interpretative History of the Mass Media*, 7th ed. (Englewood Cliffs, N.J.:Prentice-Hall, 1992), 536.
23. See Philip Meyer, "Learning to Love Lower Profits," *American Journalism Review* (December 1995): 40–44.
24. See Douglas Gomery, "In TV, the Big Get Bigger," *American Journalism Review* (October 1996): 64.
25. See William Glaberson, "Newspaper Owners Do the Shuffle," *New York Times*, February 19, 1996, pp. C1, C4.

Case Study: The Alternative Journalism of Dorothy Day and I. F. Stone, pp. 260–261

1. Stone, quoted in Jack Lule, "I. F. Stone: Professional Excellence in Raising Hell," *QS News* (summer 1989): 3.

CHAPTER 9

1. Robin Pogrebin, "No More Bubble Gum: Jane Grows Up," *New York Times*, September 7, 1997, sec. 1, p. 53.
2. John Tebbel and Mary Ellen Zuckerman, *The Magazine in America, 1741–1900* (New York: Oxford University Press, 1991), 68.
3. See Theodore Peterson, *Magazines in the Twentieth Century* (Urbana: University of Illinois Press, 1964), 5.
4. See Richard Ohmann, *Selling Culture: Magazines, Markets, and Class at the Turn of the Century* (New York: Verso, 1996).
5. See T. Peterson, *Magazines*, 5.
6. Lincoln Steffens, quoted in Justin Kaplan, *Lincoln Steffens: A Biography* (New York: Simon & Schuster, 1974), 106.
7. See discussion in T. Peterson, *Magazines*, 228; and Tebbel and Zuckerman, *The Magazine in America*, 223.
8. Alexander Graham Bell, quoted in William H. Taft, *American Magazines for the 1980s* (New York: Hastings House, 1982), 60.
9. Harold Ross, quoted in John Tebbel, *The American Magazine: A Compact History* (New York: Hawthorn Books, 1969), 234.
10. Generoso Pope, quoted in Taft, *American Magazines for the 1980s*, 226–227.
11. See S. Elizabeth Bird, *For Enquiring Minds: A Cultural Study of Supermarket Tabloids* (Knoxville: University of Tennessee Press, 1992), 24.
12. See Taft, *American Magazines*, 229.
13. See Iver Peterson, "Media: Supermarket Tabloids Lose Circulation," *New York Times*, September 9, 1996, p. C5.
14. Ibid.
15. See Deirdre Carmody, "Magazines Go Niche-Hunting with Custom-Made Sections," *New York Times*, June 26, 1995, p. C7.
16. See Robin Pogrebin, "The Number of Ad Pages Does Not Make the Magazine," *New York Times*, August 26, 1996, p. C1.
17. See Gloria Steinem, "Sex, Lies & Advertising," *Ms.*, July–August 1990, 18–28.
18. Robin Pogrebin, "Once a Renegade, Hachette Magazine Chief Gains Respect," *New York Times*, April 6, 1998, p. C1.

CHAPTER 10

1. Tahree Lane, "Couch Potatoes Turn Eyes to Books," *Denver Rocky Mountain News*, February 4, 1998, p. 10D.

2. Yvonne Zipp, "Oprah Propels Some First Novelists to the Stars," *Christian Science Monitor*, July 23, 1998, p. B4.

3. See Elizabeth Eisenstein, *The Printing Press as an Agent of Social Change*, 2 vols. (Cambridge, England: Cambridge University Press, 1980).

4. See Quentin Reynolds, *The Fiction Factory: From Pulp Row to Quality Street* (New York: Street & Smith/Random House, 1955), 72–74.

5. For a comprehensive historical overview of the publishing industry and the rise of publishing houses, see John A. Tebbel, *A History of Book Publishing in the United States*, vol. 1, 1630–1865; vol. 2, 1865–1919; vol. 3, 1920–1940; vol. 4, 1940–1980 (New York: R. R. Bowker, 1972–1981).

6. See Mary B. W. Taylor, "Two Studies See a Bull Market for Book Industry," *New York Times*, August 7, 1995, p. C7.

7. See "Student Watch: Campus Market Research," <www.nacs.org/about/csref/studentwatch.asp>, February 7, 1999.

8. For a historical overview of paperbacks, see Kenneth Davis, *Two-Bit Culture: The Paperbacking of America* (Boston: Houghton Mifflin, 1984).

9. Katie Hafner, "Net Is Not Enough: Books on Starr Report, Too," *New York Times*, September 17, 1998, p. D3.

10. See John P. Dessauer, *Book Publishing: What It Is, What It Does* (New York: R. R. Bowker, 1974), 48.

11. Patricia Nelson Limerick, "Dancing with Professors: The Trouble with Academic Prose," *New York Times Book Review*, October 31, 1993, p. 3.

12. See Doreen Carvajal, "Triumph of the Bottom Line: Numbers vs. Words at the Book-of-the-Month Club," *New York Times*, April 1, 1996, pp. C1, C5.

13. Ibid., p. C5.

14. See Doreen Carvajal, "The Other Battle Over Browsers," *New York Times*, March 9, 1998, p. C1.

15. "Research & Statistics," BookWeb.org, <www.bookweb.org/research/stats/389.html>.

16. Curtis Wilke, "The Sound and Fury of Miss. Booksellers," *Boston Globe*, December 5, 1998, p. A3.

17. See Carvajal, "Battle over Browsers."

18. Porter Bibb, "In Publishing, Bigger Is Better," *New York Times*, March 31, 1998, p. A27.

19. James Kaplan, "Inside the Club," *New York Times Magazine*, June 11, 1989, p. 62.

20. See Wilson Dizard Jr., *Old Media New Media: Mass Communication in the Information Age* (White Plains, N.Y.: Longman, 1994), 164.

21. Rosenstiel, quoted in Doreen Carvajal, "Cross-Media Deals Mean Bonanza for Publishers," *New York Times* on the Web, <www.nytimes.com>, January 25, 1999.

22. See Alvin Kernan, *The Death of Literature* (New Haven: Yale University Press, 1990).

Examining Ethics: Censorship Issues in Book Publishing, p. 338

1. See Mary B. W. Taylor, "Publishing: On Both Sides of the Political Spectrum, the Battle over Censorship . . . Continues to Rage," *New York Times*, April 3, 1995, p. C8.

CHAPTER 11

1. For a written and pictorial history of early advertising, see Charles Goodrum and Helen Dalrymple, *Advertising in America, the First 200 Years* (New York: Harry N. Abrams, 1990), 13–34.

2. Ibid., 18.

3. Michael Schudson, *Advertising, the Uneasy Persuasion* (New York: Basic Books, 1984), 165. See also Arthur Marquette, *Brands, Trademarks, and Good Will* (New York: McGraw-Hill, 1967).

4. Goodrum and Dalrymple, *Advertising in America*, 31.

5. See Schudson, *Advertising*, 164.

6. Randall Rothenberg, *Where the Suckers Moon: An Advertising Story* (New York: Alfred A. Knopf, 1994), 20.

7. Leslie Savan, "Op Ad: Sneakers and Nothingness," *Village Voice*, April 2, 1991, p. 43.

8. See Mary Kuntz and Joseph Weber, "The New Hucksterism," *Business Week*, July 1, 1999, 79.

9. Ibid.

10. Schudson, *Advertising*, 210.

11. "Adbusters TV Uncommercial: Buy Nothing Day," <http://www.adbusters.org/uncommercials/bnd.html>, February 19, 1999.

12. Vance Packard, *The Hidden Persuaders* (New York: Basic Books, 1957, 1978), 229.

13. See Schudson, *Advertising*, 36–43; and Andrew Robertson, *The Lessons of Failure* (London: MacDonald, 1974).

14. See Jay Mathews, "Channel One: Classroom Coup or a 'Sham'?" *Washington Post*, December 26, 1994, p. A1+.

15. See Michael F. Jacobson and Laurie Ann Mazur, *Marketing Madness: A Survival for a Consumer Society* (Boulder, Colo.: Westview Press, 1995), 29–31.

16. See Stuart Elliott, "Liquor Industry Ends Its Ad Ban in Broadcasting," *New York Times*, November 8, 1996, pp. A1, C5; and "Seagram Flouts Ban on TV Ads Pitching Liquor," *Wall Street Journal*, June 11, 1996, pp. B1, B5.

17. For a discussion of deceptive ads, see Jacobson and Mazur, *Marketing Madness*, 143–148.

18. G. Pascal Zachary, "Many Journalists See a Growing Reluctance to Criticize Advertisers," *Wall Street Journal*, February 6, 1992, pp. A1, A6.

19. Ibid., p. A6.

20. Kathleen Hall Jamieson, "Truth and Advertising," *New York Times*, January 27, 1996, p. 15.

21. See Stephen Ansolabehere and Shanto Iyengar, *Going Negative: How Attack Ads Shrunk and Polarized the Electorate* (New York: Free Press, 1996).

22. See Walter Goodman, "Prime Time, Politics and the Public's Right to Tune Out," *New York Times*, May 5, 1996, Arts & Leisure section, p. 28.

CHAPTER 12

1. Matthew J. Culligan and Dolph Greene, *Getting Back to the Basics of Public Relations & Publicity* (New York: Crown Publishers, 1982), 90.

2. Ibid., 100.
3. See Stuart Ewen, *PR! A Social History of Spin* (New York: Basic Books, 1996).
4. Suzanne Heck, "Multimedia Sharpshooter Brought Buffalo Bill Fame," *Public Relations Journal* (October–November 1994): 12.
5. Marvin N. Olasky, "The Development of Corporate Public Relations, 1850–1930," *Journalism Monographs*, no. 102 (April 1987): 3.
6. Quoted in Alfred McClung Lee, *The Daily Newspaper in America* (New York: Macmillan, 1937), 436.
7. Olasky, "The Development of Corporate Public Relations," 14.
8. Ibid., 15.
9. See Ewen, *PR!*, 47.
10. See Scott M. Cutlip, *The Unseen Power: Public Relations—A History* (Hillsdale, N.J.: Lawrence Erlbaum, 1994).
11. Edward Bernays, *Crystallizing Public Opinion* (New York: Horace Liveright, 1923), 217.
12. Michael Schudson, *Discovering the News* (New York: Basic Books, 1978), 136.
13. Walter Lippmann, *Public Opinion* (New York: Harcourt Brace, 1922), 345.
14. See Daniel Boorstin, *The Image: A Guide to Pseudo-Events in America* (New York: Atheneum, 1961), 11–12, 205–210.
15. Leonard Mogel, *Making It in Public Relations: An Insider's Guide to Career Opportunities* (New York: Collier Books/Macmillan, 1993), 34.
16. The author worked briefly as the assistant PR director for Milwaukee's Summerfest in the early 1980s.
17. Susan Lucarelli, "Public Relations Research," in Michael Singletary, ed., *Mass Communication Research* (New York: Longman, 1995), 357–359.
18. See Ewen, *PR!*, 28–29; and John R. McArthur, *The Second Front: Censorship and Propaganda in the Gulf War* (New York: Hill & Wang, 1992), 58–59.
19. Stanley Walker, "Playing the Deep Bassoons," *Harper's*, February 1932: 365.
20. Ibid., 370.
21. Ivy Lee, *Publicity* (New York: Industries Publishing, 1925), 21.
22. Schudson, *Discovering the News*, 136.
23. Ivy Lee, quoted in Ray Eldon Hiebert, *Courtier to the Crowd: The Story of Ivy Lee and the Development of Public Relations* (Ames: Iowa State University Press, 1966), 114.
24. See Lippmann, *Public Opinion*.
25. See Jonathan Tasini, "Lost in the Margins: Labor and the Media," *Extra!* (summer 1992): 2–11.
26. See J. David Pincus et al., "Newspaper Editors' Perceptions of Public Relations: How Business, News, and Sports Editors Differ," *Journal of Public Relations Research* 5, no. 1 (1993): 27–45.
27. Schudson, *Discovering the News*, 171.
28. Bill Walker, "Green Like Me," in Ray Eldon Hiebert, ed., *Impact of Mass Media: Current Issues*, 3rd ed. (White Plains, N.Y.: Longman, 1995), 177.
29. William Small, quoted in Walker, "Playing the Deep Bassoons," 174–175.
30. See Alicia Mundy, "Is the Press Any Match for Powerhouse PR?" in Hiebert, ed., *Impact of Mass Media*, 179–188.

Case Study: Levi Strauss and Anti-Sweatshop Public Relations, pp. 398–399
1. Public Relations Society of America, *PRSA Silver Anvil Awards* (New York: PRSA, 1994), 9–10.
2. Ibid., 10.

CHAPTER 13
1. For this section I am indebted to the ideas and scholarship of my former teacher Douglas Gomery, a media economist and historian from the University of Maryland.
2. Douglas Gomery, "The Centrality of Media Economics," in *Defining Media Studies*, Mark R. Levy and Michael Gurevitch, eds. (New York: Oxford University Press, 1994), 202.
3. Ibid., 200.
4. Ibid., 203–204.
5. David Harvey, *The Condition of Postmodernity: An Enquiry into the Origins of Cultural Change* (Oxford: Basil Blackwell, 1989), 171.
6. Ibid., 158.
7. Richard J. Barnet and John Cavanagh, *Global Dreams: Imperial Corporations and the New World Order* (New York: Simon & Schuster, 1994), 131.
8. Ben Bagdikian, *The Media Monopoly*, 4th ed. (Boston: Beacon Press, 1992), 222.
9. Roland Marchand, *Advertising the American Dream: Making Way for Modernity, 1920–1940* (Berkeley: University of California Press, 1985), 218.
10. William Paley, quoted in Robert W. McChesney, *Telecommunications, Mass Media, & Democracy: The Battle for Control of U.S. Broadcasting, 1928–1935* (New York: Oxford University Press, 1993), 251.
11. McChesney, *Telecommunications, Mass Media, & Democracy*, 264.
12. Edward Herman, "Democratic Media," *Z Papers* (January–March 1992): 23.
13. Barnet and Cavanagh, *Global Dreams*, 38.
14. Richard J. Barnet and Ronald E. Muller, *Global Reach: The Power of Multinational Corporations* (New York: Simon & Schuster, 1974), 175.

CHAPTER 14
1. Veronica Guerin, quoted in Warren Hoge, "Reporter Roused Ireland's Conscience," *New York Times*, November 23, 1996, pp. 1, 4.
2. Neil Postman, "Currents," *Utne Reader*, July–August 1995, 35.
3. Reuven Frank, "Memorandum from a Television Newsman," reprinted as Appendix 2 in A. William Bluem, *Documentary in American Television* (New York: Hastings House, 1965), 276.
4. For another list and alternative analysis of news criteria, see Brian S. Brooks et al., *The Missouri Group: News Reporting and Writing* (New York: St. Martin's Press, 1996), 2–4.
5. Horace Greeley, quoted in Christopher Lasch, "Journalism, Publicity, and the Lost Art of Argument," *Gannett Center Journal* 4, no. 2 (spring 1990): 2.

6. David Eason, "Telling Stories and Making Sense," *Journal of Popular Culture* 15, no. 2 (fall 1981): 125.

7. Jon Katz, "AIDS and the Media: Shifting out of Neutral," *Rolling Stone*, May 27, 1993, 32.

8. Herbert Gans, *Deciding What's News* (New York: Pantheon, 1979), 42–48.

9. Ibid., 42–48.

10. Ibid., 48–51.

11. See Michael Schudson, *Discovering the News* (New York: Basic Books, 1978), 3–11.

12. Code of Ethics, reprinted in Melvin Mencher, *News Reporting and Writing*, 3rd ed. (Dubuque, Ia.: Wm. C. Brown, 1984), 443–444.

13. Ibid.

14. Ibid., 443.

15. For reference and guidance on media ethics, see Clifford Christians, Mark Fackler, and Kim Rotzoll, *Media Ethics: Cases & Moral Reasoning*, 4th ed. (White Plains, N.Y.: Longman, 1995); and Thomas H. Bivins, "A Worksheet for Ethics Instruction and Exercises in Reason," *Journalism Educator* (summer 1993): 4–16.

16. Christians, Fackler, and Rotzoll, *Media Ethics*, 15.

17. See Jimmie Reeves and Richard Campbell, *Cracked Coverage: Television News, the Anti-Cocaine Crusade, and the Reagan Legacy* (Durham, N.C.: Duke University Press, 1994).

18. See David Eason, "On Journalistic Authority: The Janet Cooke Scandal," *Critical Studies in Mass Communications* 3, no. 4 (December 1986): 429–447.

19. Mike Royko, quoted in "News Media: A Searching of Conscience," *Newsweek*, May 4, 1981, 53.

20. Don Hewitt, interview conducted at *60 Minutes*, CBS News, New York, February 21, 1989.

21. Jonathan Alter, "News Media: Round Up the Usual Suspects," *Newsweek*, March 25, 1985, 69.

22. William Hoynes and David Croteau, "All the Usual Suspects: *MacNeil/Lehrer* and *Nightline*," *Extra!* Special Issue 3, no. 4 (winter 1990): 2. This article reports on the original *Nightline* study and offers a follow-up study on both *Nightline* and *MacNeil/Lehrer*, which reveals roughly the same gender patterns. See Hoynes and Croteau, "Are You on the *Nightline* Guest List?" *Extra!* 2, no. 4 (January–February 1989): 2–15.

23. William Greider, quoted in Mark Hertsgaard, *On Bended Knee: The Press and the Reagan Presidency* (New York: Farrar, Straus, and Giroux, 1988), 78.

24. Jay Rosen, "Politics, Vision, and the Press: Toward a Public Agenda for Journalism," in Rosen and Paul Taylor, *The New News v. the Old News: The Press and Politics in the 1990s* (New York: Twentieth Century Fund, 1992), 6.

25. Bluem, *Documentary in American Television*, 94.

26. Fred Friendly, quoted in Joseph Michalak, "CBS Reports Covers Assortment of Topics," *New York Times*, December 13, 1959, sec. 2, p. 21.

27. See Joe Holley, "Should the Coverage Fit the Crime?" *Columbia Journalism Review* (May–June 1996), <www.cjr.org/year/96/coverage.asp>.

28. Based on notes made by the author's wife, Dianna Campbell, after a visit to Warsaw and discussions with a number of journalists working for *Gazeta Wyborcza* in 1990.

29. Davis "Buzz" Merritt, *Public Journalism & Public Life: Why Telling the News Is Not Enough* (Hillsdale, N.J.: Lawrence Erlbaum, 1995), 113–114.

30. Rosen, "Politics, Vision, and the Press," 14.

31. Davis Merritt and Jay Rosen, "Imagining Public Journalism: An Editor and a Scholar Reflect on the Birth of an Idea," Roy W. Howard Public Lecture (Bloomington: Indiana University), no. 5, April 13, 1995, 11.

32. Ibid., 15.

33. See Jonathan Cohn, "Should Journalists Do Community Service?" *American Prospect* (summer 1995): 15.

34. Merritt and Rosen, "Imagining Public Journalism," 12.

35. Poll statistics cited in Merritt, *Public Journalism & Public Life*, xv–xvi.

36. David Broder, quoted in "Squaring with the Reader: A Seminar on Journalism," *Kettering Review* (winter 1992): 48.

37. Christopher Lasch, "Journalism, Publicity and the Lost Art of Argument," *Gannett Center Journal* 4, no. 2 (spring 1990): 1.

38. Jay Rosen, "Forming and Informing the Public," *Kettering Review* (winter 1992): 69–70.

Case Study: Reporters as Detectives on *60 Minutes*, pp. 442–443

1. Hewitt, quoted in "Father of *60 Minutes*: Taking the Heat as No. 1," *Chicago Tribune*, April 3, 1981, sec. 2, p. 15.

2. For more detail, see Richard Campbell, *60 Minutes and the News: A Mythology for Middle America* (Urbana: University of Illinois Press, 1991).

3. Hewitt, quoted in William A. Henry, "Don Hewitt: Man of the Hour," *Washington Journalism Review* (May 1986): 26.

4. Mike Wallace and Gary Paul Gates, *Close Encounters: Mike Wallace's Own Story* (New York: Berkley Books, 1984), 420.

CHAPTER 15

1. Alexis de Tocqueville, *Democracy in America* (New York: Modern Library, 1835, 1840, 1945, 1981), 96–97.

2. Steve Fore, "Lost in Translation: The Social Uses of Mass Communications Research," *AFTERIMAGE*, no. 20 (April 1993): 10.

3. James Carey, *Communication as Culture: Essays on Media and Society* (Boston: Unwin Hyman, 1989), 75.

4. Daniel Czitrom, *Media and the American Mind: From Morse to McLuhan* (Chapel Hill: University of North Carolina Press, 1982), 122–125.

5. Ibid., 123.

6. Harold Lasswell, *Propaganda Technique in the World War* (New York: Alfred A. Knopf, 1927), 9.

7. Walter Lippmann, *Public Opinion* (New York: Macmillan, 1922), 18.

8. Benjamin Ginsberg, *The Captive Public: How Mass Opinion Promotes State Power* (New York: Basic Books, 1986), 82–83.

9. See W. W. Charters, *Motion Pictures and Youth: A Summary* (New York: Macmillan, 1934); and Garth Jowett, *Film: The Democratic Art* (Boston: Little, Brown, 1976), 220–229.

10. Czitrom, *Media and the American Mind*, 132. See also Harold Lasswell, "The Structure and Function of Communication in Society," in Lyman Bryson, ed., *The Communication of Ideas* (New York: Harper and Brothers, 1948), 37–51.

11. Wilbur Schramm, Jack Lyle, and Edwin Parker, *Television in the Lives of Our Children* (Stanford, Calif.: Stanford University Press, 1961), 1.

12. See Joseph Klapper, *The Effects of Mass Communication* (New York: Free Press, 1960).

13. Schramm, Lyle, and Parker, *Television*, 1.

14. See, for example, Mark Levy, "The Audience Experience with Television News," *Journalism Monographs*, no. 55 (April 1978).

15. For an early overview of uses and gratifications, see Jay Blumler and Elihu Katz, *The Uses of Mass Communication* (Beverly Hills, Calif.: Sage, 1974).

16. See George Gerbner et al., "The Demonstration of Power: Violence Profile No. 10," *Journal of Communication* 29, no. 3 (1979): 177–196.

17. *Sex on TV: A Biennial Report to the Kaiser Family Foundation, 1999* (Menlo Park, Calif.: Henry C. Kaiser Family Foundation).

18. Robert P. Snow, *Creating Media Culture* (Beverly Hills, Calif.: Sage, 1983), 47.

19. See Maxwell McCombs and Donald Shaw, "The Agenda-Setting Function of Mass Media," *Public Opinion Quarterly* 36, no. 2 (1972): 176–187.

20. See Stephen D. Reese and Lucig H. Danielton, "A Closer Look at Intermedia Influences on Agenda Setting: The Cocaine Issue of 1986," in Pamela J. Shoemaker, ed., *Communication Campaigns about Drugs: Government, Media, and the Public* (Hillsdale, N.J.: Lawrence Erlbaum, 1989), 47–66; and Peter Kerr, "Anatomy of the Drug Issue: How, After Years, It Erupted," *New York Times*, November 17, 1986, p. A12.

21. See Craig Reinarman and Harry G. Levine, "Crack in Context: Politics and Media in the Making of the Drug Scare," *Contemporary Drug Problems* (winter 1989): 546; see also Adam Clymer, "Public Found Ready to Sacrifice in Drug Fight," *New York Times*, September 2, 1986, pp. A1, D16.

22. See Nancy Signorielli and Michael Morgan, *Cultivation Analysis: New Directions in Media Effects Research* (Newbury Park, Calif.: Sage, 1990).

23. Robert Lynd, *Knowledge for What?: The Place of Social Science in American Culture* (Princeton, N.J.: Princeton University Press, 1939), 120.

24. Czitrom, *Media and the American Mind*, 143; and Leo Lowenthal, "Historical Perspectives of Popular Culture," in Bernard Rosenberg and David White, eds., *Mass Culture: The Popular Arts in America* (Glencoe, Ill.: Free Press, 1957), 52.

25. See Stuart Hall, et al., *Policing the Crisis: Mugging, the State, and Law and Order* (London: Macmillan, 1978).

26. Horace Newcomb, *TV: The Most Popular Art* (Garden City, N.Y.: Anchor Books, 1974), 19, 23.

27. Ana Garner, Helen M. Sterk, and Shawn Adams, "Narrative Analysis of Sexual Etiquette in Teenage Magazines," *Journal of Communication* 48, no. 4 (Autumn 1998): 59–78.

28. See Janice Radway, *Reading the Romance: Women, Patriarchy and Popular Literature* (Chapel Hill: University of North Carolina Press, 1984).

29. James Carey, "Mass Communication Research and Cultural Studies: An American View," in James Curran, Michael Gurevitch, and Janet Woollacott, eds., *Mass Communication and Society* (London: Edward Arnold, 1977), 418, 421.

30. Scott Janny, "Postmodern Gravity Deconstructed, Slyly," *New York Times*, May 18, 1996, p. 1.

31. Christopher Lasch, "Politics and Culture," *Salmagundi* (winter–spring 1990): 33.

32. Scott Heller, "Humanists Renew Public Intellectual Tradition, Answer Criticism," *Chronicle of Higher Education*, April 7, 1993, p. A6.

33. Lawrie Mifflin, "Study of TV's Violence Points to Films," *New York Times*, September 20, 1995, pp. B1, 4.

CHAPTER 16

1. See Newspaper Association of America, *Facts about Newspapers* (Reston, Va.: The Newspaper Center, 1994), 27.

2. See "No Free Press," *Quill*, June 1996, 11.

3. Fred Siebert, Theodore Peterson, and Wilbur Schramm, *Four Theories of the Press* (Urbana: University of Illinois, 1956).

4. See Douglas M. Fraleigh and Joseph S. Tuman, *Freedom of Speech in the Marketplace of Ideas* (New York: St. Martin's Press, 1997), 125.

5. Hugo Black, quoted in "*New York Times* Company v. U.S.: 1971," in Edward W. Knappman, ed., *Great American Trials: From Salem Witchcraft to Rodney King* (Detroit: Visible Ink Press, 1994), 609.

6. Robert Warren, quoted in "U.S. v. *The Progressive*: 1979," in Knappman, ed., *Great American Trials*, 684.

7. See Fraleigh and Tuman, *Freedom of Speech*, 71–73.

8. See Newspaper Association of America, *Facts*, 27.

9. See Knappman, ed., *Great American Trials*, 517–519.

10. Ibid., 741–743.

11. Douglas Gomery, *Movie History: A Survey* (Belmont, Calif.: Wadsworth, 1991), 57.

12. See Eric Barnouw, *Tube of Plenty: The Evolution of American Television*, rev. ed. (New York: Oxford University Press, 1982), 118–130.

13. Dean Burch, quoted in Peter Fornatale and Joshua Mills, *Radio in the Television Age* (Woodstock, N.Y.: Overlook Press, 1980), 85.

14. See "Dummy and Dame Arouse the Nation," *Broadcasting-Telecasting*, October 15, 1956, 258; and Lawrence Lichty and Malachi Topping, *American Broadcasting: A Source Book on the History of Radio and Television* (New York: Hastings House, 1975), 530.

15. Bill Kovach, "Big Deals, with Journalism Thrown In," *New York Times*, August 3, 1995, p. A17.

GLOSSARY

A&R agents short for artist & repertoire agents, these talent scouts of the music business discover, develop, and sometimes manage performers.

absolutist ethic the principle that in a moral society legal or ethical codes must be followed without exception: no one is above the law or above a society's fundamental moral principles.

access channels in cable television, a tier of nonbroadcast channels dedicated to local education, government, and the public.

account executives in advertising, client liaisons responsible for bringing in new business and managing the accounts of established clients.

account reviews in advertising, the process of evaluating or reinvigorating an ad campaign, which results in either renewing the contract with the original ad agency or in hiring a new agency.

actual malice in libel law, to act with a reckless disregard for the truth, such as when a reporter or an editor knows that a statement is false and prints or airs it anyway.

affiliate any radio or TV station that, though independently owned, signs a contract to be part of a network and receives money to carry the network's programs; in exchange, the network reserves time slots, which it sells to national advertisers.

agenda-setting a media-research argument that says when the mass media pay attention to particular events or issues, they determine—set the agenda for—the major topics of discussion for individuals and society.

alternative rock nonmainstream rock music, which includes many types of experimental music and some forms of punk and grunge.

AM amplitude modulation; a type of radio and sound transmission that stresses the volume or height of radio waves.

analog recording a recording that is made by capturing the fluctuations of the original sound waves and storing those signals on records or cassettes as a continuous stream of magneticism—*analogous* to the actual sound.

analysis the second step in the critical process, it involves discovering significant patterns that emerge from the description stage.

anthology drama a popular form of early TV programming that brought live dramatic theater to television; influenced by stage plays, anthologies offered new teleplays, casts, directors, writers, and sets from week to week.

association principle in advertising, a persuasive technique that *associates* a product with some cultural value or image that has a positive connotation but may have little connection to the actual product.

attack ads a type of political ad that uses repeated negative assaults on another candidate's character.

audiotape lightweight magnetized strands of ribbon that allow sound editing and multiple-track mixing; instrumentals or vocals can be recorded at one location and later mixed onto a master recording in another studio.

authoritarian model a model for journalism and speech that tolerates little government criticism or public dissent; it holds that the general public needs guidance from an elite and educated ruling class.

bandwagon effect an advertising strategy that incorporates exaggerated claims that *everyone* is using a particular product so you should, too.

barter deal in TV syndication, an arrangement in which no money changes hands between the local station and the syndicator; instead, a syndicator offers a new program to a local TV station in exchange for a portion of the advertising revenue.

basic cable in cable programming, a tier of channels composed of local broadcast signals, nonbroadcast access channels (for local government, education, and general public use), a few regional PBS stations, and a variety of popular channels downlinked from communication satellites.

bits a computer term coined from *BI*nary digi*TS*, which refers to information that represents two values, such as yes/no, on/off, or 0/1.

blues originally a kind of black folk music, this music emerged as a distinct category in the early 1900s; it was influenced by African American spirituals, ballads, and work songs in the rural South, and by urban guitar and vocal solos from the 1930s and 1940s.

books on tape audiotape books that generally feature actors or authors reading abridged versions of popular fiction and nonfiction trade books.

bootlegging the illegal counterfeiting or pirating of CDs, cassettes, and videos that are produced and/or sold without official permission from the original songwriter, performer, or copyright holder.

boutique agencies in advertising, small regional ad agencies that offer personalized services.

broadcasting the transmission of radio waves or TV signals to a broad public audience.

browsers information-search services, such as Netscape's Navigator and Microsoft's Explorer, that offer detailed organizational maps to the World Wide Web.

button fatigue in TV audience measurement, the phenomenon of weary viewers failing to log on and report their viewing.

cable franchise in cable television, a local monopoly business awarded by a community to the most attractive cable bidder, usually for a fifteen-year period.

cash deal in TV syndication, an arrangement in which the distributor of a program offers a series to the highest bidder in a TV market or to a station trying to fill a particular time slot.

cash-plus deal in TV syndication, an arrangement in which the distributor of a program offers a series to the highest bidder in a TV market but retains some time to sell national commercial spots.

CATV (community antenna television) an early cable system that originated where mountains or tall buildings blocked TV signals; because of early technical and regulatory limits, CATV contained only twelve channels.

CD-ROM a computer term coined from *Compact-Disc Read-Only Memory*; a CD technology that permits the storage of vast amounts of computer software and information (one CD-ROM can store as much information as seven hundred conventional floppy disks).

channel in mass communication, a medium that delivers messages from senders to receivers.

cinema verité French term for *film truth*, a documentary style that records fragments of everyday life unobtrusively; it often features a rough, grainy look and shaky, handheld camera work.

clearance rule established in the 1940s by the Justice Department and the FCC, this rule mandated that all local affiliates are ultimately responsible for the content of their channels and must *clear*, or approve, all network programming.

coaxial cable a system for transmitting TV signals via a solid core of copper-clad aluminum wire encircled by an outer axis of braided wires; these bundles of thin wire accommodate fifty or more separate channels running side by side with virtually no interference.

codex an early type of book in which paperlike sheets were cut and sewed together along the edge, then bound with thin pieces of wood and covered with leather.

commercial speech any print or broadcast expression for which a fee is charged to the organization or individual buying time or space in the mass media.

common carrier a communication or transportation business, such as a phone company or a taxi service, that is required by law to offer service on a first-come, first-served basis to whoever can pay the rate; such companies do not get involved in content.

communication the process of creating symbol systems that convey information and meaning (for example, language, Morse code, film, computer codes).

communist or state model a model for journalism and speech that places control in the hands of an enlightened government, which speaks for ordinary citizens and workers in order to serve the common goals of the state.

compact disks (CDs) playback-only storage disks for music that incorporate pure and very precise digital techniques, thus eliminating noise during recording and editing sessions.

complementary copy positive, upbeat articles—often about food, fashion, and cosmetics—that support the ads carried in various consumer magazines.

conflict of interest considered unethical, a compromising situation in which a journalist stands to benefit personally from the news report he or she produces.

conflict-oriented journalism found in metropolitan areas, newspapers that define news primarily as events, issues, or experiences that deviate from social norms; journalists see their role as observers who monitor their city's institutions and problems.

consensus-oriented papers found in small communities, newspapers that promote social and economic harmony by providing community calendars and meeting notices and carrying articles on local schools, social events, town government, property crimes, and zoning issues.

content analysis in social-science research, a method for studying and coding media texts and programs.

continuity editing an editing technique that makes space and time seem continuous and seamless; it is used in most traditional Hollywood films.

control group in social-science research, the group that serves as a basis for comparison to the experimental group; the control group has *not* been exposed to the particular phenomenon or media content being studied.

controlled circulation the process of earning magazine revenue from advertising or corporate sponsorship by targeting captive audiences, such as airline passengers or association members, who receive the publications free.

copyright the legal right of authors and producers to own and control the use of their published or unpublished writing, music and lyrics, TV programs and movies, or graphic art designs.

cover music songs recorded or performed by musicians who did not originally write or perform the music; in the 1950s, cover music was an attempt by white producers and artists to capitalize on popular songs by blacks.

crisis management in public relations, the strategic response to uncontrolled negative publicity about an individual, client, or company; also known as *damage control*.

cultivation effect in media research, the idea that heavy television viewing leads individuals to perceive reality in ways that are consistent with the portrayals they see on television.

cultural studies in media research, the approaches that try to understand how the media and culture are tied to the actual patterns of communication used in daily life; these studies focus on how people make meanings, apprehend reality, and order experience through the use of stories and symbols.

culture the symbols of expression that individuals, groups, and societies use to make sense of daily life and to articulate their values; a process that delivers the values of a society through products or other meaning-making forms.

cyberspace the region to which the networks of computer communication transport their users—a territory that does not recognize conventional geographic boundaries or social hierarchies.

day parts in radio programming, the division of each day into time blocks—usually 6 to 10 A.M., 10 A.M. to 3 P.M., 3 to 7 P.M., and 7 to 12 midnight—in order to reach various listening audiences.

DBS (direct broadcast satellites) home-satellite dishes that for a monthly fee downlink hundreds of satellite channels and services.

deficit financing in television, the process whereby a TV production company leases its programs to a network for a license fee that is actually *less* than the cost of production; the company hopes to recoup this loss later in rerun syndication.

deliberative democracy a political culture in which citizen groups, local governments, and the news media join together to actively shape social and political agendas.

demographic editions national magazines whose advertising is tailored to subscribers and readers according to occupation, class, and zip-code address.

demographics in market research, the study of audiences or consumers by age, gender, occupation, ethnicity, education, and income.

description the first step in the critical process, it involves paying close attention, taking notes, and researching the cultural product to be studied.

desktop publishing a computer technology that allows an aspiring publisher-editor to inexpensively write, design, lay out, and even print a small newsletter or magazine.

digital audiotape (DAT) a tape format that features CD-quality sound on a machine that records as well as plays back tapes.

digital communication images, texts, and sounds that use pulses of electric current or flashes of laser lights and are converted (or encoded) into electronic signals represented as varied combinations of binary numbers, usually ones and zeroes; these signals are then reassembled (decoded) as a precise reproduction of a TV picture, a magazine article, or a telephone voice.

digital recording music recorded and played back by laser beam rather than by needle or magnetic tape.

direct payment in media economics, the payment of money, primarily by consumers, for a book, a music CD, a movie, an online computer service, or a cable TV subscription.

disassociation corollary in advertising, a persuasive technique that tries to distance the consumer from a large product manufacturer or parent company by linking new brands to eccentric, intimate, or regional places.

distribution the individuals or companies in the mass-media business that deliver media products to various regional, national, and international markets.

documentary a movie or TV news genre that documents reality by recording actual characters and settings.

domestic comedy a TV hybrid of the sitcom in which characters and settings are usually more important than complicated situations; it generally features a domestic problem or work issue that characters have to solve.

dramedy in TV programming, a narrative that blurs serious and comic themes.

drive time in radio programming, the periods between 6 and 10 A.M. and 4 and 7 P.M., when people are commuting to and from work or school; these periods constitute the largest listening audiences of the day.

economies of scale the economic process of increasing production levels so as to reduce the overall cost per unit.

electromagnetic waves invisible electronic impulses similar to visible light; electricity, magnetism, light, broadcast signals, and heat are part of such waves, which radiate in space at the speed of light, about 186,000 miles per second.

electronic publisher a communication business, such as a broadcaster or a cable TV company, that is entitled to pick and choose what channels or content to carry.

episodic series a narrative form well suited to television because main characters continue from week to week, sets and locales remain the same, and technical crews stay with the program; episodic series feature new adventures each week, but a handful of characters emerge with whom viewers can regularly identify.

ethnocentrism an underlying value held by many U.S. journalists and citizens, it involves judging other countries and cultures according to how they live up to or imitate American practices and ideals.

evaluation the fourth step in the critical process, it involves arriving at a judgment about whether a cultural product is good, bad, or mediocre; this requires subordinating one's personal taste to the critical assessment resulting from the first three stages.

evergreens in TV syndication, popular old network reruns such as the *Andy Griffith Show* or *I Love Lucy*.

exhibition the individuals or companies in the mass-media business who exhibit media products; the term usually refers to companies that control movie theaters.

experiment in regard to the mass media, research that isolates some aspect of content, suggests a hypothesis, and manipulates variables to discover a particular medium's impact on attitudes, emotions, or behavior.

experimental group in social-science research, the group under study that has been exposed to a particular phenomenon or media content.

Fairness Doctrine repealed in 1987, this FCC rule required broadcast stations to air and engage in controversial-issue programs that affected their communities and, when offering such programming, to provide competing points of view.

famous-person testimonial an advertising strategy that associates a product with the endorsement of a well-known person.

feature syndicates commercial outlets or brokers, such as United Features and King Features, that contract with newspapers to provide work from well-known political writers, editorial cartoonists, comic-strip artists, and self-help columnists.

feedback responses from receivers to the senders of messages.

fiber-optic cable thin glass bundles of fiber capable of transmitting thousands of messages converted to shooting pulses of light along cable wires; these bundles of fiber can carry broadcast channels, telephone signals, and all sorts of digital codes.

film noir French for *black film*, this film genre is usually shot in black and white, uses low-lighting techniques, shows few daytime scenes, displays bleak urban settings, and explores the sinister side of human nature.

Financial Interest and Syndication Rules (fin-syn) FCC rules that prohibited the major networks from running their own syndication companies or from charging production companies additional fees after shows had completed their prime-time runs; most fin-syn rules were rescinded in the mid-1990s.

first-run syndication in television, the process whereby new programs are specifically produced for sale in syndication markets rather than for network television.

flack a derogatory term that journalists use to refer to a public-relations agent.

FM frequency modulation; a type of radio and sound transmission that offers static-less reception and greater fidelity and clarity than AM radio by accentuating the pitch or distance between radio waves.

focus group a common research method in psychograhic analysis in which a moderator leads a small-group discussion about a product or an issue, usually with six to twelve people.

folk music music performed by untrained musicians and passed down through oral traditions; it encompasses a wide range of music, from Appalachian fiddle tunes to the accordion-led zydeco of Louisiana.

folk-rock amplified folk music, often featuring politically overt lyrics; influenced by rock and roll.

format radio the concept of radio stations developing and playing specific styles (or formats) geared to listeners' age, race, or gender; in format radio, management, rather than deejays, controls programming choices.

Fourth Estate the notion that the press operates as an unofficial branch of government, monitoring the legislative, judicial, and executive branches for abuses of power.

franchise fees the money a cable company pays a city annually for the right to operate the local cable system; these fees are limited by law to no more than 5 percent of the company's gross annual revenue.

fringe time in television, the time slot either immediately before the evening's prime-time schedule (called *early fringe*) or following the local evening news or the network's late-night talk shows (called *late fringe*).

gag orders legal restrictions prohibiting the press from releasing preliminary information that might prejudice jury selection.

gangsta rap a style of rap music that depicts the hardships of urban life and sometimes glorifies the violent style of street gangs.

gatekeepers editors, producers, and other media managers who function as message filters, making decisions about what types of messages actually get produced for particular audiences.

general-interest magazine a type of magazine that offers a wide variety of topics and is aimed at a broad national audience.

gotcha stories news reports in which journalists nab evildoers or interview subjects who were caught in an act of deception.

grunge rock music that takes the spirit of punk and infuses it with more attention to melody.

halo effect in TV audience measurement, the phenomenon of viewers reporting not what they actually watched but what they think they should have watched.

happy talk in TV journalism, the ad-libbed or scripted banter that goes on among local news anchors, reporters, meteorologists, and sportscasters before and after news reports.

headend a cable TV system's computerized nerve center, where TV signals from local broadcast stations and satellites are received, processed, and distributed to area homes.

herd journalism a situation in which reporters stake out a house or follow a story in such large groups that the entire profession comes under attack for invading people's privacy or exploiting their personal tragedies.

hidden-fear appeal an advertising strategy that plays on a sense of insecurity, trying to persuade consumers that only a specific product can offer relief.

high culture a symbolic expression that has come to mean "good taste"; often supported by wealthy patrons and corporate donors, it is associated with fine art (such as ballet, the symphony, painting, and classical literature), which is available primarily in theaters or museums.

high-definition television (HDTV) a new digital standard for U.S. television sets that has more than twice the resolution of the system that served as the standard from the 1940s through the 1990s.

human-interest stories news accounts that focus on the trials and tribulations of the human condition, often featuring ordinary individuals facing extraordinary challenges.

hypertext a data-linking feature of the World Wide Web, it allows a user to click on a highlighted word or phrase and skip directly to other files related to that subject in other computer systems.

hypodermic-needle model an early model in mass-communication research that attempted to explain media effects by arguing that the media shoot their powerful effects directly into unsuspecting or weak audiences; sometimes called the *bullet theory* or *direct effects* model.

hypotheses in social-science research, tentative general statements that predict a relationship between a *dependent variable* and an *independent variable*.

independent station a TV station, such as WGN or WTBS, that finds its own original and syndicated programming and is not affiliated with any of the major networks.

indies independent music and film production houses that work outside industry oligopolies; they often produce less mainstream music and film.

indirect payment in media economics, the financial support of media products by advertisers, who pay for the quantity or quality of audience members that a particular medium attracts.

individualism an underlying value held by most U.S. journalists and citizens, it favors individual rights and responsibilities over group needs or institutional mandates.

infomercials thirty-minute late-night and daytime programs that usually feature fading TV and music celebrities, who advertise a product in a format that looks like a talk show.

information highway the circulation of both personal communication and mass media on personal computers and modems, high-speed telephone links, communication satellites, and television screens.

ink-jet imaging a computer technique that allows a magazine publisher or advertiser to print personalized messages to individual subscribers.

instant book in the book industry, a marketing strategy that involves publishing a topical book quickly after a major event.

interactivity a communication process that allows immediate two-way communication (as via telephones or email) between senders and receivers of media messages.

Internet the vast central network of high-speed telephone lines designed to link and carry computer information worldwide.

Internet Service Provider (ISP) a company that provides Internet access to homes and businesses for a fee.

interpretation the third step in the critical process, it asks and answers the "What does that mean?" and "So what?" questions about one's findings.

interpretive journalism a type of journalism that involves analyzing and explaining key issues or events and placing them in a broader historical or social context.

invasion of privacy the violation of a person's right to be left alone, without his or her name, image, or daily activities becoming public property.

inverted-pyramid style a style of journalism in which news reports begin with the most dramatic or newsworthy information—answering who, what, where, and when (and less frequently why or how) questions at the top of the story—and then tail off with less significant details.

irritation advertising an advertising strategy that tries to create product-name recognition by being annoying or obnoxious.

jazz an improvisational and mostly instrumental musical form that absorbs and integrates a diverse body of musical styles, including African rhythms, blues, big band, and gospel.

joint operating agreement (JOA) in the newspaper industry, an economic arrangement, sanctioned by the government, that permits competing newspapers to operate separate editorial divisions while merging business and production operations.

kinescope before the days of videotape, a 1950s technique for preserving television broadcasts by using a film camera to record a live TV show off a studio monitor.

knowledge gap the growing contrast between "information haves," or digital highway users who can afford to acquire multiple media services, and "information have-nots," who cannot afford a computer much less the many options now available on the information highway.

leased channels in cable television, channels that allow citizens to buy time for producing programs or presenting their own viewpoints.

libel in media law, the defamation of character in written expression.

libertarian model a model for journalism and speech that encourages vigorous government criticism and supports the highest degree of freedom for individual speech and news operations.

limited competition in media economics, a market with many producers and sellers but only a few differentiable products within a particular category; sometimes called *monopolistic competition.*

linotype a technology introduced in the nineteenth century that allowed printers to set type mechanically using a typewriter-style keyboard.

literary journalism news reports that adapt fictional storytelling techniques to nonfictional material; sometimes called *new journalism.*

lobbying in government public relations, the process of attempting to influence the voting of lawmakers to support a client's or an organization's best interests.

low culture a symbolic expression allegedly aligned with the questionable tastes of the "masses," who enjoy the commercial "junk" circulated by the mass media, such as soap operas, rock music, talk radio, comic books, and monster truck pulls.

magazine a collection of articles, stories, and ads that appear in a nondaily periodical.

market research in advertising and public relations agencies, the department that uses social-science techniques to assess the behaviors and attitudes of consumers toward particular products before any ads are created.

mass communication the process of designing and delivering cultural messages and stories to diverse audiences through media channels as old as the book and as new as the Internet.

mass customization the process whereby product companies and content providers customize a Web page, print ad, or other media form for an individual consumer.

mass media the cultural industries—the channels of communication—that produce and distribute songs, novels, newspapers, movies, online computer services, and other cultural products to a large number of people.

mechanical royalty the copyright fee, usually about one-half cent for each CD or audiotape sold, received by songwriters and publishers when they allow their music to be recorded.

media buyers in advertising, the individuals who choose and purchase the types of media that are best suited to carry a client's ads and reach the targeted audience.

media convergence the process whereby old and new media are available via the integration of personal computers and high-speed satellite-based phone or cable links.

media-effects research the mainstream tradition in mass-communication research, it attempts to understand, explain, and predict the impact—or effects—of the mass media on individuals and society.

mega-agencies in advertising, large firms or holding companies that are formed by merging several individual agencies and that maintain worldwide regional offices; they provide both advertising and public-relations services and operate in-house radio and TV production studios.

messages the programs, texts, images, sounds, and product ads transmitted from senders to receivers.

microchips/microprocessors miniature circuits that process and store electronic signals, integrating thousands of electronic components into thin strands of silicon along which binary codes travel.

minimal-effects model a mass-communication research model based on tightly controlled experiments and survey findings; it argues that the mass media have limited effects on audiences, reinforcing existing behaviors and attitudes rather than changing them.

miniseries a serial television program that runs over a two-day to two-week period, usually on consecutive nights.

modern period a historical era spanning the time from the rise of the Industrial Revolution in the eighteenth and nineteenth centuries to the present; its social values include celebrating the individual, believing in rational order, working efficiently, and rejecting tradition.

monopoly in media economics, an organizational structure that occurs when a single firm dominates production and distribution in a particular industry, either nationally or locally.

muckraking a style of early-twentieth-century investigative journalism that referred to reporters who were willing to crawl around in society's muck to uncover a story.

multiple-system operators (MSOs) large corporations that own numerous cable television systems.

multiplexes contemporary movie theaters that exhibit many movies at the same time on multiple screens.

must-carry rules rules established by the FCC requiring all cable operators to assign channels to and carry all local TV broadcasts on their systems, thus ensuring that local network affiliates, independent stations (those not carrying network programs), and public television channels would benefit from cable's clearer reception.

myth analysis a strategy for critiquing advertising that provides insights into how ads work on a cultural level; according to this strategy, ads are narratives with stories to tell and social conflicts to resolve.

narrative the structure underlying most media products, it includes two components: the *story*—what happens to whom—and the *discourse*—how the story is told.

narrowcasting any specialized electronic programming or media channel aimed at a target audience.

network a broadcast process that links, through special phone lines or satellite transmissions, groups of radio or TV stations, which share programming produced at a central location.

news the process of gathering information and making narrative reports—edited by individuals in a news organization—which create selected frames of reference and help the public make sense of prominent people, important events, and unusual happenings in everyday life.

newsgroups organized computer conferences consisting of bulletin boards and individual messages, or postings, which are circulated twenty-four hours a day via the Internet and cover a range of topics.

newshole the space left over in a newspaper for news content after all the ads are placed.

newspaper chains large companies that own several papers throughout the country.

newsreels weekly ten-minute magazine-style compilations of filmed news events from around the world organized in a sequence of short reports; prominent in movie theaters between the 1920s and the 1950s.

newsworthiness the often unstated criteria that journalists use to determine which events and issues should become news reports, including timeliness, proximity, conflict, prominence, human interest, consequence, usefulness, novelty, and deviance.

nickelodeons the first small makeshift movie theaters, which were often converted cigar stores, pawnshops, or restaurants redecorated to mimic vaudeville theaters.

O & Os network-owned-and-operated TV stations.

objective journalism a modern style of journalism that distinguishes factual reports from opinion columns; reporters strive to remain neutral toward the issue or event they cover, searching out competing points of view among the sources for a story.

objectivity in social-science research, eliminating bias and judgments on the part of researchers.

obscenity expression that is not protected as speech if these three legal tests are all met: (1) the average person, applying contemporary community standards, would find that the material as a whole appeals to prurient interest; (2) the material depicts or describes sexual conduct in a patently offensive way; and (3) the material, as a whole, lacks serious literary, artistic, political, or scientific value.

off-network syndication in television, the process whereby older programs that no longer run during prime time are made available for reruns to local stations, cable operators, online services, and foreign markets.

offset lithography a technology that allowed books to be printed from photographic plates rather than metal casts, reducing the cost of color and illustrations and eventually permitting computers to perform typesetting.

oligopoly in media economics, an organizational structure in which a few firms control most of an industry's production and distribution resources.

option time now considered illegal, a procedure whereby a radio network paid an affiliate station a set fee per hour for an option to control programming and advertising on that station.

paid circulation the process of earning magazine revenue from consumers who either pay for regular subscriptions or for individual copies at newsstands or supermarkets.

papyrus one of the first substances to hold written language and symbols; obtained from plant reeds found along the Nile River.

parchment treated animal skin that replaced papyrus as an early pre-paper substance to document written language.

partisan press an early dominant style of American journalism distinguished by opinion newspapers, which generally argued one political point of view or pushed the plan of the particular party that subsidized the paper.

pass-along readership the total number of people who come into contact with a single copy of a magazine.

payola the unethical (but not always illegal) practice of record promoters paying deejays or radio programmers to favor particular songs over others.

pay-per-view (PPV) a cable-television service that allows customers to select a particular movie for a onetime $3 or $4 charge, payable to the local cable company, or $25 to $40 for a special onetime event.

people meters in TV audience measurement, devices that hook up a random sample of households to determine their viewing behavior.

performance royalty the copyright fee paid to songwriters and performers whenever their music is used on radio, television, or other media channels.

photojournalism the use of photos to document events and people's lives.

plain-folks pitch an advertising strategy that associates a product with simplicity and the common person.

political advertising the use of ad techniques to promote a candidate's image and persuade the public to adopt a particular viewpoint.

pop music popular music that appeals either to a wide cross section of the public or to sizable subdivisions within the larger public based on age, region, or ethnic background; the word *pop* has also been used as a label to distinguish popular music from classical music.

postmodern period a contemporary historical era usually spanning the time from the 1960s to the present; its social values include opposing hierarchy, diversifying and recycling culture, questioning scientific reasoning, and embracing paradox.

premium cable in cable programming, a tier of channels that subscribers can order at an additional monthly fee over their basic cable service; these may include movie channels and interactive services.

press agent the earliest type of public-relations practitioner, who sought to advance a client's image through media exposure.

press release in public relations, an announcement—written in the style of a news report—that gives new information about an individual, a company, or an organization and pitches a story idea to the news media.

prime time in television programming, the hours between 8 and 11 P.M. (or 7 and 10 P.M. in the Midwest), when networks have traditionally drawn their largest audiences and charged their highest advertising rates.

Prime-Time Access Rule (PTAR) an FCC rule that in 1970 took the 7:30 to 8 P.M. time slot (6:30 to 7 P.M. central) away from the TV networks and gave it exclusively to local stations in the nation's fifty largest television markets.

prior restraint the legal definition of censorship in the United States, which prohibits courts and governments from blocking any publication or speech before it actually occurs.

production the individuals or companies in the mass-media business in charge of creating movies, TV programs, music recordings, magazines, books, and other media products.

product placement the advertising tactic of buying space for a particular product so that it appears on a movie set or a program as a supporting prop.

program-length commercials controversial thirty-minute cartoon programs developed for TV syndication primarily to promote a line of toys.

propaganda in advertising and public relations, a communication strategy that tries to manipulate public opinion to gain support for a special issue, program, or policy, such as a nation's war effort.

pseudo-event in public relations, any circumstance or event created solely for the purpose of obtaining coverage in the media.

psychographics in market research, the study of audience or consumer attitudes, beliefs, interests, and motivations.

publicity in public relations, the positive and negative messages that spread controlled and uncontrolled information about a person, corporation, issue, or policy in various media.

public journalism a type of journalism, driven by citizen forums, that goes beyond telling the news to embrace a broader mission of improving the quality of public life; also called *civic journalism.*

public relations the total communication strategy conducted by a person, a government, or an organization attempting to reach and persuade its audiences to adopt a point of view.

public-service announcements (PSAs) reports or announcements, carried free by radio and TV stations, that promote government programs, educational projects, voluntary agencies, or social reform.

puffery bordering on deception, advertisements that use hyperbole and exaggeration.

pulp fiction a term used to describe many late-nineteenth-century popular paperbacks and dime novels, which were constructed of cheap machine-made pulp material.

punk rock rock music that challenges the orthodoxy and commercialism of the recording business; it is characterized by loud, unpolished qualities, a jackhammer beat, primal vocal screams, crude aggression, and defiant or comic lyrics.

qualified privilege a legal right allowing journalists to report judicial or legislative proceedings even though the public statements being reported may be libelous.

rack jobbers sales agents in the music business who contract with general retailers such as Kmart to stock their racks or shelves with the latest CDs, audiocassettes, and music videos.

random assignment a social-science research method for assigning research subjects; it ensures that every subject has an equal chance of being placed in either the experimental group or the control group.

rap music music that combines spoken street dialect with cuts (or samples) of older records and bears the influences of social politics, male boasting, and comic lyrics carried forward from blues, R&B, soul, and rock and roll.

rating in TV audience measurement, a statistical estimate expressed as a percentage of households tuned to a program in the local or national market being sampled.

receivers the target of messages crafted by a sender.

regional editions national magazines whose content is tailored to the interests of different geographic areas.

reliability in social-science research, getting the same answers or outcomes from a study or measure during repeated testing.

rerun syndication in television, the process whereby programs that stay in a network's lineup long enough to build up a certain number of episodes (usually four seasons' worth) are sold, or syndicated, to hundreds of TV markets in the United States and abroad.

responsible capitalism an underlying value held by many U.S. journalists and citizens, it assumes that businesspeople compete with one another not primarily to maximize profits but to increase prosperity for all.

rhythm and blues (R&B) music that merged urban blues with big-band sounds.

rockabilly music that mixed bluegrass and country influences with those of black folk music and early amplified blues.

rock and roll music that mixed the vocal and instrumental traditions of popular music; it merged the black influences of urban blues, gospel, and R&B with the white influences of country, folk, and pop vocals.

rotation in format radio programming, playing the most popular or best-selling songs many times throughout the day.

saturation advertising the ad strategy of inundating a variety of print and visual media with ads aimed at target audiences.

scientific method a widely used research method that studies phenomena in systematic stages; it includes identifying the research problem; reviewing existing research; developing working hypotheses; determining an appropriate research design; collecting information; analyzing results to see if the hypotheses have been verified; and interpreting the implications of the study.

scoop an exclusive story obtained by a journalist, who publicly presents the story ahead of all rivals.

search engines computer programs that allows users to enter key words or queries to find related sites on the World Wide Web.

Section 315 part of the 1934 Communications Act, it mandates that during elections broadcast stations must provide equal opportunities and response time for qualified political candidates.

seditious libel in law, defaming a public official's character in print.

selective exposure the phenomenon whereby audiences seek messages and meanings that correspond to their preexisting beliefs and values.

selective retention the phenomenon whereby audiences remember or retain messages and meanings that correspond to their preexisting beliefs and values.

senders the authors, producers, agencies, and organizations that transmit messages to receivers.

serial programs radio or TV programs, such as soap operas, that feature continuing story lines from day to day.

servers individual "host" computer centers run (or hosted) by universities, corporations, and government agencies, all of which are interconnected to the Internet by special high-speed phone lines.

share in TV audience measurement, a statistical estimate of the percentage of homes tuned to a program, compared with those actually using their sets at the time of a sample.

shield laws laws protecting the confidentiality of key interview subjects and reporters' rights *not* to reveal the sources of controversial information used in news stories.

shortwave radio a type of radio transmission, used mostly by amateur—or ham—radio operators and governments, that can bounce a radio signal off the ionosphere halfway around the world.

situation comedy (sitcom) a type of comedy series that features a recurring cast and set as well as several narrative scenes; each episode establishes a situation, complicates it, develops increasing confusion among its characters, and then alleviates the complications.

situational ethics the principle that in a moral society ethical decisions are arrived at on an individual or case-by-case basis.

sketch comedy short television comedy skits that are usually segments of TV variety shows; sometimes known as *vaudeo*, the marriage of vaudeville and video.

slander in law, spoken language that defames a person's character.

slogan in advertising, a catchy phrase that attempts to promote or sell a product by capturing its essence in words.

small-town pastoralism an underlying value held by many U.S. journalists and citizens, it favors the small over the large and the rural over the urban.

snob appeal an advertising strategy that attempts to convince consumers that using a product will enable them to maintain or elevate their social station.

social-responsibility model a model for journalism and speech, influenced by the libertarian model, that encourages the free flow of information to citizens so they can make wise decisions regarding political and social issues.

soul music music that mixes gospel, blues, and urban and southern black styles with slower, more emotional, and melancholic lyrics.

sound bite in TV journalism, the equivalent of a quote in print; the part of a news report in which an expert, a celebrity, victim, or person on the street is interviewed about some aspect of an event or issue.

space brokers in the days before modern advertising, individuals who purchased space in newspapers and sold it to various merchants.

spin doctors political consultants who manage campaigns and attempt to favorably shape the news media's image of a candidate.

split-run editions editions of national magazines that tailor ads to different geographic areas.

stereo the recording of two separate channels or tracks of sound.

stereotyping the process of assigning individuals to groups, whose members are falsely assumed to act as a single entity and to display certain characteristics, which are usually negative.

storyboard in advertising, a blueprint or roughly drawn comic-strip version of a proposed advertisement.

stripping in TV syndication, showing a program—either older network reruns or programs made for syndication—five days a week.

studio system an early film-production system that constituted a sort of assembly-line process for moviemaking; major film studios controlled not only actors but directors, editors, writers, and other employees, all of whom worked under exclusive contracts.

subliminal advertising a 1950s term that refers to hidden or disguised print and visual messages that allegedly register on the unconscious, creating false needs and seducing people into buying products.

subsidiary rights in the book industry, selling the rights to a book for use in other media forms, such as a mass-market paperback, a CD-ROM, or the basis for a movie screenplay.

superstations local independent TV stations, such as WTBS in Atlanta or WGN in Chicago, that have uplinked their signals onto a communication satellite to make themselves available nationwide.

superstore a large retail business that sells books, recordings, and new media; this contemporary trend in book-selling adapts the large retail-store concept to the publishing industry.

survey research in social-science research, a method of collecting and measuring data taken from a group of respondents.

sweeps in TV ratings, month-long measurement periods—conducted four times a year (six times in larger markets) that determine both local and national ad rates.

syndicated exclusivity (syndex) FCC rules that gave local stations exclusive rights in their area to syndicate TV programs, such as off-network reruns, which they had purchased.

synergy in media economics, the promotion and sale of a product (and all its versions) throughout the various subsidiaries of a media conglomerate.

textual analysis in media research, a method for closely and critically examining and interpreting the meanings of culture, including architecture, fashion, books, movies, and TV programs.

time shifting the process whereby television viewers tape shows and watch them later, when it is convenient for them.

Top 40 format the first radio format, in which stations played the forty most popular hits in a given week as measured by record sales.

transistor   invented by Bell Laboratories in 1947, this tiny technology, which receives and amplifies radio signals, made portable radios possible.

transponders   the relay points on a communication satellite that receive and transmit telephone and TV signals.

UHF   ultrahigh frequency; in broadcasting, the band in the electromagnetic spectrum that the FCC allocated for TV channels 14 through 69.

underground press   radical newspapers, run on shoestring budgets, that question mainstream political policies and conventional values; usually refers to a journalism movement of the 1960s.

uses and gratifications model   a mass-communication research model, usually employing in-depth interviews and survey questionnaires, that argues that people use the media to satisfy various emotional desires or intellectual needs.

validity   in social-science research, demonstrating that a study actually measures what it claims to measure.

VALS   short for values and lifestyles, a market-research strategy that divides consumers into types and measures psychological factors, including how consumers think and feel about products and how they achieve (or do not achieve) the lifestyles to which they aspire.

vertical integration   in media economics, controlling a mass-media industry at its three essential levels: production, distribution, and exhibition; the term is most frequently used in reference to the film industry.

VHF   very high frequency; in broadcasting, the band in the electromagnetic spectrum that the FCC allocated for TV channels 2 through 13.

videocassette recorders (VCRs)   recorders that use a half-inch video format known as VHS (video home system), which allows viewers to record and play back programs from television or to watch movies rented from video stores.

video news release (VNR)   in public relations, the visual counterpart to a press release; it pitches a story idea to the TV news media by mimicking the style of a broadcast news report.

virtual communities   groups of computer users who are separated geographically but connected nationally and globally by their shared interests or business and their access to an online service or the Internet.

weighting   in TV audience measurement, assigning more weight to a particular respondent in an attempt to correct the underrepresented group in the original sample.

wireless telegraphy   the forerunner of radio, a form of voiceless point-to-point communication; it preceded the voice and sound transmissions of one-to-many mass communication that became known as broadcasting.

wireless telephony   early experiments in wireless voice and music transmissions, which later developed into modern radio.

wire services   commercial organizations, such as the Associated Press, that share news stories and information by relaying them around the country and the world, originally via telegraph and now via satellite transmission.

world music   sometimes called international or ethnic songs, this category includes the many different styles of popular regional and folk music from cultures throughout the world; it usually excludes classical music and the most popular forms of American or European music.

World Wide Web   a free and open data-linking system for organizing and standardizing information on the Internet; the WWW allows computer-accessed information to associate with—or link to—other information no matter where it is on the Internet.

yellow journalism   a newspaper style or era that peaked in the 1890s, it emphasized high-interest stories, sensational crime news, large headlines, and serious reports that exposed corruption, particularly in business and government.

zapping   using a VCR to edit out commercials during the videotaping process.

zines   self-published magazines produced on personal computer programs or on the Internet.

zipping   using a VCR to fast-forward a videotaped program through the ads during the recorded viewing.

credits

Text Credits

39, Figure 2.1: "Distributed Networks" from p. 59 in *Where Wizards Stay Up Late* by Katie Hafner and Matthew Lyon. Copyright © 1996 by Katie Hafner and Matthew Lyon. Reprinted by permission of Simon & Schuster; **89**, Figure 3.2: "The Major Labels in the Sound Recording Industry" from the *Los Angeles Times*, May 22, 1998. Copyright © 1998 Los Angeles Times. Reprinted by permission; **96**, "Fans of MP3 Forced the Issue," by Lisa Napoli. From *Cyber/Times, The New York Times on the Web*, December 16, 1998. © 1998 The New York Times Company. Reprinted by permission; **103**, Figure 4.1: "The Electromagnetic Spectrum" from *The World Book Encyclopedia* (Volume 6, page 202). © 1999 World Book, Inc. By permission of the publisher; **119**, Figure 4.3 & Table 4.1: "Radio Program Log for an Oldies Station." *WQKL-FM*, Ann Arbor (1997). "The Twelve Most Popular Radio Formats." By permission of The Center for Radio Information, 19 Market Street, Cold Spring, NY 10516; **129**, "Bandwidth with Byte" by Robert Occhialini, from *Swing* magazine, November 1998. Copyright © 1998 by Robert Occhialini. Reprinted by permission of the author; **140**, "DVT: The Digital Revolution." Adapted from "Building Your Next TV: Two Industries Fight for a $150 Billion Prize" by Joel Brinkley. *The New York Times*, March 28, 1997, pp. C1–C2. Copyright © 1997 by The New York Times Company. Reprinted by permission; **147**, Table 5.1: "Selected Situation and Domestic Comedies Rated in the Top 10." Reprinted with permission; **153**, Figure 5.1: "The Fall Prime-Time Schedule Toward the End of the Network Era, 1978–79" from page 938 in *Total Television: A Comprehensive Guide to Programming from 1948 to the Present* 3e by Alex McNeil. Copyright © 1991 by Alex McNeil. Reprinted by permission of Penguin Putnam, Inc.; **163**, Table 5.2: "The Top 10 Highest-Rated TV Series, Individual Programs." Reprinted with permission; **176**, Figure 6.2: "The Rise of Cable Systems, 1970–90." Reprinted by permission of Warren Publishing, Inc., Washington, D.C.; **181**, Table 6.1: "Impact of the 1996 Telecommunications Act." Reprinted by permission of Dow Jones, Inc. via Copyright Clearance Center, Inc. © 1996 Dow Jones and Company, Inc. All Rights Reserved Worldwide. and Copyright © 1996 Time, Inc. Reprinted by permission; **222**, Table 7.3: "The Top 10 Foreign-Language Films in U.S. Theaters." Reprinted by permission; **247**, Tables 8.1 & 8.3: "The Nation's Largest Daily Newspapers" and "The Top Fifteen Daily Newspapers in the World." Reprinted by permission of Editor & Publisher; **265**, "So If You've Got It, Flaunt It" by J. D. Lasica from *American Journalism Review*, October 1998. Reprinted with permission of American Journalism Review; **297**, *Factsheet5*, © 1996 *Stay Free!, Cool Beans!, Thrift SCORE,* and *MAXIMUM ROCKNROLL*. Reprinted by permission; **300–301**, "Sex, Lies, and Advertising" by Gloria Steinem. *Ms.* Magazine (July/August 1990), pp. 18–28. Reprinted by permission of the author. First issue cover with first pages from four inside articles, Spring 1972. © 1972. Reprinted by permission of *Ms.* Magazine. "Why I Want a Wife" by Judy Syfers. © 1970 by Judy Brady. Reprinted by permission of the author; **311 & 328**, Tables 10.1 & 10.3: "Annual Numbers of New York Book Titles Published, Selected Years" and "Bookstores in the United States, 1995." Reprinted by permission of R.R. Bowker, a Reed Elsevier

Reference Publishing Company; **321**, Table 10.2: "Mass-Market Paperback Best-Sellers: The First Twenty-Five Years" from page 289 in *Two-Bit Culture: The Paperbacking of America* by Kenneth Davis. Copyright © 1984 by Kenneth Davis. Reprinted by permission of Houghton-Mifflin; **326**, Figure 10.2: "Book Economics" from page 125 in *Brill's Content*, October 1998. © 1998 Brill Media Ventures, L.P. Reprinted by permission; **434**, "Why Those Hidden Cameras Hurt Journalism" by Paul Starobin. *The New York Times*, January 28, 1997, p. A13. Copyright © 1997 by The New York Times Company. Reprinted by permission; **463**, "TV Rating Labels and the Impact of Media Research." *The New York Times*, December 20, 1996, p. A12. Copyright © 1996 by The New York Times Company. Reprinted by permission; **478–479**, "Violence Study Shows TV's Mental Block" by Ellen Goodman. © 1996 The Washington Post Writers Group. Reprinted by permission.

Picture Credits

Key: APh = Archive Photos; AP/WW = Associated Press/Wide World Photos; C/BA = Corbis/Bettmann Archive; PF = Photofest

2–3, Eric Gay/AP/WW; **7**, Gutenberg Museum, Mainz; **10**, Richard Ellis/Sygma; **12**, FPG; **14** (top), Carolyn Zlotnik/Woodfin Camp & Assoc., (bot.), Michael Gillespie; **16** (l), courtesy, General Mills, Inc., (r), PF; **21–24**, APh; **25**, Kevork Djanezian/AP/WW; **30**, Michael Coyne/Image Bank; **31**, Jeffrey Markowitz/Sygma; **34–35**, Sygma; (inset), The Image Works; **38**, Jae Shim; **42**, Dick Blume/The Image Works; **43**, The Image Works; **45**, Steven Hunt/Image Bank; **47**, Lara Jo Regan/SABA; **51**, courtesy, JenniCam; **56**, ©, August 8, 1994, US NEWS & WORLD REPORT, Art: Dave Black; **59**, R. Maiman/Sygma; **60**, Rula Halawani/Reuters/APh; **64**, Lloyd Gross/Starfile; **68**, Lundoff Collection; **72** (l), Williams Collection of The Historic New Orleans Collection; (c), Culver; (r) NYPL Music Division; **74**, courtesy, Legacy Records, Div. of SONY Music; **75–77**, C/BA; **78**, courtesy, Polygram Records; **79**, Theo Westenberger/Gamma Liaison; **81**, AP/WW; **82**, PF; **86**, Donald Greenhaus/Retna; **88**, Steve Marcus/Reuters/APh; **91** (l), Victoria Arocho/AP/WW, (r), K. Barros/Gamma Liaison; **95**, AP/WW; **96**, Eric Kamp/Index Stock Imagery; **100**, courtesy, ABC-Radio; **104**, Roger Violett/Gamma Liaison; **108**, C/BA; **114**, (t-l), Culver, (t-r), (b), PF; **115**, Culver; **116**, C/BA; **121**, Bob Child/AP/WW; **124**, Timothy Rue/C/BA; **125**, © 1993, Time Inc. Reprinted by permission; **129**, © *Steal This Radio*; **130**, Jason Grow/SABA; **134–135**, PF; **138**, Dane Penland; **140**, courtesy, SONY Electronics, Inc.; **142**, AP/WW; **148**, PF; **149**, AP/WW; **150**, PF; **156**, James Sorenson/AP/WW; **157–161**, PF; **165** (t), Henry Gris/FPG, (b), AP/WW; **166**, AP/WW; **170**, PF; **185**, courtesy, © 1996 CNN; **186**, Marty Lederhandler/AP/WW; **187** (t), Colin Braley/Reuters/APh, (b), AP/WW; **189**, Music Television, *Playa* ™, used by permission, © 1998, MTV Networks, Div. of Viacom, Intl.; **194**, © 1996, Thomson Consumer Electronics; **198**, James M. Kelley/Globe Photos; **202**, Michael Gillespie; **206**, Edison National Historic Park, Ntl. Park Service; **209–215**, PF; **215** (ctr), APh; **216**, NYPL Theater Collection; **219**, C/BA; **220**, Fotos Intl./APh;

537

AARP (American Association of Retired Persons), 291
ABC (American Broadcasting Company), 49, 412
  radio, 112
  television network, 155, 156
ABC News, 145, 433
  Walt Disney Company and, 515
ABC World News Tonight, 145
Abilene Project (Internet2), 36, 52, 62
above-the-line costs, 157
Abraham, Seth, 192
absolute privilege, 496
absolutist ethics, 433, 436
access channels, 175
account executives, 359
account reviews, advertising, 359
ACLU v. Reno, 54
A. C. Nielsen Market Research Company, 162, 414
acquisitions editors, 325, 326
Action for Children's Television (ACT), 365
Acuff-Rose Music, 493
Adams, John, 492
Adams, Judith, 421
Ad Council, 351
Adorno, T. W., 472
adult contemporary (AC) format, 123
adult standards, 124
Advanced Research Projects Agency (ARPA), 39
Advance Publications, 293, 302, 331
advances, book, 335
advances from publishers, 325–26
Adventures of Huckleberry Finn (Twain), 338
adversaries, journalists as, 445
advertising, 343–73
  alcohol, 369
  association principle, 359, 360–63
  children and, 365–66
  comparative, 370
  creative aspects of, 356, 357
  democracy and, 372–73
  early history of, 346–51
  in the 1800s, 347–50
  the Internet and, 371–72
  journalism and, 370–71
  magazine, 284, 286, 298–301
  market research and, 355
  media selection, 358–59

  modern, 351–59
  myth analysis, 363–64
  newspaper, 257–58, 264
  persuasive techniques, 359–64
  political, 372–73
  puffery and deceptive, 370
  radio, 108–9, 121–22
  regulation of, 351, 364
  saturation, 358–59
  in schools, 365–66
  for sneakers, 353, 354
  social change and, 350–51
  subliminal, 351
  television, 141, 156, 351, 355, 358, 364
  VALS (Values and Lifestyles) research, 355–57
  values and, 350–51
  visual design and, 352
  women and, 361, 362, 366, 368
Advertising Age, 366, 368
advertising agencies
  account and client management at, 359
  boutique, 353
  early, 346–47
  mega-agencies, 352–53
  structure of, 353, 355–59
advocacy journalism, 250
Advocate, 293
Ad Watch, 372
affiliate stations, 110, 111
African Americans, 11
  cigarette advertising and, 368
  film industry and, 214–15
  magazines, 293
  MTV and, 188
  newspapers, 254–55
  pop music and, 73
    rock and roll, 74–78
  radio, 123
  rap music and, 87–88
Afro-American (newspaper), 255
Agee, James, 454
agenda-setting, 470
Akwesasne Notes, 256
Albee, Edward, 229
album-oriented rock (AOR), 126
alcohol advertising, 369
Alcott, Louisa May, 334
Alexander, Charles, 275
Alfred Hitchcock Presents, 149
Alienated American, 254–55
Ali, Muhammad, 153

Allen, Woody, 146
All in the Family, 148
"All I Wanna Do," 65
Ally McBeal, 148, 149
Alter, Jonathan, 441
alternative rock, 86
Amanpour, Christiane, 185
Amazing Fish Cam, 51
Amazon.com, 43, 330, 371
Amedure, Scott, 14
American Association of Advertising Agencies (AAAA), 351
American Association of Retired Persons (AARP), 291
American Bar Association, 501
American Booksellers Association, 330
American Civil Liberties Union (ACLU), 54, 55, 498
American Express, 359
American Graffiti, 219
American Library Association (ALA), 338
American Marconi, 104–7
American Medical Association, 124
American Society of Composers, Authors, and Publishers (ASCAP), 70
American Society of Newspaper Editors (ASNE), 249
American Tobacco Company, 383
America Online (AOL), 47–49, 232
AM/FM Radio Network, 130
Amos 'n' Andy, 115–16, 136
Amsterdam News, 255
analog recording, 69
analysis, in critical process, 28
Andrew Sisters, 71
Andrus, Ethel Percy, 291
Angelou, Maya, 338
Animals, the, 84
Annenberg, Walter, 282
Annie, 217
anthology dramas, 148–50
antitrust laws and policies, 410, 412
  limits of, 419–20
AOR (album-oriented rock), 126
Apple Records, 353
A&R (artist & repertoire) agents, 90
Areopagitica (Milton), 488–89
Aristotle, 323
Arledge, Roone, 145

Armstrong, Edwin, 117–18
Arnaz, Desi, 145
ARPAnet, 39, 40
ASCAP (American Society of Composers, Authors, and Publishers), 70
As Nasty as They Wanna Be, 486
Associated Press (AP), 244, 393
association principle, 359, 360–63
As the World Turns, 151
At Home, 49
AtHome Corporation, 195
Atkinson, Samuel Coate, 275
AT&T, 49, 58, 138, 177, 381
    cable television and, 195, 196
    radio and, 106–9, 111
AT&T Broadband and Internet Services (BIS), 195
attitudes, mass-communication process and, 11
audio books, 335
Audion, 105
audiotape, 68
Audit Bureau of Circulation (ABC), 351
authoritarian model for expression and speech, 489
Avalon, Frankie, 80
Ayer, N. W., 347

Babylon, ancient, 346
Babylonians, 312
Bad Boy Entertainment, 88
Bagdikian, Ben, 419
Bailey, F. Lee, 500
Baker, LaVern, 77
balanced journalism, 444
Ball, Lucille, 145–46, 508
Band, The, 84
bandwagon effect, 360
BankAmericard, 56
banner ads, on the Internet, 371
Bantam Books, 321, 322
Banzhaf, John, 511
Baran, Paul, 39
Barbieri, Paula, 335
Barkley, Charles, 354
Barnes & Noble, 328–30, 420
Barnet, Richard J., 407
Barnum & Bailey, 380
Barnum, Phineas Taylor (P. T.), 380
Barr, Chris, 265
Barrie, Dennis, 486–87
barter deals, 162
Bartles & Jaymes, 361
Basketball Diaries, The (film), 4
Batman, 318
Bay Psalm Book, The, 314
Baywatch, 416
Bazelon, David, 511

Bazin, André, 208
BCA (Broadcasting Corporation of America), 109
B. Dalton bookstores, 328–29
Beadle, Erastus and Irwin, 314–15
Beatles, the, 81, 82, 90, 91, 353
Beauty and the Beast, 217, 230
believers, VALS research and, 356, 357
Bell, Alexander Graham, 290
Bell Laboratories, 117, 212, 213
Beloved, 221, 334
below-the-line costs, 157
Bennett, James Gordon, 243
Bentham, Jeremy, 436
Berg, A. Scott, 335
Bergen, Edgar, 146, 510
Berg, Gertrude, 508
Berkeley Barb, 257
Berle, Milton, 146
Berliner, Emile, 67
Berlin, Irving, 71
Bernays, Edward, 111, 383–84
Bernstein, Carl, 266, 431
Berry, Chuck, 73–75, 80, 85
Bertelsmann, 327, 331
best-selling books, 334–35
Betacam, 154
Betamax, 153–54
BET (Black Entertainment Television), 195
Better Business Bureau, 351
Bezos, Jeff, 330
Bhosle, Asha, 91
Big Bopper, 80
Big Issue, 264
"Big Mac" theory, 19
Bill Haley and the Comets, 76
Bird, Elizabeth, 476
Birth of a Nation, The, 219
"Bittersweet Symphony," 87–88
Blackboard Jungle, 76
Black Entertainment Television (BET), 195, 310
Black, Hugo, 487
blacklisting, 227
Blackwell, Otis, 76
Blair Witch Project, The, 226
blaxploitation movies, 215
block booking, 210, 211
block printing, 313
Bloom, Allan, 481
Bloom, Harold, 421
blue jeans, 377–78
blues, 73. *See also* rhythm and blues (R&B)
blues music, 83
"Blue Suede Shoes," 75
Bly, Nellie, 239–40, 245, 434
BMG, 89
Body Count, 11
Bok, Edward, 277
Bollywood, 223
book clubs, 327

Book of Ruth, The (Hamilton), 310
Book-of-the-Month Club, 327
book publishing industry
    colonial era, 314
    formation of publishing houses, 315–16
    organization and ownership of, 325–32
    structure of, 325–27
    trends in, 332, 334–36
books, 7–8, 309–39. *See also* book publishing industry
    alternative voices, 336
    blockbusters, 334–35
    censorship of, 337, 338
    comic, 318–19
    democracy and, 336
    dime novels (pulp fiction), 315
    e-books, 333
    history of, 312–14
    instant, 321–22
    licensing rights, 334–35
    mass-market paperbacks, 320–22
    movies and, 332–34
    paperback, 314–15
    preservation of older, 335–36
    professional, 317
    promotion and marketing of, 326–27
    reference, 323–24
    religious, 322–23
    on tape, 335
    television and, 332–34
    textbooks, 317, 320
    trade, 316–17
    types of, 316–25
    university press, 324–25
bookstores, 328–30
    online, 330
Book TV, 310
Boone, Daniel, 379
Boone, Pat, 77, 80
Boorstin, Daniel, 379, 384
bootlegging, CDs and cassettes, 94–95
Borders, 330
Borders-Walden bookstores, 328, 329
Boston News-Letter, 241
Boswell Sisters, 71
Bourke-White, Margaret, 281
boutique agencies, 353
Bowker, R. R., 324
Boy's Life, 291
Bradford, Andrew, 274
Brady, Mathew, 276
Brande, Dorothea, 320
Brave New World (Huxley), 20
Brazil, 477
Brennan, William, Jr., 487
Brenston, Jackie, 76
Brill's Content, 515
Brinkley, David, 144
Brinkley, John, 124
Britannica (EB), Encyclopaedia, 323–24
British Marconi, 104, 107
Broadband and Internet Services (BIS), 195

broadcasting, defined, 105
Broadcasting & Cable (magazine), 182
Broadcasting Corporation of America
      (BCA), 109
Broadcasting (magazine), 123
broadsides, 346
Broder, David, 454
Brokaw, Tom, 144, 332, 334
Brooks, Mel, 146
Brown, Margaret Wise, 20
Brown, Nicole, 503
Brown v. Board of Education, 73
browsers, 46, 48
Buchanan, Pat, 512
Buckley, William F., 304
Budweiser, 368
Buena Vista, 230
Buffett, Jimmy, 188
Buffy the Vampire Slayer, 156
bulletin boards, computer, 40
Burden of Proof, 503
Burke, James E., 397
Burnett, Carol, 294
Burnett, Carol, 294
Burnett, Leo, 358, 359
Burroughs, Edgar Rice, 338
Burson-Marsteller, 385–86, 397, 398
Burstein, Daniel, 36, 50
Burstyn v. Wilson, 506
Buy the Book, 310
Byrds, the, 83, 84

Cable Acts (1984 and 1992), 178–80
cable franchises, 175
Cable News Network. *See* CNN
cable radio, 193
cable television, 37, 171
   audio services, 193
   basic channels, 182–85, 188–91
   early technology and development of,
      173–74
   implications for democracy, 198–99
   interactive services, 192
   laws and regulations, 176–81
      Cable Acts (1984 and 1992), 178–80
      common carriers, 178
      electronic publishers, 178
      syndicated exclusivity (syndex) rules,
         178
      Telecommunications Act of 1996,
         180–81
   narrowcasting, 182
   ownership and business issues, 195–98
   pay-per-view services, 192
   premium channels, 191–93
   as threat to broadcasting, 174
Cablevision Industries, 195
Caesar, Sid, 146
Camel cigarettes, 366
Camel News Caravan, 144
Camel Newsreel Theater, 144
cameras in the courtroom, 501–3
Campbell-Ewald, 359
Campbell, John, 241

Campbell, Joseph, 311
Campbell, Luther R., 493
Campbell Soup, 348
Campbell v. Acuff-Rose Music, 494
Campion, Jane, 220
Canada, 189
Canadian Journalists for Free Expres-
      sions, 514
Canterbury Tales, 313–14
Cantril, Hadley, 465
"Can't Take My Eyes Off of You," 76
capitalism, 420–21
   responsible, 432
Capra, Frank, 219, 224
Capstar Broadcasting, 130
Carlin, George, 510
Carson, Lisa Nicole, 149
Carter, Bill, 158
Caruso, Denise, 512
Caruso, Enrico, 105
cash deals, 162
cash-plus deals, 162
Casiano Communications, 294
categorical imperative, 436
cathode ray tube, 138
Catholic Legion of Decency, 505
Catholic Worker, 260–61
CATV (community antenna television),
      173–74
Cavanagh, John, 407
CBS (Columbia Broadcasting System), 111
   football programming, 136
   television, 139, 149, 156
   Viacom and, 156, 412
CBS Evening News, 144
CBS News, 144
CBS Records, 68, 89, 189, 406
CBS Reports, 446
CBS/Westinghouse. *See*
      Westinghouse/CBS
CD-ROMs, 46, 332
   encyclopedias, 324
CD-Rs (recordable CDs), 46, 69
CD-RWs (rewriteable CDs), 46, 69
CDs (compact disks), 69. *See also* record-
      ing industry
   distributing and selling, 92–93
Cedar Falls, Iowa, 198
Celler-Kefauver Act of 1950, 410
celluloid, 205–6
Celluloid Closet, The, 234
censorship, 504
   of books, 337, 338
   of the Internet, 53–56
   as prior restraint, 490–92
Center for the Study of Commercialism,
      371
Century, The, 334
Chancellor Media Corporation, 130
Chan, Jackie, 223
channel, 10
Channel One, 365–66
Channel V, 189

Chaplin, Charlie, 20, 21, 209
chapter shows, 150
Charles, Ray, 73, 77
Charleston, 66
Charmin tissue, 360
Chaucer, Geoffrey, 313–14
Chayefsky, Paddy, 149
ChemLawn, 397
Cherokee Rose Bud, 256
Chess Records, 75
Chevrolet, 359, 361
Cheyenne, 151
Chicago Defender, 255
Child magazine, 298
children, advertising and, 365–66
children's magazines, 291
Children's Online Protection Act
      (COPA), 54–55
Children's Television Act (1990), 365
China, 187
   books in, 312, 313
   1989 student uprising in, 30
Chomsky, Noam, 481
Chords, the, 77
Christian gospel, 85
Christian Journal and Advocate, 274
Christian rock, 85
Chronicle of Higher Education, 480
Chuck D, 78–79, 88
Chung, Connie, 144, 430
cigarette advertising, 366, 368
Cincinnati Enquirer, 435
CinemaScope, 229
cinema verité, 224, 225
Cinemax, 191, 196
Cinerama, 229
circulation, magazine, 299
Citizen Kane, 246
Civil Action, A (Harr), 334
civil rights movement, 11
Clapton, Eric, 76
Clarissa; or, The History of a Young Lady
      (Richardson), 314
Clark, Dick, 72, 76, 80
Clarke, Arthur C., 177
Clark, Marcia, 496
Clark, Mary Higgins, 325
Clark, Roy Peter, 248
classic rock, 126
Clayton Antitrust Act (1914), 410
Clean as They Wanna Be, 494
Clear Channel Communications, 131
Clinton, Bill (Clinton administration), 10,
      11, 54, 55, 461–62
   impeachment hearings, 503
Clinton-Lewinsky affair, 10, 11, 55, 182,
      252, 295, 322
CNBC, 145

CNET, 265
CNN (Cable News Network), 31, 184–85, 188, 364
coaxial cable, 173
Coca-Cola, 348–49
Coca, Imogene, 146
Cochran, Johnnie, 503
codex, 312
Cody, William F. (Buffalo Bill), 380
Coen, Ethan, 23
Coen, Joel, 23
Cole, Nat King, 74, 159
Collier's, 278
Collier's Weekly, 280, 284
colonial era
  books, 314–15
  magazines, 274
  newspapers, 241–42
Columbia Phonograph Broadcasting System (CPBS), 111
Columbia Phonograph Company, 111
Columbia Pictures, 233, 234, 406
Columbine High School (Littleton, Colorado), 3–5
Columbus Dispatch, 251
Columbus Ledger-Enquirer, 451
Comedy Central, 171
comedy programs, television, 146–48
comic books, 318–19
Comics Magazine Association of America, 318
commercial speech, advertising and, 364, 369
Committee on Public Information (CPI), 383, 384
common carriers, 178
Common Sense, 274
communication, defined, 5
Communications Act of 1934, 508
communication satellites, 177
  direct-broadcast satellites (DBS), 193–95
  television and, 153
Communications Decency Act (CDA), 53, 54
communist model for expression and speech, 489–90
community antenna television (CATV), 173–74
community conversations, 451–52
community relations, 390, 392
comparative advertising, 370
component systems, 70
CompuServe, 48
computers, 12–13. *See also* Internet, the
  media convergence and, 44
Condé Nast, 289–90, 294, 302
conflict of interest, 435–36

conflict-oriented journalism, 253–54
Conrad, Frank, 108
consensus narratives, 235
consensus-oriented newspapers, 253–54
console systems, 70
consumer control, consumer choice vs., 421
consumer movement, 390, 392
contemporary hit radio (CHR), 122
content analysis, 469–70
continuity editing, 216
contributing writers, 298
control group, 467
controlled circulation, 299
convergence. *See* media convergence.
Cooke, Janet, 439–40
Cook, Fred, 509
cookie-and-pattern publications, 277
cookies, 57
Coolidge, Calvin, 109
COPA (Children's Online Protection Act), 54–55
cop docs, 151
"Cop Killer" (song), 11
Coppola, Francis Ford, 220
Cops, 151
copyright law, 493
Corporation for Public Broadcasting (CPB), 113, 127, 139
correlations, 468
Correll, Charles, 115, 116
Cosby, Bill, 157
Cosby Show, 158, 162, 165
Cosmopolitan, 278, 302
Cossack, Roger, 481
Costner, Kevin, 231
Coughlin, Father Charles, 124
country format, radio, 124
country & western music, 74, 77
Court TV (Courtroom Television Network), 502
cover music, 76–78
Craft, Christine, 447–48
credit cards, Internet security and, 56
Crew Cuts, 77
Crichton, Michael, 334
crime blocks, 447
critical process (critical perspective), 26–29
  benefits of, 29
  steps in, 27–29
Crockett, Davy, 379
Cronkite, Walter, 144
crooning, 71
Crosby, Bing, 71
Crow, Sheryl, 65–66
Cruz, Celia, 91
C-Span2, 310
cultivation effect, 471
cultural imperialism, 406–7, 421–22
cultural minorities
  magazines and, 292–94
  magazines for, 293–94
cultural studies, 473–75

culture
  defined, 5
  as a hierarchy, 16–19
  high, 16
  low, 16
  as a map, 19–20
  mass communication and, 5–6
  postmodern, 20, 30
  shifting values in, 22–26
Curtis, Cyrus, 277, 278–79
cyberspace, 36. *See also* information era (Information Age); Internet, the
cynical perspective, 27
Czitrom, Daniel, 461

Dallas, 152
Daly, John, 145, 445
D'Arcy Masius Benton & Bowles, 359
Dash, Julie, 221, 234
DAT (digital audiotape), 69
Dateline, 145, 158, 334, 391
Daughters of the Dust, 234
Davis, Kenneth, 320
Davis, Mike, 481
Davis, Peter, 225
Dawson's Creek, 156
Day, Benjamin, 243
Day, Dorothy, 260–61
Daye, Matthew, 314
Daye, Stephen, 314
Days of Our Lives, 151
DBS (direct-broadcast satellites), 193–95
DC Comics, 318, 319
deadheading, 381
De Armas Spanish Magazine Network, 293–94
Death of Literature, The (Kernan), 337
Death Row Records, 88
deception, media ethics and, 433–35
deejay (disc jockey), 112, 114
Deep End of the Ocean, The, 309–10
Dees, William, 494
deficit financing, 157
Def Jam, 79
Defoe, Daniel, 273
De Forest, Lee, 104–6
de Graff, Robert, 320
deliberative democracy, 454–55
Dell (publishers), 331
de Martinville, Leon Scott, 67
DeMille, Cecil B., 210
democracy, 29, 428
  advertising and, 372–73
  books and, 336–37, 339
  cable television and, 199
  deliberative, 454–55
  the Internet and, 52, 53
  magazines and, 304–5
  media economics and, 420, 422–23
  movies and, 235
  newspapers and, 266–67
  public relations and, 397–401
  representative, 454–55

Democracy without Citizens, 476
demographic editions of magazines, 286–87
demographics, 355
denim, 377–78
Denim Council, 377
Dennis, Everette E., 400
Denski, Stan, 481
De Palma, Brian, 220
dependent variable, 467
depression, Internet use and, 49
deregulation, 410–11
description, in critical process, 28
desktop publishing, 296
de Tocqueville, Alexis, 460–61
Detroit Free Press, 262
Detroit News, 262
developmental stages of new media, 38, 67
development editors, 326
Diamond Sutra (Wang Chieh), 313
Diana, Princess, 322, 438
DiCaprio, Leonardo, 4
Dickens, Charles, 243, 335
Dickson, William Kennedy, 206
dictionaries, 324
Dictionary of the English Language, 324
Diddley, Bo, 74
Didion, Joan, 216
DiFranco, Ani, 95
digital audiotape (DAT), 69
Digital Cable Radio, 193
digital communication, 9, 44
Digital Freedom Network, 514
DigitalMusic Service (DMX), 193
digital recording, 69
dime novels, 315
direct-broadcast satellites (DBS), 193–95
direct-effects model, 465
direct-mail book sales, 327–28
directors, movie, 219–20
direct payment, 408
DirecTV/USSB, 194
Dirt, 271
disassociation strategy, in advertising, 361, 363
disc jockey (deejay), 112, 114
Discovery Channel, 195
Disney. See Walt Disney Company
Disney Adventures, 291
Disney Channel, 418
Disneyland Paris (EuroDisney), 419
Distilled Spirits Council of the United States, 369
distributed networks, 39–40
diversity (cultural diversity), 26
Divx, 46
DJ Terminator X, 79
DMX (DigitalMusic Service), 193
docudrama, 22–23
documentary films, 222, 224–25
Dole, Bob, 13, 400, 515
domain names, 52
domestic comedy, 147–48

Domino, Fats, 75, 77
Donnerstein, Ed, 478
Doom (game), 4
Doomsday Flight, The, 459
Doors, the, 126
Do the Right Thing, 79
Doubleday, 327, 331, 334
Doubleday bookstores, 329
Douglass, Frederick, 255
Douglas, Susan, 148
Downs, Hugh, 515
Dragnet, 150
dramatic shows, television, 148–52
Drayton, William, 79
Dreamworks, 233
Drew and Associates, 224
Drew, Robert, 224–25
drive time, 121
Drudge, Matt, 252
drugs, psychedelic, 84
DTV (Grand Alliance digital system), 140
dumps, 326
Duncan, David, 281
Dunifer, Stephen, 128, 130
DVD (digital versatile disk, or digital videodisk), 46, 69, 230
Dworkin, Andrea, 487
Dylan, Bob, 66, 83, 85, 95, 126
Dynasty, 29, 152

early fringe, 161
Eason, David, 430
East and West (Patten), 187, 338
Eastman, George, 206, 208, 280
easy listening (EZ) format, 123, 124
Easy Rider, 219
EB Dedicated Reader, 333
Ebony, 293
e-books, 333
Echo 1, 177
Eclectic Reader, 317
e-commerce (electronic commerce), 42–43, 57
economics, media. See media economics
economies of scale, 409
Edison, Thomas, 67
    movies and, 206, 208
Editor & Publisher, 394
editors
    acquisitions, 325, 326
    development, 326
edit points, 216
Edsel, 365
Ed Sullivan Show, 12, 81–82
Effects of Mass Communication, The (Klapper), 465–66
Egypt, ancient, 312, 346
Eisenstein, Elizabeth, 314
Eisner, Michael, 412, 418, 515
elections, Section 315 rule and, 510–11
electromagnetic waves, 103
Electronic Frontier Foundation (EFF), 53–54

electronic publishers, 178
el-hi textbooks, 320
elite magazines, 292–93
Ellsberg, Daniel, 491
email, 9, 40
EMI, 89, 90
Encyclopaedia Britannica, 45–46
Encyclopaedia Britannica (EB), 323–24
encyclopedias, 323–24
Energy, U. S. Department of, 36
English Patient, The, 226, 334
entertainment systems, 70
Entman, Robert, 476
entrepreneurial stage, 67
entrepreneurial stage of media innovations, 38
episodic series, 150–52
Epitaph, 90
Epstein, Michael M., 55, 493
ER, 150, 152, 358
Espionage Acts of 1917 and 1918, 492
ESPN, 45, 48, 49
ESPN2, 180
ESPN the Magazine, 296
Esquire, 298
Essence, 293
ethics
    censorship in book publishing and, 338
    news media and, 432–38
        absolutist vs. situational ethics, 433
        conflicts of interest, 435–36
        privacy issues, 435
        resolving ethical problems, 436–38
    of online journalism, 265
    of TV talk shows, 15
    women's magazines and, 300–301
ethnic groups
    magazines for, 293–94
    newspapers for, 254–56
ethnocentrism, 431–32
EuroDisney (Disneyland Paris), 419
evaluation, in critical process, 28–29
Evans, Walker, 454
Everybook Inc., 333
"Every Breath You Take," 87
Eve's Bayou, 234
Evora, Cesaria, 91
Excite, 49
Exorcist, The, 217
experimental research, 467–68
experts, reliance on, 441, 444
Exxon *Valdez* oil spill, 397

facts, 432
Fairbanks, Douglas, 209, 505
fair comment, as defense against libel, 497
Fairness and Accuracy in Media (FAIR), 441

Fairness Doctrine, 511–12
fair use exception, 493
Falcon Crest, 152
Faludi, Susan, 429
Falwell, Jerry, 166, 323, 497–98
Falwell v. Flynt, 497
Fame, 416
famous-person testimonials, 360
Famous Players Company, 209
Fancher, Michael, 371
Fargo, 23
Farnsworth, Philo, 138
Fat Possum Records, 90
F.B.I., The, 151
feature syndicates, 258–59
Federal Communication Act of 1934, 112
Federal Communications Commission
    (FCC), 50, 54
  Fairness Doctrine and, 511
  newspapers and, 260, 261
  radio and, 112, 118, 127, 128, 509
  television and, 139, 154–55, 161, 409
    cable television, 175, 178, 179, 194,
      196
Federalist Party, 492
Federal Radio Commission (FRC), 112,
    113, 124
Federal Trade Commission (FTC), 110,
    351
feedback, 10
Fellini, Federico, 506
Fenlason, Laurie, 477
Fenske, Mark, 356
Fenton, Roger, 280
Ferber, Edna, 316
Fessenden, Reginald, 105
fiber-optic cable, 45
fiber optics, 57, 173
Field, Connie, 225
film. *See* movies (film industry)
film industry. *See* movies
film noir, 219
film review boards, 504
Financial Interest and Syndication Rules
    (fin-syn), 155
Finnegans Wake (Joyce), 20
First Amendment, 436, 488
  censorship and, 490
  commercial speech rights and, 364, 369
  movies and, 503–7
  Sixth Amendment and, 500–503
  television and, 508–12
first-run syndication, 161
flacks, 393, 394
Flagg, Fannie, 335
Flaherty, Robert, 224
Flavor Flav, 79
Fleischman, Doris, 384

Flip/Interscope Records, 120
Flockhart, Calista, 149
Flynt, Larry, 497–98
FM radio, 117–18, 125, 126
focus groups, 389–90
  advertising and, 355
folding carton, 348
folk music, 83
folk-rock, 83
Food and Drug Act (1906), 349
Food Lion supermarket chain, 434
football, on television, 136
Ford, Henry, 413
Ford Motor Co., 365
*For Enquiring Minds: A Cultural Study of
    Supermarket Tabloids* (Bird), 476
format radio, 119, 120, 122–26
Fornatale, Peter, 127
Fortune magazine, 434
"For What It's Worth," 78
Foster, Jodie, 220
Fourth Estate, the press as, 490
Fox Film Corporation, 208
Fox network, 136, 145, 155–56, 160
Fox News, 187
Fox, William, 208
franchise fee, 176
Frankenstein (Shelley), 16, 18
Frankfurt School, 472–73
Franklin, Benjamin, 241, 274, 314
Franklin, James, 241, 242
Frank, Reuven, 429
Frank's Place, 165
Frazier, Charles, 336
Frazier, Joe, 153
Freed, Alan, 73, 75, 76, 80
freedom of speech (freedom of expres-
    sion), 487–88. *See also* First
    Amendment
  in broadcast media, 507–12
  on the Internet, 53–57
  models for, 489–90
  origins of, 488–503
  pornography and, 487
  unprotected forms of expression,
    492–500
Freedom's Journal, 254
freelance writers, 298
Free Radio Berkeley, 128
Freston, Tom, 190–91
Friedkin, William, 220
Friendly, Fred, 445, 446
Friends, 148, 163, 358
fringe time, 161
fulfilleds, VALS research and, 356, 357

Gable, Clark, 506
gag orders, 501
Gallo, 361, 363
Gallup, George, 355
game shows, 143
gangsta rap, 88
Gannett newspapers, 420

Gans, Herbert, 431, 432
Gap, The, 42
Gartner, Michael, 391
gatekeepers, 10
Gates, Bill, 60
Gates, Henry Louis, 481
Gates Learning Foundation, 60
Gates, Melinda, 60
Gazeta Wyborcza, 449
Geertz, Clifford, 473
Geffen, David, 233
Gelbart, Larry, 146
General Electric (GE), 156
  radio and, 105, 106, 108–10
  RCA and, 107
General Hospital, 151
general-interest magazines, 278–79,
    282–85
General Motors (GM), 110, 363, 390, 391
Gentleman's Magazine, 273
GeoCities, 49
George, 302
Gerbner, George, 469
Gergen, David, 310
Geritol, 142
Gibbs, Georgia, 77
Gibson, Don, 77
Gifford, Kathie Lee, 398
Giles, Robert, 259
Glamour en Español, 294
glam rock, 86
Glasgow, Kentucky, 197–98
global markets (globalism), 413
global village, 30
Globe, 295
Godey's Lady's Book, 275, 276
Godkin, E. L., 276
Godzilla, 223
Goldberg, Matt, 291
Goldberg, Whoopi, 335
Golden Rule, 436
Goldman, Ron, 503
Gomery, Douglas, 58, 230, 504
Go Network, 49
Goodman, Ellen, 478–79
Good Night, Moon (Brown), 20
Goodwin, Hannibal, 205
Goodyear TV Playhouse, 149
Goosebumps books, 317, 334
Gordy, Berry, 82
Gore, Al, 384
Gosden, Freeman, 115, 116
gospel music, 85
gotcha story, 445
Gould, Stephen Jay, 481
government regulation, 410–11
GQ, 298
Graham's Magazine, 275
gramophone, 67
Grand Alliance digital system (DTV), 140
Grandmaster Flash and Furious Five, 87
Grant, Cary, 219
Grant, Hugh, 498

graphic novels (comix), 318–19
Grease, 217
"Great Balls of Fire," 76
Great Train Robbery, The, 207
Great White Wonder, The, 95
Greece, ancient, 6, 312
Greeks, ancient, 11–12
Greeley, Horace, 430
Greider, William, 444
Grierson, John, 224
Griffith, D. W., 209, 219
Grisham, John, 320
Groening, Matt, 464
grounding, 104
grunge, 86
Guerin, Veronica, 427–28
Guerra, Juan Luis, 91
Guiding Light, 115, 151
Gulf & Western Industries, 234
Gunsmoke, 150, 151
Gutenberg, Johannes, 313
Guthrie, Arlo, 126
Guthrie, Woody, 83

Hachette Filipacchi, 299, 302
Hadden, Britton, 279, 280
Hair, 217
Hale, Sarah Josepha, 275
Haley, Alex, 152
Haley, Bill, 73, 76
Hall, Stuart, 473
halo effect, 414
Hamilton, Andrew, 242
Hamilton, Jane, 310
handouts, 387
Happy Days, 148
happy talk, 448
Hare, Jimmy, 280
Hargis, Billy James, 509
Harlan County, U. S. A., 225
Harper's New Monthly Magazine, 276
Harpo Films, 221
Harris, Benjamin, 241
Harris, Christopher R., 280–81
Harr, Jonathan, 334
Hartford Courant, 371
Harvard University Press, 324
Hauptmann, Bruno, 501
Have Gun Will Travel, 151
Havel, Václav, 30
Hawaii Five-O, 151
Hayes, Isaac, 214
Hays Office, 505
Hays, Will, 505
HBO (Home Box Office), 153, 191–92, 196
HDTV (high-definition television), 140
health, advertising and, 366, 368
Hearst Magazines, 296
Hearst, William Randolph, 244, 245–46, 278, 294
Hearts and Minds, 225
Hee Haw, 161

Hefner, Hugh, 288
He Got Game (film), 78, 79
"He Got Game" (song), 78
Hemingway, Ernest, 311
Henry & June, 507
Hentoff, Nat, 97, 489
herd journalism, 441
Hero with a Thousand Faces (Campbell), 311
Hertz, Heinrich, 104
Hewitt, Don, 145, 158, 432, 440
Hicks, Wilson, 282
hidden-fear appeal, 360
Hidden Persuaders, The, 365
hierarchy
  of culture, 16
  opposition to, 22
high culture, 16
  rock and roll and, 74
high-definition television (HDTV), 140
high-fidelity systems, 70
Highlights, 291
Hilburn, Robert, 88
Hilfiger, Tommy, 53
Hill and Knowlton, 353, 385, 386, 392, 399
Hill, Anita, 11, 137
Hill, Faith, 87
Hill, Lauryn, 76, 88
Hill, Lewis Kimball, 128
Hill Street Blues, 152
Hine, Louis, 280
Historia Naturalis, 323
History Channel, 334
Hitchcock, Alfred, 219
Hit Video USA, 189
Holly, Buddy, 74, 75, 80
Hollywood, 208
Hollywood Ten, 226–27
Holmes, Oliver Wendell, 492
Holocaust, 468
Holocaust, 152
Holt, Rinehart & Winston, 331
homeless people, newspapers of, 264
Hong Kong films, 223
Hooker, John Lee, 75
Hoop Dreams, 225
Hoover, Herbert, 112
Hopper, Dennis, 219
Horgan, Stephen, 280
Horkheimer, Max, 472
horror films, 217
House of Wax, 229
House Un-American Activities Committee (HUAC), 227
HTML (Hyper-text Mark-up Language), 47
HUAC (House Un-American Activities Committee), 227
Hubbard, Gardiner Green, 290
human-interest stories, 243
Huntley-Brinkley Report, 144
Huntley, Chet, 144

Hurston, Zora Neale, 462
Hussein, Saddam, 144
Hustler magazine, 497
Hutchins Commission, 490
Hutchins, Robert Maynard, 490
Huxley, Aldous, 20
hypertext, 47
hypodermic-needle model, 464–65
hypotheses, 467

"I Can't Stop Loving You," 77
Ice-T, 11
iconoscope, 138
Ideas Publishing Group, 294
IFEX (International Freedom of Expression Exchange), 513, 514
I. F. Stone's Weekly, 260, 261
Iger, Robert A., 182
"I'll Be Missing You," 87
Illinois Central, 380
illuminated manuscripts, 313
Il Miracolo (The Miracle), 506
I Love Lucy, 145–46
image dissector tube, 138
Imagen, 294
Image, The (Boorstin), 384
Imitation of Life, 214
immigrant newspapers, 254
incentive clauses, 358
Ince, Thomas, 210
indecency, 510
Independent Film Channel, 191
independent films (indies), 225–26, 231–32
independent record labels, 89–90
independent variable, 467
India, 189
Indian film industry, 223
indirect payment, 408
individualism, 8, 21, 432
Industrial Age, 38
Infinite Jest (Wallace), 343
Infinity Broadcasting, 130
infomercials, 23, 364
information, knowledge distinguished from, 27–28
information economy. *See also* media economics
  transition to, 410–19
information era (Information Age), 36, 37
  electronic phase of, 9
  journalism and, 428–38
  telegraph and, 8–9
information highway, 37, 38. *See also* Internet, the
  alternative voices on, 52
  information access on, 41, 44–49
  knowledge gap and, 57–58

information highway (continued)
  media convergence and, 44–45
  origins of, 37–41
  problems and possibilities of, 58–61
Infoseek, 49
infotainment, 23
infotainment programs, 155
Ingram Book Group, 332, 420
ink-jet imaging, 286
instant books, 321–22
INTELSAT, 177
interactive channels, 192
interest films, 222
International Copyright Law of 1891, 320
International Data Group, 265
International Freedom of Expression
        Exchange (IFEX), 513, 514
Internet2 (Abilene Project), 36, 52, 62
Internet Explorer, 48
Internet Protocol (IP), 40
Internet Service Providers (ISPs), 46,
        47–48
Internet, the, 9, 35–62. See also informa-
        tion highway
  access issues, 41, 44
  access to, 58, 60
  advertising and, 371–72
  as decentralized system, 53
  as distributed network, 39–40
  e-commerce and, 42–43
  free expression and censorship issues,
        53–57, 512–16
  future control of, 50, 52
  highway metaphor, 36–37
  mapping, 46–49
  misinformation on, 53
  origin and development of, 38–41
  ownership issues, 49–50, 52
  photojournalism, 281
  problems and possibilities of, 58–61
  recording industry and, 89, 92–93, 96
  regulation of, 53–57
  values and, 50
interpretation, in critical process, 28
interpretive journalism, 248–50
Interpublic Group, 353
Interstate Commerce Act in 1881, 381
"In the Pines," 76
inverted-pyramid style, 247–48
Ironside, 151
irritation advertising, 360
"I Shot the Sheriff," 76
It Takes a Nation of Millions to Hold Us
        Back, 78, 79

Jackson, Bo, 353
Jackson, Michael, 188, 353
Jacobson, Michael F., 368

Jagged Little Pill, 94
Jagger, Mick, 81
James, Caryn, 137
Jamieson, Kathleen Hall, 481
Jane, 272
Japanese cinema, 223
Java, 47
Jayhawks, the, 94
jazz, 71
Jazz Singer, The, 213
J. C. Penney, 399
Jefferson, Thomas, 492
Jeffries, Bill, 434
JenniCAM, 51
Jennings, Peter, 145, 334
JenniShow, 51
Jenny Jones Show, 14, 162
Jerry McGuire, 232
Jerry Springer Show, 14, 15
Jesus Christ Superstar, 217
Jet, 293
Jewell, Richard, 436, 438, 496
Joe Camel character, 366, 368
John, Elton, 85
Johnson, Earvin "Magic," 232–33
Johnson, Jack, 504
Johnson, John H., 293
Johnson & Johnson, 397
Johnson, Lyndon, 144
Johnson, Robert, 72, 74, 76
Johnson, Samuel, 324
joint operating agreements (JOAs), 261
Jolson, Al, 213
Jordan, Michael, 353, 354
journalism. See also magazines; news;
        newspapers
  advertising's threat to, 370–71
  advocacy, 250
  conflict-oriented, 253–54
  contemporary, 251–53
  herd, 441
  in the information age, 428–38
  informational or modern model, 449
  interpretive, 248–50
  inverted-pyramid style, 247–48
  literary, 250–51
  literary forms of, 250–51
  modern, 21, 246–48
  neutrality in, 430–31
  newsworthiness criteria, 429–30
  objective, 247–48
  online, 265
  partisan and European model, 449
  photojournalism, 278, 280–82
  precision, 250
  public, 267, 450–55
  public relations and, 393–95
  rituals of, 439–45
    adversaries, journalists as, 445
    balancing story conflict, 444
    focusing on the present, 439–41
    relying on experts, 441, 444
  television and, 445–49

differences between print and televi-
        sion news, 446–48
  visual language and critical limits,
        448–49
  values in, 430–32
  yellow, 244–47
Joyce, James, 20, 499
Joyner, Tom, 101
Judas Priest, 459
jukebox, 70
Jungle, The, 278
Jurassic Park, 216, 334
Justice, Department of, 155
juvenile trade books, 316–17
J. Walter Thompson, 353

Kaczynski, Theodore, 322
Kaiser Family Foundation, 469
Kaltenborn, H. V., 114
Kane, Bob, 318
Kant, Immanuel, 436
Kapur, Shekhar, 223
Kasem, Casey, 130–31
Katzenberg, Jeffrey, 233
Katz, Jon, 240, 252–53, 431
Kazan, Elia, 227
KDKA, 108
Kelley, Kitty, 322
Kellogg's, 349
Kennedy, John F., 281
Kennedy, John F., Jr., 302
Kernan, Alvin, 337
Khomeini, Ayatollah, 338
kinescope, 146
kinetograph, 206
kinetoscope, 206
King, Larry, 31
King of Kings, The, 210
King, Rodney, 432–33
King, Stephen, 326
King World, 159
Klapper, Joseph, 465–66
Kline, David, 36, 50
KMBC television station, 447–48
Knight, Marion "Suge," 88
Knots Landing, 152
knowledge, information distinguished
        from, 27–28
knowledge gap, 57–58
Kojak, 151
Koppel, Ted, 433
Kopple, Barbara, 225
Korean War, 139
Kottak, Conrad, 477
Kovach, Bill, 514
Kraft Television Theater, 149
Krutick, Jill, 210
Kurosawa, Akira, 223
Kuwait, 392
KVUE-TV, 447

Ladies' Home Journal, 277
Ladies' Magazine, 275

Lady Chatterley's Lover (Lawrence), 338
Ladysmith Black Mambazo, 91
L. A. Law, 152
Lamb, Brian, 310
Lamb, Wally, 310
lamp black, 67
Landow, George, 332
Lapham, Lewis, 56
Lasch, Christopher, 455, 480
Lasica, J. D., 265
Lassie, 20
Lasswell, Harold, 461
"LastTime, The," 87
late fringe, 161
Latina, 294
Lawrence, D. H., 338
Lawrence Welk Show, 161–62
Leadbelly, 76
Learning Tree, The, 215
Lear, Norman, 148, 159
Lear, William, 110
leased channels, 175
least objectionable programming (LOP),
     18
Leaves of Grass (Whitman), 338
Lee, Ivy Ledbetter, 382–84, 394
Lee, Spike, 78, 79, 215, 219, 353
legal issues. *See also* First Amendment;
          freedom of speech (freedom of
          expression)
     broadcast vs. print rules, 509
     cameras in the courtroom, 501–3
     Fairness Doctrine, 511–12
     gag orders, 501
     privacy, right of, 498–99
     shield laws, 501
     unprotected forms of expression,
          492–500
          libel, 494–98
          obscenity, 499–500
Lemmons, Kasi, 234
Leno, Jay, 335
Letterman, David, 405
Let Us Now Praise Famous Men (Agee),
     454
Levi Strauss & Co., 398–99
Lewinsky, Monica, 10, 11. *See also* Clin-
          ton-Lewinsky affair
Lewinsky scandal, 137
Lewis, Edward, 293
Lewis, Jerry Lee, 76, 80
Lewis, Peter, 333
Lewis, Tom, 102
libel, 494–98
     seditious, 241–42
libertarian model for expression and
          speech, 490
Liberty and the News (Lippmann), 461
Liberty Media Corporation, 195
licenses, 334
licensing rights, book, 334–35
Life, 280–82, 284–85
Life and Times of Rosie the Riveter, The, 225

Life of an American Fireman, The, 207
Lightning Print, 332
"Like a Rolling Stone," 84
Limbaugh, Rush, 125
limited competition, 408
Limp Bizkit, 120–21
Lindbergh, Charles, 213, 501
Lind, Phil, 80
linear model of communication, 10
linotype machines, 314
Linux, 52
Lion King, The, 217
Lippmann, Walter, 249, 384, 395, 461,
     470
liquor advertising, 369
Literary Guild, 327
literary journalism, 250–51
Little, Brown, 331
Little House on the Prairie, 150
Little Richard, 74, 76, 77, 80, 85
Little Women, 334
lobbying, 392
Loeb, Philip, 508
Lois & Clark, 415
Lone Ranger, The, 136
Long, Huey, 124–25
long lines, 109
long-playing record (LP), 68
"Long Tall Sally," 77
Look, 282, 284
Lord, Daniel, 506
Lorentz, Pare, 224
Love, Amy, 290
"Love Is a Good Thing," 65
low culture, 16
Lowenthal, Leo, 472
Lucas, George, 219, 220
Luce, Henry, 279, 280, 490
Ludlow strike, 382
Lumière, Louis and Auguste, 206
Lyle, Jack, 465, 466

McCain, John, 503
McCarthy, Joseph, 150, 507
McChesney, Robert, 421
McClure's magazine, 278
MacDonald, J. Fred, 156
McDormand, Frances, 23
McGuffey, William H., 317
McKennitt, Loreena, 95
MacKinnon, Catharine, 487
McLean, Don, 80
McLuhan, Marshall, 37, 128, 204, 431
MacNeil/Lehrer Productions, 195
McWilliams, Michael, 25
Madonna, 24–25
magazine programs, on television, 141
magazines, 271–305
     advertising, 284, 286, 298–301
     advertising and sales department of, 298
     age-related, 291–92
     alternative voices, 304
     categories and types of, 287–88

     circulation and distribution department
          of, 299, 301–2
     colonial, 274
     for cultural minorities, 293–94
     in a democratic society, 304–5
     demographic editions, 286–87
     early history of, 273–76
     editorial department of, 298
     elite, 292–93
     general-interest, 278–79, 282–85
     major chains, 302–3
     modern, 276–85
     muckrakers, 277–78
     music, 290
     national, 275–76
     organization and economics of, 296,
          298–99, 301–2
     pictorial, 276
     production and technology department
          of, 296, 298
     regional editions, 286
     social reform and, 277
     Spanish-language, 293–94
     specialization of, 285–96
     sports, 289–90
     supermarket tabloids, 294–95
     travel and geography, 290–91
     webzines, 295
     women's, 275, 277, 289–90, 300–301
     zines, 296, 297
Magazines in the Twentieth Century (Peter-
     son), 292
magic-bullet theory, 465
Magnum, P. I., 150
Maher, Bill, 198
mail-order book sales, 327–28
Malone, John, 195
Mannix, 151
Manpower employment agency, 410
Manson, Marilyn, 4
manuscript culture, 313
Man with a Movie Camera, 225
map model of culture, 19–20
Marconi, Guglielmo, 104
Marconi Wireless Telegraph Company,
     104
Marco Polo, 313
Marcus Welby, M. D., 150
marketing research, 462–63
market research, advertising and, 355
Markey, Ed, 478
Marlboro, 361, 363
Marley, Bob, 76
Marshall, Penny, 220
Martin, George, 90
Martin, Ricky, 91
Martinville, Leon Scott de, 67
Marvel comics, 318, 319

Marvelettes, the, 77
mass communication
　alternative approach to, 11
　defined, 6
　global dominance of the U. S. in, 107
　linear model of, 10
　selective exposure and, 11
mass-market paperbacks, 320–22
mass media
　defined, 6
　evolution of new, 38–39
　mass-communication process and, 9–13
　　linear model of communication, 10
　role and impact of, 11–13
Mass Media and Global Communications
　　Web site, 32
mass-medium stage, 38
mass production, 410
MasterCard, 56
Masterpiece Theater, 150
Matera, Fran, 393
Matsushita, 234
Maude, 159
Maus: A Survivor's Tale (Spiegelman), 319
Maverick, 151
Maxwell House, 359
Maxwell, James, 103
"Maybellene," 75
Mazur, Laurie Ann, 368
MCA/Universal, 89, 154, 234
media buyers, 358
media convergence, 20
　content and, 45–46
　magazines and, 296
　technology breakthroughs and, 44–45
media economics (media economy),
　　405–23
　antitrust laws and policies, 410, 412,
　　419–20
　consolidation and mergers, 412
　consumer choice vs. consumer control,
　　420–21
　democracy and, 420, 422–23
　deregulation and, 410–11
　Disney as postmodern media conglom-
　　erate, 416–19
　flexible markets and, 412–13
　global markets and specialization, 413,
　　416
　organizational structures, 407–8
　performance of media companies,
　　408–9
　social issues in, 419–22
　transition to an information economy,
　　410–19
media effects (media research), 459–81
　approaches to, 466–70
　content analysis, 469–70

cultural approaches to, 472–76
early developments in, 460–63
evaluating research on, 471–72, 475–76
experimental research and, 467
explaining, 470–71
language (jargon) used in, 476, 480
marketing research, 462–63
models for, 464–66
private vs. public research, 464
propaganda analysis, 461
public-opinion research, 461–62
scientific method and, 466–67
social-psychology studies, 462
survey research, 468–69
media ethics. *See* ethics
Media Foundation, 364, 369
Media History Project, 32
Media Literacy Online Project, 32
Media Mayhem, 467
Media Monopoly, The (Bagdikian), 419
MediaOne, 196
media relations, 388
media selection, advertising, 358
Medical Question Box, 124
Meet the Press, 143
mega-agencies, 352–53
Melies, George, 207
Mencken, H. L., 29
Mercury Theater of the Air, 116
Meredith Publishing Company, 302
Merrill, John C., 400
Merritt, 452
Merritt, Davis "Buzz," 450, 451
messages, 10
"Message, The," 87
metropolitan dailies, 253
Miami Herald, 255, 256
Miami Herald Publishing Co. v. Tornillo,
　　509
Micheaux, Oscar, 214
microprocessors, 44
Microsoft, 48, 52, 324
　antitrust lawsuit against, 49–50
Microsoft Network (MSN), 48
microtechnology, 44
Middle Ages, 313
middle class, 7
Midwest Video case, 178
Miller Brewing Company, 389
Miller, Henry, 338
Miller Lite beer, 358–59
Miller, Tim, 46
Miller v. California, 500
Mill, John Stuart, 436
Mills, Joshua, 127
Milton, John, 488–89
Milwaukee Journal, 440
Mini-Disc, 69
minimal-effects model, 465–66
miniseries, 152
Minow, Newton, 143
Miracle case, 506
Miramax Films, 296

Mississippi Delta music, 83
Mitchard, Jacquelyn, 309–10
Miyazaki, Hayao, 223
Moana, 224
modernization, 20–21
Modern Maturity, 291–92
modern period, 20–21
Modern Times, 20, 21
Mod Squad, 151
Moesha, 156
Mongashkar, Lata, 91
monopolistic competition, 408
monopoly, 407–8
Monroe, Marilyn, 288
Moonlight Tobacco Company, 363
Moonves, Leslie, 172
Moore, Gordon, 44
Moore, Michael, 225
Moore's Law, 44
Morissette, Alanis, 94
Morrison, Toni, 310, 334
Morse, Samuel, 103
Mother Jones, 304
Motion Picture Association of America
　　(MPAA), 506–7
Motion Picture Patents Company (the
　　Trust), 208
Motion Picture Producers and Distribu-
　　tors of America (MPPDA), 505
Motion Picture Production Code, 229,
　　505–6
Motorola, 110
Motown, 82–83
movie rentals, 154
movies (film industry), 9, 205–35
　actors, 209
　alternative voices, 234
　attendance decline after World War II,
　　228
　classic Hollywood, 213, 216–21
　consensus narratives, 235
　directors, 219–20
　distribution, 208, 210, 231–32
　documentary, 222, 224–25
　early technology and evolution of,
　　205–8
　economics of, 230–34
　exhibition, 208, 211–12, 232–33
　First Amendment and, 503–7
　foreign, 221–23
　genres, 217–19
　HBO and, 192
　Hollywood Ten, 226–27
　implications for democracy, 235
　independently produced (indies),
　　225–26, 231–32
　interest, 222
　major studios, 233–34
　narrative, 207, 216–17
　nickelodeons, 207–8
　postmodern, 23
　production, 208, 209, 231
　rating movie content, 506–7

social and political pressure on, 504–5
sound (talkies), 212–13
studio system, 210–12
television and, 226, 228–29
vertical integration, 209, 212, 227, 234
video industry, 229–30
movie theaters, 211–12
Movietone, 213
Moyers, Bill, 166, 311
MP3, 96
MPAA (Motion Picture Association of
America), 506–7
Ms. magazine, 299
MSNBC, 48, 145
MTV India, 189
MTV (Music Television Network), 26,
93, 188–91
visual style of, 352
MuchMusic, 189
muckrakers, 277–78
Mulgrew, Kate, 161
multicultural era, 30
multimedia content, 45–46
multiple-system operators (MSOs), 195–96
multiplexes, 212
Munsters, The, 18
Murder, She Wrote, 415
Murdoch, Rupert, 107, 136, 155, 186–87,
263, 283, 295, 411
Murphy Brown, 13
Murrow, Edward R., 111, 445, 446
music. *See also* sound recording
blues, 83
folk, 83
popular. *See* popular music
rap, 87–88
world, 91
musicals, film, 217
musical wallpaper, 123–24
music business. *See* recording industry
Music Choice, 193
music clubs, 92
music industry. *See* recording industry
music magazines, 290
music videos, 93
MTV and, 188–91
must-carry rules, 175
Mutual Broadcasting System, 111–12
myth analysis, 359, 363–64

NAB (National Association of Broadcast-
ers), 130
Nader, Ralph, 390
Nanook of the North, 224
Nappy Hair, 338
narrative films, 207, 216–17
narrowcasting, 105, 182
NASA, 36
Nast, Thomas, 251
National Academy of Recording Arts and
Sciences, 84
National Association of Broadcasters
(NAB), 130, 174

National Association of Television Pro-
gram Executives (NATPE), 159
National Broadcasting Company. *See* NBC
National Enquirer, 294–95
National Football Conference (NFL), 136
National Geographic, 290–91
National Highway Traffic Safety Admin-
istration (NHTSA), 391
nationalism, 7
National Public Radio (NPR), 113, 127
National Retired Teachers Association
(NRTA), 291
National Review, 304
National Science Foundation, 36, 40, 52
National Television Systems Committee
(NTSC), 138–40
National Television Violence Study,
478–79
Nation, The, 276
Native Americans, newspapers, 256
Natural Born Killers, 460
NBC-Blue network, 109, 110, 112
NBC (National Broadcasting Company),
109–12, 141
television, 143–45, 156
NBC Nightly News, 144, 334
NBC-Red network, 109, 110
Near v. Minnesota, 490
Negro Digest, 293
Negroponte, Nicholas, 45
Nelson, Ricky, 80
Netscape, 49, 56
Netscape Communicator, 48
Network, 149
neutrality, 430–31
Nevermind, 86
Newcomb, Horace, 473, 474
New England Courant, 241
Newfield, Jack, 250
New Orleans Daily Creole, 255
news. *See also* journalism; newspapers
cable television, 444
criteria for choosing and defining,
429–30
differences between print and television, 446–48
future of, 449–55
premodern vs. modern, 21–22
radio, 112
television, 143–45
news consultants (news doctors), 448
News Corp., 136, 189, 234, 263, 283,
295, 406, 411
NewsEdge Corporation, 61
newsgroups, 40–41
newshole, 257
NewsPage, 61
newspaper chains, 263
Newspaper Preservation Act (1970), 261
newspapers, 239–67. *See also* journalism
advertising, 257–58, 264
African American, 254–55
alternative, 264, 266

alternative (underground), 256–57
business operations, 257–58
chains, 262
circulation, 259
colonial, 241–42
consensus-oriented, 253–54
democracy and, 266–67
de Tocqueville on, 460–61
electronic (online), 251, 264, 265
evolution of, 241–46
feature syndicates and, 258–59
human-interest stories, 243
immigrant and ethnic, 254
joint operating agreements (JOAs), 262
metropolitan dailies, 253
modern period, 246–51
Native American, 256
news responsibilities, 258
penny papers, 242–44
radio and, 249–50
Spanish-language, 255–56
technology and, 263–64
types of, 253
weekly, 253
wire services and, 244, 258
yellow journalism, 244–46
newsreels, 213, 222
Newsweek, 252, 281, 282, 286, 302
newsworthiness, 429–30
New York Daily Compass, 261
New Yorker, 276, 292–93
New York Journal, 242, 244–47
New York Morning Herald, 243
New York Sun, 243
New York Times, 28, 29, 55, 57, 60, 206,
246–47, 322
Pentagon Papers case and, 491
New York Times v. Sullivan, 495
New York Tribune, 430
New York Weekly Journal, 241
New York World, 239, 244–45, 247, 434
Next Generation Internet Initiative, 36
Nickelodeon, 190–91
nickelodeons, 207–8
Nielsen Market Research Company, 162
Nielsen television ratings, 414–15
Night and Fog, 225
Nightline, 24, 433, 441
Nike, 353, 354
Nipkow, Paul, 138
Nirvana, 76, 86
Nixon, Richard M., 227, 399–400
nonprofit radio, 126–28
Nordstrom, 371
North American Review, 274
North by Northwest, 219
North Star, 255
nostalgia, 19

nostalgia/big-band formats (radio), 124
Notorious B. I. G., 88
novelty stage of media innovations, 38, 67
NPR (National Public Radio), 113, 127
NTSC (National Television Systems
    Committee), 138–40
NuvoMedia, 333
N. W. Ayer, 347
NYPD Blue, 152

objective journalism, 247–48
objectivity, 467
  in journalism, 248–51, 282
obscenity, 486–87, 499–500
  on the Internet, 53–55
Ochs, Adolph, 246–47
O'Connor, Carroll, 148
off-network syndication, 161
offset lithography, 314
Ogilvy & Mather, 359
Ogilvy & Mather Worldwide, 353
"Oh, Pretty Woman," 493–94
oldies format, 119, 126
Oldsmobile, 358
oligopoly, 408
Omnicom Group, 353
Onassis, Jacqueline Kennedy, 498
Ondaatje, Michael, 334
One Life to Live, 151
online bookstores, 330
open-source software, 52
opinion, as defense against libel, 497
Oprah, 334
Oprah effect, 309
Oprah's Book Club, 309–10
Oprah Winfrey, 53
Oprah Winfrey Show, 310
option time, 111, 112
oral communication, in ancient Greece, 6
Orbison, Roy, 493, 494
Orina, Janai Robert, 53
Orman, Suze, 335
Outcault, R. F., 244, 245
Outside magazine, 290
outside sources, reliance on, 441, 444
outsourcing, 398

Pacifica Foundation, 128
packaging, 348
Packard, Vance, 365
Paglia, Camille, 25, 481
paid circulation, 299
Paine, Thomas, 274
Palestinians, 60
Paley, William, 111, 421
Palmer, Volney, 347
Pamela; or, Virtue Rewarded (Richardson),
    314

Panke, Claire, 226
paparazzi, 498
paperback books, 314–15
  mass-market, 320–22
Paper Tiger Television (PTTV), 164
papyrus, 312
Parade magazine, 302
Paramount, 162, 227–28, 233, 234
parchment, 312
Parents Music Resource Center (PMRC),
    95
Parker, Edwin, 465, 466
Parks, Gordon, 214, 215
Parks, Gordon, Jr., 214, 215
Parsons, Louella, 124
partisan press, 242
Partner, The (Grisham), 320
pass-along readership, 282
patent medicines, 347–49
Patten, Chris, 187, 338
Pauley, Jane, 391
pay-for-play, 120
Payne Fund Studies, 462
payola, 78–80, 120–21
pay-per-view (PPV) programs, 191, 192
PBS (Public Broadcasting Service), 127,
    139, 164, 166, 177
Pearce, Harry, 391
Pearl Jam, 86
Penniman, Richard Wayne. *See* Little
    Richard
Pennsylvania Gazette, 241
Pennsylvania Magazine, 274
Penn, William, 348
Pentagon Papers case, 491
People, 285
People en Español, 294
People vs. Larry Flynt, 497
Pepsi-Cola, 24
Perkins, Carl, 74–75
Perot, Ross, 31, 372
Persian Gulf War, 144, 185, 392, 481
personal computers (PCs), 44
persuasive techniques, in advertising,
    359–64
Peter Pan, 142
Peterson, Theodore, 292
Peyton Place, 151–52
Phantom Menace, The, 204
Philips Electronics, 89, 234
Philips, Stone, 391
Phillips, Sam, 75
phonographs, 67, 70
photojournalism, 278, 280–82
Pickford, Mary, 209, 505
pirate radio, 129
Pittsburgh Courier, 255
plain-folks pitch, 360
Plato, 6, 12, 312
Playboy, 288, 289
Playhouse 90, 149
"Please Mr. Postman," 77
Pliny the Elder, 323

Plow That Broke the Plains, The, 224
PMRC (Parents Music Resource Center),
    95
Pocket Books, 320
Poland, 29, 421, 449
Police Academy, 488
police dramas, 151
Policing the Crisis (Hall), 473
political advertising, 372–73
political candidates, equal opportunities
    and response time for, 510–11
political-economy studies, 475
Politically Incorrect, 198
politicians, 13
PolyGram, 89, 90
Pope, Generoso, 294–95
popular culture (low culture), 16, 18
  cultural imperialism and, 421–22
popular music (pop music), 71–88. *See also*
    jazz; recording industry; rock and
    roll
  rhythm and blues (R&B), 73, 75–77, 82,
    85, 123
  soul music and Motown, 82–83
Popular Party, 241
pornography, 13, 487
portals, 48
Porter, Edwin S., 207
Portland Oregonian, 371
Postal Act of 1879, 276
postmodern culture (postmodern period),
    20, 30
  shifting values in, 22–26
Poussaint, Alvin, 165
Powell, Colin, 326
Pratt, Jane, 271–72
precision journalism, 250
present, focusing on the, as journalistic
    ritual, 439
Presley, Elvis, 12, 74–77, 80, 85
press agents, 379
press releases, 387, 388
press, the. *See also* journalism; magazines;
    newspapers
  public relations and, 392–97
"Pretty Woman," 493–94
Prevue Channel, 283
Primary, 224–25
PRIMEDIA, 302, 366
prime time
  radio, 121
  television, 136, 157–59
Prime-Time Access Rule (PTAR),
    154–55, 161
Primetime Live, 434
printed communication, 6–8
printing press, 6–8, 313–14
print media, modern values and, 20–21
prior restraint, censorship as, 490–92
privacy, right of, 498–99
privacy, right to, 435
Procter & Gamble, 358
professional books, 317

Program, The, 459
Progressive magazine case, 491–92
progressive rock, 126
propaganda, 387
propaganda analysis, 461
Propaganda Techniques in the World War
   (Lasswell), 461
pseudo-events, 384–85
psychographics, 355
PTTV (Paper Tiger Television), 164
Public Broadcasting Act of 1967, 127
Public Broadcasting Service (PBS), 127,
   139, 164, 166, 177
Public Enemy, 78, 79, 88
publicity, 378
public journalism, 267, 450–55
   critics of, 452–53
Public Opinion (Lippmann), 461
public-opinion research, 461–62
public radio, 126–28
public relations
   community and consumer relations,
      390, 392
   defined, 379
   early developments in, 379–85
   government relations and lobbying, 392
   independent agencies, 385–86
   in-house services, 386
   media relations, 388
   practice of, 385–92
   the press and, 392–97
   pseudo-events and manufacturing news,
      384–85
   research, 389–90
   social responsibility and, 397–401
   special events, 389
public relations (PR), modern public relations agents, 381–84
Public Relations Society of America
   (PRSA), 384, 395, 396
Public Relations Student Society of
   America (PRSSA), 385
public research, 464
public-service announcements (PSAs),
   351, 387–88
Publishers Clearinghouse, 286
publishing houses. *See also* book publishing industry
   formation of, 315–16
Puff Daddy, 87
Pulitzer, Joseph, 244–45, 428
Pulitzer Prize, 445
pulp fiction, 315
Pulp Fiction, 216
punk rock, 85–86
Pure Food and Drug Act of 1906, 278

Quaker Oats, 347–48
qualified privilege, 496
Quayle, Dan, 13
Quigley, Martin, 506
Quiz Show, 142
quiz shows

radio, 115
   television, 142–43
QVC, 195

rack jobbers, 92
radio, 9, 101–31
   advertising, 121–22
   alternative voices, 128
   black/R&B format, 123
   cable, 193
   car, 110
   CBS (Columbia Broadcasting System),
      111, 408
   commercial, evolution of, 108–16
   contemporary, 121–28
   economics of, 121–26
   first voice broadcast, 105
   FM, 117–18, 125, 126
   format, 119, 120, 122–26
   free speech and, 509–10
   golden age of, 112
   government regulations, 106, 112
   Internet and, 129
   Mutual Broadcasting System, 111–12
   NBC and, 109–11
   network, 109–11
   news, 112
   newspapers and, 249–50
   news/talk format, 122–25
   nonprofit (public), 126–28
   origins and development of, 102–7
   ownership of, 128, 130–31
   payola scandals, 78–80
   pirate, 129
   programming changes, 118
   RCA monopoly, 106–10
   record industry and, 70
   rock and roll and, 73, 126
   Spanish-language, 123
   specialization of, 122–25
   technology, 103–6, 117–18
Radio Act of 1912, 106, 112
Radio Act of 1927, 112
Radio Corporation of America. *See* RCA
radio group (of radio stations), 109
radio-phonograph players, 70
Radway, Janice, 474
ragtime, 71
railroads, public relations and, 380–81
Raising Hell, 87
Rand Corporation, 40
random assignment, 467
Random House, 331, 334
Ranger Rick, 291
rap music, 26, 66, 87–88
"Rapper's Delight," 87
Rappe, Virginia, 505
Rashad, Phylicia, 157
rate cards, 299
Rather, Dan, 30, 144
ratings, television, 162–64, 414–15
Ray, Johnnie, 73
Ray of Light, 24

Ray, William J., 197–98
RCA (Radio Corporation of America)
   formation of, 107
   45-rpm record and, 68
   NBC and, 109–11
   radio and, 107–12, 117, 118
   television and, 118, 138, 139
RCA Records, 89
RCA Victor, 110
Reader's Digest, 279, 282, 286, 302
Readers' Guide to Periodical Literature, 324
*Reading the Romance: Women, Patriarchy and
   Popular Literature* (Radway), 474
Reagan, Ronald, 511
Reasoner, Harry, 145
receivers, 10
recording industry, 88–97
   alternative paths to success in, 95
   bootlegging and, 94–95
   distributing and selling CDs and tapes,
      92–93
   independent labels, 89–90
   major labels, 89
   MP3 and, 96
   MTV and, 188–91
   as oligopoly, 89
   production process, 90, 92–94
   profits and, 93–94
   radio and, 70
   rock and roll and, 80
record players, 68, 70
*Red Channels: The Report of Communist Influ-
   ence in Radio and Television*, 507
Redding, Otis, 76
Red Lion Broadcasting Co. v. FCC, 509
Reebok, 232, 354
Reed, Lowell A., Jr., 55
reference books, 323–24
regional editions of magazines, 286
Reid, Wallace, 505
Reiner, Carl, 146
Reiser, Paul, 335
reliability, scientific method and, 467
religious books, 322–23
reporters. *See also* journalism; newspapers
   types of, 258
representative democracy, public journalism and, 454
Republican Party, 323
Republic, The (Plato), 12, 312
rerun syndication, 157
research
   media. *See* media effects
   public relations, 389–90
responsible capitalism, 432
retransmission consent, 179
Review, 273
Revlon, 142

Reynolds, Frank, 145
rhythm and blues (R&B), 73, 75–77, 82, 85, 123
Rice, Anne, 325
Richardson, Samuel, 314
Rich, Frank, 136
Rich Man, Poor Man, 152
Rigler, Judyth, 265
Riis, Jacob, 280
Ringley, Jennifer, 51
Ringling brothers, 380
Ripley, Alexandra, 326
Rivard, Robert, 265
Rivera, Geraldo, 503
R. J. Reynolds, 363, 366
Road Runner, 49
Roberts, Cokie, 515
Robertson, Pat, 323
Roberts, Oral, 323
Robinson, Max, 145
Robinson, Smokey, 82, 83
rockabilly, 74, 75
rock and roll, 66, 72–82
    African Americans and, 74–75
    album-oriented (AOR), 126
    alternative, 86
    British, 81–82
    Christian, 85
    classic, 126
    cover music, 76–78
    drugs and, 84
    folk-rock, 83–84
    glam, 86
    high culture and, 74
    as mainstream culture, 84–85
    MTV and, 188–91
    northern and southern influences on, 75
    payola scandals and, 78–80
    progressive, 126
    punk and grunge, 85–86
    radio and, 73, 126
    rhythm and blues and, 75
    sexuality and, 74
"Rock Around the Clock," 76
Rockefeller, John D., 278, 382, 394
"Rocket 88," 76
Rocket eBook, 333
Rockford Files, 151
Rock the Vote campaign, 190
Rockwell, Norman, 278
Roddenberry, Gene, 161
Roger and Me, 225
Rogers and Associates, 390
Rogers, Mark C., 318–19
Rogers, Norman (DJ Terminator X), 79
Rolling Stone, 290
Rolling Stones, 76, 81–82
"Roll Over Beethoven," 74

Rome, ancient, 312
Roosevelt, Franklin, 106
    radio conversations (fireside chats), 124
Roosevelt, Theodore, 277, 384
Rooster Blues Records, 90
Roots miniseries, 152
Rorty, James, 365
Roseanne, 148
Rosenblatt, Roger, 289
Rosen, Jay, 185, 266, 445, 452, 455
Rosenstiel, Thomas, 334
Rose, Reginald, 149
Rosing, Boris, 138
Ross, Diana, 82, 83
Rossellini, Roberto, 506
Ross, Harold, 292
rotation: playing, 119
Rotenberg, Mark, 180
Rothenberg, Randall, 401
Roth v. United States, 499–500
Roundtree, Richard, 214
Rowland, Willard, 471
royalties
    book, 326
    sound recording, 94
Royko, Mike, 439–40
R. R. Bowker, 324
Run-DMC, 87
Rushdie, Salman, 338

Saatchi & Saatchi, 353
Sagan, Carl, 481
Salon, 295, 296
Sammon Communication, 176
Samudrala, Ram, 96
San Antonio Express-News, 265
Santa Barbara, 29
Sarnoff, David, 109, 110, 117–18, 141
Sassy, 271, 272
Satanic Verses (Rushdie), 338
satellites, communication, 177
    direct-broadcast satellites (DBS), 193–95
    television and, 153
"Satisfaction," 76
saturation advertising, 358–59
Saturday Evening Post, 275, 278–79, 284
Saturday Night Live, 25
Saturn automobiles, 363
Savan, Leslie, 352
Sawyer, Diane, 189, 434
scanning disk, 138
Scarlett (Ripley), 326, 327
Schenck, Charles T., 492
Schenck v. United States, 492
Schlessinger, Laura, 125
Schmidt, Harald, 405
Scholastic, 334
Scholle, David, 481
schools, advertising in, 365–66
Schramm, Wilbur, 465, 466
Schudson, Michael, 251, 346, 348, 381
Schwarzeneger, Arnold, 498

scientific method, 466–67
scientific reasoning, doubts about, 26
scoops, 440–41
Scorsese, Martin, 220
scribes, 313
Scribner's, 316
Seagram Company, 89, 234, 406, 408
    liquor advertising, 369
search engines, 48–49
Seattle Times, 371
Sebestyén, Mârta, 91
Section 315 of the 1934 Communications Act, 510
Sedition Act, 492
seditious libel, 241–42
See It Now, 445–46
Selecciones del Reader's Digest, 294
selective edits, 298
selective exposure, 11
selective exposure and selective retention, 465
Sendak, Maurice, 338
senders, 10
serial programs, 151–52
Serling, Rod, 459
servers, 40
Sesame Street Magazine, 291
(seventyeight) 78-rpm records, 68
Sex Pistols, 85
sexuality
    rhythm and blues (R&B) and, 73
    rock and roll and, 72, 74
    Web sites and, 55
Shaft, 215
Shakur, Tupac, 88
"Shame of the Cities" series, 278
Shankar, Ravi, 91
share (audience measure), 163
Share-the-Wealth Society, 125
Shaw, George Bernard, 117
Shaw, Irwin, 152
"Sh-Boom," 77
sheet music, 71, 72
Shelley, Mary Wollstonecraft, 16, 18
Sheppard, Sam, 500, 501
Sherman Antitrust Act, 410
Sheryl Crow, 66
She's Come Undone (Lamb), 310
shield laws, 501
shooters, 449
Showgirls, 507
Shriver, Maria, 498
Shuster, Joe, 318
Siegel, Jerry, 318
Silence of the Lambs, 217
Silly Symphonies, 417
Simon, Neil, 146
Simon, Paul, 91
Simon & Schuster, 325, 331
Simpson, O. J., 9, 11, 182, 281, 335, 441, 444, 462, 481, 496, 497, 500, 502–3
Sinatra, Frank, 72, 76

Sinclair, Upton, 278
Singapore, ONE (One Network for Everyone) initiative in, 35
Singing Fool, The, 213
Singletary, Michael, 468
situational ethics, 433
situation comedies, 115, 146–47
Sixth Amendment, 500–503
$64,000 Challenge, 142
$64,000 Question, 142
60 Minutes, 28, 29, 145, 158
60 Minutes II, 145
Skelton, Red, 146
sketch comedy, 146
slander, 494
Slate, 50, 295, 296
slogans, 351
small-town pastoralism, 432
Smith Brothers, 347
Smith, Hedrick, 166
Smith, W. Eugene, 281
Smoke Signals, 234
Smokey Robinson and the Miracles, 82
Smolinski, Chris, 129
sneakers, advertising for, 353
snob-appeal approach, 360
Snow White, 417
Soap Opera Digest, 289
soap operas, 115, 151–52, 421
social-psychology studies, 462
social responsibility, of journalists, 454
social-responsibility model for expression and speech, 490
Society of Professional Journalists, code of ethics of, 435, 437
Socrates, 6, 11
Socratic method, 6
SoftBook, 333
software, open-source, 52
Sokal, Alan, 480
Solomon, Michael, 43
Song of Solomon (Morrison), 310, 334
Sony, 89, 90, 117, 153, 234, 406, 408
soul music, 82–83
sound bites, 447
sound recording, 66–97. *See also* recording industry
  early technology and development of, 67–70
Souter, David, 494
South Carolina Gazette, 242
South Park, 171–72
Spanish-language magazines, 293–94
Spanish-language newspapers, 255–56
Spanish-language radio, 123
specialization, media economics and, 413, 416
spectaculars, television, 142
Spector, Phil, 81
speech, freedom of. *See* freedom of speech
Spiegelman, Art, 319
Spielberg, Steven, 219, 220, 233
split-run editions, 286

sponsors, television, 141–42
Sports Illustrated, 289, 298
Sports Illustrated for Kids, 289
Sports Illustrated for Women, 289
sports magazines, 289–90
spot ads, 141
Springer, Jerry, 15
Springfield, Buffalo, 78
Springsteen, Bruce, 85
SRI International, 355
Stained Class, 459
Standard Oil, 382
Stanford Research Institute (SRI), 355
Stanton, Edwin M., 247
Stapleton, Jean, 148
Star, 295
Starobin, Paul, 434
Starr, Kenneth, 10, 11, 55, 322
Star Trek, 150, 161
Star Trek: The Next Generation, 162
StarTV, 187
Star Wars, 203–4, 210, 223, 231
state model for expression and speech, 489–90
Stearns, Jennifer, 175
Stecklow, Steve, 41
Steffens, Lincoln, 278
Steiger, Rod, 227
Steinbeck, John, 338
Steinem, Gloria, 300–301
St. Elsewhere, 152
Stephens, Ann, 315
stereo (stereophonic sound), 68–69
stereotyping, in advertising, 362
Stern, Howard, 125, 509
Stills, Stephen, 78
Stine, R. L., 316, 317
St. Louis Post, 244
Stockham, Thomas, 69
Stone, I. F., 260, 261, 434
Stone, Oliver, 460
Storz, Todd, 119
Street News, 264
Streisand, Barbra, 220
Studio One, 149
studio system, 210–12
subliminal advertising, 351
Sub Pop, 90
subsidiary rights, 325
Sugarhill Gang, 87
Sullivan, Ed, 81–82
Sullivan, L. B., 495
Sundance Channel, 191
Sundance Film Festival, 226
Sun Microsystems, 47
Superman, 318
supermarket tabloids, 294–95
superstations, 183
superstores (bookstores), 329
Supreme Court, U. S., Communications Decency Act (CDA) and, 54
Supremes, the, 82, 83
survey research, 468–69

Surviving the Bottom Line, 166
Swayze, John Cameron, 144, 145
sweatshops, 398, 399
Swift, Jack, 451
syndicated exclusivity (syndex) rules, 178
syndication
  feature (newspaper), 258–59
  of television programs, 155, 157–62
    barter deals, 162
    cash deals, 162
    first-run syndication, 161
    independent programs, 157–58
    international syndication, 160
    off-network syndication, 161
synergy, in book publishing industry, 331
  Walt Disney Company and, 418

tabloids, supermarket, 294–95
Talk, 296
Talk Media, 296
talk radio, 122–24
talk shows, 13, 14
tango, 66
Tarantino, Quentin, 216
Tarbell, Ida, 278, 434
Tarzan series (Burroughs), 338
Taylor, Mary B. W., 337
Taylor, William Desmond, 505
TCI (Tele-Communications Inc.), 49, 171, 195, 197, 198, 407–8
Tebbel, John, 285, 313
Technicolor, 229
technology
  contemporary culture and, 26
  film, 205–8
teenagers, advertising and, 365–66
Telecommunications Act of 1996, 49, 52, 58, 128, 180–81, 196, 263, 408, 411
telegraph, 8–9, 103
telegraphy, wireless, 104
Telehit, 189
Telemedium, 32
telephone companies, cable television and, 196
telephone group (of radio stations), 109
Teletubbies, 166, 334
television, 9, 135–67
  advertising, 141, 156, 351, 355, 358, 364
  alternative voices on, 164
  anthology dramas, 148–50
  anticommunist movement and, 507–8
  Brazilian, 477
  cable. *See* cable television
  children's, 164, 166
  color, 139
  comedy programs, 146–48
  decline of network era, 152–56

television *(continued)*
  dramatic shows, 148–52
  early technology and development of, 137–43
  economics of, 156–64
    prime-time distribution, 158–59
    prime-time production, 157–58
    syndication, 159–62
  entertainment programming, 145–52
  episodic series, 150–52
  Fairness Doctrine and, 511–12
  film industry and, 226, 228–29
  free expression and, 507–12
  freeze on new licenses (1948 to 1952), 139
  future of, 167
  global markets, 416
  information culture, 143–45
  journalism and, 445–49
    differences between print and television news, 446–48
    visual language and critical limits, 448–49
  Littleton shooting and (1999), 4–5
  news, differences between print and, 446–48
  in the 1950s, 141–43
  photojournalism, 281
  prime-time, 157–59
  programming trends, 143–52
  quiz shows, 142–43
  radio programs on, 136
  ratings, 414–15
  ratings and shares, 162–64
  sponsors, 141–42
  talk shows, 13, 14
  technical standards, 138–39
  technology, 137–43, 153–54
  V-chip technology, 13
  violence on, 478–79, 481
television networks, 152–56
  emerging new, 155–56
  programs produced by, 158
Television News with Douglas Edwards, 144
television specials, 142
Telstar, 177
Texaco, 378
Texaco Star Theater, 146
Texas Instruments, 117
textbooks, 317, 320
textual analysis, 473–74
TheStreet.com, 265
Thomas, Clarence, 11, 137
Thomas, Jeremy, 234
Thomas, J. Parnell, 227
Thomas, Lowell, 114, 249

Thomson Consumer Electronics (Thomson/RCA), 194
Thornton, Willie Mae "Big Mama," 75
3-D (three-dimensional) movies, 229
Thriller, 188
Thunder on Sycamore Street, 149
Ticketmaster, 86
Time, 279–82, 286, 302
Time-Life Books, 328
time shifting, 154
Time Warner, 13, 49, 90, 97, 196, 331, 407, 408, 412, 460, 515
  magazines, 289, 294, 295, 302
Time Warner Cable, 195
Timothy, Elizabeth, 242
Tin Pan Alley, 71, 72
Titanic, sinking of, 106
Titicut Follies, 225
tobacco industry, advertising by, 366, 368
Today show, 141, 142
Toffler, Alvin, 199
toll broadcasting, 109
Tomorrow Never Dies, 186
Tonight Show, 141, 142
topless radio, 509
Top 40 radio, 119, 122
Tornillo, Pat, Jr., 509
tough-question style, 445
trade books, 316–17
trademarks, 348
Transamerica, 234
transistors, 117
travel magazines, 290–91
travelogues, 224
Travolta, John, 216
Triangle Publications, 282, 283
Tribune Company, 263
TriStar Pictures, 192
Tristar Pictures, 232
Tropic of Cancer (Miller), 338
Truman Show, The, 51
Trump Style, 299
Trust, the (Motion Picture Patents Company), 208
Truth or Dare, 25
Tucker, Ken, 82, 85
Tuesday Night Music Club, 65
Tupper, Martin Farquhar, 334
Turner, Big Joe, 75
Turner Broadcasting, 196
Turner, Ted, 153, 184, 186, 187
TV Guide, 272, 282–84, 286, 387
TV: The Most Popular Art (Newcomb), 473, 474
Twain, Mark, 338
"Tweedlee Dee," 77
Tweed, William "Boss," 250, 251
Twentieth Century Fox, 208, 233, 234
20/20, 145, 158
Twenty-One, 142
Twilight Zone, 149

2 Live Crew, 486, 493–94
Tylenol, 397–98

UHF (ultrahigh frequency) band, 139
Ulysses (Joyce), 499
Unabomber case, 322
uncommercials, 364
underground newspapers, 256–57
Ungaro, Susan, 436
United Artists, 209, 234
United Beyond 2000, 451
United Independent Broadcasters (UIB), 111
United Mine Workers, 382
United Video, 283
Universal, 233
Universal Studios (MCA), 89
University of Chicago Press, 324
university press books, 324–25
unprotected forms of expression, 492–500
  libel, 494–98
  obscenity, 499–500
Unsafe at Any Speed (Nader), 390
UPN (United Paramount Network), 156
urban contemporary (UC), 123
USA Today, 251–52
USA Weekend, 302
U. S. News & World Report, 282
U. S. Steel Hour, 149
U. S. v. Thomas, 55
Utne Reader, 304

vacuum tube, 105
Valens, Richie, 80
Valenti, Jack, 506
validity, scientific method and, 467
Vallee, Rudy, 71
Valli, Frankie, 76
VALS (Values and Lifestyles) research, 355–57
values
  advertising and, 350–51
  in American journalism, 430–32
  the Internet and, 50
  in modern culture, 20–21
  postmodern, 22–26
Van Doren, Charles, 142, 143
Vann, Robert C., 255
Van Susteren, Greta, 481
Variety, 210
variety shows, 114–15
vaudeo, 146
vaudeville, 71, 146
V-chip, 13, 478, 479
VCR Plus+, 390
vellum, 313
Velvet Underground, 85, 86
Ventura, Jesse, 400, 512
vertical integration, in film industry, 209, 212, 227, 234
Vertov, Dziga, 225

Verve, the, 87–88
VH1, 189
VHF (very high frequency) band, 139
VHS format, 154
Viacom, 162, 188, 234
Viacom/Paramount, 331
Victor Talking Machine Company, 68, 110
Victrolas, 68
videocassette recorders (VCRs), 153–54
  film industry and, 229–30
video news releases (VNRs), 387
videos, music, 93
  MTV and, 188–91
Vietnam War, 144, 261, 281, 297
Viking Penguin, 326
Village Voice, 257
vinyl records, 68
violence, on television, 478–79, 481
Virginian-Pilot, 451, 452
virtual communities, 48
Virtual Press, 333
VistaVision, 229
vitascope, 206
Vs., 86

Wagner-Hatfield Amendment, 113, 126, 127, 513
Wagon Train, 151
Wake Up and Live (Brande), 320
Waldenbooks, 329
Walker, Stanley, 392–93
Wallace, David Foster, 343
Wallace, Dewitt, 279
Wallace, Lila Acheson, 279
wall-to-wall music, 123–24
Wal-Mart, 65–66, 399
Walt Disney Company, 49, 154–56, 217, 223, 233, 334–35, 412, 459
  ABC News and, 515
  as postmodern media conglomerate, 416–19
Walters, Barbara, 145
Waltons, The, 150
Wang Chieh, 313
Ward, Ed, 77
Warner Books, 322, 326, 327
Warner Brothers (WB), 156, 212–13, 232, 233
Warner, Jack L., 227
Warner Music, 89, 352
Warner, Time, 187
War of the Worlds, The, 116, 465
Warren, Robert, 491–92
Washington Post, 439–40, 491
Wassaja, 256

Waterloo, Iowa, 198
Waters, Muddy, 75
Waterworld, 231
Watkins, Bruce, 471
WBAI radio station, 510
WB (Warner Brothers), 156
WDIA radio station, 123
WEAF radio station (now WNBC), 108, 109, 114, 115
Weavers, the, 83
Weaver, Sylvester "Pat," 141, 142
WebCams, 51
Webster, Noah, 324
Webzines, 295–96
weekly newspapers, 253
Weiden & Kennedy, 353
Welch's Grape Juice, 349
Welles, Orson, 116, 246, 465
Wells, H. G., 116, 465
Wells, Ida, 260
Wenner, Jann, 290
Wertham, Frederic, 318
Wertmuller, Lina, 220
West, Cornel, 481
Westinghouse, radio and, 108–10, 130
Westinghouse/CBS, 130, 412
West, Mae, 510
Westwood One, 122
WGCB radio station, 509
WGN radio station, 111
WGY radio station, 109
What's My Line?, 145
"White Christmas," 71
Whitman, Walt, 338
Whitmer, Clair, 265
Whittle Communications, 365
Whole Booke of Psalms, The, 314
Who's Afraid of Virginia Woolf?, 229
Why We Fight series, 224
Wichita *Eagle*, 451
Wicker, Tom, 250
Wiesel, Elie, 334
Will, George, 329
Williams, Spencer, 215
Wilson, Hugh, 488
Wilson, Woodrow, 107, 383
Winchell, Walter, 124
Winfrey, Oprah, 53, 221, 309, 334
Wireless Ship Act, 106
wireless telegraphy, 104, 106
Wireless Telephone Company, 105
wire services, 244, 258
Wiseman, Frederick, 225
WJZ radio station, 109
WLW radio station, 111
WNAC radio station, 109

Wolfe, Tom, 250–51, 335
Woman's Home Companion, 284
women
  advertising and, 361, 362, 366, 368
  film industry and, 220–21
  newspapers and, 242
  pornography and, 487
  tobacco campaign and, 383
Women Outside, 290
women's magazines, 275, 277, 289–90, 300–301
Women's Sports and Fitness, 290
Wood, Sam, 227
Woods, Tiger, 345
Woodward, Bob, 266, 431
Woo, John, 223
world music, 91
World War II documentary films, 224
World Wide Web (Web sites), 38, 46–47.
    See also Internet, the
  gathering information on users, 57
  search engines, 48–49
  sex-related, 55
WOR radio station, 111
WPP Group, 353
written communication, 6
WTBS television station, 153
WXYZ radio station, 111

X-Files, The, 135–36, 150, 152, 160, 358

Yahoo!, 49
Yahoo! Internet Life, 296
Yale University Press, 324
yellow journalism, 244–47
"Yellow Kid, The," 244, 245
Young, Owen, 107
Young & Rubicam, 355, 385
Youth's Companion, 276
You've Got Mail, 232

zapping, 154
Zenger, Anna Maul, 242
Zenger, John Peter, 241–42
zines, 296, 297
Zip disks, 46
zipping, 154
Zuckerman, Mortimer, 302
Zukor, Adolph, 208, 209, 211
Zworykin, Vladimir, 138
zzn, repeated paragraph, 260, 261

ABOUT THE AUTHOR

Richard Campbell is the director of the School of Journalism at Middle Tennessee State University. He is also the author of *60 Minutes and the News: A Mythology for Middle America* (University of Illinois Press, 1991). He is co-author of *Cracked Coverage: Television News, the Anti-Cocaine Crusade and the Reagan Legacy* (Duke UniversityPress, 1994).

He has written articles and essays on mass media for numerous publications, including *Columbia Journalism Review, Critical Studies in Mass Communication, Media Studies Journal,* and *Television Quarterly*. As a writer and media critic, he is also a frequent public speaker, including guest appearances on NPR, Wisconsin Public Radio, WJR radio, and public television.

Campbell earned a Ph.D. in Radio-TV-Film from Northwestern University where he was a national Danforth Fellow. For more than 25 years, he has taught journalism and media courses to a diverse body of students—from high school seniors in Milwaukee to Ford autoworkers in Michigan. Besides teaching at MTSU, he has also taught at Marquette University, the University of Wisconsin-Milwaukee, Mount Mary College, and at the University of Michigan. He has also worked as a print reporter and broadcast news writer.